ROSTER OF

REVOLUTIONARY SOLDIERS

IN GEORGIA

Roster

of

Revolutionary Soldiers

in

Georgia

Volume III

Compiled by

MRS. HOWARD H. McCALL
(ETTIE TIDWELL)

Vice-President General. N.S.D.A.R. 1922-1926

State Regent, Ga. D.A.R. 1916-1918

Honorary State Regent. Ga. D.A.R.

Honorary Vice-President General, N.S.D.A.R. 1948.

BALTIMORE

Genealogical Publishing Company

1 9 6 9

DEDICATED

TO THE MEMORY OF

MY HUSBAND

HOWARD H. McCALL, SR.

(1867 - 1929)

and

TO OUR SON

HOWARD H. McCALL, JR.

Captain 327th Co. - 82nd Division, U.S. ARMY

WORLD WAR - 1917-1918.

"To be a Georgian is not simply a piece of luck, it is a priceless privilege, to be paid for in loyalty and with love, and with life itself, if occasion demands. May the love of all thy children, O Georgia, encompass thee, and may God make them worthy to be called Georgians."

TABLE OF CONTENTS

iii

FOREWORD

This book is written as a dependable and authoritative reference book for libraries and patriotic organizations. The records assembled have been compiled of Revolutionary Soldiers of Georgia, whose records of service to their country in the War of the Revolution (1775 to 1783) should be easily available to all interested in genealogical research.

Care has been taken in compiling these records; the pensions, lottery lists, graves located, and the military service. All data has been verified and can be used for application papers of the National Society Daughters of the American Revolution.

Signed by,

Mrs. Howard H. McCall

Mrs. Howard H. McCall (Ettie Tidwell),
Honorary State Regent, and (War) State Regent (1916 - 1918) of Ga.
Society, D. A. R.
Vice President General, National Society, Daughters of the American Revolution (1922-1925).
State Regent Georgia Society, Daughters of the American Colonists (1937-1939).

PUBLISHER'S PREFACE

It is with considerable pride that we present this third and final volume in Mrs. Ettie Tidwell McCall's series on Revolutionary soldiers in Georgia. Before her death, Mrs. McCall had asked us to publish her works, and her son, Howard H. McCall, Jr., has most graciously cooperated with us in carrying out his mother's wishes. While her primary interest was in Georgia records (as evidenced by the first volume), Mrs. McCall's extensive researches led into countless interesting by-ways of Georgia lineages deriving from or spreading to other states. Volume II was entitled "Roster of Revolutionary Soldiers in Georgia and Other States" because so much of the material related to other areas. In this, the third volume, some of the data encompasses other states, but the majority still pertains to Georgia. This volume contains previously unpublished material given to us in the form of a copy of Mrs. McCall's typescript by the Georgia Department of Archives and History.

To facilitate access to the thousands of names in Mrs. McCall's records, we have rearranged all major entries, and many sub-entries, in alphabetical order whenever possible. In addition, we have compiled an index which contains every personal name in the book — even when the listing is a casual one. We feel that this index will greatly enhance the value of the book for all interested in their Revolutionary War heritage.

This volume no doubt contains errors which Mrs. McCall would have corrected had she lived. We have, in many instances, corrected errors when they were apparent — for the errors we did not recognize as such, we can only apologize sincerely.

As well as we can determine, there are no large-scale duplications of material from Volumes I and II. Where duplications do exist, they are usually minor, and are apparently intentional on the part of Mrs. McCall for the convenience of the reader. This volume is a completely separate and original work, but as is necessarily the case in any one author's genealogical research, there are probably many useful and desirable links between the three volumes. For this reason, the user of Volume III is advised to consult Volume I, which we reprinted in 1968, and Volume II, an original work which we also published in 1968.

GENEALOGICAL PUBLISHING COMPANY

Baltimore, Maryland, 1969

ROSTER OF
REVOLUTIONARY SOLDIERS

Many years have rolled away since the stirring scenes of the Revolution were acted, but the brilliant events of that period will live on the pages of history.

The names of those Revolutionary Soldiers who espoused the popular cause and threw the whole weight of their power and influence on the side of Liberty, are on the Nation's Roll of Honor.

While the Revolutionary Army of Georgia was small compared to many other Colonies, it was our State, Georgia, which offered land in quantity as an inducement to Revolutionary Soldiers of all the States to settle in Georgia.

Truly we can say these Revolutionary Soldiers from Georgia and the other Colonies helped to secure for us our glorious heritage.

CHARLES ABERCROMBIE (son of ROBERT ABERCROMBIE, REV. SOLDIER of N. C., b. 1715, Scotland), b. in N. C., March 4, 1742; d. 1819, Hancock Co., Ga. Served as Capt. 1778; Major 1780, N. C. Line. Received bounty land in Ga. for his services. He mar. Edwina Booth (dau. of JOHN BOOTH, private, N. C. Line, Capt. Raiford's Co., Col. Armstrong's troop. Born N. C.; d. 1804, Hancock Co., Ga.)
Children:
1. John, mar. Elizabeth Martin, widow.
2. Abner.
3. Leonard, mar. Sallie Comer.
4. Edmund (1773-1829); mar. Mary Pollard (1778-1810).
5. Anderson, Soldier of 1812; mar. Sidney Grimes.
6. James, mar. Parthenia Ann (Brown) Ross.
7. Charles, mar. Elizabeth (Grimes) Martin.
8. Jane, mar. BOLLING HALL, REV. SOLDIER, b. 1767 in Va.; d. in Ala. 1836 (son of HUGH HALL, REV. SOLDIER of Va., and his wife Mary Dixon).
9. Nancy, mar. Mr. Barnes.
10. Sarah, mar. Thomas Baines.

ROBERT ABERCROMBIE (son of ROBERT ABERCROMBIE, REV. SOLDIER of N. C.), b. Orange Co., N. C.; d. Hancock Co., Ga. Served as Major, Col. John Butler's Reg., N. C. Troops. Married Mary —.

1

JOHN ADAIR (son of JOSEPH ADAIR, REV. SOLDIER of S. C., and his wife Sarah Dillard, and grandson of JOSEPH ADAIR, REV. SOLDIER of S. C., and his (1) wife Sarah Laferty), b. Duncan's Creek, S. C., 1759; d. Morgan Co., Ga., 1812. Entered service 1779; captured near Charlotte, N. C.; in prison, Camden, S. C. (Extract from letter from Gen. Smallwood to Lord Cornwallis, Commander of the British forces, Southern Dept., Oct. 24, 1780).*
He mar. Jane Jones. She mar. (2) Green Jackson; d. 1852.
Children:
1. Joseph Alexander, mar. 1811, Elizabeth McCord.
2. John Fisher (1785-1856); mar. (1) Tylitha Brantley; (2) Mary Radcliff Slaven (dau. of Norcut Slaven and his wife Ann Holliday of Wilkes Co., Ga.
3. Hiram, Soldier of 1812. Lived Upson Co., Ga.
4. Jones, mar. (1) Miss Woods; (2) Polly Ann Shields.
5. Elizabeth, mar. Miles Garrett of Ala.
6. William, mar. —. Lived Morgan Co., Ga.
7. Mary, mar. John Apperson of Ala.
8. Farmar.
9. Susan.
10. Sarah, d. y.
11. James, mar. Sarah Dean.

---

* Sir: the prisoners taken in the neighborhood of Charlotte, N. C. Viz. ; JOHN ADAIR, RICHARD THOMAS, WILLIAM RANKIN, ANDREW BAXTER, JOHN McKAY, WILLIAM WILEY, WILLIAM WALLACE, and ALEXANDER BROWN. I understand of very desirous of obtaining an exchange. Perhaps your Lordship would have no objection to admit of a partial exchange of those persons for a like number now in our possession, whose situations and circumstances may not be altogether dissimular. If this proposition should meet with your approbation, you will be so obliging as to signify it, that the exchange may take place. "
The Henry Laurens Chapter D. A. R. of Laurens, S. C. and the Musgrove Mill Chapter, D. A. R. of Clinton, S. C. placed a tablet in the Duncan Creek Presbyterian Church, Laurens Co., S. C. (This Old Church founded by the Scotch Irish, is a veritable mother of Presbyterianism in S. C.) The tablet placed in honor of and bears the names of 16 REV. SOLDIERS, viz:

1. Joseph Adair, Sr.
2. Joseph Adair, Jr.
3. Robert Long
4. Thomas Logan
5. Leonard Beasley
6. John Copeland
7. George Young
8. Joseph Ramage
9. Thomas McCrary
10. Thomas Holland
11. Robert Hanna
12. John Craig
13. J. Bell
14. James Craig
15. James Adair, Sr.
16. William Underwood

Many of these men came to Georgia.

2

DAVID ADAMS, b. Waxhaw, S. C., Jan. 28, 1766; d. Zebulon, Ga., 1834. Served under Gen. Henderson in S. C.; was at the Battle of Eutaw Springs. Received bounty lands in Washington Co., Ga., for his services. He mar. Betsey Bradfield (1799-1833).

JAMES ADAMS (son of James and Cecily (Ford Adams), b. Albemarle Co., Va., Oct. 18, 1753; d. Elbert Co., Ga., 1835. Served as Minuteman and Orderly Sergeant, Va. Troops. Enlisted Fluvanna Co., Va., 1777, under Capt. Roger Thompson and Col. Charles Lewis. Received pension; also land, 1827 Cherokee Lottery. He mar. in Va., Jane Cunningham. Moved to Elbert Co., Ga., 1796.
Children:
1. William, mar. (1) Katherine Mansfield; (2) Sarah Head.
2. Samuel, mar. Martha Ann Thornton.
3. Ann Thompson, mar. HIRAM GAINES, REV. SOLDIER of Ga.
4. Jane, mar. Isham Teasley.
5. Elizabeth, mar. IVY SEALS, REV. SOLDIER of Ga.
6. John C., mar. Ann Dickerson.

JAMES ADAMS, b. S. C.; d. Hancock Co., Ga. Served under Gen. Sumpter in S. C. Married Mary —.
Children:
1. Robert, mar. 1815, Frances Hudson (dau. of IRBY HUDSON, REV. SOLDIER).
2. David.
3. Jonathan.
4. William.
5. James.
6. Rebecca, mar. — Hill.
7. Polly.
8. Nancy.
9. Jean.

NATHANIEL ADAMS, b. in 1747; d. in Ga., Mar. 7, 1806. A REV. SOLDIER. Qualified as a member of the Board of Commissioners of White Bluff Road, Ga. Married Anna Bolton (1752-1818).

THOMAS ADAMS, b. Fluvanna Co., Va., 1758; d. Elbert Co., Ga., 1836. Received pension as Sergeant, Va. Troops under Col. Francis Taylor. Married 1786, Sallie Ford.
Child:
1. John Adams (1798-1896), mar. Nancy Davis (dau. of JOHN DAVIS, REV. SOLDIER of Va., b. 1754, Va.; d. 1843, Elbert Co., Ga., and wife Sallie —).

WILLIAM ADDINGTON, b. 1759, S. C.; d. Union Co., Ga., 1845. Served as private and Lieut. in Col. Brandon's S. C. Regiment. His widow received pension for his services as REV. SOLDIER, 1848.

He married 1783, Delilah Duncan, b. 1765.

CHARLES ADKINS, made declaration in Ga., dated Aug. 30, 1832, and filed in Upson Co., Ga., when he was 72 years of age. Served in N. C. Applied for pension.

WILLIAM ADKINS, received land April 6, 1784 upon certificate of Col. Elijah Clarke, "that he hath steadfastly done his duty and is entitled to bounty land as a REV. SOLDIER, of 250 acres in Ga."

JAMES AIKENS, b. 1762, Penn. (near Md. line), lived in Mecklinburg Co., N. C. Served as private, N. C. Regiment, enlisted 1778. Served under Captains Brownfield, Hugh Parks and Charles Polk. Granted a pension, Sept. 5, 1832, while a resident of Coweta Co., Ga., where he died April 12, 1843. Married in Greene Co., Ga., Frances —, Mar. 16, 1791. She was granted a pension 1844, she being eighty years old.

JOHN ALBRITTON, b. Hanover Co., Va., Dec. 6, 1747. Private in Capt. George's Co., Col. Charles Scott's Va. Reg. Then in S. C. Reg. Taken prisoner at siege of Augusta. Died in Ga., 1833.

DAVID ALDERMAN, b. in New Jersey, 1749 (son of DANIEL ALDERMAN, REV. SOLDIER of N. C., and his wife Abigail Harris), came with his parents to Duplin Co., N. C. Served as a REV. SOLDIER with N. C. Troops. Married 1773, Jemina Hall of N. C. Moved to Bullock Co., Ga., where he died 1815.
Children:
1. David, mar. Nancy Morgan.
2. Isaac, mar. Elizabeth Morgan.
3. Elisha, mar. his cousin, Rebecca Alderman.
4. Ann (Nancy), mar. John Carlton (son of THOMAS CARLTON, REV. SOLDIER of N. C., and wife Martha).
5. Timothy, mar. Sarah Williams.

LODOWICK ALFORD, b. N. C., 1715; d. in Ga., 1789. Served in the Gen. Assembly of N. C. from Wake Co. A PATRIOT. Married Rebecca Ferrell.
Children:
1. Jacob.
2. James, mar. Lurania Boykin.
3. Lodwick, Jr., mar. Judith Jackson.
Perhaps others.

DREWRY ALLEN, b. Dec. 1, 1749, Orange Co., N. C.; d. Pike Co., Ga., Jan. 20, 1826. Served as REV. SOLDIER, N. C. Troops. Married in Greene Co., Ga., Elizabeth Yarbrough (1753-1823).
Children:

1. Josiah, mar. Elizabeth Browning.
2. Clement, mar. Mary McKissick.
3. Stokes, mar. Susan Jane Fouche.
4. Nancy, mar. (1) — West; (2) James Ravens; (3) — Yarborough.
5. Martha (1782-1853); mar. (as (2) wife), William Pyron.
6. Young David, mar. Jane Moore.

JAMES ALLEN, b. Belfast, Ireland, 1750; d. Burke Co., Ga., 1835. Private, Ga. Militia. Received land grant in Washington Co. Married 1784, Francis Simmons.

JOHN ALLEN, b. 1760; d. 1828 in Ga. Served as private, Ga. State Troops. Married 1777, Elizabeth Inman, b. 1762.

PHILIP ALLEN, drew bounty land for Revolutionary services in Va., while living in Clarke Co., Ga., 1835, age 76.

ROBERT ALLEN, b. in N. C.; d. in Ga. Received a grant of land for his services as a REV. SOLDIER of N. C. Married (1) near Hepzibah, Ga.), Elizabeth Anderson (dau. of Elisha Anderson, and his (1) wife, Miss Brack).
Children:
1. Martha, mar. Judge William Rhodes.
2. Jane, mar. Edmund Palmer.
3. Elizabeth, mar. (as (1) wife), Alexander Murphy.
4. Rosa, mar. Benjamin Wooding.
5. Polly Crawford.
6. Sarah.
7. Jackson.
8. Emily.
9. Robert A., mar. (1) Priscilla Wood; mar. (2) Caroline Walker, widow.
10. Elisha A., mar. Jeanette Evans (dau. of Daniel Evans).
ROBERT ALLEN mar. (2) —.
Child:
11. Hattie, mar. Henry Washburne of Savannah, Ga.
(From "Lost Arcadia" by Clark)

DR. ADAM ALEXANDER, b. Mar. 13, 1738, Inverness, Scotland; came to America and settled at Sunbury, Ga., 1776. Served as Surgeon in the Continental Army, Ga. Troops. Married (2) Louisa F. Schmidt (1775-1846).
Children:
1. Adam Leopold, b. Jan. 29, 1803; mar. Sarah Hillhouse Gilbert (dau. of FELIX GILBERT, REV. SOLDIER, and his wife Miss Hillhouse, and granddaughter of David and Sarah (Porter) Hillhouse of Conn. and Ga.).
2. Louisa, b. 1807; mar. Major Anthony Porter.

HUGH ALEXANDER, b. 1747; d. in Ga., 1835. Served as Lieut., Ga. Troops. Was at the Siege of Savannah, Ga. Married, 1769, Molly Woods (1751-1837).

JOHN ALEXANDER, b. in S. C.; d. 1830, Gwinnett Co., Ga. Served in S. C. Troops. Married Miss Williamson (dau. of THOMAS WILLIAMSON, REV. SOLDIER, "who commanded the troops 1776 that checked the invasion of the Tories and Cherokees". JOHN ALEXANDER and his three brothers joined the "Tiger Irish Co.", under Gen. Francis Marion.

SAMUEL ALEXANDER, b. 1757, N. C.; d. in Ga., 1817. In Col. Elijah Clarke's Reg. of Rifle Corps. Received 287.5 acres of land for his services as a REV. SOLDIER in Franklin Co., Ga. Married Olivia Wooten (or Norton), b. 1759.
Children:
1. Asa, mar. Fathia Wooten of Greene Co., Ga.
2. Mary, mar. James Simmons, b. 1774.
3. Asenith, mar. Dr. Willis Roberts.

NOTE: From House Journal of Ga., 1796, page 113:
"Capt. Samuel Alexander prays compensation for balance due him while serving as Capt. in Col. Elijah Clarke's Reg. Rifle Corps. Raised to aid Gen. Wayne in 1782. Capt. Alexander satisfied claims for GEORGE BARNHARD, LEWELLYN INLOW, and WILLIAM CLINTON, privates in his Co. The Governor of Ga. was authorized to draw warrant out of taxes of 1794, for sum due him." Feb. 13, 1796.

WILLIAM ALEXANDER, b. in Va.; d. Elbert Co., Ga., 1806. Received bounty land in Wilkes Co., Ga., 1784, for his services as a REV. SOLDIER in Continental Army of Va. and Ga. Also drew land as a REV. SOLDIER in Elbert Co., 1806. Married (1) —; mar. (2) Nancy —.
Children:
1. Peter, mar. Nancy Shackelford (dau. of HENRY SHACKELFORD, REV. SOLDIER.
2. James.
3. John.
4. George.
5. Elijah.
6. Ezza, mar. as (1) wife, Standley Jones. He mar. (2) Frances Rucker (dau. of WILLIAM RUCKER, REV. SOLDIER).
7. Milly, mar. Willis Rucker.
8. Dau., mar. William Page.
9. Frances, mar. 1810, Bardin Rucker.
10. Dau., mar. Reuben Cleveland.

HENRY ALLISON (from Greene Co. Records), and wife Martha,

of Richmond Co., Ga., Oct. 10, 1787, sold to Anderson Crawford of Richmond Co., Ga., 460 acres on the Oconee River, Washington Co., on lands reserved by an act of the Assembly of the State, Feb. 12, 1784, for the payment of bounties and gratuities to the Officers and Soldiers of the Continental Establishments and the above mentioned tract of 460 acres of land being a gratuity ordered by the General Assembly of Ga. to Henry Allison, formerly a Lieut. in the Continental Troops, land in Greene Co. (formerly Washington Co.), Ga., granted April 1784, by his Honor, Governor Mathews.

JAMES ALSTON, b. Chowan Co., N.C., about 1746; d. Elbert Co., Ga., 1815. He was an officer in N.C. Regiment. Married Orange Co., N.C., 1774, Grizell (Gilly) Yancey, b. 1752, N.C. ; d. 1845, Monroe Co., Ga.
Children:
1. Nathaniel (1775-1852); mar. Mary Grey Jeffrys.
2. Charity, mar. James Banks.
3. Sarah, mar. Joseph Groves.
4. Martha, d. unmarried.
5. John, mar. (1) Charity Tate; mar. (2) Miss McGinty.
6. Hannah, mar. James Jones Banks (son of Ralph and Rachel (Jones) Banks).
7. Elizabeth, mar. John O. Glover.

LIEUT. COL. WILLIAM ALSTON, b. in N.C., Dec. 25, 1736; d. 1810, Elbert Co., Ga. Member N.C. Provincial Congress, 1775; of the Constitutional Convention, Halifax Co., N.C., 1776. Lieut. Col., 3rd Reg., N.C. Troops under Gen. Jethro Summer. Married his cousin Charity Alston, d. 1823.
Children:
1. James, mar. Catherine Hamilton (dau. of MAJOR ANDREW HAMILTON, REV. SOLDIER of Va., and his wife Jane McGara).
2. William H., mar. Elizabeth Rucker.
3. Philip Rucker, mar. Miss Woolfolk.
4. Solomon.
5. George.
6. Mary, mar. Capt. James Clark.
7. Elizabeth, mar. — Thompson.
8. Christine.
9. Ann, mar. — Tait.
10. Sarah, mar. Thomas Chambers.

NICHOLAS ANCIAUX, who came to Ga., where he died. First came to this county with the French army, under command of Capt. DuPonte. He held a Captain's commission signed by Louis XVI of France. Born at Frankfort on the Main, Germany, son of Chevalier De Wilterino.

GEORGE ANDERSON, b. in New York; d. Savannah, Ga. Served as a REV. SOLDIER from Ga. Married in New York, Feb. 18, 1761, Deborah Grant (1736-1812). Moved to Ga., 1763.
Child:
> 1. George Anderson, Jr., b. Savannah, Ga., 1767; d. 1847. Married 1794, Elizabeth (Clifford) Wayne.

WILLIAM ANDERSON, b. S. C., 1763; d. Walton Co., Ga., 1837. Received pension 1836, for his services as private, Va. Troops. Married 1786, Elizabeth Lewis.

WILLIAM ANDERSON, b. in Va., Jan. 8, 1763; d. Baldwin Co., Ga., May 6, 1844. Enlisted Wilkes Co., Ga., under Capt. Burwell, Col. Elijah Clarke's Ga. Line. At Siege of Augusta. Enlisted later at Wrightsboro, Ga., as a Volunteer Rifleman, stationed at Philip's Fort, Wilkes Co., Ga. Pension: Widow's file No. 6855. Married (1) Wilkes Co., Ga., Sarah Finch (dau. of CHARLES FINCH, REV. SOLDIER, d. 1795, Franklin Co., Ga., and his wife Joyce —). He mar. (2) Baldwin Co., Ga., Mar. 5, 1806, Mary Hunnicutt, d. 1844. She drew a Pension as widow of REV. SOLDIER, 1844. They had 15 children, 13 living in 1844, and mentioned in Pension.
Children:
> 1. Louisa.
> 2. Sarah.
> 3. Allen G.
> 4. Thomas B.
> 5. Lazarus G.
> 6. Henry F.
> 7. David M.
> 8. Gilbert M.
> 9. Mary Ann.
> 10. Martha S., mar. George W. Rowell.
> 11. Ann Mariah, b. May 19, 1825; mar. 1857, Thomas Parham Redding. She was a Real Daughter of the U. S. D. A. R.
> 12. Lucy Ann, b. 1829; mar. T. Marion Gibson. She was a Real Daughter of the U. S. D. A. R.
> 13. George Washington.

JOHN ANDREW, after the Revolutionary War, was the first itinerant Methodist preacher in Ga., who was a native Georgian. He was the son of James Andrew, a member of the Puritan Dorchester settlement in Ga. This was the only congregation of Puritans south of New England. They removed in a body from Mass. to S. C., then to Ga., and formed the famous "Midway Church" in St. John's Parish (now Liberty Co.). John Andrew left an orphan when young, was brought up at the home of Pastor Osgood, in charge of the Midway Congregation.

JOHN ANDREW, b. Midway, Ga., 1758; d. Mar. 10, 1830, Clarke Co., Ga. Served as private under Gen. Samuel Elbert, Ga. Troops; Ensign under Gen. Wade Hampton. Married (1) in S. C., Feb. 10, 1779, Ann Lambright.

Child:

1. Ann, b. Jan. 20, 1780; mar. Abram J. Roberts.

JOHN ANDREW married (2) at Colonels Island, Ga., Sept. 20, 1785, Mary Buer Andrews.

Children:

2. Mary Buer, b. 1786; mar. 1807, Samuel Le Seuer.
3. Matilda Hull, b. 1792; mar. 1809, George C. Spencer.

JOHN ANDREW married (3) in Elbert Co., Ga., Dec. 11, 1791, Mary Overton Cosby.

Children:

4. James Osgood, b. May 3, 1794, Wilkes Co., Ga.; mar. May 1, 1816, Ann Amelia McFarland of Charleston, S. C. He was Bishop of Methodist Episcopal Church, South.
5. Charles Godfrey (1795-1796).
6. Lucy Garland, b. 1799; mar. (1) 1830, John Wright; mar. (2) 1844, William R. Henry.
7. Betsey Sidnor, b. 1800.
8. Scynthia Fletcher (1802-1803).
9. Caroline Wesley, b. 1804.
10. Patsey Evelina, b. 1806.
11. Judy Harvey (1809-1833).
12. Hardy H. (1811-1854).
13. William Harvie.

GARNETT ANDREWS, b. June 11, 1764; d. Oct. 5, 1807, Oglethorpe Co., Ga. Married Jane (called Ginny) Woodson on Jan. 1, 1787. She was b. Mar. 26, 1767.

Children:

1. William, b. 1787.
2. Susanna, b. 1789.
3. Betsey W., b. 1790.
4. Thomas, b. 1800.
5. Wyatt, b. Feb. 6, 1794; d. 1831; mar. 1816, Johanna Smith (dau. of Anthony Garnett Smith, and his wife Polly Allen).
6. Jacob Woodson.
7. Thomas Garnett, b. 1802.
8. Nancy.
9. Ave Pollard, b. 1807.

JOHN ANDREWS, b. in Va., May 4, 1762; d. Oglethorpe Co., Ga., May 2, 1816; REV. SOLDIER of Va. Married Mar. 17, 1789, Nancy Goode, in Va. She died after 1816.

Children:
1. Marcus, mar. Ann Connell.
2. Frances Garnett, mar. James Daniel.
3. John Garnett, mar. Mary Ann Polhill.
4. Garnett, mar. Annulet Ball.
5. Sarah Martha, mar. Dr. Isaac Bowen.
6. Elizabeth, d. y. (1800-1804).
7. Elizabeth, b. 1805; mar. Dr. Willis Green.
8. Emily, mar. Richard Jones.
9. James A.
10. Daniel Marshall, mar. Martha A. Wylie.

WILLIAM ANDREWS (son of DR. MARK ANDREW, REV. SOLDIER of Va., and his wife Avis Garnett), b. in Va., 1758; d. Oglethorpe Co., Ga., May 3, 1821. Allowed pension for his services as Sergeant in Capt. Mayo Carrington's Co., Va. Troops. Wounded at the Battle of Brandywine, 1777. Married Mary Gaines.
Child:
1. William, b. 1796; d. 1875; married Elizabeth —.

THOMAS ANSLEY, b. 1737; d. 1809, Warren Co., Ga. Served as private, Ga. Troops. Received bounty land for his services. Married 1760, Rebecca Harrison, widow, d. 1804.
Children:
1. Thomas, Jr. (1767-1837); mar. Henrietta Ragland.
2. Abel, mar. Lydia Morris.
3. Samuel, mar. 1809, Mary Tillman.
4. Miller.
5. William.
6. James.
7. Joseph.
8. Rebecca, mar. — Duckworth.
9. Nancy.
Step-son of Thomas Ansley:
1. Benjamin Harrison.

CHRISTOPHER ANTHONY, b. in Va., 1744; d. 1815, on a visit to Cincinnati, Ohio. Served as a REV. SOLDIER in Va., and drew land for his services in Wilkes Co., Ga. Married (1) Judith Moorman.
Children:
1. Mary, mar. David Terrell.
2. Joseph, mar. Rhoda Moorman.
3. Charles, mar. Elizabeth Harris.
4. Elizabeth, mar. William Ballard.
CHRISTOPHER ANTHONY married (2) Mary Jordan of Nansemond Co., Va. (dau. of Samuel and Mary (Bates) Jordan).
Children:
5. Christopher, mar. Annie H. Couch.

6. Samuel, mar. Mary Irwin.
7. Hannah, mar. (1) — Johnson; (2) John Davis.
8. Sarah, mar. Henry Davis.
9. Jordan.
10. Penelope.
11. Charlotte, mar. Eph Morgan.
12. Rachel, mar. Lot Pugh.

JAMES ANTHONY, b. 1747, Bedford Co., Va.; d. 1827, Wilkes Co., Ga. Served in Capt. Stubblefield's Co., Col. Parker's Reg. 5th Va. Married Ann (Nancy) Tate.

JOSEPH ANTHONY, b. Mar. 28, 1750 in Va.; d. 1810 in Wilkes Co., Ga. He served as a REV. SOLDIER of Va. and drew bounty land for his services in Wilkes Co., Ga. Married (1) Rhoda —.
Children:
1. Samuel P.
2. Thomas C.
3. Charles.
4. Judith.
JOSEPH ANTHONY mar. (2) Ann Elizabeth (called Betty) Clark (dau. of MICAJAH CLARK, REV. SOLDIER of Va. and his wife Judith Adams).
Children:
5. Mary, mar. Armistead Ellis Stokes.
6. Mark.
7. Anselin (1778-1868); m. (1) 1806, Sarah Menzies of N. C.; mar. (2) 1836, Catherine Blakely of Wilkes Co.
8. Joseph.
9. Micajah.
10. Ann, mar. — Early.

JOHN APPLING, JR., b. in Va.; d. in Richmond Co., Ga. Private, Ga. Troops, and granted land for his services. Member Constitutional Convention from Richmond Co. Married Rebecca Carter (dau. of LANGDON CARTER, REV. SOLDIER of Va.). Their son, Col. Daniel Appling was a Soldier of 1812.

JOHN APPLING, SR., REV. SOLDIER of Va. Married Martha. After his death, Martha Appling moved with her children to Richmond Co., Ga. (now Columbia Co.) and was given two tracts of land as the widow of a REV. SOLDIER in 1785. Made will Aug. 17, 1788.
Children:
1. JOHN, JR.
2. Daniel.
3. William.
4. Elizabeth.
5. Lucy.
6. Patty.

JEAN PIERRE ARNAND, b. 1751 in Marseilles, France; came to America and settled in Maryland. He died 1833, Savannah, Ga. Served as private in Capt. Williamson's Co. Md. line. Later served as privateer, was captured and confined on the "Jersey" prison ship. Married Elizabeth Leland (1760-1853).
Child:
1. Elizabeth Cecil Virginia (1801-1839), mar. 1820, John James Penfield Boisfeuillet (1703-1864).

JAMES F. ARNOLD, b. Halifax Co., Va., 1754; d. 1825, Monroe Co., Ga. Served as Major, N. C. Line. Married 1770, Bethany Bailey (1758-1850).
Children:
1. Elijah B., mar. Susan Ware.
2. Jesse.
3. Malina.
4. James.
5. Fielding.
6. Augustus.

JAMES ARNOLD, b. Augusta Co., Va., 1760; d. Wilkinson Co., Ga., 1823. Served as Corporal under Capt. John Gillison, Col. Stephens and Col. Russell, 6th and 10th Va. Regiment. Married Elizabeth Stroud (dau. of JOHN STROUD (1745-1813) served as private under Capt. Meriwether, 1st Va. Reg. and his wife Mary Margaret Dozier (1750-1812), dau. of WILLIAM DOZIER, REV. SOLDIER of Va. and his wife Elizabeth).

RICHARD ASBURY, b. Richmond Co., Va., 1761; d. Taliaferro Co., Ga., 1845 (son of HENRY ASBURY, REV. SOLDIER and Patriot of Va. and his (1) wife Emily Reade). Served as 2nd Lieut. under Major Redmond, Va. Troops. Married 1780, Elizabeth (called Betty) Thornton.

WILLIAM ASHE, b. in Penn.; d. Burke Co., Ga., 1831. Served in the Snow campaign; in 1777 under Capt. Bratton, Col. Neal, and Col. Lacey. Married 1783, Jane Fleming, d. 1854. She received a pension as his widow, 1834 for his services.
Children:
1. John, mar. Miss Newton; moved to Ala.
2. Alexander (1785-1848), mar. 1824, Elizabeth McCracken (dau. of WILLIAM McCRACKEN who served with N. C. Troops, and received bounty grant of land for his services 1784 in Franklin Co., Ga. and his wife Elizabeth McCord).
3. James.
4. Dobey.
5. William, Jr., mar. Cynthia Turk.
6. Robert Rutherford

7. Mary Hunter.
8. Janet.
9. Elizabeth.
10. Elijah.
11. Isabella.
12. Rachel.

ICA ATKINS (son of ICA ATKINS, REV. SOLDIER of Cumberland, N. C. Private N. C. Line and his wife Nancy Hutchins), b. Mar. 7, 1763; d. in Dodge Co., Ga., 1832; married Mary Gordon. (His grave as a REV. SOLDIER was marked by the Col. Wm. Few Chapter, D. A. R. of Eastman, Ga.)
Children:
1. Ann (1795-1885), mar. (1) William Martinleer; (2) John Miers; (3) Wm. Colbert.
2. Sarah.
3. Littleberry.
4. Ica.
5. Janet.
6. Mary.
7. Lillie.
8. Grace.
9. Richard Gordon.   10. Elizabeth.

JOHN ATKINSON, b. Northampton Co., Va.; d. 1808, Camden Co., Ga. Private Capt. Bentley's Co., Col. Thomas Marshall, 3rd Va. Reg. 1777. Married 1756, Elizabeth Gardner.

NATHAN ATKINSON, b. in S. C.; d. Greene Co., Ga. Served with S. C. Troops and received bounty land for his services in Ga. Married Betsey Whitehead. Moved to Greene Co., Ga.
Children:
1. Betsey.
2. Patience.
3. Rhoda.
4. Thomas.
5. Jane.
6. Lazarus, b. 1791; d. in Ala. Married July 13, 1813, Mary Ellen Lane (dau. of WILLIAM D. LANE, served with Ga. Troops; d. Putnam Co., Ga., before 1785. Grant made to William Lane's heirs (dec.) Feb. 15, 1785 on Certificate of service in 3d Ga. Continental Batt. Nathaniel Pearce, Lieut. and Adj.)

JOSEPH AVANT, b. 1720, Paris, France; d. 1798, Washington, Ga. Enlisted in Col. George Mathew's Va. Reg.; was at Germantown and Brandywine. Married Melinda Davis.

JOHN AVERY, b. in Va.; d. Columbia Co., Ga., 1847. (Had two sons Archer and Isaac Avery). Was given grant of land for his services. Married Mary Loggett.
Children:
1. John.
2. Martha, mar. — Wellborn.
3. Elizabeth, mar. — Smith.
4. Miller.
5. Herbert.
6. Archer.
7. Asa, mar. Sarah Jones.

DR. SAMUEL JACOB AXON, b. S. C., 1751; d. Liberty Co., Ga., 1827. Served as Surgeon 1st S. C. Reg. Married (1) Mary Ann Giradeau at "Midway" Church. Three daughters. She d. 1799. He mar. (2) Ann (Lambright) Dicks (or Dix) in 1806.
Child:
1. Saccharissa, mar. Moses Jones.

RICHARD AYCOCK, b. in Va., 1740; d. Wilkes Co., Ga., 1791. Served with Ga. Troops. Had grant of land for his services, Washington Co., Ga. Married (1) Mary —; (2) Rebecca Thurman (1741-1791).
Children:
1. Burwell.
2. Henry.
3. Joel.
4. Rebecca.
5. Richard, mar. Nancy Bradford.
6. Winefred.

WILLIAM AYCOCK, b. in Va.; d. Elbert Co., Ga., 1807. Served with Ga. Troops. Received grant of land in Wilkes Co., Ga., for his services. Married Patty Easter (dau. of James and Sarah Easter of Elbert Co., Ga.).
Children:
1. James.
2. Richard.
3. Melton.
4. Juda.
5. Tabitha.
6. Terrell.

DANIEL AYERS, b. 1763; d. 1827 in Ga. Drew land in Ga. for his services as a REV. SOLDIER. Married Rhoda Holton.
Children:
1. Joseph.
2. Obediah.
3. Mary

4. Priscilla.
5. John.
6. Rhoda.

MOSES AYERS, b. Snowden, Wales, 1747. Came to Va., then N. C.
Served at the Battle of King's Mt. and Yorktown. Lived in Franklin
(now Hart Co.) Co., where he died. Married many times. Last wife,
Abigail Payne.

JOHN BACHLOTT, b. St. Milo, France, 1760; d. June 6, 1833, Camden Co., Ga. Came with LaFayette to America. Was at the Battle of
Yorktown. Drew land in Camden Co., Ga. for his services. Married
1785, Mary Conrad in Va. Came to S. C., then Amelia Island, Fla.,
1799. Settled at St. Mary's, Ga., 1800.
Child:
    1. Joseph Bachlott, b. in Va., 1792; d. St. Mary's, Ga., 1822. Mar-
       ried Mary Frances Rudolph, b. 1805 (dau. of THOMAS RU-
       DOLPH, b. 1760; buried St. Mary's, Ga., a REV. SOLDIER, and
       his wife Elizabeth, who as his widow drew a Pension for his
       services.)

NOTE: The grave of John Bachlott has been marked by the Brunswick
Chapter D. A. R., Brunswick, Ga.)

JOHN BACON, b. in S. C., 1739; d. in Ga., 1786. Served as Capt. Co.
of Riflemen Liberty Co., Ga., 1777. Member Provincial Congress
from St. John's Parish, Ga., 1775. Married (1) Feb. 17, 1761, Ann
Andrew; (2) April 12, 1778, Sarah Bacon; (3) in Carolina, 1779, Elizabeth More. She mar. (2) William Kirkland.

THOMAS BACON, b. 1743 in S. C.; came to Ga., 1755; d. Liberty Co.,
Ga., Jan. 26, 1812. Served as 3d Lieut. under Col. John Bacon, 1776;
1st Lieut. Liberty Co. Riflemen. Received bounty land for his services
1784. Married (1) June 7, 1770 at Midway Church, Catherine Winn, d.
Jan. 4, 1778; mar. (2) June 1, 1778, Sarah Baker; mar. (3) 1779, Martha
Wheeler in Carolina.
Children by (1) wife:
    1. John.
    2. Thomas, mar. (1) Elizabeth Sumner; mar. (2) Sarah Holcombe.
    3. William.
Child by (2) wife:
    4. Sarah.
Children by (3) wife:
    5. Catherine.
    6. Joseph.
    7. Henry.
    8. Eliza Winn.

GEORGE BAGBY, b. 1751 in Va.; d. Jackson Co., Ga., 1807. Drew bounty land in Ga. for his services as REV. SOLDIER. Married Mariana (or Miriam).

Children:

1. An.
2. John.
3. Joseph.
4. Flumes.
5. Abner.
6. Dicey.
7. Sally.
8. Rachel.
9. Henry.
10. William.
11. George W.
12. Betty.
13. Jeffries.

JOHN DANIEL BAGWELL, b. N. C.; d. Gwinnett Co., Ga., buried seven miles from Lawrenceville, Ga., Primitive Baptist Church Cemetery. Served as REV. SOLDIER of N. C.

BEAL BAKER, b. Baltimore, Md., 1756; d. in Ga., 1842. Served as a REV. SOLDIER of Md. Married 1782, Sarah Brown, b. Burke Co., N. C., 1759; d. in Ga., 1850. They moved to Hall Co., Ga.

Children:

1. John, b. Oct. 15, 1784, mar. Amelia Brawner.
2. Polly, mar. Isaiah Pritchet.
3. James, mar. Mary Sewell.
4. Joshua (1792-1842), mar. 1814, Mary (called Polly) Parks (1797-1876) (dau. of HENRY PARKS, b. Albemarle Co., Va., 1758; d. in Ga., 1825 and his wife Martha Justice. He was a REV. SOLDIER and drew bounty land for his services in Franklin Co., Ga.).

COL. JOHN BAKER, b. Dorchester, Mass., 1722 (son of Benjamin Baker of Dorchester, Mass., who came to Midway (Liberty Co.) 1752). He d. June 3, 1792, Liberty Co., Ga. He was appointed member of the committee which met in Savannah, Ga., July 1774, to discuss the British Port Bill. Appointed Colonel and served in Continental Army. Member Provincial Congress of Ga. Married (1) Elizabeth Filbin; (2) Mary (Jones) Lapin (widow of CAPT. MATHIAS LAPIN, REV. SOLDIER of Ga. Line, who lived at Sunbury, Ga.).

Child by (1) wife:

1. Mary Ann Baker, mar. John J. Maxwell (son of CAPT. MAXWELL, REV. SOLDIER of Ga.)

Child by (2) wife:

2. Sarah Baker, mar. in Liberty Co., Ga., MICHAEL RUDOLPH, b. Elkton Co., Md.; d. at sea. Served as REV. SOLDIER; Capt. 1781 of Ga. Dragoons under Col. Henry Lee, Ga. Line.

   Child:

   1. Amelia Rebecca Rudolph (1788-1814), mar. John Francis William Courvoisier, Jr. (son of JOHN FRANCIS WILLIAM COURVOISIER, b. 1750 in Switzerland; d. 1811, Savannah, Ga. A REV. PATRIOT, a Signer of the Resolutions presented

16

by the City of Savannah about the condition of the Colonies in 1775. He mar. 1778, Mary Fox (1762-1816)
Child:
1. Mary Fox Courvoisier, b. 1810; d. 1850; mar. Robert Lundy (or Lunday) (1798-1860) (son of THEOPHILUS LUNDAY, b. in Va.; d. in Ga. Served as 2nd Lieut. Volunteer Co. of St. George's Parish, Ga. Received grant of land for his services in Effingham Co., Ga. He mar. 1790, Frances McLinn.).
3. Matilda Amanda Baker, mar. Thomas Huston Harden (son of WILLIAM HARDEN, REV. SOLDIER of S. C.)

ABRAHAM BALDWIN, b. in Guilford, Conn., Nov. 6, 1754; d. Mar. 4, 1807 in Washington, D. C., while serving in Congress as a Senator from Ga. He served as Chaplain in the Continental Army from Conn. Moved to Savannah, Ga., 1784; sent to Continental Congress, 1785. A member of the Congress, 1787, at the convention which framed the Constitution of the United States. He was the father (acknowledged in this manner) of the educational system of Ga. (See Life of Abraham Baldwin by Dr. Harry C. White, Prof. of Chemistry at the University of Georgia 1870-192).

AUGUSTUS BALDWIN (cousin of Abraham Baldwin of Ga.), b. Aug. 27, 1764, Goshen, Conn.; d. May 23, 1808, Savannah, Ga. Served as Chaplain REV. WAR. Married Rebecca Cooke, widow, 1799. She d. May 25, 1828, Augusta, Ga.
Children:
1. Louise, mar. Dr. Alexander Cunningham.
2. Augustus Collins, mar. Mary E. Allen.
3. William Henry.

DAVID BALDWIN, b. in N. C.; commanded a Co. at the Second Siege of Augusta, Ga., where he and his son, DAVID, JR., REV. SOLDIER, both died of fever, 1783. Married Sarah Owen.
Child:
2. WM. BALDWIN, b. 1746 in N. C.; d. Columbia Co., Ga., 1819. Served as Sergeant in Ga. Troops. Married Elizabeth Kimbrough (dau. of JOHN KIMBROUGH, REV. SOLDIER who served under Col. Elijah Clarke, 1775-1779, Morgan Co., Ga., and his wife Ann Le Grande.

DAVID BALDWIN, SR. and DAVID BALDWIN, JR. each drew 287. 5 acres of land as bounty grant for their services as REV. SOLDIERS in Washington Co., Ga.

EDWARD BALL, b. in S. C.; d. in Ga., 1779. Came to St. John's Parish, Ga., 1767. Member of Provincial Congress 1775 from St. John's Parish. Lieut. in Capt. John Bacon's Co. of Riflemen 1777.

Married 1773, Rebecca Baker.

JOHN BALL, b. near Fredericksburg, Va., about 1740. Moved to
Camden Dist., S.C. Died 1815, Warren Co., Ga. Served with Ga.
Troops, as private, Col. John Stewart's Reg. Married Miss Robinson.

ABNER BANKSTON, REV. SOLDIER. (Grave marked by the D.A.R.
in Ga., on Indian Springs Road to High Falls, Butts Co.

LAURENCE BANKSTON, b. in Va., 1748; d. Wilkes Co., Ga., 1844.
Served in Continental Army with Va., N.C., and Ga. Troops. Received
grant of land in Wilkes Co., Ga. for his services. Married Nancy Henderson, b. 1758 in Va.; d. Sept. 26, 1849, Wilkes Co., Ga. (dau. of JO-
SEPH HENDERSON, REV. SOLDIER of N.C., d. 1809 Wilkes Co., Ga.
and his wife Isabella Delphia Lea).
Children:
  1. Isabella Lea (1784-1874), mar. 1800, Isaiah Tucker Irvine
     (1783-1855) (son of CHRISTOPHER IRVINE, REV. SOLDIER
     of Va., and grandson of WILLIAM IRVINE, REV. SOLDIER of
     Va.).
  2. Priscilla, mar. William Matthews.
  3. Elizabeth, mar. Samuel G. Mozley (Ancestor of Miss Ruth
     Blair, State Historian of Ga., 1936).
  4. Martha, mar. Caleb Sappington.
  5. Delphia, mar. Jacob Shorter.
  6. Esther, mar. Isaac Whitaker.
  7. Hiram, mar. Susanna —.

MAJOR JOHN BARNARD (son of Col. John Barnard of the British
army who came about 1743 to Savannah, Ga., in command of a Regiment called the "Rangers", held commission until his death.), was
b. Nov. 12, 1750, Wilmington Island, Ga.; d. in Ga. Member Provincial
Congress, 1775. Assisted in raising the "Liberty Pole" in Savannah.
Commanded a Co. which attacked the crew of a British frigate, which
had landed on Wilmington Island. Was taken prisoner, exchanged, and
served until the end of the War. Married Lucy Turner (dau. of Lewis
and Jeston Turner of Savannah, Ga.),
Children:
  1. Timothy, b. 1775, mar. Amelia Guerard.
  2. Lucy W., mar. (1) Henry Charles Jones; (2) Charles O. Screven.
  3. Mary E.
  4. John W.
  5. James, mar. Catherine Guerard.
  6. Henrietta, mar. Stephen Williams.
  7. Georgia A., mar. Murdock Chisolm.

ABRAHAM BARNETT, b. 1751, Orange Co., N.C.; d. Greene Co.,
Ga., 1792. Served in Capt. Wm. Johnston's Co. 11th Va. Reg. and N.C.

Troops. Received bounty grant of land for his services. Married Mecklenburg Co., N. C., Mary Broomfield (1757-1818).
Children:
1. William, moved to Miss.
2. Martha, b. 1798; d. 1851, Henry Co., Ga.; mar. Dr. John S. Fall as (2) wife.
3. Mary, mar. — King.
4. Margaret (called Peggy).
5. Ann, mar. — Dale.
6. Jane, mar. (1) — Elliot; (2) — Broomfield.
7. Elizabeth, mar. — Hart.

JOEL BARNETT, b. 1762, Amherst Co., Va. Moved to Ga.; d. on a visit to Miss. (Son of NATHANIEL BARNETT, REV. SOLDIER of Va. and Ga.). Served as private Ga. Line; received bounty grant of land for his services in Washington Co., Ga. Married (1) Elizabeth Crawford; mar. (2) Mildred Meriwether.
Child by (1) wife:
1. Joel, Jr.
Children by (2) wife:
2. Susan, mar. (1) John Gresham; (2) John Gilmer.
3. Charles (1800-1890), mar. Eliza Williamson Gresham.
4. Frank, mar. Eliza Goolsby.
5. Emily, mar. (1) Craven Totten; (2) — Stewart.
6. Ann, mar. — Burke.
7. Rebecca, mar. Michael Johnson.
8. Nathaniel.
9. Daughter, mar. — Crawford.

JOHN BARNETT (son of NATHAN BARNETT, REV. SOLDIER of Va. and his wife Lucy Webb), b. in Va., 1762; d. Clark Co., Ga., Mar. 1814. Served as private Ga. Troops under Gen. Elijah Clarke and in S. C. Troops under Gen. Francis Marion. Received bounty grant of land. Married 1782, Columbia Co., Ga., Caroline Fleming Tindall (1762-1842) (dau. of WILLIAM TINDALL, REV. SOLDIER of Ga. and his wife Betsey Ann Booker).
Children:
1. Nathan (1783-1810), mar. Sarah Lumsden.
2. William, mar. Miss Blakeley; moved to Ky.
3. Lucy Greene (1791), mar. Elijah Brown.
4. John F., b. 1793; mar. Nancy Briscoe. Moved to Miss., then to Texas.
5. Mary Booker, mar. 1815, William Griffin, of Henry Co., Ga.
6. Sarah Caroline, mar. John Griffin (brother of William).
   Child:
   1. Gen. Thomas Griffin, mar. Sarah Colbert.

NATHAN BARNETT, b. New Kent Co., Va., 1729; d. Greene Co., Ga.,

1805. Served as REV. SOLDIER from Ga. in the Battle of Kettle Creek, Feb. 14, 1779 under Gen. Elijah Clarke. Was given land for his services. Married 1757 in Va., Lucy Webb, b. 1731. Came to Ga., 1768, settled on Little Kioka Creek, St. Paul's Parish.
Children:
1. NATHAN, JR., b. 1758, REV. SOLDIER.
2. MIAL, b. 1760, Va.; living Greene Co., Ga., 1814. REV. SOLDIER. Married Polly —.
3. JOHN, REV. SOLDIER.
4. CLAIBORNE, REV. SOLDIER. Land, Greene Co., Ga. Living 1806, Logan Co., Ky.
5. Leonard, living 1828, Greene Co., Ga.

NATHANIEL BARNETT, b. Amherst Co., Va., 1727; d. 1824, Wilkes Co., Ga. Served as private Ga. Troops. Was a prisoner of the British, confined at Augusta, Ga., when the Tories drove the Whigs into upper Ga. Married 1748, Susanna Crawford, b. 1728; d. before 1824.
Children:
1. Nelson, d. 1803.
2. David.
3. WILLIAM, mar. (1) Mary Meriwether; (2) Sally (Wyatt) Bibb. REV. SOLDIER.
4. JOEL, mar. (1) Elizabeth Crawford; (2) Mildred Meriwether. REV. SOLDIER.
5. Ann, mar. Joel Crawford.
6. Elizabeth, mar. — Spears.
7. Peter.

ROBERT BARNETT, b. 1754, Sumpter, S. C.; d. 1827, Wilkinson Co. Received land in Carroll Co., Ga. for his services. Married (1) 1778, Sarah Love (1755-1806).

SION BARNETT, REV. SOLDIER, was present at Battles of Stony Mt. and Cowpens; published the first proclamation connected with the Mecklenburg Declaration. Died 1854, age 82, at Jasper Co., Ga.

WILLIAM BARNETT, b. 1747 in N. C.; d. 1834, Wilkes Co., Ga. Commanded a troop of Horsemen of Mecklenburg Co., N. C., later served in S. C., under Gen. Sumpter. Received bounty land for his services, Wilkes Co., Ga. (He was son of JOHN BARNETT, b. in Ireland, 1717; d. N. C., 1804; REV. SOLDIER of N. C. and his wife Ann Spratt (1718-1801). He mar. 1772, Jean Jack (1750-1811), (dau. of PATRICK JACK, REV. PATRIOT and his wife Lillis McAdough (Adoo) of N. C.).
Children:
1. Samuel, mar. (1) —; (2) Elizabeth (Worsham) Welles, widow of Thomas Welles.
2. John, mar. Mary Jack.

3. William, mar. Nancy (or Mary) Ray.
4. Lilly.
5. Patrick, mar. Nancy Beall.

WILLIAM BARNETT, b. Ulster Province, Ireland, 1715; d. N. C., 1778. REV. SOLDIER of N. C. Married 1749, Mary Spratt (dau. of Thomas Spratt of N. C.)
Children:
1. WILLIAM, REV. SOLDIER.
2. John.
3. Thomas, Caswell Co., N. C.
4. Abraham.

WILLIAM BARNETT (son of Nathaniel Barnett and Susanna Crawford), b. Amherst Co., Va. Lived in Ga. Died in Ala., 1830. Served in Va. Troops; was given bounty land in Columbia Co., Ga. for his services. Married (1) Mary Meriwether (dau. of FRANCIS MERIWETHER, REV. SOLDIER of Va. and his wife Martha Jameson), b. 1766; d. 1805. He mar. (2) Sally (Wyatt) Bibb, widow William Bibb (no issue).
Children by (1) wife:
1. Thomas Meriwether, mar. Margaret Micon.
2. Martha, mar. Francis M. Gilmer.
3. Mary, b. 1797, mar. David Taliaferro (brother of Capt. BENJAMIN TALIAFERRO, REV. SOLDIER).
4. Nathaniel, b. 1793; mar. 1814, Polly Hudson (dau. of DAVID HUDSON and his wife Mary Cobb Booker. DAVID HUDSON was a REV. SOLDIER, placed on pension roll 1833 from Elbert Co., Ga. for service in Major Andrew Pickens S. C. Regiment).
5. Lucy, mar. George Mathews.
6. Frances, mar. Isaac Ross.
7. Elizabeth, mar. William Mathews.
8. Peter, mar. Miss Saffold.

WILLIAM BARNETT, b. in Va.; d. Greene Co., Ga. Served with Va. Troops, received bounty land in Ga. for his services. Married Mary Hewey.
Child:
1. John Barnett, b. 1784 in Greene Co., Ga.; mar. Elizabeth Butrill (dau. of WILLIAM BUTRILL, REV. SOLDIER of Va. and Ga., and his wife Martha). They moved to Heard Co., Ga., 1827.

JAMES BARR, b. Feb. 7, 1762, Guilford Co., N. C. Served in Capt. Daniel Gillespie's Co. of Minute men, in Col. John Paceley's N. C. Reg. Allowed pension claim 1832 (S. 31537) while a resident of Jackson Co., Ga. His father was living 1781, Pittsylvania Co., Va.

JOHN BARRON (brother of William) was a Captain at the Siege of Augusta; wounded and captured by the British; beheaded by the Tories.

SAMUEL BARRON, b. Ga., Mar. 16, 1768; d. 1826, Washington Co. (now Jones), Ga. Served as a private, N. C. Regiment; received bounty grant of land Washington Co., Ga. for his services. Married Joanna Braswell.
Children:

1. Rebecca.
2. Nancy.
3. Sally.
4. Willis.
5. Jonathan.
6. Wiley.
7. Greene.
8. Abner.
9. Benjamin, mar. Sarah Barron.
10. William.
11. Thomas.
12. James.

WILLIAM BARRON, b. about 1740 in Ireland; married there 1760, Prudence Davis. She died 1815. They removed with their family to America and settled 1766 in Warren Co., Ga. He served as Captain in REV. WAR and was wounded at the Siege of Augusta, Ga. He fell into the hands of the Tories and they lured the Indians to behead him. The Tories put his head as a trophy of war on a pole, placed erect in the center of Augusta, where it remained three weeks, until the Whigs regained control of the town and took it down.
Children:

1. John, b. about 1763 in Ireland.
2. WILLIAM, JR., b. in Ga. 1767; mar. Martha Farr. He was a REV. SOLDIER.
3. SAMUEL BARRON, mar. Joanna Braswell. He was also a REV. SOLDIER of Ga.
4. (Mary) Elizabeth, mar. Jacob Garrard.

JAMES BARROW, b. Edgecomb Co., N. C., Jan. 31, 1757; d. in Ga., Jan. 20, 1828. Served as private N. C. Line under Col. Jethro Summer. Served at Valley Forge, Brandywine, Savannah, and Charleston. Received bounty grant of land on Bark Camp Creek, Burke Co., Ga., 1784. Married 3 times; (1) 1785, Anne; (2) 1802, Nancy Hardwick; (3) 1814, Patience Crenshaw, b. May 15, 1779; d. 1817 (dau. of Jesse Crenshaw and his wife Precious Cain).
Children:

1. David Crenshaw, b. July 26, 1815; d. 1879; mar. (1) 1838, Sarah Eliza Pope.
2. Precious Patience, mar. Wm. McKinley.

NOTE: David Crenshaw Barrow, Jr. (1852-1929) was Chancellor of the State University, Athens, Ga.; the only living man for whom a county in the State of Ga. was named, Barrow Co., 1915.

MOSES BARROW, b. 1755 in N. C.; d. in Ga., 1801. Served as private in Capt. Bacot's Co., 10th Reg. N. C. Line. Married 1790, Mildred Powell (1770-1812).

WILLOUGHBY BARTON, b. 1750 in Scotland; d. 1800, Wilkes Co.

...eived bounty grant of land for services as private under Gen.
...ke. Married Rebecca McCoy.

JOHN HICKS BASS, b. 1763, Brunswick Co., Va.; d. 1850, Putnam
Co., Ga. Served as private, Va. Troops. Received bounty land in Ga.
Married 1791, Rebecca Pattillo (1774-1835).

REDDICK BASS, d. Warren Co., Ga., 1828. Received bounty grant
of land in Warren Co., Ga., 287.5 acres for his services. Married
Obedience Persons.
Children:
    1. Buckner.
    2. Elizabeth, mar. — McTyre.
    3. Nancy.
    4. Larkin.
    5. Perkins Persons.

JESSE BATTLE, b. Hertford Co., N. C., July 8, 1738; d. Hancock Co.,
Ga., Aug. 25, 1805. A Patriot; furnished supplies for the American
troops. Came to Ga., 1787. Married 1756, Susanna Faucette (or For-
sett), b. in France 1738; d. Hancock Co., Ga., May 8, 1819.
Children:
    1. John.
    2. William Summer, mar. Sarah Whitehead.
    3. Benjamin, mar. Christian Wyatt.
    4. Priscilla.
    5. Bathsheba.
    6. Lewis.
    7. Jesse
    8. Susan Faucette, mar. (1) John Ragan; (2) — Fairchild.
    9. Mary (1774-1842), mar. 1793, William Rabun.
        Child: Governor of Ga., 1819.
   10. Lazarus, mar. (1) Miss Cook; (2) Margaret (Porter) Fannins.
   11. Isaac, mar. Martha (Patsey) Rabun.
   12. Reuben Taylor (1784-1805), mar. Bethia Alexander.

WILLIAM SUMNER BATTLE, b. Nansemonde Co., Va., Oct. 26,
1761; d. Taliaferro Co., Ga., 1828. Came to Greene (now Hancock) Co.,
Ga. and served with Ga. Troops. Received grant of land for his ser-
vices. Married Edgecombe Co., N. C., Sarah Whitehead, b. N. C.,
Mar. 9, 1766 (dau. of Lazarus Whitehead).
Children:
    1. Elizabeth (1784-1803).
    2. Joseph John (1786-1858), mar. Rhoda Henrietta Whitehead.
    3. Jesse Brown, mar. Martha Battle Rabun.
    4. Sarah Whitehead, d. in Texas, 1811; mar. Christopher Anthony
       Carter.
    5. John William, mar. (1) Elizabeth Atkinson; (2) Miss Asbury;

(3) Sidney Lane Tuggle.
6. Mary Hale, mar. Herman Mercer.
7. Serena A. Hagan, mar. William Stroud.
8. Lazarus Whitehead, mar. Nancy Chevers.
9. Susan Faucetta, mar. Col. William Henry Long.
10. Selina C., mar. (1) Albert G. Bunkley; (2) Richard Felton.
11. Bennett W., d. y.
12. Betsey, d. y.

ANDREW BAXTER, JR. (son of ANDREW BAXTER (1725-1781)
REV. SOLDIER of S. C., Lieut. and Major, killed by the Tories, and
his wife Frances), was born in S. C., Dec. 21, 1750; d. Wilkes Co. (now
Greene), Ga., 1816. Served in Continental Army. Received bounty
grant of land in Ga. for his services. Married 1784, Elizabeth Harris
(1764-1844) (dau. of Charles and Elizabeth (Thompson)(Baker) Harris.
Children:
1. Thomas W. (1781-1844), mar. Mary Wiley (1798-1869) (dau. of
   Moses Wiley and his wife Ann Jack, dau. of JOHN JACK, REV.
   SOLDIER and his wife Ann Barnett).
2. Eli H., mar. Julia Richardson.
3. Andrew.
4. John.
5. Cynthia.
6. Eliza T.
7. James.
8. Richard.
9. Mary, mar. Wm. Green Springer.

THADDEUS BEALL, b. 1745, Frederick Co., Md.; d. 1815, Hancock
Co., Ga. Private in Capt. Edward Burgess' Co.; 1st Lieut., Capt.,
Major on Gen. Resin Beall's Staff. Flying Camp., Md. Troops. Married
1767, Amelia Jane Beall.
Children:
1. Frederick, mar. Martha Beall.
2. Jeremiah, mar. Elizabeth Catten.
3. Josiah, mar. Miss Colton.
4. Thaddeus, Jr.
5. Samuel.
6. Elias, mar. Mary Neal.
7. Walton, mar. William Reese.
8. Amelia, mar. William Dent.
9. Anna, mar. Thomas Dent.
10. Major, mar. Mr. Catron.

JOHN BECK, b. Albemarle Co., Va., 1756; d. Buckersville, Ga., 1821.
Served as Ensign 9th Va. Reg. Married 1784, Sarah Wansley (1766-
1860) (dau. of JOHN WANSLEY, b. 1738, Louisa Co., Va.; d. 1842, Ruck-
ersville, Ga.; married 1762, Amelia Barber, b. 1744, Va. Served as

private Va. Line; received a pension for his services).

SAMUEL BECKHAM, b. Nov. 24, 1760; d. near Milledgeville, Ga., Nov. 2, 1825. His record as a REV. SOLDIER found on his tombstone, erected by the State of Ga. (grave marked by D. A. R.) Married Feb. 18, 1790, Elizabeth Houghton (1769-1805).
Children:
1. Nancy, mar. — Mitchell.
2. Mary B.
3. Elizabeth H.
4. Erasmus G.
5. Susan, mar. — Burch.
6. Albert G.

ROBERT BELCHER, b. 1758, S. C.; d. 1848, Twiggs Co., Ga. Enlisted 1776 in Capt. James Foster's Co., S. C. Served in Battles of Brandywine and Monmouth. Received pension for three years service Va. Line. Married Nancy Hopkins.

FRANCIS BELL, b. Lynchburg, Va., 1750; d. Jackson Co., Ga., 1838. Served in N. C. Troops, in the Battle of Guilford Court House. Married 1770, Esther Montgomery (1754-1834).
Children: (known)
1. Sarah, mar. Curtiss Greene.
2. Mary, mar. John Bell.
3. Joseph Scott, mar. Rachel Phinizy.

JAMES BELL, b. in N. C., Oct. 4, 1747; d. Elbert Co., Ga., Oct. 23, 1809. Married 1776, Olive Moseley, b. in N. C., Jan. 1, 1760; d. Elbert Co., Ga., Oct. 22, 1822. Served in N. C. Continental Line. Moved to Ga., 1788. He also served as J. P., Elbert Co., 1792. (Record for Society Daughters of the War of 1812).
Children:
1. Joseph, mar. Mary —.
2. James (1789-1848), mar. Susan Key (dau. of WILLIAM BIBB KEY, REV. SOLDIER, b. in Va., 1759; d. in Ga., 1836, and his wife Mourning Clark).
3. William, mar. Elizabeth Thornton.
4. Thomas, mar. Polly (Hubbard) Dye.
5. David, mar. Elizabeth Snellings.
6. Polly.
7. Elizabeth, mar. William Moore.
8. Nancy.
9. Polly, mar. — Moore.
10. Martha, mar. Harmon Lovingood.

JOSEPH BELL, b. in N. C.; d. 1818, Elbert Co., Ga. Served in N. C. Line. Received bounty grant of land for his services in Elbert Co.

(formerly Wilkes), Ga., 1784. In 1825 his widow drew land in Land Lottery as widow of REV. SOLDIER. Married in N. C., Elizabeth Moseley, b. in N. C., 1765.
Children:
1. Anna, mar. 1807, Tapley Bullard (son of THOMAS BULLARD, REV. SOLDIER of Ga., and his wife Ann).
2. Thomas.
3. Mary.
4. Joseph, Jr.
5. Rebecca, mar. John Gunter.
6. Eleanor, mar. William W. Downer.
7. Elizabeth, mar. Burrell Dye.
8. Milly L., mar. Peter B. Butler.

SAMUEL BELLAH, b. 1752, Rowan Co., N. C.; d. 1833, Morgan Co., Ga. Served as private N. C. Line. Married in N. C., July 18, 1776, Jane Morgan.
Children:
1. James.
2. Robert.
3. Tempee.
4. Rachel.
5. Morgan, mar. Elvey Price.
6. Peggy.
7. Walter.
8. Steele.

JOHN BENNEFIELD, b. in N. C., 1731; d. 1779, Wilkes Co., Ga. REV. PATRIOT. Member of Committee of Correspondence at Savannah, Ga. Married Martha —.
Child:
1. Mary Ann Bennefield, mar. 1772, Dempsey Hinton (1745-1779).

NATHAN BENTON, b. 1764, Orange Co., N. C.; d. 1826, Columbia Co., Ga. Served as private N. C. Line. Married 1796, Susanna Crawford (1776-1804).
Children:
1. Nelson Moore, mar. (1) Lucy Jones; (2) Martha Ann Wooding.
2. Parmelia Frances, mar. James Luckie.
3. Thomas H.
4. George Constantine.
5. Eugenius.

MAJOR GEN. JOHN BERRIEN, b. 1759, Princeton, N. J.; d. 1815, Savannah, Ga. Came to Ga., 1775. Served as private, Lieut., Capt., Major 1782. Served at Valley Forge and Monmouth. Was Brigadier Gen., Northern Army, Sol. of 1812. Married (1) Margaret McPherson (1763-1785) (dau. of JOHN McPHERSON, REV. SOLDIER, an officer in the Provincial Navy). He mar. (2) Williamenia Sarah Eliza Moore.
Child by (1) wife:
1. John McPherson, b. Rockhill, N. J., 1781; d. in Ga., 1856. Married (1) Eliza Richardson Anciaux, d. 1828 (dau. of MAJOR

NICHOLAS ANCIAUX, REV. SOLDIER who came to America with LaFayette and was under command of Count Duponte, was at the surrender of Cornwallis at Yorktown. Lived and died in Ga.). He mar. (2) 1833, Eliza G. Hunter.
Children by (2) wife:
2. Richard.
3. Thomas.
4. Sarah.
5. Eliza.
6. Weems.
7. Ruth Lowndes, mar. Dr. James Whitehead.
8. Julia, mar. John Whitehead.

JOHN BERRY, b. 1762; d. 1817, Effingham Co., Ga. Served as private from Effingham Co., Ga. Line. Married Mary Reisser.
Children:
1. John.
2. Bananza.
3. Obediah.
4. Naomi.
5. Salome, mar. 1811, Emanuel Rahn (son of JONATHAN RAHN, REV. SOLDIER of Effingham Co., Ga.).

PAUL BEVILLE, b. in Va., 1755; d. 1836 in Ga. Served as private Ga. Line. Received bounty land for his services. Married 1780, Sarah Scruggs (dau. of RICHARD SCRUGGS, REV. SOLDIER of Ga.).
Children:
1. Paul, Jr. (1788-1819), mar. 1810, Mary Pearce (1793-1816) (dau. of STEPHEN PEARCE, REV. SOLDIER of Ga., and wife Mary Mills).
2. James, mar. Delia Dell (dau. of PHILIP DELL, REV. SOLDIER of Ga.)
3. Frances, mar. — Garnett.

ROBERT BEVILLE, b. 1752, Henrico Co., Va.; d. 1838, Screven Co., Ga. Served as private Ga. Line. Received bounty of land in Ga. for his services. Married Sarah Williams Hudson.
Children:
1. Robert.
2. Granville (1785-1850), mar. Sarah Ann Bonnell (1800-1854) (granddau. of ANTHONY BONNELL, REV. SOLDIER, served as Lieut. Ga. Line, and wife Mary. He d. 1805, Screven Co., Ga.)
3. Claiborne (1781-1852), mar. 1802, Susannah Daly (1784-1844) (dau. of BENJAMIN DALY (D'Oilly), REV. SOLDIER of Ga., and his wife Susanna Garnett, sister of THOMAS GARNETT, REV. SOLDIER).

WILLIAM BIBB, b. Hanover Co., Va., 1735; d. Wilkes Co., Ga., 1796.

(now Elbert Co.). Served in the Va. Continental Army. Member Va. Convention 1774. Committee of Safety of Va. 1775. Married (1) in Va., Mrs. Booker (nee Clark); (2) Sallie Wyatt, b. 1750, Charlotte Co., Va.; d. 1826, Autauga Co., Ala. She mar. (2) William Barnett.
Children by (1) wife:

1. Elizabeth, mar. (1) Capt. John Scott; (2) — Clarke.
2. Lucy.
3. Hannah, mar. (1) Peyton Wyatt; (2) Major John Tull.
4. Sallie Booker, mar. (1) Marable Walker; (2) Archelaus Jarrett.

Children by (2) wife:

5. William Wyatt, mar. Mary Freeman (dau. of HOLMAN FREEMAN, REV. SOLDIER of Ga.) (He was appointed first Governor of the Territory of Alabama, then elected first Governor of the State of Alabama.)
6. Thomas, mar. Parmelia W. Thompson. He was also Governor of Alabama.
7. Peyton, mar. Martha Cobb.
8. John Dandridge, mar. Mary Xenia Oliver.
9. Joseph Wyatt, mar. (1) Louise DuBose; (2) Martha Daucy.
10. Benajah Smith, mar. Sophia Lucy Ann Gilmer.
11. Delia, mar. Alex Pope.
12. Martha, mar. Fleming Freeman (son of HOLMAN FREEMAN, REV. SOLDIER of Ga.).
13. Lucy.

WILLIAM BIRD, b. in Penn.; d. in Warren Co., Ga., 1813. Served 1775 in Col. William Thompson's Batt. of Riflemen, the first troops south of New England to join Gen. Washington's troops at Cambridge. Came to Warren Co., Ga., 1794. Married (1) Miss Wood of Penn.; (2) Catherine Dalton of Va.
Children:

1. William.
2. Wilson.
3. John.
4. Fitzgerald.
5. Ariana.
6. Eliza, mar. 1808, James Lesley.
7. Emily, mar. as (3) wife, Rev. Robert M. Cunningham.
8. Caroline, mar. Benjamin Cudsworth Yancey.
9. Louisa, mar. Capt. Robert Cunningham, a Sol. of 1812.
   Child:
   1. Ann Pamela Cunningham, founder and first Regent of the Mount Vernon Ladies Memorial Association.
10. Catherine.

WILLIAMSON BIRD, SR., b. in Va., 1728; d. Wilkes Co., Ga., 1802. Married 1750, Phoebe Price, b. 1732. Served as Captain of the Militia of Prince Edward Co., Va., in 1779, in place of Charles Venable, re-

signed. He came with his family to Wilkes Co., Ga., 1788, and received bounty grant of land for his services as a REV. SOLDIER.
Children:
1. Price.
2. Philémon.
3. Betsey (or Elizabeth), mar. — Woodall.
4. Fanny, mar. — Price.
5. Tabitha.
6. Caty.
7. Dice.
8. Williamson.
9. John.

WILLIAM BIVINS, b. April 2, 1738; buried Dec. 11, 1828, in Bivens Estate, Wilkinson Co., Ga. Married Polly Melson Hall, b. Sept. 17, 1770; d. Nov. 28, 1838, buried Marion Co., Ga. (8 miles from Buena Vista, Ga.) He was a REV. SOLDIER.
Child:
1. Martin Luther, b. July 18, 1816; d. 1878. Married Winifred Powell (1818-1841) (dau. of William Powell, Jr. (1778-1852), and his wife Nancy Edwards (1780-1857), mar. 1802).

DAVID BLACKSHEAR, b. Jones Co., N. C., 1764; d. 1837, Laurens Co., Ga. Served as private N. C. Militia at the Battle of Moore's Creek, 1776. Moved to Ga. 1790, and was a Ga. Soldier of the War of 1812. Married Frances Hamilton. (Grave marked by D. A. R.)
Children:
1. James H., mar. Caroline L. Floyd (dau. of Col. John Floyd, a Soldier of War of 1812, and granddau. of CHARLES FLOYD, REV. SOLDIER of Va. and Ga.).
2. Mary.
3. William T.
4. Edward Jefferson.
5. Ann Elizabeth.
6. Eliza Ann.
7. David, Jr.
8. Everard.
9. Joseph.
10. Floyd.
11. Elijah.
12. John Duke.

JAMES BLAIR, b. in Va., 1761; d. Habersham Co., Ga., 1839. Served as private under Col. McDowell at King's Mountain, N. C. Line. Married Elizabeth Powell.

PHILIP BLASENGAME, b. in S. C.; d. 1825, Greene Co., Ga. Served as a REV. SOLDIER. Married Frances —. Left in his will to his son James, two draws of land received for his services as REV. SOLDIER. Other children mentioned in will were:
2. Benjamin.
3. Polly, mar. Absolom Awtrey.
4. Nancy, mar. — Awtrey.

5. Elizabeth, mar. — Bradshaw.

MILLER BLEDSOE, b. 1761, in Va.; d. 1845, Oglethorpe Co., Ga. Enlisted Henry Co., Va. at 15 years of age, under Capt. Ambrose Dudley, 2nd Va. Reg. He was severely wounded at the capture of "The Hook". Was at Battle of Camden. In charge of Co. ordered to Henry Co., Va. and was at the surrender of Yorktown. Granted land 100 acres in Ky. as private Va. Line. Married Jean Bowling (Bolling). Children mentioned in will:

1. Polly, mar. — Swanson.
2. Sidney, mar. — Derby.
3. Jane (1791-1861), mar. William Landrum.
4. Unie, mar. Whitfield Landrum.
5. Nancy, mar. Lemuel Edwards.
6. Betsey, mar. — Elder.
7. Moses.
8. Peachy.
9. Miller, Jr.

SAMUEL BLOODWORTH (brother of Thomas), drew land as a REV. SOLDIER in Washington Co., Ga.

THOMAS BLOODWORTH, b. 1755, Wilmington Dist., N. C.; d. 1836, Morgan Co., Ga. Appointed Major Continental Army N. C.; Member N. C. Assembly 1781. Married Francis Proctor (1774-1868) in 1802. Children:

1. Hiram.
2. Solomon (1806-1890), mar. (1) Lucy Thornton.
3. David Madison.
4. Thomas S. M., mar. Caroline Maxey.
5. Fanny, mar. — Brand.
6. Lymise Proctor, mar. (1) James McNab; (2) Joe Hale.
7. Mary Ann, mar. — Yarborough.
8. Simeon Peter, mar. Elizabeth Crawford.

MATTHEW BOLTON, b. in Va. about 1760; d. 1824, Columbia Co., Ga. Served in the Va. Line. His widow drew land in Warren Co., Ga. in 1827 for his services. Married Mar. 26, 1788, Mary Chapman. Children:

1. Martha, mar. James Mappin.
2. Mary, mar. Willis Roberts.
3. Robert, mar. Lydia —.
4. Thomas, mar. Martha Smithson.
5. Samuel, mar. Jane Phelps.
6. Elizabeth, mar. (1) H. T. Wade; (2) Joseph Elliott.
7. Nancy P., mar. Robert Markes.
8. John T.
9. Millie (1812-1813).

10. Elisha P., mar. Elijah Burbridge.

ANTHONY BONNELL, b. about 1752; d. 1805, Screven Co., Ga.
Served as Lieut., Ga. Line. Married Mary —.
Children:
1. William, mar. 1795, Rebecca Magee.
2. Daniel.
3. Elizabeth.

HENRY BONNER, b. in Va. 1724; d. Warren Co., Ga., 1822. Served
as Captain, Va. Continental Army. Married Ann Cate.
Children: (known)
1. Robert.
2. Henry.
3. Richard.

JOHN BOOTH, b. in N. C.; d. 1804, Hancock Co., Ga. Served as
private, N. C. Line.

ISAAC BORING, b. in N. C., Mar. 8, 1762. Served as private, N. C.
Troops. Given land for his services. Died 1831, Wilkes (now Jackson)
Co., Ga. Married 1780, Phoebe Browning (dau. of JOHN BROWNING,
REV. SOLDIER of N. C.) d. 1851 in Jackson Co., Ga.
Children:
1. David.
2. John.
3. Elizabeth, b. 1784; mar. Wm. Lyle.
4. Susannah.
5. Sarah (or Senah), b. 1789; mar. James Wafer.
6. Robert.
7. Rebecca.
8. Isaac, Jr.
9. Phoebe.

CHESLEY BOSTICK, b. in Va.; d. Richmond Co., Ga., 1801. Served
as Capt., 1st Ga. Reg., Jan. 1776. Was taken prisoner at Savannah, Ga.
Living in Augusta, Ga., 1786. Married Jane Gervais.
Children:
1. John, mar. Betsey Bostic.
2. Chesley, Jr., mar. (1) Susanna Cobb; (2) Ann Matilda Hargrove.
3. Elizabeth, mar. Thomas P. Carnes.
4. Sarah Maria, mar. — Shellman.
5. Mary Ann, mar. — Thompson.
6. Henrietta, mar. John Guyton.

LITTLEBERRY BOSTICK, SR., b. Goochland Co., Va., July 10, 1751;
d. in Ga., Sept. 10, 1823. Served as private in Col. James McNeill's
Ga. Regiment. Received bounty land grant for his services. Married

July 27, 1773 (1) Rebeckah Beal (1752-1791); mar. (2) Nov. 6, 1792, Mary Birdsong (1773-1820).

Children by (1) wife:

1. Littleberry, Jr., mar. (1) 1812, Margaret Rudd Hancock; (2) 1820, Mary Ann Martha Walker.
2. Jacob, mar. Rebeckah Beal.
3. Betsey, mar. John Bostick (son of Chesley).
4. Nathaniel, mar. Sarah J. B. Brown.
5. Jeremiah.

Children by (2) wife:

6. Mary, mar. Jesse Roberson.
7. Susanna Addison, mar. (1) Nicholas Connelly; (2) Marcus Flournoy.
8. Matilda Golden, mar. (1) Jacob Beal; (2) Don Frederick Bostick.
9. Caroline Verlinda, mar. — Todd.

NATHANIEL BOSTICK (called Nathan), b. Jan. 26, 1746 in Va.; d. in Jefferson Co., Ga., Feb. 14, 1818. Served as private in Co. under Col. James McNeill, Ga. Regiment. Married Martha Gwinn, b. 1750.
Children:

1. Elizabeth (1770-1835); mar. 1798, WILLIAM WALKER, REV. SOLDIER, b. in Va., 1762; d. Jefferson Co., Ga., 1818. He served as private in Col. John Twiggs Regiment in Ga.
2. Hillery.
3. John Rufus.
4. Nathan.
5. Fillmon.
6. Polly.
7. Homer.

JOHN BOSTON, b. in N. C., 1737; d. Effingham Co., Ga., May 8, 1810. Served as Major in Onslow Co., N. C. troops. Married Rebecca Randal (1740-1790).
Child (only child living to maturity):

1. James Boston, b. 1767 in N. C.; d. 1837, Effingham Co., Ga. A Soldier of the War of 1812. Married (1) 1794, Elizabeth Dell Briggs; (2) 1814, Sarah Kettles, widow. He had 11 children by (1) wife and 2 children by (2) wife.

EDMUND BOTSFORD, b. Woburn, Bedfordshire, England, 1745. Arrived Charleston, S. C., 1766. Came to Ga. At this time, June 1771, there was only one ordained Baptist minister in Ga., viz. DANIEL MARSHALL, REV. SOLDIER). But in 1771, he preached his first sermon in Ga. and was ordained in Charleston, S. C., Mar. 14, 1773. He lived in Burke Co., Ga., but travelled over Ga. He served as Chaplain in the American Army, in S. C., N. C., and Va. Married (1) 1773, Susanna Nun at Augusta Ga. She was born in Ireland. He died in Georgetown, S. C., Dec. 25, 1819.

OLIVER BOWEN, b. in Rhode Island, 1741; came to Savannah, Ga.; d. Augusta, Ga., July 11, 1800. Member of Council of Safety; Captain of Ga. Continental Troops; Commodore of the Navy. Placed in command of the first vessel, "The Dauntless", commissioned during the Revolution. His vessel officered by Commodore Bowen and Major Joseph Habersham, made the first capture of the Rev. War, a British Schooner, a part of whose cargo was 14,000# of gun-powder. He married Mar. 21, 1798, Ann Dorsey, widow, of Liberty Co., Ga.

BIUS (or Bias) BOYKIN, d. in Ga., 1812. Served in N. C. Line and received bounty grant of land for his services. Married Sarah Peeples, b. in Va.; d. in Ga. after 1812.
Children:
1. Thomas (1785-1829), a Soldier of the War of 1812, mar. Elizabeth Fennell (dau. of NICHOLAS FENNELL, a REV. SOLDIER of N. C., and his wife Margaret Robinson). He received bounty grant of land in Ga.
2. John
3. Solomon.
4. Nancy.
5. Jeany.

BURWELL BOYKIN, b. 1752 in Va.; d. 1817 in S. C. He mar. (1) Elizabeth Whitaker; (2) Mary Whitaker. He had 17 children. (Brother of Major Francis Boykin).

NOTE: In 1785 MAJOR FRANCIS BOYKIN, CAPT. JAMES CANTEY of Camden, S. C., and ENSIGN HUDSON WHITAKER of N. C., all REV. SOLDIERS, came to Baldwin Co., Ga. CAPT. SAMUEL BOYKIN and CAPT. BURWELL BOYKIN, brothers of MAJOR BOYKIN, remained in S. C.

MAJOR FRANCIS BOYKIN, b. in S. C., 1745; d. Baldwin Co., Ga., 1821. Served as Major in the "Mounted Rangers" of S. C. (Grave marked by the Nancy Hart Chapter, Milledgeville, Ga.) Married Catherine Whitaker.
Children:
1. Samuel (1786-1848), mar. (1) Sarah Maxwell; (2) Narcissa Cooper.
2. James, mar. (1) Miss Owens; (2) Miss Rutherford.
3. Elizabeth, mar. William Rutherford.

JOHN BRADDOCK, of McIntosh Co.; d. at Darien, Ga., 1797. He commanded a Co. of Ga. Troops. Married Lucy Ann Cook.

NATHANIEL BRADFORD, 287.5 acres of land in Franklin Co., Ga., for services as REV. SOLDIER.

JOHN BRADLEY, b. 1755, St. George's Parish, Ga.; d. 1837, Oglethorpe Co., Ga. In 1780 he served as Captain of a Galley from St. George's Parish. Married Mary Noil (or Neil).
Children: (known)
1. John A., mar. Martha Jameson Meriwether.

2. Mary Ardis, mar. 1820, Isham Weaver.

WILLIAM SCOTT BRANCH, b. Chesterfield Co., Va., 1760; d. 1838, Clarke Co., Ga. Served in the Va. Line. Drew land in 1827 Ga. Lottery for his services as a REV. SOLDIER. Married Dicey Jane Calicutt.
Children:
1. John, mar. Sarah Broughton.
2. James, mar. Leah —.
3. Arnistead, mar. Julia.
4. Marcellus, mar. Malcom Dawson.
5. Sarah, mar. William Walker.
6. Emily, mar. Malcom O'Neill.
7. Judith
   and others.

SPENCER BRANHAM, b. in Goochland Co., Va.; d. 1803, Wilkes Co., Ga. Served as private, Va. Line. Married 1785, Elizabeth Richardson.

JACOB BRASWELL, b. Mar. 7, 1763, Edgecombe Co., N. C.; d. July 25, 1839 in Ga. Served with N. C. Troops. Married July 9, 1789, Nancy Cotton, b. Dec. 1772.
Children:
1. Elizabeth.
2. Micajah, d. y.
3. Jacob, Jr.
4. Priscilla Macon.
5. Sallie.
6. Willie.
7. Peggy.
8. Tempsey.
9. Alexander Cotton.
10. Maria.
11. Micajah, b. 1811.
12. Rodia.

JACOB BRASELTON, of N. C., b. in Wales, June 27, 1749; d. 1825, Jackson Co., Ga. Served in Va., N. C., and Ga. Continental Troops. Granted bounty land in Ga. 1790. Married 1772, Hannah Green, b. April 8, 1757.
Children:
1. John (1774-1850), mar. Elizabeth Brown.
2. Elizabeth, b. 1775.
3. Henry, b. 1777.
4. William, b. 1779.
5. Hannah, b. 1781.
6. Mary (or Mart), b. 1783.
7. Jacob, Jr., b. 1785.
8. Green, b. 1786.
9. Reuben, b. 1788.
10. David, b. 1790.
11. Job, b. 1792; mar. Sallie Dowdy.
12. Rebecca, b. 1795.
13. Amos, b. 1797.
14. Sarah, b. 1799.

CHARLES BRAWNER, REV. SOLDIER of Ga., received certificate from Lieut. Col. James Jackson of Ga., July 30, 1784, "That he served in the Ga. State Legion Infantry from the reduction of Augusta to the evacuation of the State by the British", and received 287. 5 acres of land in Washington Co., Ga.

ADAM FOWLER BRISBANE, b. in Charleston, S.C., 1754; d. in Ga., 1799. Delegate to the First Provincial Congress held in Savannah, Ga. 1775. Married 1775, Mary Cumber, d. 1820.

ALLEN BROOKS, JOAB BROOKS, JOHN H. BROOKS, JAMES BROOKS, and MICAJAH BROOKS. These five brothers, all REV. SOLDIERS, were born near Fayetteville, N.C. (sons of John Brooks of Va., who moved to N.C., 1736). They moved to Ga., and all received land grants in Ga. for their services in REV. WAR. One brother ISAAC BROOKS, REV. SOLDIER, remained in N.C. (Grave of MICAJAH BROOKS, REV. SOLDIER, marked by Ga. D.A.R. in Polk Co., five miles west of Rockmart, Ga.)

JOHN H. BROOKS, b. in N.C.; d. 1811, Jones Co., Ga. (Grave marked by D.A.R.) Married Jane Terrell of N.C.
Children:
1. Philip H., Soldier of the War of 1812.
2. Charles E., Soldier of the War of 1812.
3. Samuel, Soldier of the War of 1812.
4. William T., Soldier of the War of 1812.
5. John, mar. 1816, Alice Waldrop of Jones Co., Ga.
6. Isham.
7. Sarah, mar. Richard C. Shirley.

BENJAMIN BROWN, REV. SOLDIER, served with N.C. Regiment. (Grave marked by Atlanta Chapter D.A.R.) He is buried Brown's Cemetery, 11 miles from Fayetteville, Ga.

EZEKIEL BROWN, REV. SOLDIER, b. 1769; d. 1863, Harris Co., Ga. Married Elizabeth Merritt.

JOHN BROWN, b. in Scotland, 1729; d. 1786, Burke Co., Ga. Served as private, Burke Co., Ga. Militia, under Col. Elijah Clarke. Married 1754, Rebecca Yates (1732-1795).

JOHN BROWN, b. Kingston, R.I., 1764; d. St. Mary's, Ga., 1826, and was a REV. SOLDIER. He lies buried in the ancient Burial Ground of St. Mary's, Camden Co., Ga.

NATHAN BROWNSON, b. Woodbury, Conn., May 14, 1742. Removed to St. John's Parish, 1764. Member Provincial Congress; delegate from Ga. to Continental Congress. Surgeon, Ga. Brigade, Continental Army. Elected Governor of Ga., 1781. Died Oct. 18, 1796, Liberty Co., Ga. Married Elizabeth, d. 1775.

BLAKE BRYAN (son of WILLIAM BRYAN, REV. SOLDIER of N.C.) was b. Johnston Co., N.C.; d. Twiggs Co., Ga. Served as private in Capt. Bryan Whitfield's Co., N.C. Militia. Married Elizabeth Blackshear, 1791.

JONATHAN BRYAN, b. 1708 in S. C.; d. 1788 at "Brampton", near Savannah, Ga. Member Provincial Congress and Committee of Safety, Ga. Together with his son JAMES BRYAN, REV. SOLDIER, he was captured by the British, 1779, and was a prisoner in New York two years. Married Oct. 13, 1737, Mary Williamson (1722-1781).
Children:
1. HUGH, a REV. SOLDIER.
2. Jonathan, d. y.
3. Joseph.
4. WILLIAM, REV. SOLDIER.
5. JAMES, REV. SOLDIER, mar. Elizabeth Langley.
6. Mary, mar. JOHN MOREL (1733-1776), REV. SOLDIER.
7. Josiah (1746-1774), mar. 1770, Elizabeth Pendarvis. After his death, his widow married (2) LIEUT. JOHN SCREVEN, REV. SOLDIER, and they had 13 children.
8. John.
9. Elizabeth.
10. Hannah, mar. JOHN HOUSTON, a REV. SOLDIER and Governor of Ga. (son of Sir Patrick Houston of Ga.)
11. Ann.
12. Sarah Jenet.

BENJAMIN BRYANT, b. N. C., 1760; d. in Jackson Co., Ga., 1796. Served as private Ga. troops. Married 1782, Sarah Whitfield.
Children:
1. William Lane, mar. Eliza H. Trout.
2. Hugh.
3. John, mar. Elizabeth Crockett.
4. Martha, mar. John Keith.

BENJAMIN BUCHANAN, b. Newberry Dist., S. C., 1754; d. 1821, Jasper Co., Ga. Served as private and corporal S. C. Continental Line. Married Mary Wood.

WILLIAM BUGG, REV. SOLDIER, b. 1757; d. Jan. 29, 1804. Buried in the Bugg cemetery near Augusta, Ga.

SHERWOOD BUGG, b. 1720, New Kent Co., Va.; d. 1782. Commanded a Co. in Col. James Jackson's Ga. Regiment, was captured and confined prison ship. His home at Beech Island, S. C., was raided by the British and Tories. Married ELIZABETH HOPSON, a REV. PATRIOT.
Children:
1. Obedience (1753-1841), mar. 1790, William Newsome (1750-1851).
2. Sherwood, Jr., mar. Sarah Ann Jones.
3. Mary Elizabeth, mar. John Lamar.

THOMAS BULLARD, of Va. and Ga., b. in Va.; d. 1823, Elbert Co., Ga. Drew land for his services in Wilkes Co., Ga. In 1825, his widow drew land as widow of REV. SOLDIER. Married Ann —, d. 1827. Children: (mentioned in will)
1. Elizabeth, mar. Aug. 22, 1811, William Dye.
2. Temperance, mar. John Woodly.
3. Thomas P., mar. Eliz P. Gunter.
4. Sarah, mar. — Murphy.
5. Delilah, mar. — Cooks.
6. Tapley, mar. Ann Bell.
7. Nancy, mar. — Butler.
8. Allen.

ARCHIBALD BULLOCH, b. in Charleston, S. C., 1731; d. in Ga., Feb. 1777. Buried in the Colonial Cemetery, Savannah, Ga. Was President of the first Provincial Congress assembled in Tondee's Tavern, Savannah, Ga., 1775. Delegate to Continental Congress 1775-1776. He was the leader of the party who burned every house on Tybee Island to prevent its use by the British Seamen from the Men-at-War anchored in the Roads, and first read the Declaration of Independence to the townspeople of Savannah. Was the President of the new Republic of Ga. from 1776 to 1777. Was Commander-in-Chief of the Army in Ga. and headed the famous "Liberty Boys" of Ga. He married Oct. 9, 1764, at "Argyll", Ga., Mary (called Polly) DeVeaux (1748-1818) (dau. of COL. JAMES DE VEAUX, REV. SOLDIER of Ga., in command of 1st Ga. Regiment of Militia 1775, and his wife Ann Fairchild). Children:
1. James, mar. Anne Irvine.
2. Archibald Stobo, mar. 1793, Sarah Glen.
3. Jane, mar. Benjamin Maxwell (son of Wm. Maxwell).
4. William Bellinger, mar. (1) 1798, Harriet De Veaux (dau. of Jacob De Veaux and his wife Elizabeth Barnwell); mar. (2) Mary Young (dau. of Benjamin Young and his wife Martha Allston and his wife Esther Marion, sister of GEN. FRANCIS MARION of S. C., REV. SOLDIER).

JAMES BULLOCH (son of Archibald Bulloch), b. in Ga., 1765; d. Feb. 9, 1806, Savannah, Ga. He was a REV. SOLDIER of Ga., and Capt. of Va. Garrison Troops 1778-1780, under Col. George Mister. Hon. member Ga. State Society of the Order of the Cincinnati. Married April 13, 1786, Anne Irvine (dau. of Dr. John Irvine and his wife Ann Elizabeth Baillie).
Children:
1. John Irvine, mar. Charlotte Glenn.
2. James Stephens, mar. (1) Esther Amerinthia Elliott; (2) Martha (Stewart) Elliott.
3. Jane, mar. 1808 in Liberty Co., Ga., John Dunwoody (1786-1856) (son of JAMES DUNWOODY, b. Chester Co., Penn., 1741;

In front of Tondee's Tavern, Savannah, Ga., June 5, 1775, was erected the famous LIBERTY POLE, which became the rallying center of Savannah; and from the porch, Archibald Bulloch, then President of the Council of Safety, read the Declaration of Independence to the assembled populace, after which 13 guns were fired from the old Battery on Bay Street.

Peter Tondee, owner of this famous Tavern, was a loyal Patriot.

During the latter part of Feb. 1777, the President of Georgia died and Button Gwinnett was elected President and Commander-in-Chief.

* * *

In a beautiful spot in the heart of Liberty Co., Ga., the Congress of the United States reared a Memorial to the joint memory of GEN. JAMES SCREVEN and GEN. DANIEL STEWART, REV. SOLDIERS of Ga. (Gen. Daniel Stewart was the great-grandfather of President Theodore Roosevelt and the great-great-grandfather of Eleanor (Roosevelt) Roosevelt, the wife of the President of the United States, Franklin Delano Roosevelt).

Gen. James Screven was wounded and later died, Nov. 28, 1778, at the home of John Elliot, Sr., whither he had been taken after being wounded.

This Monument stands in the Old Midway Cemetery, next to the Old Midway Church, at the edge of the old Stage Road from Savannah to Darien. Upon the altars erected in this historic church were kindled the fires of Georgia's resistance to the dominion of England, and as a rebuke for her primacy in the cause of country, this Church and Parish sustained the full measure of royal vengeance. At Sunbury, near this place, was fought one of the most stubbornly contested engagements of the Revolution.

"The old Church stands now (1938) like a sentinel in its isolated grandeur, at the intersection of two Colonial roads with a prospect down an avenue of ancient oaks, beneath which the Red coats marched more than one hundred and fifty years ago, and under which the heavy tramp of the Union Army in the War between the States, awoke the echoes of the quiet woods many years later. The most historic highway in Georgia.

The present Church was built in 1792 upon the ruins of the edifice burned by the British.

The people of Midway, known as the Dorchester settlement, but called Midway, by reason of its equal distance from two of the principal rivers, came originally from Dorchester, S. C., to which point they had emigrated from Dorchester, Mass.

* * *

Archibald Bulloch, Noble Wimberly Jones, John Houston, and George Walton were the "Famous Quartette of Libery" in Georgia.

d. Liberty Co., Ga., 1807, REV. SOLDIER, and his wife Esther
Dean Splatt.
(N. S. D. A. R. 94587)

JAMES BULLOCH, b. in Scotland, 1701; came to S. C., 1729; d. 1780,
Savannah, Ga. He was J. P., Colleton Dist., S. C. 1735-1737. Received
a Royal Grant of land in Ga. 1765. Was a Member of the Patriotic
Provincial Congress of 1775 for the Sea Island Dist. of Ga., and received permission to raise a company of Continental Soldiers. He
married (1) Jean Stobo (dau. of Archibald Stobo from Scotland to S. C.
1700 and his wife Elizabeth Park); mar. (2) Mrs. Ann Ferguson, widow;
mar. (3) Mrs. Ann (Cuthbert) Graham; mar. (4) Mary Jones (dau. of
Hon. Noble Jones and Miss Wimberly.
Among the children by (1) wife were:
1. ARCHIBALD BULLOCH, mar. Mary De Veaux.
2. Jean Bulloch, mar. Josiah Perry.
3. Christina Bulloch, mar. Hon. Henry Yonge.

JAMES STEPHENS BULLOCH, b. in Ga., d. suddenly in the "Old
Presbyterian Church", Roswell, Ga. Married (1) Dec. 31, 1817, Esther
Arnarinthia Elliott, b. 1797 (dau. of John Elliott and his (1) wife Esther
Dunwoody); mar. (2) Martha (Stewart) Elliott, widow of the above John
Elliott as (2) wife, and dau. of GEN. DANIEL STEWART, REV. SOL-
DIER of Ga. (see Stewart family) and his wife Susanna Oswald.
Child by (1) wife:
1. James D. Bulloch.
Children by (2) wife:
2. Charles Irvine, d. y.
3. (Lieut.) Irvine Stephens, mar. Ella Sears.
4. Martha (see below).
5. Anna, mar. James K. Gracie.

MARTHA BULLOCH (sometimes called Mitty), b. Hartford, Conn.,
July 8, 1834; d. Feb. 12, 1884. She married at Roswell, Ga., Dec. 22,
1853, Theodore Roosevelt, b. 1831 in New York City, d. 1878. They
lived in New York City. (The old Bulloch mansion is still standing
[1934] in Roswell, Ga.)
Children:
1. Theodore Roosevelt, Lieut.-Col. of the "Rough Riders" during
the Spanish-American War; President of the United States of
America. Married (1) Alice H. Lee; (2) Edith Kermit Caron.
2. Elliott Roosevelt, mar. Anna R. Hall.
Child:
1. Ann Eleanor Roosevelt, mar. 1905, her cousin, Franklin
Delano Roosevelt, b. in Hyde Park, N. Y., Jan. 30, 1882.
(1937) President of the United States of America.
3. Anna Roosevelt, mar. Commodore W. S. Cowles.
4. Corinne Roosevelt, mar. Douglas Robinson, Jr.

HAWKINS BULLOCK, b. in N. C.; d. Oglethorpe Co., Ga. (Wilkes), Nov. 1, 1833. Served under Capt. Twitty, Gen. Nathaniel Greene. Received bounty land in Wilkes Co., Ga., for his services. Married Mar. 12, 1789, Frances Roy Gordon (dau. of CAPT. ALEXANDER GORDON who received bounty land in Wilkes Co., Ga. for his services as a REV. SOLDIER).
Children:
1. John Gordon (1790-1835).
2. Mary Wyatt, b. 1791; mar. Richard A. Sims.
3. Alexander Gordon, b. 1797; mar. Milly Sorrells.
4. Nathaniel H., b. 1798; mar. Setty Colbert.
5. William Gordon, b. 1802; mar. Elenor Sorrells.
6. Richard Henley, b. 1810; mar. (1) Mary H. R. Griffeth; mar. (2) Malinda Thompson.
7. Frances Roy, b. 1806; mar. Hiram Hampton.
8. Hawkins Sherman, b. 1812.
9. Louise Nance.

NOTE: His sister Susanna Bulloch mar. George Gordon.

HAWKINS BULLOCK (son of Nathaniel Bullock and his wife Mary Hawkins), was b. in Ga. Moved to Ga. during the REV. WAR and served as a REV. SOLDIER in Ga., where he died.

DANIEL BULLOCK, b. in S. C., Oct. 25, 1762; d. in Columbia Co., Ga., June 1834. Enlisted Edgefield Dist., S. C. Served as private in Capt. Tutt's and Capt. Maxwell's Companies, under Col. Hammond. Served under Gen. Pickens and Gen. Greene. Received Pension File W. 8403. Married Columbia Co., Ga., Jane Finquefield.
Children: (known)
1. Zacheriah, b. 1790; mar. Frances Edrington.
2. John.
3. Daniel, Jr.
4. Lucy L.
5. David.

NATHANIEL BULLOCK, REV. SOLDIER of N. C. Drew land for his services Wilkes Co., Ga., where he died. Married Mary Hawkins.

CHARLES BURCH and EDWARD BURCH came to Ga., and settled on the Waters of Big Spirit Creek. Their names appear on the payroll of the Burke Co., Ga. Rangers, commanded by Col. Patrick Carr of Jefferson Co., Ga., 1782.
Children of Charles Burch:
1. Charles, Jr.
2. Joseph E.
3. Blanton.
4. Kilt of Richmond Co., Ga.

JOHN BURFORD of Wilkes Co., Ga., and wife Phoebe. He drew
287.5 acres of land for his services as a REV. SOLDIER in Greene
Co., Ga.

WILLIAM BURGAMY, b. in France, 1739; d. 1819, Ga. Served as
private, Ga. Line. Married, 1759, Susan Hawkins.

JOHN BURKHALTER, b. 1760, Edgefield Dist., S. C.; d. in Ga., 1861.
Served as private Ga. Troops at Kettle Creek. Married 1798, Sarah
Hardin Loyless. Buried near Buena Vista. (Grave marked by Ga.
D. A. R. The grave of his brother, JOSHUA BURKHALTER, REV.
SOLDIER, also marked by D. A. R.)

MICHAEL BURKHALTER, b. in Germany, 1725; d. Jones Co., Ga.,
1828. Served as private Ga. Troops, under Col. Elijah Clarke, at Battle
of Kettle Creek and at Siege of Augusta. Was living in Wilkes Co.
(now Warren), Ga. Married MARTHA NEWSOME, a REV. PATRIOT,
who nursed the wounded soldiers.
Children:
    1. JOHN BURKHALTER, mar. Sarah —. He was a REV. SOLDIER
       at 13 years of age. (Grave marked by the Lanahassee Chapter
       D. A. R., Buena Vista, Ga.).
    2. Michael, Jr.
    3. Joshua.   6. Isaac.
    4. Jacob.   7. Mary.
    5. Jeremiah.   8. Barbara.

HENRY BURNLEY, b. Bedford Co., Va., 1756; d. Columbia Co., Ga.,
Jan. 1835. He enlisted 1776, Bedford Co., Va. Served two years under
Capt. Henry Terrell, Capt. William Jones, Col. Daniel Morgan. Then
Ensign of Volunteers, Oct. 28, 1782. Commissioned Lieut. in Militia,
Campbell Co., Va. Was at the Battles of Guilford Court House, Chest-
nut Hill, and others. Married (1) 1782 in Va., Lucy (Barksdale) Daven-
port (widow of JOHN DAVENPORT of Va., REV. SOLDIER killed at
Battle of Guilford Court House. Married (2) Widow Todd.
Children by (1) wife:
    1. Richmond, b. 1789; mar. Sally Veazey.
    2. Sarah, mar. Hiram Hubert.
    3. Lucy Barksdale (1799-1864), mar. J. Turner Dickson (1790-
       1864).
    4. Elizabeth, mar. Spencer Seals.
    5. Ann, mar. Archibald Seals.
    and others.

ISRAEL BURNLEY, b. in Va., 1725; d. in Wilkes Co., Ga., 1792.
(Will recorded Mar. 15, 1793). Married in Va., Ann (Hannah) Overton
(1727-after 1793). He was a REV. PATRIOT, furnished supplies to the
Continental Army in Campbell Co., Va. Was granted bounty lands in

Ga. for his services.
Children:
1. Susan, mar. John Barksdale.
2. Daughter, mar. John Colbert.
3. Daughter, mar. George Smith.
4. HENRY (1756-1835), mar. Lucy (Barksdale) Davenport. He served as a REV. SOLDIER of Va. Received bounty land in Ga.
5. Stephen G., mar. Partheny Garrett, 1810 in Warrenton, Ga.

JOHN BURCH, b. 1750 in Va.; d. 1818, Hancock Co., Ga. Served in Henry Co., Va. on muster roll of Capt. Jones Tarrant's Co. and Col. Abraham Penn's Regiment. Married in Va., Sarah Phillips (1753-1840).
Children:
1. Gerard, b. 1782, in Va.; mar. (1) Susan Simms (dau. of ROBERT SIMMS, a REV. SOLDIER and his wife SARAH DICKINSON, a REV. PATRIOT, for whom the Sarah Dickinson Chapter D. A. R. of Newman, Ga., is named). He mar. (2) Elizabeth Beckham.
2. John, mar. (1) Miss Sampson; (2) Obedience Dutiful (Bugg) Cobb.
3. William P.
4. Richard C., mar. 1822, Martha Matilda Jernigan.
5. Jane, mar. Richard L. Watson.
6. Elizabeth, mar. Arthur Fort.
7. Seleta, mar. Needham Jernigan.
8. Morton Newman, mar. Mary (Ballard) Figg.

MOODY BURT, from Edgefield Dist., S. C., received 287.5 acres of land in Greene Co., Ga., for his services as REV. SOLDIER.

THOMAS BURTON, b. in Va.; d. 1828, Elbert Co., Ga. Served as private under Col. Elijah Clarke. Married Nancy Nunnellee.

HEZEKIAH BUSSEY and Amey, his wife, sold to JONATHAN RAGAN, REV. SOLDIER of Wilkes Co., Ga., Jan. 30, 1788, 287.5 acres of land granted to said Hezekiah Bussey for his services as a REV. SOLDIER. Land on Oconee River, Washington Co., Ga., 1785.

EDMUND BUTLER, b. 1755; d. 1802, Hancock Co., Ga. Private under Col. Elijah Clarke, Ga. Troops. Received bounty land for his services. Married Fanny Garrett.

EDWARD BUTLER, b. Hanover Co., Va., 1748; d. in Ga., 1809. Served as private, Va. Continental Line. Married 1770, Elizabeth Wingfield (1752-1823). They came to Wilkes Co., Ga., 1706.
Children:
1. John W., mar. Polly Wingfield.
2. Zacheriah (1786-1837), mar. 1810, Massie Terrell.
3. David (1788-1822), mar. Frances W. Shackelford.

4. Elizabeth, mar. Thomas Wingfield.
5. Kitty, mar. Richard Terrell.
6. Frances, mar. Joel Terrell.
7. Nancy, mar. Osbourne Stone.
8. Lucy, mar. William Terrell.

PATRICK BUTLER, b. Mar. 1, 1760, Hanover Co., Va.; d. 1838, Elbert Co., Ga. Enlisted from Mecklenburg Co., Va. Served as private under Capt. James Anderson, Col. Nelson's Va. Reg. Received pension for services in 1833. Married Rebecca —.
Children:
1. John (1780-1830), mar. 1806, Elizabeth Hubbard.

WILLIAM BUTTRILL, b. in Va., 1763; d. Butts Co., Ga., 1858. Served under Gen. Nathaniel Greene in Ga. Married Mary Williams of Va. Lived in Jasper Co., Ga.
Children:
1. Thomas, mar. Luranie Bonner.
2. William, mar. Mary Fold.
3. Elizabeth, mar. — Barnett.
4. Nancy, mar. Dr. Jesse George.
5. Mary, mar. — Ford.
6. Burwell, mar. Marion Elizabeth Moseley.
7. Asa, mar. Lucile Manley.
8. Brittain, mar. (1) Louise Hudson; (2) Emmaline McCord.
9. John, mar. Anne Allston.
10. Jesse.

SAMUEL BUXTON, b. in Va.; d. in Ga. On muster roll of militia belonging to the upper counties of Ga.; served under Gen. Wayne at Ebenezer 1782. Married Nancy Plummer.
Child:
1. William Buxton, b. 1791, Burke Co., Ga.; married Rebecca Heath (dau. of JORDAN HEATH, b. in S. C.; d. Burke Co., Ga., a REV. SOLDIER, wounded at the Siege of Charleston, and his wife Christian Wimberly).

GEORGE CABANISS, b. in Va.; d. in Baldwin Co., Ga., 1815 (son of NATHAN CABANISS, REV. SOLDIER of Va.) Served as a REV. SOLDIER. Married Palatia Harrison (dau. of Henry Harrison of Berkeley Co., Va.).
Children:
1. Henry.
2. Elijah.
3. H. B.
4. Mathew.
5. George.
6. Eldridge Guerry.
7. Mary.
8. Sandall.
9. Rebecca.
10. Palatia.
11. Dau., mar. Elisha Greer.

JOHN CALDER (Caulder), b. in S.C., 1762; d. McIntosh Co., Ga.,
Jan. 24, 1845. Received pension for his services as a REV. SOLDIER
1832. Served as private Ga. Militia, commanded by Gen. Elijah Clarke;
was at the Siege of Augusta. Served as a Soldier in S.C. (Light Horse)
under Capt. Harvie, Col. Samuel Hammond. Was wounded at Battle of
Eutaw Springs. Joined Col. Hammond's Reg. at Saluda. Marched in
Indian Expedition at Battle of Little Terrapin under Gen. Pickens.
Served under Captains Jesse and William Thompson and was discharged
at Perkins Mill, S.C. (Record certified to by Allen B. Powell, of
McIntosh Co., Ga., Nov. 21, 1833). He mar. (1) Dec. 24, 1787, Phoebe
Haughton (or Horton) in Ga., d. McIntosh Co., Ga., May 17, 1803; mar.
(2) Mar. 15, 1804, Winwood F. Rickey, d. Feb. 10, 1854.
Children by (1) wife:
1. Sarah, b. Oct. 4, 1788.
2. William Horton Hazzard.
3. Mary, b. Nov. 9, 1790; mar. Allen Beverly Powell.
4. Ann, b. Mar. 8, 1792.
5. Esther, b. Mar. 1, 1794.
6. Henrietta, b. Feb. 3, 1796.
7. Maria, b. July 1, 1798.
8. Alexander H., b. July 6, 1801.
9. John, b. 1803.
Children by (2) wife:
10. John Morrison, b. Mar. 28, 1807; d. 1834.
11. James Rickey, b. Oct. 22, 1808; d. 1837.
12. Catherine A., b. Oct. 21, 1810.
13. Robert Patrick, b. Nov. 23, 1813; d. 1818.
14. William McKay, b. Jan. 10, 1816; d. 1839.
15. Margery, b. Mar. 6, 1818.
16. Hugh P., b. April 20, 1820; d. 1822.
17. Allen Powell, b. June 25, 1822; d. 1824.
18. A. Seraphina, b. Dec. 8, 1824; d. 1824.
19. George W., b. May 27, 1827.
20. Eugene M., b. Sept. 9, 1830.
(The grave of JOHN CALDER, REV. SOLDIER has been marked
through the Atlanta Chapter, D.A.R. by his descendants, Mrs. DeLos
L. Hill and Mrs. Thomas C. Mell, Atlanta, Ga. They also marked the
grave of ALLEN BEVERLY POWELL of McIntosh Co., Ga., a Soldier
of 1812).

JOHN CALLAWAY, b. Bedford Co., Va., 1750; d. Wilkes Co., Ga.,
1842. Served as Major, Bedford Co. Militia, Va. Received bounty land
for his services in Ga. Married 1770, Bethany Arnold (1752-1842).
Children:
1. John, Jr.
2. Joseph.
3. Jacob.
4. Isaac, mar. Polly Barnett

5. Pheribee, mar. REUBEN STROZIER, REV. SOLDIER.
6. Mary, mar. — Thrash.
7. Nancy, mar. Daniel Carrington.
8. Addah.
9. Bethany, mar. Joseph Talbot.
10. Enoch (1792-1859), mar. 1811, Martha Reeves.
11. Job (1780-1819), mar. Tabitha Lawrence.
    3 other children.

JAMES CAMERON, b. 1761; d. in Ga., 1840. Served as REV. SOL-
DIER. Received land in Cherokee Land Lottery 1827 for his services
while living in Jasper Co. Married Sarah Brown.
Children:
1. David (1796-1849), mar. Mary Lyle.
2. Thomas, mar. Nancy Stephens.
3. James Hawthorne (1800-1850), mar. Emma Castleberry.
4. Flora, mar. — Lorrance.
5. Benjamin H., mar. Mrs. Eliza Gilmer.
6. Janie, mar. James Lloyd.
7. Susie, mar. Benjamin Wilson.
8. William.
9. Sarah, mar. James Wilson.

BENJAMIN CAMP, b. in Va., 1757; d. in Jackson Co., Ga., 1832.
Served as private in Capt. Nathaniel's Welch Co., Col. Wm. Brent, 2nd
Va. Reg. Married 1776, Elizabeth Dykes.
Child:
1. Joseph Camp (1779-1854), mar. 1799, Elizabeth Camp (dau. of
   THOMAS CAMP, JR., b. in Va.; d. in S. C., private 2nd Va. Reg.,
   and his wife Susan Wagner; and granddau. of THOMAS CAMP,
   SR., b. in Va., 1717; d. in N. C., 1798, a REV. SOLDIER and
   PATRIOT and his wife Winifred Starling. They had 5 sons who
   fought at the Battle of King's Mt. One son, JOHN CAMP (son
   of Thomas Camp, Sr.) b. Brunswick Co., Va.; d. 1818, Jackson
   Co., Ga. Served as private Va. Troops. Married Mary Tarpley.)

SAMUEL CAMP (son of ICHABOD CAMP, b. 1726, Milford, Conn.;
d. 1786 in Illinois, a REV. SOLDIER of Conn., and his wife Content
Ward), was b. Durham, Conn., May 14, 1752; d. Warren Co., Ga., Aug.
18, 1827. Quartermaster in Col. Gabriel Penn's Va. Reg. Albermarle
Barracks, 1779. Also served Quartermaster Va. Troops. Married
Amherst Co., Va., Mary Banks, 1776.
Children:
1. Madden.
2. Cecilius.
3. Chander, mar. Mary Harwell.
4. Sarah, mar. James Ledbetter.
5. Nancy, mar. — Williams.

6. Elizabeth, mar. John Smith of Warren Co., Ga.
7. Mary, mar. Sims Kelly; moved to Ala.
8. Telemachus, d. Evansville, Ill.
9. Hyppupile (called Lucy), mar. — Johnson.
10. Gerard, mar. Martha Lacey.
11. Claudely, mar. 1806, Ann Harry.

DAVID CAMPBELL, b. 1750 in Va.; d. 1812 in Tenn. Served in Va. under Gen. Nathaniel Greene of R. I. and Ga. Married 1780, Elizabeth Outlaw (dau. of ALEXANDER OUTLAW, b. 1738 in N. C.; d. 1826 in Tenn. Served as private N. C. Reg. under Col. William Campbell at King's Mt., and his wife Penelope Smith).
Children:
1. Alexander.
2. Penelope.
3. Polly.
4. Betsey.
5. Mary.
6. Thomas J., mar. 1817, Sarah Bearden
7. Victor.
8. Moreen.
9. Caroline.
10. Letitia.
11. Margaret
12. Harriet.

WILLIAM CANDLER, b. in Ireland 1735; d. Richmond Co., Ga., 1787. Served as Colonel of a Reg. known as the "Regiment of Refugees of Richmond Co., Ga." Served at Siege of Augusta, King's Mt., and Siege of Savannah. Married Elizabeth Anthony (dau. of JOSEPH ANTHONY, REV. SOLDIER of Va. and Ga., and his wife Elizabeth Clark). She married (2) Cornelius Dysart.
Children:
1. Mary, mar. MAJOR IGNATIUS FEW, b. in Md. 1748 (a brother of WILLIAM and BENJAMIN FEW, all three REV. SOLDIERS of Ga.)
2. HENRY, REV. SOLDIER, mar. Miss Oliver.
3. JOSEPH, REV. SOLDIER.
4. WILLIAM, a REV. SOLDIER, mar. Miss Guthrie.
5. JOHN, a REV. SOLDIER.
6. Charles, d. y.
7. Amelia.
8. Falby.
9. Elizabeth, mar. John A. Devereux.
10. Mark Anthony, mar. (1) —; (2) Lucy White.
11. Daniel, b. Columbia Co., Ga., 1779; d. there 1816. Married 1799, Sarah Slaughter (dau. of SAMUEL SLAUGHTER of Va. and Ga., a REV. SOLDIER. A brother of REUBEN SLAUGHTER,

also a REV. SOLDIER of Baldwin Co., Ga.)

NOTE: Field Officers of the "Regiment of Refugees" Richmond Co., Ga. at the organization 1780. COL. WILLIAM CANDLER, LIEUT.-COL. DAVID ROBESON, MAJOR JOHN SHIELDS (killed in battle), ADJ. JOHN McCARTHY, and REV. LOVELESS SAVAGE, Chaplain. Some of the Line Officers were: CAPT. ROBERT SPURLOCK, CAPT. EZEKIEL OFFUT, CAPT. ABRAHAM AYERS, CAPT. JOHN SHACK-ELFORD, CAPT. JAMES STALLINGS, LIEUT. EDMUND MARTIN. This was the only Ga. Regiment distinguished as "Refugees".

JAMES CANTEY, b. Camden Dist., S. C., 1755; d. near Milledgeville, Ga., Oct. 9, 1817. Served as Lieut. and Captain under Col. William Thompson's S. C. Rangers. Married in S. C., Martha Whitaker (1765-1806).
Children:
  1. John (1786) mar. Emma Susanna Richardson.
  2. Zacheriah.
  3. Mary, mar. William Whitaker (son of HUDSON WHITAKER, REV. SOLDIER).
  4. Sarah, mar. Henry Crowell; moved to Columbus, Ga.
  5. James, mar. Camilla F. Richardson, a Soldier of 1812.

NOTE: See "Our Children's Ancestry" by Sarah Cantey (Whitaker) Allen (Mrs. H. D.) of Milledgeville, Ga. Regent Nancy Hart Chapter, D. A. R.

DUDLEY CAREY, b. in Va.; d. in 1808, Clarke Co., Ga. Served as Lieut., Gloucester Co., Va. Militia. Married Lucy Tabb.

JOHN CARGYLE, b. in Va.; d. Greene Co., Ga. Served as private under Capt. Porterfield, Col. Daniel Morgan, Va. Continental Line. Married 1746, Catherine Reneau (1726-1774).

MRS. ELIZA (MAJORS) CARLTON, Real Daughter U. S. D. A. R. of Senoia, Ga., member Joseph Habersham Chapter, Atlanta, Ga. (The dau. of SAMUEL D. MAJORS, served as private, age 16, in the Halifax Co., Va. troops; also served in War of 1812). She married Thomas W. Carlton of Va.; they removed to Oglethorpe Co., then Coweta Co., Ga. They had 13 children.

THOMAS PETERSON CARNES, b. Prince George Co., Md., 1762; will made Athens, Ga., Aug. 2, 1816; probated 1822. Served in the Md. Line and was given bounty land for his services in Franklin Co., Ga. He d. in Milledgeville, Ga. Married (1) Elizabeth Bostwick (dau. of CHESLEY BOSTWICK (Bostic), REV. SOLDIER of Ga.); mar. (2) Susan Screws of Milledgeville.
Children by (1) wife:

1. Robert Watkins
2. William W.
3. Ann Low
4. Julia, mar. Augustin N. Clayton of Athens, Ga.
Children by (2) wife:
5. Thomas P., Jr.
6. Peter Johnson.
7. Nancy Clarke.
8. Richard S.
9. Susan King.

THOMAS CARR, b. Spottsylvania Co., Va., 1758; d. 1820, Columbia Co., Ga. Served under Marion, was twice wounded; was Col. of Militia. Married (1) —; (2) Frances Bacon (1771-1812).
Children:
1. Alexander Walter, b. 1787.
2. Susanna Brooks (1789-1870), mar. Nickolas Ware.
3. Thomas Dabney, mar. Annie Belle Watkins.
4. Selina Agnes, mar. Rev. Ignatius Few (first President of Emory College, Oxford and Atlanta Ga.).
5. William Anthony, mar. (1) Cynthia Walker; (2) Jane Aikens.

WILLIAM CARRAWAY, age 78 in 1832. Applied for Pension. Entered service Camden Dist., S. C. A resident of Cumberland Co., N. C. Served under Capt. John Moore, 3rd Co. Was Orderly Sergeant at Siege of Savannah, Ga. A resident of Ga.

JOHN CARSON, b. Neury, Ireland; d. Crawford Co., Ga. Served as a minute man under Col. Elijah Clarke. Received bounty land for his services. Married Isabella M. Gough.
Child: (known)
1. Joseph Jefferson (1802-1875), mar. Martha Raines.

ALEXANDER CARSWELL, b. in Ireland 1727; d. Burke Co., Ga. (formerly St. George's Parish), 1803. Served as private from Ga. under Gen. Twiggs. Received bounty grant of land in Burke Co., Ga. for his services. Married Lady Isabella Brown.
Children:
1. Edward, b. 1755; mar. Jane Trimble.
2. Agnes, b. 1757; mar. Andrew Templeton.
3. JOHN, b. 1760; d. Burke Co., Ga., 1817. Served as REV. SOLDIER with his father, Ga. Line under Gen. Twiggs, 4th Ga. Reg. Married Sarah Wright.
   Children:
   1. Alexander (1789-1848); mar. 1813, Mary Palmer (dau. of GEORGE PALMER (1753-1821), Burke Co., Ga. REV. SOLDIER who obtained bounty grant of land for his services, and his wife Mary Cureton).

2. Mathew (1795-1844); mar. Adelaide M. Williams.
4. Alexander, Jr., b. 1762; mar. Elizabeth Stiles.
5. James.
6. Matthew, mar. Sarah Martin.

DAVID CARTER, b. in New Jersey, Feb. 20, 1752; d. Franklin Co.,
Ga., Dec. 16, 1849. Enlisted as private 1775 under Col. Morgan. Private Pickens Dist., S. C. Captured and confined on prison ship "Concord" 1781. Received pension for services. Buried Mt. Zion Methodist Church Yard, Elbert (now Hart) Co., Ga. Married Mehitable Cobb.
Children: (known)
1. Micajah, mar. (1) Nancy (Goolsby) Garrett.
2. Mehitable.
3. David, Jr.

JOHN CARTER, b. in Va., Dec. 18, 1761; d. Aug. 1820. Buried City
Cemetery, Augusta, Ga. Married Anne Wray.

THOMAS A. CARTER, b. 1750 in Va.; d. 1811, Elbert Co., Ga.
Served as private Va. Line. Married (1) 1774, Miss Faris (1755-1795).

WILLIAM CASON, b. April 17, 1749 in S. C.; d. Warren Co., Ga.
Enlisted Fairfield Co., S. C.; drew pension for services 1833 while
resident of Warren Co., Ga. Drew land as REV. SOLDIER Cherokee
Lottery 1838.

BENJAMIN CATCHING, b. in Va., Oct. 31, 1748; d. Wilkes Co., Ga.,
1798. Served with Ga. Troops, promoted to Major on the Battlefield
of Kettle Creek. Received bounty lands for his services. Married
1769, Mildred Criddle Carleton, b. 1749.
Children: (known)
1. Joseph (1782-1852), mar. 1801, Mary Holliday (dau. of THOMAS
   HOLLIDAY, b. in Va. 1750; d. Wilkes Co., Ga., 1798. Served as
   private Ga. Troops, and his wife Martha Dickerson).
2. Philip, mar. Jincey Barnes.

JOSEPH CATCHINGS, b. 1762, Md.; d. 1805, Greene Co., Ga. Received bounty grant of land Wilkes Co., Ga. for services as private.
Married Martha Townsend.

JOHN CHAPMAN, b. in Va.; came to Richmond Co., Ga. He enlisted
in the Ga. Troops, was Sergeant of Minute Men. Received grant of land
in Wilkes Co., Ga. 1784 for his services. He married Mary Thompson.
They died in Wilkes Co., Ga.
Children: (known)
1. Nathan, b. S. C., Feb. 11, 1777; mar. Elizabeth Hart, b. Jan. 30,
   1780 (dau. of SAMUEL HART, REV. SOLDIER of Ga., and his
   wife Susanna Boring).

2. Benjamin, mar. Susanna Hart.
3. Thomas, mar. Sarah Hart.

JOSIAH CARTER, b. 1735 in England; d. 1827, Putnam Co., Ga.
Served as private Ga. Line under Col. Elijah Clarke. Married Mary
Anthony.
Children:
1. Josiah, Jr.
2. Anthony.
3. James.
4. John.
5. Loula.
6. Wellen.
7. Nancy.
8. Christopher, mar. Sarah Whitehead Battle.

WILLIAM CHEEKE, b. 1752, Randolph Co., N. C.; d. Franklin Co.,
Ga., 1845. Placed on pension roll 1833 for service as private Va.
troops. Married (1) 1775, Mary (called Polly) Vines (1750-1818).

TULLY CHOICE, b. in Va., June 17, 1753; d. Dec. 19, 1837, Hancock
Co., Ga. Enlisted 1776 in Capt. Thomas Dillard's Co., Col. Charles
Lewis Va. Regiment. 2nd Lieut. 1775; in Col. Mason's Va. Reg. 1779;
and Capt. Henry Co., Va. Militia 1780. Married Aug. 15, 1791, in
Laurens Co., S. C., Rebecca Sims. They moved to Ga. 1792.
Children:
1. John.
2. Fenton.
3. Ann.
4. William.
5. Tully, Jr.
6. Ruth.
7. Jesse.
8. Catherine.
9. Martha.
10. Rebecca.

ROBERT CHRISTIE, b. 1750 in Scotland; d. 1801, Savannah, Ga.
Served as Lieut. in Capt. Zachray Smith Brooks Co. S. C. Cavalry.
Married Ann Marshall (1755-1817).
Child:
1. Robert, Jr. (1787-1822), mar. 1814, Hannah Rahn (dau. of
JONATHAN RAHN, REV. SOLDIER (1762-1840), Effingham Co.,
Ga. Served as corporal, 2nd Co., Reg. of Ga., and his wife
Christiana Buntz (1763-1824).

NOTE: Other REV. SOLDIERS connected with this family are JAMES
McCALL, S. C.; FRANCIS McCALL, N. C.; THOMAS McCALL, S. C.;
and JACOB CASPAR WALDHAUER of Ga.

JOHN CHRISTIAN, b. in Va.; d. 1820, Franklin Co., Ga. Served as
private and Captain in Col. Vance's Va. Troops. Married Mary —.

ALONZO CHURCH (1793-1862); President of University of Ga. (1830-1860) (then Franklin College), Athens, Ga. (grandson of TIMOTHY CHURCH, b. 1736, South Hadley, Mass.; d. 1823, Brattleboro, Vermont, REV. SOLDIER of Vermont, and Abigail his wife), married Sarah Trippe (1800-1861) of Putnam Co., Ga.

CHRISTOPHER CLARK, b. in Va., April 20, 1737; d. 1803, Elbert Co., Ga. Served with Va. Troops; received bounty land for services. Married Mildred Terrell, b. June 7, 1741; d. 1800.
Children:
1. Micajah, b. 1758; mar. Penelope Gatewood.
2. CHRISTOPHER (1760-1819); mar. Rebecca Davis. REV. SOLDIER.
3. David (1762-1846); mar. Mary Clark.
4. Mourning (1764-1840); mar. 1783, WILLIAM BIBB KEY, a REV. SOLDIER. They had 15 children.
5. Judith (1766-1812); mar. PETER WYCHE, REV. SOLDIER.
6. Rachel, b. 1768; mar. (1) JOHN BOWEN, REV. SOLDIER of Va. (1758-1790); she mar. (2) John Daley.
7. Agatha, mar. George Wyche.
8. Mary, mar. Thomas W. Oliver.
9. Samuel.
10. Joshua.
11. Millie, mar. Shelton White.
12. Terrell, b. 1781 in Va.
13. Susan, b. 1783 in Ga.; mar. F. McCarty Oliver.
14. Lucy, mar. as (2) wife, James Oliver.

CHRISTOPHER CLARK (son of Christopher Clark and his wife Mildred Terrell), b. in Va., Jan. 6, 1760; d. Elbert Co., Ga., Sept. 21, 1819. Served in Va. Line and received bounty grant of land in Ga. for his services. Married Oct. 17, 1799, Rebecca Davis (dau. of WILLIAM DAVIS, REV. SOLDIER of Va., and his wife Mary Chisolm), b. 1780; d. 1857.
Children:
1. Samuel (1800-1862); d. in Ala.
2. Margaret Ann, b. 1803; d. in Texas 1866; married 1821, James Opher Clark, her cousin (son of Micajah Clark, Jr.).
3. William Davis (1805-1882); mar. 1830, Elizabeth Jane Hearn (dau. of Thomas Hearn).
4. Christopher Hill (1807-1848).
5. Thomas Jefferson.
6. George Washington.
7. Mary (1812-1848); mar. Thomas B. Burge.

DAVID CLARK, b. in Va., April 8, 1762; d. Elbert Co., Ga., Sept. 10, 1846. Served as private, Ga. Militia. Received bounty grant of land for services. Married Dec. 10, 1794, Mary Clark (his cousin) (dau.

of John and Mary (Moore) Clark (1775-1840).
Children:
1. Elizabeth, mar. Philip Matthews.
2. Mary, mar. Thomas Edwards.
3. Eliza, mar. Madison Hudson.
4. Lucinda, mar. Henry Cosby.
5. Christopher.
6. John T.
7. Mildred, mar. Thomas F. Willis.

JOSEPH DAVID CLARK, b. in Va., April 12, 1752; d. in Orange Co., Va., Feb. 5, 1839. After Rev. War, he moved to Elbert Co., Ga., where he remained until shortly before his death. Enlisted Culpepper Co., Va., served as matross in Capt. William Murray's Co., in Capt. Eddin's Co., 1st Va. Artillery Regiment, Col. Charles Harrison. His children obtained pension Feb. 20, 1851 (No. S. 8208). Married (1) Ann Haynes, b. 1758; (2) 1812, Catherine (no issue).
Children by (1) wife:
1. Larkin, lived Morgan Co., Ga.
2. James, b. Orange Co., Va., 1779; came to Elbert Co., Ga., where he died. Soldier of 1812. Drew land in Lottery of 1806. Lieut. of Militia 1809; Capt. 1812. Married April 8, 1812, Mary Alston (1783-1871), dau. of LIEUT.-COL. WILLIAM ALSTON, REV. SOLDIER, and his wife Charity Alston).
3. Mary, mar. Col. Barnard Heard, Wilkes Co., Ga.
4. Ann P., mar. Adj. Gen. John C. Easter.
5. Elizabeth, mar. Col. Thomas White, Jones Co., Ga.
6. Sallie T., mar. Lewis Shirles of Va.
7. Tabitha, mar. Cuthbert Reese of Jones Co., Ga.
8. Eunice H., mar. Solomon H. McIntyre of Va.
9. William David of Orange Co., Va., mar. Jane Mary Eliason.
10. Bathsheba.

JUDITH (ADAMS) CLARK, a PATRIOT (dau. of Robert and Mary (Lewis) Adams of Va., and widow of MICAJAH CLARK, REV. SOLDIER of Va.), b. in Va.; d. in Ga. After the death of her husband, the widow Clark moved to Ga. with her children; received land. Five sons were REV. SOLDIERS.
Children:
1. CHRISTOPHER (1737-1800), mar. Millicent (sometimes spelled Mildred) Terrell. A REV. SOLDIER.
2. ROBERT, b. 1738; mar. Susanna Henderson. REV. SOLDIER.
3. WILLIAM, mar. Judith Cheadle. REV. SOLDIER.
4. Judith, mar. 1770, ANDREW MOORMAN, REV. SOLDIER.
5. MICAJAH, JR., mar. Mildred Martin. REV. SOLDIER.
6. JOHN (1743-1819), mar. Mary Moore. REV. SOLDIER.
7. Penelope, mar. (1) Reuben Rowland; (2) Jonathan Sanders.
8. Bolling, mar. Elizabeth Cheadle.

9. James C., mar. Lucy Cheadle.
10. Elizabeth, mar. JOSEPH ANTHONY, REV. SOLDIER.

LARKIN CLARK, b. Orange Co., Va., 1760; d. 1843, Elbert Co., Ga.
Served as private Major Allen's Ga. Troops. Married Lucy Simpson
Welch (1780-1852).

WILLIAM CLARK (son of John Clark, b. in Va., 1728; d. S. C., 1794,
and wife Judith), was b. 1763; d. 1831, Putnam Co., Ga. Served as
private Ga. Line and received bounty for his services in Washington
Co., Ga. Married 1792, Mary Harvey (1776-1830) (dau. of EVAN and
Rachel HARVEY. Evan Harvey b. 1753; d. Putnam Co., Ga., served in
S. C. Line and received bounty grant of land in Wilkes Co., Ga. for
his services in Ga. Line under Col. Clarke. He had four sons REV.
SOLDIERS: Jeremiah, James, Benjamin).

NOTE: Connected with the WILLIAM CLARK line are REV. SOLDIERS
THOMAS WELLBORN, EVAN HARVEY, EVANS LONG, ARTHUR FORT.

GENERAL ELIJAH CLARKE, b. Edgecomb Co., N. C., 1736; d. Rich-
mond Co., Ga., Dec. 15, 1799. Married in N. C., 1760, Hannah Arrington
(1737-1827). He moved with his family to the "Ceded Lands" of Ga.,
1774 (now Wilkes Co.). Both are buried at the home plantation in now
Lincoln Co., Ga. "Woburn". (Their graves were marked by the Elijah
Clarke Chapter, Athens, Ga. and Hannah Clarke Chapter, Quitman,
Ga. D. A. R.)
He was a REV. SOLDIER of Ga., and the story of his life and brav-
ery is told in detail in every history of Ga. He was the Col. at the
Battle of Kettle Creek, and it has been said that this Battle made pos-
sible Cornwallis' defeat. Was at the Siege of Augusta and King's Mt.
Served as Captain of Rangers, Colonel and then Brigadier-General.
His wife was one of the REV. heroines of Ga. Her home was burned
by the Tories while her husband was in the field, and she, too, was at
the Siege of Augusta.
Children:
1. JOHN CLARKE, b. 1766, N. C.; d. Fla., Oct. 15, 1832. Married
   Mary Williamson (dau. of COL. MICAJAH WILLIAMSON, REV.
   SOLDIER of Ga.). Served as a REV. SOLDIER under his father;
   distinguished himself at the Battle of Jack's Creek; became
   Major Gen. in the War of 1812; was placed in charge of all
   forces destined for the protection of the Seacoast and Southern
   boundaries of the State. Elected Governor of Ga. 1819, re-
   elected 1821. In 1827 he removed to Fla., where he died.
   Children:
   1. Son.
   2. Daughter, mar. Col. John Campbell.
2. Gibson Clarke (1772-1820); married Susanna Clark. Moved to
   Miss.

3. Elijah Clarke, Jr., mar. Margaret Long.
4. Nancy Clarke, mar. Jesse Thompson, b. 1754, Amelia Co., Va.
Moved to Ga. with his brother Robert Thompson and sister
Elinor (mar. Samuel Watkins). They settled in Wilkes Co. He
served as REV. SOLDIER, Ga. Line under Gen. Clarke. Received bounty land for his services. Died 1819.
5. Elizabeth Clarke, mar. BENAJAH SMITH, a REV. SOLDIER of
Ga. Served under Gen. Clarke.
6. Sarah Clarke, mar. (1) COL. CHARLES WILLIAMSON (son of
Col. Micajah Williamson) a REV. SOLDIER of Ga. She mar. (2)
William J. Hobby of Augusta, Ga.
7. Frances Clarke, b. 1781; married EDWIN MOUNGER, a REV.
SOLDIER of Ga.
8. Susan Clarke, d. y.

DAVID CLAY, b. Duplin Co., N. C.; d. 1818, Wilkinson Co., Ga.
Served as private N. C. Troops under Capt. Hall and Capt. Komegay.
Widow applied and received pension 1852. Married 1792, Eve Hardin
(1772-1855).

JOSEPH CLAY (son of Ralph Clay and Elizabeth Habersham of
England), b. Beverly, England, 1741; d. 1805, Savannah, Ga. Member
Provincial Congress Ga. 1777, and of Council of Safety. Served as
Paymaster of the Southern Division Continental Army. Married Ann
Legardiere (1745-1821).
Children:
1. Joseph, mar. Mary Ann Savage.
2. Ann, mar. Thomas Cummings.
3. Elizabeth, mar. Thomas Young.
4. Betsey, mar. Dr. James Box Young.
5. Sarah, mar. William Wallace.
6. Kitty, mar. 1793, Joseph Stiles.

BENJAMIN CLEVELAND, b. in Prince Wm. Co., Va., May 26, 1738;
d. Wilkes Co., Ga., 1806. Served as Ensign Ga. Troops. Removed to
Ga. N. C. Troops Howe's Reg. Married Mary Graves. They had several children.
Child:
1. Jemina, mar. James Wiley.
    Child:
    1. James Rutherford Wiley of Ga., married Sarah Hawkins
    Clark (dau. of William Clark and his wife Elizabeth Sevier,
    dau. of Gen. John Sevier of Tenn.).

LARKIN CLEVELAND, brother of Benjamin Cleveland, b. in Va.,
1748; d. in Ga., 1814. Married Frances —. He served as Lieut. under
his brother as Colonel.

GEORGE CLIFTON, b.1761; d.1840, Clarke Co., Ga. Applied for pension, which was allowed. Enlisted 1777 with the Delaware troops under Capt. Dagget, Col. Vaughan's Regiment. Married (1) Elizabeth Dickenson.

EZEKIEL CLOUD, b. Wilkes Co., N.C., 1762; d.1850, Henry Co., Ga. Served as private Ga. Line. Received pension for his services 1831. Married Elizabeth Harmon.
Children: (known)
1. Nancy (Ann), mar. Col. William Hardin (son of Valentine and Margaret (Castleberry) Hardin). A Soldier of the War of 1812. They lived at New Echota (house built for the Moravian Missionaries). They had 7 children.
2. Levi, mar. Elizabeth Brown.
3. Mary Elizabeth, mar. Jacob Hale Stokes.

JEREMIAH CLOUD of Wilkes Co., Ga. (wife Sarah), drew 287.5 acres of land on Rocky Creek, Washington Co., for his services as a REV. SOLDIER.

JEREMIAH CLOUD, b. in Va.; d. Wilkes Co., Ga., 1783. Served with Ga. Troops under Col. Elijah Clarke. Married (1) 1742, Ann Bailey; mar. (2) Sarah —.

DANIEL CLOWER (son of Geo. Clower and his wife Elizabeth Morgan, sister of GEN. DANIEL MORGAN, REV. SOLDIER of Va.), was b. July 18, 1762 in Penn.; d. Gwinnett Co., Ga., Sept. 30, 1842. (Grave marked by Atlanta Chapter, D.A.R.) Enlisted Orange Co., N.C. and drew pension 1835 for his services, while residing in Gwinnett Co. He was a Methodist preacher.
Children:
1. Sarah, b.1787; mar. John Moorman Venable of Jackson Co., Ga. Ten children.
2. Elizabeth, d.y.
3. Jonathan, d.y.
4. John, b.1794; mar.1816, Nancy Winn. Ten children.
5. Nancy, b.1799; mar.1824, John W. Stell.
6. Jane, b.1802; mar. George Witherspoon.
7. Daniel, Jr., b.1805; mar. Parthenia Carter Brandon.
8. Mary, b.1807; mar. John Brown.
9. Searcy, d.y.

GEORGE CLOWER (brother of Daniel), moved from Penn. to Jasper Co., Ga., then Wilkerson Co., Ga. He was a REV. SOLDIER. Also his brother JONATHAN CLOWER enlisted as a REV. SOLDIER, Orange Co., N.C. Moved to Jasper Co., Ga.; d. Bibb Co., Ala. Married Berks Co., Penn., Mary Sular.

From Augusta Chronicle:

"CAPT. THOMAS COBB, age 110 years, a native of Buckingham Co., Va. Came to Ga. 1784. A REV. SOLDIER. His patriotism induced him to take part with his country for the Independence of these States and he was often associated in the Councils of the Chiefs in those startling times."

ZEBULON COCKE, b. in N. C., 1734; d. Burke Co., Ga. Served in N. C. and Ga. Line. Married Sarah (Perry) Field and moved to Burke Co., Ga., 1764.
Children: (others)
1. CALEB, a REV. SOLDIER.
2. Isaac Perry, mar. Almeda Griffin (dau. of WILLIAM GRIFFIN, REV. SOLDIER, and his wife Mary Booker Barnett of Henry Co., Ga.).
3. John, b. 1784. Soldier of War of 1812. Mar. Lydia Davis, b. 1791, Burke Co., Ga. (dau. of BENJAMIN DAVIS, REV. SOLDIER of Ga., and his wife Elizabeth Daniell).
   Child:
   1. Benjamin E. Cocke, mar. 1841, Margaret Cameron (dau. of ALEXANDER CAMERON, REV. SOLDIER of N. C., and his wife Nancy McCarty). They moved 1828 from Cumberland Co., N. C. to Early Co., Ga., where they died.

PETER COFFEE, b. 1750, landed in America from Ireland; d. in Hancock Co., Ga., 1820. Served in the Va. Continental Army, private Capt. Benjamin Casey's 12th Va. Regiment; also Capt. Michael Bower's Co., Col. James Wood Regiment. Drew pension for his services. Married Sarah Smith of Prince Edward Co., Va.
Children:
1. Elizabeth, b. 1775; mar. (1) Charles Daniels.
2. Susanna, mar. T. Randall.
3. Nancy, mar. (1) Abram Heard; (2) —.
4. John, mar. Ann Penelope Bryan (dau. of JOHN HILL BRYAN, REV. SOLDIER). He was Gen. in the War of 1812.
5. Sarah, mar. William Harris.
6. Joshua.
7. Mary, mar. Henry Gibson.
8. Cynthia, mar. Thomas Stocks.
9. Martha, mar. George Heard.
10. Joshua.

NOTE: JOSHUA COFFEE, brother of PETER COFFEE came with him to America. Was a REV. SOLDIER. Both Peter and Joshua Coffee had a son John Coffee; both of whom were Generals in the War of 1812.

BLANCHARD COLDING, b. 1756, S. C.; d. 1816. Served as Soldier

S. C. Line. Married Ann Gibbon (1756; d. 1818, Screven Co., Ga.).
Child:
1. Thomas Colding (1773-1847), mar. Ann Dell (dau. of PHILIP DELL, REV. SOLDIER of Ga.).

THOMAS COLE, b. 1758, Warren, Rhode Island; d. Savannah, Ga. Served as private in Capt. Thomas Allen's Co. of Rhode Island Troops. Married 1781, Anna Vose.

JONATHAN COLEMAN (son of THOMAS COLEMAN, REV. SOLDIER of Va., and his wife Mildred Richards), b. in Va., came to St. George's Parish (now Burke Co.), Ga. Served as Soldier Ga. Line, under Gen. Wayne. Buried at Old Bark Camp Church, near Midville, Ga. Married Mildred (Milly) Pittman.
Children:
1. Charles, mar. Amelia Garner.
2. Lindsey, lived Jefferson Co., Ga.
3. Elisha, mar. (1) Miss Whitfield; (2) Mary L. Scott (dau. of Brig. Gen. John Scott, granddau. of CAPT. JAMES SCOTT, REV. SOLDIER and his wife Frances Collier).

JOHN W. COLLEY, b. in Va.; d. near Washington, Ga. Served in Va. Line, received 1784 bounty grant of land in Ga. for his services.

VINES COLLIER, b. Brunswick Co., Va.; d. in Oglethorpe Co., Ga., Sept. 1795. Served as private Va. Line. Received grant of land Wilkes Co., Ga. for his services. Married 1760, Elizabeth Williamson (dau. of Benjamin Williamson of Va.).
Children:
1. Elizabeth.
2. Sarah.
3. Maria.
4. Ann, mar. John Hardman.
5. Isaac.
6. John.
7. Thomas.
8. William.
9. Vines.
10. Benjamin.
11. Williamson.
12. Robert, mar. Martha M. Bookes.
13. Cuthbert.
He is buried at Old Salem Churchyard, 6 miles N. E. of Lexington, Ga.

JOHN COLLINS, b. Frederick Co., Md.; married Burke Co., Ga., Nov. 30, 1786, Phoebe Sailors. She received a pension as widow of a REV. SOLDIER, Jan. 31, 1853, while a resident of Cobb Co., Ga.

JOHN COLQUITT, b. in Va.; d. in Ga., Oglethorpe Co., 1800. Served as private Va. Troops. Married Elizabeth Hendricks.
Child:
   1. ROBERT, b. in Va., d. Oglethorpe Co., Ga. Served as private Va. Troops. Drew land as a REV. SOLDIER 1827 Lottery in Ga. Married Susan Hubbard.

JAMES THOMAS COMER, b. 1729 in Va.; d. 1837, Jones Co., Ga. Served as private Ga. Line. Married 3 times.

WILLIAM CONE, b. 1745 in N. C.; d. 1815, Bulloch Co., Ga. Served as private McLean's Reg. Ga. Troops. Married 1765, Keziah Barber. They had 3 sons and 9 daughters.
Children: (known)
   1. Aaron (1766-1830), mar. Susanna Marlow.
   2. Joseph, removed to Thomas Co., Ga.
   3. William, Jr. (1777-1857), mar. Sarah Haddock, moved to Camden Co., Ga.
   4. Sarah, mar. Wm. A. Knight.
   5. Nancy, mar. Edwin Morris.

THOMAS CONNALLY, b. in Va., 1718; d. at the age of 82 (in 1800), in Gwinnett Co., Ga. (Buried in the Strickland grave yard near Sewanne, Ga.) He married Polly Price (dau. of John E. and Elizabeth (Lindsey) Price), b. in Va.; d. Madison Co., Ga. He served as a recruiting Officer in Va. during REV. WAR.
Children:
   1. John, mar. Biddy King.
   2. Thomas, mar. (1) Temperance Porter; (2) Susan Bagley.
   3. Charles, mar. Nancy Stokes.
   4. George.
   5. David, mar. in Va., Elizabeth Christian, b. Oct. 31, 1776, in Orange Co., N. C.; d. Fulton Co., Ga., 1848.
   6. Abner, mar. Lucy Bagley.
   7. Nathaniel, mar. Eliz Nailer.
   8. Price, mar. Sally Corker.
   9. William, mar. Cenas Christian.
   10. Christopher, mar. Elizabeth McIntyre.
   11. Samuel, mar. Pyrene Christian.
   12. Elizabeth, mar. Thomas Gaddis.
   13. Margaret, mar. Thomas Jones.
   14. Sallie, mar. Abner Barnes.
   15. Mary, mar. Wilson Strickland.

THOMAS CONNER, JR. (son of Thomas Conner, Sr., b. 1678, d. Aug. 4, 1768), b. in Md., 1726; d. in Ga., Sept. 12, 1802. Married about 1751, Margaret —. Served as private in Capt. Nathaniel Ewing's Co., 1st Maryland Regiment. Enlisted Dec. 10, 1776; his name appears on roll for the month of Feb.1779, dated at Middlebrook, Mar.3,1779. Came to Ga.

Children: (known)

1. Elizabeth, d.1809; mar. Ananias Lang.
2. James, b.1755.
3. Lewis, b.1756.
4. Ann.
5. William.
6. WILSON, REV. SOLDIER

WILSON CONNER (son of Thomas Conner, Jr.), b. in Md., July 7, 1768; d. in (Screven) Montgomery Co., Ga. His grave as a REV. SOLDIER was marked in 1922 at the Dead River Cemetery in Montgomery Co., Ga., by the Brier Creek Chapter D.A.R., Sylvania, Ga.) He was also Soldier of the War of 1812; Capt. of Co. of Riflemen in the Fla. Indian War. Married Oct. 8,1809, Tattnall Co., Ga., Mary Cook, b. Aug. 4,1774.

Children:

1. Martha, mar. Jesse Wall.
2. Louisa, mar. John Wilcox.
3. Wilson, Jr., mar. Annie Johnson.
4. Eliza, mar. William Ryals.
5. James, mar. Penelope Ryals.
6. Nancy, mar. George Cooper.
7. Harriet Elizabeth, mar. John Griffin.
8. Thomas, mar. Sarah Wall.
9. Lucy Ann, mar. Joseph Ryals.
10. Mary J., mar. Thomas Sullivant.
11. Maria, mar. John Ryals.
12. Elizabeth

PIERRE CONSTANTINE, b. Toulouse, France, 1736; d. Savannah, Ga.,1811. Came from France with Count Rochambeau and served as a grenadier with him at Yorktown. Married Marie Louise Bidot.

JAMES COOK, REV. SOLDIER, Elliott's Dist., Jefferson Co., Ga.

JOHN COOK, b. in Va.; d. in Hancock Co., Ga. Served as Captain under Gen. William Washington throughout the War. Was at the Battles of Eutaw Springs, Cowpens, Guilford Court House and others. Married (2) Martha Pearson.

Children: (known)

1. Philip, b.1775, S.C.; d.1841, Twiggs Co., Ga. Married Martha Wooten.
2. Martha, mar. John Daniel.

REUBEN COOK, b.1740, Hanover Co.,Va.; d.1820, Elbert Co., Ga. Served as private Va. State Troops. Married Molly Daniel, d. 1828.

HENRY COOPER, b. in New York, 1759; d. 1840, Putnam Co., Ga. Served as private in Capt. Jonathan Lawrence's Co.; Col. Harper's Reg. of Levies, N. Y. Married Frances Peery.

JOHN COOPER, b. Henry Co., Va., 1742; d. Wilkes Co., Ga., 1835. Served as private Ga. Line. Received bounty grant of land for services. Married 1778, Elizabeth Wilson.

JOHN COOPER, b. Frederick Co., Va., 1742; d. 1835, Wilkes Co., Ga. Received grant of land for his services as private Henry Co., Va. Mil. 1777. Married 1778, Elizabeth Wilson.

JOHN COOPER, b. 1751 in Ga.; d. in Ga., 1816. Raised the Company known as "The Liberty Independent Troop", and served as Lieut. and Captain. Married Elizabeth Giginillat.

RICHARD COOPER, b. Duplin Co., N. C., 1758; d. Screven Co., Ga. Served as private under Capt. Wm. Kenson, Col. Charles Ward, N. C. Regiment. Married in S. C., Lucretia Howard.
Children: (known)
1. David.
2. William.
3. Jane, mar. James Middleton.
4. Rachel, mar. Rev. Richard Parker.
5. George (1783-1862), mar. Mary Conner (dau. of REV. WILSON CONNER, REV. SOLDIER of Ga., and his wife Mary Cook).

THOMAS COOPER, b. 1733, Frederick Co., Va.; d. 1796, Greene Co., Ga. Served as Capt., Va. Troops. Also gave civil service. Married 1762, Sarah Anthony, b. 1742 (dau. of JOSEPH ANTHONY, REV. SOLDIER of Va., and his wife Elizabeth Clark). His will in Hancock Co. Children:
1. Penelope, mar. James Nisbet.
2. Elizabeth, mar. Thomas Stovall.
3. Joseph.
4. Agnes.
5. Thomas, mar. Judith Harvey (dau. of James and Sarah Harvey).
6. Polly.
7. John.
8. Sarah.
9. Micajah.

WILLIAM CORAM, b. 1756 in Va.; d. Wilkes Co., Ga. Married Mar. 1783, Ann Hodo (1755-1829) (dau. of PETER HODO, REV. SOLDIER of Warren Co., Ga.) He was a REV. SOLDIER and served as Sergeant.

CARY COX, b. in S. C.; d. Mar. 24, 1814, Putnam Co., Ga. Served as private S. C. Troops. Married 1762, Mary Horne, d. 1823.

JOHN COX, b. Jan. 6, 1737; d. Oct. 1, 1793 in Ga. Received grant of land for his services as a REV. SOLDIER. Married Francinia —, b. July 25, 1737; d. Dec. 2, 1811.
Children:
1. Thomas (1759-1817).
2. Mary.
3. Nancy Clark, b. 1763; mar. REUBEN RANSOME, a REV. SOLDIER. (His grave in Clarke Co., Ga. marked by the Elijah Clarke Chapter D. A. R., Athens, Ga.)
4. Letitia, mar. — Mattox.
5. John.
6. Francinia (1769-1801), mar. THOMAS GREER (1760-1843), a REV. SOLDIER. They had 10 children.
7. Elizabeth, mar. — Turner.
8. Richard (1776-1837), mar. Eliza Massey Mead.
9. Martha, mar. — Colleran; moved to La.
10. Bolling, d. 1842 in Ala.

JOHN CRAPS, b. 1765 in S. C.; d. 1853, Terrell Co., Ga. Served as private, 4th S. C. Artillery Regiment. Married Catherine Lowman, b. 1770, S. C.; d. in Ga., 1850.
Children:
1. George, b. 1799; mar. Harriet Rogers.
2. Elizabeth, mar. Martin Stampes.
3. John Jacob.
4. Anna Barbara, b. 1796; mar. MAJOR DAVID KAIGLER. (Grave marked by the Stonecastle Chapter D. A. R., Dawson, Ga.)

NOTE: Connected with the Craps family are ANDREW KAIGLER, REV. SOLDIER, d. in Tenn.; JACOB SAYLOR, REV. SOLDIER, d. in S. C.; and Jack Dennard, d. at Jeffersonville, Ga.

JOHN CRATIN, b. in Md.; d. 1826, Wilkes Co., Ga. Served as Lieut. 2nd Md. Reg. Married 1780, Marcia Ann Lanham, d. 1835.

CHARLES CRAWFORD, b. 1738 in Amherst Co., Va.; d. 1813 in Ga. Captain; commanded a Co. under Gen. Robert Howe, 2nd N. C. Reg. Married Jane Maxwell in 1763. She was b. 1743.

JOEL CRAWFORD, b. 1736, Amherst Co., Va.; moved to Edgefield Dist., S. C., 1779; d. Wilkes Co., Ga., 1788. Enlisted Amherst Co., Va.; removed to Chester Dist., S. C., 1780. Soon after this was captured by the British, placed in Camden jail, released several months later. Removed 1783 to Kioka Creek, Columbia Co., Ga. Married Fannie Harris (dau. of BENJAMIN HARRIS, REV. SOLDIER).
Children:
1. Ann.
2. Robert.

3. Joel, Jr.; Soldier of 1812.
4. Lucy.
5. William Harris.
6. Elizabeth.
7. Charles.
8. Fannie.
9. Nathan
10. Bennett.
11. David, mar. Mary Lee Wood.

WILLIAM HARRIS CRAWFORD, one of the most prominent and important men in Ga. History, was b. Amherst Co., Va., Feb. 24, 1772; d. in Ga., Sept. 16, 1834. Settled 1799 in Lexington, Oglethorpe Co., Ga. Married 1804, Susanna Gerdine. (See Life of Wm. Harris Crawford).

STEPHEN CROW, b. N. C., 1750; d. 1830, Clark Co., Ga. Served as private Ga. Militia. Married Margaret Stroud (1757-1834) (dau. of JOHN STROUD, REV. SOLDIER of Ga.).
Child:
1. Rachel Crow, mar. Jeremiah Burnett.

DAVID CULBERTSON (son of JOSEPH CULBERTSON, REV. SOLDIER of Va., and his wife Agnes), b. 1762 in Va.; d. Greene Co., Ga., 1796. Served in N. C. Troops. Received bounty lands in Ga. for his services Franklin Co. Pension granted to his widow for his services in 1830. Married Caswell Co., N. C., 1782, Clara Browning (dau. of JOHN BROWNING, REV. SOLDIER of N. C., who d. in Ga.). She mar. (2) Jonathan Haralson.
Children:
1. Isaac, mar. Mary Houston.
2. Jeremiah.
3. John.
4. James, mar. (1) Sarah M. Wilkerson; (2) Libby Ashford, widow.
5. David, mar. Lucy Wilkerson.
Children of Jonathan Haralson and Clara Browning (Culbertson) Haralson:
1. Jonathan.
2. Kinchen.
3. Hugh A.

NOTE: Allied with this family are ROBERT MORROW, REV. SOLDIER, Md.; THOMAS EWING, REV. SOLDIER, Md.; JOHN WILKERSON, REV. SOLDIER, Ga.

JAMES CULBERTSON, b. 1764; d. 1823 (son of Joseph Culbertson), served with N. C. Troops. Received Pension. Married Mary Kilgore.

ALEXANDER CUMMINS, b. in Va.; d. 1811, Oglethorpe Co., Ga. Commanded a Co. under Col. Thomas Meriwether, Bedford Co., Va. Militia. Married Elizabeth —.

ANSEL CUNNINGHAM, b. in Ireland, 1763; d. Jackson Co., Ga., 1837.

Received pension 1832 as a private, Va. Troops, under Col. Tucker.
Mar. (1) —; (2) Mary —.

MICHAEL CUP, b. 1740, N. C.; d. 1821 in Ga. Served in Ga. Troops
under Col. Elijah Clarke. Married Barbara Layle.
Child:
1. Mary, mar. Lazarus Summerline.

RICHARD CURD, b. in Va.; d. May 16, 1827, Henry Co., Ga. Served
in Va. Troops. Was a Juror in the trial of Aaron Burr at 65 years of
age. (From records at Milledgeville, Ga.)

HENRY CUYLER, b. 1754, New York City; d. 1781, Savannah, Ga.
Commissioned Captain of Light Infantry Rev. War by Governor John
Houston. Married 1778, Dorothy Martin, d. 1786.

BENJAMIN DALEY, b. in S. C., 1750; d. in Ga. Served in Ga. Militia.
Received bounty grant of land in Effingham Co. for his services. Mar-
ried in Effingham Co., Ga., Jan. 6, 1774, Susanna Garnett (sister of
THOMAS GARNETT, REV. SOLDIER, Lieut. of Ga. Troops and under
Capt. Abraham Pavot of Ga.).
Children: (known)
1. Elizabeth, b. Effingham Co., Ga., Dec. 22, 1774.
2. Susanna, mar. Clayborne Beville (son of ROBERT BEVILLE,
REV. SOLDIER of Ga.).

JOHN DALLAS served as private, Va. Infantry. Born 1748 in Va.;
d. 1815, Wilkes Co., Ga. Married 1774, Mary Walker.

ALLEN DANIEL, b. in Va., 1738; d. Madison Co., Ga., 1814. Served
as Captain, 8th Va. Reg. J. P., Elbert Co. Representative from Elbert
Co., Ga. Also War of 1812 record. Married Mary Allen.
Children:
1. Elizabeth, mar. Aaron Johnson.
2. Allen, Jr., b. in Va. 1772; d. in Ga. 1836. Brig.-Gen. in War of
1812. Representative 1821. Married Mary Jones (dau. of
Russell Jones).
3. James, mar. (1) Elizabeth Jones (dau. of James and Elizabeth
Jones); (2) Delilah Eurenice Wilson.
4. Charity, mar. Elisha Johnson.

BENJAMIN DANIEL, b. in N. C., 1740; d. Laurens Co., Ga., 1818.
Served in Ga. Line, certified to by Col. James McNeill. Married
Lucretia Bergamont, d. 1830.
Children:
1. William.
2. James.
3. John, mar. Elizabeth Hudson.

4. Mary.
5. Elizabeth, mar. Benjamin Brantley.

FREDERICK DANIEL, b. Brunswick Co., Va., 1755. Enlisted Nash Co., N.C. Moved to Ga., 1795. Applied for Pension.

JEPTHA DANIEL, b. Va. Certified to by Gen. John Twiggs. Married Nov. 12, 1808, Sarah Rowland.

JOHN DANIEL, b. 1757; d. Washington Co., Ga., 1788. Served as private, Ga. Troops. Received bounty land for his services in Washington Co., Ga. Married 1787, Mary Mason.

JOHN DANIEL (Daniell), b. Wake Co., N.C., May 23, 1760; d. Elbert Co., Ga., 1841. Enlisted Wake Co., N.C., Captain in Col. Malmadges N.C. Reg. Served under Col. Farmer 1780. Granted pension, File No. 31638. Married Marguerite Means.
Children:
1. James J.
2. David.
3. John.
4. Allen.
5. Nancy, mar. — Cunningham.
6. Mary, mar. — Craft.
7. Sarah, mar. — Cunningham.
8. Lucinda, mar. —Prewitt (Pruitt).

JOHN DANIEL, b. Marlboro Dist., S.C., 1760; d. Dodge Co., 1830. Served as private in Capt. Moses Pearson's Co., Col. Marion's S.C. Regiment. Married 1799, Rebecca Stephens.
Children:
1. Jack, mar. Eliza Mitchell.
2. Moses, mar. Lucinda Evans.
3. Matthew.
4. James, mar. Elizabeth Wilcox.
5. Nancy, mar. 1827, Simeon Bishop, b. N.Y., 1799; d. Ga. 1836.
6. Sallie, mar. George Wilcox.
7. Mary, mar. John Wilcox.
8. Sophronia, mar. Norman McDuffie.
(Grave marked by the Col. Wm. Few Chapter, D.A.R., Eastman, Ga.)

WILLIAM DANIEL, b. in N.C., 1747; d. Laurens Co., Ga., 1807. Served as private, S.C. Line under Gen. Sumpter. Married Lucretia Bell.
Children: (from will)
1. John.
2. Elizabeth, mar. Philip Raiford.
3. Martha, mar. — Marsh.
4. Jesse.
5. James.
6. Mary, mar. — Hatcher.
7. Catherine, mar. (1) Lewellyn Threwitz; (2) — Griffin; (3) —Ball.

STEPHEN BEADON DANIELL, b. in N.C., 1745; d. in Ga. Served as Ensign 1776; was transferred Aug. 1777 from N.C. to S.C. Reg. Member Committee of Safety Brunswick Co., N.C. (Home on Little River, N.C., burned by the British). Married 1769, Rebecca Howe (dau. of GEN. ROBERT HOWE, REV. SOLDIER of N.C., and his wife Sarah Grange). Died in Ga. about 1820. Six children.
Children: (known)
1. George W., b. in N.C., 1782; d. Laurens Co., Ga., 1845. Married (1) Lucrety Smith; (2) Mary Gonto; (3) Sarah Garnett, widow. 12 children by (2) wife; 1 child by (3) wife. Soldier of 1812.
2. Amos.
3. Robert Howe.

NOTE: For history of the Daniell family, see "McCall-Tidwell and Allied Families" by Ettie Tidwell McCall.

WILLIAM DANIELL, b. Nov. 25, 1743, N.C.; d. in Clarke Co., Ga., Sept. 5, 1840. Married (1) Rachel —; (2) June 11, 1787, Mary Melton, b. Mar. 11, 1770; d. Oct. 3, 1843 (dau. of Moses and Nancy (Keen) Melton). Served as private, N.C. Troops. Certified to by Col. Elijah Clarke, Feb. 2, 1784, that "WILLIAM DANIELL was a Refugee Soldier of N.C. and entitled to draw a bount grant". He received 287.5 acres of land in Franklin Co., Ga. (Grave marked by the Elijah Clarke Chapter, D.A.R., Athens, Ga.) He had 26 children; 12 by (1) marriage, 14 by (2) marriage.
Children by (1) wife: (known)
1. William, Jr., b. Sept. 22, 1767; mar. Elizabeth Davis.
2. Elizabeth
3. Mary
4. Rebecca
5. Nathaniel, mar. — Brantley.
6. Isaac, b. 1781; mar. Polly Johnson.
7. George, mar. Ellen Barber.
Children by (2) wife:
1. Rachel, mar. William Barber.
2. Josiah (1792-1845), mar. (1) Sarah Ann (Owen) Burrough; (2) Elizabeth Jeffries.
3. Susannah, mar. Treman Fuller.
4. Jeremiah Melton, mar. (1) Nancy Burnett; (2) Sarah Wise.
5. Eleanor, mar. — Bradley.
6. Beadon, mar. Patsey Hodges.
7. Masters, d. at sea.
8. Clarissa, mar. John Hodges.
9. Alfred, mar. (1) Mary Hodges; (2) Mary Dinard.
10. Stephen, mar. (1) Elizabeth Melton; (2) Louise Hodges.
11. Moses (1811-1892), mar. Eliza Hamby.
12. Robert, mar. (1) Naomi Burnett; (2) Margaret Fleming.
13. Olive, mar. David Hamby.
14. Cary, mar. — Hodges.

WILLIAM DANIELL (Daniel), b. 1745 in Ireland; d. 1836, Washing-

ton Co., Ga. Served as private, Ga. Line. Married 1772, Elizabeth Skinner, d. 1837.
Children:

1. William, mar. Temperance Ellis.
2. Elizabeth, mar. — McConald.
3. Thomas M.)
4. Theophilus) twins
5. Frances, mar. Delano Renfroe.
6. Young.
7. Thomas.
8. Kenoth.
9. Abel (1794-1885); mar. 1825, Penelope (Jones) Sullivan (dau. of THOMAS JONES, b. 1755 in England; d. 1809, in Ga., REV. SOLDIER, and (2) wife Elizabeth Boyd).

WILLIAM DANMARK, b. N. C.; d. age 102 years, Warren Co., Ga. Served as REV. SOLDIER. Married (1) Miss Moye; (2) Emma Moye.
Children:

1. Redden, b. Screven Co., Ga., 1770; d. in Ga., 1814. Married Lavinia Wise (dau. of WILLIAM WISE, REV. SOLDIER of Va. who settled in Screven Co., Ga.). She mar. (2) Mr. McNeely.
   Children:
   1. Elizabeth, mar. James Groover.
   2. Clarissa.
   3. Sarah, mar. William Lastinger.
   4. John, d. 1844, Perry, Fla.
   5. Thomas Irving, b. 1809; mar. Amanda Groover (dau. of Charles Groover).

CYRUS DART, b. Haddon, Conn., June 11, 1764. Drowned near St. Simons Island, Ga., 1817. (He was the son of JOSEPH DART, a REV. SOLDIER of Conn., and his wife Abigail Brainerd.) Enlisted as private in Capt. Stillwell's Co., 1st Conn. Reg., April 1, 1782. Came to Glynn Co., Ga., 1792, and lived in the "old town of Frederica". Married May 7, 1796, Ann Harris; they lived at "Coleraine", Dead town of Ga.
Children:

1. Erastus.
2. Horace.
3. Urbanus, b. 1800; d. Brunswick, Ga., 1883; mar. 1836, Eliza Moore. They had 8 children.
4. Alfred.
5. Theodore.
6. Ann Maria, mar. Dr. Du Pree.
7. Eliza Ann, mar. (1) Cyrus Paine; (2) Schupert Burns.
8. Edgar C. P., mar. Ellen Moore.

NOTE: "Coleraine" was an Indian town (now a dead town of Ga.) on the North side of St. Mary's River where the Treaty of Peace and

Friendship was made June 29, 1796, between the President of the United States and the Kings, the Chiefs, and Warriors of the Creek nation of Indians, ratified March 18, 1797.

The Commissioners on the part of the U. S. were Benjamin Hawkins, George Glymer, and Andrew Pickens. (The Lyman Hall Chapter, D. A. R., of Waycross, Ga. marked the site of Coleraine.)

CHRISTIAN DASHER, served as private in Ga. Troops under Col. Jenkins, Cols. Davis and Howell. Died in service. Married Anna Christiana Moyer.

JOHN MARTIN DASHER, b. 1738, N. C.; d. 1802 in Effingham Co., Ga. Served as private under Capt. Kubler in St. Mathew's Parish, Ga. Married Susanna Shaffer (dau. of BELTHASAS SHAFFER (Schaffer), REV. SOLDIER of Ga.).
Children:
1. John.
2. Solomon (1791-1854); mar. Maria Wylly (dau. of THOMAS WYLLY, b. 1762, West Indies; d. 1846, Effingham Co., Ga. Asst. Quartermaster under his uncle RICHARD WYLLY, REV. SOLDIER of Ga.).
3. Naomi, mar. 1802, William C. Wylly.
4. Susanna, mar. — Franklin.
5. Martin, mar. Lydia Wiltman.
6. Christopher, mar. Ann Bird.
7. Joshua, mar. Dolly Moore.

THOMAS DAVENPORT, b. Charlotte Co., Va.; d. 1808 in Ga. Served as private, Ga. Line and received bounty grant of land for his services in Ga.

JOHN DAVIS, b. 1754, King William Co., Va.; d. 1843, Elbert Co., Ga. Placed on Pension roll, Elbert Co., 1833 for services as private, Va. Militia. Married Sarah —.

JOHN DAVIS (From Pension). REV. SOLDIER of Va., pension issued April 5, 1833, service private. Applied Sept. 30, 1830, age 100 years, living then in Gwinnett Co., Ga. Served from Prince William Co., Va., 1777, 4 years, 4 months, under Capt. Andrew Leach, Lieut. Valentine Peyton, Col. Philip Lee's Brigade. Removed to Pendleton Dist., S. C., settled 1824, Gwinnett Co., Ga.

JOHN DAVIS, b. in N. C., 1759; d. 1818, Morgan Co., Ga. Private, N. C. Line. Married Nancy Patterson.

JONATHAN DAVIS, b. in England about 1730; d. in Wilkes Co., Ga., 1818. Served in Va. Line. Married Lucy Gibbs, 1756.
Child:

1. WILLIAM DAVIS, b. Orange Co., Va., Jan. 7, 1765. Served under Gen. de La Fayette and was present at the surrender of Cornwallis. Married Nancy Easton of Philadelphia, Penn., d. 1841. He d. Wilkes Co., Ga., Oct. 31, 1831. Received bounty grant of land in Ga. for his services. Baptist preacher. They had 12 children.
Children: (known)
1. Rev. James (1805-1859; mar. Louise Hudson.
2. Rev. Jesse, b. 1808; mar. (1) Sophia Burton; (2) Mrs. Elizabeth Gilbert; (3) widow McGouldrick. He d. 1868, Blakely, Ga.
3. Rev. Jonathan, mar. Mary E. Johnston.
4. Jeptha.
5. William, Jr.

WILLIAM DAVIS, b. 1748; d. in Ga., 1801. Served in S. C. Regiment. Received bounty grant of land for his services. Married in S. C., Anne McLeod.
Children:

1. John.	5. Jane.
2. Charles.	6. Martha.
3. Rebecca.	7. Elizabeth.
4. Ulysses.	8. Maria.

WILLIAM DAVIS, b. in Va., 1748; d. Wilkes Co., Ga., May 14, 1818. Served as Lieut.-Col. in 5th Va. Regiment. Moved to Wilkes Co., Ga., 1795. Married Brunswick Co., Va., Aug. 28, 1769, Agnes Lanier, d. Feb. 21, 1813 (dau. of Sampson Lanier of Va.). They had 11 children.
Child:
1. Lewis Lanier Davis (1792-1832); mar. 1818 in Wilkes Co., Louise Tucker Irvine (dau. of Isaiah Tucker Irvine and his wife Isabella Lea Bankston).

STEPHEN DAY, b. 1742 in Penn.; d. 1825 in Columbia Co., Ga. Received bounty land in Ga. for his services upon certificate of Col. James McNeil. Married Margaret Jones, b. 1744 (dau. of JAMES JONES, REV. SOLDIER of Ga., and his wife Mary).
Children:
1. John, mar. Feribee Bulloch.
2. Stephen, Jr.
3. Jonathan.
4. Joseph.
5. Daughter, mar. Thomas Kendrick.
6. Rebecca, mar. John Kendrick, b. Frederick Co., Md., 1759; d. Pike Co., Ga., 1843. Served as Lieut., REV. SOLDIER, and received bounty land in Ga. for his services. Granted pension No. 4255.
Children:

1. Sylvanus K., mar. Elizabeth Park.
2. John, mar. Nancy Locklin.
3. William A., mar. Mary McLean.
4. Adeline Eliza, mar. William Freeman.
5. Sarah Rebecca, mar. Jonas Shivers.
6. Theodate, mar. Daniel Carroll.
7. Cornelia.

(Above record of JOHN KENDRICK, REV. SOLDIER).

REUBEN DE JARNETTE, b. in Va.; d. 1830, Putnam Co., Ga. Served in the Va. Continental Line. Married Miss Bird.

JAMES DE LAUNAY, buried City Cemetery, Milledgeville, Ga. A REV. SOLDIER.

RAYMOND DEMERE, b. in Ga., 1742; d. Jan. 2, 1829, Ga. (Grave marked by the Brunswick Chapter, D. A. R.) He was a member of Provincial Congress which met in Tondee's Long Room, Savannah, Ga., July 4, 1775. Was captured and made prisoner by the British. Was exchanged Mar. 1776. Served on staff of Lord Stirling as aide-de-camp, and later with Gen. Washington; in the campaigns of New Jersey. Married Ann —, b. in S. C., 1744; d. Dec. 17, 1808. Mentions in Will: Son Raymond, Jr.; 3 daughters; and grandsons Joseph, Lewis, John, and Paul.

JOHN DENMAN, an Englishman who came to America about 1760. Served as a REV. SOLDIER, and after the War, he removed to Franklin Co., Ga., where he died.

JACK (John) DENNARD, b. in S. C., 1750; d. in Ga., 1810. Enlisted in S. C. 6th Regiment 1776. Served as Lieut. in Capt. McBee's Co.; also Capt. Mapps Co., Col. Roebuck's S. C. Reg. Married Harriet —. Children: (known)
1. Shadrack.
2. Isaac, mar. Mary Harris. Soldier of 1812.
3. William.
4. Thomas.
5. John.
6. Bird, b. 1780; mar. Rhoda Marshall. Soldier of 1812.

GEORGE DENT, b. 1756 in Md.; d. in Ga. 1813. Served as Lieut. 1776, 3rd Md. Flying Camp.

PETER DE VEAUX, b. in Ga., 1752; d. in Ga., 1826. Member Provincial Congress. Served in S. C. and Ga. Militia. Married Martha Box.

DAVID DICKSON, b. 1750 Pendleton Dist., S. C.; d. May 23, 1830 in

Fayette (now Clayton) Co., Ga. Served at Snow Camps, Speedy River, 1775. Commanded a Volunteer Co., under Gen. Williamson, 1776, in the Cherokee Nation against the Indians and Tories. Commanded a Co. of Minute Men on the Frontier. Received bounty grant of land in Ga. for his services. He married (1) Sarah — (1750-1785); (2) Martha Cureton (1764-1796); (3) Anne Allen (1772-1840).
Children: (mentioned in will).
1. William H.
2. Michael.
3. David.
4. John Orr, mar. Mary Glass.
5. Nancy Campbell, mar. — Smith.
6. Martha Easley, mar. — McConnell.
7. Thornton Smith.
8. Robert David.
9. (Step-son) Chandler Aubrey.
(Grave marked by the Ga. D. A. R.)

MICHAEL DICKSON, b. Lunenburg, Va., 1743; will filed Sparta, Hancock Co., Ga., 1803. Served as Capt. in Ga. Militia. Married Lucy Crawford Atwood.
Child:
1. Eliza Sarah DeVeaux, mar. John Morel.

JOHN DIXON, b. 1758 in N. C.; d. 1835 in Ga. Served as private, 1st Batt. of N. C., under Capt. McRee and Col. Clark. Married 1796, Elizabeth Poythress (1771-1842).

JOHN DOBY, b. Sussex Co., Va., 1755; d. 1836, Jasper Co., Ga. Served as private in Capt. Cade's Co., Col. Keenan's N. C. Reg. Married 1784, Sarah White (1757-1815) (dau. of WILLIAM WHITE, a REV. SOLDIER, and his wife Sarah Lucas.).

JOHN DOLLAR, b. 1742; d. Oct. 20, 1797 at his plantation home "Antrim" near Sunbury, Ga. A REV. SOLDIER. Captain of Continental Artillery in the American War. (From Ga. Gazette Funeral Notice).

JOHN DOOLY, b. in N. C.; came from S. C. to the Ceded Lands of Ga. (now Wilkes Co.) with a wife, 3 sons and 3 orphan nephews in 1762. Served as Captain of the 2nd Continental Ga. Brigade, and was later Colonel. Was killed by the Tories 1780. Several of these Tories crossed the Savannah River and were later captured by the "War Heroine of Ga., Nancy Hart".

NOTE: Others were also captured and hung at Tory Pond in Wilkes Co. (Dooly Co., Ga. was named for Col. Dooly, founded in 1821.) His brother THOMAS DOOLY, REV. SOLDIER, was killed July 22, 1776, in a skirmish with the Indians while returning to Ga. with a band of recruits fro the Ga. Continental Army.

JAMES S. DOZIER, b. Lunenburg Co., Va., 1739; d. 1808, Warren Co., Ga. Served as Sergeant, Va. Militia and in Artillery. Married Mary Dunwoody (or Dinwoody), b. 1740.
Child:
1. Leonard Wesley Dozier, b. in Va.; d. Warren Co., Ga. Married Nancy Staples.

WILLIAM DRANE, REV. SOLDIER, b. in Va.; d. in Ga. Married Cassandra Magruder.
Children: (known)
1. Eleanor, b. in Columbia Co., Ga.; d. Coweta Co. Married Anselm B. Leigh, a Soldier of 1812.
2. William, Jr., b. Columbia Co., Ga., 1800; married Martha H. Winfrey (dau. of JESSE WINFREY, REV. SOLDIER).

ISAAC DuBOSE, b. in S. C.; d. Columbia Co., Ga. Served in S. C. as Lieut. under Gen. Morgan and Gen. Sumpter. Married his cousin, Sarah DuBose.

AMBROSE DUDLEY, b. 1750, Spotsylvania Co., Va.; d. 1825, Fayette Co., Ga. Commanded a Co. of Va. Troops. Married 1773, Ann Parker.

ANDREW DUKE, b. 1730, Cabarrus Co., N. C.; d. in Ga., 1798. Served as Lieut., N. C. Line. Married Keziah Anderson. They lived in Hancock Co., Ga.

JAMES DUNWOODY, b. 1741, Chester Co., Penn.; d. Liberty Co., Ga., 1807. Came to Ga. 1770. Member Ex. Council of Ga. Married 1774, Esther (Dean) Splatt (dau. of Abraham Dean and his wife Ann Du Pont).
Children:
1. James, Jr., mar. Elizabeth West Smith.
2. John, mar. Jane Bullock.
3. Esther, mar. Sen. John Elliott as (2) wife.

NOTE: JAMES DUNWOODY was the son of John Dunwoody of Chester Co., Penn., and his wife Susanna Cresswell, dau. of William Cresswell of Fogg's Manor Penn.

ROBERT DUNWOODY, b. Chester Co., Penn., 1744; d. 1794, Screven Co., Ga. Served as private 1781 in Capt. Allen's Co., Chester Co., Penn. Militia. Married Mary Cresswell.
Child:
1. Mary Dunwoody (1793-1870); mar. Benjamin Archelus Saxon (1796-1855).

MAJOR NATHANIEL DURKEE, buried in "Old Redwine Cemetery", d. 1823 in Franklin Co. (now Hart Co.), Ga. Married Malinda —. (Grave marked by the John Benson Chapter, D. A. R., Hartwell, Ga. He was a nephew and namesake of Gen. NATHANIEL GREENE, REV. SOLDIER.)

ELISHA DYAR (or Dyer), b. in Va., 1763, near the Potomac River; d. in Ga., 1836. Enlisted Granville Co., N. C., 1778, under Gen. Abram Potter and Col. Farrow. Was at the Battle of Briar Creek. Enlisted 1780 under Capt. Peter Burnett; Col. Ambrose Dudley. Came to Ga., 1800. Received land in Cherokee Land Lottery 1827 as a REV. SOLDIER. Married Malvina Wheeler (1760-1820).
Children:
1. Martin.
2. John.
3. Joel H., mar. Rachel Sanders.
4. Rebecca, mar. 1820, William S. P. Crawford.
5. William.
6. Polly, mar. William Smith.
7. Elizabeth, mar. Jeremiah Wells.
8. Melvina, mar. George Hornbuckle.

JACOB EARLY (son of JEREMIAH EARLY, REV. SOLDIER of Va.), d. 1794 in Ga. Served as Capt., Va. Line. Received bounty grant of land for his services in Wilkes Co., Ga. Married 1767, Elizabeth Robertson. His will was probated Clarke Co., Ga.   —
Children:
1. Ann (called Nancy), b. 1769; mar. BUCKNER HARRIS, a REV. SOLDIER (son of WALTON HARRIS, REV. SOLDIER, and his wife Rebecca Lanier).
2. Mary.   4. Alicey.
3. Elizabeth.   5. Sally.

JOEL EARLY (son of JEREMIAH EARLY, REV. SOLDIER of Va.), b. in Va.; d. 1807 at his home "Early's Manor", now Greene Co., Ga. (formerly Wilkes Co.) Served in Va. Line, Lieut. stationed 1781 at Travis Point. Delegate to Va. Convention from Culpeper Co. Moved to Ga., 1791. Married 1772, Lucy Smith.
Children:
1. Peter, b. 1773; elected Governor of Ga., 1813. Married Ann Adams Smith. She mar. (2) Rev. Adiel Sherwood.
2. Elizur, mar. Miss Patterson.
3. Mary (called Polly), mar. Major George Watkins.
4. Clement, mar. Sarah Terrell.
5. Joel, Jr., mar. Miss Singleton.
6. Jeremiah, mar. (1) Jane Sturgis; (2) Ann Billups (she mar. (2) John Cunningham).
7. Lucy, mar. Col. Charles Lewis Mathews (youngest son of

Governor George Mathews of Ga.).

JAMES EASTER, b. in Va.; d. Elbert Co., Ga. (Will made May 19, 1791, probated Feb. 11, 1792). Served in Va. Line. Received 287.5 acres of bounty land in Franklin Co., Ga. 1784. He married Sarah —. She mar. (2) 1792, Edmund Brewer; (3) Robert Moore.
Children: (mentioned in Will)
Daughters
1. Mary Ann.
2. Elizabeth.
3. Dolly.
4. Lotty.
5. Sophia.
6. Tere.
7. Patty, mar. William Aycock.
8. Tabitha (Tabby), mar. Thomas Napier.
9. Marjery.
Sons
10. William Thompson.
11. Booker Burton, mar. Catherine Youmans.
12. Lewis.
13. Champion.

ELI EAVENSON, b. Chester Co., Penn., Jan. 12, 1760; d. Elbert Co., Ga., July 29, 1829. Married 1781, Rachel Seal, b. April 25, 1760; d. after 1829. He was a REV. SOLDIER and drew two lots in Lottery of 1806; one 1825 for REV. service in Elbert Co. Was also a Soldier of 1812. Came to Ga., 1791.
Children:
1. George, b. Nov. 7, 1782; mar. Polly Hilly.
2. Susanna, b. Jan. 4, 1784; mar. John Higgenbotham.
3. Hannah, b. Nov. 2, 1786; mar. Matthew Pulliam.
4. Elizabeth, mar. Beverly Teasley.
5. Polly, b. 1791.

NEHEMIAH EDGE, b. 1754 in Md.; d. 1806 in Ga. Served in N.C. Troops. Received land in Wilkes Co., Ga. Married Elizabeth Doster.
Children:
1. John, b. 1784; d. Cave Spring, Ga., 1844; mar. Sarah Miller (1780-1840).
2. James.
3. Reason, mar. (1) —; (2) Susan J. Deloney (1816).

ISAAC EDMONDSON, b. in England 1760; came to America. Served in S.C. Line. Moved to Bulloch Co., Ga.; d. Savannah, Ga., 1811. Married 1785, Nancy Cox (1765-1842). Moved to Brooks Co., Ga.
Children:
1. Susanna, mar. John Mathis.

2. Elizabeth, mar. William Holoway.
3. James.
4. John, b. 1806; mar. Martha Strickland (dau. of Archibald Strickland of Tattnall and Brooks Co., Ga.).
5. David, mar. Tabitha Tillman.
6. Sally, mar. William Alderman.

JOHN EDWARDS, b. 1759 in England; d. 1833, Meriwether Co., Ga. Served as private, Ga. Troops, Capt. Eldredge's Co., Col. Elliott's Reg. Married 1786, Elizabeth Rainey.
Children:
1. Sterling (1788-1853), mar. 1816, Susan Hicks.
2. Patsey.
3. Paulina, mar. John Rainey.
4. Mary, mar. George Crinder.

SOLOMON EDWARDS, b. 1756 in Va.; d. Clarke Co., Ga., 1844. Served as private, Va. Line. Received bounty land in Ga. for his services. Married Sarah Matthews.
Children:
1. William, mar. Kate Coleman.
2. Sarah Matthews, mar. Wylie Jones. She mar. (2) Mr. Dennis. 10 children.
3. Richard, mar. (1) Polly Harper; (2) Amanda Cunningham.

WILLIAM EDWARDS, b. about 1741; lived in N. C.; d. Effingham, Ga., 1833. Served in Capt. Elliott's Co., Col. Charles Pinckney's S. C. Reg. Enlisted 1775. Served also in Col. William Caldwell's S. C. Reg. Drew land as a REV. SOLDIER in Cherokee Lottery 1827. Married 1761, Chloe Stokes (1744-1803).
Children: (known)
1. William (1770-1833); mar. Elizabeth Beall.
2. Obediah, mar. 1799, Tabitha Pitts (dau. of JOHN PITTS, REV. SOLDIER of N. C., and his wife Frances Griffin).
3. Henry.
4. Chloe.
5. Beall.

SAMUEL ELBERT, b. in Prince William Parish, Va., 1740; d. at Great Ogechee, Ga. Moved to Savannah, Ga. Made Captain of Grenadiers 1774; member Council of Safety 1775; Lieut.-Col. 1776; Commandant of a Brigade at the Battle of Brier Creek, Ga. Was appointed Major-General of the Ga. Militia. Was Governor of Ga. 1785. He d. Nov. 1, 1788. (Grave marked by Sons of the Revolution.) Married Nov. 29, 1769, Elizabeth Rae.
Children: (known)
1. Kitty, mar. 1791, Capt. John Burke.
2. Betsey, mar. 1798, Dr. M. Burke.

SHADRACK ELLIS, age 80, drew pension in 1840 for his services as a REV. SOLDIER while a resident of Talbot Co., Ga.

STEPHEN ELLIS (and wife Agnes), of Richmond Co., drew land 287.5 acres, Greene Co.

DAVID EMANUEL, b. 1744 in Wales or Penn.; d. 1808, Burke Co., Ga. Served in the Ga. Line under his brother-in-law Brig.-Gen. John Twiggs of Ga. Was captured but escaped from the Tories. He was Governor of Ga., 1801. Married Ann Lewis.
Children:
1. Rebecca, mar. Jacob Walker.
2. Ruth.
3. Martha.
4. Asenath, mar. Francis Wells.
5. Ann, mar. as (2) wife, James Welch.
6. Mary, mar. Thomas Blount.

JESSE EMBREE, b. Wilkes Co., Ga., 1750; d. 1800, Oglethorpe Co., Ga. Served as private, Ga. Line. Married 1773, Nancy Embry (1755-1805).

JOHN EMBREE, b. 1721, Little Egg Harbor, New Jersey; d. June 1826, Wrightsboro, Ga. Was a PATRIOT 1775. Married 1752, Elizabeth Harrison, Columbia Co., Ga.

JOHN EPPINGER, b. May 8, 1730, Werender, Wurtenburg. Came to London 1749; and to America, Oct. 15, 1749. Settled in N. C. Came to Savannah, Ga. He was a REV. PATRIOT and many patriotic meetings were held in his home, "The Eppinger Tavern," Savannah. He d. 1776. Married Barbara Mayers (dau. of Jacob Mayers), b. in Wurtenburg, July 10, 1732; d. Savannah, Ga., Jan. 1776.
Children:
1. Margaret, b. Wilmington, N. C., Jan. 1, 1775; d. 1793. Married BALTHAZER SCHAEFFER, May 30, 1772. He was a REV. SOLDIER.
2. Anna Magdalina, d. y.
3. Wenafoothu (Winifred), b. Savannah, Ga., July 1, 1763. Married Joseph Roberts.
4. John, b. July 21, 1769; d. July 23, 1823. Married Hannah Elizabeth Cline. He was U. S. Dist. Marshall 1808-1812. (1812 Rec.)
5. Sarah, mar. (1) John Miller; (2) John Jones.
6. James, mar. Elizabeth Shandley.
7. George.
8. Matthew.

JAMES ESPY, b. Cumberland Co., Penn., Dec. 7, 1759; d. Athens, Ga., 1834. Served in Col. Charles McLain's N. C. Reg. as private from Tryon Co., N. C. Drew pension for his services in 1832. Married (1) Sarah Baker, d. 1829.

DANIEL EVANS, a REV. SOLDIER of Burke Co., Ga., whose name appears on the "Roster of Capt. Patrick Carr's Co. of Burke Co. Rangers" 1782. Married Mary Jones (dau. of William and Mary Jones). Child:
    1. Martha Jones Evans, mar. Reuben Walker (son of THOMAS WALKER, REV. SOLDIER of Ga.).

JOHN EVANS, b. 1765 in Ga.; d. in Ga. 1821. Served as a private, Ga. Line. Received grant of land for his services. Married 1795, Elizabeth Murray (McMurray) (d. 1845).

JOHN EVANS, a native of N. C., came to Ga., 1800, and settled in Franklin Co., Ga. A REV. SOLDIER of N. C.

WILLIAM EVANS, b. 1746 in Va.; d. 1806, Wilkes Co., Ga. Served as private, Va. Line. Received bounty grant of land 1784 in Washington Co., Ga. for his services. Married Susanna Clement (dau. of Benjamin Clement of Pittsylvania Co., Va.). Widow mar. (2) Daniel Slaton. Children:
    1. John (1772-1825); mar. Bessie Morton.
    2. Stephen, mar. (1) Elizabeth Bennett; (2) — Jackson.
    3. James, mar. Sallie Bennett.
    4. Arden, mar. Elizabeth —.
    5. William (1776-1828), mar. Elizabeth Combs.
    6. Susan, mar. Kellis Slaton.
    7. Annie, mar. Jonas Starke.
    8. Sallie, mar. (1) Samuel Slaton; (2) William Combs.

EBENEZER FAIN, b. Chester Co., Penn., 1762; d. Habersham Co., Ga., 1842. Served as private with Penn., S. C., and Ga. troops, under Capt. James Montgomery, Capt. William Trimble, and Col. Elijah Clarke. Married 1781 in Tenn., Mary Black, d. Gilmer Co., Ga., 1846. Children:
    1. David, b. 1782 of Gilmer Co., Ga.
    2. Margaret.
    3. Mercer, moved to Texas.
    4. Elizabeth, b. 1791; mar. John Trammell of Habersham Co., Ga. (son of WILLIAM TRAMMELL, REV. SOLDIER of Ga.).
    5. Mary Ann.
    6. Sallie.   8. Rebecca Ann.
    7. John.   9. Polly.

THOMAS FAIN (only child of WILLIAM FAIN, REV. SOLDIER of Tenn., and his wife Miss Knox). (Grave marked by Tenn. Society D. A. R.) Was b. in N. C., 1760; d. Decatur Co., Ga., 1832. Place of

residence during REV., Orange Co., N.C. Served as private, N.C. Line. Married 1781, Mary Parramore (1762-1832).
Children: (names copied from Bible owned by Rebecca Jane Lewis Pollard and statement from Laura (McCall) (Cook) Leverette of Brooks Co., Ga.)

1. Matthew, b. Aug. 11, 1782.
2. Betty, b. Feb. 17, 1785.
3. Lavinia, b. 1787; mar. William McMullen.
4. Nancy, b. 1789.
5. Mary, b. 1791; mar. — Martin.
6. Rebecca, b. 1793; mar. James McMullen.
7. Clara, b. 1795; mar. — Strickland.
8. Ann, b. 1788; mar. — Whiddon.
9. Luvenicia, b. 1801; mar. George R. F. McCall (son of WM. McCALL, REV. SOLDIER).
10. Thomas, Jr., b. 1802; mar.
11. William, b. 1807.
12. Levice, b. 1810; mar. — Marshall.
13. L., b. Jan. 15, 1817.

JOHN FAIR, b. 1760; d. in Ga. 1850. Served as a REV. SOLDIER. Received grant of land. Married Polly Waldener.
Children:

1. Sally.
2. Nancy.
3. William.
4. Alexander.
5. Elizabeth.
6. Rhoda.
7. Rebecca.
8. Polly.
9. Susan.
10. Effie.

PETER FAIR, b. in France, came to America and served under La Fayette. Married Susanna Bone of Charleston, S.C. On his tombstone in Milledgeville, Ga., 1824, "A Frenchman who came to S.C., later to Ga."

ANDERSON FAMBROUGH, d. Clarke Co., Ga., Nov. 1815. Served as REV. SOLDIER. Drew bounty land in Ga. Married Elizabeth —.
Children:

1. Gabriel.
2. John Anderson.
3. Joshua.
4. Jesse.
5. Jane.
6. Lucy.
7. Polly, mar. — Thompson.
8. Nancy, mar. — Thompson.
9. Susanna, mar. — Ward.
10. Elizabeth, mar. — Cole.

JAMES FANNIN, b. Nov. 28, 1739; d. in Ga., Nov. 4, 1803. Served in REV. WAR and received bounty land in Ga. for his services. Married Elizabeth Saffold (1748-1814).
Children:

1. Ann, mar. Littleton Mapp.

2. Sarah, mar. James Allison.
3. William, mar. C. Martin.
4. Joseph Decker (1776-1817); mar. Betsey Lowe.
5. John H., mar. Mary Wright.
6. James W., mar. Ann P. Fletcher.
7. Jeptha, mar. Katie Porter.
8. Eliza, mar. Stephen Bishop.
9. Isham (1778-1819); mar. Patsey Porter.
10. Abram, mar. Jane Williamson.

ROBERT FARQUHAS, b. 1743 in Scotland; d. 1784, Charleston, S. C. Was a REV. PATRIOT and who loaned money to the State of Georgia during REV. WAR to help "carry on".

JOHN FARR, served as private, Ga. Troops at the Battle of Kettle Creek; d. 1850, Newton Co., Ga. Married Polly Waldener (1761-1852).

THOMAS FARRAR, b. Farrar's Island, Va.; d. 1810, at the home of his son Abner, Franklin Co., Ga. Served as Colonel, S. C. Militia. Married Eliza Howard.
Children: (known)
1. Abner, mar. Katie Malone
2. Absolom, mar. Phoebe Avary.

JOHN FAVER of Va.; d. in Wilkes Co., Ga. Served at the Battle of Kettle Creek and was granted land for his services in 1784. (A monument has been erected at his grave by the Sarah Dickinson Chapter, D. A. R., Newnan, Ga.) He mar. in Va., Mary Bolton.

WILLIAM FEARS, b. in Va., Feb. 16, 1746; d. in Jasper Co., Ga., May 13, 1820. He served in the Va. Line and in the Cherokee Lottery 1827 in Ga., drew two lots of land for his services as a REV. SOLDIER and for being wounded in the service. Married 1771, in Va., Ann Bulger, b. in Va., Feb. 13, 1752.
Children:
1. James, b. April 28, 1772; mar. Mary Anthony Porter.
2. William, b. Jan. 31, 1774; mar. (1) Mary (Polly) Griffin; (2) Joicy T. Bowdre.
3. Mary, b. Nov. 20, 1775; mar. (1) — Crenshaw; (2) Henry Fulke of Va.
4. Elizabeth, b. Dec. 18, 1777; mar. — Petty.
5. Rebecca, b. May 20, 1779; mar. Bartholemew Roberts.
6. Ezekiel, b. Sept. 30, 1781; mar. Alice Stringfellow.
7. Thomas, b. Oct. 30, 1783; mar. 1833. (no issue).
8. Frances, b. Nov. 5, 1786; mar. — Parks.
9. Zacheriah, b. July 3, 1789; mar. Elizabeth Mathews.
10. Samuel, b. Oct. 13, 1791; mar. Mary Ballard.
11. Robert, b. Aug. 21, 1793; mar. — Smith.

12. Sarah, b. 1796; mar. — Chaplaine; moved to Tenn.
13. Nancy, b. Oct. 30, 1799; mar. William Roberts.

ISAAC FELL, d. in Ga. Was serving in a Co. stationed at the Springfield Redoubt when Savannah, Ga. was besieged by the British. He lost an arm in the conflict; was captured; placed aboard a ship; and conveyed to England. He was also a Soldier of the War of 1812. Married Mar. 10, 17--, in Savannah, Ga., Elizabeth Susannah Shick (dau. of JOHN SHICK, a REV. SOLDIER of Ga., and his wife Margaret Ritter).

WILLIAM FEW, SR., b. 1714, Kennett, Penn. Came to Ga. from N. C.; d. near Wrightsboro, Ga. Married 1743, Mary Wheeler. Received bounty land for his services in N. C. Line in Washington Co., Ga.
Children:
1. BENJAMIN, b. 1744 in Md. Came to Ga.; d. on a visit to Ala., 1805. Married in N. C., Rachel Wiley. Served as Col. in Richmond Co., Ga. Militia.
2. WILLIAM, JR., b. June 8, 1748 in Md.; d. July 16, 1828 at Fishkill on the Hudson, N. Y. Married Catherine Nicholson (dau. of COMMODORE JAMES NICHOLSON, N. Y., a REV. SOLDIER). Served as Lieut.-Col., Richmond Co., Ga. Militia. Member of Executive Council 1777-78; and of Continental Congress 1780-82. Moved to N. Y. One of the first Trustees of the University of Ga.
3. James, b. 1746, was murdered by the Tories during the Regulator movement. Married Sarah Wood.
4. IGNATIUS, b. 1750 in Md.; d. 1810. Served as 1st Lieut., Capt., and Major, Ga. Troops. Mar. Mary Candler.
5. Hannah, mar. RHESA HOWARD, REV. SOLDIER of Ga.
6. Elizabeth, mar. COL. GREENBERRY LEE, REV. SOLDIER

NOTE: Rev. Ignatius Alphonso Few, b. 1789, Columbia Co., Ga.; d. 1845, was the first President of Emory College (now Emory University, Atlanta, Ga.).

MATTHEW FINLEY, b. 1758 in Ireland; d. 1818 in Ga. Served as private under Col. Elijah Clarke. Married Jane McCord.

BENJAMIN FITZPATRICK, b. 1746 in Va.; d. at Buckhead, Morgan Co., Ga., 1821. Served as private, Va. Line. Received bounty grant of land in Ga. for his services. Married (1) Mary Perkins; (2) Sarah Jones.
Children by (1) wife:
1. James, mar. Sarah Harris.
2. Constantine (1771-1845), mar. —.
3. Frances, mar. — Stewart.

4. Nancy, mar. — High.
Children by (2) wife:
5. Elizabeth, mar. Samuel Clay.
6. William, mar. Nancy Green.
7. Joseph, mar. Nancy Hunter.
8. Alexander, mar. Nancy Hill.
9. Susan (mar. twice).
10. Bennett, mar. Eliza Shackelford.
11. Mary, mar. Thomas Brown.

RENEE FITZPATRICK, b. in S. C.; d. Catoosa Co., Ga., 1839. Served as private, Ga. Line. Received bounty grant of land in Ga. for his services. Married 1797, Mollie Hardwick (dau. of WILLIAM HARDWICK, REV. SOLDIER, and his wife Cynthia Parker).

LEWIS FLEMISTER, b. Essex Co., Va., 1746; d. Wilkes Co., Ga., 1807. Enlisted 1775 Chesterfield C. H., Va. Served as private, 7th Va. Reg., Capt. William Moseley; transferred to Morristown, N. J., Capt. Caleb Gibbs Co. Sergeant 1783. Discharged Newburg, N. Y., 1783. (Grave marked by Joseph Habersham Chapter, D. A. R., 1930). Married Feb. 27, 1790, Ellender Chism (dau. of James and Barbara Chism), b. Halifax Co., N. C., 1773; d. near Monticello, Ga., 1855. Children:
1. William L., mar. Micha Wilson.
2. James, mar. Ailsa Wilson.
3. Lewis Fielding, mar. Lucy Wilson.
4. John, mar. Huldah Woodruff.
5. Catherine, mar. John Lindsay.
6. Euramie Elizabeth, mar. Isaac Parker.

JOHN FLERL (or Floerl), b. in Saltzburg, Austria, Germany; d. in Ga., 1776. Came to America, settled in Ebenezer, Ga. (Salzburger Colony). Member First Provincial Congress of Ga., 1775. Capt., Ga. Troops 1776, under Gen. Samuel Elbert. Married (1) Jan. 15, 1765, Harriet Elizabeth Brandner (1743-1773); mar. (2) 1774, Dorothy Kieffer.
Children:
1. Judith, d. y.
2. Margaret (or Mary), b. 1767; mar. J. C. WALDHAUER, a REV. SOLDIER.
3. John, d. y.
4. Israel (1771-1813); mar. Sarah Salome Waldhauer. She mar. (2) Lewis Weitman.

JOHN FLETCHER, b. in S. C., Jan. 14, 1765; d. in Gadsen, Fla., May 30, 1860. Served 1780 under Capt. James Gregg, Lieut.-Col. Thomas Davis, Col. Hugh Giles, Gen. Francis Marion. After Gates' defeat, he was under Major David Thornley, Col. Baxter and others.

Applied for pension Nov. 9, 1832. Served as private to 1782. Lived in Marion Dist., 50 miles above Georgetown. Moved to Ga., 1784; to Gadsen, Fla., 1825. Was living as a minor with his father during REV. All were REV. SOLDIERS; his father WILLIAM FLETCHER and three brothers. He was Capt., Bullock Co. Mil., Ga. 1796. Soldier 1812 record. He was H.R., Telfair Co., Ga., 1816-17. Married Telfair Co. (formerly Bulloch), Susan Mizell.
Children: (known)
1. Zecheriah.
2. John, moved to Opelika, Ala.
3. Nancy, mar. Leonidas Lott.
4. Sarah.
5. Zabud.
6. Ziba, mar. Blanche Reese.

WILLIAM FLETCHER, b. in Accomac Co., Va., 1729; d. in Telfair Co., Ga., after 1837. He is buried in Telfair Co. Place of residence during the REV. was Marion Dist., S.C., 50 miles above Georgetown. He served as REV. SOLDIER and is recorded in the Pension claim (granted) of his son JOHN FLETCHER in 1832. He was given land in the Cherokee Land Lottery in Ga., 1827, as a REV. SOLDIER of Telfair Co. He married (1) in Va. (name unknown); mar. (2) Elizabeth McIntosh in Georgetown, S.C. (St. Philips Parish Church); mar. (3) Louisa Hendricks.
Children by (2) wife:
1. GEORGE, b. Dec. 28, 1752. S.C. REV. SOLDIER. Moved to Effingham Co., Ga.
2. JOSEPH, mar. Elizabeth Lanier. Lived in Bulloch Co., Ga.
3. JOHN, b. S.C., 1765; mar. Susan Mizell. REV. SOLDIER. Moved to Ga., then Fla.
4. Ann (called Nancy), mar. WILLIAM McCALL, REV. SOLDIER of S.C. Moved to Ga. (Effingham and Screven Counties).
5. Elizabeth, mar. (1) — Barton; (2) Joseph Morrison.
6. Rebecca, mar. JOSHUA HODGES, REV. SOLDIER. They lived in Screven and Bulloch Counties.
Children by (3) wife:
7. Sarah.
8. Thomas.
9. Wiley.

ABNER FLEWELLYN, b. Baldwin Co., N.C., 1760; d. 1815, Bibb Co. Served as a private and his tombstone gives record as a man and a REV. SOLDIER. Married Ann Lane.

JAMES FLOURNOY, b. Chesterfield Co., Va., 1763; d. 1858 in Ga. Received a pension for his services as private in Capt. Cheatham's Co., Col. Robert Good's Reg. Married 1785, Peggy Cundiff.

JOHN FLOURNOY, b. Chesterfield Co., Va.; d. in Ga. Served as private, Ga. Line. Married his cousin, Mary Ashurst.

ROBERT FLOURNOY, b. 1763, Prince Edward Co., Va.; d. 1825, Lexington, Ga. Served at age of 17 years as a private in Ga. Militia. Married 1780, Mary Willis Cobb, d. 1830. Record on tombstone, Sparta, Ga.

CHARLES FLOYD, b. Northampton Co., Va., Mar. 4, 1747; d. "Bellevue", Camden Co., Ga., Sept. 9, 1820. Came to Charleston, S. C. Served with the "Liberty Boys" of Ga.; was captured by the British; carried to Savannah, then Charleston, and remained a prisoner until the end of the WAR. Married 1768, Mary Fendin of Greene's Island, S. C., b. 1747; d. McIntosh Co., Ga., 1804.
Child (only):
1. Major Gen. John Floyd of the War of 1812, b. 1769; d. 1839. Married 1793, Isabella Maria Hazzard of S. C. They had 12 children

OWEN FLUKER (son of Thomas Fluker of Mass., and his wife Hannah Waldo of Boston, Mass.), b. 1756; d. 1815, Wilkes Co., Ga. Served as private, Ga. Troops, under Col. Clarke. Received bounty land in Wilkes Co., Ga. for his services. Married Mary Ann Baldwin (called Nancy).

THOMAS FORSTON, b. Orange Co., Va., May 1, 1742; d. Feb. 15, 1824, Wilkes (now Elbert) Co., Ga. Received bounty land in Wilkes Co. for his services, Va. Troops. Married (1) in Va., Rachael Wynn.
Children:
1. Benjamin, mar. Elizabeth —.
2. William, mar. Eliza Lane.
3. Jesse (1783-1827); mar. Mary B. White.
4. Richard (1778-1836); mar. (1) Lucy Arnold.
5. Elizabeth (1810), mar. William Gibbs.
6. Milly, mar. JOHN WILLIS, d. 1822, A REV. SOLDIER. She drew land as widow of REV. SOLDIER in Elbert Co., Ga. 1837; also drew land for her orphan children:
   1. Benjamin.
   2. Eliz C.
   3. Louisa Willis.
7. John (1794), mar. (2) Elizabeth Gaines.

ROBERT FORSYTH (buried in St. Paul's Churchyard, Augusta, Ga.) From tombstone record: "Sacred to the memory of ROBERT FORSYTH Federal Marshall of Ga. Who in the discharge of the duties of his office fell a victim to his respect for the laws of his Country and his resolution in support of them on the 11th of January 1794, in the 40th Year of his Age.

"His virtues as an Officer of rank and unusual Confidence in the War which gave Independence to the U. S. and in all the tender and endearing relations of social life, have left impressions on his Country and his Friends, more durably engraved than this monument." His wife, Fanny Forsyth, d. at Louisville, Ga., Sept., 1805, age 46; buried in Summerville Cemetery, Augusta, Ga.
Child:
1. John Forsyth, was Governor of Ga.

NOTE: The act granting the Charter to Franklin College (now the State University at Athens, Ga., Clarke Co.) was passed Jan. 27, 1785. (The first of American State Universities. Ref.: "Abraham Baldwin" by Prof. Henry C. White, Prof. of Chemistry, University of Ga.)
Abraham Baldwin, the first President, called in 1800 to be Prof. of Mathematics at Franklin College, Josiah Meigs of Conn. He was later President of the College. Born in Middletown, Conn., Aug. 21, 1757 (son of RETURN MEIGS, REV. SOLDIER of Conn., and Elizabeth Hamlin); d. 1822. He married Clara Benjamin, b. May 5, 1762, Stratford, Conn. (dau. of JOHN BENJAMIN (1730-1796), REV. SOLDIER of Conn., and his wife Lucretia Backus).
Their dau., Clara Meigs married John Forsythe, Governor of Ga. (son of Robert Forsythe of Va., and Augusta, Ga.).

ARTHUR FORT, b. Jan. 15, 1750; d. Twiggs Co., Ga., June 15, 1833. Served Ga. Troops, living in Burke Co., Ga., 1775. Married Susanna (Tomlinson) Whitehead (1755-1820), widow of Richard Whitehead by whom she had one son, Richard Whitehead, Jr., b. 1776.
Children:
1. Sarah, b. 1779; mar. Appleton Rossiter (son of TIMOTHY ROSSITER, a REV. SOLDIER, b. 1752; d. Hancock Co., Ga., 1848, and his wife Mary Dinsmore).
2. Moses, mar. Eudlocia Walton Moore.
3. Arthur, mar. Mary Newson (or Munson).
4. Tomlinson, Soldier of 1812; mar. Martha Fannin. They had 13 children.
5. Susanna, mar. (1) Robert Jamison; (2) Samuel B. Hunter.
6. Elizabeth, mar. Lovett B. Smith.
7. Zachariah C., mar. Amanda Beckham.
8. Owen Charlton, b. 1798; d. 1829.

JOHN FOSTER, b. 1761, Southampton Co., Va.; d. 1821, Columbia Co., Ga. Served as Sergeant in Capt. Augustin Tabb's Co., 2nd Va. Reg., under Cols. Gregory, Smith, and William Brent. Married 1785, Elizabeth Savage (1769-1830).

SAMUEL FOSTER, a REV. SOLDIER, buried in Lincoln Co., Ga. on the Savannah River.

FRANCIS FARRAR, REV. SOLDIER of Wright's Dist., Clarke Co., Ga.

MAJOR JONAS FOUCHE, REV. SOLDIER, Greene Co., Ga. (Grave marked by Ga. D. A. R.)

REV. GEORGE FRANKLIN, b. in Va., 1744; d. Jan. 1816 (son of Rev. William and Sarah (Boone) Franklin, who moved from Va. to Currituck Co., N. C., 1780). He was a REV. SOLDIER. Married Vashti Mercer (half-sister of Rev. Silas Mercer of Ga.).
Children:
1. Vashti, mar. (1) — Boyd; (2) Daniel Harris as (2) wife.
2. Owen, mar. Eliza Floyd.
3. George.
(His grave was marked by the Major Gen. Samuel Elbert Chapter, D. A. R., of Tennille, Ga.)

GEORGE FREEMAN (son of Holman Freeman, Sr.), b. in Va., 1758; d. Wilkes Co., Ga., May 12, 1796. Married Frances (called Fanny) Taylor in Va. Moved to Wilkes Co., Ga. (then the "Ceded Lands") in 1772. Served under Gen. Elijah Clarke in Ga. Militia and was at the Siege of Augusta. She d. 1820.
Children:
1. Wesley.
2. Allen.
3. Henry, moved to Fayette and Coweta Co. Married (1) Elizabeth Hinton; (2) —; (3) Nancy Moody.
4. Elizabeth.
5. Alicy.
6. George, Jr.
7. Joseph.

HOLMAN FREEMAN, JR. (son of Holman Freeman, Sr.), b. in Va., came with his parents to the "Ceded Lands", now Wilkes Co., Ga., 1772. He served during the REV. under Gen. Elijah Clarke; was at the Siege of Augusta and served throughout the War. He was also a Soldier of the War of 1812, as Col. of Batt. He married about 1783, Peninah Walton (sister of Josiah Walton of the Broad River Settlement) b. in Va.; d. in Ala., where she removed after her husband's death in Wilkes Co., 1817.
Children:
1. Fleming, mar. Sally Bibb; moved to Ala.
2. John, mar. Miss Callaway; moved to Ala.
3. Mary, mar. Dr. William Bibb, the Territorial Governor of Ala., 1816.

JOHN FREEMAN (son of Holman Freeman, Sr.), b. in Va., 1756; d. "Poplar Grove", Wilkes Co., Ga., Jan. 7, 1807. Served under Gen. Elijah

Clarke; was at the Siege of Augusta and Charleston, S. C.; fought under Pickens, Sumpter, and Morgan in S. C. Was with Count D'Estaing at Savannah, Ga. After Savannah, seized by the British, the Freeman brothers joined the Va. Army. He was made Captain. Later joined Gen. Greene and was at Battle of '96. Also served in Col. Holman's Freeman's Batt. during the War of 1812. He married 1785, Catherine Carlton (dau. of Robert and Rebecca Carlton of Va. and Wilkes Co.). Only child:

    1. Rebecca Freeman (1786-1843), mar. Oct. 6, 1803, Shaler Hillyer (son of ASA HILLYER, REV. SOLDIER of Conn., and his wife Rhoda Smith). He was b. Aug. 2, 1775 in Conn.; d. Mar. 22, 1820, Wilkes Co., Ga.

JAMES FREEMAN (son of Holman Freeman, Sr.), mar. Rhoda —. He was a REV. SOLDIER of Ga.

WILLIAM FREEMAN (son of Holman Freeman, Sr.), mar. Sally —. Lived in Augusta, Ga. He was a REV. SOLDIER of Ga.

RICHARD FRETWELL, b. in Va., 1752; d. 1843 in Ga. Received pension for services as private, 4th Va. Reg., under Capt. Holcombe, Col. Robert Lawson. Moved to Ga. 1784. Married Frances —. His will mentions: grandsons Richard, Leonard, William A., and Philip Z. Fretwell; granddaus. Patsey Brown, Frances Kennon (wife of M. L. Kennon), Nancy Fretwell, and Elizabeth Fretwell; son Leonard and wife Polly; daus. Lucy Clifton, Nancy Burge and Patsey Harwell.

WILLIAM FURLOW, b. in Ireland; d. Greene Co., Ga. Came to Md., then to S. C. Served with Col. Elijah Clarke at the Siege of Augusta. Married Margaret (or Elizabeth) Nidy.
Children:

    1. James.
    2. John.
    3. William.
    4. David.
    5. Charles.
    6. Sallie, mar. — Neal.
    Two other daughters.

WILLIAM GAINER, b. 1758, Petersburg, Va.; d. Washington Co., Ga., buried near Sandersville, Ga. Served as private, 12th Va. Reg., under Capt. Benjamin Speller, Col. Smith, and William Brent Reg. Married 1778, Martha Williams, b. 1762.
Children: (known)

    1. Mary (1779-1846); mar. Jordan Smith.
    2. Rebecca (1794), mar. Jesse Wall.
    3. Penelope, mar. Jason Bryan.

DANIEL GAINES, b. in Va., 1745. Moved to Ga. 1785, Wilkes Co. He d. 1803 in Wilkes Co., Ga. He was a REV. SOLDIER of Va. Major of Batt. of Minute Men from the Counties of Albemarle, Amherst, and

Buckingham, Va. Served under Col. Charles Lewis and Gen. La Fayette in Yorktown and Va. Married (1) Mary Hudson (dau. of John and Anne (Jones) Hudson of Va.); mar. (2) Mary Gilbert (dau. of Henry Gilbert of Amherst Co., Va.).
Children:
1. Bernard, the eldest (1767-1839); mar. 1812, Sarah Force Cook.
2. Gustavus.
3. Hippocrates.
4. Zenophen.
5. Daniel.
6. Archimedes.
7. Henry Gilber.

PRIOR GARDNER, b. 1755; d. 1808, Warren Co., Ga. Served in N. C. Troops, Rifleman; was at the Battle of Guilford Court House.

HENRY GARLAND received a Pension for his services as a REV. SOLDIER, while a resident of Upson Co., Ga.

THOMAS GARNETT (Garnet), b. Essex Co., Va., 1750; d. Chatham Co., 1793. Married at the Ebenezer Jerusalem Church, Effingham Co., Ga., Jan. 8, 1772, Rachel Willson. (She mar. (2) WILLIAM G. PORTER, REV. SOLDIER of Effingham Co., Ga.)
Child:
1. John Garnett, b. 1776; mar. 1794, Mary Bostwick (dau. of Samuel Bostwick and his wife Ann Mary Maner). He was a Soldier of War of 1812.

NOTE: At a meeting of the Ga. Council of Safety, June 25, 1776, Commissions were issued to: "ABRAHAM RAVOTT, Captain; THOMAS GARNETT, First Lieut.; DANIEL HOWELL, 2nd Lieut.; JAMES DELL, 3rd Lieut. of a Co. of Militia, Second Battalion, First Reg, Upper District of St. Mathews Parish, Ga."

ANTHONY GARRARD, b. in Va., 1756; d. Wilkes Co., Ga., 1807. Served in N. C. Continental Army. Was given a grant of land in Ga. for his services.

JACOB GARRARD, b. Sept. 4, 1763; d. 1819, Putnam Co., Ga. (Baldwin). Served as private, Ga. Troops; was at Battle of Cowpens. Received bounty grant of land in Ga. for his services. Married, June 22, 1786, Mary Elizabeth Barron, d. Baldwin Co., Ga., 1827.
Children:
1. Nancy, b. 1787; mar. (1) Thomas Roquemore; (2) Samuel Johnson; (3) Green Simmons.
2. William, b. 1791; mar. (1) Delilah Clements; (2) Mary Ann (Roquemore) Allen.
3. John, b. 1790.
4. Jacob, b. 1794.
5. Mary Rebecca.
6. Hiram.

7. Zillah Ann, b. 1802; d. in Texas. Married Rev. James Roquemore.
8. Eliza Maria.
9. Anna Lucinda.

JOHN GARRARD, b. 1730; d. Jones Co., Ga., 1807. Served as private. Received 287.5 acres of land for his services in Wilkes Co., Ga. Married (1) 1758, in S. C., Mary Bolt; mar. (2) Elizabeth —.
Children by (1) wife:
1. Robert.
2. Frances, mar. John Barron
3. Nancy.
4. JACOB, REV. SOLDIER; mar. Mary Elizabeth Barron.

ALLEN GAY, b. Northampton Co., N. C., 1765; d. Coweta Co., Ga., June 18, 1847. Served as private in Capt. Robert Raiford's Co., Col. Dickerson N. C. Reg. (He was son of JOHN THOMAS GAY, REV. SOLDIER of N. C.) He married (1) Sept. 5, 1787, Celia Rae Elbert of Savannah, Ga., d. 1793; mar. (2) in Ga., Abigail Castleberry; mar. (3) widow Annie Benton of Coweta Co., Ga.
Children by (1) wife:
1. John William.   2. Elizabeth.
Child by (2) wife: (known)
3. Gilbert, b. 1811; mar. Sarah Stamps.

HEROD GIBBES, b. in Va.; d. Morgan Co., Ga. Served seven years in Va. Continental Army. Removed to Pickens, S. C., then to Morgan Co., Ga. Married Lucy Anderson in Va.
Child:
1. Thomas A., b. 1786, S. C.; mar. Martha Maddox of Greene Co., Ga.; d. Walton Co., Ga.

JOHN GIBSON, b. 1750; moved to Cheraw Dist., S. C., then Warren Co., Ga., 1784. Served in S. C. Line. Married (1) 1777, Ann Crawford; (2) widow Fuller.
Children by (1) wife:
1. Thomas, b. 1786; mar. Martha Neal.
2. John, b. 1778.
3. Susan G., b. 1780.
4. William, b. 1783.
Children by (2) wife:
5. Mary Anne.
6. Ferriby.   8. Elizabeth.
7. Lucy.   9. David Neal.

JOHN GIBSON (son of Gideon Gibson), b. 1759 in S. C.; d. 1832, Campbell Co., Ga. Served as private, S. C. Reg., under Col. Charles Pickney. Married (1) 1779, Fannie Flewellyn, d. 1807 (dau. of ABNER

FLEWELLYN, REV. SOLDIER); mar. (2) 1809, Elizabeth Dozier; mar. (3) Clara Butts (widow of Wm. Butts), d. 1842.
Children:
1. John.
2. Churchell.
3. Nancy, b. 1796; mar. John Gorman; moved to Gwinnett Co., Ga.
4. Wylie Jones (1801-1868); mar. Sarah Ann Bennett.
5. Sarah, mar. Isaiah Tucker, b. in Amherst Co., Va., 1761; came to Warren Co., Ga., 1794.
6. Ann, b. 1810; d. 1863; mar. Horatio Whitfield.

FELIX GILBERT, b. in Scotland; came to Va.; d. Wilkes Co., Ga. Served as a private, Va. Troops. Married Miss Grant (dau. of Peter Grant of the Broad River Settlement, Ga.)
Children:
1. Dau., mar. Henry Gibson.
2. Ann, mar. John Taylor.
3. Elizabeth, mar. Dr. Gilbert Hay.
4. Maria, mar. (1) — Christmas; (2) Andrew Shepherd.
5. William.
6. Felix, b. Rockingham Co., Va.; mar. Miss Hillhouse.

THOMAS GILBERT, b. in Orange Co., Va., 1730; d. in Ga., 1820, age 90 years. A REV. SOLDIER and a Baptist preacher.

WILLIAM GILBERT, b. 1758, Va.; d. 1830, Gwinnett Co., Ga. Served in Va. and Ga. Troops. Received bounty grant of land in Ga. for his services. Married 1785, Tamar Strickland, b. 1768.
Children:
1. Isaac (1790-1863); mar. 1813, Elizabeth Allbright. 9 children.
2. Jacob.
3. Nancy.   5. William.
4. John.   6. Oliver.

PETER GILLIAM, b. 1737 in Va.; d. 1809, Wilkes (now Elbert) Co., Ga. Served as a REV. SOLDIER from Pittsylvania Co., Va., under Gen. Daniel Morgan. Received grant of land in Wilkes Co., Ga. for his services. Married Ann Heard (dau. of Stephen Heard and Mary Falkner), b. in Va., 1744; d. Greene Co., Ga., 1821.
Children:
1. Charles.
2. Sarah, mar. Ewing Morrow (son of ROBERT MORROW, b. in Ireland 1742; d. in Md., 1782. A REV. SOLDIER, Ensign in 2nd Md. Batt. Flying Camp and his wife Margaret Ewing (1751-1803), dau. of COL. THOMAS EWING (1730-1790), REV. SOLDIER, Col., 3rd Batt. Flying Camp. Md. and his wife Margaret).
3. Mary, mar. — Reeves of Va.
4. Patsey, mar. — Williams of Greene Co., Ga.

5. Elizabeth, mar. — Price.
6. Ann, mar. Joseph Morrow (brother of Ewing Morrow).

EZEKIEL GILLIAM, b. in Va.; d. in Ga., Oglethorpe Co. Served as private, S. C. Troops. Married Sarah Clemens.

JOHN BLAIR GILMER (son of GEORGE GILMER and his (3) wife Harrison Blair, REV. PATRIOT of Va.), b. Williamsburg, Va., 1748; d. 1793, Broad River settlement of Ga. Served under Marquis de La Fayette. Was at the Siege of Yorktown. Received bounty grant of land Wilkes Co., for his services. Married 1770, Mildred Thornton Meriwether, d. 1826.
Children:
1. John Thornton (1774-1831); mar. 1803, Martha Gaines Harvie. Moved to Kentucky, then to Illinois.
2. Nicholac, b. 1776; mar. Amelia Clarke.
3. Francis Meriwether (1785-1864); mar. 1808, Martha Barnett (1790-1855) (dau. of WM. BARNETT, REV. SOLDIER, and his wife Mary Meriwether); 5 children.
4. George Oglethorpe, mar. Martha Johnson (dau. of Nicholas Johnson).
5. David H., mar. Virginia Clark.
6. Harrison Blair, mar. 1808, Gabriel Christian.
7. Betsey, mar. Thomas McGehee.
8. Sally, mar. Burton Taliaferro.
9. Jane, mar. (1) Thomas Johnson; (2) Abner McGehee of Ala.

THOMAS MERIWETHER GILMER (son of Peachy Ridgeway Gilmer and his wife Mary Meriwether of Va.), b. in Va. 1760; d. 1817, Broad River Settlement, Ga. Served as private under Marquis de La Fayette and also had active service in Ga. Received grant of land for his services. Married Elizabeth Lewis (1765-1855) (dau. of THOMAS LEWIS, REV. SOLDIER of Va. (1718-1790), and his wife Jane Strother).
Children:
1. Peachy, mar. (1) Mary Bontwell Harvie; (2) Caroline Thomas, widow. Moved to Ala.
2. Mary, mar. (1) Warren Taliaferro (son of ZECHERIAH TALIAFERRO, b. 1730 in Va.; d. 1811 in S. C., a REV. SOLDIER, and his wife Mary Bontwell). She mar. (2) Nicholas Powers.
3. Thomas Lewis, mar. (1) Nancy Harvie; (2) Ann Harper.
4. George Rockingham, b. 1790; mar. Eliza Frances Grattan (dau. of ROBERT GRATTAN, REV. SOLDIER of Va., and his wife Elizabeth Gilmer). He was a Soldier of 1812, and also Governor of Ga.
5. John (1792-1860); mar. (1) Lucy Johnson; (2) Susan (Barnett) Gresham.
6. William Benjamin Strother; mar. Elizabeth Marks. Moved to Ala.

7. Charles L., mar. (1) Nancy Marks; (2) Matilda Kyle, widow.
8. Lucy Ann Sophia, mar. Senator B. S. Bibb of Ala.
9. James Jackson, mar. Elizabeth Jordan.

JAMES GILMORE, b. Cumberland Co., N. C., 1755; d. 1835, Washington Co., Ga. Received a pension for his services as a private, corporal, and Sergeant, N. C. Troops, under Capt. Gilmore and Welch. Married 1779, Mary Hughs.

HENRY GINDRAT, b. 1740, Purysburg, S. C.; d. 1801, Effingham Co., Ga. Served as an officer under Gen. Nathaniel Greene and was wounded at Eutau Springs. Received bounty land in Ga. for his services in S. C. and Ga. Married (1) Mary May (dau. of John May and his wife Mary (Stafford) Patterson, dau. COL. WILLIAM STAFFORD, REV. SOLDIER of S. C.; she mar. (3) James Mullet and d. 1820, age 106 yrs.). He mar. (2) Dorcas (Williams) Stafford (widow of COL. SAMUEL STAFFORD, REV. SOLDIER of S. C.).
Children by (1) wife:
1. Abraham, mar. Barbara Clark, widow of William Clark.
2. John.
3. Mary, mar. Dr. Benjamin St. Mark.
4. Rhoda, mar. William Gilleland.
Children by (2) wife:
5. Dorcas, mar. — Washburn.
6. Henrietta, mar. 1823, JOSIAH CLARK, a REV. SOLDIER, served as officer under Gen. Nathaniel Greene; lived at Beech Island, S. C., and Effingham Co., Ga.).
7. Henry, Jr.

THOMAS GLASCOCK (son of William Glascock, the "Rebel Counsellor" of Ga., and his wife Elizabeth, both buried on the Glascock plantation near Augusta, Ga.). He was Captain in the famous Legion of Cavalry under Count Pulaski. He was made a Brigadier-General in the Continental Army. He d. age 54 at his country home, "The Mill", near Augusta, Ga.

WILLIAM GLOVER, b. in Prince George Co., Md., 1760; d. in Ga. Enlisted Wilkes Co., N. C., 1778; private under Capt. Shephard and Col. Gordon. Received a Pension for his services. Grave in Elbert (now Hart) Co., Ga. marked by the U. S. Government.

WILLIAM GOBER, b. in N. C., 1744; d. 1826, Newton Co., Ga. Private in N. C. and Ga. Militia. Married 1762, Lucy —.

JAMES GOLDWIRE, b. in Augusta, Ga., 1747; d. Mt. Pleasant, Ga. Commanded a company of Ga. Militia, 1776, from St. Matthew's Parish (now Effingham Co.), Ga. Married Sarah King, b. 1749.
Child:

1. John Goldwire (1779-1830); mar. 1809, Frances Offutt (dau. of JESSE OFFUTT (1760-1830), a REV. SOLDIER, and his wife Obedience Jones, dau. of JOHN JONES and Susanna Strobhar).

COL. AMBROSE GORDON, b. in New Jersey, June 28, 1751; d. Augusta, Ga., June 28, 1804. He was a REV. SOLDIER.

THOMAS GORDON, b. in Spotsylvania Co., Va., 1758; d. 1826, Gwinnett Co., Ga. Served as private, S. C. Line. Received land grant in Ga. for his services. Married 1776, Mary Buffington (1760-1837).

MOSES GRANBERRY, b. Norfolk Co., Va.; d. 1807, Warren Co., Ga. Served as private, N. C. Line. Married Susanna Dykes.

DANIEL GRANT, b. 1724 in Va.; d. Wilkes Co., Ga. (will dated July 4, 1793). Removed to N. C., 1765. Served with N. C. Troops. Received bounty grant of land in Ga. for his services. Married 1750, Elizabeth Tait.
Children:
1. Amelia, mar. Lieut. John Owen.
2. Fanny, mar. — Gafford.
3. Thomas, mar. Frances Owen.
4. Isabella, mar. — Davis.
5. Anna, mar. — Wilkins.

DR. ROBERT GRANT, b. July 15, 1762, Scotland; came to S. C. Served as Surgeon on Gen. Marion's Staff, S. C. He d. 1843 at St. Simon's Island, Ga. Married April 5, 1799, Sarah Foxworth, b. 1778, S. C.; d. 1859, New York.
Children:
1. Robert.
2. Elizabeth Helen, mar. Dr. Robert Hogan.
3. Amelia.
4. Harry.
5. Charles, mar. Cornelia Bond.
6. Hugh F., mar. Mary Elizabeth Fraser.
7. Harry Allen, mar. (1) Louisa Bloodgood; (2) Laura Thompson.
8. Sarah Ann.
9. James Couper.
(Ref.: Old family Bible owned by Mrs. David Banks, New London, Conn.)

THOMAS GRANT, b. Hanover Co., Va., 1757; d. Nov. 27, 1827 in Jasper Co., Ga. Served as Lieut. in N. C. Troops with his father DANIEL GRANT, REV. SOLDIER. They received land in Ga. and moved there with their families. Married Frances Owen (dau. of John and Mildred (Grant) Owens).
Children:
1. Daniel, mar. Lucy Crutchfield.

2. Mildred, mar. J. Billingsley.
3. Thomas, Jr., mar. Mary Baird.
4. William, mar. Ritura Mills.
5. Elizabeth, mar. William Love.

JOHN GRAVES, b. 1748, Culpepper Co., Va.; d. 1824, Wilkes Co., Ga. Received bounty grant of land for his services. Married Catherine West.

LEWIS GRAVES, b. 1760, Spotsylvania Co., Va.; d. Newton Co., Ga., 1839. Served as private, S. C. Troops, under Capt. Griffeth and Col. Murphy. Married 1781, Ruth Graves.

WILLIAM GRAVES, b. 1746; d. 1802 in Ala. Received land in Ga. for his services. Moved later to Ala. Married Sarah Smith.
Child:
1. Dorothy Graves, mar. as (1) wife, Bird Fitzpatrick (son of WILLIAM FITZPATRICK (1746-1809), received bounty grant of land in Ga. for his services, lived in Savannah, Ga., and his wife Anne Philips, dau. of JOSEPH PHILIPS, REV. SOLDIER of Ga., who served under Col. Elijah Clarke, (1734-1800 in Ga.), and his wife Sarah Lynde).

JAMES GRAY, b. 1758 in S. C.; d. 1834 in Ga. Served as private, Ga. Line. Received bounty land in Ga. for his services. Married Mary — (1769-1836).
Child:
1. Susan Gray, married Robert Howe (1782-1858).

ISAAC GRAY, b. in S. C., 1750; d. Franklin Co., Ga., 1831. Served in S. C. Troops, under Capt. John A. Patrick in Chandler's Batt. Drew land as a REV. SOLDIER in the Lottery of 1825.

HENRY GRAYBILL, b. Lancaster Co., Penn., 1734; d. 1816, Washington Co., Ga. Served as private, Ga. Line, under Gen. Elijah Clarke. Received bounty land in Ga. for his services. Married Mary Rutherford.

JAMES GREEN, b. 1762 in Va.; d. Hancock Co., Ga., 1839. Served as private, Ga. Line, under Col. Elijah Clarke. Received bounty grant of land in Ga. for his services. Married Elizabeth Bass in Va.
Children:
1. Allen B.
2. Mary B.
3. Polly B.
4. Susan B.
5. Thomas B.
6. Hartwell B.
7. Dolly B.
8. James, Jr.
9. William, mar. Patience Clarke Wyche.

JOHN GREEN, mar. Martha Rebecca. Claims as a REV. SOLDIER paid to him Jan. 27, 1784, then Sheriff of Effingham Co. He d. 1819 in Effingham Co., Ga., age 55 years.

McKEEN GREEN, JR. (son of McKEEN GREEN, SR., REV. SOL-DIER of Ga.), d. Tattnall Co., Ga. On certificate of Col. Caleb Powell, he received bounty grant of land on the Altamaha River, Washington Co., Ga., for his services as a REV. SOLDIER, June 9, 1784. Married at Ogechee, Ga., July 3, 1786, Elinor McCall (dau. of CHARLES McCALL, REV. SOLDIER of S. C. and Ga., and granddau. of FRANCIS McCALL, REV. SOLDIER of N. C.).
Children:
1. Harris.
2. Selete, mar. Daniel Sauls, April 24, 1811.
3. Ann.
4. William.
5. Jane, mar. CAPT. MICHAEL HENDERSON, REV. SOLDIER.
6. Sarah Hull, mar. BASIL O'NEAL, REV. SOLDIER.
7. James.

NOTE: McKeen Green and John Green were appointed Members of the Ex. Council of Ga., Jan. 5, 1786. McKEEN GREEN, Jr., JOHN GREEN, and BENJAMIN GREEN, of Ga., REV. SOLDIERS, were brothers.

MAJOR GEN. NATHANIEL GREENE, b. in Warwick, Rhode Island, May 27, 1741; d. June 9, 1786 at his plantation home "Mulberry Grove" in Ga. (Plantation presented to him for his REV. service by the State of Ga., formerly the confiscated estate of Lieut. Gov. of Ga., John Graham, 14 miles from Savannah, Ga.). He served as Col., was made Major Gen. by act of Legislature and in 1783 was voted a resolution of thanks for his services by the Congress of the U. S. Monument erected to his memory, Savannah, Ga. Inscribed on monument, "Major Gen. Nathaniel Greene. Soldier, Patriot, and friend of Gen. George Washington". (Gen. George Washington was a REV. SOLDIER and later President of the U. S.) Married July 20, 1774, Catherine Littlefield. She mar. (2) at Philadelphia, Penn., 1796, Phineas Miller.
Children:
1. George Washington, d. unm.
2. Martha Washington, mar. (1) 1795, John Nightengale of War-wick, R. I. 3 children. Mar. (2) Henry Turner. 4 children.
3. Cornelia Lott, mar. (1) Peyton Skipwith; (2) Edward Littlefield.
4. Nathaniel R., mar. Ann Maria Clark.
5. Louisa Catherine.

WILLIAM GREENE, JR., b. in N. C., 1764 (son of William and Sarah Ann (Alston) Greene); d. in Greene Co., Ga., Dec. 13, 1819. Will on record, made Dec. 8, 1819. Served as private in N. C. and Ga. Militia

of the First Batt., Richmond Co., Ga. Mil. Received 287.5 acres of
bounty land for his services, in Greene Co., upon certificate of Gen.
Elijah Clarke, 1785. He was also a Soldier of the War of 1812 from
Greene Co., Ga. Married June 17, 1784, Ruth Hunter, b. in Warren Co.,
N. C., Sept. 24, 1764; d. Greene Co., Ga., May 15, 1826 (dau. of JESSE
HUNTER, REV. SOLDIER of N. C., and his wife Ann Alston, dau. of
SOLOMON ALSTON, REV. SOLDIER of N. C., and his wife Nancy
Hinton).
Children:
1. Lemuel, b. Mar. 29, 1785; mar. (1) Ann Merritt; (2) Eliza
   Coleman.
2. Sarah, b. June 12, 1786; mar. (1) Douglass Watson; (2) Drury
   Towns; (3) John Mercier.
3. Alston Hunter, b. Mar. 31, 1788; Soldier of War of 1812; mar.
   Cynthia (Clay) Barrett (dau. of James and Margaret (Muse)
   Clay).
4. Nancy, b. 1790; mar. Wm. Fitzpatrick.
5. Nathaniel, d. y.
6. William (1795-1818).
7. Augustine, mar. (1) Phoebe Burke; (2) Mrs. Baldwin; (3) Miss
   Fisher (or Fish).
8. Elizabeth, mar. — Sledge.
9. Philip, d. Dec. 2, 1871, La Grange, Ga.; mar. Mildred Washington Sanford.
10. Ruth Hunter, b. Feb. 26, 1804.

WILLIAM GREENE, SR., b. 1734 in Va., removed to Warren Co.,
N. C. Married there, Sarah Ann Alston. Served in 1st N. C. Regiment
as Captain. Was granted 500 acres bounty land as an officer for services, in Washington Co., Ga., Jan. 24, 1784.

JOHN GRESHAM, b. in Va., 1759; d. 1818, Oglethorpe Co., Ga. Received bounty land for his services 3 years Va. Line in Ga.   Mar. 1784,
dau. of JOHN SCOTT, REV. SOLDIER, and his wife Elizabeth Upshaw,
and granddau. of THOMAS SCOTT, REV. SOLDIER of Va. (1730-1801),
and his wife Elizabeth Wingfield).
Children: (known)
1. Eliza Williamson (1801-1876); mar. 1824, Charles Barnett.
2. John, Jr. (1799-1827); mar. Susan Crawford Barnett (1798-
   1874) in Miss. (dau. of JOEL BARNETT (1762-1851), REV.
   SOLDIER of Ga., and his wife Mildred Meriwether).

JAMES GRIFFIN, b. in Edgecomb Co., N. C., 1753; d. Irwin Co.,
Ga., Dec. 1836. Enlisted in Continental Army at Edgecomb Co., N. C.,
1777 and as Corporal served in companies under Captains Blount and
Euglas, Colonels Buncombe and Harney's N. C. Reg. He was in the
Battles of Brandywine, Monmouth, Guilford Court House; and was with
Gen. George Washington at Valley Forge. Discharged 1783. Married

April 1, 1780, Sarah Lodge of N. C. They had 9 children. They moved to Irwin Co., Ga., 1815, from N. C. His wife d. near Hahira, Ga., after 1836. Both are buried 8 miles from Ocilla, Ga., in Irwin Co.
Children:
1. Noah.
2. Joshua.
3. Thomas.
4. Rhoda.
5. Shadrack, mar. Nancy Bradford (dau. of REV. SOLDIER, THOMAS BRADFORD, b. Edgecomb Co.; buried by the side of James Griffin. He served as Lieut. in N. C. Regiment with Corporal James Griffin. (Their graves were marked by the Gen. James Jackson Chapter, D. A. R., Valdosta, Ga., in 1938).
6. Solomon.
7. Elizabeth.

JOHN GRIFFIN, b. Powhatan Co., Va., Sept. 3, 1740; d. in Oglethorpe Co., Ga., Feb. 1819. Served as Sergeant in Capt. William Earl's N. C. 1st Reg., then as Lieut. and Captain. From N. C., he moved to Wilkes Co., Ga., where he received bounty land for his services. Married Powhatan Co., Va., Nov. 19, 1772, Mary Ann Andrews, b. 1754; d. before 1816. His will is on file at Lexington, Ga.
Children:
1. Sarah, b. Sept. 1, 1773.
2. Ann Garnett, b. June 20, 1776; mar. — Barnett.
3. David, b. 1778 (twin).
4. Jesse Andrews, b. 1778 (twin).
5. Mary, b. Sept. 11, 1781; mar. as (1) wife, William Fears (son of WILLIAM FEARS, REV. SOLDIER, d. Jasper Co., Ga., and his wife Ann Bucher).
6. William, b. Jan. 21, 1790; mar. Mary Booker Barnett.
7. Thomas, b. Sept. 24, 1787.
8. John, b. Jan. 21, 1790; mar. Sarah Caroline Barnett.
9. Wyatt Andrews.
10. George W., b. 1796.
11. Susanna, mar. — Hubbard.

JOHN GROOVER (spelled Gruber), b. in America, 1738; was a REV. SOLDIER; killed by the Tories at his home on Cowpens Branch, Effingham Co., Ga., in 1780. The State at this time was over-run by the British. He married at Ebenezer, Jerusalem Church, June 4, 1765, Mary Magdalen Kalcher (dau. of Rupert Kalcher of Ebenezer, from London, England).
Children: (all baptized at Jerusalem Church)
1. John, b. 1766; d. Brooks Co., Ga.; married Hannah Lastinger.
2. Joshua, b. 1772.
3. Solomon, b. 1769.
4. William, b. 1780.

STEPHEN GROVES, b. 1740, England; d. 1839, Madison Co., Ga. Placed on Pension Roll of Madison Co. for services as private in Penn. Mil. Married Isabella Weakley.

MOSES GUEST, b. 1750; d. in Ga. 1837. Received pension for his services as a REV. SOLDIER while a resident of Franklin Co., Ga. Married Mary Blair.
Children:

1. Sanford.	10. Barton.
2. Susanna.	11. Giles.
3. Morgan.	12. Elizabeth.
4. William.	13. Mary.
5. Moses, Jr.	14. Celia.
6. John.	15. Cynthia.
7. Hall.	16. Susan.
8. Nathaniel.	17. Annie.
9. Cobb.	

DANIEL GUNN, b. in N. C., 1757; d. 1825 in Jones Co., Ga. Served as Orderly and Sergeant in Capt. Lawson's N. C. Co. Married 1786, Susan Street. Had issue.

GEORGE GUNN, b. in Va.; d. 1807, Wilkes Co., Ga. Served as private Augusta Co., Va. Militia. Received bounty grant of land for his services Wilkes Co., Ga. Married Anne —; d. 1819. Had several children.

JACOB GUNN, b. in Va.; d. in Ga. Served as Major, 2nd Reg., Augusta Co., Va. Militia. Buried near Milledgeville, Ga. Inscription on tombstone "Major Jacob Gunn".

JAMES GUNN, b. 1739 in Va.; d. Louisville, Ga., July 30, 1801. Enlisted in Va. Continental Army, as Captain of Dragoons. Served under Gen. Anthony Wayne at the Siege of Savannah, Ga., 1782. Was Colonel and General State Militia after War. Member Continental Congress, 1787. Senator U. S. in 1795. Married Sarah —. Had children.

RICHARD GUNN, SR., b. June 6, 1761, Brunswick Co., Va.; d. Taliaferro Co., Ga., June 30, 1840. Served in the Va. Continental Line. Received bounty land in Ga. for his services in Oglethorpe Co. Married in Va. about 1784, Elizabeth Radford, b. in Va., May 16, 1671; d. Taliaferro Co., 1847.
Children:
1. Jane (called Jincy, b. July 31, 1785; mar. 1805, Jeremiah Holden.
2. Nelson, b. 1787; mar. Jane Reynolds.
3. William, b. 1789; mar. Pleasance Stephens.
4. John, d. y.
5. Richard, Jr., b. 1795: moved to Ala.

5. Radford, b. in Va., 1797; mar. (1) Peggy Rhodes, Oglethorpe Co.; (2) Ann J. S. Beck, Warren Co.
6. Elizabeth, b. in Ga., 1799; mar. Mr. Rhodes.
7. Larkin R., b. 1802; mar. Cynthia Darden; moved to Ala.
8. Jonathan, b. 1809; mar. 1830, Elizabeth D. Wynne.

WILLIAM GUNN, b. in Va.; d. after 1814, Wilkes Co., Ga. Served in the Augusta Co., Va. Militia. Received bounty grant of land for his services in Wilkes Co., Ga. Married in Va., —.
Children:
1. Elizabeth, mar. 1807, Harrison Mallory.
2. John, mar. 1810, Catherine Hammack.

BUTTON GWINNETT, baptized Gloucester Co., England, April 10, 1735. Married Ann Bourne in England, April 19, 1757. Came to America 1765; his wife joined him in 1767 in Savannah, Ga. He bought St. Catherine's Island on the Ga. coast (formerly owned by Mary Musgrove). The "Olde House" was his plantation home. Feb. 2, 1771, he was elected a delegate from Ga. to the Continental Congress. Was elected Mar. 5, 1777, President and Commander-in-Chief of the Continental Army at the death of President Archibald Bulloch. He was one of the three signers from Ga. of the Declaration of Independence. He was fatally wounded in a duel with Gen. Lachland McIntosh, and d. May 19, 1777 at Savannah, Ga. His wife d. 1780.
Children: (all born in England)
1. Ann, b. 1759.
2. Amelia, b. 1758.
3. Elizabeth, b. 1762; mar. Peter Belin of S. C.
(Ref.: "Button Gwinnett" by Charles Francis Jenkins)

JAMES HABERSHAM, b. 1744, Ga.; d. Savannah, Ga. Served as Lieut., Ga. Batt., under his brother JOSEPH HABERSHAM. Made Major; served throughout the War. Was known as the "rebel financier". Married Sept. 20, 1769, Esther Wylly.
Children:
1. Richard Wylly, mar. 1808, Sarah Elliott.
2. John, mar. 1812, Ann Middleton Barnwell (dau. of CAPT. JOHN BARNWELL, REV. SOLDIER of S. C.).
3. Alexander.
4. Mary, mar. Benjamin Maxwell.
5. Esther, mar. Hon. Stephen Elliott.
6. Joseph Clay, mar. Ann W. Adams.

JOHN HABERSHAM, b. Dec. 23, 1754, Ga.; d. Nov. 19, 1799, Charham Co., Ga. Served as 1st Lieut., Ga. Batt., 1776. Brigade. Major under Gen. Lachlan McIntosh and Col. Samuel Elbert. Member Continental Contress. Married 1782, Sarah Ann Camber, of Bryan Co., Ga.
Children:

1. Ann, d. y.
2. James Camber, d. y.
3. Joseph Clay, mar. Ann Wylly Adams, 1795.
4. John Harris, d. y.
5. John Bolton, d. y.
6. Mary Butler, mar. her cousin, Joseph Habersham.
7. Susan Dorothy.

JOSEPH HABERSHAM, b. Savannah, Ga., 1751; d. same place, Nov., 1815. Served as Major, Lieut.-Col. of 1st Ga. Reg., Ga. Line Continental Troops throughout the War. Member Provincial Congress. Charter member, Order of the Cincinnati. Married May 19, 1776, at "Brampton", Isabella Rae (sister of Elizabeth Rae, who mar. Gen. Samuel Elbert, Rev. Soldier).
Children:
1. James.
2. John.
3. Mary.
4. Isabella.
5. Joseph.
6. Robert, mar. (1) Mary O'Brien; (2) Elizabeth Neyle.
7. William, mar. Mary Elliott.
8. Eliza A.
9. Susan Ann.

NOTE: James, John and Joseph Habersham were sons of JAMES HABERSHAM, ROYALIST of Ga.

WILLIAM HALEY (or Hailey), b. 1748 in Va.; d. 1830. Living on Cody's Creek, Elbert Co., Ga., 1792. Drew land in Wilkes Co., Ga. for his services in Continental Army. Also drew land 1806 and 1825 Lottery as a REV. SOLDIER. A Soldier of the War of 1812. Married 1779, Mary Turman.
Children: (mentioned in will made Oct. 2, 1830)
1. John, mar. Polly Underwood.
2. Thomas.
3. James.
4. William.
5. Reuben, mar. Sally Wood.
6. Mary, mar. Jesse Cash.
7. Ritta (or Polly), mar. James B. Adams.
8. Tabby (Tabitha), mar. Eason Forston.
9. Lucy, mar. Benajah Teasley (son of Isham Teasley).
10. Sally, mar. Henry Mann.
11. Betsey, mar. John A. Teasley.
He also mentions in will the children of THOMAS LANE, Dec. 1829, a REV. SOLDIER who drew land in Ga. 1784 as a Refugee Soldier, viz.: John and Eliza (Lane) Forston, wife of William Forston (son of Thomas

Forston).

HUGH HALL, b. in Ireland; d. Greene Co., Ga. Served as private, N. C. Line. Married in Penn., Mary Reid.
Child:
1. Alexander Hall, b. in N. C.; d. 1828, Meriwether Co., Ga.; married Elizabeth Brown (dau. of Reuben and Betsey (Lange) Brown).

JAMES HALL, late of N. C. Reg., Capt. John Richards Co., appoints Francis Baldwin, Attorney to ask and receive his pay as a REV. SOLDIER, N. C. Line. Lived in Greene Co., Ga.

LEWIS HALL, b. 1746 in N. C.; d. in Ga., 1822. Served as Lieut. in Ga. and N. C. Troops. Captured by British, wounded, in prison, Charleston, S. C. Released and served again until close of War. Married (1) —; (2) Nancy Colley, 1790, (1767-1858).
Children:
1. Instance, b. 1797.
2. James, of Montgomery Co., Ga.
3. Seaborn of Tattnall Co., Ga., b. 1808; mar. (1) Ann Gannay; (2) Chrissie Quinn.
4. W. L.
5. Flora, mar. James Kemp.
6. Polly, mar. Henry Cook.
7. Priscilla, mar. Benj. H. Smith.
8. Rebecca, mar. D. D. David.
9. Elpheus.
10. Mary, mar. George Wilcox.
11. John.

LYMAN HALL, b. Wallingford, Conn., April 24, 1724. Came to Dorchester, S. C., later to Ga. with the famous Puritan Colony which formed the Midway settlement in the Parish of St. John. Was sent from this Parish as a delegate to the Continental Congress in Philadelphia. Signer of the Declaration of Independence on behalf of Ga., with George Walton and Button Gwinnett. His property at Sunbury, Liberty Co., was confiscated by the British government. Returned South in 1782; settled at Savannah, Ga. Was called to the office of Governor of Ga. Married Mary Osburn. Died Oct. 19, 1790, at his plantation home, Shell Bluff, Burke Co., Ga. Buried at same place. His remains were re-interred 1848, under the monument at Augusta, Ga., erected to the three Signers of the Declaration of Independence for Ga.

BENJAMIN HAMBRICK, 1839 Pension; b. Prince Edward Co., Va., July 9, 1739. Lived Wilkes Co., N. C., then Wilkes Co., Ga., Jasper Co. and Upson Co., Ga. Entered service under Capt. John Cleveland, Co.

of Light Horse, under Col. Benj. Cleveland, Col. Wm. Lenoir, and Gen. Rutherford, N.C. Line. Was at Battle of Kings Mt.

JOHN HAMES, b. 1735; d. 1852, buried Murray Co., Ga.; re-interred 1911, in National Federal Cemetery, Marietta (by D.A.R.). Served as private, Capt. and Major, Ga. Troops. Married Miss Jasper (sister of SERGEANT JASPER, killed in battle. Monument to his memory erected on Bull St., Savannah, Ga.).

GEORGE HAMILTON, b. 1722 in Md.; d. in Ga., 1798. Served as Captain, Md. Militia. Received bounty grant of land for his services in Washington Co., Ga. Married Elizabeth Schuyler.
Child:
1. GEORGE HAMILTON, JR., b. 1754 in Md.; d. 1826, Wilkes Co., Ga. Served as private in his father's Co. Received land for his services in Wilkes Co., Ga. Married Agnes Cooper (dau. of THOMAS COOPER, REV. SOLDIER, b. 1753 in Va. Served in Va. Militia, and wife Sarah Anthony. They removed to Ga. 1794. He d. 1797, Greene Co., Ga.).

JAMES HAMILTON, b. in Ireland; d. 1788 in Ga. Served as Ensign, 1777; Lieut. 1778, 6th Va. Reg. Prisoner at Charleston, S.C. Married Ann Fox Napier.
Children: (known)
1. Thomas Napier, mar. Sarah Sherwood Bugg (dau. of Sherwood Bugg, Jr. and wife Sarah Ann Jones; granddau. of SHERWOOD BUGG, REV. SOLDIER of Ga. and S.C., and his wife Elizabeth Hopson, a Patriot).
2. Ann Eliza, mar. Samuel Goode.
3. James Fox, mar. (1) Frances Harris; (2) Emily Bowden.

JOHN HAMILTON, b. Amelia Co., Va., 1747; d. Hancock Co., Ga., 1829. Served in Va. Troops. Married Tabitha Thweatt, b. in Va., 1747; d. in Ga., 1805 (dau. of James Thweatt and wife Sarah Studevant of Va.).
Children:
1. Marmaduke (1770-1832); mar. Elizabeth Scott.
2. James Thweatt.
3. John.
4. Thomas P., mar. Elizabeth Freeman.
5. George, mar. Elvira Eavens.
6. Sarah Thweatt (1775-1850); mar. ROBERT RAINES of Hancock Co., Ga., d. 1816, a REV. SOLDIER, Ga. Troops.
7. Frances (1781-1827); mar. Brig.-Gen. David Blackshear, Laurens Co., Ga.
8. Martha.
9. Mary, b. Hancock Co., Ga., 1778; d. Thomas Co., Ga. Married George White Hayes.
10. William, mar. (1) Mary —; (2) Elizabeth Bryan.

11. Everard. Soldier of 1812. Married Mary H. Floyd (dau. of
Gen. John Floyd, Soldier of 1812).

STEWART HAMILTON, b. in N. C.; d. Montgomery (now Telfair)
Co., Ga., 1831. Served as private, Capt. Bailey's 10th N. C. Reg. He
married Clarissa Stringer, d. 1840.
Children:
1. Benjamin.
2. Solomon.
3. Rebecca, mar. — Stoney.
4. Strotho.
5. Josiah.
6. William, mar. Elizabeth Brown.
7. Sarah, mar. Benj. Burch.
8. Rosannah, mar. — Gillis.

JOHN HAMMOCK, b. in Va., 1758; d. Lincoln Co., Ga., 1831. Served
as private, Va. Troops. Received bounty land for his services 1784,
Washington Co., Ga. Married (1) 1778, Phoebe Paschall (1760-about
1808); mar. (2) Sarah Thornton, widow. Lived in Wilkes (now Lincoln)
Co., Ga.
Children by (1) wife:
1. Samuel, mar. Elizabeth.
2. Paschall, mar. (1) Zilpha Green; (2) Miss Hughes.
3. William.
4. John, mar. Ann —.
5. Elijah, mar. Polly Chapman.
6. Charles.
7. Thomas.
8. Feraby, mar. — Mumford.
9. Margaret, mar. — Green.
10. Elizabeth, mar. Roling.
11. Reliance.
12. David.

ROBERT HAMMOCK, b. in Va.; d. Wilkes Co., Ga., July, 1779. (Will
made July 9, 1779). Was a REV. SOLDIER, a Patriot Wife Millenor.
Children:
1. Lewis
2. Robert.
3. McFarlane.
4. Joshua.
5. Wm.
6. Edward.
7. Anna, mar. — Ray.
8. Betsey, mar. — Moncreif.
9. Lucy.
10. Polly.
11. Lurina.
12. Katie.
13. Millie, mar. — Bentley.

ABNER HAMMOND, b. 1762; d. Milledgeville, Ga., 1829 (son of
CHARLES HAMMOND, REV. SOLDIER of S. C., and his wife Elizabeth
Steele. They had four sons who were REV. SOLDIERS: ABNER;
CHARLES, killed as REV. SOLDIER; LeRoy; and SAMUEL; and one
dau. Elizabeth). ABNER HAMMOND raised a Volunteer Co., joined
his brother SAMUEL at the Siege of Augusta, Ga. Was Lieut., S. C.

Troops, later Captain. Married (1) Ann Jones; (2) 1803, Sarah Dudley. Children by (2) wife:
1. John, m. (1) —; (2) Caroline Fort.
2. Anne, mar. Peter Stubbs.
3. Eliza, mar. Baradell Palmer Stubbs.
(Grave marked by Nancy Hart Chapter, D.A.R., Milledgeville, Ga.)

JOHN HAMMOND, b. 1722, Richmond Co., Va.; d. 1781, Jackson Co., Ga. Served as Capt. under Col. Le Roy Hammond and Gen. Andrew Williamson in Drayton's Campaign. Married Ann Coleman.

LE ROY HAMMOND, b. in Va.; d. Beech Island, S.C. Lived at Augusta, Ga. Served under Gen. Andrew Williamson. Appointed 1778. Married Miss Tyler.
Child:
1. LE ROY HAMMOND, JR., a REV. SOLDIER at the age of 16 years.

SAMUEL HAMMOND, b. Richmond Co., Va., Sept. 21, 1757; d. Sept. 11, 1842, at his home on Horse Shoe Creek, Beech Island, S.C. Monument erected to his memory in Augusta, Ga. He served as aide to Gen. Hand. Fought at King's Mt., and the Siege of Augusta. Was Military Governor of Missouri, 1805; later Governor. Married (1) Rebecca, widow of John Rae, d. 1788. He mar. (2) May 5, 1802, Eliza Amelia O'Keefe. Eight children.
1. Mary Ann, mar. James R. Washington. Charter member U.S. D.A.R., of Mary Hammond Washington Chapter, D.A.R., Macon, Ga., which bears her name.

HENRY HAND, b. 1753 in Va.; d. 1835, Talbot Co., Ga. Received bounty land in Ga. for his services as private. Married Elizabeth Harrison.
Children: (known)
1. William.
2. John.
3. Henry Harrison.
4. James.
5. Rev. Thomas.
6. Joel.
7. Rev. Joseph.

GEORGE HANDLEY, b. in England, Feb. 9, 1752; came to America; d. Richmond Co., Ga., Sept. 17, 1793. Served as 1st Lieut., 1st Ga. Reg. 1776; Captain, Lieut.-Col. Moved to Glynn Co., Ga., soon after the Revolution. Charter member of the Society of the Cincinnati. Was elected Governor of Ga., 1788. Married Sarah Howe (niece of MAJOR GEN. SAMUEL ELBERT).
Child:
1. George Thomas Handley.

JAMES HANES (Haines), b. Oct. 12, 1762, New Castle Co., Delaware;

d. Clayton Co., Ga., 1862. Served as private. Enlisted May 18, 1781, under Recruiting Officer Thomas Keane, in New Castle Co., for the Del. Reg., as per Muster Roll in Dept. of Public Archives, Del. Married 1790, New Castle Co., Del., Jemina Callaway.
Children:

1. Ephriam, b. Sept. 13, 1791; killed at Savannah, Ga. Soldier of War of 1812.
2. Joshua, b. Aug. 1796; mar. Miss Allen. Had 11 children.
3. Elijah, b. Aug. 1798; mar. Celia Rountree.
4. James, b. Jan. 5, 1808; mar. Malinda Lasseter.
5. David (1803-1866); mar. (1) Elizabeth Lasseter; (2) Martha Barnes.

JOHN HARDEE, b. Pitt Co., N. C., 1747; d. 1809, Camden Co., Ga. Served as private and Captain of Continental Galley on the Coast of Ga. for 3 years. Later Capt., Ga. Militia. Given bounty grant of land, 1360 acres, in Camden Co., 1786. He married 1768, in Pitt Co., N. C., Sarah Ellis (1774-1848).
Child:

1. John Hardee, d. Camden Co., Ga., 1838. A Soldier of 1812.

HENRY HARDIN, b. May 8, 1750, Johnston Co., N. C.; d. 1843, Walton Co., Ga. Served in the N. C. Continental Line under Capt. Smith, Col. Brevard, and Col. Hunter. Married (1) Sarah Cook; (2) Matilda Jones.
Children:

1. Effie, mar. Richard Fletcher.
2. Judith, mar. Thomas Stephens.
3. Elizabeth, mar. (1) — Eads; (2) — Taylor.
4. Mark, mar. Mary Hadley.
5. Benjamin Cook.
6. Edward J., mar. Jane Louise Barrett.
7. Clarissa Warren, mar. Few Gordon.
8. Harriet Hargrove, mar. Wiley Thornton.

MARK HARDIN, b. 1750, Fanquin Co., Va.; d. Warren Co., Ga. Served as private Va. Mil. Married (2) 1797, Martha Frances Newsome.

WILLIAM HARDIN, b. in S. C., 1741; d. 1810 in Ga. Served as private, S. C. Militia, under Gen. Francis Marion. Married Sarah Bledsoe.

CHARLES HARDMAN, b. in Va.; d. 1822, Oglethorpe Co., Ga. Took the Oath of Allegiance in Henry Co., Va. Married Rhoda —.

WILLIAM HARDWICK, b. June 6, 1727, S. C.; d. Greene Co., Ga., Feb. 24, 1803, buried near Davisboro, Ga. Served as private, 3rd S. C. Troops, and Sergent, 6th S. C. Troops. Married Cynthia Parker,

April 22, 17--.
Children: (not in order of birth)
1. Martha, mar. — Jones.
2. Nonaly, mar. — Dawkins.
3. Nancy, mar. — Daniell.
4. Molly, b. 1763, mar. Renee Fitzpatrick.
5. WILLIAM, JR., b. 1760; mar. Nancy Shipp.
6. Garland, b. May 22, 1768.
7. James, b. Dec. 16, 1750.
8. George, b. 1766.
9. Peggy, b. June 7, 1773.

WILLIAM HARDWICK, JR., b. 1760; d. Ga., Mar. 1, 1826. Received bounty land in Ga. for his services as a REV. SOLDIER. Married April 22, 1780, Nancy Shipp.
Children:
1. Betsey, mar. 1808, Allen Roberts.
2. William.
3. Franky.
4. Richard.
5. Eliza, mar. — Hart.
6. Nancy, mar. James Barrow.
7. Jefferson.
8. Patsey, mar. 1809, David Lewis.
9. Sophie Garland, mar. Stephen Jones.
10. Polly, mar. Adam Jones.

JOHN HARDY, b. Tyron Co., N. C., 1756; d. Warren Co., Ga., 1818. Member of a Co. of Patriot Troops, under Col. Elijah Clarke. Received bounty land in Ga. for his services. Married 1778, Sarah Sutton (1758-1812).
Children: (known)
1. John, Jr.
2. Jesse.
3. Penelope.
4. Sutton.

GEORGE HARLAN, b. Chatham Co., S. C., 1756; d. 1813 in Ga. Served as private in Capt. Henry Key's Penn. Militia. Married Ann Breede.

ROBERT HARPER, served as a REV. SOLDIER under Gen. Elijah Clarke at the Battle of Kettle Creek, Wilkes Co., Ga. Brother of WILLIAM HARPER.

WILLIAM HARPER, b. Halifax Co., Va.; d. Wilkes Co., Ga. Served at Battle of Kettle Creek, under Gen. Elijah Clarke. Received bounty land in Washington Co., Ga., 1785. Married Ann Philada Hudson (dau. of Charles and Mary Hudson of Wilkes Co., Ga., and granddau. of Samuel Hudson of Va.).

WILLIAM HARPER, REV. SOLDIER. Buried in Family Cemetery, Hancock Co., Ga. Drew pension. Born in Va. Married Mary Ingram.

JACOB HARRELL, b. in N. C., 1763; d. Decatur Co., Ga., Feb. 1837. Served as a REV. SOLDIER in N. C. Line. Married Polly Whiddon, b. in N. C.; d. 1838, Decatur Co., Ga.
Child:
    1. John.

ABSOLOM HARRIS (son of BENJAMIN HARRIS (1732-1812), REV. SOLDIER of Va.), b. 1750, Greenville Co., Va.; d. 1824, Hancock Co., Ga. Enlisted 1778 as private, Va. Line. Lieut., Brunswick Co., Va. Militia. Married (1) Elizabeth (Lowe) Tarver; (2) Sarah Clare Jeter.

BENJAMIN HARRIS, b. in Sampson Co., N. C., 1761; d. 1840, Walton Co., Ga. Served as private, N. C. Line. Received bounty grant. On Pension Roll, 1832.

JOHN HARRIS, b. 1738 in Va., d. 1810, Walton Co., Ga. Served as gunner in Col. Charles Harrison's Va. Reg. of Artillery. Married Mary Walker.

SAMUEL HARRIS, b. in Va.; d. 1789, Greene Co., Ga. Served as a REV. PATRIOT. Married Martha —.
Children:
    1. Robert.
    2. James.
    3. Thomas.
    4. Samuel, Jr.
    5. John.
    6. William.
    7. Laird.
    8. Mathew.
    9. Dau., mar. Samuel Ross.
    10. Jane, mar. THOMAS McCAULE (son of James McCall), REV. SOLDIER.
        Child:
        1. Dau., mar. William Wylie.

THOMAS HARRIS, b. Necklinburg Co., N. C., 1740; d. 1790, Greene Co., Ga. Served as Capt., 4th N. C. Reg. Married:
Child:
    1. Elizabeth Harris, mar. ANDREW BAXTER, JR., REV. SOLDIER of N. C. (1750-1814) (son of Andrew Baxter, Sr., of N. C.).

WALTON HARRIS, b. 1739 in Va.; d. Greene Co., Ga. 1809. Served as private, Ga. Line, under Gen. Elijah Clarke at the Battle of Kettle Creek. Was made prisoner Augusta, Ga. Married Rebecca Lanier

(dau. of Sampson Lanier of Va.).
Children:
1. BUCKNER HARRIS, b. in Va. 1761; d. in Ga. 1821. Served as private, under Gen. Elijah Clarke, Ga. Line. Lived Wilkes Co., Ga. Married Nancy Matilda Early.
2. SAMPSON, b. 1763. Served as a REV. SOLDIER. Married Susan Terrell Willis.
3. Joel.
4. Edwin.
5. Nathan.
6. Simeon.
7. Augustine (1767-1836); mar. Ann Byne.
8. Walton, mar. Virginia Beverly Billups. Had 11 children.
9. Elizabeth.
10. Littleton.
11. Jeptha V. (1778-1856); mar. Sarah Hunt.

EDWARD HARRISON, b. in England; d. Hall Co., Ga. Served as private, Ga. Troops. Received bounty land for his services. Married (3) Susan Gideon.

BENJAMIN HART (son of Thomas Hart and his wife Susanna Rice), was b. in Hanover Co., Va., 1730; d. Brunswick, Glynn Co., Ga., 1802. He moved with his parents to Orange Co., N. C.; then to Edgefield Co., S. C., and in 1771 moved with his family to the "Ceded Lands" of Ga. formerly Wilkes Co., now Elbert Co., Ga. He is buried in the old Cemetery, Wright's Square, Glynn Co. He served as Lieut., Ga. Mil., 1777 to Nov. 9, 1782. Was also a musician (cornet), and served as regimental quartermaster of the 3rd Continental Dragoons, July 26, 1778. Married Ann (called Nancy) Morgan (dau. of Thomas and Rebecca (Alexander) Morgan of Bucks Co., Penn.), d. in Henderson Co., Ky., 1840. (Her grave has been marked by the Samuel Hopkins Chapter, D. A. R., of Henderson, Ky. Grave in Hart Cemetery, 12 miles from Henderson.
Children:
1. THOMAS MORGAN (called Morgan), name appears on list of Georgians who fought at the Battle of Kettle Creek, at War Hill, Wilkes Co. (adjoins Elbert), together with the names of BENJAMIN HART and NANCY HART.
2. JOHN, b. 1762; d. 1821, Henderson Co., Ky. He was a REV. SOLDIER of Ga., and also a Soldier of 1812. Lived Oglethorpe Co., Ga., 1788, Sparks Fort near Athens, Ga. 1791. Married 1787, Patience Lane (dau. of JESSE LANE, REV. SOLDIER of Ga., and his wife Winifred Aycock).
3. Sally, mar. — Thompson.
4. Keziah.
5. Benjamin, Jr., mar. Mary —.
6. Mark

7. Lemuel.
8. Sukey (Susanna) (The Sukey Hart Chapter, C. A. R., of Milledgeville, Ga., bears her name).

NANCY HART moved to Kentucky after her husband's death
and lies buried in the Blue Grass State. Among the heroines of the
Revolution, an exalted place must be assigned to Nancy Hart of Ga.
The story of her bold capture of a band of Tories, single-handed,
electrified the whole theatre of War, during the troublous times of
Toryisms in Upper Georgia. In the dangerous, infested districts in
Ga., in the darkest hour of the struggle for Independence, she not only
outwitted and out-braved the whole band of Tories, but added another
name to the heroic Roster of the Revolution.

On another occasion, she built a raft of logs and crossed to the
Carolina side of the Savannah River to obtain information for the Ga.
Troops. While in the fort with other women and children, while the
men were away in the field, she ably defended it many times from the
Tories and Indians who attacked it.

In Elbert Co., Ga., there is a small tributary of Broad River,
which acquired the name of "War Woman's Creek" during the Revolution. It was near this stream that Benjamin Hart, the husband of
Georgia's Revolutionary heroine, Nancy Hart, lived; and the name was
conferred on the creek because of the heroic deeds of Nancy Hart, who
was known among the Indians of that section as the "War Woman".

Georgia is very proud of her "Nancy Hart" and her name is
commemorated in the State. She is known as the Heroine of the Battle
of Kettle Creek, Hart Co., the only county in Ga. named for a woman,
which is named for her. Also, the "Nancy Hart Highway" and the
Nancy Hart Chapter, D. A. R., of Milledgeville, Ga., bear her name.
A splendid picture of "Nancy Hart capturing the Tories" hangs on the
wall of the Genealogical room at the State Department of Archives,
Atlanta, Ga. A memorial built by the Federal Government at Hartwell,
Ga. was unveiled and dedicated by a descendant of the heroine.

JOHN HART, b. in S. C.; d. in Ga. Served as an officer in the 2nd
S. C. Reg. Was taken prisoner at Charleston, May 12, 1780. Married
Mary Screven (dau. of GEN. JAMES SCREVEN, REV. SOLDIER of Ga.,
killed at the engagement at Midway Church, Nov. 24, 1778).
Child:
1. Elizabeth, mar. CAPT. JOSEPH JONES of Liberty Co., Ga. (son
   of MAJOR JOHN JONES, a REV. SOLDIER who served on the
   staff of Gen. McIntosh and was killed at the Siege of Savannah,
   Ga.

REV. OLIVER HART, b. July 5, 1723 at Warminster, Penn.; d. Dec.
31, 1795 at Hopewell, N. J. As a minister of the First Baptist Church,
Charleston, S. C. He was appointed by the Council of Safety to recon-
cile the settlers on the frontier. He served as Chaplain in the Contin-

ental Army. Married (1) Sarah Breese (1729-1772); mar. (2) 1774, Ann Marie (Sealy) Grimball.

SAMUEL HART, b. Caswell Co., N. C., about 1748; d. Hancock Co., Ga., 1808. Served as a REV. SOLDIER of N. C., and received bounty grant of land in Ga. for his services. Inventory of his estate in Hancock Co., Ga., made July 8, 1808. Married Susannah Boring (dau. of Joseph and Elizabeth Boring of Caswell Co., N. C.), d. 1837 in Taliaferro Co., Ga.
Children:
1. William.
2. Samuel, Jr.
3. Eli.
4. James, mar. —. Moved to Ill.
5. Elizabeth, mar. Nathan Chapman.
6. Sarah, mar. Thomas Chapman.
7. Susannah, mar. Benjamin Chapman.
8. Martha, mar. James Veazey.
9. Mary.
10. John.

WILLIAM HARTSFIELD, b. 1748; d. Oglethorpe Co., Ga., 1830. Served as private, N. C. Line. Received bounty land in Ga. for these services. Married 1771, Anna —.
Children:
1. Henry.
2. Mary.
3. John.
4. Becky.
5. Jacob.
6. Tempe.
7. Sally.
8. Betsey.
9. James.
10. Haskey.
11. Andrew.
12. William, Jr.

JOHN HARVIE, b. in Scotland, 1706; came to Va., 1730; d. in Va., 1767. Married Martha Gaines, b. in Va., 1719; d. Oglethorpe Co., Ga., 1801. In 1780, during the Revolution, MARTHA HARVIE, widow, a PATRIOT during the Revolution, moved with most of her children to Ga. and settled on the Broad River, Wilkes Co.
Children:
1. JOHN, JR., REV. SOLDIER; remained in Va. Married Margaret Jones.
Other children were: (all came to Ga.)
2. Richard.
3. Daniel, mar. Sally Taliaferro (sister of COL. BENJAMIN TALIAFERRO, REV. SOLDIER).
4. WILLIAM, REV. SOLDIER of Va.; mar. Judith Cosby.
5. Martha, mar. John Moore.
6. Mary, mar. DAVID MERIWETHER, REV. SOLDIER.
7. Martha, mar. John Davenport.

8. Genette, mar. Reuben Jordan.
9. Elizabeth, mar. JAMES MARKS, REV. SOLDIER.

JOSIAH HATCHER, b. 1761, Va.; d. 1847 in Pike Co., Ga. Served as private, Ga. Line. Married Levinia Clay.

WILLIAM HATCHER, b. 1755 in Va.; d. 1833 (?), Wilkinson Co., Ga. Served as private and received bounty land for his services. Married 1782, Priscilla Stout (?).

BENJAMIN HAWKINS, b. 1754, Butte (now Warren) Co., N. C.; d. June 8, 1816 in Ga., at his home "Creek Agency" on the Flint River, Crawford Co. (son of Col. Philemon and Delia Hawkins; their 4 sons JOHN, PHILEMON, BENJAMIN, and JOSEPH were Colonels in the REV. WAR). BENJAMIN was a member of the Senior Class at Princeton when selected by Gen. George Washington as French interpreter on his official staff. Was at the Battle of Monmouth; afterwards a Soldier of 1812. Member Continental Congress 1782. He was buried on a bluff overlooking Flint River in Crawford Co., and his grave was marked by the Ga. D. A. R. He married Lavinia Downes (1782-1858). Children: (2 sons, 5 daus., but only 3 daus. reached maturity).
1. Jeffersonia, youngest dau., mar. (1) Francis Bacon of Mass.;
   (2) Dr. Jeremiah C. Harvey.
2. Sarah, mar. John B. Hardin.
3. Virginia, mar. William A. Carr.

NOTE: Fort Hawkins on the Ocmulgee River, Macon, Ga. is named in his honor. The Benjamin Hawkins Chapter, D. A. R., Cuthbert, Ga. bears his name.

NOTE: JAMES, WILLIAM, STEPHEN, and JOHN HAWTHORNE, Ga. Soldiers of the Line. JOHN HAWTHORNE drew land as REV. SOLDIER in 1820, Twiggs Co.; WILLIAM HAWTHORNE drew land as REV. SOLDIER, Decatur Co., in Lottery of 1827.

BENJAMIN HAYGOOD, b. in Va. or N. C., 1758; d. in Ga., 1849. Served under Capt. George Herndon, Gen. Folsom's N. C. Brigade. Married 1777, Mary Stewart (dau. of JAMES STEWART, REV. SOLDIER of N.C., and his wife Elizabeth.

PARMENAS HAYNES (son of HENRY HAYNES (1701-1782), REV. SOLDIER of Va., and wife Mary), b. Bedford Co., Va., July 1, 1742; d. Oglethorpe Co., Ga., Mar. 1, 1813. Served as Captain, Va. Continental Line. Married (1) Dec. 15, 1767, Elizabeth Baber (1749-1813); mar. (2) Delia Greer, Dec. 2, 1781 (dau. of Aquilla Greer, b. 1719, Surry Co., Va., a Patriot who signed the Oath of Allegiance in Henry Co., Va., 1777, and with his wife Elizabeth, moved to Greene Co., where he died.

Children by (1) wife:
1. Nancy, b. Dec. 10, 1768; mar. (1) James Shackelford; (2) Jesse Eley.
2. Robert, b. 1770; mar. 1794, Lucy Phelps.
3. Richard, b. 1773; mar. 1800, Abi Ragin (dau. of JONATHAN RAGAN, REV. SOLDIER of Ga.).
Children by (2) wife:
4. Parmenas, Jr. (1783-1849); mar. 1807, Jane Phelps.
5. Sally, b. 1785; mar. Woody Jackson.
6. Delia, b. 1788; mar. 1808, William Greer of Greene Co., Ga.
7. Polly, mar. John Thorington of Oglethorpe Co., Ga.
8. Jasper, mar. Lucy Slaton.
9. Henry.

MOSES HAYNES, b. in Va.; d. 1829, Wilkes (now Hart) Co., Ga. Served in Va. Continental Line. Received bounty land in Wilkes Co., Ga. for his services. Married Sarah —.
Children:
1. Stephen.
2. William.
3. Moses, Jr.
4. Thomas.
5. Nancy.
6. Elizabeth.
7. Polly.
8. Sarah.
9. Jane.

THOMAS HAYNES, b. 1748, Mecklenburg Co., N. C.; d. 1823, Columbia Co., Ga. Member Council of Safety, Halifax Co., N. C. Married 1782, Frances Stith.

GEORGE HAYS, REV. SOLDIER, Miles Dist., Jackson Co.

JOHN HAYS, b. Nov. 2, 1731; d. June 2, 1839. His wife Mary, b. Dec. 19, 1760; d. June 19, 1839. Tombstone marked "A Revolutionary Soldier", Decatur, Ga.

JAMES HEAD, b. Orange Co., Va.; d. Elbert Co., Ga. (Will made Oct. 23, 1795, Pro. Jan. 7, 1796). Lived on Kettle Creek, Wilkes Co. Served as REV. SOLDIER of Va. Received bounty land in Ga., 1793. Married Elizabeth Janet Powell (dau. of SIMON POWELL, REV. SOLDIER, Sergeant in Co. of Rangers under Capt. Hogg, Orange Co., Va.).
Children:
1. Lucy, mar. James Allen (son of DAVID ALLEN, b. 1755 in Va.; d. after 1827, Morgan Co., Ga., REV. SOLDIER, and his wife Eliza Caroline. Drew land in Cherokee Land Lottery, Ga., 1827).
2. Elizabeth, mar. Reuben White.
3. Martha, mar. John Lewis.
4. James, mar. Elizabeth Seals.
5. Sarah, mar. Benjamin Forston.
6. Benjamin.   7. Simon.

BARNARD HEARD, b. 1739; d. Wilkes Co., Ga., 1798. Served as Major, Ga. Troops. Made prisoner by the British, escaped, and was at the Siege of Augusta. Married Nancy Germany.

JESSE HEARD, b. Augusta Co., Va., 1749; d. Wilkes Co., Ga., 1803. Served as private, Ga. Troops, under Gen. Elijah Clarke. Received bounty grant of land for his services in 1784. Married (1) Judith Wilkinson; (2) Elizabeth —.
Children by (1) wife:
1. Stephen.
2. Lucy Wilkinson (1779-1843); mar. 1806, Wm. Weare Harman.
3. Sarah, mar. Stephen Martin; moved to Mo.
4. Judith, mar. her first cousin, William Smith; moved to S. C.
5. Mary, mar. — Grier. Moved to Ala.
6. Jesse Falkner, b. 1785; mar. Caroline Wilkinson (dau. of BENJAMIN WILKINSON, of Wilkes Co., Ga., REV. SOLDIER, fought at Battle of Kettle Creek).
7. Elizabeth, mar. John Stanton; moved to Mo.
8. Susan, mar. (1) Thomas Beatty; (2) — Robbins.

STEPHEN HEARD (son of JOHN HEARD, REV. SOLDIER, and his wife Bridget Bouton of Va. and Ga.), b. in Va., 1740; d. Elbert Co., Ga., 1815. Commanded a Co., member of Ex. Council and also President. Was elected Governor of Ga., and for a time the seat of the Government of Ga. was at his home, Heard's Fort, Wilkes Co., while Savannah was in the hands of the British. He was also taken prisoner by the British. Married (1) Jane Garmany; she was driven from her home by the Tories and died from exposure; mar. (2) Aug. 25, 1785, Elizabeth Darden (called Betsey) (1766-1848).
Children:
1. Barnard, b. 1787; mar. Mary Hutson.
2. Martha Burch, b. 1788; mar. Bartlett Tucker.
3. George Washington, b. 1791.
4. John Adams, b. 1793;
5. Bridget Carroll, b. 1795; mar. (1) Simeon Henderson; moved to Miss.; mar. (2) — Thompson.
6. Jane Lanier, b. 1797; mar. Singleton W. Allen.
7. Pamela Darden (1799-1816).
8. Thomas J., b. 1801; d. 1876; mar. Nancy Middleton.
9. Sarah Hammond, b. 1804; mar. Dr. Jarrett.

THOMAS HEARD, b. 1742 in Va.; d. 1808, Greene Co., Ga. Served as Capt., Va. State Troops. Married 1766, Elizabeth Fitzpatrick (1750-1790) (dau. of JOSEPH FITZPATRICK, REV. SOLDIER of Va., b. 1720 in Va.; d. Greene Co., Ga., and his wife Martha Napier, d. age 106 years). Married (2) Mary Veazy.
Children by (1) wife:
1. Catherine, mar. (1) Isaac Stockes; (2) Pressly Watts.

2. Abram (1769-1822); mar. Nancy Coffee.
3. Joseph, mar. (1) — Smith; (2) — Clark;   (3) Mary Allen.
4. Mary, mar. John Cook.
5. Thomas, mar. Polly Whatley.
6. Elizabeth, mar. (1) — Peeples; (2) Whatley.
7. Polly, mar. Wilson Whatley.
8. Woodson, mar. Mary Peeples.
9. George, mar. Martha Coffee.
10. Falkner, mar. Mary Robinson (dau. of RANDALL ROBINSON, REV. SOLDIER and his (1) wife Lydia Walker).

ELISHA HEARN, b. 1754, Somerset Co., Md.; d. Putnam Co., 1812, Ga. Served as a private and a sailor in Va. Widow received bounty land for his services in Va. in 1831. Married Fereby Johnson. Children:
1. Elisha, Jr.
2. Francis, mar. Elizabeth White.
3. Joshua.
4. Huldah.   6. Benjamin.
5. Polly.   7. Thomas.

JOHN HEARN, b. 1767, Va.; d. Putnam Co., Ga., after 1808. Served as a REV. SOLDIER of Va., 1781-1782. Came to Hancock Co., Ga. Married Nancy Lynch.

ROBERT HENDERSON, b. 1750, Augusta Co., Va.; d. 1839, Jackson Co., Ga. Served in Augusta Co., Va. Militia under Capt. William Robinson and Capt. Henry Watterson. Removed to Jackson Co., Ga. in 1796. Drew land as a REV. SOLDIER, 1838, in Ga. Married Mary Carroll.

WILLIAM HENDLEY, b. in Scotland; came to Va. Served in the Va. Continental Line. Settled in Bulloch Co., Ga., then Telfair Co. Married Millie Ann Horton.
Children:
1. William, mar. — Harrell.
2. Sophia, mar. W. I. Harrell.
3. Nancy, mar. — Roundtree.
4. Jeanet, mar. Daniel McCranie.
5. Horton, mar. Polly Ann Daniel.
6. Dau., mar. — Fletcher.
7. Dau., mar. — Posey.
8. Dau., mar. — Jarnigan.

JOHN HENDRICK, b. 1754, Lincoln Co., N. C.; d. 1820, Monroe Co., Ga. Served as private Capt. Robert Porter's Co., Col. John White Va. Reg. Married 1793, Lucy Hunt (1760-1808).

WYATT HEWELL, b. Spottsylvania Co., Va., 1756; d. in Ga., 1842. Received Pension 1832 for services as private and Sergeant, Va. Troops. Married 1777, Sarah Wortley.

ROBERT HENDRY, b. in Scotland, 1752; came to Hanover Co., N. C.; d. in then Liberty Co., Ga., 1830. Served as private under Light Horse Harry Lee at Yorktown. Married 1772, Anne Lee (1752-1830).

DAVID HICKS, b. 1739, Brunswick Co., Va.; d. 1812, Elbert Co., Ga. Served as Sergeant, Va. Infantry. Married 1763, Mary Johnson, d. 1820.

NATHANIEL HICKS of Ga. Courier on the staff of Gen. Nathaniel Greene, and lived after the War on the Ohoope River (now in Emanuel Co., Ga.). Married —.
Child:
1. James Hicks, b. in Ga., 1799; mar. Mary Hightower (dau. of JOSHUA HIGHTOWER of Laurens Co., Ga., a REV. SOLDIER of Va.; d. in Ga.).

THOMAS HIGHTOWER, b. Amelia Co., Va.; d. Greene Co., Ga. A REV. SOLDIER.

ABRAHAM HILL, b. Chowan Co., N. C., 1732; d. Wilkes Co., Ga., Feb. 4, 1792. Served as private under Lieut. John Cropper in Va. Troops. Moved from Wake Co., N. C., 1785, to Wilkes (now Oglethorpe) Co., Ga. Married Christian Walton (dau. of Thomas Walton, member N. C. House of Assembly).
Children:
1. John.
2. ABRAHAM, b. 1759; d. 1818. Murdered in Oglethorpe Co., Ga. Served as private in Capt. John Reid's troops of Light Dragoons, Lieut.-Col. Wade Hampton's N. C. Reg., Gen. Sumpter's Brigade. Married May 5, 1791, Elizabeth McGehee (1773-1816). Children: (known)
   1. Abram Scott (1807-1866); mar. Susan F. Halsey.
   2. Elizabeth Ann, b. 1810; mar. Blanton Meade Hill.
3. Judith, mar. Josiah Jordan.
4. Clara (1763-1798); mar. Henry Augustus Pope.
5. Sarah (1765-1816); mar. Benjamin Blake.
6. Henry (1767-1829); mar. Betty Andrew (dau. of BENJAMIN ANDREW, a REV. PATRIOT and Member of Council of Safety, Ga.).
7. Theophilus (1769-1829); mar. Polly Jordan.
8. Noah (1771-1805); mar. Ann Pope (1780-1805) (dau. of BURWELL POPE, a REV. SOLDIER, b. 1752 in Va.; d. Wilkes Co., Ga., and his wife Priscilla Wooten).
9. Miles (1774-1844); mar. Tabitha Pope (dau. of BURWELL and Priscilla (Wooten) POPE).

10. Wylie Pope (1775-1844); mar. Martha Pope (dau. of BURWELL and Priscilla (Wooten) POPE).
11. Mary (1777-1849).
12. Thomas, mar. Sally McGehee. She mar. (2) Dyonosius Oliver.

HENRY HILL, b. 1730 in N. C.; d. 1804, Wilkes Co., Ga. Served as REV. SOLDIER. Married Sarah Cotten, d. 1814.
Children:
1. John.
2. Abram (1778-1852); mar. 1806, in Wilkes Co., Ga., Clarissa Callaway (1790-1855) (dau. of Joseph Callaway; granddau. of JOB CALLAWAY and JONATHAN RAGAN, both REV. SOLDIERS).
3. Theophilus.
4. Henry, Jr.
5. Nancy (1770-1839); mar. COL. WILLIAM JOHNSON (1755-1821), Wilkes Co., Ga., a REV. SOLDIER who was granted bounty land for his services in Washington Co., Ga.
   Children:
   1. Elizabeth, mar. Drury Cunningham.
   2. Mary, mar. Henry Spratlin.
   3. Susan, mar. Judge James Dabney Willis.
   4. John Pope, mar. Prudence Irvine.
   5. Nancy, mar. her cousin, Col. Lodwick M. Hill, as (1) wife.
   6. William.
   7. Stephen.
   8. Martha Pope, mar. as (2) wife, Burwell Pope Hill.
   9. Catherine.
   10. Sarah.

ISAAC HILL, b. Charles Co., Md., 1748; d. Warren Co., Tenn., 1825. Served as drummed 3rd Md. Reg. Married 1772, Lucy Wallace (1746-1798). Grandfather of Senator Benjamin Harvey Hill. J. E. Hill of Decatur, Ga. is not a relative.

ISAAC HILL, b. 1748; d. Clarke Co., Ga. (will made Nov. 9, 1829; pro. Oct. 7, 1833). Served as REV. SOLDIER. Married Nancy Crain (a Patriot and wounded in War).
Children:
1. Middleton.
2. Isaac, Jr.
3. Elender, mar. — Hopkins.
4. Charlotte, mar. — Burney.
5. Olivia, mar. — Harvey.
6. Elizabeth, mar. Joseph Lane, Jr.
7. Sally, mar. John Love.
8. Catherine, mar. John Love as (2) wife.
9. Nancy, mar. — Seavers.
10. Eudocia, mar. — Anderson.
11. Roderick.

WILLIAM HILL of Ga., b. 1760; d. 1850. Served as private, Ga. Line. Married 1782, Phoebe Flournoy (1764-1819).
Children:
1. John.
2. Robert.
3. Frances, mar. John Ashurst.
4. Phoebe, mar. Frederick Crow.
5. Winifred, mar. Eli Lester.
6. Virginia, mar. Harmon Hubert.
7. William, Jr.

CHRISTOPHER HILLARY, b. 1735; d. St. Simons, Ga., Feb. 18, 1796. Served in Ga. Line under Gen. Elijah Clarke. Captured by the British 1781, exchanged 1782. Received bounty land in Glynn Co., Ga., 1787. Married March 20, 1787, Agnes Hightower. She mar. (2) as (2) wife, COL. JOHN McINTOSH, REV. SOLDIER of Ga.
Child:
1. Marie Hillary, b. in Ga., 1788; mar. Major William Jackson McIntosh (son of COL. JOHN McINTOSH and his (1) wife Sarah Swinton).

DAVID HILLHOUSE, b. in Conn.; d. Wilkes Co., Ga. Moved before 1787 from New Haven, Conn. to Washington, Wilkes Co., Ga. He owned and edited the "Monitor" of Washington, Ga. (This was the first town in the U. S. to be named in honor of President George Washington, and the "Monitor" was the first newspaper to be published in Ga.) He married Sarah Porter (dau. of ELISHA PORTER, b. 1742 in Hartford, Conn. (or Hadley, Mass.) and d. in Springfield, Mass., 1796, a REV. SOLDIER who commanded a Reg. at the Lexington alarm, was at the Battle of Saratoga, and escorted Gen. Burgoyne to Boston; mar. Sarah Jewett).
Children: (known)
1. Dau., mar. Felix Gilbert of Wilkes.
2. Mary, mar. Andrew Shepherd as (2) wife.

JAMES HINES, b. 1760; d. 1804, Effingham Co., Ga. Served in N. C. Line from Pitt Co., N. C. Married Drucilla —. They had 10 children.

MATHEW HOBSON, a REV. PATRIOT, at whose house the Council of Safety of Ga. held their meeting in Augusta, Ga.
Child:
1. AGNES, swam the Savannah River at Augusta, to carry important information to the American forces.

JOSEPH HODGES, b. in N. C., 1762; d. Bullock Co., Ga., 1842. Married June 13, 1799, Sarah Carr (1770-about 1840). He served as Lieut. in Ga. Militia. Received grant of land in Burke Co., Ga. for his services.
Child: (only one known)

1. James Carr, b. Mar. 18, 1800; d. Jan. 17, 1865; mar. 1826, Sarah Ann Newton (1802-1903).

JOSHUA HODGES, SR., b. N. C., Oct. 13, 1736; d. Bulloch Co., Ga., Mar. 13, 1809. Served in the Militia from Martin Co., N. C., under Capt. Kenneth McKenzie on a tour of duty, 1780. Received land grant in Burke Co., Ga. for his services. Married Ann Raiford in N. C. All of their children, except Alcy, lived and died in Bullock Co., Ga.
Children:
1. Alcy, mar. —; removed to Lowndes Co., Ga.
2. JOSEPH, mar. — Denmark; he was REV. SOLDIER.
3. Catherine, b. 1762; mar. Jarvis Jackson.
4. Benjamin, mar. Dorothy Carr.
5. Joshua, Jr., b. 1766; mar. Rebecca Fletcher (dau. of WILLIAM FLETCHER, REV. SOLDIER of S. C. and Ga., and his (2) wife Elizabeth McIntosh.
6. Essenurer (called Alcy), b. 1776; mar. 1801, John Dampier; removed to Lowndes Co., Ga.
7. Rhoda, mar. Lemuel S. Lanier.

BENJAMIN HODNETT, b. in Va., 1761; d. 1820, Jasper Co., Ga. Served as private, Va. Troops. Married (1) 1784, Elizabeth Wyatt Collier.

LEWIS HOGG, b. 1750 in S. C.; d. 1820, Ga. Served as private, S. C. Militia. Married 1777, Clara Smith (1747-1838).

JESSE HOLBROOK, b. 1764 in Va.; d. 1844, Elbert Co., Ga. Placed on Pension Roll for services in REV. WAR, as private, Va. Line. Resident of Elbert Co., Ga. Married Susanna —.

NATHAN HOLBROOK, b. Burlingham, Mass., 1745; d. Savannah, Ga., 1819. Served as Lieut. and Capt., Mass. Troops. Married Susanna Wadhams (1760-1839) (dau. of JONATHAN WADHAMS, b. 1730, Wethersfield, Conn.; d. 1812, Goshen, Conn., a REV. SOLDIER of Conn.; Volunteer from Goshen for relief at Danbury, Conn. He mar. 1754, Judith Howe (1730-1818)).
Child:
1. Ann (1786-1878); mar. 1806, Rev. Thomas Goulding of Ga. (1786-1848).

HENRY HOLCOMBE, b. Prince Edward Co., Va., Sept. 23, 1762. Removed with parents to S. C. Served as an Officer in S. C. Line. Married 1786, Frances Tanner. Was called to the First Baptist Church, Savannah, Ga., 1799; then to Philadelphia, Jan. 1, 1812; and d. Philadelphia, Penn., May 22, 1821.
Child:
1. Robert, mar. Elizabeth Witter.

JORDAN HOLCOMBE, b. Nov. 19, 1762 in Bute Co., N. C. Moved in 1776 to Spartanburg Dist., S. C. (His father was killed in an engagement with the Tories during the REV. WAR.) Served as private in Capt. John Lawson's Co., Col. Thomas's S. C. Reg. Discharged April 1, 1781. Served four months in Capt. Jeremiah Dixon's Co., Col. Roebuck's S. C. Reg. Also private in S. C. Rangers in Capt. Culverson's Co. Allowed Pension, 1836. Moved to Hall Co., Ga., where he d. Married. Children:
A son and a daughter.

THOMAS HOLLIDAY, b. 1750 in Va.; d. in Ga. Served in Ga. Troops under Gen. Elijah Clarke. Received bounty land for his services, Washington Co., Ga. Married Elizabeth Rae.

WILLIAM HOLLIDAY, JR., b. in Ireland, 1750; came to America before the Revolution and settled in Laurens Co., S. C. Moved to St. Paul's Parish, Richmond Co., Ga. He d. Laurens Co., S. C., Nov. 1826. Served as private, Ga. Troops, under Gen. Elijah Clarke. Fought at the Battle of Kettle Creek. Received bounty land for his services, Wilkes Co., Ga. Married Jane Cooper.
Children:
1. Wm., b. in S. C., moved to Miss.
2. Robert Alexander, b. 1787 in S. C., moved to Ga., where he d. Nov. 1862. Married Rebecca Burroughs. They had 12 children.
3. Mathew, mar. Miss Dean, moved to Cass Co., Ga.; moved to Miss.
4. Martha Ann (called Nancy), mar. John Russell, moved to Cass Co., Ga.
5. Margaret.

WILLIAM HOLLIDAY, SR., b. in Ireland; d. 1786, Wilkes Co., Ga. Will made July 7, 1786. Served as private, Ga. Line. Received bounty grant of land for his services, in Wilkes Co., Ga. Married Ann —.
Children:
1. WILLIAM, mar. Jane Cooper.
2. Thomas, mar. Rebecca Ragan.
3. Robert.
4. Abraham.
5. Ayers.
6. John.
7. Jane.
8. Mary.
9. Ann.
10. Elizabeth.
11. Margery.

DAVID HOLLIMAN, b. 1757; came to Wilkes Co., Ga. (then Washington) from N. C. Will made Oct. 30, 1779, pro. July 1, 1783. Served in N. C. Line. Received grant of land, Wilkes Co., Ga. Married Mary —.
Children:
1. Sarah.
2. Elizabeth.
3. Nancy.
4. David, Jr.
5. Mark.
6. Samuel.

JOHN HOLMES, b. Caroline Co., Va., 1747; came to the Carolinas, then Ga.; d. Wilkes Co., Ga., 1806. Served in Ga. Militia. Received grant of land in St. Andrew's Parish, Ga., and was licensed to teach English and Latin at Savannah, Ga. Rector of Burke Co., Ga., Church, 1776, and on Feb. 16, 1776 was appointed Chaplain of 1st Ga. Reg. He married 1767, Chloe Bentley (1747-1813) (dau. of WILLIAM BENTLEY, b. Fairfax, Va.; d. DeKalb Co., Ga., 1802. Served as Lieut., then Capt. Received land grant for services. Married Mary Elliott).
Children:
1. Apsylla (1770-1815); mar. 1789, Pitt Milner (son of JOHN MILNER, a REV. SOLDIER, and his wife Elizabeth Godwin).
2. Penelope, mar. Benjamin Milner (son of Pitt Milner).
3. Mary, mar. (1) — Parks; (2) Elisha Kendall.
4. Elizabeth.
5. Josiah.   7. James.
6. John, Jr.   8. Moses.

WILLIAM HOLT, b. 1757, Louisa Co., Va.; d. 1826, Elbert Co., Ga. Served as Surgeon in Va. Militia, with the rank of Captain. Married 1784, Lucy Sanders (1765-1847).

JOHN HOOD, b. Amelia Co., Va.; d. Wilkes Co., Ga. Served in the Va. Continental Line; discharged at Augusta, Ga. Received bounty land, Wilkes Co., Ga. Married Rebecca Reeves of Wilkes Co.
Child:
1. Joel, b. 1789, Wilkes Co., Ga.; d. Meriwether Co., Ga., 1861. Married Martha Dowdy (dau. of MARTIN DOWDY, REV. SOLDIER of Va., who d. Oglethorpe Co., Ga., and his wife Mary Temple).

WILLIAM HOOD, b. N. C., 1739; d. 1809, Washington Co., Ga. Enlisted 1782 in Capt. Brevard's 10th N. C. Reg. Married Christina Hood (1746-1807).

JOHN HOUSTON, b. in the Parish of St. George, Ga., 1744; d. near Savannah, Ga., July 20, 1796. Member Continental Congress. Signed the famous "Card" which called the Ga. Patriots together at Tondee's Tavern. A leading Patriot; forwarded supplies to the closed port of Boston, Mass. Was elected Governor of Ga., 1778. Married —.

JOHN HOUSTON, b. in Ireland, 1760; d. Coweta Co., Ga., 1835. Served as private under Capt. Thomas Dugan and Col. John Purvis. He was allowed Pension, 1832. Married 1788, Mary Wilson (1768-1849).

JOHN HOWARD, b. in S. C., Oct. 4, 1761; d. in Baldwin Co., Ga., April 18, 1822. Served as a private in Capt. Putnam's Co., under Brig. Gen. Sumpter, S. C. Troops. Rose to rank of Major. (Grave marked

by the Nancy Hart Chapter, D. A. R., Milledgeville, Ga.) Married Jane Vivian (1770-1837).
Children:
1. Mary, mar. Seaborn Jones.
2. Elizabeth, mar. (1) Robt. Rutherford; (2) Edward Cary.
3. John Harrison, mar. Caroline Bostick.
4. Thacker, mar. Elizabeth Thweatt.
5. Homer, mar. Eleanor Sewell.
6. Augustus, mar. (1) Miss Wimberly; (2) Ann Lindsay.
7. Ann.
8. Melton.
9. Sarah.

NEHEMIAH HOWARD, living in Edgefield Dist., S. C., was a REV. PATRIOT. Married Edith Smith, b. 1733. Moved to Elbert Co., Ga., where he d. 1798.
Children:
1. Nehemiah, Jr.
2. Mark.
3. Benjamin.
4. James.
5. Joseph.
6. John, mar. Jane Vivian.
7. Isaiah, mar. — Pittman
8. Hester, mar. — Torrance.
9. Nancy, mar. Elisha (?) Owens.
10. Mary, mar. (1) — Woodward; (2) John Barrett.

SOLOMON HOWARD, b. Bertie Co., N. C., 1758; d. Washington, Ga., 1834. Record of service, Bureau of Pensions, Washington, D. C. Married Moaning Barron.

JOSEPH HOWELL (son of Joseph and Margaret Howell), b. in N. C., 1733; d. in DeKalb Co., Ga., 1835, age 102 years. Member N. C. Assembly. Served in the Mecklinburg Co., N. C. Militia. Fought at Guilford Court House and King's Mt. Married Anson Co., N. C., 1768, Margaret Eleanor Garmon, d. after 1795.
Children:
1. John, mar. Essena Osbourne.
2. Joseph, mar. Sylva Robinson.
3. Elizabeth, d. Ala.; mar. (1) Eli Green; (2) Jacob Smith.
4. Eli, mar. 1801, Nancy Love.
5. Margaret, d. Ala.; mar. Edmund Smith.
6. William, mar. Elizabeth Sides.
7. Isaac, d. Ga.; mar. 1805, Margaret Tucker.
8. Evan, b. Cabarrus Co., N. C., 1781; d. 1868, Ga. Married (1) Martha Love; (2) Mary Elliott; (3) Harriet Humes; (4) Jane Brooks; (5) Teziah Brown.
9. Michael, d. Ark.; mar. Mary Freeman.
10. Eleanor, d. Ga.; mar. John Kiser.

JOHN HUBBARD, lived in Petersburg, Elbert Co., Ga., where he d.

Feb. 15, 1800. Received 287.5 acres bounty land on certificate of Gen. Elijah Clarke for his services. Married Sally.
Children: (mentioned in will)
1. Mary, mar. — Puryear.
2. Joseph.
3. Rhoda, mar. — Burton.
4. Benjamin.
5. Susanna.
6. John, mar. (1) Betsey Cook; (2) Ann Nunnellee.
7. Richard, mar. Patsey Jones.

JOHN HUBBARD, b. 1763, Va.; d. in Ga., 1831. Received bounty land in Ga. for his services as private, Ga. Troops. Married 1785, Elizabeth Flint.

JOSEPH HUBBARD, b. in Va., 1760; d. 1830 in Ga. Married 1778, Cynthia Bennett, b. 1763; d. 1835. Served as REV. SOLDIER and also in the War of 1812.
Children:
1. Elizabeth (1778-1840); mar. Jacob Wise of Butts Co., Ga.
2. Susan.
3. William.
4. Susannah.
5. Bennett.
6. John.
7. Mildred.

MATTHEW HUBERT, b. 1757 in Va.; d. 1812, Warren Co., Ga. Served as private under Captains Edmunds and Gregory in Va. Lived Caswell Co., N. C.; moved to Wilkes Co., Ga. Married 1775, Martha Wallace (1753-1835) (dau. of Robert Wallace).
Children:
1. Nancy, b. in N. C., 1776; mar. William Flournoy of Putnam Co., Ga.
2. Hiram, mar. Sarah Burnley.
3. Mary, mar. John Vining; moved to Ala., then Texas.
4. Benjamin (1782-1812).
5. Archibald.
6. Elizabeth.
7. William, b. in Ga., 1784; mar. Rebecca Hawkins of Putnam Co., Ga.; moved to Texas.
8. John, mar. Sally Wright.
9. Harman, mar. Virginia Hill.

WILLIAM HUDGINS, age 70 years in 1832. Had wife and 13 children living (Upson Co., Ga.). Served as a REV. SOLDIER in N. C., under Capt. Oldham, Col. Wm. Moore. Received Pension.

CUTHBERT (called Cutbird) HUDSON, b. in Va.; d. 1801, Elbert Co., Ga. Served as REV. SOLDIER and received bounty grant of land on Eastanollee Creek, Franklin Co., Ga., 1785. His widow received

land as widow of REV. SOLDIER, 1827 Cherokee Lottery. Married
Elizabeth —.
Children: (mentioned in will)
1. Christopher.
   Child:
   1. Cuthbert.
2. Joacim.
3. Joshua.
4. Gilliom.
5. Thomas.
6. Amphelady, mar. Stephen Westbrook.
7. Elizabeth, mar. — Northington.
8. Mary, mar. Richard Burton.
9. Bathsheba, mar. Abraham Burton, Jr.
10. Susanna.

DAVID HUDSON, b. Prince Edward Co., Va., 1762; d. 1831, Elbert
Co., Ga. Placed on Pension Roll for services as private in Capt.
Moore's Co., Major Picken's S.C. Reg. Married Mary Cobb Booker
(1765-1830).
Children: (known)
1. Charles.
2. Wm.

IRBY HUDSON, SR., b. 1750; d. Hancock Co., Ga., 1806. Married
Dec. 4, 1778, Orange Co., Va., Phoebe Featherstone (1754-Dec. 16,
1821). Served in Capt. Robert Bolling's Dinwiddie Co., Va., under Col.
Parker and Gen. Mecklenburg's Brigade.
Children:
1. Elizabeth (1779-Jan. 5, 1834); mar. Thomas Little.
2. William, Mar. Aug. 23, 1806, Frances Long.
3. Sarah, mar. July 17, 1806, Woodlief Scott.
4. Thomas, mar. Jan. 20, 1809, Sophia Thurmond.
5. Irby, Jr., mar. Dec. 22, 1812, (1) Jane Frances Flournoy; mar.
   (2) Martha (Flournoy) Marshall.
6. Charles, mar. Elizabeth Reese.
7. Mary, mar. Oct. 1808, Frederick Scott.
8. John (Jan. 4, 1794-June 5, 1859); mar. (1) June 8, 1820, Nancy
   Gaither; (2) Elizabeth D. Jarrett.
9. Lewellyn (1795-1836); mar. 1821, Evelina Alexander.
10. Frances, mar. Robert Adams.

HENRY HUGHES, b. in England; d. Burke Co., Ga., April 27, 1814.
Served as Capt., Va. Line. Married Jane Cooper (dau. of Thomas
Cooper), d. 1826.

HOPE HULL, b. Somerset Co., Md., Mar. 13, 1763; d. Athens, Ga.,
1818. Served as a REV. SOLDIER, together with his two brothers,

THOMAS HULL and JOHN HULL. Moved to Salisbury Dist., N.C., 1785; then to Wilkes Co., Ga., 1788. Married in Va., Ann Wingfield of Hanover Co., Va.

JENNENS HULSEY, b. King's Mt., N.C., 1765; d. 1850, Henry Co., Ga. Served as private at the Battle of King's Mt. Married 1806, Rebecca Pate (1788-1827).

THOMAS HUMPHRIES, REV. SOLDIER, Baldwin Co., C.H., Milledgeville, Ga. (Name found in list in old book labelled "Watson's Batt. District". Registered by Robert Winn, Mar. 15, 1819.)

JAMES HUNT, JR., b. in Va., June 6, 1762; d. Elbert Co., Ga., Mar. 23, 1832. Served as a SOLDIER, Va. Continental Line. Married in Va., Jemina Carter, b. 1772; d. Jan 7, 1869, Hart Co., Ga.
Children:
1. Elizabeth, b. 1791; mar. Jesse M. Redwine.
2. Henry.
3. William, b. 1795.
4. Sion, mar. Priscilla Thornton.
5. James (1800-1838).
6. Moses, b. 1802.
7. Drucilla, mar. Nicholas M. Adams.
8. Willis, b. 1808; mar. Priscilla Teasley.
9. Hullium, mar. Harriet C. Ward.
10. Richard Carter, b. 1813, Elbert Co., Ga.; d. Arkansas. Married (1) Mary Harris.
11. Mary, mar. 1826, Wm. (Buck) Page.

MOSES HUNT, b. June 8, 1760; d. Elbert Co., Ga. Served in Major Dobbs Battalion. Received bounty land for his services, Ga. Militia. Married Mary Tamar Tyner (1760-1840). She was captured as a girl and held in captivity several years by the Indians.
Children:
1. Mary (1779-1863); mar. James Adams.
2. James.
3. John S., mar. 1825, Mary Gaines.
4. Nancy, mar. Lawrence M. Adams.
5. Joel.
6. Henry.
7. Joshua.
8. Richard.
9. George.
Will made June 6, 1839, pro. Mar. 12, 1842.

TURNER HUNT, b. 1756, N.C.; d. 1847, Monroe Co., Ga. Served as private, N.C. Line. Married Mary —.

WILLIAM HURT, b. in N. C.; d. in Hancock, Ga., 1812. Served as private, Ga. Line, where he was wounded. Received bounty land in Ga. for his services. Married (1) Priscilla Yancey; (2) 1794, Polly (Bass) Hunnicutt.

DANIEL INMAN, b. 1751, N. C.; d. Burke Co., Ga., 1837. Served in Burke Co., Ga. Troops. Married (1) Ava Allen; (2) Mary McPheeters. Children:

1. Alfred.
2. Rachel, mar. Levi Spain.
3. Elizabeth.
4. Allen.
5. Sophie.
6. Mary.
7. Jeremiah.
8. Daniel, Jr.

SHADRACK INMAN, b. 1750; killed at the Battle of Musgrove's Mill. Entered service as Lieut., Ga. Line. His widow, Elizabeth was granted land in Ga., as the widow of a REV. SOLDIER.

CHRISTOPHER IRVINE, b. in Ireland, 1725; d. Wilkes Co., Ga., 1815. Served as Captain of Co., 5th Ga. Reg., 1776. Received bounty land for his services in Wilkes Co., Ga. Married (1) 1779, Louisa Tucker of Amherst Co., Va. (dau. of Mathew Tucker of Va.), d. 1795; mar. (2) 1797, Prudence Echols of Wilkes Co., Ga., d. 1821.
Children by (1) wife: (known)

1. Isaiah Tucker, b. 1783 in Va.; d. 1855 in Ga. Soldier of 1812. Married 1801, Isabella Lea Bankston (dau. of LAWRENCE BANKSTON, REV. SOLDIER of Va. and Ga., and his wife Nancy Henderson). Ten children.
2. Charles Mallory.

Children by (2) wife:

3. John.
4. William.
5. David (1808-1865); mar. Sarah Baldwin Royston of Greene Co., Ga.
6. Christopher, Jr.
7. Smith, killed by Indians.

HUGH IRWIN, b. in Ireland, 1727; emigrated to America and settled in N. C. Moved to Ga., 1757. He d. Burke Co., Ga., 1805. Married —. Was a PATRIOT during the Revolution and was given a grant of land in Ga. for his services, Aug. 20, 1781.
Children:

1. Jared.
2. John Lawson.
3. Alexander.
4. William.
5. Margaret.

JARED IRWIN, b. in N. C., 1750; d. Union Hill, Washington Co., Ga., Mar. 1, 1818. Entered the Continental Army as Captain, promoted to Colonel, then General. Was twice elected Governor of Ga. As Governor

he signed the rescinding of the Yazoo act, Feb. 13, 1796. Married his cousin Isabella Erwin.
Children:

1. John, a Soldier of 1812.   3. Jane.
2. Thomas.   4. Elizabeth, mar. Simeon Whitaker.

NOTE: With his three brothers, JOHN LAWSON, ALEXANDER, and WILLIAM IRWIN, all of whom were REV. SOLDIERS, he built a fort near Union Hill, his home, to protect this section of Ga. from the Indians, called Fort Irwin. The first monument ever erected by the State of Ga., was erected to the memory of Gov. Jared Irwin at Sandersville, Ga.

JOHN LAWSON IRWIN, b. Mecklinburg Co., N. C., Aug. 29, 1755; d. Jan. 1, 1822. Was one of the first settlers of Washington Co., Ga. Served under his brother JARED IRWIN and was with his command at the seiges of Savannah and Augusta and in the Battles of Camden, S. C., Briar Creek, Ga., and Black Swamp, S. C. Married Rebecca Sessions, b. Mar. 30, 1773; d. June 8, 1839, mar. 1790. He was son of HUGH IRWIN, b. 1725 in Ireland; d. 1805; granted bounty land for his services in Ga. Line, and his wife Martha Alexander.
Child:

1. Alexander (1792-1843); mar. 1824 Margaret Moore Lawson (1798-1853) (dau. of ANDREW THOMPSON LAWSON, b. 1760 in Ga.; d. 1822 in Augusta, Ga., REV. SOLDIER of Ga., and his wife Mary Moore Barry, dau. of ANDREW BARRY, b. 1746 in Penn.; d. 1811 in S. C., REV. SOLDIER, commanded a Co. of S. C. Rangers; mar. MARGARET MOORE, a PATRIOT of the Revolution).

JOHN GODHILP ISRAEL, b. 1755; d. in Ga., June 4, 1820. Served as a REV. SOLDIER. Received bounty land for his services. Married Christinia (Kieffer) Mingledorf (1755-1851).
Children:

1. Christinia, mar. Charles Ryall.
2. Hannah Elizabeth, mar. Matthew Carter.
3. Sarah, mar. James Bird of Bryan Co.
4. David.   6. Joshua.
5. Solomon.   7. Susannah.

JAMES JACK (son of PATRICK JACK, Lieut., 3rd Lancaster Co., Penn. Batt., and member of N. C. Council of Safety, REV. SOLDIER of Penn. and N. C., and his wife Lillis McAdoo), b. 1731 in Penn.; d. in Wilkes (now Elbert) Co., Ga., 1826. Served in N. C. Line. Carried the "Mecklinburg Declaration of Independence" to Philadelphia for the Congress. Received bounty land for his services in Wilkes Co., Ga., 1784. Married Margaret Houston.
Children:

1. William, mar. Miss Cummings.
2. Patrick (1769-1820), Soldier of 1812; mar. Harriet Spencer. They had 8 children.
3. Catherine, mar. Sidnor Cosby.
4. Archibald.
5. James.

JOHN JACK (son of PATRICK JACK), b. in N. C.; d. in Wilkes Co., Ga. Served in N. C. Line. Received bounty land for his services in Wilkes Co., Ga. Married Mary Barnett (dau. of JOHN BARNETT, REV. SOLDIER of N. C., and his wife Ann Spratt, b. 1725, the first white child born in N. C. between the Yadkin and Catawba Rivers).

COL. SAMUEL JACK (brother of JOHN and JAMES JACK), a REV. SOLDIER. Married Kitty Jack.

ABSOLOM JACKSON, came from Wilkes Co., Ga. to Millers Bluff, Camden Co., Ga. A SOLDIER in Continental Army.

BENJAMIN JACKSON, b. in Ga.; d. Hancock Co., Ga. Private, Va. Received bounty land for his services in Hancock Co., Ga.

CHARLES JACKSON, REV. SOLDIER of Mass., b. Newton, Mass., 1767; d. Cumberland Island, Ga., 1801, at the home of Phineas Miller.

DANIEL JACKSON, b. 1735 in S. C.; d. 1812, Wilkes Co., Ga. Served as private under Col. John Brandon in S. C. Married 1770, Nancy High. Children: (known)
1. Samuel (1786-1830); mar. 1807, Orrie Cox.
2. Elizabeth (1792-1872); mar. Jack Wilburn (son of THOMAS WILBURN (or Wellborn), REV. SOLDIER of Ga., and his wife Martha.

DRURY JACKSON, b. in England; d. in Wilkes Co., Ga., 1794. Served as private, S. C. Troops. Received bounty land in Ga. for his services. Married 1768, Nancy Mayfield (1749-1837).
Children:
1. Nancy.
2. Greene.
3. Edward.
4. Hartwell (1777-1859); mar. (1) 1801, Elizabeth Bostic (Bostwick); mar. (2) Margaret Bradford.

EDWARD JACKSON, b. in S. C.; d. 1845, Walker Co., Ga. Name appears in Rev. War Claims W. 2119. On Pension Roll 1830. Living in Gwinnett Co., Ga.

ISAAC JACKSON, b. in Ireland; d. 1790, Hancock Co., Ga. Served as a REV. SOLDIER. Received land in Hancock Co., Ga., for services as Major, Ga. Line.

JAMES JACKSON, b. 1757, Devonshire, England; d. Washington, D. C., Mar. 19, 1806, while serving in Congress as Senator from Ga. Served from Savannah, Ga., as a REV. SOLDIER, as Captain, Brigade Major, and Colonel, Legionary Corps, Ga. State Line. Escaped from the British at the capture of Savannah, Ga.; was at the Battle of Cowpens; later served with Gen. Washington. Member Provincial Congress of Ga. Elected Governor, 1788 (but declined). Served as Governor 1799 to 1801. Married 1785, Mary Charlotte Young (dau. of Wm. Younge (1743-1776) and his wife Sophia Chappelle). Had issue.

NOTE: The story of the past played by Gen. James Jackson in the exposure of the Yazoo fraud can be found in all Histories of Ga. The Gen. James Jackson Chapter, D. A. R., at Valdosta, Ga., bears his name.

LEWIS JENKINS, b. 1760, d. Meriwether Co., Ga. Received Pension for service as private, 5th N. C. Reg., under Capt. Tidd and Major Tiller. Married Mary Jones.

WILLIAM JENKINS, b. 1746 in Md.; d. 1806, Morgan Co., Ga. Served as private, Ga. Line. Married Demarius Roberts.

ROBERT JENNINGS, b. in Va.; d. Oglethorpe Co., Ga. Served as private, Va. Line. Received bounty land in Ga. for his services. Married (1) Eloise Brown; (2) Elizabeth Arnold.

JOHN JOHNSON drew land as a REV. SOLDIER in Ga. Married Elizabeth Ashfield. Both d. in Ga.
Child:
1. Silas Johnson, a Soldier of the War of 1812, b. 1795; d. 1864; mar. Mary B. Lankford.

JOHN JOHNSON, b. in Va.; d. in Ga., 1792. Served in Ga. Line and received land for his services on Shoals Creek, Franklin Co., Ga. Married Sarah —, d. after 1792.
Children:
1. Walter.
2. Joseph.
3. Isaiah.
4. Darcus.
5. Upton.
6. Elizabeth.
7. Precious, mar. — Cash.
8. Sarah.

JOHN JOHNSON, b. in Va.; d. in Elbert Co., Ga., 1802. Received bounty grant of land in Ga. for his services, certified to by Col. Elijah Clarke, Feb. 2, 1784. Married Catherine Johnson (sister of two REV. SOLDIERS who drew land in Ga. for their services, Monroe

Co. Lottery, ANGUS JOHNSON and ARCHIBALD JOHNSON).
Children:
1. Mary.
2. Elizabeth.
3. Angus.
4. Nancy.
5. Alexander.
6. Peter.
7. Donald.
8. John, Jr.
9. Malcom.
10. Neil.

JONATHAN JOHNSON, REV. SOLDIER, d. Tattnall Co., Ga.
Child:
1. Benjamin Johnson, of Tattnall Co., Ga.; mar. Patsey Lane.

LITTLETON JOHNSON, b. in 1761, Worcester Co., Md.; d. Jasper
Co., Ga., 1842. Served as Corporal, 3rd Co., Worcester Co., Md.
Troops, also as Sergeant under Capt. Child's N. C. Co. Married (1)
Lucy Childs.

NATHAN JOHNSON, b. 1720 in Ireland; d. 1805 in Oglethorpe Co.,
Ga. Served as private, Ga. Line. Received bounty grant of land for
his services. Married Elizabeth Hutchins.
Children:
1. Aaron, b. 1762; mar. Elizabeth Daniel (dau. of ALLEN DANIEL,
a REV. SOLDIER of Va., and Madison Co., Ga., and his wife
Mary Allen).
2. Thomas, mar. Mary Susan Griffeth (dau. of JOHN GRIFFETH,
a REV. SOLDIER, and his wife Ann McCraft).
3. Nathan, Jr., mar. Rebecca Elliott.
4. Elisha, mar. Charity Daniel (dau. of ALLEN DANIEL, REV.
SOLDIER).
5. Luke, mar. Elizabeth Ellsbury.
6. Mary.

NICHOLAS JOHNSON, b. in Va.; d. in Ala. Lived on the Broad River,
Wilkes Co., Ga. Served in Ga. Line. Received bounty grant of land for
his services (son of THOMAS JOHNSON (1735-1803), REV. SOLDIER
of Va., and his wife Elizabeth Ann Meriwether of Va.). Married Mary
Marks of the Broad River Settlement, Ga. (dau. of JAMES MARKS,
REV. SOLDIER of Va., b. in Amherst Co., Va., 1745; d. in Ga., 1816,
and his wife Elizabeth Harvie).
Children:
1. Nancy, mar. — Reuben Jordan.
2. Betsey, mar. Louis Bourbon Taliaferro.
3. Martha, mar. George Oglethorpe Gilmer.
4. Lucy, mar. George Gilmer.
5. Barbara, mar. — Fraser.
6. Rebecca, mar. Charles Jordan.
7. Sarah, mar. Morgan Smith.
8. Frank.
9. James.
10. Edward.

THOMAS JOHNSON, with wife Agnes, sold to Thomas Standley, 287.5 acres of land, Greene Co., granted to him for his services as a REV. SOLDIER.

THOMAS JOHNSON, b. in Va.; d. 1805, Oglethorpe Co., Ga. Served as a private, Ga. Line, in Capt. James McNeil's Co. Received bounty land in Ga. for his services. Married 1765, Penelope Sanders, d. 1839.

WILLIAM JOHNSON, b. in Scotland, 1734; d. in Ga., 1806. Served as private and received bounty grant of land for his services. Married Margaret Scott.
Children:
1. William.
2. Samuel.
3. Laban Scott.
4. Margaret.

WILLIAM JOHNSON, b. 1753, in Amelia Co., Va.; d. Bibb Co., Ga., 1839. Placed on Pension Roll, 1835, for services 1777 in Capt. Wm. Lewis's Co., Col. Richard Parker's Va. Reg.; also served 1781, under Captains Payne and Archer. Married —.
Child:
1. Martha Johnson (1818-1894); mar. 1834, John Holliman, d. 1849.

WILLIAM JOHNSON, b. 1755; d. 1821, Wilkes Co., Ga. Will pro. Sept. 1821. Was granted land for his services as a REV. SOLDIER in Washington Co., Ga., 1785. Married in Wilkes Co., Ga., Nancy Hill, b. 1770; d. 1839, Meriwether Co., Ga.
Children:
1. Elizabeth, mar. Drury Cunningham.
2. Mary, mar. Henry Spratlin.
3. Susan, mar. Judge James Dabney Willis.
4. William, Jr., d. unm.
5. John Pope, mar. Prudence Irvine.
6. Nancy (1808-1846); mar. 1824, Col. Lodowick Meriwether Hill; he mar. (2) Martha Strother Wellborn.
7. Martha Pope (1814-1893); mar. (1) 1829, Burwell Pope Hill as (2) wife; mar. (2) Rev. Wm. D. Martin.
8. Catherine, mar. George W. Chatfield.
9. Stephen, d. unm.
10. Sarah, d. unm.

ABRAHAM JONES, b. about 1749 in Va.; lived in Halifax Co., N.C.; then Florida, and 1773 moved with his widowed mother to St. George's Parish, Ga. (son of Abraham and Martha (Jones) Jones of Prince George Co., Va. They had seven sons, all REV. SOLDIERS: JOHN, ABRAHAM, JAMES, BATTE, SEABORN, WILLIAM, THOMAS). He served as Lieut., 2nd Ga. Reg., at the fall of Charleston, S.C., 1780; was taken prisoner by the British. He d. Montgomery Co., Ga., 1811.

Married (1) Sarah Bugg of Beach Island, S. C.; mar. (2) the widow of Zephamiah Beale.

Children by (1) wife:

1. Martha Bugg, b. 1785; mar. Dr. Thomas Moore of Md. and Augusta, Ga.
2. Seaborn, d. 1874, Columbus, Ga.; mar. in Milledgeville, Ga., Mary Howard.
3. John A. (1790-1880); mar. Martha Jenkins.
4. Eliza Agnes.
5. Eliz.
6. Sarah Keziah Paris, mar. Dr. Charles Williamson.

ADAM JONES, b. in Va., 1775. A REV. SOLDIER, he settled near Long Creek at Meeting House (he was a preacher), on the Ogechee River in 1785. He d. Oct. 1, 1830.

BATTE JONES, b. Edgecombe Co., N. C., Mar. 4, 1754; d. 1821, Burke Co., Ga. Served as 1st Lieut., 6th Co. Ga. Militia, under Col. John Thomas. Granted bounty land for his services. Married his first cousin, Mary Jones (dau. of HENRY JONES, REV. SOLDIER of Ga.).

Children:

1. Harriet Eliza (1791-1863); mar. 1822 (2) wife, Rev. James Hall T. Fitzpatrick.
2. Henry Seaborn (1793-1838); mar. Margaret Torrence.
3. Mary Thomas, mar. (1) James E. Hines; (2) Everet Sapp.
4. Sarah M.
5. James Burwell.
6. Jane Margaret.

BRIDGES JONES (name sometimes written Bridgeon), b. Aug. 11, 1759 in N. C.; d. in Ga. (will pro. Nov. 12, 1819). He mar. Rachel Barry, b. 1762. Lived in Bullock Co., Ga. Served as private in Continental Line.

Children: (mentioned in will)

1. Briant.
2. Barry, mar. Rebecca Wise.
3. Josiah.
4. Buckner.
5. Bazil.
6. John T.
7. Lucy.
8. Nancy, mar. — Jones.
9. Mary, mar. — Everett.
10. Rachel (1791-1871); mar. John Wise.

FRANK JONES, an early settler of Screven Co., Ga.; b. in Wales; was a REV. SOLDIER, as were his sons: FRANK, JAMES, and JOHN and PHILIP JONES, of Ga.

GEORGE JONES, b. 1743 (son of Hugh and Elizabeth Jones); d. in Ga. Served as a private, Ga. Line. Married 1769, Phoebe Foster, b. 1749.
Children:
1. Delphia Garnett (1770-1857); mar. 1808, Andrew Bryan. They had 8 children.

2. Edmund.	8. Phoebe.
3. George.	9. Hugh.
4. Larkin.	10. Elizabeth.
5. Catlett.	11. Lucy.
6. John.	12. Thomas.
7. Ann F.	13. Matilda.

HENRY JONES, b. in Va., 1727; moved to Ga., 1770; d. Burke Co., Ga., 1803. One of the two representatives from St. George's Parish to the Provincial Congress, meeting in Savannah, Ga., 1774-1775. Appointed Magistrate by the Committee of Safety. On July 6, 1780, his name appears as the "Rebel Colonel". Married Keziah Jones.
Children:
1. Sarah, b. Amelia Co., Va., 1761; mar. her first cousin, James Jones.
2. Mary, b. 1764; mar. her first cousin, Batte Jones.
3. Henry, b. 1766; mar. Fannie (Miller) Jones (widow of his uncle Robert Jones).
4. Thomas.
5. Daniel.
6. Margaret, b. 1772; mar. (1) Capt. John Evans of Ga.; (2) Dr. Job S. Barney of Philadelphia, Penn.

HENRY JONES (son of Henry and Winny (Elder) Jones), b. 1762, near Petersburg, Va.; d. on a visit to Ala., 1818. Removed after the War to Guilford Court House, N. C., then to Hancock Co., Ga. Served three enlistments under Capt. B. Jones in Va., and was at the Battle of Camden, S. C. Married (1) Sarah Lightfoot; (2) Mary Hogan; (3) Nellie Payne.
Child by (1) wife:
1. Henry L.
Children by (2) wife:
2. William.
3. Thomas.
4. Cannon.
5. Seaborn.
6. John.
7. Reuben.
8. Allen, mar. Mary Jane Moody and moved to Wisconsin.
9. Nancy.

10. Sarah.
11. Mary.
Children by (3) wife:
12. Joseph.
13. Minnie.
14. Benjamin.

JAMES JONES (son of Abraham Jones), b. Edgecomb Co., N. C., about 1752; d. near Waynesboro, Ga., 1810. Enlisted from St. George's Parish, Ga. Captured at the fall of Charleston, S. C., and confined as a prisoner at Augusta, Ga., until that place was captured by the Americans. Married his first cousin Sarah Jones.
Children:
1. Mary, mar. Alexander W. Allen.
2. Jane Ann, mar. Thomas Cooper Butler of New York. They moved to Ohio.
3. Seaborn, mar. Margaret A. Jones.
4. James W., mar. Elizabeth H. Blount.

JAMES JONES, b. in Va., April 28, 1764; d. 1807, Elbert Co., Ga. Served in the Va. Continental Line and received bounty grant of land in Ga. for his services. Married —.
Children:
1. James, Jr.
2. John.
3. Stanby.
4. George.
5. Thomas.
6. William.
7. Nancy.
8. Polly, mar. Gillam Hudson.
9. Dau., mar. Richard Hubbard.
10. Dau., mar. Shadrick Floyd.

JAMES JONES, b. April 28, 1764 in S. C.; d. 1822 Screven Co., Ga. (son of Francis Jones). Served as private, Ga. Line. Received bounty grant of land for his services. Married 1791, Elizabeth Mills, b. June 1774; d. 1836.
Children:
1. Francis, b. Jan. 27, 1792; mar. Rachel Spain.
2. Matthew, b. Oct. 11, 1795; mar. Elizabeth Inman Benjamin (Benny), Sept. 10, 1797.
3. Thomas, b. May 14, 1802; mar. Lavinia Young.
4. Brady Michael, b. Sept. 27, 1805.
5. Lavinia, b. July 9, 1795; mar. James Young.
6. Harriet, b. Mar. 21, 1817; mar. James B. Blackshear.
7. Elizabeth, b. April 20, 1813; mar. Joseph S. Neely.

JOHN JONES, b. 1720, Penn.; d. 1782 in Wrightsboro Township, Ga. Served in S. C., and received bounty land for his services in Ga. upon certificate of Col. Lee. Married Mary —.
Children:
1. Richard.

2. Ann, mar. — Brown.
3. Phillipine, mar. — Stanfield.
4. Margaret, mar. STEPHEN DAY, a REV. SOLDIER.
5. Mary, mar. — Anglin.
6. James.
7. Jonathan.
8. Nathan.

JOHN JONES, b. in N. C., 1745; d. 1817 in Ga. Served in Ga. Line under Gen. Clarke, and received bounty grant of land for his services. Married 1769, Susanna Strobhar.
Child:
1. Obedience (1764-1832); mar. JESSE OFFUTT, b. 1760 in Ga.; d. 1830, Richmond Co., Ga. He served as a private in Ga. Militia, under Col. Few.
   Child:
   1. Frances Offutt (1787-1833); mar. John Goldwire (1779-1830) (son of JAMES GOLDWIRE, b. 1747 at Augusta, Ga.;d. 1810, Mt. Pleasant, Ga.; commanded a Co. of Militia, 1777, from St. Mathews Parish (now Effingham Co.), Ga.; mar. 1763, Sarah King, b. 1749; d. 1810).

JOHN JONES, b. 1749, lived at Sunbury, Liberty Co., Ga. Major, Ga. Line Continental Troops, and killed at the assault on Spring Hill Redoubt near Savannah, Ga., Oct. 9, 1778. Married Mary Sharpe (dau. of James and Mary (Newton) Sharpe).
Child:
1. Joseph Jones, commanded the Liberty Co. Independent Troops in the War of 1812. Married Elizabeth Hart (dau. of JOHN HART, REV. SOLDIER of S. C., and his wife Mary Esther Screven, dau. of BRIGADIER GEN. JAMES SCREVEN, REV. SOLDIER of Ga., who was killed at Midway Church, Ga.).

MOSES JONES, b. 1765 in Va.; d. 1830, Wilkes Co., Ga. Served as private, Ga. Militia. Received grant of land, Wilkes Co., Ga. for his services. Married Mary Florance, d. 1826.
Children:
1. Solomon.
2. Mason.
3. Anderson.
4. Moses, Jr., d. Harris Co., Ga., 1864.
5. Sarah, mar. John Mays (son of WILLIAM MAYS, REV. SOL-DIER, granted land in Ga., and his wife Mary Wadkins).
6. Genevieve.
7. Armand.
8. Lucinda.
9. Toliver, mar. Hannah Gideon (dau. of FRANCIS GIDEON, Capt. Ga. Line, and his wife Elizabeth Hopkins, of Wilkes Co., Ga.).

NOBLE WIMBERLY JONES, b. 1725; d. 1805 in Ga. Signed the call for the earliest meeting of the Patriots of Ga., held in Savannah. Member House of Assembly. Married Sarah Davis.
Children:
1. John.
2. Edward.
3. Sarah.
4. Catherine.
5. George.

PHILIP JONES, b. 1759 in N. C.; d. 1789, Burke Co., Ga. Served as private, N. C. Line. Received bounty grant of land for his services in Ga. Married Elizabeth Jones.

SARAH ANN JONES (sister of Seaborn Jones), b. 1763, N. C.; mar. 1788, SHERWOOD BUGG, JR., REV. SOLDIER of Augusta, Ga., and Beach Island, S. C. She was a PATRIOT.

SEABORN JONES (son of Abraham and Martha (Jones) Jones), b. in Halifax Co., N. C., June 15, 1759; d. Augusta, Ga., July 24, 1815. Served in the Va. Continental Line; was taken prisoner at Charleston, S. C.; discharged and fought as a Refugee Soldier, 1781. Married (1) Wilkes Co., Ga., Sarah Harwood Wilkinson, d. Nov. 1806; mar. (2) 1807, Elizabeth Harris, widow. Lived at Augusta and Screven Co., Ga. Children by (1) wife: (who reached maturity)
1. Augustus Seaborn, mar. Emily Robert of S. C.
2. Martha Melvina Milledge, mar. Rev. Mr. Woderwell.
3. Sarah Seaborn Rebecca Weed, mar. Governor Charles J. Jenkins of Ga.
Child by (2) wife:
4. Elizabeth, b. 1816; mar. Dr. John Valentine Freeman Walker.

SOLOMON JONES, b. in Va., 1760; of Liberty Co., Ga. Applied for a Pension as a REV. SOLDIER and musician. He enlisted in the REV. WAR in Va., in Continental service, 1776. Andrew Getle, Recruiting Sergeant, brought him from there to Savannah, Ga.; served under Capt. Andrew Getle, Col. Stark, commander of Reg. 3 yrs. Discharged at Charleston, S. C., by Gen. McIntosh. Returned to Va. Re-enlisted in N. C. in Co. of Militia and came to Charleston on 9 month tour. Re-enlisted with Col. William Washington, served as trumpet major in Col. Washington's Dragoons. Discharged at end of Rev. War at High Hills of Santee. Was in battles of Eutau Springs and Cowpens; horse shot from under him in the first, and wounded in the second. Wife (living 1826, b. 1772). One dau., now in S. C.; one son in Miss. (on file in records of Bryan Co., Ga., May 25, 1826.)

WILLIAM JONES and wife Abigail, on Oct. 10, 1785, sold to Robert Flournoy of Augusta, Ga., 287. 5 acres of land in Washington Co., on Shoulderbone Creek, granted to the said William Jones by his Honor, the Governor of Ga., Samuel Elbert, Oct. 13, 1784, for his services as a REV. SOLDIER (Greene Co. Records)

WILLIAM JONES, b. in Va.; d. in Ga. Served in the first Co. (Volunteers of Va.). Was in the Southern campaign. His commission signed by Benjamin Harrison. Married Susan Wilson.

WILLIAM JONES, b. 1762, King and Queen Co., Va.; d. 1834, Columbia Co., Ga. Served in the Va. Continental Line in Va. and Ga. Received bounty grant of land in Ga. for his services. He married 4 times and had 21 children. Married (4) 1826, Elcie V. (Tankersly) Pace (dau. of JAMES TANKSERSLY, REV. SOLDIER of Va., and his wife Susan Brooks).
Children: (known)
1. Edwin Thomas (1831-1867); mar. Martha Dillon Wright.
2. Mary S., b. Columbia Co., Ga., Dec. 18, 1828; d. Dec. 6, 1809. Was a "Real Daughter", National Society, D. A. R. She mar. 1846, John M. Cutliff (1823-1907) (son of John Cutliff and Lucinda Ragan; grandson of ABRAM CUTLIFF, JONATHAN RAGAN, and JOHN RAY, all REV. SOLDIERS of Ga).

WILLIAM JONES, b. in Va., 1759; d. Feb. 1841, Jasper Co., Ga. Enlisted Sept. 1, 1776 in Va., as private and Sergeant in Capt. Joseph Parnell's Co. Served in Col. Samuel Elbert's Rev., later in Col. Meriwether's Va. Reg. Applied for Pension, April 21, 1829, age 70 years. Pension granted. His widow was allowed pension as a widow of a REV. SOLDIER. Married in Va., Mary —.
Children: (known)
1. William, Jr., b. in S. C.; moved to Ga.
2. Mary Amelia, b. 1786 in S. C.; mar. Putnam Co., Ga., William Tidwell (son of WILLIAM TIDWELL, REV. SOLDIER, d. in S. C., and his wife Mary De Gaffenreid). He mar. (2) Emilia Patterson and had five children: Jane, Lucy, Nancy, Milly, and Joseph. (Ancestor of Ettie Tidwell McCall [Mrs. Howard H.] McCall.)

WILLIAM JONES, b. Amherst Co., Va.; d. in Ga., Feb. 12, 1809. Served as private, S. C. Troops under Gen. Nathaniel Greene. Served in Va. and S. C. throughout the War. Married 1781, Ann Freeman (dau. of James and Ann Freeman). She mar. (2) John Parker, d. 1831. She d. June 3, 1847.
Children:
1. Elizabeth Jones made application for services of William Jones while a resident of Sumpter Dist., S. C., Feb. 2, 1854. Granted. She was b. Dec. 5, 1784.
2. James.

3. Mary.	6. Eli.	9. Wylie.
4. Peggy.	7. William, Jr.	10. Betsey Ann.
5. Nancy.	8. Leonard.	11. Sarah.

JOHN JORDAN, b. in Va., 1756; d. in Washington Co., Ga., Aug. 20, 1828. Married in N. C., 1786, Winifred Jordan, his cousin. Served in N. C. Troops; joined Gen. Samuel Elbert's Reg. in Ga. Was taken prisoner and exchanged. Was at the surrender at Yorktown. Received grant of land for his services, Washington Co., Ga. Pension granted to his daughter Mary (Jordan) Newton of Athens, Ga. Buried near Sandersville, Ga.
Children:

1. Britton (1787-1806); mar. 1814, Peggy (Margaret) Bell. Had 7 children.
2. Green, mar. Elizabeth Sanford.
3. Burwell, mar. Lavinia Holland.
4. John (1800-1852); mar. Eliza Smith.
5. Patience, mar. Isom Saffold.
6. Persilla, mar. William Tennille (son of LIEUT. COL. FRANCIS TENNILLE, REV. SOLDIER, and wife Elizabeth Dixon).
7. Mary, mar. John H. Newton.

REUBEN JORDAN, b. 1754 in Va.; d. 1816, Broad River Settlement, Wilkes Co., Ga. Served as a REV. SOLDIER. Received bounty grant of land in Ga. Married (1) —; (2) Genette Harvie.
Children:

1. Martha, mar. Dr. Bradley.
2. Reuben, Jr., mar. (1) Nancy Johnson (dau. of COL. NICHOLAS JOHNSON, REV. SOLDIER of Ga.); mar. (2) Martha (dau. of William Williamson and his wife Mary Terrell).
3. Fleming, mar. Anna Meriwether (dau. of THOMAS MERIWETHER, REV. SOLDIER of Ga.), they moved to Jasper Co., Ga.
4. Margaret, mar. —.
5. Betsey, mar. Dr. George Meriwether.
6. Mortimer, mar. dau. of Hezekiah Gray.
7. Charles, mar. (1) Rebecca Johnson (dau. of COL. NICHOLAS JOHNSON, REV. SOLDIER); mar. (2) Elizabeth Yancey Reid.

WILLIAM JORDAN, b. in Va., Mar. 31, 1744; d. in Ga., Sept. 23, 1826. Served as Lieut., Continental Army, and received land grant for his services, Warren Co., Ga. Married 1786, Anne Medlock (1756-1817).

DEMPSEY JUSTICE (1766-1827), REV. SOLDIER, buried in family cemetery near Salem Church, Baldwin Co., Ga.

JACOB KELLY, b. 1755, Robinson Co., N. C.; d. 1835, Jasper Co., Ga. Served as private 1779 in Col. Elijah Clark's Ga. Troops. Married Susanna —.

MICHAEL JOHNSTON KENAN, b. in N. C., 1746; d. 1817, Hancock Co., Ga. Served in N. C. Troops and was a member of the N. C. Con-

vention, 1777. Took Oath of Allegiance, 1775, in N.C. Married Ann Holmes of N.C. (He had two brothers. JAMES KENAN rose to rank of General in N.C. OWEN KENAN, N.C., killed by the Tories.)
Children:
  1. Thomas Holmes Kenan, mar. Amelia (Gray) Powell.

HENRY KENDALL, MAJOR JOHN KENDALL, and DR. JAMES KENDALL, three brothers, all REV. SOLDIERS, are buried in Upson Co., Ga.

JOHN WALTER KEY, b. in Va., May 11, 1751; d. Franklin Co., Ga., 1827. Served as private, Va. Line. Received grant of land for his services in Franklin Co., Ga. Married Virginia (called Jenny) Wade.
Children:
  1. Lucinda, mar. — Fields.
  2. Agnes, mar. Bradley Harrison.
  3. Elizabeth, mar. — Embry.
  4. Patty (Martha), mar. Beasley Thomas.
  5. Peirce (Price), mar. Sarah Hix.
  6. Winney, mar. Boley Embry.
  7. Tolbert, mar. (1) 1816, Elizabeth Embry; (2) Effie Burgess; (3) 1850, Mary Wooten.
  8. Sarah, mar. — Bailey.
  9. George W., mar. Delilah Embry.

WILLIAM BIBB KEY, b. Albemarle Co., Va., Oct. 2, 1759; d. Dec 7, 1836, Elbert Co., Ga. Served as a REV. SOLDIER. Received bounty grant of land for his services. Married Mourning Clark, b. Aug. 12, 1764 (dau. of CHRISTOPHER CLARK, REV. SOLDIER of Ga., and his wife Millicent Terrell).
Children:
  1. Charles, b. 1784; mar. Mary Ann Clark.
  2. Martha, mar. Nicholas Good.
  3. James, b. 1788; mar. Rebecca Grizzle.
  4. Milly, b. 1790; mar. Humphrey Posey.
  5. Nancy, mar. Simeon Glenn.
  6. Elizabeth, mar. Thomas Bell.
  7. Margaret, mar. Thomas Good.
  8. Keturah, mar. James Hamm.
  9. Mary (Polly), mar. Joseph Bell.
  10. Henry, d. y.
  11. Thomas, d. y.
  12. Susan, b. 1799; mar. James Bell, Jr.
  13. Jane, b. 1801; mar. John Grizzle.
  14. Sarah, b. 1803; mar. Thomas C. Elliott.
  15. Lucy, b. 1809; mar. Nathan Mattox.

JOHN KIMBROUGH, b. Anson Co., N.C., 1745; d. 1799, Wilkes.

Served as Lieut., under Gen. Elijah Clarke. Married Anne Le Grande.

WILLIAM KIMBROUGH, d. 1803 in Greene Co., Ga. Served as private, Ga. Line, under Gen. Clarke.

JOHN KING, b. 1754 in Va.; d. 1840, Jackson Co., Ga. Received pension for his services as a private, Va. Troops. Married 1792, Eleone Karr (1770-1860).

ROSWELL KING, b. in Sharon, Conn., May 3, 1765. Served as private, 1782. Moved to Darien, Ga., McIntosh Co. Married Catherine Barrington (dau. of Josiah Barrington, a kinsman of James Edward Oglethorpe, the Founder of the Province of Georgia (1733). (Fort Barrington on the Altamaha River in Ga., an outpost built long before the Revolution for defense against the Spaniards, was named for him.)
Child:
1. Barrington, b. 1798, moved to Roswell, Ga. (named for his father); married Catherine Nephew (dau. of JAMES NEPHEW, REV. SOLDIER of Ga., Lieut. in Col. John Baker's Reg. of Liberty Co., Ga., Militia).
(In 1937, the James Edward Oglethorpe Chapter, Daughters of the American Colonists in Ga., placed a marker at the home built by Barrington King in Roswell, Ga., a beautiful colonial home.)

PETER KITTLES, b. in S. C.; d. in Ga. Served as private under Gen. Francis Marion. Married Sarah Williamson.
Child:
1. John R., of Screven Co., Ga.; mar. Clarky Lovett (dau. of Fens Lovett, and granddau. of THOMAS LOVETT, REV. SOLDIER of S. C. and Ga.).

PETER KOLB, b. Craven Co., S. C., 1762; d. Dec. 8, 1835, Meriwether Co., Ga. Served with S. C. Troops under Capt. Abel Kolb and Gen. Francis Marion. Married Theresy Gales.
Children:
1. Martin.
2. Elizabeth.
3. Nancy.
4. Mary.
5. Wilds.
6. Valentine.
7. William.
8. Linnie.
9. Hariot.

THOMAS LACKEY, b. 1756, Hanover Co., Va.; d. 1824, Wilkes Co., Ga. Received bounty land for his services in Ga. Troops under Gen. Elijah Clarke. Married Janett Lackey.

ARCHIBALD LACY, b. in Va., 1758; d. 1822, Warren Co., Ga. Received pay 1783 as a Va. Soldier for services in Va. Continental Line.

His widow, living Newton Co., Ga., drew land in 1827 Lottery in Ga., as a widow of REV. SOLDIER. He married in Va., 1787, Sarah Martin; came to Wilkes (now Warren) Co., Ga.
Children:

1. Polly, b. in Va., 1788; mar. as (2) wife, Fisher Gaskin.
2. Betsey, b. Wilkes Co., Ga., 1791; mar. Wm. Smith.
3. John Butler, d. Thomas Co., Ga., 1878.
4. Martha, b. 1796, Warren Co.; mar. Gerard Camp.
5. Nancy, b. 1799; mar. 1814, William Candler.
6. Pleasant Martin, mar. Nancy Reynold.
7. Sally, mar. John K. Johnson. Moved to Miss.
8. Randolph Grief (1807-1825).

RICHARD LAKE, b. in New Jersey; d. 1800 in Ga. Served as private in Capt. Longstreet's Co., 3rd Reg. Middlesex Co., N.J. Married Sarah Landon.

BASIL LAMAR (son of John Lamar and Priscilla Bugg), b. 1764; d. in Ga., May 5, 1827. Served in Ga. Militia. Received grant of land for his services. Married 1794, Rebecca Kelly (1762-1829).
Children:

1. Priscilla, b. 1795.
2. John Thomas, b. 1797.
3. Gazaway Bugg, b. 1798.
4. James Jackson, b. 1800.
5. George Washington (1801-1892); mar. 1841, Sarah Walker Harlow (dau. of Dr. Southwell Harlow of Plymouth, Mass.).
6. Oswald.
7. Zecheriah.
8. Rebecca J., mar. Hugh McLeod.
9. Thomas Jefferson.

CAPT. JOHN LAMAR, b. 1740; killed 1799 near his home in Hancock Co., Ga. Served in Ga. Militia and received bounty grant for his services as a REV. SOLDIER. Married (1) Elizabeth Bugg (dau. of SHERWOOD BUGG, REV. SOLDIER of S. C. and Ga., and his wife Elizabeth Hopson, a Patriot); mar. (2) Priscilla Bugg (dau. of SHERWOOD BUGG, JR., a REV. SOLDIER of Ga., and his wife Obedience Jones); mar. (3) Lucy Appling.

JOHN LAMAR, b. 1763, S. C.; d. Jones Co., Ga., 1842. Served as private, S. C. Troops, under Gen. Marion and Gen. Pickett; twice wounded. Married Frances Breedlove (1766-1841).

ZECHERIAH LAMAR, b. 1752; d. 1825 in Ga. Served under Gen. Elijah Clarke.

THOMAS LANDRUM, b. Orange Co., Va., Oct. 6, 1759; d. near

Lexington, Oglethorpe Co., Ga., 1833. Enlisted Feb. 23, 1778, private in Va. Co., under Capt. Burnley, Lipscomb, Col. Heath, Parker, and Morgan. While a resident of Oglethorpe Co., Ga., 1832, he was allowed a Pension for his services. He served as Col., Ga. Troops, War of 1812. Married 1784, Nancy Bell of Orange Co., Va.
Children:
1. Elizabeth, b. 1785; mar. Bledsoe Brockman.
2. John, b. 1787.
3. James B., b. 1789.
4. William H. (1793-1867); mar. 1820, Jane Bledsoe.
5. Mary, b. 1791; mar. — Norton.
6. Joseph, b. 1795.
7. Hay T., b. 1799.
8. Whitfield, b. 1797; mar. Eunice Bledsoe.
9. Nancy, b. 1801; mar. — Jennings.
10. Sarah B., b. 1803; mar. — Wray.

ABRAHAM SHEPHERD LANE, b. 1759, Raleigh, N. C.; d. 1849, Emanuel Co., Ga. Served as private, Ga. Troops. Received bounty grant of land in Ga. for his services. (Grave marked by the Sylvania Chapter, D. A. R.) Married 1782, Betsey Mills.
Children:
1. Benjamin Lane (1797-1860); mar. Jane Bonnell (1804-1861) (granddau. of ANTHONEY BONNELL, REV. SOLDIER).
2. Edward Wood (1788-1851); mar. Susanna Lanier.

JESSE LANE, b. Halifax Co., N. C., July 3, 1733; d. on a visit to his children in Ky., Oct. 18, 1804. He served as an Officer in 3rd N. C. Reg. Was given bounty grant of land in Ga. for his services. Married Halifax Co., N. C., 1755, Winifred Aycock (dau. of WILLIAM AYCOCK of N. C. and Wilkes Co., Ga., a REV. SOLDIER, and his wife Rebecca (Pace) Bradford), b. April 11, 1741; d. Dec. 16, 1794 of pleurisy, caused from exposure of being driven from home by the Indians. He moved with his family, 1784 to Wilkes (now Elbert) Co., Ga., then to Sparks Fort (now Clarke Co.), Ga.
Children:
1. CHARLES, b. Oct. 2, 1756; mar. Elizabeth Mallory. A REV. SOLDIER.
2. Richard, b. 1759; mar. Mary Flint.
3. Henry, d. y.
4. Caroline, b. May 26, 1761; mar. (1) DAVID LOWRY, a REV. SOLDIER; (2) George Swain.
5. Rhoda, b. May 1, 1763; mar. John Rakestraw.
6. Patience, b. May 8, 1765; mar. John Hart (son of BENJAMIN HART, REV. SOLDIER of Ga., and his wife NANCY MORGAN (known in history as the heroine "Nancy Hart").
7. Jonathan, b. April 3, 1767; mar. (1) Patience Rogers; (2) Mary Colley.

8. Jane, b. Dec. 25, 1769; mar. Elizabeth Street. They were the parents of Gov. Joseph Lane of Oregon.
9. Simeon, b. 1771; mar. Judith Humphries.
10. Rebecca, b. Mar. 5, 1773; mar. James Luckie.
11. Joseph, b. Mar. 28, 1775; mar. Elizabeth Hill.
12. Mary, b. June 18, 1777; mar. Thomas Kirkpatrick; moved to Ill.
13. Sarah, b. June 18, 1777; mar. John Kirkpatrick; moved to Ill.
14. Winifred, b. Oct. 11, 1780; mar. James Peleg Rogers. (Ancestors of Mrs. Herbert M. Franklin, State Regent, D. A. R. of Ga.)
15. Jesse, Jr., b. June 12, 1782; mar. Rhoda Jolly.
16. Elizabeth, b. Sept. 6, 1786; mar. William Montgomery; moved to Mississippi.

WILLIAM LANE, b. Fairfax Co., Va.; d. Elbert Co., Ga., a REV. SOLDIER. Married Nancy Allen.

BENJAMIN LANIER (son of Byrd Thomas Lanier and wife Mary), b. Dec. 14, 1740 in N. C.; d. Aug. 1817, Screven Co., Ga. Served in Ga. Line from Effingham Co. Appointed to purchase supplies for American Army, 1778. Was a member of the Ga. Assembly. Married (1) Susanna Ann Jones (1744-1805).
Children:
1. John Lewis, b. 1774; mar. Hannah Mills (dau. of THOMAS MILLS, REV. SOLDIER of Ga., and his wife Lucy).
2. CLEMENT, a REV. SOLDIER of Ga.
3. Mary, b. Dec. 25, 1759.
4. Berryman, b. 1776.
5. Bird.
6. Betsey.
7. Hannah, mar. Robert Dickson.
8. Lucy, mar. Philip Newton.
9. Nancy, mar. Thomas Mills, Jr.

LEWIS LANIER, b. in Sussex Co., Va., 1756; d. Screven Co., Ga., 1839. Enlisted Essex Co., Va., as private; promoted to Captain. Was taken prisoner and held for nine months on a British vessel. (His son Thomas B. Lanier applied for pension of Lewis Lanier, 1846. BENJAMIN TAYLOR of Screven Co., Ga., in the application stated that he knew him and had served with him as a REV. SOLDIER of Va.) He married (1) Sept. 21, 1788, Ann Butler (dau. of THOMAS BUTLER, REV. SOLDIER of Va.); mar. (2) 1803 in Ga., Esther (called Hester) Thorn (1775-1855). Will of Lewis Lanier recorded Screven Co.
Children by (1) wife:
1. James.
2. Mary (called Polly), mar. Robert McCall (son of CHARLES McCALL, REV. SOLDIER of S. C. and Ga., and grandson of FRANCIS McCALL, REV. SOLDIER of N. C.).
3. Elizabeth, mar. Charles McCall, Jr.
Children by (2) wife:
4. Noel (1811-1890); mar. 1839, Sarah Tullis.
5. Isaac (1806-1885); mar. Miss Hurst.

6. Sarah, mar. Henry Strickland.
7. Amy, mar. (1) James Johnson; (2) — Kelly.
8. Clarissa, mar. William S. Jackson.

JAMES LASSITER, b. Halifax Co., N. C., 1759; d. in Ga. Enlisted
N. C., 1776. Served later as private in Lieut. John Pope's Co., Col.
Marbury's Ga. Reg. of Light Dragoons. Married 1782, Elizabeth Butt,
b. 1760, Halifax Co., N. C.

JOHN LASTINGER, b. in Germany about 1740, came to America,
landed at Charleston, S. C., then settled at Ebenezer, Ga. Served as
private, Ga. Troops. Received bounty land. Married 1765, Anna
Barbara —. She came to America on the same ship with him.
Children:
1. Hannah, b. Aug. 25, 1768; mar. JOHN GROOVER (or Gruber),
REV. SOLDIER of Ga.).
2. John George, b. Nov. 24, 1776.
3. Barbara, mar. James English. Had 9 children.
4. Abner, mar. Ann Beasley.
5. Andrew, b. Feb. 12, 1778; mar. Mary Parker.
6. Elizabeth, b. Feb. 12, 1778; mar. — Millen.
7. Mary, b. May 22, 1780.
8. David, mar. Sarah —. Lived Bullock Co., Ga.
9. Tabitha.
10. Sarah.

ROGER LAWSON, b. in Va., 1730; d. Aug. 6, 1803 in (now Jefferson
Co.), Ga. Lived in Rowan Co., N. C. Served with Ga. Troops and re-
ceived bounty grant of land in Ga. for his services, Washington Co.
Married (1) 1752, Hannah Thompson (dau. of Rev. John Thompson of
Penn., N. C., and Ga.); mar. (2) Margaret McGill.
Children by (1) wife:
1. HUGH LAWSON, b. 1755; d. 1802 in Ga. Served as Capt., Ga.
Militia. Wounded at Augusta, Ga. Mar. (1) Ann —; (2) Sarah
Whitaker.
2. JOHN THOMPSON, b. Brunswick Co., Va., 1757; d. Twiggs Co.,
Ga., 1816. Served as Capt., then Colonel, Ga. Militia. Was
given bounty grant of land in Liberty Co., Ga. Married Columbia Co., S. C., Sept. 1, 1778, Alice Moore, b. 1760; d. 1798.
She was a REV. PATRIOT; deeds recorded in S. C. History.
Children:
1. Roger, b. 1779; mar. Lucy Smith.
2. Charles Moore.
3. Andrew.
4. Hannah, b. 1785; mar. 1804, Archibald McIntyre, b. N. C.,
1776; d. Thomas Co., Ga., 1830.
3. ROGER, Jr., A REV. SOLDIER.
4. WILLIAM, killed as a REV. SOLDIER of Ga.

5. ANDREW THOMPSON, b. 1760 in Ga.; d. 1822, Augusta, Ga. Served in Ga. Militia. Was a refugee after the fall of Charleston, S. C. Received bounty land in Ga. for his services. Married (1) 1792, Mary Moore Barry (1779-1802) (dau. of ANDREW BARRY, REV. SOLDIER, b. 1746 in Penn.; d. 1811 in Spartanburg, S. C., and his wife MARGARET CATHERINE MOORE, a REV. PATRIOT). He mar. (2) Elizabeth Eakin.
Children by (1) wife:
1. Margaret, mar. Alexander Nevin.
2. Mary Barry (1802-1869); mar. Benjamin Sessions.
3. Elizabeth Hannah.
4. Andrew Barry, b. 1794.
6. Andrew Barry Lawson; mar. Jane Patterson; lived in Jefferson Co., Ga.
7. Mary, mar. Michael Burke.
8. Hannah Thompson, mar. Moses Speer.
Child by (2) wife:
9. Margaret McGill Lawson, mar. JOHN GAMBLE of Jefferson Co., Ga. He was a REV. SOLDIER.

ROBERT LAWTON, b. 1753, S. C.; d. 1819, S. C., a REV. SOLDIER of S. C. Married Mar. 18, 1773, Sarah Robert (1755-1839). Children:
1. Wm. Henry, mar. Catherine Maner (dau. of WM. MANER, REV. SOLDIER of S. C.).
2. Joseph J., mar. Phoebe Mosse.
3. Rev. Winborn Asa, mar. (1) Mary (Cater) Rhodes; mar. (2) Mrs. Perry; mar. (3) Lucinda Landrum.
4. Thirza, mar. as (1) wife, Thomas Polhill. He mar. (2) Matilda Rebecca Jaudon.
5. Benjamin Themistocles Dion, mar. Jane Mosse.
6. Charlotte Ann, mar. her first cousin, James Jehu Robert.
7. Alexander James, mar. Martha Mosse.

ANDREW LEBEY was one of six brothers who came with Count d'Estang's fleet from France to assist the Continental Army in its efforts to take Savannah, Ga., from the British in 1779. He was wounded in the assault on the British at Springfield Redoubt near Savannah, and his five brothers, JEROME, LOUIS, PHILIP, AUGUSTINE, and JOHN LEBEY, were all killed. After the war he settled at Ebenezer, Ga. Married Mary (Hines) Anderson. Had issue. Died Savannah, Ga.

RICHARD LEDBETTER, REV. SOLDIER, 100 years of age. Buried Lumpkin Co., Ga.

HENRY LEE, JR. (son of HENRY LEE, REV. SOLDIER of Va.), b. Prince William Co., Va., 1756; d. 1818 Cumberland Island, Ga., at "Dungeness". Served as Capt. of Cavalry and Lieut. Col., Va. Troops.

Known as "Light Horse Harry Lee".

JAMES LESTER, d. 1820, buried Smith-Lester Cemetery, Baldwin Co., Ga. Name found on record book, Baldwin Co. Court House, labelled Watson's Batt. Dist. He was a REV. SOLDIER and a Soldier of 1812. He was also J. P., Burke Co., Ga.

ROBERT LEVERETT, d. Lincoln Co., Ga., 1806. Received grant of land for his services as a REV. SOLDIER. Married Patsey Hammock. Children:
1. Nancy.
2. Jordan.
3. Patsey.
4. Betsey.
5. Absolem.
6. Sallie.
7. Robert.
8. Hardy.
9. Polly.
10. Gricy.
11. Peggy.

THOMAS LEVERETT, b. 1755; d. 1834, Troup Co., Ga. Served as private, Ga. Line, under Capt. John Clarke, Col. Alexanders' Reg. Married 1789, Mary Griffin.

WILLIAM LEVERETT, b. 1760; d. 1812, Putnam Co., Ga. Served as private. Received bounty grant of land in Cherokee Co., Ga. Married Celia Ann Moseley.

JOHN LEWIS, b. 1753 in Va.; d. 1817 in Ga. Served as a private in Va. and Ga. Line. Married 1776, Elizabeth Kennore (1754-1826). Children:
1. Elizabeth (1801-1858); mar. Wm. Desarix Stone.
2. Ulysses (1799-1856); mar. Sarah Abercrombie.

JOHN LEWIS, b. Chowane Co., N. C., 1733; d. Jan. 3, 1818, Burke Co., Ga. Married 1768, Nancy Lavinia Ward, b. 1744, N. C.; d. 1784, Ga. He served as private, N. C. Line.
Children: (known)
1. Jesse.
2. Mary.
3. James.
4. Matthew.

JOHN LEWIS, b. Albermarle Co., Va., 1757; d. in (now Cass Co.) Ga., 1849 (son of John Lewis and his wife Sarah Taliaferro of Va.), served in the Va. Army at Brandywine, Monmouth, and Yorktown, under Marquis de La Fayette. Married 1786, Ann Berry Earle, d. 1845, Cass Co., Ga. (dau. of JOHN EARLE, b. 1737 in Va., a REV. SOLDIER of S. C. Rangers, and his wife Thomasine Berry). (Grave of John Lewis marked by Ga. D. A. R. Inscription on tomb, "A Soldier of the Revolution).

RICHARD LEWIS, b. in Va., 1747; d. 1809, Greene Co., Ga. Was

Sergeant, Capt. Lytle's Co., 10th Reg. N. C. Troops. Married Caroline Booker.

WM. LEWIS, granted a Pension while a resident of Stewart Co., Ga.

REV. ELIJAH LINCH, b. in S. C.; d. in Ga. He and four brothers were REV. SOLDIERS. He married Miss Chapman.

JOHN LINDSAY, b. Halifax Co., Va., 1750; d. Wilkes Co., Ga., 1808. Served as Major and Colonel. Wounded and known as "Old Silver Fist". Placed on Invalid Pension Roll for his services in S. C. and Ga. Married Clarissa (Bullock) Sims (dau. of NATHANIEL BULLOCK, REV. SOLDIER, and wife Mary, lived in Walkes Co., Ga.).
Children:
1. Clarissa Harlow Bullock Lindsay.
2. Munesis Creswell Christmas Lindsay.
3. Matilda Marbury Somerville Lindsay (1789-1826); mar. Andrew Baskins Stevens.
4. Sallie Collier Billingsea Lindsay.
5. Jackson Clark Watkins Lindsay.
6. Jennie M. Lindsay of St. Mary's, Ga.
7. Benjamin Few Hamilton Lindsay.

JAMES LITTLE, b. in Va., 1737; d. Franklin Co., Ga., 1807. Served as Capt., Ga. Militia. For a time in charge of a block-house at Cherokee Ford, on Savannah River. Fought in 22 battles. Received bounty grant of land in Franklin Co., Ga., for his services, June 6, 1784. Married Isabella Hamilton (1741-1821).
Children: (known)
1. James H.
2. John.
3. Ellen.
4. William.

MICAJAH LITTLE, b. in Martin Co., N. C.; d. 1809, Wilkes Co., Ga. Served as Lieut. in Capt. William Brinkley's Co., 3rd N. C. Reg. Received bounty land in Ga. for his services. Married 1781, Mary Brackenberry.
Children: (known)
1. Cherry, mar. 1801, John Bethune.
2. Littleberry.
3. John E.
4. William.

MATTHEW LIVELY (son of Abraham Lively, who came from Scotland), b. in Ga., 1750; d. Burke Co., Ga., 1834. Served in Ga. Line. Received bounty land in Ga. for his services. Married Elizabeth Odom.

ADAM LIVINGSTON, b. in Ireland. Served as a REV. SOLDIER in Penn. Removed to Va., then Green Co., Ga., where he was killed by

Indians. He had 13 children, living in Greene Co., Ga.

EVANS LONG, b. Culpeper Co., Va.; d. Twiggs Co., Ga., 1819. (He was the youngest of five brothers who all served as REV. SOLDIERS: GABRIEL, ANDERSON, NICHOLAS, and NIMROD LONG.) He served as private, Capt. Long's Co., Col. Morgan's Reg., 11th Va. Married Lucy Apperson.
Children:
1. Mary (1783-1872); mar. William Crocker (1777-1835).
2. Margaret, mar. Elijah Clarke, Jr. (son of GEN. ELIJAH CLARKE of Ga.).
3. Frances, mar. William Hudson.
4. Lunceford, mar. Nancy Jackson.
5. Lucinda, mar. John Owens.
6. Sarah Ann, mar. Tuttle Moreland.
7. Nimrod Washington, mar. Catherine Davis of Lewis Co., N. C.

NICHOLAS LONG, b. in N.C.; d. in Wilkes Co., Ga., 1819. Served in the N.C. Line and received bounty land in Ga. for his services. He also served as Col. of the 43rd Ga. Reg. in the War of 1812. Member Provincial Congress. Married (1) —; (2) Mary McKinney.
Children:
1. Margaret, mar. Thomas Telfair (son of Gov. EDWARD TELFAIR of Ga., a REV. SOLDIER), lived at Savannah, Ga.
2. Sarah Rebecca, mar. James Rembert.
3. Eliza, mar. — DuBose.
4. Eugenia, mar. Lock Weems.
5. Richard H., mar. Nancy Hay.
6. John, lived in Washington Co., Ga.

REUBEN LONG, b. in Va.; d. 1792. Served as a PATRIOT of Va. Married Mary —.
Children:
1. Gabriel.
2. Evans.
3. Anderson.
4. Nicholas.
5. Nimrod.
6. Fannie, mar. Daniel Richardson.
7. Peggy, mar. Robert Kay.
8. Polly, mar. John Nash.

SAMUEL LONG, b. in Ireland, 1753; came to Penn., 1762. Served in the Penn. Army; also as Captain under Marquis de La Fayette, and was at the surrender of Cornwallis at Yorktown. Married Ann Williamson, b. in Ireland. They moved to Madison Co., Ga., 1792, where he died.
Children:
1. James, b. in Penn., 1781; mar. in Ga., Elizabeth Ware.
Child:
1. Crawford W. Long (1815-1876), mar. 1842, Mary Caroline Swain (dau. of George Swain). A statue of Dr. Crawford W.

Long has been placed by Ga. in "Statuary Hall of Fame", National Capitol, Washington, D. C., as the "Discoverer of Anesthesia".

2. Thomas
3. Ann.   5. Joseph.
4. Mary.   6. Samuel, Jr.

DAVID LOVE, b. in Anson Co., N. C., 1740; d. Greene Co., Ga., Nov. 30, 1798. Served as Lieut. Col. N. C. Troops. Member Provincial Congress. Married Oct. 22, 1772, Jean Blewett (1756-1817).
Children:
1. d. 6.
2. Robertus.
3. Acksah, mar. Thomas Sparks.
4. Vertus Mary.
5. Beloved.
6. Chaste Esther, mar. Abner Turner; had 15 children.
7. Allelujah, mar. 1812, Henry Rogers.
8. Ovid Blewett.
9. Josephus, mar. —.

ISAAC LOW, SR., b. —; d. Richmond Co., Ga., May 17, 1790. Was a J. P. in Richmond Co., 1782. Received a bounty grant of land in Ga. upon certificate of Col. James McNeil. Mar. —.
Children: (mentioned in will)
1. Esther, mar. Samuel Hart.   5. Hickenbotham.
2. William.   6. Grace.
3. Ann   7. Isaac, Jr.
4. Burrey.   8. George.

CHARLES LOWRY (son of CHARLES LOWRY, REV. SOLDIER of Va.), was b. in Va.; d. 1847, Cass Co., Ga. Served in the Va. Continental Army and moved to Ga., 1812, Franklin Co. Married in Va., Miss Reese. Had 15 children, 5 d. y.
Children:
1. David, Soldier of 1812.   6. Elizabeth.
2. James, Soldier of 1812.   7. Mary.
3. Solomon, Soldier of 1812. 8. Martha.
4. John, Soldier of 1812.   9. Sarah.
5. Samuel.   10. Thomas.

DAVID LOWRY, b. 1764; d. Jackson Co., Ga., 1848. Served as a REV. SOLDIER and received bounty land in Ga. for his services, Married 1806, Martha McLeuller.

GEORGE LUMPKIN, b. 1723, King and Queen Co., Va.; d. 1799 in Wilkes Co., Ga. Served as Captain in Rev. Army of Va. Removed to Ga., 1784. Married (1) 1748 in Va., Mary Cady (1728-1799). His will

on file, Wilkes Co., Ga.
Child:
1. John, b. 1763 in Va.; d. 1834 in Ga. Married 1780, Lucy Hopson
   (1764-1820) (dau. of HENRY HOPSON, REV. SOLDIER of Va.,
   and his wife Martha Nevil (Neville).
   Children:
   1. William.
   2. Wilson.
   3. Jack.
   4. George.
   5. Henry Hopson.
   6. Samuel.
   7. Robert.
   8. Martha.
   9. Joseph Henry (1799-1867); mar. Callender Grieve.
   10. Thomas Jefferson
   11. James Nevil.

JEREMIAH LUMSDEN, b. in Va., 1753; d. in Ga., Jan. 18, 1837.
Served as a private, Va. Troops. Received bounty grant of land for his
services. Married Elizabeth Belcher (1757-1830).
Children:
1. Wilmoth, b. 1779.
2. Lucy, b. 1780.
3. Elizabeth.
4. Sally.
5. Amy.
6. Polly.
7. Susanna.
8. Phoebe.
9. John, mar. Susanna Jones.
10. Nelly P.
11. Jeremiah, Jr.
12. Charles W.
13. Jesse M.

BENJAMIN MADDOX, b. in Va., July 4, 1760; d. Atlanta, Ga., 1864.
Served as private, Va. Reg. Settled in Elbert Co., Ga., 1804. Married
Elizabeth Waldroop.
Children:
1. Fielding.
2. Sarah, mar. John Bush.
3. Themie, mar. — Prior.
4. Stansfield.
5. Posey.
6. James A., mar. Martha Tate.
7. Walter.
8. John.
9. Henley.

NINIAN OFFUTT MAGRUDER (McGruder), b. in Md., 1744; d.
Richmond Co., Ga. (now Columbia Co.), 1800. Enlisted Montgomery
Co., Md. Sergeant, 2nd Co. Md. Troops. Married 1765, Mary Harris
(1748-1820).
Children:
1. ZADOC, b. 1766, Montgomery Co., Md.; d. 1820, Columbia Co.,
   Ga. Served as private, Md. Troops as a REV. SOLDIER. He
   mar. (1) Miss Talbott; mar. (2) Tracy Rearden.
   Children by (1) wife:
   1. Ninan.
   2. Sophronia.
   3. Selina.

Child by (2) wife:
4. Martha.
2. George (1772-1836); mar. (1) Elinor Shaw; (2) 1805, Susanna Williams.
3. Archibald.
4. John, mar. Sarah Prior.
5. Eleanor, mar. Williamson Wynne.
6. Sarah, mar. John Oliver.
7. Basil, mar. Elizabeth McGruder.

SAMUEL MAGRUDER, b. 1708, Prince George Co., Md.; d. 1786, Columbia Co., Ga. Served as Captain, Md. Militia. Member of Observation for Frederick Co., Md. Took Patriots' Oath. Married Margaret Jackson (1712-1806).
Children:
1. NINIAN BEALL, b. in Md., 1735; d. Columbia Co., Ga., 1807. Took patriotic Oath, Montgomery Co., Md., 1778. Appointed Sergeant, Md. Reg., 1780. Married Rebecca Young (1739-1811).
2. Ann.　　　　　　　　　5. Sarah.
3. Ruth.　　　　　　　　6. Elizabeth.
4. Margaret.　　　　　　7. Samuel B.

GIDEON MALLETTE, b. Purysburg, S. C., June 14, 1759; d. Effingham Co., Ga., Sept. 3, 1822. Served under Gen. Francis Marion, S. C. Troops. Married 1783, Hanna Elizabeth A. De Rocke (1767-1848).
Children:
1. Gideon, Jr.
2. Mary Ann.
3. Abraham (1790-1867); mar. Catherine Kennedy.
4. Daniel, mar. Susanna Zeigler.
5. Lewis.
6. John Henry.
7. Margaret.
8. Jeremiah (1802-1865); mar. (1) Emma Metzger; (2) Mary Porter (dau. of William G. Porter).
9. Eliza M., mar. John William Exley.

WILLIAM MANLEY, b. Cecil Co., Md., Nov. 24, 1761; d. Oconee Co., Ga., 1824. Served as private in Capt. Price's Co., Md. Line. Married 1785, Lucy Freeman (1767-1830), in Dinwiddie Co., Va.
Children:
1. William, mar. Mary Robinson Brown.
2. Joseph Parson, mar. 1814, Elizabeth Calhoun Bailey.
3. John.
4. Greene.
5. Infant.
6. Nancy, mar. — Morton.
7. Lourraine, mar. — Gresham.

8. Mary, mar. — Gill.
9. Elizabeth, mar. — Jackson.
10. Puss, mar. — Atkins.

JAMES MANN, d. 1816, Elbert Co., Ga. Served as REV. SOLDIER.
Married Judith —.
Children: (mentioned in will)
1. John, mar. 1816, Polly Harper.
2. Joel.
3. Jeremiah.
4. Asa, mar. Nancy White.
5. James, Jr., mar. Esther Lewis.
6. Henry, mar. Sarah Haley.
7. Martha, mar. HENRY SHACKLEFORD of Elbert Co., Ga., b. in
   Orange Co., Va. REV. SOLDIER.
8. Elizabeth, mar. (1) George Roebucks; (2) Johnston Maley.

JOHN MANN, b. 170-; d. Liberty Co., Ga., 1789. Member Provincial Congress 1775. Married 1732, Anne Vincent, d. 1797.
Children:
1. Mary Sophy.
2. LUKE, b. 1736 in Ireland; d. Apr. 7, 1802 at Great Ogechee, Ga.
   Member Provincial Congress from Parish of St. Philips (now
   Bryan Co.), Ga. Served as Captain in Gen. Greene's Army.
   Married Anne Butler, d. 1788, Great Ogechee, Ga.
   Children:
   1. Mary, mar. Samuel Sleigh.
   2. Sarah, mar. (1) Josiah Stewart (son of JAMES STEWART,
      REV. SOLDIER of Ga. ; mar. (2) Mr. Foster; mar. (3)
      Grover.
      Child by (1) husb. :
      1. Sarah Elizabeth Stewart, mar. William H. Mell.
   3. Martha, mar. William A. Dunham.
   4. Jane, mar. 1803, James P. Heath. Living Baltimore, 1808.
   5. Thomas, b. 1780; mar. (1)—; (2) Harriet —.
   6. Susan, mar. 1805, Samuel Lewis of Liberty Co.
   7. Frances, mar. Arthur M. Charlton of Wilkes Co. (son of
      THOMAS CHARLTON, REV. SOLDIER, and wife Lucy
      Kenan).
   8. Rebecca, mar. Thomas Day.
   9. Harriet, mar. Samuel Dewse.
   10. Ann, mar. John Pray.
   11. Luke, Jr., mar. (1) Margaret —; (2) Eliza —.

JAMES MARKS, b. 1745 in England. Came to Albemarle Co., Va.
He d. 1816, Wilkes Co., Ga. Signed Oath of Allegiance, Albemarle Co.,
Va. Served with Va. Army. Was given grant of land in Ga. for his
services. Married 1771, Elizabeth Harvie (1754-1793).

Children:
1. John, b. 1773; mar. Susan M. Tompkins.
2. Meriwether, mar. Ann Mathews; moved to Ala.
3. Martha, mar. James Watkins.

REV. DANIEL MARSHALL, b. in Windsor, Conn., 1706; d. in Ga., 1784. He was the famous Pastor of the First Baptist Church in Ga., the Kiokee Church on Kiokee Creek. He moved through Conn. to Va., and the Carolina to Ga. He was an ardent PATRIOT; imprisoned several times by the British. Served as Chaplain. Married (1) Hannah Drake; (2) Martha Stearns in 1747.
Children by (1) wife:
1. DANIEL MARSHALL, REV. SOLDIER.
Children by (2) wife:
2. ABRAHAM MARSHALL, b. in Windsor, Conn., 1748; d. in Ga., 1819. Served as Chaplain in Col. Stewart's Reg. of Minute Men from Augusta, Ga. Married Ann Waller.
3. LEVI MARSHALL, b. Winchester, Va., 1754; d. 1809, Columbia Co., Ga. Served as private, Ga. Troops. Received bounty grant of land for his services. Married Sarah Wynne.
4. Mary Marshall, mar. ELIAS WELLBORN, REV. SOLDIER.
   Child:
   1. James M. Wellborn (1809-1879); mar. Louisa Cody (dau. of Michael Cody and Rebecca Rogers, dau. of REUBEN ROGERS REV. SOLDIER of Ga.).
5. Eunice Marshall, mar. JOHN PITTMAN, REV. SOLDIER of Ga.
6. JOHN, REV. SOLDIER.
7. Joseph.
8. ZACHERIAH, REV. SOLDIER.

NOTE: The graves of the five sons: JOHN, ABRAHAM, LEVI, JOSEPH and ZACHERIAH MARSHALL, all REV. SOLDIERS of Ga., have been marked by the Ga. D. A. R.
The grave of DANIEL MARSHALL, who organized the Kioka Baptist Church in 1772, in the town of Appling, the County seat of Columbia Co., is a little south of the Court House, on the side of the road to Augusta, Ga.

ELIJAH MARTIN, b. 1751 in Penn.; d. Jones Co., Ga., 1819. Served in Penn. Troops; private, S. C. Militia. Married in Penn., 1774, Mary Van Der Burg (1753-1833).
Children:
1. Elya.
2. Shadrack.
3. Israel, mar. Grace Warren.
4. Levi, mar. Jemina Harris.
5. Nancy, mar. — Coulter.
6. Rachel, mar. — Witt.

7. Elizabeth, mar. — Chapman.
8. Martha, mar. — Lambert.
9. Dau., mar. Robert Henderson.
   Two other daughters.

ELIZABETH (MARSHALL) MARTIN was a Heroine of the Revolution and lived to be 96 years of age.

JAMES MARTIN, b. 1749 in Va.; d. 1785 in Ga. Served as Col., Va. Army. Married Obedience Bugg (dau. of SHERWOOD BUGG, SR., REV. SOLDIER of S. C. and Ga.).
Children:

1. Prudence.	4. Letitia.
2. Keziah.	5. Mary.
3. Elizabeth.	6. James, Jr.

JOHN MARTIN, d. Augusta, Ga., Feb. 14, 1843, aged 105 years. On monument, St. Paul's Churchyard, Augusta, Ga. "He served in the Cherokee War 1735. Was wounded in the head by a tomahawk. He served throughout the whole of the Revolution with honor. Erected as a tribute of respect by the Ladies of Augusta, Ga."

MARSHALL MARTIN, d. Augusta, Ga., 1819 (son of Abram Martin and his wife Elizabeth Marshall. They had seven sons who were REV. SOLDIERS.) He was wounded at the Siege of Augusta.

WILLIAM MARTIN (brother of MARSHALL MARTIN), was b. in S. C.; killed at the Siege of Augusta, Ga. Married GRACE WARING of Dorchester, S. C., one of the Heroines of the REV.

JOHN MASON, b. 1755 in Ga.; d. in Ga., 1795. Served as Sergeant-Major, Ga. Line. Married Elizabeth Hix, b. 1765.

TURNER MASON, b. in Va. In 1793, he moved to Jefferson Co., Ga., where he d. Served as Lieut. in Continental Army of Va. Married (1) in Va., Elizabeth Burns, d. 1783, three children; mar. (2) 1785, Halifax Co., N. C., Mary Lowe, had 14 children.

GEORGE MATHEWS, b. 1739 in Amherst Co., Va.; d. Aug. 30, 1812 in Augusta, Ga. Buried in old St. Paul's Churchyard. Served as Lieut. Col., 1775, 9th Reg., Va. Troops, stationed at Chesapeake Bay under Gen. Andrew Lewis. Was at Brandywine and Germantown; was taken prisoner, sent to British prison in New York, exchanged and placed in command of 3rd Va. Reg. Removed to Goose Pond Tract, Wilkes Co., Ga. Elected Governor of the State of Ga., 1786. Representative from Ga. to the First Continental Congress. Again elected Governor of Ga., 1794-95. Removed to Florida, then returned to Ga. Married (1) Ann (called Polly) Paul (dau. of John Paul and half-sister of COL.

JOHN STUART, REV. SOLDIER of Va.). He mar. (2) Mrs. Reed of Va.; mar. (3) Mrs. Flowers of Miss.

Children by (1) wife:

1. John, mar. his cousin Elizabeth Mathews (dau. of Archer Mathews), 5 children.
2. William, mar. Elizabeth (Meriwether) Thornton (dau. of Frank Meriwether of Wilkes Co.).
3. George, mar. his step-sister, Miss Flowers; moved to Miss.
4. Charles Lewis, mar. Lucy Early (sister of Gov. Peter Early of Ga.); moved to Ala.
5. Ann, mar. Samuel Blackburn; moved to Va.
6. Rebecca (1770-1825); mar. THOMAS MERIWETHER (1750-1831), a REV. SOLDIER; lived Jasper Co., Ga.
7. Jane, mar. Mr. Telfair.

MOSES MATHEWS, b. 1725, Halifax Co., Va.; d. 1806, Wilkes Co., Ga. Learned the trade of gun-maker in Va. Moved to S. C., and made guns for Gen. Sumpter. Received bounty grant of land in Ga. for his services in S. C. Troops. Married 1749, Sarah Findley, b. in Va.

Child:

1. JAMES MATHEWS, b. in Va., Oct. 15, 1755; d. in Wilkes Co., Ga. 1828. Enlisted 1775 in 2nd S. C. Reg., under Col. Wm. Thompson and Gen. Francis Marion. Married (1) widow Jenkins, one son. Moved to Ga., 1782, a Baptist preacher. Mar. (2) 1786, Rebecca Carleton (1762-1840) (dau. of ROBERT CARLETON, a REV. SOLDIER of Va., and his wife Miss Wafford, who moved to Wilkes Co., Ga., 1785).

   Children:

   1. James, mar. Keturah Pope (dau. of John Pope). She mar. (2) Henry Long. (JOHN POPE was REV. SOLDIER of N. C. and Ga., mar. Elizabeth Smith, and was son of JOHN HENRY POPE, REV. SOLDIER of N. C., and Mary Burwell.)
   2. Elizabeth Rebecca, mar. (1) Ephraim Smith Vernal; (2) Augustua F. Griggs.
   3. Jacob Gibson, b. 1790; mar. Winny Jordan.
   4. Philip, b. 1792; mar. (1) 1814, Elizabeth Clark (dau. of DAVID CLARK, REV. SOLDIER of Va. and Wilkes Co., Ga.); he mar. (2) 1852, Mrs. Wilkes.
   5. William, mar. Alice Gaither.
   6. Abram, mar. Elizabeth Burrus.

JEREMIAH MATTHEWS, b. Halifax Co., N. C.; d. in Ga. Served as private, N. C. Troops. Married Sarah Brinkley.

WILLIAM MATTHEWS, b. in England; d. in Baldwin Co., Ga. Served as private, REV. SOLDIER. Married Dorcas Wright.

JOHN MATTOX, petitions for bounty grant of land for services as

Minute Man, Ga. Militia certified to by Col. Patrick. Land granted, 1785.

JOHN MATTOX, b. S. C., about 1765; d. Tattnall Co., Ga., 1826. Married —. Received bounty land, Mar. 20, 1784, in Washington Co., Ga., for his services as a Minute Man in Ga. Militia, while a resident of S. C. He also served as a Soldier of 1812 from Tattnall Co., Ga. Children: (known).
   1. Elijah, mar. Lavinia Johnson.
   2. Michael.
   3. Allen.
   4. John.

McKENZIE MATTOX, b. in S. C., moved from the Colleton Dist., S. C., about 1800 to Tattnall Co., Ga. Married in S. C., Elizabeth Hartridge. He was a REV. SOLDIER of S. C.
Child:
   1. Elijah Mattox, mar. Candace Tippins.

MICHAEL McKENZIE MATTOX (brother of JOHN MATTOX), b. in Colleton Dist., S. C. Moved to Tattnall Co., Ga. Served as REV. SOLDIER and received payment for 104 days in S. C. Militia. Married Elizabeth Hartridge.
Children: (from will, Tattnall Co.)
   1. Aaron.
   2. John.
   3. Elijah, mar. Candace Tippins.
   4. Elizabeth, mar. — Addison.
   5. Dau., mar. William Eason.

AUDLEY MAXWELL, d. in Ga. Served as Colonel, Ga. Troops. Member of First General Assembly of Ga. Married Mary Stevens (dau. of John and Mary Stevens). In 1756, John Stevens deeded to Audley Maxwell and others, 2-1/2 acres of land on which the "Old Midway" Church was built.
Child:
   1. JAMES MAXWELL, a Colonel in Ga. Reg. Member Provincial Congress which met at Savannah, Ga., 1775. Secretary of State, 1778. Married Ann Way.

WILLIAM MAXWELL, b. 1739, Amelia Township, S. C.; d. Bryan Co., Ga., 1807 (son of James Maxwell and his wife Mary Simons of S. C., who came to Ga., 1752, and settled on Midway River (now Bryan Co.), Ga.) He served as Capt. and as privatiersman, commanding his own armed vessel, 1779; was captured, kept under parole by the British until after the evacuation of Savannah, Ga., July 11, 1782. Married 1763, Constantia Butler of Great Ogechee, Ga.
Children:

153

1. Elizabeth.
2. John Jackson (1784-1855); mar. Mary Anne Baker (dau. of COL. JOHN' BAKER, REV. SOLDIER of Ga.).

WILLIAM MEAD, b. Va., 1727; d. 1805, Augusta, Ga. Gave active service, Bedford Co., Va. Troops. Col. in Va. Married (2) Martha Ann Haile, d. 1769.
Child:
1. JOHN HAILE MEAD, b. 1755, Bedford Co., Va.; d. Augusta, Ga., 1798. Served as Ensign, 14th Va. Reg. Mar. Elizabeth Crump, d. 1813.

DAVID MELSON, b. in Md.; d. Hancock Co., Ga. Served as private, Md. Line. Married Mary Grace.

SILAS MERCER, b. 1745, Currituck Co., N. C.; d. 1793, Wilkes Co., Ga. Served as Chaplain, N. C. Troops. Married Dorcas —, d. 1791.
Child:
1. Mount Moriah Mercer (1784-1822); mar. 1816, Nancy (Ann) Edge.
   Child:
   1. Herman, mar. Elizabeth Andrews of Greene Co.

DAVID MERIWETHER, b. Albemarle Co., Va., 1755; d. Clarke Co., Ga., Nov. 16, 1822. Served as Lieut., Va. Troops. Was at the Siege of Savannah, Ga.; was taken prisoner at Charleston, S. C., realeased and served until the end of the War. Received bounty grant of land, Wilkes Co., Ga., for his services. Married 1782, Frances Wingfield of Wilkes Co., Ga.
Children:
1. John, moved to Ala.
2. James, moved to Tenn.
3. William, mar. Sarah Malloy.
4. Francis.
5. George, mar. Martha Williams.
6. David, b. 1800; mar. (1) Henrietta Collier; (2) Eliza Dabney.
7. Judith, mar. Rev. Mr. Hemming.

DAVID WOOD MERIWETHER, b. 1754, Louisa Co., Va.; d. 1797, Clarke Co., Ga. Served as private and Lieut., Va. Line. Married 1782, Mary Lewis, d. 1801.

FRANCIS MERIWETHER (son of Thomas Meriwether and wife Elizabeth Thornton), b. Oct. 3, 1737 in Va.; d. 1803 in Ga. Served with the Va. Troops and received bounty grant of land for his services in Ga. Married Martha Jameson (dau. of James and Mary (Gaines) Jameson). They moved to Wilkes Co., Ga., 1784.
Children:

1. THOMAS, REV. SOLDIER, mar. Rebecca Mathews.
2. Valentine, b. 1768; mar. Barbara Cosby.
3. Nicholas, mar. Mary D'Yempest.
4. Mary, mar. William Barnett.
5. Mildred, mar. Joel Barnett.
6. Elizabeth, mar. William Mathews.
7. Margaret, mar. Dr. John A. Bradley.
8. Nancy, mar. William Glenn.
9. Sarah, mar. James Olive.
10. Lucy, mar. Grover Howard.

JAMES MERIWETHER, b. in Va., 1755; d. 1817, Louisville, Ga. Served in the "Silk Stocking" Co. of Richmond, Va. Received bounty grant of land in Ga. Married Susan Hatcher.
Children:
1. James, Jr.
2. Alexander.
3. Dau., mar. Thomas M. Berrien.
4. Dau., mar. Eleazur Early (brother of Gov. Peter Early).
5. Dau., mar. Daniel Sturgiss.

THOMAS MERIWETHER (son of Francis Meriwether and his wife Martha Jameson), b. in Va., 1766; d. Jasper Co., Ga., 1831. Served as a private under Gen. La Fayette. Received bounty land for his services in Wilkes Co., Ga. Married Rebecca Mathews (dau. Gov. George Mathews).
Children:
1. Frank, mar. Miss Butler.
2. George, mar. (1) Miss Jordan; (2) Miss Watkins.
3. Ann, mar. Fleming Jordan of Jasper Co., Ga.
4. Mary, mar. Dr. David Reese.
5. David, mar. 4 times.

WILLIAM MERIWETHER, b. in Va., 1730; d. 1790. Mar. —.
Children:
1. Elizabeth, mar. Nicholas Meriwether.
2. DAVID WOOD, REV. SOLDIER; mar. Mary Lewis.
3. William, Jr., mar. Sarah Oldham.
4. Mildred, mar. Thomas Mitchell.
5. Sarah, mar. Gen. D. L. James.
6. Valentine, mar. Priscilla Pollard.
7. Ann, mar. Major John W. Hughes.

NOTE: Thomas Meriwether, b. 1714 in Va.; d. 1756 in Va.; mar. Elizabeth Thornton.
Children:
1. Nicholas, REV. SOLDIER; mar. Margaret Douglas.
2. Francis, REV. SOLDIER; mar. Martha Jameson.

3. David, REV. SOLDIER; mar. Mary Harvie.
4. Mildred, mar. JOHN GILMER, REV. SOLDIER.
5. Elizabeth, mar. THOMAS JOHNSON, REV. SOLDIER.
6. Sally, mar. Michael Anderson.
7. Mary, mar. PEACHY R. GILMER, REV. SOLDIER.
8. Nancy, mar. Richard Anderson.
9. Lucy, mar. (1) WILLIAM LEWIS, REV. SOLDIER; mar. (2) JOHN MARKS, REV. SOLDIER; moved to Ga.
   Children by (1) husb.:
   1. Meriwether Lewis, Gov. of Missouri.
   2. Reuben Lewis, mar. Mildred Dabney.
   3. Jane Lewis, mar. Edmund Anderson.
   Children by (2) husb.:
   1. John Marks.
   2. Mary Marks.
10. Jane, mar. Samuel Dabney; 11 children.

JAMES McAFEE, b. N. C., 1762; d. Habersham Co., Ga., 1844. Enlisted 1776, N. C. Troops. Served until close of War. Married Margaret Cole.

CHARLES McCALL (son of FRANCIS McCALL, REV. SOLDIER of N. C.), b. 1732 in Penn. (on Va. line); d. Bullock Co., Ga., 1816. He was a PATRIOT who rendered material aid during the REV. WAR, and also served in S. C. Troops at the "Battle of McCall's Field", his home place in S. C. He received bounty land in Effingham Co., Ga. for his services. Also served as H. R. and in civil offices in Ga. (Record for Society of War of 1812). Married in S. C. (1) 1755, Celete Ann (called Nancy) William (dau. of Rev. Robert Williams, 1st Pastor Welch Neck Baptist Church, Society Hill, S. C., and his wife Ann Boykin). Mar. (2) Bullock Co., Ga., Hannah Everett.
Children by (1) wife:
1. JOHN, REV. SOLDIER; remained in S. C.
2. DAVID, REV. SOLDIER; mar. Frances —; moved to Ga.
3. GEORGE, REV. SOLDIER of S. C.; mar. (1) Elizabeth Burnett; (2) Elizabeth Sanders; removed to Ga., then to S. C., where he died.
4. WILLIAM, REV. SOLDIER; mar. (1) Ann (called Nancy) Fletcher (dau. of WILLIAM FLETCHER, REV. SOLDIER of Ga., and his wife Elizabeth McIntosh); mar. (2) Mary Pearce (dau. of JOSHUA PEARCE, JR., REV. SOLDIER of Ga.).
5. HENRY, private S. C. Troops from Cheran Dist.
6. Eleanor, mar. Ogechee, Ga., 1786, McKEEN GREEN, JR., a REV. SOLDIER of Ga.
7. Nancy, mar. STEPHEN McCOY, a REV. SOLDIER.
8. Robert, mar. Bullock Co., Ga., Mary (called Polly) Lanier (dau. of LEWIS LANIER, REV. SOLDIER of Ga.).
9. Francis, mar. (1) Sarah Pearce (dau. of JOSHUA PEARCE, JR.,

REV. SOLDIER); mar. (2) Sarah Mattox, widow, of Tattnall Co., Ga.

10. Charles, Jr., mar. Betsey B. (Lanier) Stith (dau. of LEWIS LANIER, REV. SOLDIER).
11. Nathaniel, mar. 1807, Mary Johnson.
12. Mary, mar. William Wright. He mar. (2) Hannah Everett, and had two children by (2) wife:
    1. Sarah.
    2. John.

NOTE: Grave of CHARLES McCALL, REV. SOLDIER located by Mrs. Julian Lane of the Briar Creek Chapter, D. A. R., Sylvania, Ga., in the Everett graveyard, Bullock Co., Ga. (See "McCall-Tidwell and Allied Families" by Ettie Tidwell McCall (Mrs. Howard H.)

DAVID McCALL (son of CHARLES McCALL, REV. SOLDIER of S. C. and Ga.), b. in S. C.; d. in Ga. Served as private 1782, in Capt. Giles Co., Col. William Hill's Reg., S. C. Received land 1786 in Effingham (now Bullock) Co., Ga. for his services. Married Frances (called Fanny).
Children:
    1. Selaway, moved to Irwin Co. (Telfair Co.).
    2. John, moved to Irwin Co., Ga.
    3. David, Jr., mar. Ellender Johnson.
    4. James, mar. Rebecca McMullan; moved to Lowndes Co., Ga.

GEORGE McCALL (son of CHARLES McCALL), b. on Lynch's Creek, S. C., Pedee Dist., Mar. 10, 1760; came to Effingham Co., Ga., 1786; returned to S. C., where he d. at Society Hill, Jan. 9, 1837. He served under Capt. James Gregg, Major Thornby; later together with his three brothers: JOHN, HENRY, and WILLIAM, joined the command under Gen. Francis Marion. Married (1) Elizabeth Burnett; (2) Elizabeth Sanders (dau. of NATHANIEL SANDERS, REV. SOLDIER of S. C.).
Children by (1) wife:
    1. Nathaniel, mar. Sabrina B. Long.
    2. Elhannon.   5. Robert.
    3. David.   6. Francis.
    4. Harriet.   7. William.
Children by (2) wife:
    8. James Sanders, mar. Elizabeth Ellen Lucretia Muldrow.
    9. Moses Sanders, mar. Elizabeth Gregg.
    10. George Jay Washington (1801-1871); mar. (1) Harriet Harlee; (2) Louisa Caroline Huggins.

HUGH McCALL (son of JAMES McCALL, REV. SOLDIER of N. C. and his wife Janet Harris, and brother of CAPT. JAMES McCALL, REV. SOLDIER of S. C.), was a REV. SOLDIER of N. C. Received bounty grant of land in Wilkes Co., Ga., for his services. He was an uncle of HUGH McCALL (son of COL. JAMES McCALL) who was a

Soldier of 1812, and State Historian of Ga.; d. in Savannah, Ga., unm.

JOHN McCALL (son of THOMAS McCALL, REV. SOLDIER, and his wife Rachel McCall), b. in S. C.; d. in Ga. Served as private in Capt. Giles Co., Col. William Hill's S. C. Reg. State Troops. Served 10 months in Sumpter's Brigade. Married Sarah —.
Children:
1. James.
2. Elizabeth, mar. Rev. Mann Dutton of Gloucester Co., Va.
   Child:
   1. Henrietta Dutton, mar. Robert Raines Terrell.
3. Henrietta.

SHERROD McCALL (son of THOMAS McCALL, REV. SOLDIER, and his wife Rachel McCall), b. in S. C., 1766; d. in Gadsen Co., Fla. Moved to Ga., where he received a grant of land in Effingham Co., Ga. for his services as a REV. SOLDIER of S. C., Dec. 1784. Was a member of Ga. State Legislature, 1808-1813 (Record for papers for War of 1812). Married Margaret — of Bullock Co., Ga.
Children:
1. Elizabeth, mar. Eli Kennedy of Bullock Co., Ga. (son of FRANCIS KENNEDY, REV. SOLDIER of S. C. and Ga., and his wife Sarah McGee).
2. William.
3. Sarah.
4. Jesse.
5. Thomas.
6. Allen.
7. Seaborn.
8. John.
9. Margaret
10. Sherrod, Jr.
11. George.

THOMAS McCALL (son of FRANCIS McCALL, REV. SOLDIER of Mecklenburg Co., N. C.; mar. his cousin Rachel McCall, dau. of JAMES McCALL, REV. SOLDIER of Mecklenburg Co., N. C.), b. in Va. (near Penn. line), 1740. Moved with his parents to N. C. Served in the S. C. Militia and received in 1784, bounty grant of land in Effingham Co. for his services. He d. Bullock Co., Ga., 1818. His wife d. 1821 at the same place.
Children:
1. ALEXANDER, REV. SOLDIER of S. C. Received bounty grant of land in Wilkes Co., Ga.
2. JOHN, REV. SOLDIER; mar. Sarah —.
3. SHERROD, REV. SOLDIER; mar. Margaret —.
4. George.
5. Francis, mar. Miss Rawls.
6. Thomas, Jr., mar. Sarah —.
7. Jesse, mar. Mary —.
8. Marcia, mar. JOHN MOORE, REV. SOLDIER of S. C. and Ga., private in Capt. Giles Co., Col. Wm. Hill's Reg. Moved to Ga.
9. Ann, mar. — Musgrove.

10. Sarah, mar. Henry Williams.
11. William.
12. Abraham.
13. Eliza.

THOMAS McCALL (son of CAPT. JAMES McCALL, REV. SOLDIER,
b. in Penn., 1741; d. in S. C., April 16, 1781, and his wife Elizabeth Mc
Call), b. Mecklenburg Co., N. C., Mar. 19, 1764; d. Laurens Co., Ga.,
1839. He served as private, S. C. Troops and received bounty grant of
land in Ga. for his services. Was appointed Surveyor General of Ga.
and also served as a Soldier of the War of 1812. He mar. (1) April 1,
1787, Henrietta Fall (1767-1797); mar. (2) July 1798, Elizabeth Mary
Ann Smith (1775-1831).
Children by (1) wife:
    1. Eliza Henrietta.
    2. Selina Mary Ann, mar. Virgil H. Vivien.
    3. Louisa Freeman, mar. George Gaines.
    4. Thomas William.
    5. James.
Children by (2) wife:
    6. Sarah Georgiana, mar. Col. Eli W. B. Spivey.
    7. Elizabeth Smith, mar. as (3) wife, Dr. Thomas Moore.
    8. Margaret, d. y.
    9. Harriet Moore, mar. Major Luke Mizell.
   10. Janet Harris, mar. Ira Stanley.
   11. Margaret Sanders, mar. Jeremiah H. Yopp.

REV. THOMAS McCALL (changed his name to McCaule while at
college) (son of James McCall and Janet Harris), b. in Penn.; d. in
Savannah, Ga., Sept. 13, 1796. Served as Chaplain in S. C. Reg. "He
fanned, while preaching, the flames of patriotism in his Church and
cherished the spirit of Independence". (From funeral notice). He
married (1) Jane Harris; (2) Mar. 8, 1796, Eliza H. Montfort (widow of
Robert Montfort of Savannah, Ga.).

WILLIAM McCALL (son of CHARLES McCALL, REV. SOLDIER of
S. C. and Ga., and his wife Celete Ann Williams), b. 1766 at Lynche's
Creek, near Society Hill, S. C.; d. in Screven Co., Ga., Jan. 12, 1830.
Served as private under Gen. Francis Marion in S. C.; was at Snow
Island. Moved with his family to Effingham Co. (now Screven), Ga.
Received land grant for his services. Soldier of 1812. Married in
S. C., 1789, Ann (called Nancy) Fletcher (dau. of WILLIAM FLETCHER,
REV. SOLDIER of S. C. and Ga., and his (2) wife Elizabeth McIntosh);
mar. (2) 1800, Mary Pearce (dau. of JOSHUA PEARCE, JR., REV.
SOLDIER of Effingham Co., Ga., d. in Miss).
Children by (1) wife:
    1. Selete.
    2. William, d. y.

3. George Robert Francis, mar. Luvincia (dau. of THOMAS FAIN, REV. SOLDIER of Ga.).
4. Moses Nathaniel (1792-1885); mar. (1) 1820, Caroline Griner (dau. of PHILIP GRINER, REV. SOLDIER of Ga.); mar. (2) April 1836, Catherine (Porter) Dopson. He was Soldier of 1812.

Children by (2) wife:
5. Joshua William Pearce (1801-1864); mar. Mary Trowell.
6. Mary.
7. William.
8. Charles H., mar. (1) Miss Boynton; mar. (2) Lucinda (Tharpe) Lowe.
9. Francis Stephen, mar. Ann Dopson.
10. John G., mar. Jane Dopson.
11. Sarah, mar. James Griner.

(His grave, as a REV. SOLDIER, has been marked by the Briar Creek Chapter, Ga., D. A. R., Sylvania, Ga.)

NOTE: For McCall history, see "McCall-Tidwell and Allied Families" by Ettie Tidwell McCall.

ISAAC McCLENDON, b. 1754 in Scotland; d. Jasper Co., Ga., 1823. Lived in N. C. Moved to Wilkes Co., Ga. Married 1776, Mary Fincher. Was a REV. SOLDIER. Received bounty grant of land in Wilkes Co., Ga. for his services. Had issue.
Child:
1. Freeman (1807-1877), mar. Frances Watts.

NOTE: THOMAS, SR., JACOB, and ISAAC McCLENDON were brothers.

JACOB McCLENDON, b. 1725; d. in Ga. Served as REV. SOLDIER of Ga., under Gen. Clarke and received bounty grant of land for his services. Married Martha —.
Children:
1. Isaac.
2. Samuel.
3. Francis.
4. Dennis.
5. Amos.
6. Jenina.
7. Laney.
8. Penelope.
9. Nancy, b. about 1758; mar. WILLIAM HEARD, REV. SOLDIER of Va.
10. Bartheny.

JOSEPH McCLENDON, JR., b. June 1751; d. Coweta Co., Ga., 1837. Served as private, Ga. Militia, under Gen. Elijah Clarke. Married Olive Blake (dau. of WILLIAM BLAKE, REV. SOLDIER, and his wife Lucy (Allen) Mobley of Elbert Co., Ga.). He was also a Soldier of the War of 1812.

THOMAS McCLENDON, b. Edinburg, Scotland, 1734; d. Henry Co., Ga., 1798. Place of residence during the War was Montgomery Co., N.C. Served in N.C. Militia and received grant of land in Ga. for his services. Married Sarah Cooper, d. in Ala.
Children: (known)
 1. Jacob.
 2. Jeptha.   4. Cynthia.
 3. Wylie.   5. Lydia.
 6. JOSEPH, b. June 1751; d. in Ga., 1837. Served in Ga. as REV. SOLDIER. Received grant of land in Ga. for his services. Mar. (2) Olive Blake.
 7. THOMAS, JR., b. 1758; d. in Ga. Served in N.C. Line as REV. SOLDIER. Married Elizabeth —.
    Child:
    1. Sophia, mar. Joseph Jesse Lasseter (son of TOBIAS LASSETER, REV. SOLDIER of Ga.).

THOMAS McCLENDON, JR., b. 1758; d. in Ga. Served as private, Ga. Militia under Gen. Elijah Clarke. Received bounty grant of land in Ga. for his services. Married Elizabeth —.
Child:
 1. Sophie McClendon, mar. Henry Co., Ga., Joseph Jesse Lasseter.

NOTE: THOMAS, JR. and JOSEPH McCLENDON were sons of THOMAS McCLENDON, SR., REV. SOLDIER of N.C. and Ga.

JAMES McCORMICK, d. Baldwin Co., Ga., 1813. Served in S.C. Militia. Received land in Wilkes Co., Ga. for his services. Married (1) Mary Ann Fletcher, b. 1759, Santee, S.C.; mar. (2) Katherine Oliver.
Child by (1) wife:
 1. Patsey, mar. Samuel Neal.

STEPHEN McCOY, b. in S.C.; d. in Ga. Married Jan. 27, 1792, Nancy McCall (dau. of CHARLES McCALL, REV. SOLDIER of S.C. and Ga.). He was a REV. SOLDIER of S.C. in 1782.
Children: (known)
 1. Robert.
 2. Mary (called Polly), b. 1798; mar. (1) — Ellerbe; (2) Jan. 16, 1820, Reuben H. Jones. Had 9 children.

DAVID McCULLOUGH, b. 1738 in Ireland; d. 1795 in Savannah, Ga. Served as Captain on the cruiser "Rattlesnake" and captured many prizes from the British. Married 1765, Phoebe Boyd.

JOHN McCULLOUGH was an early school teacher in Savannah, Ga. A REV. SOLDIER. Married Nancy Butt; settle in Hancock Co., Ga.

DAVID McCURDY, b. county Antrim, Ireland, 1709; came to America and located in Penn. Was a PATRIOT and REV. SOLDIER of Penn. Married Susan Madden. In 1787 he moved with his son John's family to Ga., where he d. 1833 at the age of 124 years.
Children: (all REV. SOLDIERS of Penn.)
1. JOHN, b. in Westmoreland Co., Penn.; moved to Madison Co., Ga., 1787. Served as private, Penn. Militia. Married Elizabeth Groves.
   Children:
   1. Stephen.
   2. John S., b. 1790; mar. (1) Rebecca Woods; (2) Mary Kelly.
   3. William.
   4. James.   6. Samuel.
   5. Alexander   7. Robert.
2. DAVID.
3. ROBERT.
4. SAMUEL.
5. DANIEL.

ANGUS McCURRY, SR., b. in Scotland; settled in N.C., 1774. Served as private, N.C. Militia. Received bounty land in Elbert (now Hart) Co., Ga. for his services. (Grave marked by the John Benson Chapter, D.A.R., Hartwell, Ga.) Buried Mt. Zion Churchyard. Mar. Catherine.
Children:
1. Margaret, mar. John McDonald.
2. Sarah, mar. John Gordon.
3. John, mar. his cousin Sarah McCurry.
4. Daniel L.
5. Angus, Jr., mar. Elizabeth Davis (dau. of JOHN DAVIS, REV. SOLDIER of Va., and his wife Nancy Womack).

NOTE: Children of John Davis were:
1. John.   7. Nancy.
2. Elizabeth.   8. Polly.
3. Julia.   9. Frances.
4. Lucy.   10. James.
5. Sally.   11. Richard Davis.
6. Lucretia.

WILLIAM McCUTCHEON, b. 1760, Augusta Co., Va.; d. 1827, Spalding Co., Ga. Served as private, Va. Militia. Married (2) Ann Shaw (1772-1832).

ALEXANDER McDONALD, b. 1750; d. McIntosh Co. Served as Sergeant, 2nd S.C. Reg., under Lieut. Col. Francis Marion. Enlisted Nov. 4, 1775. Name on Pay Rolls to Nov. 1, 1779. Married 1771, Christine McLeod. They lived and died in McIntosh Co., Ga.
Children: (known)

1. William, b. 1772; d. in McIntosh Co. Married (1) Feriby Farrar; mar. (2) Zilpha Farrar.
2. Daniel, mar. Margaret Buchan. They d. in Thomas Co., Ga.
3. Alexander.

NOTE: WILLIAM and DANIEL McDONALD were both Soldiers of the War of 1812; enlisted at Darien, Ga.

DANIEL McGEHEE, b. 1747, Amelia Co., Va.; d. 1839, Augusta, Ga. Served as REV. SOLDIER. Married 1770, Jane Brooke Hodnett.

MICAJAH McGEHEE, b. 1735, Augusta Co., Va.; d. July 31, 1811, at the Broad River Settlement, Wilkes Co., Ga. Served with Va. Troops. Received bounty land in Wilkes Co., Ga. for his services. Married 1769, Ann Baytop Scott (dau. of CAPT. JAMES SCOTT, REV. SOLDIER of Va., and later of S. C., and his wife Frances Collier).
Children:
1. Thomas, mar. Betsey Gilmer; moved to Ala.
2. James.
3. Frank.
4. Abner, b. 1779, Prince Edward Co., Va.; d. 1855 in Ala. Mar. (1) Charlotte Spencer; (2) Jane (Gilmer) Johnson (dau. of John Gilmer and his wife Mildred Meriwether, and widow of Thomas Johnson); he mar. (3) Mary Russell Graves.
5. William, mar. (1) Miss Taliaferro; (2) Miss Watkins. Moved to Miss.
6. Edmund, mar. Miss Cosby. Moved to La.
7. Jack, mar. Melinda Hill (dau. of Miles Hill); settled in Wilkes Co., Ga., then Miss.
8. Abram.
9. Hugh, mar. Miss White.
10. Betsey, mar. Abram Hill.
11. Sally, mar. (1) Thomas Hill; mar. (2) as (2) wife, Dyonsius Oliver.
12. Lucinda, mar. Dyonosius Oliver.

NOTE: MICAJAH McGEHEE was the first of the settlers of Wilkes Co., Ga., to plant a peach orchard on the waters of Broad River, and to turn the fruit unto brandy; it was said too that he built the first comfortable house on Broad River.

JOHN McGOUGH, b. in Ireland, 1750; d. 1847, White Plains, Greene Co., Ga. Served in the S. C. Militia from Abbeville Dist. Received bounty land in Ga. Married Elizabeth Carson (dau. of Wm. Carson and Margaret Mill of Abbeville Co., S. C.) (See will of Wm. Carson, 1802).
Child:
1. Robert, b. S. C., Mar. 28, 1786; d. in Ga. Soldier of War of

1812. Married 1810, Sandall Cabaniss. They had 10 children.

JOHN McINTOSH, b. 1755 in McIntosh Co., Ga.; d. in same county, 1826. Served as Capt. and Lieut. Col., Ga. Troops. Married (3) 1781, Sarah Swinton (1761-1799).
Child:
1. William Jackson McIntosh (1782-1863); mar. 1808, Maria Hillary.

MAJOR GEN. LACHLAN McINTOSH, b. in Scotland, Mar. 17, 1725; d. Savannah Ga., Feb. 20, 1806. Came to Ga., 1735. Served as Colonel of the 1st Batt. of Troops appointed from Ga. by the Continental Congress, Jan. 6, 1776. Member of the Council of Safety. Transferred, after his duel with Button Gwinnett at Savannah, Ga., 1779, for services in Va., under Gen. Washington's immediate command. His son CAPT. LACHLAN McINTOSH, Jr. and JOHN BERRIEN were with him, serving as Staff Officers. Served with troops in Western Va. and Penn. Was returned to Ga. as second in command under Gen. Lincoln at the Siege of Savannah. When Charleston, S. C. was surrendered to Gen. Clinton, he was taken prisoner and later exchanged for Gen. O'Hara. Delegate to Continental Congress 1784. Married Mary Threadcraft. Left no descendants in male line.
Children:
1. Catherine McCauley, mar. Charles Harris.
2. Hetty, mar. 1793, John Peter Warde.
3. Lachlan, Jr., d. at Camden Co., Ga., Feb. 15, 1783.

NOTE: In Jan. 1775, a District Congress was held in St. Andrew's Parish, Ga., endorsing the "Resolutions of the Great American Congress). LACHLAN, WILLIAM, and GEORGE McINTOSH, brothers, signed this endorsement.

COL. WILLIAM McINTOSH, b. in Scotland; d. McIntosh Co., Ga. Served as Capt., later Col. of Ga. Continental Troops. Member Provincial Congress 1775. Married Mary Mackey.
Children: (known)
1. Margery (1754-1818); mar. James Spalding. They lived at St. Simons Island, Ga.
2. John, a Soldier of the War of 1812; mar. (1) Agnes Hightower Stevens; (2) Mrs. C. Hillary; (3) Sarah Swinton.

NOTE: (From the "Ga. Gazette") "Died on Sunday last, Dec. 1, 1799, at St. Simon's Island, MAJOR WILLIAM McINTOSH, REV. SOLDIER of Ga. He was born in Ga. 1759, and was just entering his 40th year of age. He obtained his rank and was a distinguished officer in the late Continental Revolution Army of America from the beginning of that war to the end of it. Alas! our firm disinterested PATRIOTS of 1776 are daily decreasing."

JOHN McLAUGHLIN, b. Jan. 1756 in Ireland; came to N. C.; d. in
Warren Co., Ga., 1836. Enlisted 1776; served under Capt. Robert
Smith, Col. Polk, 4th N. C. Reg. In Battles of Sullivan's Island, Brandy-
wine, Germantown. Sergeant under Gen. Davidson and Gen. Rutherford.
On Pension Roll, Warren Co., Ga., 1832. Married Oct. 1825, Eleanor
Williams, widow. She mar. (3) John Matthews. She drew Pension 1856
as widow of a REV. SOLDIER in Ga.

JAMES McMULLEN, SR., b. in Scotland, 1758; came to Halifax,
N. S., then to Mass. Served with Mass. Troops as drummer boy at
Lexington, Mass. Moved to S. C. and served with S. C. Troops. Re-
ceived bounty grant of land. Moved to Bullock Co., Ga. Married Sarah
Minton of S. C., b. 1765. Died Bullock Co., Ga.
Children:
    1. William, b. in S. C., 1782; d. 1847; mar. 1803, Lavinia Fain.
    2. James, b. in Ga., Mar. 6, 1788; mar. 1811, Rebecca Fain.
       Both brothers moved to Lowndes (now Thomas) Co., Ga. (now
       Brooks Co.) 1846.

JOHN McMULLEN, b. 1740 in Dublin, Ireland; came to Orange Co.,
Va.; d. Elbert (now Hart) Co., Ga., Dec. 1817. Served in Col. William
Johnson's Va. Reg. (11th). Was granted land for his services on Swift
Run, Orange Co., Va., by the Commonwealth of Va. Married (1) 1759,
Theodosia Elizabeth Beasley; mar. (2) Elizabeth Stowers (1763-1848
Ga.) (dau. of MARK STOWERS, REV. SOLDIER).
Children by (1) wife:
    1. James.
    2. Mary, mar. Lewis Powell.
    3. PATRICK, REV. SOLDIER; b. 1761 in Va.; d. in Ga.
    4. Catherine.
    5. John.
Children by (2) wife:
    6. Neal.
    7. Jeremiah.
    8. Lewis.
    9. Thomas.
   10. Fielding.
   11. Nancy.
   12. Sinclair, mar. Clarissa Richardson (dau. of AMOS RICHARD-
       SON, REV. SOLDIER of Va. and Ga., and his wife Susan Smith).
   13. Daniel.
   14. Elizabeth.
   15. Lavinia (1806-1896); mar. Archibald Smith
       (Last four children born in Elbert Co., Ga.)

DANIEL McMURPHY, b. 1735 in Ireland; d. Oct. 27, 1817 in Augusta, Ga. (From inscription, City (now Magnolia) Cemetery, Augusta,
Ga.) "Capt. Daniel McMurphy, d. Oct. 27, 1817, aged 82 years. Born

in Antrim, Ireland. Came to Ga. 1756". In 1780 was a member of the Council when it was decided to evacuate Augusta. Removed to Va. with his family, then returned South with Gen. Nathaniel Greene's Army. He was a Captain. Received public thanks for his care of the wounded at Cowpens, Eutaw Springs, and Guilford Court House. Married 1778, Susanna Crossley.
Children:
1. George G. A. Y., mar. Keziah Martin.
2. Ann, mar. Henry Ware.
3. Jane, mar. William A. Cobb.
4. Daniel, mar. Mary Lamb.
5. Barbara, mar. David Reid.

DAVID McNAIR, b. in Scotland, 1748; d. Richmond Co., Ga., 1811. Buried near the old Martin McNair house, near Blythe, Ga. First settled in Va., then N. C., then Ga. He served in the Ga. Militia and Jan. 1, 1784, he received 287.5 acres bounty land for his services in Washington Co., Ga. Married (1) Catherine; (2) Eleanor Martin.
Children by (1) wife:
1. Samuel, mar. Anna McNair.
2. John (twin); mar. Mary Lucky.
3. Daniel (twin).
Children by (2) wife:
4. Anna, mar. Andrew McDonald.
5. Martin, mar. Mary Donnelly.
6. Robert, mar. Mary —.
7. Harriet, mar. John Patterson.
8. James S., mar. Martha Fudge.

ISAAC MIDDLEBROOKS, b. in Md., 1755; d. 1823, Morgan Co., Ga. Served as private, Ga. Troops. Married 1780, Elizabeth Perkins (dau. of ARCHIBALD PERKINS, b. N. C., 1748; d. 1840, Greene Co., Ga.; private N. C. Troops, and his wife Elizabeth Gibbs).
Children:
1. Isaac, Jr., mar. Elizabeth Thompson.
2. James, mar. Miss Hays.
3. Bethenia, mar. Jesse Wade (son of PEYTON WADE, REV. SOLDIER).
4. Fannie, mar. — Thompson.
5. Elizabeth, mar. — Chaney.
6. Lea, mar. — Chaney.
7. Polly, mar. Jeremiah Boggess.

JOHN MIDDLEBROOKS, b. 1755, Caswell Co., N. C.; d. 1830, Newton Co., Ga. Private, Capt. Root's Co., Col. Lytle's Caswell Co., N. C. Troops. Married (1) Mary Ware; (2) Milly Sutton.
Child by (2) wife:
1. Elizabeth (1790-1865); mar. Aquilla Cheney, Jr. (1790-1867)

(son of AQUILLA CHENEY, a REV. SOLDIER of Mass.; and grandson of LEVI CHENEY, a REV. SOLDIER of Mass.).

CHARLES MIDDLETON, b. 1750, Westmoreland Co., Va.; d. Dooly Co., Ga. Served as 2nd Lieut., Ga. Troops. Married 1773, Margaret —.

JOHN MILLEDGE, b. in Savannah, Ga., 1757; d. Feb. 9, 1818. Buried Summerville Cemetery, Augusta, Ga.

ELISHA MILLER, b. 1715 in N. C.; d. 1800 in Ga. Served as private, Ga. Line. Married 1736, Martha Colson (1720-1790).
Child:
1. Sarah Miller (1737-1835); mar. 1755, JOHN CONYERS, b. in Ga., 1725; d. Screven Co., Ga., 1814. Served as Captain under Col. John Thomas in Ga. Militia. REV. SOLDIER.
    Child:
    1. Lucy Conyers, d. 1822; mar. 1790, ROBERT WILLIAMSON, d. 1810, Screven Co., Ga. He received a grant of land in Ga. for his services as a REV. SOLDIER, Ga. Line as Colonel.
        Child:
        1. Benjamin Williamson (1792-1881); mar. 1821, Elizabeth Roberts (1790-1829) (dau. of JAMES ROBERTS (1744-1814) Screven Co., Ga. Served as Lieut., Ga. Militia, and his wife Emily Williamson).

JACOB MILLER, b. in England, 1752; d. Columbia Co., Ga., about 1820. Settled with his parents in Fredericksburg, Va.; there to N. C. and S. C. Served as a private in Capt. George Liddell's S. C. Militia. Received land in Camden Dist., S. C., for his services. Later removed to Columbia, S. C. Married in S. C., Catherine Maloy.
Children:
1. Francis, b. 1773 in S. C.
2. John.
3. Elizabeth, mar. James Bradley.
4. Flora, mar. Harry Skinner.
5. William, mar. Phyllis Ellis.
6. Jacob, Jr., mar. Martha Newsom.
7. Mary, mar. Samuel McNair.
8. Catherine, mar. Hugh Smith.
9. Nancy, mar. William Newsome.
10. Francis II, mar. Hannah Mercer.
11. John II, mar. Mary Dayon.
12. Margaret.

JESSE MILLER, b. 1750, York Co., S. C.; d. 1819 in Ga. Married about 1780, Martha (called Patsey) Rose (dau. of WILLIAM ROSE, REV. SOLDIER of S. C. and Ga., and his wife Amy Langston). Served under Col. Greenberry Lee and received bounty grant of land in Wash-

ington Co., Ga. for his services.
Children: (mentioned in Will)

1. Amy.
2. Susan.
3. Empson.
4. Archibald.
5. William.
6. George.
7. James.
8. Howell.
9. Rebecca.
10. Mary.
11. Margaret.

WILLIAM MILLER, b. in N. C., April 8, 1759; d. in Ware Co., Ga.,
Nov. 27, 1837. Served as private, N. C. Line and in Ga. Militia. Married 1785, Amey Barker, d. Oct. 23, 1831. Buried Kettle Creek
Churchyard, Ware Co., Ga. Received Pension at Jackson Co., Ga.
Children: (known)

1. Mary Ann, b. 1790 in S. C.; mar. as (1) wife, Daniel Blackburn.
2. Barbara, b. Bullock Co., Ga.; mar. as (1) wife, Gen. Thomas
   Hillard, b. Appling Co., Ga., 1805.
3. Elsie, b. 1785; mar. Benjamin Fordham.

THOMAS MILLS, b. Rowan Co., N. C., 1740; d. Screven Co., Ga.
Served as 2nd Lieut., 1st Reg., 2nd Batt., Ga. Militia, 1776. Married
1760, Lucy —.
Child: (others not known)

1. Hannah, mar. 1792, John Lewis Lanier (1762-1812).

JOHN MILNER, b. in England, May 16, 1746; d. Wilkes Co., Ga.,
1812. Served under Gen. Pickens and Gen. Sumpter in S. C., as Capt.
Received bounty grant of land for his services, in Wilkes Co., Ga.
Married 1765, Elizabeth Godwin of Va., d. 1812.
Children:

1. Willis (1768-1790); mar. Sarah Ballard.
2. Pitt, mar. Apsyllah Holmes.
3. Simeon.
4. Benjamin.
5. John (1775-1841); mar. Eunice Callaway; 12 children.
6. Jonathan.
7. Lucy.
8. Nancy.
   Two other daus.

JOHN HAMILTON MILNER, b. in Va., 1769; was a REV. SOLDIER
of Va., at the age of 14 years, and was present at the Battle of Yorktown. Married Miss Fairfax of Va. Moved to Pike Co., Ga., and d.
at Cleola, Harris Co., Ga.

JOHN MILTON, b. 1740, Halifax Co., N. C.; d. Jefferson Co., Ga.,
1803. Moved early to Ga., and was Secretary of the State, 1777, and
in charge of the Great Seal of Ga. After the red-coats overran Ga.,

he secured the State official Records, removed first to Charleston, then New Bern, N.C., then to Md., where they remained until after the war. Obtained in N.C., a commission of Lieut., later Lieut. Col. in Continental Army from Continental Congress. Was taken prisoner at the surrender of Fort Howe and was in prison at St. Augustine, Fla. Was Secretary of State again 1781-3-9. Married Hannah E. Spencer. Charter member of the Cincinnati.

Children:
1. Homer Virgil, Soldier of 1812; mar. Elizabeth Robinson.
2. Anna Maria, b. 1781 in Ga.; mar. Benjamin F. Harris of Ga.

PHILIP MINIS, b. Savannah, Ga., July 11, 1734 (the first male white child born in Ga.); d. there Mar. 6, 1789. Gave active support to the Colonists and named in the Royal Disqualifying Act of 1780. Married Judith Pollock of Rhode Island.

Child:
1. Isaac Minis, b. in Charleston, S.C. (after the British captured Savannah); d. in Philadelphia, Penn., 1856. Married Dinah Cohen of Georgetown, S.C., b. 1787; d. Savannah, Ga., 1874. He was a Soldier of the War of 1812.

NOTE: The parents of Philip Minis were Abraham and Abigail Minis, who, with their daus. Esther and Leah, arrived in Savannah, Ga., July 11, 1733. The history of their organization for the journey in London, England, their trials and tribulations, as well as their successes, until they landed on Ga. soil in 1733, forms one of the interesting romances of the Colonization of the New World.

Judith Pollock was a member of one of the first Jewish families that settled in Rhode Island. It is an interesting fact that Rhode Island and Georgia were the only Colonies where Jews were not prohibited from settling.

THOMAS MITCHELL, b. in England, 1755; d. Henry Co., Ga., 1840. Served as Lieut. in Col. Elijah Clarke's Reg. Married Mary Barnett.

Child:
1. William Mitchell (1777-1859); mar. Eleanor Thompson (1780-1860) (dau. of JOHN THOMPSON, REV. SOLDIER. Served as Corporal of Artillery, N.C. Troops; d. 1831 in Ala., and his wife Eleanor Diamond).

HENRY MITCHELL, Governor of the State of Ga.; d. May 7, 1837, age 75 years. Lived in Warren Co., Ga.; d. in Hancock Co., Ga. Served as Ensign at 18 years of age, in Va. Was wounded and captured at Hanging Rock, N.C.

THOMAS G. MITCHELL, b. 1756 in Va.; d. 1826, Thomas Co., Ga. Served in the 11th Va. Reg., under Col. Daniel Morgan. Received bounty grant of land for his services, in Montgomery Co., Ga. Mar.

1779, Anna Raines (1762-1832) (dau. of NATHANIEL RAINES, REV. SOLDIER; served in Va. Troops; d. 1789 in Va., and his wife Susanna Parham).
Children:
1. Susanna (1785-1850); mar. Littleton Wyche.
2. Amy Goodwin, b. 1782; mar. Gen. Edward Blackshear.
3. Hartwell, mar. Martha Jordan.
4. Nathaniel Raines, mar. Temperance Jordan.
5. Richard (moved from Va. to Old Hartford, Pulaski Co., Ga.); mar. Sophronia Dickey.
6. Thomas Goodwin, Jr. (1793-1862); mar. 1818, Elizabeth Alston (1796-1880) (dau. of JAMES ALSTON (1761-1825), REV. SOLDIER, and his wife Jane Wilcox; and granddau. of PHILIP ALSTON, Col. in REV. Army of N. C.).
7. Tabitha, d. y.
8. John, d. y.
9. Robert, d. y.
10. Nancy, mar. (1) Thomas Gallin; (2) — Stone; (3) E. Alexander.

WILLIAM MITCHELL, b. 1748 in Va.; d. 1819 in Carnesville, Ga. Served as private, Ga. Line. Married 1770, Henrietta Randolph (1752-1824). REV. SOLDIER and Soldier of War of 1812.
Children:
1. Robert, b. 1771.
2. James, b. 1772.
3. William, b. 1772.
4. John, b. 1774.
5. Joseph, b. 1776.
6. Martha, b. 1779.

JAMES MONTGOMERY, b. 1736 in Scotland; d. 1808, Franklin Co., Ga. Served as 2nd Lieut., Ga. Troops. Received bounty land grant in Ga. for his services. Married (1) 1756, Elizabeth McConnell; (2) Susannah Strange.

JAMES MOORE, and wife Alys, of Richmond Co., sold 1787, to Thomas Mitchell, 287.5 acres of land granted him in Greene Co., Sept. 30, 1784, for his services as a REV. SOLDIER.

WILLIAM MORAN, b. in Ireland, came to N. C., removed to Ga. Buried in family cemetery, Hancock Co., Ga.

SAMUEL MORDECAI, b. in S. C.; d. 1820, Savannah, Ga. Served with the S. C. Troops as a grenadier. Married Miss Andrews.
Children: (known)
1. Rachel Mordecai, mar. Isaac Harby (son of Solomon Harby and his wife Rebecca Moses, dau. of MEYER MOSES, b. 1735 in Eng.; d. 1800 in Charleston, S. C.; rendered material aid to the REV. Army and to the cause of the Colonies, and his (2) wife Rachel Andrews).

170

THOMAS MORGAN, b. Buck's Co., Penn.; moved to Orange Co., N. C., then to Ga.; and d. Savannah, Ga., 1778 (son of James Morgan of Penn.). Married in Md., Rebecca Alexander (dau. of Martin and Susanna Alexander of Md.). He served as a REV. SOLDIER and received a bounty grant of land for his services. His wife d. before 1778. Children: (from Will on file, Savannah, Ga.)

1. John.
2. Thomas.
3. Luke.
4. Lemuel.
5. Sarah, mar. John Blair.
6. Ann (called Nancy); mar. BENJAMIN HART, REV. SOLDIER, whose name appears on the Monument erected by the U. S. Government for the men who fought at Kettle Creek on the Kettle Creek Battleground.

NOTE: The Daughters of the American Revolution accept the statement that Thomas, James and Sarah were children of James Morgan.

Sarah Morgan mar. Squire Boone, and they were the parents of Daniel Boone of Ky., b. in Bucks Co., Penn., Feb. 11, 1734 or 1735. The family settled on the Yadkin River, Orange Co., N. C., 1750.

James Morgan, d. in 1782. Married Eleanora —. They were the parents of GEN. DANIEL MORGAN, REV. SOLDIER, b. in 1736. He mar. Abigail Bailey.

Thomas Morgan was the father of Ga.'s War Heroine, NANCY HART.

ROBERT MORROW, b. in Va.; came to Ga., 1785. Obtained bounty land for his services as a REV. SOLDIER. Married in Va., Nancy Herley.
Child:

1. William H. Morrow, b. 1788, Morgan Co., Ga. He was a Soldier of 1812. Married Nancy Elliott, b. Jasper Co., 1790 (dau. of George and Mary (Cloud) Elliott).

OLIVER H. MORTON, b. in Boston, Mass., 1763; d. in Clinton, Ga., 1848. Served on board the Brigantine "Independence", commanded by Col. Simeon Samson, 1776-77. Later he joined the Militia at Plymouth, Mass., under Capt. Partridge. Married Sarah Everette of Ashe Co., N. C.
Children:

1. Silas, mar. (1) Miss Hunter; (2) Selina Archer.
2. Daniel E., mar. Salome Hearst.
3. Mary, mar. Anthony Everett.
4. Ann Elizabeth, mar. Thomas Sharpe.
5. Martha.
6. Sarah.
7. Jesse.

8. Oliver H., Jr., mar. Catherine Harris.
9. Lemuel B. (Samuel), mar. Sarah Feagin.
10. Jane, mar. Edward Chapman.
11. Thomas, mar. Martha Cole.

DR. GEORGE MOSSE, b. in England, 1741; d. in Savannah, Ga., 1807. He settled at St. Helena's Island, S. C. Served in S. C.; was taken prisoner but escaped from the prison ship at Charleston, S. C., and returned to his duties as Surgeon in the Continental Army. Married (1) Miss Martin; (2) Dorothy Phoebe Norton (dau. of Jonathan Norton and his wife Mary Ann Chaplin).
Children:
1. Esther, b. 1772; mar. PAT McKENZIE, served in the Md. Line REV. SOLDIER.
2. Elizabeth, mar. James Stoney.
3. Phoebe, mar. Joseph J. Lawton.
4. Jane, mar. Benjamin Themistocles Dion Lawton.
5. Mary, mar. ADAM FOWLER BRISBANE, REV. SOLDIER.
6. Martha, mar. Alexander J. Lawton.
7. Sarah, mar. Robert G. Norton.

NOTE: Closely connected with the Mosse family is the Lawton family of S. C.

HENRY MOUNGER, d. Wilkes Co., Ga. Served under Gen. Elijah Clarke. Received bounty land for his services. Married —.
Children:
1. Thomas, mar. Lucy Grimes (dau. of JOHN GRIMES, REV. SOLDIER, and his wife Elizabeth Wingfield of Wilkes Co., Ga.).
2. Edwin, b. 1781; Treasurer of the State of Georgia; mar. Frances Clarke, b. 1787 (dau. of COL. ELIJAH CLARKE of Ga., REV. SOLDIER).
3. Henry, moved to Ala.
4. Sidney, mar. Dr. Thomas Wingfield.
5. Mary Ann, mar. Gen. David Terrell.
6. Lucy, mar. Mr. Woodruff.
7. Julia, mar. Mr. Bozeman.
8. Elizabeth, mar. Matthew Talbot.

WILLIAM MURDOCK, b. in Ireland, 1759; d. Franklin Co., Ga., 1840. On Pension Roll, Elbert Co., for services as private. Married Mary Mills.

JOHN MURPHREE, b. 1735, Dublin, Ireland; d. Burke Co., Ga., 1798. Served as private in Capt. John Johnson's Co., Col. John Collins N. C. Reg. Married Martha —.

EDMUND MURPHY (son of Nicholas Murphy, who settled in Augusta,

Ga., 1736), b. 1745, Augusta, Ga.; d. Dec. 10, 1821 in Ga. Enlisted Ga. Troops; was captured by the British, imprisoned at Fort Grierson, later at Fort Augusta, and was only released when Fort Augusta was captured and its garrison surrendered to Gen. Pickens and Lee in 1782. Married (1) Betsey Ann; mar. (2) Feb. 10, 1785, Nancy Rhodes (sister of Aaron Rhodes).
Children by (1) wife:

1. James.   2. Nancy, mar. Aaron Rhodes.

Children by (2) wife:
3. Nicholas, mar. (1) Nancy Collins, d. Mar. 20, 1819; mar. (2) 1820, Nancy Carswell (dau. of JOHN CARSWELL, REV. SOLDIER, and granddau. of ALEXANDER CARSWELL, REV. SOLDIER).
4. Alexander, mar. (1) Elizabeth Kinlow; (2) Elizabeth Allen; (3) Margaret Jones, widow of Henry Seaborn Jones.
5. Leroy, mar. Lucinda Brown.
6. John.
7. Edward.
8. Elizabeth Ann, mar. Robert Evans.
9. Levicy, mar. — Hull.
10. Mary, mar. Charles Rheny.
11. Maria, mar. — Brown.
12. Harriet.

JOHN MYRICK, b. 1751, York Co., Va.; d. 1835, Baldwin Co., Ga. Served as private, Ga. Line. Received bounty grant of land for his services. Married 1778, Amy Goodwin (1755-1786).
Children:
1. Goodwin (1779-1831); mar. 1809, Martha Parham.
2. John.
3. Polly, mar. — Jones.
4. Martha, mar. — Horton.
5. Elizabeth, mar. — Green.
6. Lucy, mar. Drury Jackson.
7. Amy, mar. Thomas Stith Parham.

RENE NAPIER, b. Goochland Co., Va., 1742; d. Elbert Co., Ga., 1807. Married 1765, Rebecca Hart. Received bounty grant of land in Washington Co., Ga., for his services as a REV. SOLDIER of Va., and for services in Ga., under Col. Elijah Clarke.
Children:
1. Thomas, b. Nov. 1, 1768; d. 1839; mar. (1) Tabitha Easter; (2) Nancy Hopson Moultrie. He was a REV. SOLDIER.
   Child:
   1. Leroy, mar. Mathilda L. Moultrie.
2. Skelton, d. unm.
3. Sarah Garland, mar. Matthew Duncan.
4. Walker, mar. Miss Minter.

5. Chloe, mar. — Kelsey.
6. Dollie, mar. — Shorter.
7. Lucy.

THOMAS NAPIER, b. in Va., 1758; d. Bibb Co., Ga., Sept. 30, 1838. Married (1) 1790 in Va., Tabitha Easter, b. 1771, Goochland Co., Va.; d. 1800 (dau. of JAMES EASTER, REV. SOLDIER); he mar. (2) Nancy Moultrie. He was a REV. SOLDIER of Va., and received bounty grant of land in Ga. for his services. Also Soldier of 1812.
Children by (1) wife:
1. Leroy S., mar. Jane Gage.
2. Thomas.   4. Tabitha.
3. Martha.   5. Freeman.
Child by (2) wife:
6. Wm.

BASIL NEAL, b. in Md., 1758; moved to Va., 1775; came to Ga., 1780; d. in Columbia Co., Ga., Oct. 14, 1849. Served as private, Va. Militia, Henry Co., Va., Sept. 20, 1777. Served under Capt. Daniel Chadwell, 1778, Major John Graves. Served two terms in Va., one in Ga. (Grave marked by Ga. D. A. R.) Married (1) Ellen Briscoe (dau. of Dr. Briscoe and Ann Stuart of Va.); mar. (2) 1825, Sarah Hull Greene (1798-1875) (dau. of McKEEN GREENE, JR., REV. SOLDIER of Ga., and his wife Eleanor McCall, dau. of CHARLES McCALL, REV. SOLDIER of S. C. and Ga.).
Children by (2) wife:
1. Sarah Jane, mar. Lycurgus Rees.
2. Amanda, mar. Simpson Booker.
3. Fannie, mar. Jeremiah Jones.
4. Basil Lewellyn, d. 1927; mar. Martha Palmer.
5. Augustus A., mar. Scott Forston.

DAVID NEAL of Warren Co., Ga. Served as Capt., 1st Ga. Batt., under Major John Lawson, Commander Ga. Troops.

JAMES NEAL, d. Warren Co., Ga. A REV. SOLDIER. Married Mary Rucker.

THOMAS NEAL, d. Warren Co., Ga., 1799.

THOMAS NEAL, b. N. C.; d. in Ga., 1807. Served as a REV. SOLDIER. Married Sarah —.
Children:
1. Polly Gardner.
2. Diana.   6. Rebecca.
3. Esther.   7. Patsey.
4. Betsey.   8. Drucilla.
5. Sally.   9. Elisha.

JOHN NEELY, b. in Ireland, 1744; d. Coweta Co., Ga., 1837, at the age of 93. Enlisted as a REV. SOLDIER while a resident of Waxham Settlement, S. C., 1776. Private under Capt. Eli Kershaw, 3rd S. C. Reg.; was in Ga., 10 months, under Capt. Pettigrew, Col. Jack's Reg.; with State Troops in S. C., wounded in an engagement with the Tories At Camden, S. C. Received Pension in 1832, while a resident of Coweta Co., Ga.

JEREMIAH NELSON, REV. SOLDIER. Received bounty grant of 490 acres of land for Rev. services in Irwin Co., Ga., Mar. 28, 1820, signed George M. Troup, Governor. He was living in Lucas Dist., Hancock Co., Ga., 1820.

THOMAS NELSON, b. Rutherford Co., N. C.; d. Pike Co., Ga., 1846. Took Oath of Allegiance in S. C., 1776. Served with S. C. Troops. Received bounty grant of land in Ga. Married Susan Woodward.

WILLIAM NEVER, b. in 1758; d. on a visit to Ala., 1852. Served as a private in Va. Troops, seven years. Also Soldier of the War of 1812. Came to Ga., 1787, and settled in Putnam Co. Married Miss Ballard in Va. (1768–1850).
Children:
1. William.
2. Elizabeth, mar. Capt. Jones.
3. John, mar. (1) Garnett Smith; (2) Julia Smith (dau. of David Smith of Va. and Jones Co., Ga.).
4. Alsy.
5. Mary, mar. William Hardin.
6. Charlotte.
7. Daniel.

JOHN NEVILLE, JR., b. in Va., 1750; d. in Bullock Co., Ga., July 30, 1804. Was a REV. SOLDIER, private. Place of residence during the Rev. War, Va. and S. C. Married about 1768, Frances Ann Nixon (1752–1815). Children mentioned in Will made April 12, 1803 were: son Jacob and four daughters.
Children:
1. Jacob Neville, b. 1769; d. 1873 (age 104 years) at Statesboro, Ga.; mar. Nov. 11, 1798, in Bullock Co., Nicey Henderson (1780–1889, age 109 years).

JOHN NEWTON, b. in Penn., Feb. 20, 1759; d. in Lexington, Oglethorpe Co., Ga. Buried under the pulpit of the Presbyterian Church at Lexington, Ga. Served as private and Chaplain, N. C. Troops. Mar. in N. C., 1783, Catherine Lourance, b. 1756; d. Athens, Ga., 1846. They had 3 sons and 3 daus.

REV. JOHN NEWTON, b. Aug. 7, 1732; d. Nov. 20, 1790. Served as a

REV. SOLDIER. Married 1753, Keziah Dorsett.
Children:
1. JOHN, JR., b. July 5, 1755; d. as a REV. SOLDIER, in a British prison. A monument was erected to his memory by the City of Savannah, Ga.
2. Jemina, b. 1757.
3. Philip Dorsett, b. 1760.
4. James.
5. MOSES, b. Aug. 14, 1766; d. 1826. Married 1793, Elizabeth Hudspeth. He was a REV. SOLDIER, served under his father, REV. JOHN NEWTON; was at Savannah, Ga., and was taken prisoner at Charleston, S. C.
    Children:
    1. Mary Early, mar. James Marcellus Johns.
    2. John Hamlin, mar. Mary Jordan.
    3. Isaac.
    4. Nancy.
    5. Elizabeth, mar. Andrew Howard.
    6. Grace, mar. George Baskerville Lewis.
    7. Sarah Baker.
    (His grave was marked by Ga. D. A. R.)

WILLIAM NIBLACK, b. 1761 in N. C.; d. Camden Co., Ga., 1828. Served as private, N. C. Line. Married Diana Tison.

JOHN NICHOLSON, b. in Scotland; d. in Oglethorpe Co., Ga., 1818. Moved to Mecklinburg Co., N. C. Served as private, N. C. Troops. Married (1) 1770 in N. C., Penelope Mann of Edgecomb Co., N. C., d. before 1802. They moved to Oglethorpe Co., Ga. He mar. (2) Susan Brown.
Children by (1) wife:
1. John.
2. George.
3. Joseph.
4. Jennie (or Jane), mar. David McLaughlin.
5. Peggy.
6. Sally.
7. Mary.
8. Ann.

WILLIAM NORMAN, b. in Fauquier Co., Va.; d. Lincoln Co., Ga. Enlisted as a private, 1776, in Capt. George Stubblefield's Co., 5th Va. Reg., under Lieut. Col. Josiah Parks. Wounded at the Battle of Brandywine. Married Miss Shepherd.

WILLIAM NORTHERN, b. in Va.; came to Edgecombe Co., N. C. Served with N. C. Troops. Married Margaret Dicken of N. C. They moved to Powellton, Ga., 1800.

Child:
1. Peter Northern, b. 1794 in N. C.; d. 1863 in Ga. Was Soldier of War of 1812. Married, 1817, Maria Davis.
   Child:
   1. William Jonathan Northern was Governor of Ga.

THOMAS NORTON, b. in N. C.; d. 1801, Oglethorpe Co., Ga. (Will made June 18, 1801 on file Lexington, Ga.) Served as private in N. C. Line, under Capt. Carr. Drew land for his services in Griffin's Dist., DeKalb Co., Ga., in Cherokee Lattery. Married Mary —, about 1760.
Children: (mentioned in will)
1. John.
2. James.
3. William (1765-1843); mar. Mary Landrum.

WILLIAM NORTON, b. in S. C., 1744; d. Savannah, Ga., 1800. Served with S. C. Troops. Married Mary Godfrey in S. C.
Children:
1. Alexander.
2. Robert Godfrey, b. Bluffton Beaufort Dist., S. C.; married his cousin Sarah Mosse (dau. of GEORGE MOSSE, REV. SOLDIER, and his wife Dorothy Phoebe Norton). He served as private, S. C. Troops.
   Child:
   1. Alexander Robert Norton, b. in S. C., 1812; d. 1869. Married Julia Elizabeth Green (dau. of Dr. John Green of Screven Co., Ga. He and his wife are buried in Burke Churchyard on Briar Creek, Screven Co., Ga.).

GEORGE W. NORWOOD, b. 1760 in N. C.; d. 1840 in Ga. Drew a Pension 1833, living in Campbell (now Fulton) Co., Ga. Served as Orderly Sergeant in Capt. James Richard's Co., Col. Benj. Seawell's N. C. Reg. Married Marish Wall.

JOHN NUNNALLY, b. Va., Feb. 12, 1758; d. June 10, 1825, Clarke Co., Ga. Served in the 1st and 11th Va. Reg. Married Susan Virginia Burton (called Sukey), b. Oct. 25, 1766; d. Mar. 14, 1849. Both are buried in Old Cemetery near Bishop, Oconee Co., Ga. His widow received Pension for his services as a REV. SOLDIER. They had issue.

JAMES FRANKLIN NUNNELEE, b. in Va., Jan. 3, 1760; d. in Elbert Co., Ga., Feb. 12, 1838. Served as a REV. SOLDIER. Married (1) Keziah —; mar. (2) Oct. 28, 1810, Jane Nash.
Children by (1) wife:
1. Willis.
2. Howell.
3. Osamin.
4. Simeon.
5. Charlotte, mar. — Bentley.
6. Sarah, mar. — Bolton.
Children by (2) wife:

7. Elizabeth (1812-1888); mar. 1825, Nicholas Burton.
8. Nancy (1813-1880); mar. 1830, Abraham Burton.
9. Martha, mar. 1830, Bud Wall.
10. Sophia, mar. 1833, Henry P. Mattox.
11. James Franklin, Jr., mar. 1836, Rachel McKinley.
12. Jane, mar. James Nelms.
13. Frances Elizabeth, mar. Richard Ware Snellings.

WILLIAM NUNNELEE (name also spelled Nunnally), b. Chester-field Co., Va.; d. 1804 Elbert Co., Ga. Served as a REV. SOLDIER of Va. Married in Va., Susanna Hubbard (dau. of Thomas Hubbard).
Children:
1. JAMES FRANKLIN, b. in Va., Jan. 3, 1760; d. Elbert Co., Ga., Feb. 12, 1838; mar. (1) Keziah —; (2) Jane Nash.
2. Elizabeth, mar. Col. Robert Middleton.
3. Nancy, mar. THOMAS BURTON, b. in Va.; d. 1828, Petersburg, Ga. He served as private, Ga. Troops, under Col. Elijah Clarke.
   Children:
   1. Leroy.   3. Malinda, mar. John Chillers.
   2. Nicholas.   4. Sophia.
4. Priscilla, mar. WILLIAM HATCHER, REV. SOLDIER.
5. Walter.

WILLIAM OAKMAN was living in Savannah, Ga. during the Rev. War; served in 2nd Ga. Reg., under Lieut. Francis Tennille. Married Mary Lilybridge. They had twin sons, b. in Savannah, Ga., Oct. 12, 1792.
Children:
1. William Henry, d. 1860; married 1820, Eliza Ann Hagood, b. 1800 near Barnwell, S. C. They had 15 children.
2. Henry William, d. 1821; married Frances Jennings; 2 children.

THOMAS OGLESBY, b. in Va. 1750; d. Elbert Co., Ga., 1832. Served as private, Ga. Troops. Drew bounty land. Married 1776, Miss Parteis, d. 1825.
Children:
1. William (1777-1852); mar. (1) Mary Christian; (2) Paulina Wiley.
2. Leroy.
3. Garrett, mar. Ruth Bradley.
4. Drury.
5. Thomas, Jr.
6. Lindsay.
7. George.
8. Robert.
9. James.
10. Mary Lucinda, mar. William C. Morgan, 1819.

WILLIAM OGLETREE (or Oglitree), b. in Scotland, 1764; d. in Wilkes Co., Ga., 1837. (Grave marked by Ga. D. A. R.) Served as private, Va. Line. Married Mary (or Martha) Elizabeth Bird (1766-1830), Wilkes Co., Ga.
Children:
1. Philemon, mar. (1) Miss Harper; (2) Miss Harper; (3) Elizabeth Crawford Glynn Tigner.
2. Absolem, b. 1811 in Ga.; mar. Matilda Stewart (dau. of Thomas and Nancy (Russell) Stewart of Oglethorpe Co., Ga.).
3. James.
4. John.
5. Fannie.
6. David, mar. Frances Fletcher.
7. Elizabeth Bird, mar. Hiram Phinazee.
8. Mary, mar. Harris Phinazee.

DYONISIUS OLIVER (son of Thomas Oliver and wife Mary Mc Carty), b. in Va., 1735; d. in Wilkes Co., Ga., 1808. He lived from 1793 on Wahatchie Creek near Stencombs Meeting House, where he d. and was buried. Served as Captain of a privateer of Ga.; was with Gen. Lincoln at Kettle Creek, was captured and imprisoned by the British. Married (1) in Va., 1758, Mary Ann Winfrey (dau. of Valentine Winfrey of Chesterfield Co., Va.); they moved before 1779 through S. C. to Wilkes Co. (now Elbert Co.), Ga. She was b. 1740 in Va.; d. 1802, Elbert Co., Ga. He mar. (2) Jane Jackson of S. C.
Children by (1) wife:
1. Peter, b. 1763; mar. his cousin Betty Oliver (dau. of Francis Oliver of Va.
   Child: (only son)
   1. Dyonisius Oliver, moved to Miss.
2. John (1765-1816); mar. his cousin Frances Thompson (dau. of William and Mary (Wells) Thompson).
3. James, b. 1767; mar. (1) Mary Thompson (dau. of William and Mary (Wells) Thompson); mar. (2) Lucy Clark (dau. of Christopher Clark).
4. Dyonisius, Jr., b. 1768; mar. his cousin Frances Oliver (dau. of Francis Oliver of Va.). They lived Edgefield Dist., S. C.
5. Thomas Winfrey, mar. Mary Clark (dau. of Christopher Clark), both are buried in the yard of the "Old Tavern", Elberton, Ga.
6. William, mar. (1) Barbara Tait; (2) Frances Ragland.
7. Eleanor, mar. John Goss of Ga.
8. Martha, b. 1773; mar. her cousin, Thomas Hancock of S. C.
9. Florence McCarty, a Methodist minister, b. in Va., 1775; mar. 1796, Elbert Co., Ga., Susanna Clark (dau. of Christopher Clark); moved to Ala.
10. Frances, mar. William T. Cook of Va.
Child by (2) wife:
11. Jackson, mar. Polly Maxwell.

MAJOR JAMES BRUSH OLIVER of London, England. He assembled and equipped his own Co. of REV. SOLDIERS. Buried in old St. Paul's Churchyard, Augusta, Ga.

WILLIAM OSBORNE, b. in Ga., 1749; d. in Ga., 1796. Served as private, 3rd Batt., Ga. Reg. Married Mary — .

THOMAS PACE, b. in N. C., 1745; lived in N. C. until 1768, when he moved to Ga., and was ganted land in St. Paul's Parish. He. served as an Officer in Ga. Troops and was on the British Black list in Ga. as a "Rebel Officer". Was granted land in Washington Co., Ga. He moved back to N. C., and died there 1795. Married Cebelle Mathews. She mar. (2) Benjamin Carr, and moved back to Ga., settled in Newton Co. with her 8 children by (1) husband.
Children:
1. William.
2. Nannie.
3. John.
4. Mary.
5. Martha.
6. James.
7. Elizabeth.
8. Hardy.

MAJOR WILLIAM PAGE of St. Simon's Island, a REV. SOLDIER of S. C.
Child: (only)
1. Anna Matilda Page, mar. 1824, Thomas Butler King, b. 1797, Mass.; d. Waresboro, Ga., 1864 (son of CAPT. DANIEL KING, b. 1749 in Mass.; d. 1815, Mass., REV. SOLDIER at the Alarm at Lexington, and his wife Hannah Lord of New London, Conn.).

GEORGE PALMER, b. 1750, N. C.; d. 1826, Burke Co., Ga. Served as private in 4th Ga. Batt. Married Mary Cureton.

RICHARD PARHAM, REV. SOLDIER of Ga., buried in family Cemetery, 13 miles east of Milledgeville, Baldwin Co., Ga.

EZEKIEL EVANS PARKE, b. in Va., 1757; d. Greensboro, Ga., 1826. Served under Gen. Nathaniel Greene; wounded at the Battle of Guilford Court House. Married Susan Smythe.
Children:
1. James, mar. Frances Wingfield.
2. Griffen, mar. Louise Starke.
3. Richard, mar. Frances Redd.
4. Joseph.
5. Thomas Payton, mar. Caroline Russell.
6. Katherine, mar. Eugene Van Valkinburg.
7. Lucinda, mar. Peter Jones Williams.

DANIEL PARKER, b. in Albemarle Co., Va.; d. in Ga., Aug. 14, 1844. Entered service at Chatham Co., N. C., Sept. 15, 1780, under Capt. Mark

Patterson; also served under Capt. William Griffin. Received Pension for his services. Married Mary Lucy White, b. in Va., 1766; d. Upson Co., Ga., Nov. 14, 1845. Mentions his wife Lucy and the following children in his will, made Dec. 15, 1840, pro. Sept. 6, 1844.
Children:
1. Mary, mar. — Hudman.
2. Nancy, mar. — Meadows.
3. Faythia, mar. — Dark.
4. Stephen.
5. Daniel, Jr.
6. Philemon.
7. Sherwood.
8. Lucy.
9. Thomas.
10. Susanna, mar. — Meadows.

DAVID PARKER of Baldwin Co., drew 287.5 acres of land for his services as a REV. SOLDIER. Paid taxes also, 1809, in Hancock Co.

JACOB PARKER (son of George and Sarah Parker of Md.), b. Somerset Co., Md., 1724; d. Greene Co., Ga., 1791. Served in 2nd Md. Reg. Moved to Hancock Co., Ga., on Rocky Creek, 1790. Married 1748, Mary Smith (dau. of George and Judith (Turner) Smith of Md.).
Children:
1. Elisha, remained in Md.
2. George, mar. 1780, Rhoda Evans of Md.
3. Jacob, Jr., mar. widow Spurlock of Ga.
4. Nancy, mar. Wm. Beauchamp of Md. They came to Ga.
5. Rhoda.
6. Polly, mar. 1793, Chris Simmonds in Ga.
7. Judith, mar. 1786 in Md., PHILIP TURNER, REV. SOLDIER. They came to Ga. He was the youngest son of ZADOC TURNER, SR., REV. SOLDIER of Md., who d. at the home of his son in Hancock Co., Ga., 1819, and his wife Sarah Hicks).

JOHN PARKER, b. 1740, Sussex Co., Delaware; d. 1825 in Ga. Served as private under Captains Vaughan, Moore and Pope, Col. Haskett, Del. Line. Married 1760, Sarah Gordy (1743-1793).
Children:
1. Hannah.
2. Jacob.
3. Priscilla.
4. John.
5. Elizabeth.
6. Mary.
7. William.
8. Peter.
9. Elisha.

MOSES PARKER, b. in Mass., 1725; came to Chowan Co., N. C., about 1750, then Cheran Dist., S. C., 1760. Served as private, S. C. Militia and also furnished forage and provisions to the Militia. Married Susanna —. Moved to Greene Co., Ga., where ʰ⌐ d. Dec. 1798.
Child:
1. MOSES PARKER, JR., b. 1748 in Mass.; d. Greene Co., Ga., 1799. Served as private, S. C. Militia. Married (1) Miss Breedlove; (2) Ann Parker.

Children by (2) wife:
1. John.
2. Daniel.
3. Priscilla Ann (1796-1880).

HENRY PARKS, b. Albemarle Co., Va., May 31, 1758; d. May 18, 1845 in Franklin Co., Ga. Served with the Continental Army in Va. Received land grant in Ga. for his services. Married (1) 1782, Martha Justice (1753-1818); mar. (2) Emma Crutchfield; mar. (3) Sarah Pullian. Children by (1) wife:
1. John, b. 1784; mar. Betty Meadows.
2. Henry, Jr., mar. Mary Ann Dorsey.
3. Mary (Polly), b. 1797; mar. 1814, Joshua Baker (1794-1834).
4. Elizabeth, mar. James Hargroves.
5. Charles, d. y.
6. William Justice, mar. (1) Naomi Pickett; (2) Dolly Varden, widow; (3) Mrs. Burgess.
   Children by (2) wife:
   1. Frank A.
   2. Sallie, mar. Levi Shankle.

SAMUEL PARSONS, b. 1762 in Va.; d. 1832, Fayette Co., Ga. Served as private, Va. Line. Was at the Battle of Guilford Court House and was at the surrender at Yorktown. Married Ann —.
Child:
1. Catherine Parsons (1784-1855); mar. Pernal Patrick, b. in Md., 1776; d. in Ga., 1856 (son of JOHN PATRICK, b. in Ireland, 1751, a REV. SOLDIER of S. C.).

WILLIAM PATMAN, b. 1760 in Henrico Co., Va.; d. Lexington, Ga., 1821. Served as Sergeant of Artillery 3 years, Va. Line. Obtained grant of land in Ga. for his services. Married Susanna Biggers.
Children:
1. Mary.
2. John.
3. Elizabeth.
4. Watson.
5. James.
6. Nancy.
7. Susannah.

JOHN PATTERSON, b. in Ireland, 1736; d. Burke Co., Ga., 1822. Served as private in Capt. Abner Beckham's Co., Col. John Twiggs Ga. Reg. Married Catherine Mossman.

WILLIAM PATTERSON, b. in Ga., 1743; d. in Jefferson Co., Ga., 1843. Enlisted from St. George's Parish, Ga., at the beginning of War. Married 1765, Nancy Mossman.

RICHARD PAULETT, b. 1753, in Va.; d. 1835, Campbell Co. Ensign 1778; Lieut. under Col. Francis Taylor, Va. Continental Line. Married

Catherine Smith.

JOHN PEACE, b. on the voyage of his parents to America; d. Hancock Co., Ga. Served as private, Va. Continental Line. Married in N. C., Elizabeth Wade, b. in Wales. Moved to Ga. and received bounty grant of land for his services. They had 8 children.
Children:
1. Major, b. 1790, N. C.; d. 1854; mar. (1) Biddy Gilleland; (2) Sarah Vincent.
2. John.
3. Daniel.
4. Elizabeth, mar. — Johnson.
5. Nancy, mar. Lemuel Lovett.
6. Jane, mar. Peter Bray.
7. Martha, mar. Robert McCook.
8. Temperance, mar. Wm. Brewster.

JOSHUA PEARCE, JR. (son of Joshua and Hannah Pearce) (name sometimes spelled Pierce), was b. in St. Mathews Parish (now Screven Co.), Ga.; d. 1810 on a visit to his brother WILLIAM PEARCE, REV. SOLDIER of Ga., who moved to Miss., and his wife Sarah Bray. They moved later to La. His brother STEPHEN PEARCE was also a REV. SOLDIER of Ga. All lived in Effingham Co., Ga. (later Screven Co.). Joshua Pearce, Jr. mar. (1) Hannah —.
Children:
1. Mary, mar. as (2) wife, WILLIAM McCALL, REV. SOLDIER of Ga.
2. Sarah, mar. his brother Francis McCall, as (1) wife.
JOSHUA PEARCE, JR. was a REV. SOLDIER of Ga. and S. C. Received a grant of land in Effingham Co. for his services. He mar. (2) Miss Ann Bray.

WILLIAM PEARMAN, b. in Va., 1760; d. after 1802 in Ga. Served as Sergeant, Capt. Ree's Co.; also under Capt. John Peyton's Va. Troops. Married Miss Weakley.
Children:
1. Elizabeth, mar. W. S. Douglas.
2. Robert, mar. Elizabeth (Worthington ?).
3. Mary, mar. A. M. Duke.
4. Sarah, mar. Henry Duke.
5. Susan, mar. Thomas Douglas.
6. William.
7. Samuel.
8. Weakley.

JOHN PECK, b. in Va., 1743; d. in Ga., 1800. Was in Ga. Troops under Col. Elijah Clarke and was at the Siege of Augusta. Married Tabitha Peck.

HENRY PEEK, b. in Va., Dec. 25, 1764; d. 1855 in Ga. Married Taliaferro Co., Ga., 1798, Polly Lockett. Enlisted Jan. 7, 1781 in Capt. John Peck's Co., Col. Elijah Clarke's Reg., Ga. Troops. Was at the Siege of Augusta.
Children:
1. William Winfrey, mar. Elizabeth Reed.
2. James, mar. Polly Swain.
3. Thomas, mar. Miss Jarrold.
4. Elizabeth.
5. Sarah, mar. Adam Hunter.
6. Mary, mar. — Trippe.

WILLIAM PENN, b. 1760, Charles City, Md.; d. 1836 in Ga. Served in Ga. Line. Buried Baptist Cemetery, Monticello, Ga. Engraved on his tombstone is an account of his services as a REV. SOLDIER. He married Martha A. Slade (1793-1883).

ARCHIBALD PERKINS, b. in N. C., 1746; d. in Greene Co., Ga. Served as private, N. C. Troops. Married Elizabeth Gibbs.
Child:
1. Elizabeth Perkins, b. 1766; mar. 1780, ISAAC MIDDLEBROOKS, b. 1755 in Va.; d. 1823, Morgan Co., Ga., a REV. SOLDIER.

JOHN PERKINS, and wife Sarah, of Richmond Co., granted 287. 5 acres of land in Washington Co., 1785.

JAMES PERRY, b. 1759 in N. C.; d. 1843, Jasper Co., Ga. Served as private, N. C. Line. Received bounty grant of land for his services in Jasper Co. (formerly Baldwin), Ga. Married Elizabeth Valentine (1768-1853).

JONES PERSONS, b. 1760, Bute Co., N. C.; d. 1850, Upson Co., Ga. Served as private, N. C. Line from Bute Co. Received bounty land in Ga. for his services. Married Diana Neal in 1790.
Children:
1. Thomas, mar. Nancy Freeman.
2. Pinckney, mar. Sarah Ann Williams.
3. Benjamin.
4. Lovett, mar. Malinda Lyons.
5. Jones, Jr., mar. Miss Neal.
6. Martha, mar. Stanley Purefoy.
7. Mary, mar. — Allison.
8. Sarah, mar. — Smith.

WILLIAM PETERS, an original settler of Lowndes Co., Ga., was granted Pension 1846 as a REV. SOLDIER, while residing in Lowndes Co., Ga.

ISHAM PHILIPS, b. in Ga., 1741; d. in Henry Co., Ga., 1837. Served as a private under Col. Clarke, Ga. Militia. Married Mary Dawson.

GEORGE PHILLIPS, b. in Va., 1758; d. 1849 in Ga. Served as private, Va. Line. Married 1790, Sarah Lavell.

ISAAC PHILLIPS, b. 1741, Savannah, Ga.; d. 1837, Henry Co., Ga. Served as private, Ga. Troops. Married Mary Dawson.

MARK PHILLIPS, b. in Ireland, 1755; d. 1839 in Ga. Applied for Pension, 1819, which was granted. Served as private, N. C. Militia, under Capt. Samuel Jones. Married Raney Moore, b. 1753.

JOHN PHINAZEE, b. in Ireland, 1760; d. Harris Co., Ga., 1837. Served as private, S. C. Line. Received bounty grant of land for his services, in Ga. Married 1788, Sarah Harris (1765-1856).
Children:
1. William, mar. Jane Potts.
2. James, mar. Polly Baldwin.
3. Harris, mar. Mary Ogletree.
4. Jonathan, moved to California.
5. Hiram (1802-1883); mar. Elizabeth Bird Ogletree (1803-1884). They had 9 children.
6. Rachel, mar. Joseph Bell.
7. Margaret, mar. George Bell.
8. Sallie, mar. Nathan Bramblett.
9. Polly, mar. Griffin Read.
10. Elizabeth, mar. Benjamin Read.
11. Mahala, mar. (1) Arthur Herring; (2) — Watts.

WILLIAM PIERCE (or Pearce), b. in Ga., 1740; d. Dec. 10, 1789, Savannah, Ga. He entered the Continental Army and became aide-de-camp to Gen. Nathaniel Greene. Member Sons of Liberty, Savannah, Ga. Charter member, Society of the Cincinnati. Married Charlotte Fenwick (dau. of Edward Fenwick of S. C.). After his death, she mar. (2) EBENEZER JACKSON of Mass., REV. SOLDIER (son of GEN. MICHAEL JACKSON of Mass.). In 1781, Continental Congress presented a sword to MAJOR WILLIAM PIERCE for his services.
Child: (only)
1. WILLIAM LEIGH PIERCE, of Savannah, Ga., a REV. SOLDIER of Effingham Co., Ga. His homestead was built on the original grant of land given to him by George III of England. This home was made doubly historic, for in 1825, his son Stephen Pearce entertained Marquis de La Fayette on his visit to the South.

NOTE: In 1791, Gen. George Washington, on his memorable visit to Georgia, spent the night at the home of JOSHUA PEARCE (Pierce), brother of MAJOR WILLIAM PIERCE.

WILLIAM PILCHER, b. in N. C.; came to Wilkes Co., Ga. Killed by the Tories. Buried in (now Glascock Co.), Ga.

WILLIAM PINDAR, b. in Wales; d. 1793, Savannah, Ga. Was a PATRIOT. Supplied the Continental Troops with provisions during the Siege of Savannah. When the British captured Savannah, they burned his home and made him prisoner. He was sent to Nassau Island where he remained until the end of the War. He married Rebecca Huchins, d. 1799.

JOHN PITTMAN, b. 1723 in Va. Settled in S. C., 1771; d. Richmond Co., Ga., April 19, 1785. Served in 4th Artillery, S. C. Reg., under Capt. Harman Davis. Married 1747, in Va., Mary (called Polly) Rowe (or Bow). She was a REV. PATRIOT and was crippled by the Tories. Children:

1. BUCKNER PITTMAN, b. 1738; d. after 1805, Adams Co., Mo. A REV. SOLDIER of Ga.
2. Lucy (1750-1774).
3. Sarah (1763-1771).
4. JOHN PITTMAN, JR., b. 1752. A REV. SOLDIER. Mar. Eunice Marshall (dau. of REV. DANIEL MARSHALL, REV. SOLDIER of Ga.).
5. Mary Pittman, b. 1754; mar. PELEG ROGERS, a REV. SOLDIER. Had 10 children.
6. JAMES PITTMAN (1756-1850). Received Pension as a REV. SOLDIER. Mar. Martha Taylor. Had 13 children.
7. Patsey, b. 1760; mar. David Langston of S. C.
8. Zilpha, b. 1762; mar. Blanton Nobles.
9. PHILIP PITTMAN (1765-1849, Decatur Co., Ga.). A REV. SOLDIER at 16 years of age. Married 1792, Epsie Jasper.
10. Timothy, b. 1767; d. 1854 in Ga.
11. Grace, mar. Jamerson Andrews.

JAMES PITTMAN, b. Amelia Co., Va., Mar. 4, 1756; d. Madison Co., Ga., 1850. Enlisted Columbia Co., Ga. Served under Capt. Germaine, Col. Marbury's S. C. Reg., under Capt. Wm. Grier and under Col. Clarke on his expedition to Fla. Served in Va., 1781. Pensioned as private and Lieut., 1833 at Madison Co., Ga. Married July 5, 1781, Martha Taylor, b. May 4, 1763; d. 185-, in Va. (dau. of JAMES and Nancy (Owen) Taylor of Henry Co., Va., a REV. SOLDIER of Va., d. in Tenn.).
Children:

1. John Green (1782-1873); mar. 1804, Polly Moore (dau. of JOHN MOORE, REV. SOLDIER).
2. Pleasant Owen, mar. Susanna Benton.
3. Martin Hughes, mar. Nancy Smith.
4. James, d. in Miss; mar. Nancy Benton.
5. Elizabeth Alice, d. in Ala.; mar. Samuel Barnett.

6. Nancy, mar. Silas Smith.
7. Lucinda, mar. Henry Harris.
8. Timothy F., mar. Mary Ann Harris.
9. Sarah Ann, mar. Sampson Lay.
10. Martha Diana, mar. Abner Wells.
11. Noah Washington, mar. (1) Lucinda Strickland; (2) Martha Smith.
12. America Taylor (1805-1872); mar. Benjamin Woods.
13. Teresa, mar. Wilson Strickland.

JOHN PITTS, b. in N. C., 1740; was murdered by the Tories in (Effingham Co.), Ga., 1787. Served as Capt., 1st Reg., N. C. Militia, under Col. Samuel Jarvis. Married 1781, Frances Griffin. She mar. (2) — Marks.
Children:
1. Tabitha (1782-1863); mar. 1799, Obediah Edwards (1777-1857) (son of WILLIAM EDWARDS, a REV. SOLDIER, and his wife Chloe Stokes).
2. Lorena.
3. Daniel, moved to Tenn.
4. Hardy Griffin (1787-1840); mar. (1) widow Porter (she received part of Benjamin Porter's estate); mar. (2) Elizabeth Scruggs (dau. of Gross Scruggs). Buried Colonial Cemetery, Savannah, Ga.
5. Elizabeth, mar. DANIEL DAMPIER (1757-1847), a REV. SOLDIER.

WILLIAM POLLARD, b. 1737; d. 1802, in Ga. A REV. SOLDIER.
Married Tabitha Collins.
Children:
1. Frances, b. 1784; mar. John S. Shorpshire.
2. Joseph.
3. Sallie, mar. John Jeffries.

JAMES PONDER, b. in S. C.; d. Screven Co., Ga., 1826. Married Rebecca —, d. Screven Co., Ga. He served as Commissary and Wagon Master, S. C. Troops. Received pay for REV. service in S. C., June 10, 1785.
Child:
1. Mary Ponder, mar. (1) Thomas Roberts, Soldier of 1812 (son of ELIAS ROBERTS, REV. SOLDIER of S. C. and Ga., and his wife Mary Rue); mar. (2) George Smith of Screven Co., Ga.
   Children:
   1. Elias, mar. Nancy Nevils.
   2. Elizabeth, mar. Charles H. Johnson.
   3. Patience, mar. Charles H. Nessmith.
   4. Polly Ann, mar. James Cone.

DUDLEY POOL, b. in Va., 1753; d. 1826, Wilkes Co., Ga. Received bounty land grant in Wilkes Co., Ga. for his services. Married Elizabeth Hyde.

HENRY POOL, b. in England, 1759; d. 1850. Married (1) in England, Susan Ratchett. They came to America. He mar. (2) Mary Hutchinson; mar. (3) Eleanor Hutchinson. Had many children. He served as REV. SOLDIER and was present at the Battles of Kettle Creek, King's Mt., Cheraw, Cowpens, and others. He drew land as a REV. SOLDIER in Warren Co., Ga., in the Cherokee Land Lottery of 1827. (His grave marked by the D. A. R.)
Children: (known)
1. Mary, mar. Arch Newsom. She d. Feb. 11, 1939.
2. Sarah, d. 1937.
   Both became members of the National Society Daughters of the American Revolution as "Real Daughters".

BURWELL POPE, b. in N. C., 1751; d. Wilkes Co., Ga., Jan. 9, 1800. Served in N. C. Line and received bounty grant of land in Ga. for his services, Oglethorpe (formerly Wilkes) Co. Married 1772, in N. C., Priscilla Wooten (1756-1806). He was a Soldier of 1812.
Children:
1. Robert (1775-1831).
2. Tabitha Christian (1778-1852); mar. 1795, Miles Hill.
3. Ann (1780-1805); mar. 1796, Noah Hill.
4. Martha (called Patsey) (1782-1853); mar. Wylie Hill.
5. Wylie, mar. Sallie Davis; moved to Ala.
6. Sarah, mar. Robert Holmes.
7. Burwell, Jr., b. 1790; mar. 1815, Sallie Key Strong. He was Brig.-Gen., War of 1812.

CHARLES POPE, b. 1748 in Smyrna, Del.; d. 1803, Columbia Co., Ga. Served as Lieut. Col., Del. Reg. Was wounded 1776. Married (1) Jane Stokeley (1752-1793); mar. (2) 1799, Sarah Simpson (dau. of Thomas and Janet Simpson).
Children by (1) wife: (known)
1. Benjamin Stokeley, mar. Eliza Wyatt.
2. Alexander (1777-1845); mar. Dorothy Bibb.
3. William, d. 1803, Petersburg, Ga.

HENRY AUGUSTINE POPE, b. Aug. 6, 1760; d. 1801, Oglethorpe Co., Ga. Served as REV. SOLDIER, and received bounty land in Ga. Mar. (1) Clara Hill (1763-1798); mar. (2) 1799, Mary Davis, d. 1843.

JOHN POPE (brother of Henry Augustine Pope), b. 1755; d. 1819, Wilkes Co., Ga. Was also a REV. SOLDIER and received bounty land in Ga. He mar. Elizabeth Smith (dau. of John and Elizabeth Smith).

WYLIE POPE (brother of Henry Augustine Pope), b. 1758; d. in Ga., 1808. Served as private under Gen. Elijah Clarke at Kettle Creek.

JESSE POPE, b. in Chowan Co., N. C.; d. Hancock Co., Ga., 1820. Received bounty grant of land in Ga. for his services, in N. C. Troops. Married Mary Fort.

JOHN POPE, b. 1755, Halifax Co., N. C.; d. 1819, Wilkes Co., Ga. Served as Capt., Ga. Troops. Received bounty grant of land in Ga. for his services. Married Elizabeth Smith, d. 1829.
Children:
   1. Huldah, mar. Henry Jossey, Jr.
   2. Keturah, mar. James Mathews, Jr.
   3. Mary L., mar. — Henderson.
   4. Wylie.
   5. Rowena.
   6. Louisa.
   7. Martha, mar. Rev. Wm. A. Callaway.
   8. Augustine Burwell.

JOHN HENRY POPE, b. 1756; d. 1821, Wilkes Co., Ga. Received bounty land in Ga. for his services with N. C. Troops. Married Mary Burwell.

OLIVER PORTER (son of JOHN PORTER, REV. SOLDIER of Va. and Mary Anthony), b. Prince Edward Co., Va., 1763; d. Greene Co., Ga., 1838. Enlisted in the Reg. of his brother WILLIAM PORTER, and was at the Siege of Yorktown. Received land in Greene Co., Ga. for his services. Married Margaret Watson, b. 171- (dau. of DOUGLASS WATSON, b. 1750 in Va.; d. 1797, Wilkes Co., Ga. Served in Va. and received bounty grant of land in Wilkes Co., Ga. for his services, and his wife Margaret Parker).
Children: (known)
   1. Ann (1793-1875); mar. 1815, Adam Goudylock Saffold (son of WILLIAM SAFFOLD, REV. SOLDIER who received land in Ga. for his services; d. in Ga.; mar. Ann Goudelock).
   2. Douglass Watson, mar. Annabelle Burwell (dau. of JOHN BUR-WELL, REV. SOLDIER, and his wife Ann Powell).
   3. James, b. Greene Co., Ga.; mar. Athline (or Abijah) Cox, b. Morgan Co., Ga. (dau. of John Cox and his wife Elizabeth Hyde, dau. of JAMES HYDE, REV. SOLDIER who d. from effects of wounds received in service).

WILLIAM PORTER, b. in Va.; d. May 1791, Effingham Co., Ga. Served in Va. Line. Received bounty grant of land as a Refugee Soldier in Effingham Co., Ga. Married Elinor Stewart (?) (His estate was administered by his son David Porter, and appraised by Christian Treutlen, Samuel Bostwick, and John Boykin.)

Children:
1. Susanna, mar. Wm. Cox of Barnwell, S. C.
2. James, mar. Elizabeth —.
3. William, Jr., mar. (1) Miss Treutlen; (2) Rachel (Wilson) Garnett (widow of THOMAS GARNETT, REV. SOLDIER of Effingham Co., Ga.).
4. Benjamin, mar. Elizabeth —.
5. David, mar. 1797, Sally Bostwick (dau. of Samuel Bostwick and his wife Ann Mary Maner).

DR. ANTOINE POULLAINE, b. in France; d. in Washington, Wilkes Co., Ga., 1794. Sailed to America from Bordeaux, France. Served as REV. SOLDIER, Surgeon, and private physician to Marquis de La Fayette. Married about 1787, Sarah Garland Wingfield, at Hanover Co., Va.
Child: (only)
1. Dr. Thomas Noel Poullaine (1792-1889, Greensboro, Ga.); mar. 1814, Harriet Bryan Wray.

LEWIS POWELL, b. 1750, Bladen Co., N. C.; d. Dooly Co., Ga. Received Pension as private, N. C. Troops, under Col. Thomas Robeson. Married Martha Thompson.

MOSES POWELL, b. in S. C., about 1755; d. in Jasper Co., Ga., 1821. Served as private, Ga. Troops, under Gen. Elijah Clarke. Married Sarah —.
Children:
1. George.
2. William.
3. Evan.
4. Charity.
5. Catherine.
6. Martha.
7. Sarah.
8. Nancy.
9. Sivility.
10. Benjamin.

JAMES POWERS, b. in N. C., 1747; d. in Ga., 1818. Served in Col. Hogan's 7th N. C. Reg., as Lieut. Married Penelope Hardy.

OTEY PROSSER, REV. SOLDIER, buried in Family Cemetery, Hancock Co., Ga.

GEORGE PURVIS, b. in England; settled in Del.; came to Glynn Co., Ga., 1789, where he d., 18--. Enlisted Del. Reg., 1775; Second Lieut. in Capt. Patten's Co., Col. Hall's Reg., April 1777; First Lieut., Oct. 1777. Was in Battles of Monmouth, Germantown, and Brandywine. Captured at Camden, S. C., and exchanged. Made Captain, 1782. Member of the Cincinnati. Married Eliza —.
Children:
1. Polly, mar. Benjamin Franklin.
2. Sarah A., mar. 1821, John Flinn.

3. Martha Eliza, mar. James Hatcher.
4. William G., mar. Martha Goodwin Bills (dau. of Jonathan and Lucy Bills, who came 1819 to Glynn Co. Ga., from Middletown, Conn.).

JOHN QUATERMAN of Liberty Co., Ga., a REV. SOLDIER. Married Elizabeth. Four of their sons: JOHN, JR., ROBERT, THOMAS, and WILLIAM QUATERMAN, were all REV. SOLDIERS.

ROBERT QUATERMAN, b. 1744; d. Liberty Co., Ga., 1786. Served as private in Ga. Militia. Mar. (2) 1771, Elizabeth Baker, b. 1756. Children:
1. Mary Ann, mar. 1797, Micajah Andrews (son of ISHAM AN-DREWS, REV. SOLDIER, Va. Troops, and his (1) wife Rebecca Way).
2. Elizabeth, b. 1776; mar. as (1) wife, Joseph Quaterman.
3. Rebecca.
4. Joseph.
5. Sarah.
6. William.
7. Thomas.
8. John.
9. Susannah.

THOMAS QUATERMAN, b. in S. C., 1738; came with his parents to (now Liberty Co.), Ga., 1754; d. Medway, Ga., 1791. Served as private, Ga. Militia. Married (1) 1758, Rebecca Bacon, d. 1775; mar. (2) 1776, Rebecca Smallwood.
Children by (1) wife:
1. Rebecca, mar. 1775, John Norman.
2. JOSEPH (1764-1801); mar. his cousin Elizabeth Quaterman. He served as private, Ga. Mil.
   Child:
   1. Joseph (1796-1863); mar. Harriet Stevens.
3. Thomas, Jr., mar. 1787, Renchie Norman.
4. William.
5. Sarah.

NOTE: At the beginning of the Revolution, the British occupation drove the inhabitants away from Medway and the famous Medway (Midway) Church.

WILLIAM QUATERMAN, b. 1746; d. 1794 in Ga. Served as REV. SOLDIER, Ga. Line. Received bounty land for his services. Married Sarah Stewart (1751-1832).
Children:
1. William, Jr.
2. Susanna.
3. John Stewart.
4. Cynthia B.
5. Sarah.
6. Richard.
7. Elizabeth.
8. Rebecca, mar. John Stacy.
9. Arlissa (a son).

MATTHEW RABUN, b. Halifax Dist., N. C., May 15, 1744; d. Hancock Co., Ga., May 14, 1819. Served with N. C. Troops. Commissioner of specific supplies and Assistant Quartermaster General Commissioner for Halifax Co., N. C., 1781. Mentioned as Staff Officer, N. C. Records. Married Sarah Warren in N. C.; came to Ga.
Children:
1. Jane (1766-1855); mar. 1790, JOHN VEAZEY (1760-1847), a REV. SOLDIER.
2. Elizabeth, d. y.
3. Sarah, mar. (1) — Moss; (2) Nathan Morris.
4. Martha, mar. Isaac Battle.
5. Mary, mar. (1) — Biggers; (2) — Brown; (3) Rev. Haygood; (4) John Bishop.
6. William, b. 1771; mar. Nov. 21, 1793, Mary Battle. In 1819, William Rabun was elected Governor of Georgia.

JONATHAN RAGAN, b. in Nottoway Co., Va., April 11, 1744; d. Washington Co., Ga. Will made in Wilkes Co., Ga. (now Oglethorpe Co.) April 6, 1813, pro. Mar. 1814. Served as private, Ga. Line under Gen. Elijah Clarke. Received bounty land for his services. Married Ann, b. in Va., 1745; d. in Ga., before 1813.
Children: (mentioned in will)
1. Nathaniel, b. 1762; mar. Elizabeth (Ray) Griffen.
2. Polly, mar. — Phillips.
3. John.
4. Nancy, mar. Joseph Callaway.
5. Rebecca, mar. — Callaway.
6. Winnie, mar. Isaac Callaway.
7. Abigail (Abi), mar. Richard Haynes.
8. Elizabeth, mar. William Lumpkin.
9. Asa.
10. Jonathan, Jr.
11. Jeremiah.
12. David, mar. (1) Elizabeth Simmons.
13. Jehn.
14. Marcus B.

JONATHAN RAHN, b. 1762; d. Effingham Co., Ga., 1840. Corporal, 2nd Ga. Batt. Married 1783, Christiana Buntz (1763-1824) (dau. of URBAN BUNTZ, REV. SOLDIER of Ga.).
Children: (known)
1. Emanuel Rahn, b. 1789; mar. 1811, Salome Berry (dau. of JOHN BERRY, b. 1762; d. 1817, Effingham Co., Ga. Served as private, Effingham Co., Ga. Militia, and his wife Mary Reisser).
2. Susannah Rahn (1798-1863); mar. 1820, John Wilson (son of JAMES WILSON (1745-1825), REV. SOLDIER of N. C., and Effingham Co., Ga.

JOHN RAIFORD, b. 1750, in N. C.; d. 1812, Jefferson Co., Ga. Married 1769, Lucy Spell. He served as Lieut., in the 2nd Reg., N. C. Troops 1780-81.

ROBERT RAINES, b. 1766; d. 1816, Twiggs Co., Ga. Served as private, Ga. Line. Married Sarah F. Hamilton (dau. of JOHN HAMILTON, b. Amelia Co., Va., 1747; d. Hancock Co., Ga. Served as private, Ga. Line and his wife Tabitha Thweatt).

WILLIAM RAMSEY, and wife Jemina, of Wilkes Co., Ga., sold 287.5 acres of land, granted him by his services as a REV. SOLDIER, Sept. 18, 1784, to Thomas Daniell of Greene Co., Ga., May 1, 1787.

REUBEN RANSOME, d. Clarke Co., Ga. (near Athens), 1833. (Will made Oct. 11, 1832, pro. Mar. 4, 1833). He was REV. SOLDIER. Drew land as a REV. SOLDIER in 1827 Cherokee Land Lottery. (Grave marked by Elijah Clarke Chapter, D. A. R., Athens, Ga.) Married Nancy C. —.
Children:
1. Dudley.
2. Reuben, Jr.
3. Nancy, mar. — Perkins.
4. Polly.
5. Jane, mar. — Turner.
6. Joseph.
7. Elizabeth, mar. — Cook.
8. Richardson D.
9. William.
10. Dau., mar. Isaac Knowles.

ABRAHAM RAVOT, b. in S. C.; d. in Ga. (son of Gabriel Frances Ravot and his wife Louise Catherine Malette). Served as Captain, Effingham Co., Ga., Mil. Married (1) —, d. July 16, 1795; mar. (2) Mary Mikell, widow, d. 1811.
Children by (1) wife:
1. Abraham, Jr., b. 1773.
2. Henrietta, b. 1775; mar. 1795, John Porter.
Children by (2) wife:
3. Margaret Marie, mar. William King, Jr.
4. Mary.
5. Elizabeth, mar. John Palmer.

HENRY RAWLINGS, b. in Va.; d. 1807, Hancock Co., Ga. Served as Capt. in Va. Militia, under Col. Bowman. Married 1769, Sarah Allen.

ABRAHAM REDDICK, d. in Jasper Co., Ga., age 94 years. Married Hannah —. He sold 287.5 acres of land, granted for his services as a REV. SOLDIER in 1786, to James Harvey, Greene Co., Ga., 1788.

ANDERSON REDDING, b. 1764, Va.; d. 1845, Monroe Co., Ga. Buried Salem Churchyard, near Bolingbroke, Ga. Served as private, Va. Line; was at the surrender at Yorktown. Married Delilah Parham.
Children:

1. William Chambless, mar. Margaret Flewellyn (dau. of ABNER FLEWELLYN, REV. SOLDIER).
2. Elizabeth, mar. John Green.
3. Rowland.
4. Thomas (1794-1877); mar. Maria Searcy.
5. Lourania.
6. Mary.
7. James M.

WILLIAM REDDING, b. in Va., 1736; d. in Ga., 1822. Served with Va. Troops and received bounty land in Ga. for his services. Moved to Ga., 1785. Married Patty Parham.
Children: (known)
1. CHARLES, b. in Va., 1756; d. in Ga., 1815. A REV. SOLDIER. Married Edith —.
2. Arthur, mar. Frances Wynne.
3. ANDERSON, b. 1764 in Va.; d. 1845 in Ga.; a REV. SOLDIER. Married Delilah Parham.

JACOB REDWINE, b. Oct. 12, 1751; d. Coweta Co., Ga., 1840. Removed from Montgomery Co., N. C. Served as private in Capt. John Johnston's Co., Col. John Collier's Reg. of Militia. Moved to Ga. 1784. Married Rowena Rhineheart, b. 1755; d. Elbert Co., Ga., July 4, 1831.
Children:
1. Elizabeth, b. 1778; mar. John W. Carroll.
2. Mary, b. 1777; mar. William Ballinger.
3. Jemina, mar. —McGee.
4. Sally, mar. — Larramore.
5. Kate, mar. — Hearn.
6. Barbara, mar. Joseph Parker.
7. Nancy, mar. — Underwood.
8. Lewis, mar. Mary Merritt.
9. Jacob, mar. — Tuble.
10. Michael, mar. — Hart.
11. John, mar. — Crawford.

ISHAM REESE, b. 1748, Dinwiddie Co., Va.; d. Ga., April 17, 1816. Served as a REV. SOLDIER. Buried in Jones Co., Ga. Married Susan Coleman, b. Dec. 1755.
Children:
1. William C., b. 1775.
2. Isham, Jr.
3. Cuthbert (1781-1855); mar. Tabitha Clarke (dau. of JOSEPH CLARK, REV. SOLDIER of Va.).
4. Joseph.
5. John C.
6. Percilla.
7. Susan, b. 1790; mar. Dr. Amos.

8. Sarah P., mar. Dr. Cook.
9. Henry L.
10. Jordan.

SAMUEL REID, had Pension granted him as a REV. SOLDIER.
Enlisted Abbeville Dist., S. C. He was b. Lancaster, Penn., Jan. 26,
1749; d. in Gwinnett Co., Ga., Feb. 5, 1843. Received Pension 1832,
with his children, in St. Clair, Ala.

SAMUEL REID, b. 1728, Rowan Co., Ala.; d. 1810, Putnam Co., Ga.
Lived in Iredell Co., N. C.; a member of the Council of Safety; Capt.
in Col. Alexander's Reg.; Gen. Rutherford's N. C. Brigade. Received
bounty land in Ga. for his services. Married Agnes Kay (or McKay)
(1753-1806).
Children:
    1. Samuel, Jr. (1758-1842, Jasper Co., Ga.); mar. Emily Elizabeth
       Hurt.
    2. Alexander (1769-1810); mar. Elizabeth Brewer.
    3. William.

4. James.	8. Margaret.
5. John.	9. Jean.
6. Andrew.	10. Agnes.
7. Mary Hall.	11. Sarah.

JOHN REMSHART, b. in England; came to Ga. with Gen. James
Edward Oglethorpe on his second voyage to Ga. Joined the Salzburger
Colony at Ebenezer. Made Will, Aug. 15, 1782, pro. Nov. 20, 1782, Ef-
fingham Co., Ga. Was a REV. PATRIOT. Married Feb. 14, 1764, Anna
Margaret Mueller.
Children:
    1. Daniel, b. Oct. 26, 1765; mar. Elizabeth Waldhauer.

2. Catherina.	5. Christine.
3. Judith.	6. Christian.
4. Asa.	7. Elizabeth.

AMOS RICHARDSON, d. in Elbert (now Hart) Co., Ga. Served as
private Ga. Line. (Grave in Sardis Churchyard, Hart Co., marked by
the D. A. R.) Married Susan Smith.
Children:
    1. Mahbon, mar. Sallie Self.
    2. Clarissa, mar. Sinclair McMullen.
    3. James, mar. (1) Milly Bobo; (2) Elizabeth McMullen.
    4. Willis, mar. Drucilla Gaines.
    5. Annie, mar. John Farmer.

DANIEL RICHARDSON, b. in England; came to America; settled in
Culpeper Co., Va. Moved to S. C., then to Ga.; d. Hancock Co., Ga.,
1796. Enlisted in Capt. Levine's Co., 9th Va. Reg., Col. George Mathews,

as Lieut. Married Frances Long, d. in Ga., 1796 (dau. of REUBEN LONG, a REV. SOLDIER, who had 7 sons as REV. SOLDIERS. She was granddau. of COL. BLOOMFIELD LONG, REV. SOLDIER of Va.).
Children:
1. Thomas.
2. Obediah, mar. Jane Bush.
3. Polly, mar. — Thomas.
4. Elizabeth, mar. — Harris.
5. Katie, mar. — Lamar.
6. Nancy, mar. Sam Dent.
7. Margaret, mar. — William.
8. Gabriel.
9. Sally.
10. Julia, mar. — Baxter.
11. Armistead, b. 1788; d. Putname Co., Ga. Soldier of 1812. Mar. Elizabeth Griggs, Putnam Co., Ga.

JOHN RICHARDSON, b. in Va., 1760; d. in Oglethorpe Co., Ga. Served in the Va. Line and received bounty land in Oglethorpe Co. for his services. Married 1790, Elizabeth Tate.

WALKER RICHARDSON, b. in Va.; d. Elbert Co., Ga. (will made Mar. 13, 1819, pro. 1822). Served as Lieut. in 1st Va. Reg., commanded by Col. Charles Harrison. Came to Ga., 1792. Married Prudence —.

CATO RIDDLE, b. 1755, Chatham Co., N. C.; d. 1823, Washington Co., Ga. Served as Capt., N. C. Troops. Was at Cowpens and Guilford Court House. Married Martha Tomlinson (1770-1840).

ELIAS ROBERTS (Robert), b. in the Santee Dist., S. C., 1745; d. Screven Co., Ga., after 1815. Served in the S. C. Militia. Married Mary Rue in S. C. She was b. in France; d. at Yamacraw Bluff, Ga., 1815 "leaving 5 adult children". They were living in Savannah, Ga., 1789.
Child: (only one known)
1. Thomas Roberts, b. 1787 in S. C.; d. in Screven Co., Ga., about 1816. Was a Soldier of the War of 1812. Married Mary Ponder (dau. of JAMES PONDER, REV. SOLDIER of Ga.). She mar. (2) George Smith of Screven Co., Ga.
Children:
1. Elias, mar. —.
2. Patience, mar. Charles Nessmith.
3. Elizabeth.

JAMES ROBERTS, b. 1744, Screven Co., Ga.; d. at the same place, 1814. Served as Lieut., Ga. Troops. Received bounty grant of land for his services. Married 1785, Emily Williamson (dau. of — WILLIAMSON, REV. SOLDIER of Ga., and his wife Lucy Conyers).

FREDERICK ROBINSON, b. in N. C.; d. Wayne Co., Ga. Served in
N. C. Line. Married Jane Thomas in N. C., and moved to Ga.

JOHN ROBINSON (or Roberson), b. May 6, 1756; d. Baldwin Co., Ga.,
Dec. 18, 1832. Applied for Pension, Nov. 1832. Served in Va. Enlisted
after Battle of Trenton for 3 years with Wm. Porter, Recruiting Officer. Served in Capt. William Taylor's 2nd Va. Reg. Taken prisoner
at Charleston, but escaped. Married Mar. 27, 1788, Jeriah, b. Aug. 19,
1769, in Columbia Co., Ga. His wife applied for Pension, May 8, 1839,
as the widow of a REV. SOLDIER. (Pension Claim W. 5747).
Children:
1. Solomon, b. 1789.
2. John, b. 1792.
3. Sally, b. 1794.
4. Luke, b. 1797.
5. William, b. 1798.
6. Maria, b. 1801
Jeriah Robinson, widow, was living, Baldwin Co., Ga., Dec. 6, 1843.

RANDAL ROBINSON, b. Granville Co., N. C., May 2, 1762; d. in
Newnan, Ga., Feb. 27, 1842. Served in N. C., Jan. 1, 1777 to Nov. 15,
1778. Moved to Edgefield Dist., S. C., 1779; and served 189 days in
Capt. Waters' S. C. Reg. Married (1) 1789, Lydia Walker, d. 1790;
mar. (2) Pheriby Hill (1767-1847).
Child by (1) wife:
1. Mary, mar. Falkner Heard.
Children by (2) wife:
2. Martha.
3. Elizabeth, mar. Peyton Prichard.
4. Samuel, d. y.
5. Alma, mar. Turner Persons.
6. Permilia, mar. Caleb Cook.
7. John Evans, mar. (1) 1829, Mary Wingfield; (2) 1835, Sarah
Ramey.

BRITTAIN ROGERS, b. Oct. 11, 1761, N. C.; d. April 22, 1835, Monroe Co., Ga. Married 1782, Elizabeth Lockett (1767-1845). Soldier
of 1812 as well as REV. SOLDIER.
Child:
1. Osborne (1783-1857); mar. 1813, Mary Thorn (?).

REUBEN ROGERS, b. Northampton, N. C., Nov. 1, 1735; d. 1794,
Warren Co., Ga. Served as private under Col. Elijah Clarke. Captured
by British and held as prisoner of War. Name appears on monument
erected by the Government and D. A. R. at Kettle Creek. Received
bounty land for his services in Wilkes (now Warren) Co., Ga. Married
Dec. 15, 1767, Temperance James, b. Aug. 24, 1751.
Children:

1. John, b. 1769; mar. 1802, Nancy Swain.
2. Faith, b. 1771; mar. — Darden.
3. Mary.
4. Clary.
5. Nancy, mar. — Saxon.
6. Reuben, Jr., mar. Elizabeth Emerson. She mar. (2) Elias Wilson.
7. Phoebe, mar. Frederick Brown.
8. Temperance, mar. as (2) wife, Thomas Lockett.
9. Joseph, b. 1784; mar. Frances Gardner. She mar. (2) — Stafford.
10. Rebecca, b. 1786; mar. Michael Cody.
    Children:
    1. Michael Cody.
    2. Louise Amanda Cody, mar. James M. Wellborn (son of ELIAS WELLBORN, REV. SOLDIER).

JAMES ROQUEMORE, b. in France; d. Warren Co., Ga. Served as private, Ga. Line. Married Elizabeth —.

WILLIAM ROSE, b. about 1725 in N.C.; d. in Ga. Enlisted 1776 in Capt. Nelson's Co., Col. Thomas Polk's N.C. Reg. of Militia. Married Amy Langston.
Children: (from Will; brother-in-law James Langston, Ex. of will)
1. JOHN ROSE, b. in N.C., 1746; d. in Ga., 1846. Served as private in Col. Thomas Polk's Reg., N.C. Militia and also with Ga. Troops under Col. Elijah Clarke. Married 1778, Mary Washington.
2. Frederick.
3. William.
4. Howell.
5. Martha (called Patsey); mar. JESSE MILLER, REV. SOLDIER of S.C., who received land grant in Ga. for his services.
6. Sarah.
7. Elizabeth.
8. Winifred.

RICHARDSON ROUNTREE, b. 1751; d. 1819 in Ga. Married 1777, Mildred Hart. Served as a REV. SOLDIER.
Children:
1. Maria.
2. James.
3. Martha, mar. Cary Cox., Jr.
4. Isabella, mar. William Stephens, Jr.
5. Mildred (Elizabeth), mar. William Goldsmith.
6. William.
7. Daniel, mar. Fanny Nelson.
8. Thomas, mar. — Nesbit.

JAMES ROWAN, b. in Ireland, 1752; d. 1795, Warren Co., Ga. Served as private, S. C. Troops. Received bounty land in Ga. for his services. Married Ann —, b. 1758.

GEORGE RUDICIL, a native of Wurtemburg, Germany, accompanied the celebrated Baron de Kalb to America during the Rev. War, and fought throughout that struggle for American Independence. Joined the Continental Army at Trenton and was present at Valley Forge. Three of his brothers were in the Continental service and all four brothers were wounded. He saw further service under Gen. Nathaniel Greene in the Carolinas, and was present at the surrender of Yorktown. Settled near Lincoln Co., N. C. Married Miss Johnson of Va. They had seven children.

JOHN RUSHIN (Rushing), b. Cheraw, S. C., 1764; d. in Ga., on Flint River, 1843. Buried near Montezuma, Ga. Served as Lieut. in Col. Benton's S. C. Reg. Was also a Soldier in War of 1812. Married 1780, Rachel Renfroe (1765-1833).
Children:
1. Joel, b. 1785.
2. John, b. 1791.
3. William (1794-1843); mar. Mary (Polly) Cox.
4. Mary, b. 1801.   7. Matilda, b. 1797.
5. James, b. 1787.   8. Caroline, b. 1807.
6. Elizabeth, b. 1792.   9. Evelyn, b. 1805.
(Grave marked by Archibald Bullock Chapter, Montezuma, Ga., D. A. R.)

JOHN RUTHERFORD, b. 1760, S. C.; d. 1833, Baldwin Co., Ga.
Served under Gen. Nathaniel Greene and received bounty grant of land in Wilkes Co., Ga., for his services. Married (1) Mary (Polly) Hubert (dau. of BENJAMIN HUBERT, REV. SOLDIER of Warren Co., Ga.); mar. (2) Sally Gordon, widow; mar. (3) Elizabeth Barron.
Children:
1. William, mar. Eliza Boykin (1806-1837) (dau. of MAJOR FRANCIS BOYKIN, REV. SOLDIER who moved from S. C. to Milledgeville, Ga. Grave marked by the Nancy Hart Chapter, D. A. R., Milledgeville, Ga.).
2. Dorothy, mar. (1) Samuel Wiggins; (2) Joshua Bigham; (3) Francis Jeter.
On his tombstone, 3 miles from Sandersville, Ga., on Milledgeville Rd., is the following inscription, "To the memory of JOHN RUTHERFORD a Soldier of the Revolution who lived long to share the honors of his countrymen. Died Oct. 31, 1833. Buried at his request by the side of his first wife, Polly Hubert."
He was the son of ROBERT RUTHERFORD of N. C., REV. SOLDIER.
(His brother Thomas, mar. Nancy Harvey).
Children mentioned in will of JOHN RUTHERFORD, Baldwin Co., Ga.:
Present wife Sally Gordon, widow and her son John W. Gordon.

Children:
1. John G.
2. Nathaniel; the heirs of son.
3. Robert, dec.
4. Benjamin.
5. William, and dau.
6. Dorothy Wiggins, and the children by her first husband, Samuel Wiggins.

WILLIAM RYALS, b. 1748 in N. C.; and d. 1828, Montgomery Co., Ga. Served as private, 2nd and 10th N. C. Reg., under Capt. Hall and Col. John Patten. Married Edith Childs (1765-1835). (Grave marked by Oconee Chapter, D. A. R., McRae, Ga.)

PHILIP RYAN, b. Henry Co., Va.; d. 1822, Jackson Co., Ga. Served as private, Ga. Troops. Buried in the old Ryan Cemetery, 4 miles from Athens, Ga. Married Obedience —.
Children:
1. Christiana, mar. John Nance.
2. Matilda, mar. Phinizy.
3. Angelica, mar. Lewis Lampkin.

JESSE SANDERS, b. 1743, Lancaster Co., Va.; d. in Ga. Capt. 6th Reg., N. C. Troops. Married 1765, Ann Yancey.

MOSES SANDERS, b. 1742 in England; d. in Ga., 1817. Served as a REV. SOLDIER. (From tombstone): "A Baptist preacher and REV. SOLDIER". Married Sallie Hamilton (1745-1816).

JEREMIAH SANFORD, b. Loudon Co., Va., Nov. 4, 1739; d. Greensboro, Ga., Aug. 11, 1825. The epitaph on his tombstone reads: "A REV. SOLDIER, a Friend of Gen. George Washington, An Honest Man". Served as private, Ga. Militia. Married 1766, Mary Modessett (1746-1793).
Children:
1. Vincent, b. April 17, 1770; mar. Priscilla Palmer.
2. Benjamin, b. Nov. 26, 1771; mar. Jane Armour.
3. Jeremiah, Jr., b. Sept. 24, 1772; mar. 1798, Ada Palmer (1776-1864).
4. Daniel, b. Jan. 28, 1778; mar. Elizabeth Totley.
5. Mildred Washington, b. July 12, 1781; mar. Israel Palmer.
6. Thomas, b. 1783; d. y.

DILL SAPP, and wife Lydia, of Burke Co., drew 287.5 acres of land on Rocky Creek, Washington Co., for his services as a REV. SOLDIER.

BALTHAZER SCHAEFFER, b. at Seckback, Frankfort on the Main,

Germany, April 1, 1742; came to Savannah, Ga., 1770. Married there
(1) May 30, 1772, Margaret Eppinger, b. Wilmington, N. C., Jan. 14,
1755; d. Savannah, Ga., Oct. 1793; mar. (2) widow Unselt. Died in Savannah, Ga., May 1, 1811. Served as a REV. SOLDIER as private, Ga.
Troops, under Gen. Lachlan McIntosh.
Children:
1. John W., b. 1773; mar. Mary Lawrence.
2. George, b. 1775; mar. Mary Morgan of N. Y.
3. James, b. 1777; mar. Susan Dasher.
4. Frederick, b. 1779; mar. Mary Cole.
5. Margaret, b. 1781; mar. Mr. Gugle.
6. Jacob, mar. the widow of his brother John W.
7. Sarah, b. 1787.
8. Hannah Eppinger, b. 1789.
9. Elizabeth.
10. Simon Peter (1792-1849 in N. Y.).

THOMAS SCOTT, WOODLIEF SCOTT, and FREDERICK SCOTT,
three brothers, b. in Va., were REV. SOLDIERS, Va. Line. Came to
Ga., and settled in Hancock Co.

WILLIAM SCOTT, b. 1754, Louise Parish, Va.; d. 1806, Monroe Co.,
Ga. Served as Capt., Ga. Troops, under Gen. Elijah Clarke. Married
1784, Jane Thomas (1763-1808).
Children:
1. Annie (1785-1850); mar. 1806, Charles H. Willingham.
2. Daniel, b. 1787; mar. Jemina Walker.
3. Jane, mar. — Sanford.
4. Polly, mar. — Welch.   8. John.
5. Darius.   9. Sarah.
6. James.   10. Samuel.
7. Isaac.   11. Benjamin.

BRIG.-GEN. JAMES SCREVEN, b. James Island, S. C., 1744; d.
Nov. 24, 1778 from a wound received in a skirmish with British sol-
diers near Midway Church, Ga. Married 1764, Mary Esther Odingsell,
d. Jan. 6, 1779 (dau. of Charles Odingsell).
Children:
1. Esther (1765-1801); mar. Thomas Smith.
2. Mary Esther (1767-1845); mar. Capt. John Hart (son of REV.
   OLIVER HART, REV. SOLDIER, and his wife Sarah Breese).
   CAPT. JOHN HART, a REV. SOLDIER, was b. 1758; d. 1814;
   Lieut. 1777, 7th S. C. Reg.; then Capt. Captured at Siege of
   Savannah. In 1815, his widow moved to Liberty Co., Ga., where
   she died. Received Pension as widow of REV. SOLDIER.
   Children:
   1. Oliver James.   3. Martha Lee.
   2. Esther Mary.   4. John S.

          5. Charles T.   8. Odingsell W.
          6. Henry William.   9. Smith Screven.
          7. Elizabeth Screven Lee.
       3. Martha.
       4. James.
       5. Charles Odingsell, b.1773; d.1830, N.Y. Married (1) Lucy
          (Barnard) Jones; (2) Barbara Rankin Golphin. They lived at
          Sunbury, Ga.
       6. Thomas.

NOTE: In 1915, U.S. Congress erected a monument jointly to the
memory of GEN. SCREVEN and GEN. DANIEL STEWART, and this
monument marks the spot where Gen. Screven was buried in Old Midway Churchyard, near Darien, Ga.

   JOHN SCREVEN (brother of GEN. JAMES SCREVEN), b. James
Island, S.C., 1750; d.1801 in S.C. Lived in Ga. and are known as the
"Ga. Screvens". Served as Lieut. of the St. John Rangers of Liberty
Co., Ga. Married (1) 1772, Patience Holmes; mar. (2) 1776, Elizabeth
(Pendarvis) Bryan (widow of Josiah Bryan).
Children by (2) wife:
       1. John (1777-1830); mar. Hannah Proctor.
       2. Richard Bedon, mar. (1) Alice Pendarvis, (2) —.
       3. Sarah (1780-1841); mar. as (2) wife, Major Wm. Hazzard of
          S.C. (1759-1821), served as Aide to Gen. Anthony Wayne and
          was wounded at Siege of Savannah.
       4. Martha, mar. James West of S.C.
       5. Elizabeth, mar. John Brooks Posey (son of GEN. POSEY, REV.
          SOLDIER of Orange Co., Va.).
       6. Mary Bedon, mar. Stephen Royer Proctor.
       7. Thomas Edward, mar. Cornelia Ann McNich.

   WILLIAM SCURLOCK, b. in Va., 1763; d.1840 in Ga. Placed on
Pension Roll, 1833. Served under Col. Benjamin Cleveland, N.C. Reg.
Married 1796, Rhoda Simmons (1771-1831).

   JOHN SEAY, b.1758; d. in Ga. Served in Ga., under Gen. Micajah
Williamson. Married (1) Miss West; (2) Sarah McAlpin.

   THOMAS SEMMES, b.1753 in Md.; d. Wilkes Co., Ga., 1824. Served
in Capt. Walter Hanson's Co., as Lieut., Md. Reg. Married Feb. 1779,
Mary Ann (Radcliff) Brawner.

NOTE: Two brothers of THOMAS SEMMES were JOSEPH SEMMES,
REV. SOLDIER of Md.; mar. Henrietta Thompson; and ANDREW
SEMMES, killed at one of the Battles on Long Island.

   SAMUEL SENTELL, b.1759; d. in Ga., 1844. Received bounty grant

of land in Ga. Married Nancy Stephens.
Children:
1. William, b. 1783.
2. Nathan.
3. Elizabeth, mar. Larkin Cardin.
4. Samuel, Jr.
5. John.
6. Sarah, mar. Andrew Griffin.
7. Brittain.
8. Hetty Louise, mar. Rev. Edmund R. Reynolds.
9. Martin.
10. Nancy, mar. Ingram Love.

JOHN SESSIONS, b. 1758, N. C.; d. 1836, near Griffin, Ga. Served
in the N. C. Troops, under Capts. Bright and Heritage. Married
Mary —.

EDMUND SHACKELFORD, b. in Va.; d. Elbert Co., Ga., 1821.
Served in Va. Militia. His widow drew land as widow of REV. SOLDIER
in Cherokee Land Lottery 1827, while a resident of Jackson Co., Ga.
Married Judith —.
Children: (mentioned in will)
1. Philip.
2. Edmund.
3. John, mar. Martha Mann.
4. Reuben.
5. Jefferson.
6. Nancy, mar. Drury Oglesby.
7. Elizabeth, mar. John Seal.
8. Judith, mar. Mordecai Alexander.
9. Polly, mar. John Harris.

HENRY SHACKELFORD, b. in Va.; d. Elbert Co., Ga. Will made
April 5, 1808, pro. Jan. 5, 1819. Was a REV. PATRIOT. Married —,
who d. before 1808.
Children: (mentioned in will)
1. Henry, Jr.
2. Edmund, mar. Judith.
3. Nancy.
4. Betsey.
5. Jenny.
6. Fanny.
Grandchild:
1. Edmund Alexander.

JOHN SHACKELFORD (son of Roger and Cary (Baker) Shackelford), b. Hanover Co., Va.; d. April 13, 1800, Hancock Co., Ga. Served
as private, Va. Troops and received bounty land for his services in
Ga. Married Frances Wade Butler (dau. of Edmund and Susanna Butler of Va.).
Children:
1. Elizabeth (1781-1860); mar. GEN. J. EPPS BROWN (1766-
1827), REV. SOLDIER.
2. Polly, mar. — Wingfield.
3. Ann.

4. Nancy, mar. George S. Rives (son CAPT. GEORGE RIVES,
   REV. SOLDIER of Va.).
5. James.
6. Patsey.   8. John, Jr.
7. Edmund.   9. Susanna.

JOHN SHARPE (Sharp), b. 1762, Halifax Co., Va. Served as private,
Ga. Troops, under Capts. Lewis and Grant, Col. Emanuel and Col.
Jackson. Married Betsey Wynn, d. 1835. He d. Tattnall Co., Va., 1835.

JOHN SHEFFIELD, b. in Penn.; d. in Moore Co., N. C. Married
1748, Hannah —.
Child:
   1. Mary Sheffield (1760-1862); mar. Isaac Dunn.

NOTE: JOHN SHEFFIELD, WEST SHEFFIELD, ABRAHAM HILL,
NATHANIEL RAINES, and THOMAS MITCHELL, all REV. SOLDIERS
and related families.

WEST SHEFFIELD (son of JOHN SHEFFIELD, a REV. SOLDIER of
N. C., and his wife Elizabeth Grady), b. in N. C., 1747; d. Wayne Co.,
Ga., 1830. Private from St. George's Parish (now Wayne Co.), with
Ga. Troops. Received bounty grant of land for his services. Married
(1) 1774, Susanna Sherrard, b. 1752; mar. (2) Elizabeth —, b. 1765, in
1803.
Children:
   1. Sidnah, b. Nov. 11, 1776; mar. Job Tison, b. 1770.
   2. Aaron.
   3. Sherrard, b. 1782.
   4. Bryant (1784-1855); mar. Elizabeth Ogden (1804-1887).
   5. Pliny.
   6. Flora.
   7. Catherine.
   8. Randal.
   9. John (1804-1883); mar. 1825, Sarah Ann Cook (1806-1895).

LEVI SHEFTALL, b. in Ga., Jan. 11, 1739; d. Savannah, Ga. Enlisted
and served in Ga. Troops. Married in the West Indies, Sarah De
Lemotta. Had 7 sons.
Children: (known)
   1. Benjamin.
   2. Mordecai.
   3. Solomon.

JOHN SHELLMAN, b. 1756 in Md.; d. 1838, Savannah, Ga. Granted
a Pension, 1836, for his services in the Md. Line. Married Clarissa
Montford, d. 1845.

JOHN SHICK, b. in Germany, 1726; d. Savannah, Ga., 1797. Served as Lieut. in Continental Army of Ga. Was wounded and lost his right arm. Was prisoner on British ship. Married Margaret Ritter. Received bounty grant for services.
Child:
    1. Elizabeth Susanna, mar. ISAAC FELL, REV. SOLDIER.
        Child:
        1. Peter.

NOTE: When the British took Savannah, one of their prisoners was ISAAC FELL, the fiancee of Elizabeth Susanna Shick, and in her efforts to secure his freedom, the British officers offered her wine and insisted upon a Toast. She gave the following toast impromtu. "Here's to those who were turned out and not to those who turned them out; I hope to see a turn about of those turned in who were turned out." She secured the release of her lover.

JOHN SHINE, b. 1759, Jones Co., N. C.; d. 1832, Twiggs Co., Ga. Served as private 1780, N. C. Troops, under Col. Caswell. Married Clarissa Williams, d. 1819.
Children: (known)
    1. Daniel W., mar. (1) Mary Womble; (2) 1826, Nancy Glenn.
    2. Cassandra, b. 1788; mar. 1806, James Harrison.
    3. Sarah Williams, b. 1784; mar. James Miller.

WILLIAM STUBLEY SHIRLEY, b. in Washington Co., Ga., 1757; d. in Ga., Oct. 10, 1833. Served as private, Ga. Troops. (son of Richard Shirley who came with his brother William, from Augusta Co., Va., and settled in Ga.). Married 1780, Washington Co., Ga., Elizabeth Maxwell.
Children:
    1. Richard Charles, b. 1781; mar. (1) Sarah Brooks; mar. (2)
        Nancy Porter.
    2. James   )
    3. John.   )   triplets, born 1783.
    4. Samuel)
    5. Edward.
    6. Mahaley Parker.
    7. Mary.
    8. William S., Jr.) twins
    9. Elizabeth   )

JONAS SHIVERS, d. Warren Co., Ga., 1826. Will made Sept. 6, 1825, pro. Dec. 1826. Married Lilliory Godwin, d. Aug. 8, 1826. Served as private, Ga. Line. Received grant of land in Ga., for his services.
Children:
    1. Barnaby.   3. William.
    2. Willis.   4. Thomas.   5. James.

SPENCER SHROPSHIRE, REV. SOLDIER. Settled in Oglethorpe Co., Ga. Married Miss Pollard. They had 9 children.
Child:
1. Wesley Shropshire, b. 1801, Oglethorpe Co., Ga.; mar. Nancy Swanson, 1827. Was one of the pioneers of Chattooga Co., Ga.

SAMUEL SHY (Shi), b. 1765; d. Dec. 13, 1830, Jasper Co., Ga. Buried about a mile from Pennington, Morgan Co., Ga. Served as a private. Received land in Hancock Co., Ga., for his services. Married Jane —, d. Sept. 12, 1843.
Children:
1. Sarah, mar. Thomas Tyler.
2. Nicey, mar. Thomas Aikens.
3. Eleanor, mar. Joseph Howard.
4. Polly, mar. James Aikens.
5. Eliza, mar. Samuel Pennington.
6. Mariah, mar. Ransom Harwell.
7. Seaborn.

JOHN SIMMONS, b. in Va. (son of John Simmons and (1) wife); moved to Wilkes Co., Ga., where he d. Served as private, Va. Continental Army. Married Ann Freeman (dau. of Holman Freeman, Sr., of Wilkes Co., Ga.). (Six of his brothers, all REV. SOLDIERS of Va., came to Wilkes Co., Ga. They were: WILLIAM, JAMES, HENRY, STERNE, ADAM, RICHARD SIMMONS).
Children: (mentioned in will)
1. Moses W.
2. John, Jr.
3. Holman F.
4. Susanna, mar. John L. Richardson of Nacoochee, Ga.

JOHN SIMMONS, b. in Va.; moved to N. C., then Ga. He d. Talbot Co., Ga., 1837. Wounded at Battle of Cowpens. Served in N. C. Militia. Married Miss Nutt in 1756.
Children: (known)
1. WILLIAM, JR., b. 1758 in N. C. Served N. C. Militia. Obtained bounty land in Ga. for his services. Obtained a Pension (not granted by U. S.) and was living in Ga., 1832. He changed his name to Isaac for his uncle ISAAC NUTT, a REV. SOLDIER of N. C., killed at the Battle of Cowpens.
2. Rhoda.
3. Winnie.   5. John.
4. Sarah.   6. Wm.

JOHN SIMMONS, b. in Scotland, 1712; came to America and settled in Va. Married (1) —. He moved to Wilkes Co., Ga.; mar. (2) Rebecca —. He served as REV. SOLDIER of Va. and in Ga. Served under Gen. Elijah Clarke at the Battle of Kettle Creek. Received a bounty grant of land, 287.5 acres, for his services, on Shoulderbone Creek, Washington Co., Ga. (now Hancock Co.) On Sept. 1, 1794, he willed "the 650 acres where I now reside (formerly Wilkes Co.) and the 287.5 acres in Hancock Co." received for his service as a REV. SOLDIER to his children by (2) wife. He d. 1797; his wife d. before him. Children by (1) wife: (known)

1. William.
2. John, Jr.
3. Richard.
4. James.
5. Adam.
6. Asa.
7. Jesse Sterne.
8. Henry.

These sons were all REV. SOLDIERS of Va. and N. C. They moved with their families to Wilkes Co., Ga., where they received bounty lands for their services.

Children by (2) wife:

9. Thomas, lived in Lincoln Co., Ga.
10. Rebecca, mar. Joseph Westmoreland.
11. Elizabeth, mar. Ishmael David.
12. Keziah, b. in Wilkes Co., Ga., 1784; d. "Poplar Grove", DeKalb Co., Ga., Mar. 8, 1868; married Feb. 14, 1805, in Miss., as (2) wife, Reuben Westmoreland (son of JOSEPH WESTMORELAND, REV. SOLDIER of Va., and his wife Martha Shores, Ancestors of Ettie Tidwell McCall).
13. Susannah.
14. Ruth.
15. David, moved to Miss.
16. Elijah, moved to Miss.

(The grave of JOHN SIMMONS, REV. SOLDIER, has been marked by the Nancy Hart Chapter, D. A. R., Milledgeville, Ga. Grave located 8 miles from Sparta, Ga., Hancock Co.)

STERNE SIMMONS, b. in Va.; d. in Wilkes Co., Ga. Will on file made Oct. 18, 1828, pro. Jan. 1829. Received a land grant in Wilkes Co., Ga., for his services as a REV. SOLDIER of Ga. Married Gracey —.
Children:

1. John.
2. Thomas.
3. Sterne, Jr.

WILLIAM SIMMONS, b. 1745 in Va.; d. 1828 in Ga. (Jasper Co.) Received bounty land in Ga. for services in Va. Line. Married 1793, Ann King (1759-1810).
Children:

1.. William, Jr.
2. Allen G., mar. 1820, Mary Cleveland.

ROBERT SIMMS, b. 1757 in N. C.; d. in Hancock Co., Ga., 1815. Served as private in Capt. John Dickinson's Co., N. C. Troops. Mar.

(1) 1774, Sarah Dickerson (dau. of CAPT. JOHN DICKERSON, REV. SOLDIER of N. C., and his wife Mary Barnes).

ARCHIBALD SIMPSON, b. 1750 in Va.; d. 1828 in Ga. Served under Col. Elijah Clarke, Ga. Troops at Kettle Creek. Married Catherine Nelson.

HENRY SLAPPEY, b. in S. C., 1758; d. 1820, Twiggs Co., Ga. Served in S. C. Light Dragoons, under Capt. William Alexander. Wounded at King's Mt. Married Ann Rutherford.
Children: (known)
    1. Dorothy, mar. Capt. Ezekiel Wimberly.
    2. John G., mar. Margaret Monroe.

EZEKIEL SLAUGHTER, b. in Va., 1727; d. Greene Co., Ga., 1792. Served as private in Col. Thweatt's Va. Reg. Received bounty grant of land for his services in Ga. Married Sarah Butler (dau. of Samuel and Barsheba Butler of Hanover Co., Va.), b. Oct. 1, 1727.
Children:
    1. Mary, b. Oct. 15, 1748; mar. — Worsham.
    2. JOHN (1750-1805); mar. Mary Hendricks. He was a REV. SOLDIER of Va. Died in Va.
    3. Sallie, mar. Peter Robert.
    4. James.
    5. Betty, b. Jan. 11, 1753; mar. — Jones.
    6. Juda, b. Oct. 17, 1754; mar. — Hill.
    7. Samuel, mar. Fanny —.
    8. Ann (or Nancy), b. July 5, 1760; mar. — Stillwell.
    9. Patty, b. July 3, 1764; mar. John Gill.
    10. Susanna, b. 1768; mar. SAMUEL HAWKINS, REV. SOLDIER of Ga., brother of BENJAMIN HAWKINS, Col. of Ga. Reg.
    11. Lucy, b. April 30, 1769.
    12. Ezekiel, b. April 30, 1756.
    13. Reuben, mar. (1) Ann; (2) Polly Lawson.

GEORGE SLAUGHTER, b. in Va., 1764; d. 1840, Greene Co., Ga. Served as private, Va. Line. Placed on Pension Roll. Married 1788, Martha Smith, d. 1813.

REUBEN SLAUGHTER, b. in Va., Nov. 4, 1766; d. after 1792 in Greene Co., Ga. Served as private, Bedford Co. Militia. Received grant of land in Ga. for his services. Married (1) Ann —; mar. (2) Polly Lawson. Had issue.

SAMUEL SLAUGHTER, b. in Va.; d. 1821, Baldwin Co., Ga. Will made April 5, 1820, pro., July 4, 1821. Served in the Bedford Co., Va. Militia and received land grant in Ga. for his services. Married Fanny —.

Children:
1. Daniel.
2. John.
3. Reuben.
4. Prudence A., mar. Isaiah Chapman.
5. Sally, mar. (1) 1799, Daniel Candler; mar. (2) 1819, D. S. Chapman.

NOTE: Nancy Hart Chapter, D. A. R. of Milledgeville, Ga., marked graves of SAMUEL SLAUGHTER, 3 miles from Milledgeville; COL. DAVID LOWE, JAMES PARK, GEORGE DAWSON, and MICAJAH WILLIAMSON, all REV. SOLDIERS.

ABNER SMITH, b. in Ireland; settled in S. C. Wounded in Battle at Sullivan's Island. Received Pension as a REV. SOLDIER while a resident of Coweta Co., Ga., where he d.

ALEXANDER SMITH, granted a Pension as REV. SOLDIER, 1840, while a resident of Meriwether Co., Ga.

CHARLES SMITH, b. 1760 in Md.; d. 1822, Morgan Co., Ga. Served as 2nd Lieut., Md. Line. Received bounty land in Ga. Married Jane Pinckard.

CHARLES SMITH, b. 1764 in S. C.; d. Jan. 28, 1843, Cherokee Co., Ga. Enlisted 1781; served two months as private in Cavalry under Capt. Jacob Barnett, Col. Hampton's S. C. Reg. He was living in Habersham Co., Ga., 1838. His widow was granted Pension for his services, April 10, 1847, Claim W. 6122. Married Elizabeth Gillespy, d. 1865.
Children: (mentioned in Pension)
1. Jemina, b. Dec. 11, 1785; mar. — Hyde.
2. James, b. 1788.
3. Anna, b. 1790; mar. — Conn.
4. Elizabeth, b. Mar. 21, 1793; mar. — Boling.
5. Edward G., b. 1798; mar. Elizabeth —.
6. Charles, Jr., b. 1800.
7. John, b. 1803.
8. Noah.

COLESBY SMITH, b. in Va., 1765; d. Washington Co., Ga., 1840. Served as private, Va. Militia. Granted bounty in Ga. for his services. Married 1792, Anna Henry. (Grave marked by Ga. D. A. R.)

DANIEL SMITH, b. in Conn.; d. Savannah, Ga., 1814. A REV. SOLDIER. A Custom Officer of Savannah. Left wife and children.

FRANCIS SMITH, b. in Va.; came to Ga., and d. on Fishing Creek,

Wilkes Co., Ga. Received grant of land in Ga. for his services as a REV. SOLDIER. Married Lucy Wilkerson.
Children:

1. John, mar. Miss Walker; moved to Tenn., then Mo.
2. Ebenezer of Wilkes Co., mar. Frances Anderson.
3. William Wilkerson, mar. Judith Heard; moved to Ala.
4. Thomas, mar. Cynthia White; moved to Mo.
5. Francis, mar. Mrs. Toombs (formerly Miss Kelne. She mar. (3) Andrew White of Tenn; mar. (4) Gov. Blount of Tenn. She mar. 4 times before she was 21 years of age).
6. Reuben, mar. —; moved to Mo.
7. Ann Adams, mar. Gov. Peter Early of Ga.
   Children:
   1. Augustus.
   2. Thomas   5. Peter.
   3. Alexander.   6. Lucy.
   4. Francis.   7. Cynthia.
   She mar. (2) Rev. Adiel Sherwood.

HARDY SMITH, b. 1757, Johnson Co., N. C.; d. 1852, Laurens Co., Ga. Served as private, N. C. Troops, under Col. Armstrong and Col. Johnson. Received bounty land in Ga., on Oconee River and was also granted Pension for his services. Mar. (1) —; (2) 1796, Rebecca Thompson, d. 1835.
Children by (2) wife: (known)

1. Hardy, Jr. (1801-1864); mar. (1) —; (2) 1836, Ann Anderson (dau. of Gaillard Anderson of N. C.
2. Thompson.
3. Loftin.

ISAAC SMITH, b. New Kent Co., Va., 1758; d. Monroe Co., Ga., 1834. Enlisted as Sergeant, 1st Va. Reg. In 1831 he was placed on the Pension Roll of Ga. Married Rebecca Gilmore.

JAMES SMITH, b. in N. C.; was a Soldier in the N. C. Continental Line. He was at the Battle of Cowpens and other engagements. He removed to Lincoln Co., Ga., then Greene Co., Ga., where he d. Mar. Elizabeth Cowan, b. in Scotland; d. at more than 100 years of age, in Cobb Co., Ga.
Children: (known)

1. Ebenezer, mar. Cynthia Lewis.
2. Dau., mar. Jesse Oslin.
3. Dau., mar. Rev. William Collins.

JOHN SMITH, b. in England; d. Washington Co., Ga. Served as Lieut., Va. Militia, under Col. Thomas R. Walker. Married Elizabeth Taylor.

JOHN GOTTLEIB ISRAEL SMITH, b. 1755; d. 1820 in Ga. Served as private, Ga. Troops. In 1782, he petitioned Council of Safety for a discharge in order to help the suffering in Savannah after the evacuation by the British. Married at Ebenezer, Ga., Christiana Kieffer (1755-1841). His will on record, Bryan Co., Ga.
Child:
1. Christiana Smith, mar. Charles Ryals.

LARKIN SMITH, b. 1760 in Va.; d. Oglethorpe Co., Ga., Oct. 20, 1834. Received Pension for his services as private in Capt. James Baytop's Co., Col. Heth's Va. Reg. Married Avey Bradley (1767-1807).

ROBERT SMITH, b. Feb. 20, 1760; d. and was buried near Cork, Butts Co., Ga. He was a REV. SOLDIER. Married Ferguson Wilson,* b. Nov. 1767 on ship-board in passage from Ireland to America.
Children:
1. Hugh, b. Nov. 27, 1787.
2. Elizabeth, b. July 4, 1789.
3. Jane, b. May 19, 1792.
4. Robert Wilson, b. Mar. 10, 1794. Soldier of War of 1812.
5. Ann Adair, b. Aug. 16, 1796.
6. Mary, b. Dec. 14, 1798.
7. David, b. Sept. 16, 1801.
8. Rosannah, b. May 4, 1804.
9. William, b. June 12, 1811.

THOMAS SMITH, b. in Va.; d. 1785, Warren Co., Ga. A REV. SOLDIER. Received bounty land in Ga., for his services. Married Phoeby.

GEORGE SNELLINGS, b. in Va.; came to Elbert Co., Ga., 1797, where he d. Oct. 1818. Served in Va. Militia. (Grave marked by the Stephen Heard Chapter, D. A. R., Elberton, Ga.) Married Rebecca Hudson of Nottoway Co., Va., d. Elbert Co., Ga., Sept. 1826.
Children:
1. John (1787-1856); mar. Nancy Butler.
2. Hannah (1788-1839); mar. Peter Patrick Butler.
3. Elizabeth, mar. Joseph Brawner.
4. Samuel (1793-1876); mar. 1815, Elizabeth Neal Burton (dau. of Thomas and Rhoda (Hubbard) Burton).
5. Rebecca, mar. John Taylor.
6. Martha, mar. John Hudson.
7. Mary, mar. (1) Richard Burton; (2) Richard D. Hudson.
8. Richard Ward, mar. Elizabeth Nunnellee.

LAZARUS SOLOMON, b. Washington Co., N. C., 1765; d. 1837, Jeffersonville, Ga. Enlisted 1781, 9th N. C. Reg. Married Elizabeth

---

* Supplied by Marjorie Thomas Schairer, descendant; Aug. 1938.

Bedgood.
Children:
1. Delilah (1789-1815); mar. — Finch.
2. Henry, b. 1791; mar. Lucinda Griffin.
3. William, b. 1792.
4. Mary, b. 1795.
5. John, b. 1797.
6. Dicey, b. 1799.
7. James, b. 1800.
8. Sarah, b. 1802

9. Fannie, b. 1804.
10. Peter, b. 1806.
11. Hardy, b. 1808.
12. Carol, b. 1810.
13. Lewis, b. 1812.
14. Elizabeth, b. 1814.

JAMES SPANN, b. Red Banks, S. C., 1754; d. Savannah, Ga., 1796. Served as Lieut. in Col. Samuel Hammond's S. C. Reg. Married Elizabeth Fox (1758-1827).

JOHN SPARKS, b. 1755 in N. C.; d. 1834, Washington Co., Ga. Enlisted Wilkes Co., N. C. Received Pension for his services. Buried near Sandersville, Ga. Married 1779, Margaret Hampton.

JOHN SPEARMAN, b. Caroline Co., Va., 1764; d. 1827, Jasper Co., Ga. Received bounty grant of land for services in Ga. Troops. Married 1787, Mary Witherspoon.

JOHN SPRINGER, b. 1744 in Del.; d. 1798, Washington, Ga. He served as a REV. SOLDIER. Married Ann Green (dau. of WILLIAM GREEN, REV. SOLDIER of N. C., and his wife Mary Christmas).

JOHN STACY, b. St. Mary's Co., Md., 1725; d. in Ga., 1788. Was a member of the "Sons of Liberty", of the Committee of Confidence. Lived in the "Old Midway Colony", Liberty Co., Ga. Married Sarah Dunham Way, d. June 15, 1782.
Children:
1. JOHN STACY, JR., b. Dec. 10, 1761 in Ga.; d. April 7, 1817. Served as REV. SOLDIER with Ga. Troops. Mar. (1) May 3, 1787, Margaret W. Quaterman; mar. (2) Nov. 23, 1797, Sarah Quaterman.
2. James, b. 1763.
3. Margaret, b. 1765.
4. Mary, b. 1767.
5. William, b. 1769.
6. Jonathan, b. 1771.

7. Elizabeth, b. 1773.
8. Susanna, b. 1775.
9. Thomas, b. 1776.
10. Sarah, b. 1778.
11. Robert, b. 1780.

JOHN STANTON, b. 1756, Prince George Co., Va.; d. in Ga., 1832. Buried near Sandersville, Ga. Served as private in Capt. Howell Tatum's Co., N. C. Line. Sergeant 1780. Married 1778, Elizabeth Short.

STEPHEN STAPLES, b. Hanover Co., Va., about 1749; d. Wilkes Co., Ga., 1805. Served as private, Ga. Line, under Gen. Elijah Clarke and Col. Stephen Heard. Married 1778, Mary Starke, b. 1762 (dau. of JOHN STARKE, Col. of Hanover Co., Va. Militia, 1775 and member of Va. Assembly, and his wife Ann Wyatt). They had 14 daughters and 2 sons.

ALEXANDER STEVENS, b. 1726 in England; d. 1813 in (now Taliaferro Co.), Ga. Served seven years as Capt. of Penn. Troops. Buried 2 miles from Crawfordville, Ga. Married in Penn., Catherine Baskins, d. in Ga., 1794.
Children: (not in order of birth)
1. Nehemiah, moved to Tenn.
2. James, b. 1778; mar. 1800, Elizabeth Garrett.
3. Jane.
4. Mary.
5. Catherine.
6. Elizabeth.
7. Andrew Baskins (1782-1846), lived on Kettle Creek, Ga. Mar. (1) Margaret Greer (dau. of AARON GRIER, REV. SOLDIER, who moved to Ga. from Penn., and sister of Robert Grier of "Grier's Almanac". He mar. (2) 1814, Matilda M. Lindsey.
   Children by (1) wife:
   1. Mary.
   2. Aaron.
   3. Alexander Hamilton Stevens, Vice President of the Confederate States of America, and Governor of Georgia in 1882.
   Children by (2) wife:
   4. John.
   5. Andrew B., Jr.
   6. Benjamin.
   7. Linton.
   8. Catherine, mar. 1833, Thomas Grier.

JOHN STEVENS, b. in S. C., 1737; d. Liberty Co., Ga., 1777. Delegate to Provincial Congress, 1775. Married Margaret McCarty.
Children:
1. Elizabeth.
2. Mary.
3. Margaret.
4. John, Jr., mar. Araminthia Way Munroe.

DANIEL STEWART, b. St. John's Parish (now Liberty Co.), Ga., Dec. 20, 1760; d. 1829, and is buried at the Cemetery of Midway Church. At 15 years of age, he enlisted and served under Col. Harden, Gen. Marion, and Gen. Sumpter. At Pottalego, S. C., he was taken prisoner, made his escape and served throughout the War. He was a General in the War of 1812. (The British Army laid waste St. John's Parish, and burned the famous Midway Church of the Dorchester Settlers). He married (1) at Dorchester, S. C., Feb. 20, 1783, Martha Pender,

b. there, Nov. 1763. He mar. (2) Jan. 1, 1786, Susanna Oswald, b. Nov. 2, 1770 at Newport, Liberty Co., Ga. He mar. (3) Mar. 6, 1810, Sarah (Hines) Lewis (widow of Capt. Elijah Lewis).
Child by (1) wife:
1. John, b. 1784, d. y.
Children by (2) wife:
2. Mary, b. Feb. 12, 1788; mar. Major Josiah T. Wilson.
3. Daniel McLaughlin, b. Oct. 4, 1791; mar. 1824, Elizabeth Eichenberger of Glynn Co., Ga.
4. Sophia, b. 1792.
5. Susanna, b. 1794.
6. Joseph Oswald, b. 1797.
7. Martha, bap. Aug. 15, 1799; mar. (1) Jan. 6, 1818, Sen. John Elliot; mar. (2) 1832, Major James S. Bullock
8. John, mar. Hepworth Carter.
9. Sarah Caroline, d. y.
10. Georgia Drusilla, d. y.

NOTE: Martha (Stewart) (Elliott) Bullock was the material grandmother of President Theodore Roosevelt, and a great grandmother of Eleanor Roosevelt, wife of Franklin Delano Roosevelt, the President of the United States.

GRAVERNER STEWART, REV. SOLDIER, received bounty grant of 287.5 acres of land in Washington (now Greene) Co., Ga. for his services as a REV. SOLDIER. He married Jane —.

HENRY STEWART (son of MATTHEW STEWART, b. in Scotland, 1720; d. in N. C., 1808; a REV. SOLDIER of N. C., and his wife Elizabeth McCall of N. C.), was b. in Anson Co., N. C., 1759; d. 1861 in Ga. Enlisted in N. C., Aug. 1776, under Capt. Charles Polk; transferred to Capt. Thomas Ray; and then served under his father CAPT. MATTHEW STEWART. After the War, removed with his brother JAMES STEWART, also REV. SOLDIER, Wilkes Co., Ga. Received for his services, land in this Co. Removed to Greene (now Taliaferro) Co. Applied and was granted a Pension.

JAMES STEWART, b. Aug. 3, 1732, Dorchester Co., S. C.; came to Liberty Co., Ga., 1752; then to St. John's Parish. Served in Ga. Militia from Liberty Co. Member of the House of Assembly and of Executive Council, 1783. (Name sometimes spelled Stuart). He mar. (1) Susanna —; mar. (2) 1782, Elizabeth Jackson. She mar. (2) Sept. 1785, as (2) wife, Thomas Stone, and d. Dec. 1785. James Stewart d. 1784, and his bounty grant of land (250 acres) on certificate of Col. John Baker, Liberty Co., was receipted for by his son James M. Stewart.
Children:
1. William.
2. John, b. 1764; mar. 1798, Susanna Graves.

3. James M., b. Oct. 31, 1766; mar. Sarah Mann.
   Child:
   1. Elizabeth, mar. 1818, William H. Mell.
4. Josiah (1771-1805).
5. Charles, mar. Christian Graham.
6. Susanna, mar. William Thompson.

JAMES STEWART, b. in Va., 1737; d. 1794, Chatham Co., N. C.
Served as private, 9th N. C. Reg. Married 1758, Elizabeth —
Child:
   1. Mary Stewart (1760-1851); mar. 1777, BENJAMIN HAYGOOD,
      b. in Va., 1758; d. 1849 in Ga. Enlisted 1775 and served in
      Capt. Geo. Herndon's Va. Reg.

JOHN STEWART, b. 1740 in S. C.; d. 1815, Liberty Co., Ga. A
member of "Legionary Corps" of Ga. Was at the Battle of Midway
Church and also at the Siege of Savannah.

JOHN STEWART, came to Wilkes Co., Ga.; made will there, June
26, 1829, pro. Sept. 1, 1829. Received grant of land for his services
as a REV. SOLDIER. Married Mary —.
Children: (from will)
   1. Dogel (or Dugald).
   2. James.   4. Dau., mar. Wylie Pope.
   3. Charles.   5. Ann, mar. William Smith.

JOHN STEWART, b. Feb. 23, 1726, S. C.; d. in Liberty Co., Ga.,
Sept. 4, 1776. Served as Col. Artillery, Ga. Brigade. Married (1)
Susanna —, d. Oct. 21, 1766; mar. (2) Aug. 7, 1769, Sarah Nichols.
Children by (1) wife:
   1. Sarah, b. 1751; mar. William Quaterman.
   2. Ann, d. y.
   3. Susanna, b. 1758; mar. Joseph Fox.
   4. Daniel, mar. (1) Martha Pender; (2) Susanna Oswald; (3) Sarah
      (Hines) Lewis.
   5. Mary, d. y.
   6. John, d. y.
Child by (2) wife:
   7. Elizabeth, b. 1774; mar. John Jones.

NOTE: Heirs of JOHN STEWART, dec. REV. SOLDIER, Nov. 2, 1786,
sold to Joseph Philips, 287.5 acres of land in Greene Co., granted
him for his services, 1785. Heirs were his children: James, Robert,
Charles, and Lydia Stewart.

WILLIAM STEWART, b. 1762; d. Monroe Co., Ga., 1848. Served as
private and Sergeant of Va. Militia; placed on Pension Roll for his
services, 1834. Married Mary (called Molly) Penn, d. 1816 (dau. of

Joseph Penn and wife Mary Taylor, dau. of JOHN TAYLOR of Va.
(1696-1780), a PATRIOT and his wife Catherine Pendleton).
Children:
1. John.
2. Thomas (1792-1871); mar. Nancy Russell.
3. Charles.
4. James, mar. Jane Russell.
5. Blanton, mar. Regina Maria Dyson.
6. Richard (1808-1850); mar. Elizabeth Booty.
7. Nancy.
8. Frances, mar. — McCommon.
9. Polly

SAMUEL STILES, b. in the Bermudas; settled in Bryan Co., Ga.,
1769. Was a REV. SOLDIER and was at the Siege of Savannah, Ga.
Married Catherine Clay (dau. of JOSEPH CLAY, REV. SOLDIER,
Savannah, Ga.).

THOMAS STONE, b. in S. C.; came to St. Philip's Parish (now
Bryan Co.), Ga. Was a J.P. 1774-1778. Was appointed on the com-
mission for confiscated estates from Chatham Co., 1782, to the House
of the Assembly. Gave material aid and support to the cause of the
Colonies. He mar. (1) May 3, 1759, Frances Guerin; mar. (2) 1785,
Elizabeth (Jackson) Stewart (widow of James Stewart of Midway, Ga.);
mar. (3) May 19, 1799, in Glynn Co., Ga., Elizabeth Clubb (widow of
Thomas Clubb of St. Simons, Ga.). They lived in Brunswick, Glynn
Co., Ga., where he d.
Children by (1) wife:
1. Susanna.
2. Elizabeth Frances, mar. 1791, William Maxwell.
3. Henry Dassex, mar. (1) 1788, Susanna McClelland; mar. (2)
Ann (Maxwell) Oswald.

HENRY STONEHAM, b. Amherst Co., Va.; d. Jan. 18, 1815, Jackson
Co., Ga. Served as private, Va. Troops, under Capt. Campbell. Wounded
at Guilford Court House. Married Jane Dillard (1759-after 1856); she
was living 1856 in Grimes Co., Texas, when she was allowed 160 acres
of bounty land as the widow of a REV. SOLDIER.
Children: (known):
1. George, b. in Va., 1786.
2. John D., b. 1795.

ANTHONY STORY (son of GEORGE STOREY, REV. SOLDIER of
Penn. and S. C., and his wife Nancy Cantor), was b. 1746; d. Jackson
Co., Ga., 1799. Served in Capt. Robert Farris Co., Col. Brandon's S. C.
Reg. Married Sarah Farris (1748-1795).
Child:
1. Edward Storey (1772-1852); mar. Margaret Thompson (dau. of

JOHN THOMPSON, REV. SOLDIER of S. C. and his wife Margaret Ann Wallace).

JAMES STOVALL, b. in Va.; d. Elbert Co., Ga., of wounds received during REV. WAR. Served with Va. Troops. Received land grant in Elbert Co., Ga. for his services. Married Miss Bradley and moved to Ga., 1787.

JOSIAH STOVALL and BENJAMIN STOVALL, both REV. SOLDIERS from Granville Co., N. C. (sons of JOHN STOVALL, REV. SOLDIER of N. C.), received land in Wilkes Co., Ga. for their services. Josiah d. 1798, Lincoln Co., Ga.; Benjamin d. 1828, Oglethorpe Co., Ga.

THOMAS STOVALL, b. Henry Co., Va.; d. 1806, Hancock Co., Ga. Served under Gen. Clark, Va. Line. Married (1) 1781, Elizabeth Cooper (1762-1843) (dau. of CAPT. THOMAS COOPER, b. in Va.; d. Greene Co., Ga. Served as Capt., Va. Line, and his wife Sarah Anthony). Children: (born in Henry Co., Va.)
1. George, b. 1783; mar. Elizabeth Jeter.
2. Joseph, mar. Mary Pleasant Bonner.
3. Pleasant, mar. (1) Miss Lucas; (2) Miss Trippe; (3) Mrs. Hill.
4. Sallie, mar. Benjamin Simmons of Sparta, Ga.
5. Ruth, mar. Mr. Hunt.
6. Polly.

LEWIS STOWERS, b. Orange Co., Va., 1764; d. 1844, DeKalb Co., Ga. Served as private in Capt. Richard White's Co., Col. Taylor's Va. Reg. Married 1786, Joyce Sheflett (1765-1842).

JACOB STRICKLAND, b. 1741, N. C.; d. 1804, Franklin Co., Ga. Served in N. C. Line. Received bounty grant of land, 1784, in Franklin Co., Ga., for his services. Settled there with his brothers Henry, Isaac, and Solomon Strickland of N. C., on Rocky Comfort Creek. Married in Guilford, N. C., 1765, Priscilla Young. Children:
1. Faith, b. 1767; mar. — Myers; moved to Miss.
2. Tamar, b. Oct. 13, 1768; mar. WILLIAM GILBERT, REV. SOLDIER, living in Wilkes Co., Ga.
3. Isaac (1770-1857); mar. 1799, Mary Hargrove. Settled in Madison Co., Ga.
4. Jacob, b. May 6, 1772; mar. widow Sanders.
5. Mary, b. 1773; mar. (1) JOHN GILBERT, a REV. SOLDIER. Settled Franklin Co., Ga. She mar. (2) James Allen of Habersham Co.
6. Hardy, b. 1775; mar. Susan Pyron of Jackson Co., Ga. Settled in Madison Co.
7. Priscilla, mar. her cousin Hardy Strickland. Settled in Jackson Co., Ga.

8. Celia, mar. Robert Young of Hill Co.
9. Henry, b. 1781; mar. Elizabeth Wilkins of Franklin Co. Settled in Hall Co.
10. Wilson, mar. Polly Connally. Settled Gwinnett Co.
11. Betsey, mar. — Eubanks. Moved to Tenn.
12. Nancy, mar. James Rylee of Franklin Co.
13. Sarah, mar. Berry Vaughn.

SOLOMON STRICKLAND, b. 1735 in N. C.; d. 1818 in Ga. Served N. C. Line. Married Amy Pace (Marriage bond on file, Raleigh, N. C.). She was b. 1739 in N. C.; d. in Ga., 1815. He served in N. C. Militia at the Battle of King's Mt. He mar. (2) Elizabeth Hodge, 1760.
Child:
1. Eunice.

CHARLES STRONG, b. Hanover Co., Va., Jan. 18, 1764; d. Clarke Co., Ga., Oct. 16, 1848. Served as private, Va. Line; later Captain. On Pension list of Ga., 1831, from Oglethorpe Co. Married Nov. 29, 1785, Sarah Thompson (sister of JOHN THOMPSON of Ga., REV. SOLDIER), b. July 25, 1764; d. May 27, 1849.
Children:
1. Elizabeth (1787-1807); mar. Obediah Echols.
2. William (1789-1795).
3. Elisha (1792-1879); mar. Ann Scott Hill (dau. of Thomas Hill).
4. Sarah Key (1795-1877); mar. Burwell Pope.
5. Ann T., mar. Ebenezer Newton.
6. Susan (1799-1875); mar. Thomas W. Golding.
7. Charles (1801-1870).
8. Nancy, d. y.
9. Martha (1805-1877); mar. 1824, John D. Moss, Athens, Ga.

FRANCIS STROTHER, b. Culpeper Co., Va.; d. Lincoln Co., Ga., REV. SOLDIER. Married Sarah Holliday, Wilkes Co., Ga.

JOHN STROTHER, b. in Va.; d. 1796, Hancock Co., Ga. Received pay for services, N. C. Line at Hillsborough Dist., Orange Co., N. C. Moved to Franklin Co., then Hancock Co., Ga. Married Jane Fussell, will probated May 1830.
Children:
1. David.
2. Aaron.
3. John, mar. Hannah —.
4. James.
5. Richard.
6. Anna, mar. — Moody.
7. Elizabeth, mar. — King.
8. Martha, b. in Va., 1765; d. Clarke Co., Ga. She mar. (1) Amos Thompson; mar. (2) MARK STROUD, a REV. SOLDIER, d. Hancock Co., Ga.

JOHN STROUD, b. 1732, Amwell, New Jersey; d. by drowning, in

Ga., 1837, buried Mars Hill Cemetery, Clarke Co., Ga. (Grave marked by Ga. D. A. R.) Joined the Colonial Army in Penn.; fought in the French and Indian Wars; served as REV. SOLDIER in N. C., under Major John Ashe, 1st N. C. Reg., 1777-1779. Moved to Burke Co., Ga., then Hancock Co., Ga., then to Clarke Co., Ga. He married 1756, Sarah Connally (Connelly).

Children: (not in order of birth)
1. Margaret (1757-1834); mar. STEPHEN CROW (1750-1830), a REV. SOLDIER of Ga.
2. William.
3. John.
4. Betty.
5. Hannah, mar. — Melson.
6. Mary, mar. William Haygood.
7. Rachel, mar. Jeremiah Burnett.
8. Sarah.
9. James.
10. Mark.
11. Tabitha.

MARK STROUD, b. Hillsborough Dist., N. C., Feb. 27, 1763; d. Hancock Co., Ga., while enroute to Clarke Co., July 2, 1798. Member N. C. State Reserves, and was at the Battle of Guilford Court House. Married 1784, Martha (Strother) Thompson.
Children:
1. William, mar. Serena A. Ragan Battle.
2. Levi, mar. Fannie Haygood.
3. Eli.
4. Mary (twin), mar. William Haygood.
5. Sarah (twin), mar. James Haygood.
6. Albion.
7. Orion.
8. Tillitha.

PETER STROZIER, b. 1748 in Germany; d. 1823, Wilkes Co., Ga. Served as private, Ga. Militia, under Col. John Dooly at Kettle Creek. Married Margaret Dozier.

JAMES STUBBS, b. in Va., 1746; d. Putnam Co., Ga., 1822. Served as private, Ga. Line. Married 1770, Mary Eliza Scott (1750-1820).

JOSEPH SUMNER, SR., a REV. SOLDIER of Emanuel Co., Ga. Drew land for his services, and also in Lottery of 1827.

WILLIAM SUTTLES, b. in Va., 1731; d. 1839 in Ga. Received bounty land in Ga. for his services as a private in Va. Troops. Married Margarette Harley.

STEPHEN SWAIN, b. Chowan Co., N. C.; d. 1796 in Montgomery Co. (formerly Laurens), Ga. Married Tyrrell Co., N. C., Ann Elizabeth —. Served as a REV. SOLDIER of N. C., as Ensign, 1775, 8th Co.Reg. Batt. of Foot. Resigned Aug. 1777. Received land, 1790, on the Oohoope River.
Children: (known)
1. Stephen, served as a member of the Ga. Legislature 33 years, from Montgomery and Emanuel Counties, Ga.
2. Canneth, b. 1770; married Rebecca Johnson. He d. Thomas Co., Ga.
3. Sherrod, mar. Mary Lane.

JOHN TALBOT, b. in Va., July 15, 1735; d. Wilkes Co., Ga., Aug., 1795. One of the Signers of the Declaration of Independence at Williamsburg, Va., 1774. Served as PATRIOT. Married (1) Sarah Anthony (no issue); mar. (2) Phoebe Mary Mosely (dau. of COL. WILLIAM MOSELEY of Va.); they moved to Wilkes Co., Ga., 1783.
Children:
1. Elizabeth Cresswell.
2. Mathew, mar. Elizabeth Munger.
3. Ann Williston, mar. MAJOR JOHN TRIPLETT, REV. SOLDIER of Md.
4. Phoebe, mar. COL. DAVID CRESSWELL (son of Rev. James Cresswell of Va.), REV. SOLDIER of Va., and was granted bounty land for services under Gen. Nathaniel Greene, in Franklin Co., Ga. He d. in Ga.

MATHEW TALBOT, b. Bedford Co., Va., 1729; d. Morgan Co., Ga., 1812. Served in Bedford Co., Va. Militia. Married Mary (Haile) Day. As a PATRIOT, settled 1778 on the Watauga River, Ga. Fort Wautauga was built for his place.
Children:
1. Hale, b. 1754.
2. Mathews, b. 1756.
3. Thomas.
4. William, b. 1760; mar. Mary Bailey.
5. Edward.
6. Clayton.
7. Mary.

BENJAMIN TALIAFERRO (son of ZACHARIAH TALIAFERRO, REV. SOLDIER of Va., and his wife Mary Boutwell), was b. 1750 in Va.; d. Wilkes Co., Ga., Sept. 3, 1821. Served as Col. under Gen. Lee and Gen. Lincoln in Southern Army. Captured at Charleston, S. C. He married (1) Martha Meriwether; mar. (2) Miss Cox.
Children by (1) wife:
1. Emily, mar. Isham Watkins.
2. Louis Bourbon, mar. Betsey Johnson.

3. Betsey.
4. Mary.
5. Benjamin, Jr., mar. Martha Watkins (dau. of James Watkins, Sr. of Elbert Co., Ga.).
6. Martha, mar. William McGehee.
7. David, mar. Mary Barnett.
8. Thornton, mar. (1) — Green; (2) widow Lamar.
9. Margaret (1794-1836); mar. (1) John Brown; (2) Joseph Green.
10. Nicholas M. (1801-1871); mar. 1824, Ann Hill (1804-1868) (dau. of Miles Hill and Tabitha Pope; granddau. of ABRAHAM HILL, REV. SOLDIER of N. C. and Ga., and Christian Walton; also granddau. of BURWELL POPE, REV. SOLDIER of Va. and Ga., and Priscilla Wooten).

Child by (2) wife:
11. Zacheriah.

NOTE: Rev. Dabney Jones, Preacher and First Ga. Temperance Lecturer of Coweta Co., Ga. (1791-1866); mar. Mary Penn (1798-1858) (dau. of William Penn, and his wife Frances Taliaferro, dau. of ZECHERIAH TALIAFERRO, REV. SOLDIER, and his wife Mary Boutwell.

JOHN TALIAFERRO, b. in Caroline Co., Va., 1733; d. 1791 in Ga. Served as Captain of Minutemen of Va. Troops. Married Mary Hardin (dau. of HENRY HARDIN, REV. SOLDIER of Va., and his wife Judith Lynch).
Children:
1. RICHARD, b. 1759, Amherst Co., Va.; d. 1781 in N. C., a REV. SOLDIER of Va. Married Dorcas Perkins.
2. Charles.
3. Benjamin.
4. Judith.
5. Rosa.
6. Elizabeth.
7. Anna.
8. Betheland.
9. Sally.
10. Lucy.

CALEB TALLEY, b. Hanover Co., Va.; d. Greene Co., Ga. Served as private, Va. Line. Married Elizabeth Stuart, and moved to Lincoln Co., Ga., in 1797.
Children: (Five of the sons were Methodist Ministers).
1. Dau.
2. William.
3. Nicholas.
4. Alexander.
5. Caleb.
6. Elknah.
7. Nathan.
8. John Wesley, b. 1800; d. 1885 in Texas. Married Rosetta Ralston.

ABSOLOM TARVER, b. in N.C., 1757; d. Hancock Co., Ga., 1831. Served as private, N.C. Continental Line and received grant of land in Ga. for his services. Married 1776, Ursula Smith.

JOHN TATE, b. in Ireland, 1758; d. 1838 in Ga. Received a Pension for service as a private, Penn. Troops, under Col. Dunlap. Married 1790, Anne Olipharit (1768-1841).

JOSIAH TATTNALL (son of Josiah Tattnall, the Loyalist), was b. at Bonaventure, near Savannah, Ga., 1762; d. at Nassau, New Providence, Bahama Island, 1803. His remains were removed to the family burial ground at Bonaventure (now Chatham Co.), Ga. His father, during the Rev. War, removed with his family to the Bahama Island. But, despite his father's care, Josiah Tattnall escaped from home, and in 1782 joined the Colonial Troops, under Gen. Anthony Wayne in Ga. In 1801, he was elected Governor of Ga.
Child:
1. Commodore Josiah Tattnall, Jr., served the United States with distinction upon the high seas.

CLARK TAYLOR, b. Mecklenburg, Va., 1759; d. 1846, Oglethorpe Co., Ga. Served as a REV. SOLDIER and received a bounty grant of land in Ga. for his services. Married 4 times. One wife was Elizabeth Whitehead (1766-1819).

WILLIAM TAYLOR, b. 1760 in N.C.; d. 1812 in Ga. Served as private, 1777, N.C. Troops, 10th Reg., under Col. Abraham Shepard. Married 1780, Mary Billingsley, d. 1804.

WILLIAM TAYLOR, JR., b. 1765, Edgefield Dist., S.C.; d. in Ga. (son of WILLIAM TAYLOR, REV. SOLDIER of S.C., and his wife Nancy Johnson). Served as private and Sergeant in Capt. Joseph Harley's Co., 3rd Reg., S.C. Troops. Married Molly Clarke (dau. of GEN. ELIJAH CLARKE, REV. SOLDIER of Ga., and his wife Hannah Arrington).

JOHN TEASLEY, b. 1755 in Va.; d. Wilkes Co., Ga. Served as private, Va. Troops, and in N.C. Lived Washington Co., N.C. Moved to Wilkes Co., Ga., where he received bounty grant of land for his services. Married Lucy Hunt.
Children:
1. Isham, b. Wilkes Co., Ga.; d. 1834, Elbert Co., Ga. Married Jane (called Jency) Adams (dau. of JAMES ADAMS, a REV. SOLDIER).
2. John.
3. James.
4. George.
5. Peter.
6. Aquilla.
7. Priscilla, mar. Lemuel Rucker.
8. Thomas.

WILLIAM TEASLEY, b. in Va.; d. 1824 in Ga. Served as private, Va. Line. Married Sarah —. She received land, 1825, as the widow of a REV. SOLDIER in Elbert Co., Ga.
Children: (mentioned in his will)
1. Anna, mar. Wesley Christer.
2. Amelia, mar. William Lumsford.
3. Winny, mar. John Horton.
4. Elizabeth, mar. Thomas Horton.
5. Levi.
6. Thomas J.

EDWARD TELFAIR, b. in Scotland, 1735; came to Va., 1758, then to N. C., and later, 1758, settled in Savannah, Ga. Was a "Son of Liberty", Member Ga. Assembly, 1776; Member Continental Congress; and on July 24, 1778, signed the ratification of the Articles of Confederation. Was elected Governor of Ga., 1786; and as Governor, entertained George Washington, President of U. S., on his memorable visit to Ga. in 1791. He d. Savannah, Ga., Sept. 17, 1807. Married Sarah (dau. of WILLIAM GIBBONS, REV. PATRIOT of Ga.
Children:
1. Edward.
2. Thomas, mar. Margaret Long (dau. of Col. Nicholas Long).
3. Josiah G.
4. Alexander.
5. Mary.
6. Sarah.
7. Margaret.

FRANCIS TENNILLE, b. Prince William Co., Va., 1747; d. in Ga., 1812. Enlisted Washington Co., Ga., 2nd Batt. Served as Lieut., Capt., and Lieut. Col., Ga. Militia. Married Mary Elizabeth Bacon Dixon (dau. of ROBERT DIXON, a REV. SOLDIER, and his wife Ann Bacon of Ga.).
Children:
1. Francis (1799-1877); mar. Miss Jordan.
2. William, mar. Priscilla Jordan.
3. Robert.
4. John.
5. Benjamin.
6. Algernon.
7. Sidney, mar. Louise Dunbar Roe.

RICHMOND TERRELL, b. 1760, Charlottesville, Va.; d. Newton Co., Ga., 1856. Served at the Battle of King's Mt. Married Cecilia Darracott.

SIMON TERRELL, b. 1755, Orange Co., N. C. Placed on Pension Roll, 1836, of Franklin Co., Ga., for services as Dragoon, N. C. Mil.

Married Ann Sarah Thompson. He d. Franklin Co., Ga. 1836.
Children: (known)
1. William, b. 1784; mar. Sarah Kendrick.
2. Thompson, mar. Miss Baker.
3. Hannah, mar. James Allen.
4. Timothy, b. 1777; mar. Mary (Polly) Davis.
5. Elizabeth, mar. — Martin.
6. Amelia, mar. Thomas Hollinsworth.

VINCENT A. THARPE, b. in Wales, 1760; came to Va., then S. C.,
and d. Twiggs Co., Ga., 1825. Served as private in S. C. Troops under
Gen. Francis Marion. Was a gunsmith by trade and was detailed to
make guns for Continental Army. After the war was a Baptist minister of Ga. Married (1) —; (2) Sarah Persons.
Children: (known)
1. Jeremiah Allen, mar. Jane Dunn, a Soldier of 1812.
2. William, mar. Martha Davis.
3. Chadwick, mar. Elizabeth —.
4. John, mar. Obedience Elizabeth Hatcher.

JAMES THOMAS, b. in Va.; settled at Augusta, Ga. Was presented
a sword "for his gallant service" under Gen. Nathaniel Greene. He d.
1844, and is buried in Baldwin Co., 8 miles from Milledgeville, Ga.

PHILIP THOMAS, b. 1753, Charles Co., Md.; d. 1821, Franklin Co.,
Ga. Served as Corporal in Capt. Yates Co., Col. Josiah Hawkins,
Charles Co., Md. Reg. Married Elizabeth Covington Wailes.
Children:
1. John W.
2. Philip W.
3. Elizabeth.
4. Edward Lloud (1778-1850); mar. Mary Hogue.
5. James L.; mar. Rebecca Avery.
6. Levin Wailes, mar. Thursa Farrar.

WILLIAM THOMAS, b. 1763, Culpeper Co., Va.; d. 1835, Franklin
Co., Ga. Served as private, Capts. Leah, Chapman, and Varnum, under
Col. Paisley.

ALEXANDER THOMPSON, b. in Penn.; d. in Wilkes Co., Ga.
Served as a REV. SOLDIER of N. C., from Burke Co. Received grant
of land for his services in Ga. Married 1760, Elizabeth Mary Hodge.
Children: (known)
1. William, mar. Mary Tillman (dau. of William and Mary (Farrow) Tillman).
2. Alexander, Jr. (1771-1845); mar. Eunice Strickland (dau. of
SOLOMON STRICKLAND, b. 1735; d. 1818 in Madison Co., Ga.,
REV. SOLDIER, and his wife Amy Pace).

ANDREW THOMPSON, b. 1762 in S. C.; d. 1819. Served in the S. C. Militia, and was captured by the British. Married Mary McBride. Child:

1. Mary McBride Thompson, b. Union Dist., S. C., Nov. 30, 1807; d. in Coweta Co., Ga., Oct. 2, 1902. She was a "Real Daughter" of the National Society D. A. R.

BENJAMIN THOMPSON, b. in Ireland; d. in Hancock Co., Ga., 1796. Served as private, Ga. Line. Received land grant for services. He married Ann —, d. after 1802.
Children: (known)

1. John.
2. William, moved to Miss.
3. Jesse.

DANIEL THOMPSON, b. in Ireland, 1759; d. Moreland, Ga., 1841. Served in the Va. State Line for 3 years; was given bounty grant of land, 1783, in Ga., for his services. Married 1785, Jane Boyd, b. 1760. Child:

1. James Thompson (1793-1847); mar. 1820, Elizabeth Carmichael (1804-1866) (dau. of Arthur Carmichael and his wife Frances Bell, dau. of JOHN BELL, REV. SOLDIER of S. C., and his wife Sophia Patrick Carmichael).

ISHAM THOMPSON, b. Chesterfield Co., Va.; d. 1795, Elbert Co., Ga. Served as private in Gen. Elijah Clarke's Reg. Received bounty land in Ga. for his services. Married Mary Ann Oliver, b. 1742.

JOHN THOMPSON, b. in Va., 1762; d. Clarke Co., Ga., 1810. Served 2 years, Va. Continental Line. Married Sarah Strong (sister of CHARLES STRONG, REV. SOLDIER of Ga.).
Children:

1. Richard.
2. Frances, mar.— Price.
3. Elizabeth, mar. — Middleton.
4. Polly.
5. Sarah.
6. Martin.
7. William.

JOSEPH THOMPSON, b. Spartanburg Dist., S. C., 1765; d. in Ga., July 1, 1802. Served in S. C. Troops, under Gen. Francis Marion. Received bounty grant in Ga. for his services upon certificate of Gen. John Twiggs at New Savannah, 1785. Married Jane Dill, b. in Penn., 1770; d. in S. C., April 7, 1802.
Children:

1. Alexander (1791-1877); mar. (1) Betsey Alexander; (2) Elizabeth Pedon.
2. James, d. unm.
3. John, d. unm.

4. Joseph, b. Sept. 29, 1797 in S. C.; d. Aug. 21, 1885 in Atlanta, Ga. Married May 21, 1827, Mary Ann (Tomlinson) Young (dau. of George Tomlinson and his wife Avaline Reynolds of DeKalb Co., Ga.). They had 9 children. He mar. (2) 1851, Mrs. Reeder; (3) Mrs. Thomson.

WILLIAM THOMPSON (buried in St. Paul's Churchyard, Augusta, Ga.). From tombstone, "Member Order of the Cincinnati. Here lies the body of William Thompson, Esq. Who was an Officer in the 9th Pennsylvania Regiment of the late American Army. From its formation in 1776 to its dissolution and amongst his American Bretheren made an offering of his blood on the Altar of Liberty. He departed this life on the 19th of March 1794. Aged 45 years. And as a Testimony of regret, and in remembrance of him, his disconsolate widow hath caused this stone be placed as a covering to his Bed of Rest." Granted bounty land, Mar. 9, 1785.

CHARNEL HIGHTOWER THORN, b. Buncombe Co., N. C.; d. Gwinnett Co., Ga. Buried near Lawrenceville, Ga. Served as a REV. SOLDIER in the Brigade of Light Horse Harry Lee.
Child:
1. Ann Thorn, b. Edgefield Co., S. C., Jan. 1804; d. April 20, 1858. Married William Sanders Howard (1793-1885), A Soldier of 1812 (son of JOHN HOWARD, b. Granville Co., N. C., Aug. 23, 1756; d. 1832; REV. SOLDIER of S. C., and his wife Margaret Fudge, b. in S. C.; d. 1834.

DOZIER THORNTON (son of Mark and Susanna (Dozier) Thornton), was b. in Lunenburg Co., Va., April 14, 1755; d. in Franklin Co., Ga., Sept. 1843. Enlisted from Surry Co., N. C., then Wilkes Co., N. C. Served in N. C. Pension granted to him for his services while a resident of Franklin Co., Ga. He was a Baptist preacher and a Missionary to the Cherokee Indians. Received land grant, 1825, as a REV. SOLDIER, recorded in Elbert Co., Ga. Married (1) Lunenburg Co., Va., Feb. 6, 1779, Lucy Hill, b. Jan. 13, 1760; mar. (2) Jane (Gilbert) Pulliam (dau. of Rev. Thomas Gilbert).
Children:
1. Jeremiah.
2. Reuben, mar. (1) Elizabeth Adams; (2) Katherine Richardson; (3) Elizabeth Waters.
3. Green.
4. Sanford.
5. Jonathan.
6. Dozier, Jr.
7. Evans.
8. Benjamin (1781-1854); mar. (1) Sarah Upshaw; (2) Rebecca Upshaw.
9. Percilla.

10. Martha Ann, mar. Samuel Adams (son of James and Jane (Cunningham) Adams).

SOLOMON THORNTON, b. in Va., 1745; d. 1809, Savannah, Ga. Served as private, Ga. Line. Received bounty grant of land, 1785, in Wilkes Co., Ga. for his services. Married Sarah —.
Children: (mentioned in will)
    1. William (1765-1825); mar. Mary Carter.
    2. Martian.
    3. Nancy.   7. Polly.
    4. Judy, mar. Samuel Hunter. 8. Aggy.
    5. John.   9. Caty.
    6. Joshua.   10. Samuel.

JOHN TILLMAN, b. 1751, Somerset Co., Md.; d. 1830, Bullock Co., Ga. Served in the 2nd Batt., N. C. Continental Line. Received land for his services. Settled in 1810, Bullock Co., Ga. Married Sarah Eggerton (or Ergarton).
Children:
    1. James (1776-1855); mar. Martha Marlow.
    2. John, b. 1777.
    3. Mary, b. 1780; mar. 1800, Henry Simmons.
    4. Elizabeth, mar. William Rushing.
    5. Nancy, b. 1782; mar. 1811, Daniel Simmons.
    6. Henry (1790-1851); mar. Aleph Simmons.
    7. Joseph Isaiah, mar. (1) Catherine Chewing; (2) Cassandra C. Everett.

WILLIAM TILLMAN (son of George and Goudeth Tillman of Va. and N. C.), was b. 1739, Bristol Parish, Va.; d. Burke Co., Ga., 1786. A REV. PATRIOT of S. C., who gave material aid. Removed to Burke Co., Ga. Married in Va., 1768, Mary Farrow.
Children:
    1. William (1770-1825); mar. Polly —.
    2. James (1778-1837); mar. Nancy Vinson.
    3. Sarah (1769-1837); mar. 1772, Nathaniel Trout.
    4. Polly, mar. William Long.
    5. Penelope, mar. James Carithers.
    6. Nancy, mar. 1800, William Thompson of Madison Co., Ga.

WILLIAM TINDALL, b. in Va., 1717; d. Columbia Co., Ga., July 22, 1804. Served in the Va. Continental Army. Received a bounty grant of land for his services in Franklin Co., Ga. Married about 1758, Betsey Ann Booker, d. Sept. 24, 1804, age 62 years.
Children:
    1. John, b. 1759; mar. Mary —.
    2. Caroline Fleming, b. 1762; mar. 1782, JOHN BARNETT (son of NATHAN BARNETT), both John and Nathan were REV.

SOLDIERS of Ga.

3. William, b. 1764; mar. Elizabeth —.
4. Jonathan, b. 1766; mar. Betsey —.
5. Pleasant, mar. Polly Hobbs of Richmond Co., Ga.
6. Sealy Ann, mar. (1) — Davis; (2) — James.
7. Elizabeth.
8. Bird Booker, mar. Nancy —.

JAMES TINSLEY, b. in Richmond, Va., 1764; d. Columbia Co., Ga.
Moved to S. C., near Charleston. Served as private, Va. and S. C.
Troops. Came to Ga., 1790. Married (1) Elizabeth Zachery of S. C.
Had 7 children. Married (2) Lucy Ann (Crawford) Richards (sister of
Hon. William Harris Crawford), and had 3 children.

GABRIEL TOOMBS, b. in Va.; d. Wilkes Co., Ga. A REV. PATRIOT,
too old for active service. Moved to Ga., 1784. Married Ann —, d.
before 1807.
Children:
1. Robert.
2. Dawson Gabriel, mar. Mary.
3. Mary, mar. Dr. Lewis Barrett.
4. Elizabeth.
5. Sallie D., mar. Robt. Dawson.
6. Ann D., mar. John Spearman.

ROBERT TOOMBS, b. in Va.; d. 1815, Wilkes Co., Ga. Served as
Major, commanding a Reg. of Va. Troops. Moved 1783 to Wilkes Co.,
Ga., where he received bounty grant of land for his services. Married
(1) Miss Sanders, no issue; mar. (2) Sarah Catlett; mar. (3) Catherine
Huling (dau. of JAMES HULING, REV. SOLDIER of Va. and Wilkes Co.,
Ga.).
Children by (2) wife:
1. Laurence Catlett Toombs, mar. 1822 in Wilkes Co., Ga., Harriet E. DuBose (dau. of EZEKIEL DuBOSE, REV. SOLDIER of
Lincoln Co., Ga., and his wife Mary Rembert).
Children by (3) wife:
2. Sarah Ann, mar. Henry J. Pope.
3. Robert A. (1810-1885); mar. 1830, Mary Julian DuBose. He
was the famous "Bob Toombs" of Ga. History and a Confederate Soldier.
4. Gabriel.
5. James H.
6. Augustus.

ANDREW NICHOLSON TORRANCE, b. in Scotland; settled in Va.,
1766. Served as private, Va. Troops, and as quartermaster. Moved to
S. C., then Baldwin Co., Ga., where he d. July 1811. Married 1789,
Hester Howard.

Children:
1. William Howard, Soldier of War of 1812; mar. Miss Crawford; both d. 1837.
2. Aurelins.
3. Mansfield.
4. Harriet.
5. Clara.
6. Maria.
7. Matilda.

JOHN TOWNS, b. in Va., 1758; moved to Wilkes Co., Ga.; d. 1825, Morgan Co., Ga. Served as Lieut. in Capt. John Cropper's Co., Col. Daniel Morgan's Va. Reg. Married Margaret Hardwick (widow of JAMES HARDWICK, REV. SOLDIER, killed in battle). He received bounty land in Wilkes Co., Ga. for his services. They had 4 sons and 3 daughters.
Child:
1. George Washington Bonaparte Towns, b. 1801, Wilkes Co., Ga. Moved to Greene Co., then Morgan Co., where he d. Married (1) Miss Campbell; (2) Mary Jones. He was elected Governor of the State of Georgia.

THOMAS TRAMMELL, b. 1747 in S. C.; d. 1823, Upson Co., Ga. Served as private in Capt. Hughes Co., Col. Brandon's S. C. Reg. He married 1775, Mary Turner (1759-1859).

FREDERICK TREUTLEN, b. in Holland; came with his brother to America, settled at Frederica, St. Simons Island, Ga., then in 1735, moved to Savannah, Ga. Made will Feb. 17, 1798, probated Nov. 15, 1798. Served with Ga. Troops. Married Margaret Schadd, b. in Switzerland 1728; d. 1807, St. Simons Island, Ga. (dau. of COL. SOLOMON SCHADD, REV. SOLDIER of Ga. Lived at Wilmington Island).
Children:
1. Catherine, mar. John Tebeau (son of JAMES TEBEAU, REV. SOLDIER of Ga.).
2. Ann, mar. Peter Provost.
3. Elizabeth.
4. Frederick.
5. Charles.
6. Edmund.

NOTE: JAMES TEBEAU, REV. SOLDIER of Ga., mar. Susan Henks. They had six children:
1. John.
2. Samuel.
3. Norris.
4. Charles
5. Daniel.
6. Ann Mary.

JOHN ADAM TREUTLEN, b. in Berectegaden, Austria, 1726; killed by Tories, buried near Metts Cross Roads, S. C. (Grave marked by D. A. R., Chapter St. Matthew, S. C.) He came from Holland to America in 1735; was at Frederica, St. Simons Island; later Vernonsburg, near Savannah, Ga. He was a REV. SOLDIER; member of the First Provincial Congress of Ga.; and was elected as First Governor of Ga. under the Constitution of 1776, on May 8, 1777. Married (1) 1756, Margaretta —, of Purysburg, S. C.(across the Savannah River from Ebenezer, Ga.); mar. (2) Mrs. Ann Unselt (widow of David Unselt). Children by (1) wife:

1. Christiana.
2. Jonathan.
3. Dorothea.
4. Elizabeth, b. April 8, 1760; mar. WILLIAM KENNEDY, b. Aug. 12, 1757 REV. SOLDIER (son of Hugh Kennedy).
5. Mary, mar. (1) Edward Dudley; (2) John G. Morel.
6. Hannah.
7. Christian, mar. Mary —.
8. John Adam, Jr., b. Aug. 29, 1770; mar. 1793, Ann Margaret Miller (dau. of JOHN MILLER, REV. SOLDIER of S. C., under Col. Wm. Thompson).

JOHN TRIPLETT, b. 1756 in Va.; d. Richmond Co., Ga. Served as private, Ga. Troops, under Col. Elijah Clarke. Married Rachael Brock.

PURNAL TRUITT, b. in Delaware, Feb. 26, 1757; d. Wilkes Co., Ga., 1844. Served as private from Del., in Capt. John Patten's Co., Col. David Hall's Reg., 1778. In 1779, transferred to Col. Charles Pope's Reg. Received Pension for his services. Moved to Wilkes Co., Ga. Married (1) Polly Godfrey, b. Jan. 26, 1758, 7 children; mar. (2) Rachel Render, b. 1762, Wilkes Co., Ga.
Children:

1. Sarah, b. 1784; mar. — Montgomery.
2. Nancy, b. 1786; mar. — Collins.
3. Riley, mar. Bonetta Smith.
4. Thomas.
5. Nathan.
6. John.
7. Purnal, Jr., b. Dec. 24, 1795; mar. 1819, Nancy Callaway, b. b. 1796. 10 children.

ISAIAH TUCKER, b. Amherst Co., Va., about 1761; d. in Ga. Served in Va. Militia; was given grant of land for his services in Wilkes Co., Ga. Married Sarah Gibson. Children.

WILLIAM TURK, b. in Ireland 1744; came with his parents James and Mary Turk, to America, and settled, 1757, in S. C. Served as Express Courier under Gen. Pickens of S. C. Married Margaret Archibald (dau. of John Archibald of Rowan Co., N. C., moved to Elbert Co., Ga. Died Franklin Co., 1795).

JAMES TURNER, b. Orange Co., Va., 1752; d. 1804, Franklin Co., Ga. Served as private, Ga. Troops, under Capts. Davis and Burroughs. Married 1772, Martha Seals (1754-1812).

JOSEPH TURNER, b. Dinwiddie Co., Va., July 27, 1764; moved to Hancock Co., Ga., d. Putnam Co., after 1807. Served as Major in Va. Line. Married Rhoda Hines.

ZADOC TURNER, b. 1729, Worcester Co., Md.; d. 1820, Hancock Co., Ga. Served as private, 2nd Reg., Md. Militia. Came to Ga., 1793, and settled at Mt. Zion, Hancock Co., Ga. Married (1) Sabra Hicks; mar. (2) Eliza.—.
Children: (known)
  1. Philip.
  2. Henry.
  3. Joshua.
  4. Zadoc, Jr.

NOTE: ZADOC TURNER came with his family and household goods on a sailing vessel from Chesapeake Bay. After a stormy passage, the vessel was driven to the West Indian Islands, and finally landed at Savannah, Ga. One of the daughters died at sea and is buried in the Colonial Cemetery at Savannah. From Savannah, the Turner family took boats on the Savannah River to Augusta, Ga., whence they crossed Georgia on horseback and in wagons, and finally settled in Hancock Co., east of the Oconee River, just after the Indians had removed a little farther west. He was in the Battles of Brandywine, Trenton, and Valley Forge.

JOHN TWIGGS, Major General of Ga. Troops; b. in Md., June 5, 1750; d. Richmond Co., Ga., Mar. 29, 1816. Served with Ga. Troops also as Capt., Col., and was made Brigadier General in 1781. Married Ruth Emanuel, b. 1744 (a sister of DAVID EMANUAL, a REV. SOLDIER and Governor of the State of Georgia).
Children: (mentioned in will and not in order of birth)
  1. Abraham.
  2. Levi.
  3. Asa.
  4. George, mar. Sarah Lowe.
  5. David Emanuel, b. 1790, Richmond Co., Ga. Soldier of the War of 1812 and Brig. Gen. in the War with Mexico. Married (1) Elizabeth Hunter; mar. (2) Miss Hurt of New Orleans, La.
  6. Asenath, mar. Frances Wells.
  7. Ruth, mar. Harry Greenwood.
  8. Sarah, mar. as (2) wife, Henry Greenwood.

WILLIAM TWITTY, b. 1761 in S. C.; d. 1816 Broad River Settlement. Aided in the defense of Graham's Fort when it was attacked by the Tories. Served with the Lincoln Co. Boys at King's Mt. Married 1784, Frances Rhodes Lewis (1768-1838).

MATTHEW VARNER, b. 1765 in Md.; d. Oglethorpe Co., Ga. Served as private in Col. Wade's Reg., N. C. Married 1787, Susanna Henley.

JAMES VEAZEY, b. in Md., 1725; d. Powelton, Ga. A PATRIOT and private, Ga. Line. Married Elizabeth (Hollinsworth) Johnson (1727-1812).
Children:
1. Zebulon (1751-1827); mar. Nancy Cain.
2. Mary, mar. (1) Dr. Wilson; (2) John Tapperly; (3) Thomas Heard.
3. William (1756-1806); mar. Ann Armistead.
4. Ezekiel (1759-1837); mar. Elizabeth Veazey.
5. Jesse (1762-1813); mar. Sarah Peek.
6. Francinia, mar. William McClellan.
7. JOHN (1760-1847), REV. SOLDIER. Married Jane Rabun. He served as private, Ga. Line and received bounty land in Ga. for his services. His wife was dau. of MATHEW RABUN, REV. SOLDIER of N. C., and (1) wife Sarah Warren.

JOHN VENABLE, b. in Va., 1740; d. in Jackson Co., Ga., 1811. Served with the rank of Captain and was the assistant Commissioner of Provision Laws, Bedford Co., Va. Was at the Battle of Guilford Court House. Married 1780 in Va., Agnes Moorman (dau. of CHARLES MOORMAN of Va.) They moved to Wilkes Co., Ga., where he received a bounty grant of land for his services in Va.
Children:
1. Robert, Soldier of War of 1812. Married Judith Jackson.
2. Charles.
3. Abram.
4. William.
5. John Moorman, mar. Sarah Clower.
6. Nathaniel, mar. Sarah Montgomery.
7. Mary, mar. Jacob Venable.

JOHN VERNER, SR. (son of JOHN VERNER, SR., REV. SOLDIER and his wife Mary Pettigrew), was b. Granville Co., N. C., Mar. 5, 1763; d. Elbert Co., Ga., 1853. Was a REV. SOLDIER and drew bounty land for his services. Married (1) 1785, Jane Edmundson (1767-1792); mar. (2) July 18, 1793, Rebecca Dickey (1774-1849).
Children by (1) wife:
1. Mary P., b. 1786; mar. William Cockerman.
2. William, mar. Elinor Hooper.
3. James, b. 1790.
Children by (2) wife:
4. Nancy, d. y.
5. Jane, b. 1796; mar. Thomas Humphries.
6. John Augustus, b. 1799.
7. David O., b. 1799.
8. Charles, b. 1801; mar. Mary L. Davis.

9. Rebecca.
10. Lemuel H.
11. Samuel, b. 1808; mar. Malinda Crawford.
12. George W., b. 1810; mar. 1833, Harriet Harris.
13. Anna, mar. W. L. Stribling.
14. Ebenezer Pettigrew, mar. Emma Foster.

JOHN VERNER, SR., was a REV. SOLDIER of S. C. He married
Mary Pettigrew and they had 8 children.
Children:

1. David.
2. John, Jr.
3. Samuel.
4. George.
5. Charles.
6. Dinah.
7. Nancy.
8. Jane.

EDWARD WADE, b. in Va.; d. 1790, Greene Co., Ga. Was a
PATRIOT. Took the Oath of Allegiance, Pittsylvania Co., Va., 1770.
Also was private in Va. Troops, under Capt. William Witcher. He
married 1746, Mary —.
Child:

1. PEYTON WADE, b. in Halifax Co., Va., 1755; d. Morgan Co.,
   Ga., 1831. Took Oath of Allegiance and also served under Capt.
   Wm. Witcher. Married Martha Perkins.
   Children:
   1. Archibald.
   2. Jesse.
   3. Peyton L.
   4. Edward.
   5. Frances, mar. Henry Vidette.

THOMAS WAGNON, b. in Va., 1727; d. in Ga., 1810. Served as private, Ga. Line. Married 1748, Frances Vaughn (1730-1805).

JACOB CASPAR WALDHAUER, b. in Austria before 1734; d. Savan-
nah, Ga., May 1804. Married Mary Virginia Flerl (dau. of Capt. JOHN
FLERL, REV. SOLDIER, and his wife Dorothy Brandens). He came to
America with Gen. James Edward Oglethorpe. Represented St. Math-
ew's Parish in the First Provincial Congress of Ga., assembled at
Savannah, Ga., 1775. Served as Capt., Ga. Militia, 1776. Member of
Council of Safety, 1776.
Children:

1. Salome, mar. Israel Floerl.
2. John C., mar. Margaret Floerl.
3. Israel.
4. Elizabeth, mar. Daniel Remshart, b. Oct. 2, 1765 (son of JOHN
   REMSHART, REV. SOLDIER, and his wife Anna Margaret
   Mueller).
5. Hannah, mar. Lewis Weitman.
6. Margaret, mar. David Gugel.

ELISHA WALKER, b. about 1761 in Va.; d. in Washington Co., Ga., 1802. Married 1787, Elizabeth Bowers, d. 1839. She drew land in Lottery as the widow of a REV. SOLDIER. He served as private, 1777, 1st Batt., Richmond Co., Ga., Militia, commanded by Col. James McNeill. Drew bounty land for his services in Washington Co., Ga.
Children:
1. Noah, b. 1790; mar. Charlotte Calhoun.
2. Jeremiah, mar. Joanna —.
3. Henry, mar. Charity Fox.
4. Judy, mar. — Johnson.
5. Perusilia, mar. Arthur Rawls.
6. Annie, mar. — Parker.
7. Lott, mar. Mary (Polly) Walters.

ISAAC WALKER, SR., b. 1707; d. Jefferson Co., Ga., 1781. Served with Ga. Troops and was a PATRIOT. Married Mary Morgan.
Child:
1. ISAAC WALKER, JR., b. 1730; d. 1810, Sump. Co., Ga. Served as private, Ga. Troops. Married Ida Wolf.
   Child:
   1. Henry I. Walker (1789-1862); mar. Winifred Jackson.

JAMES WALKER, b. in N. C., 1753; d. 1848, Upson Co., Ga. He commanded a Brigade at the Battle of Cowpens. Received bounty land in Ga. for his services. Married Charity Smith. They moved to Washington (now Putnam) Co., Ga.
Children:
1. N. C. (1783-1823); mar. Susan N. Palmer.
2. William.
3. Benjamin.
4. Allen.
5. Lucretia, mar. Martin Stamper.
6. Mary, mar. Elisha Perryman.
7. Sarah, mar. Daniel Grant.
8. Amanda, mar. Enoch Womble.

JEREMIAH WALKER, b. 1747, N. C.; d. in Elbert Co., Ga., Oct., 1792. Mar. (1) —; (2) Milly (widow of Jacob Colson). He served as a REV. SOLDIER of N. C., and a Soldier of 1812 in Ga. (1st wife d. before 1780, N. C.)
Children:
1. Polly, mar. John Coleman.
   Children:
   1. Elizabeth.
   2. Narcissa.
   3. Melanda.
2. Henry Graves.
3. Memorable, d. 1803; mar. Sallie —.

4. James Sanders.
5. Elizabeth, mar. — Marshall.
6. John Williams.
7. Jeremiah.

JOEL WALKER, b. Mar. 10, 1733; d. Jefferson Co., Ga., Jan. 19, 1796. Served as a REV. SOLDIER. Received bounty land in Ga. Married (1) Judith — (1733-1782); mar. (2) 1784, Barbara Beal.
Children by (1) wife:
1. Arthur, b. 1756.
2. Joel, Jr., b. 1758.
3. William (1762-1815); mar. 1798, Elizabeth Bostic.
4. David, b. 1765; mar. Elizabeth —.
5. Charles.
6. Elizabeth, b. 1760.
7. Betsey
8. Sarah.
9. Mary, b. 1773.
Children by (2) wife:
10. Jeminah.
11. Peggy)
12. Patty) b. 1787. Twins.
13. Henry.
14. Nancy.
15. Sally)
16. Grace) b. 1795. Twins.

JOEL WALKER, b. Franklin Co., N. C., 1756; d. in Ga., 1800. Served in Ga. Militia. Was at the Battle of Guilford Court House. Received bounty land in Warren Co., Ga., for his services. Married Holly Berry Persons (1765-1846) (sister of JOSIAH PERSONS, REV. SOLDIER of N. C., and his wife Rachel; and dau. of John and Prudence (Jones) Persons).

JOHN WALKER, b. in Va., Dec. 7, 1766; d. Oct. 10, 1826 in Wilkes Co., Ga., near Danburg, Ga. Served as private, Ga. Line, under Gen. Elijah Clarke. Was granted bounty land Wilkes Co., Ga., 1784, for his services. He was Senator, U. S. Congress, 1796. Married Feb. 11, 1790, Martha Smith, b. in Va., Nov. 17, 1770; d. in Wilkes Co., Ga.
Children:
1. William (1792-1823).
2. John S., b. May 12, 1793.
3. Taylor (1795-1817).
4. James, b. Aug. 6, 1798.
5. Nancy, b. Feb. 24, 1801.
6. George (1803-1824).
7. Richard, b. May 13, 1805.
8. Robert, b. Oct. 10, 1807.

9. Sophia, b. Aug. 13, 1810.
10. Martha, b. April 14, 1813; mar. 1830, Thomas Smith (1800-1864).

JOHN H. WALKER, b. 1763, Prince Edward Co., Va.; d. in Ga., 1836. Buried in family cemetery, Monroe, Ga. Enlisted London Co., Va.; served as private, Va. Reg., under Capt. John Henry, Col. Alexander's Va. Reg.; then transferred to Capt. Call's Light Infantry. Married (1) —; mar. (2) 1797, Elizabeth Johns; mar. (3) 1814, Maria Leverett.

WILLIAM WALKER (son of Joel and Judith Walker), b. 1762, Buckingham Co., Va.; d. Jefferson Co., Ga., 1818. Private in Ga. Militia, under Major Gen. John Twiggs. Married Elizabeth Bostic (1770-1835) (dau. of NATHAN BOSTIC (or Bostwick), b. Suffolk Co., Va., 1746; d. 1818 in Jefferson Co., Ga. Received bounty grant of land for services as private, Ga. Militia. Married Martha Gwinn, b. 1750).
Children:
1. Charles Hillary, b. 1812; mar. Caroline E. Jones.
2. Arthur.
3. William H.
4. Anthony Winston.
5. Martha Ann, b. 1806; mar. Littleberry Bostic, Jr.

JOHN WALL (wife Mary), had a bounty grant of 287.5 acres of land granted him for REV. SERVICE, 1785, Washington (now Greene) Co., Ga.

WILLIS WALL, b. in Va.; d. Wilkes Co., Ga. (now Elbert Co.), Ga. REV. SOLDIER. Married Martha Page.

JOHN WALLER, SR., b. Mar. 13, 1749 in Md.; d. 1808, Hancock Co., Ga. Served as private, Md. Troops. Married Elizabeth Rhodes (Rodes).
Children:
1. HANDY, b. in Md.; d. 1845, Putnam Co., Ga. Served as private, Md. Troops. Married 1792, Martha Teasley. Received bounty land.
2. James Waller mar. Elizabeth Ellis (dau. of LEVIN ELLIS, a REV. SOLDIER, b. in Va.; d. Hancock Co., Ga., and his wife Isobel). He was Soldier of 1812; b. Dec. 15, 1768; d. Hancock Co., Ga., 1817. She was b. 1772; d. 1845.
   Children:
   1. Mary Elizabeth.   5. James B.
   2. Martha.   6. Phyllis.
   3. Ellis M.   7. Ibby C.
   4. Elizabeth K.   8. Irwin.
3. Daniel.
4. John.
5. William.

6. Charles R.
7. Elizabeth.
8. Nathaniel E.

GEORGE WALTON, one of the three Signers of the Declaration of Independence of Georgia. He was b. in Va., 1741; came to Savannah, Ga., 1759; and d. at his home in Augusta, "Meadow Garden". Married Dorothy Camber of Chatham Co., Ga., d. Sept. 12, 1832 in Pensecola, Fla. He purchased a country seat (in Augusta, Ga.), 1791, which he called "Meadow Garden", where he spent the last 14 years of his life. He lies buried under the Monument erected to "the Signers", George Walton, Lyman Hall, and Button Gwinnett, in Augusta, Ga.
Child:
1. George Walton, was the first Secretary of State of the Territory of Florida.

NOTE: "Meadow Garden" was purchased by the National Society, D.A.R., for memorial purposes. They have made it a patriotic museum for relics of the Revolutionary period. The Augusta Chapter, D.A.R. of Ga., are in charge of the home.

GEORGE WALTON, b. Prince Edward Co., Va., 1724; d. Columbia Co., Ga., 1796. Served as 1st Lieut. in Col. McIntosh's command, Ga. Line. Married (1) Martha Hughes (1734-1815); mar. (2) Elizabeth Hughes (?).
Child:
1. Nancy Hughes (1760-1809); mar. 1776, THOMAS MOORE, REV. SOLDIER, b. 1756, Prince Edward Co., Va.; d. Columbia Co., Ga., 1806.

JOHN WALTON, b. 1743 in Va.; moved to Richmond Co., Ga. He was member of Provincial Congress of Ga. Married Elizabeth Claiborne.

NOTE: JOHN, ROBERT, and GEORGE WALTON, the Signer, were REV. SOLDIERS of Ga., and were the sons of Robert Walton and Sallie Hughes of Va.

WILLIAM WALTON, b. in Va.; d. Columbia Co., Ga. Served in Va. Continental Army, and received grant of land for services. Moved to Ga., 1790. Married Sallie Grinage.

JOHN WANSLEY, b. 1738, Louisa Co., Va.; d. Elbert Co., Ga., 1833. Allowed Pension as a private, Albemarle Co., Va. Line. Enlisted 1776. Married 1761, Amelia Barber, b. 1744.
Children: (known)
1. Sarah (1766-1800); mar. John Beck.
2. Martha (1781-1868); mar. Benjamin Davis, Jr.

WILLIAM WARD, b. 1757 in Va.; d. 1850 in Ga. Served as REV. SOLDIER. Married Sarah Vernon.
Children: (known)
    1. Sarah.
    2. Vernon.
    3. Nancy.

ROBERT WARE, REV. SOLDIER of Va.; moved to Ga.
Child:
    1. Nicholas Ware, b. Caroline Co., Va., 1769.

NOTE: WILLIAM ALEXANDER WARE, EDWARD WARE, and JAMES WARE, brothers, b. Amherst Co., Va., REV. SOLDIERS who were present at the surrender of Cornwallis at Yorktown, came to Georgia.

EDWARD WARE, b. Amherst Co., Va., 1742; d. Danielsville, Ga., Nov. 3, 1836. Pension granted him 1826 for his services. Enlisted Va., 1776 under Capt. James Higgenbothem; 1778 under Capt. Rucker, Col. Fontaine. In 1780, Sergeant under Capt. Samuel Higgenbothem, Capt. Dillard and Col. Lynch; Second Lieut. Came to Ga. about 1790; lived in Richmond Co., then Madison Co. Married 1781, Sarah Thurmond (dau. of Philip Thurmond of Va.).
Children: (known)
    1. Philip (1786-1853); mar. Mary (Polly) Strickland.
    2. Henry (1788-1822); mar. Melinda Strickland.
    3. Elizabeth, mar. James Long.
       Child:
       1. Dr. Crawford W. Long of Ga., the famous discoverer of "Anesthesia".
    4. Letty, mar. her cousin James Ware, Jr.

JAMES WARE, b. 1745 in Va.; d. Madison Co., Ga. Moved to Ga., about 1790. Commissioned Second Lieut., 1775 in Va. Continental Line. Married Mary Veal.
Children: (known)
    1. Edward, mar. Sarah Daniel Penn.
    2. James, Jr., mar. his cousin Letty Ware. They had 14 children.

WILLIAM ALEXANDER WARE never married. He lived on Line Creek, Fayette Co., where he died.

JESSE WARREN, b. Va.; d. Hancock Co., Ga., 1827. Will made Jan. 16, 1826, pro. Feb. 12, 1827. Served as REV. SOLDIER of Va. Drew land for his services in Lottery 1827. Married Elizabeth —.
Children:
    1. Jeremiah.   4. Jesse, mar. Timley —.
    2. William.   5. Sally, mar. Lott Harton.
    3. Robert.   6. Mary.

7. Susannah.
8. Elizabeth, mar. — Smith.

JOSIAH WARREN, b. in Va.; moved to Onslow Co., N. C.; d. 1806 in Burke (now Laurens) Co., Ga. Served as Capt. at the Coast of Ga. for its defense. Received pay for his services in 1782, and 287. 5 acres of land in 1785. Married 1774, Nancy Doty, b. in New Jersey. Children: (first 2 born in Onslow Co., N. C.)

1. Josiah, Jr.
2. Richard
3. Benajah.
4. Hinchey.
5. Kittrell.
6. Silas.
7. Eli, Soldier of 1812. Gen. in Ga. State Militia.
8. Rachel.
9. Sarah.
10. Mary.
11. Lott, b. 1797.

WILLIAM WARTHERN, b. 1761 in Va.; d. Washington Co., Ga. Served as private, Va. Line. Received bounty land for his services. Married Rebecca Beckham.

JAMES WATKINS, REV. SOLDIER, b. 1728 in Va.; d. Dec. 21, 1798 and is buried Peterburg, Ga., on the North side of the Broad River, just before the waters empty into the Savannah River. He married Martha —, d. Nov. 22, 1803, age 69 years.

MOSES WATKINS, b. Mar. 1745 in Va.; d. 1814, Oglethorpe Co., Ga. Served in Va. Continental Line. Received bounty land in Ga., Feb. 12, 1784. Married Margaret —.

THOMAS WATKINS, JR., b. in Va. (son of THOMAS WATKINS, REV. SOLDIER of Powhatan Co., Va.), was a REV. SOLDIER, killed by the Indian Allies of the British.. Married 1763, Sallie Walton of Richmond Co., Ga. (a sister of GEORGE WALTON, Signer of the Declaration of Independence from Ga.). She mar. (2) Joshua Morris of Ky.
Children by (1) husband:

1. Robert, mar. Elizabeth Walton (dau. of John Walton), lived Richmond Co., Ga.
2. Thomas III, Lieut. in Indian Wars.
3. Anderson, mar. Catherine Eve.
4. George, b. 1770; mar. Mary (called Polly) Early (dau. of Joel Early). Lived in Wilkes Co., Ga.
5. Claiborne, mar. Elizabeth Craig (dau. of CAPT. ROBERT CRAIG, REV. SOLDIER of Va.). She mar. (2) Mr. Clapp.
6. Isaac, mar. twice. Settled in Ark.
7. Polly, mar. William Nichols of Ky.

JOHN WATSON, buried in old Family Cemetery, West Baldwin Co.,

Ga. (Name found in old Land Lottery Book 1819, Baldwin Co., Ga.) He was a REV. SOLDIER.

JOHN WATSON, b. in S. C., 1753; d. 1848, Franklin Co., Ga. Served as private in Capt. Wm. Butler's Co., S. C. Reg. Married Charity Hillen (1752-1850).

ROBERT WATSON of Habersham Co., Ga. REV. SERVICE certified to Jan. 9, 1837. Witt: by Absolem Holcome J. I. C. and John H. Sterrett J. P. Enlisted Jan. 1781 in Co. A. S. C. under Capt. William Alexander and Col. Wade Hampton, Continental Line. Discharged from service, Orangeburg, S. C. A resident of Ga., Mar. 8, 1818.

MOSES WAY, b. 1734 in S. C.; d. Liberty Co., Ga., 1786. Came to Ga. 1754; settled at Midway. Served as Lieut., then Capt., Ga. Militia. Married (1) 1756, Lydia Mitchell, d. 1765; mar. (2) 1766, Ann Winn. Children by (1) wife:
1. Lydia, mar. (1) 1774, Peter Sallens; (2) John Foster.
2. John, mar. 1790, Sarah Goulding.
3. William.
Children by (2) wife:
4. Mary, b. 1767; mar. Samuel Jones, Jr. (son of Samuel Jones and Rebecca Baker, dau. of William Baker and Sarah Osgood).
5. Susanna, mar. — White.
6. Patty.
7. Moses, Jr., mar. widow Susanna Dowse.
8. Rebecca T., mar. — Shearer.

ANTHONY WAYNE, b. in Penn., Jan. 1, 1745. Was made Colonel in REV. WAR and saw service in the North. Took part in the operations in the South and Dec. 1782, took possession of Charleston. After the War, he settled in Ga., and was a delegate to the Convention that framed the first State Constitution after the Independence of the Nation was established. In 1792, he succeeded Gen. Harman as General-in-Chief of the Army. He was called "Mad Anthony Wayne" because of his success in the Northwest against the Indians. He d. in Penn., Dec. 15, 1796. Wayne Co., Ga., named in his honor, was laid out under the Lottery Act of 1803.

BENJAMIN WEAVER, b. 1760, Halifax Co., N. C.; d. 1816, Greene Co., Ga. Served as private in Capt. Raiford's Co., N. C. Reg. Married (1) Miss Drewry, one son and two daus.; mar. (2) Elizabeth Daniel. Children by (2) wife:
1. William Wylie, mar. Caroline Mounger.
2. Travis A. D., mar. Caroline Cook.
3. Henry, d. y.

CLAIBORNE WEBB, b. 1760, Albemarle Co., Va.; d. Elbert Co.,

Ga., 1813. Name appears in list of REV. SOLDIERS of Va., who received pay for their services, 1784, and also received grant of land in Wilkes Co., Ga., 1785. Married Margaret —, b. in Va., 1765. Received land 1827 as widow of REV. SOLDIER. Living in 1832.
Children:

1. Bridges, Soldier of 1812.
2. Margaret, mar. Joseph Glenn.
3. William.
4. Claiborn, Jr.
5. Milton Pope, mar. Alice Deadwyler.
6. Abner, mar. Nancy Deadwyler.
7. Evelina, mar. Mial Smith.
8. Elijah, mar. Ann B. Deadwyler.
9. Martha P., mar. 1825, Joseph Deadwyler.

FRANCIS WEBB, b. Essex Co., Va., 1759; d. 1811, Hancock Co., Ga. Served as Midshipman in Navy, under command of Capt. Travis, on the ship "Dragon". Was wounded. Married 1786, Frances Walker (1764-1809) (dau. of Freeman Walker and his wife Frances Belfield). They moved to Ga., 1810, where he received land.
Children:

1. Bathurst, d. y.
2. Thomas.
3. James (1792-1853); mar. 1813, Rachel Elizabeth Lamar (dau. of Col. Thomas Lamar of Hancock Co., Ga.).
4. John, b. 1794; d. Aug. 19, 1870; mar. Ann (Nancy) Thomason (dau. of John Connor Thomason and his wife Narcissa Jane Lewis). He was a Soldier of 1812.
5. Frances Belfield, d. y.
6. Richard W., d. y.
7. Wm. Meriwether.
8. Frances W., d. y.

ELIAS WELLBORN, b. 1759, Randolph Co., N. C.; d. 1836, Columbia Co., Ga. Placed on Pension Roll. Served as private, N. C. Militia. Received land in 1827 Lottery. Married Mary Marshall. Received Pension.
Children:

1. Ruby, mar. Dr. Davis.
2. Marshall H., mar. (1) Miss Hill; (2) F. Hardaway.
3. Stephen.
4. Lucy, mar. (1) George Lewis; (2) — Morrow.
5. James Madison, mar. Louise Amanda Cody.
6. Martha, mar. William Briscoe.
7. Selina H., mar. Theophilus Hill.
8. Mary, mar. — Fleming.
9. Abner W., mar. — Heard.
10. Nancy, mar. Nathaniel Bailey.

WILLIAM WELLBORN, b. 1733 in N. C.; d. in Ga., 1792. Served as private, N. C. Militia. Was at the surrender of Cornwallis at Yorktown. Married Hepzibah Stearns (dau. of Isaac Stearns and his wife Rebecca Johnson).
Children:
1. Abner, mar. Martha Render.
2. ELIAS, b. 1759, Randolph Co., N. C.; d. 1836, Columbia Co., Ga. Received Pension as REV. SOLDIER. Married Mary Marshall. They had 10 children.
3. Johnson, mar. Sallie Render.
4. Clara, mar. — Dennis.
5. James.
6. William.
7. Chapley.
8. Samuel.
9. Isaac.
10. Mary.

JAMES WEST, b. 1735 in England; d. 1800 in Ga. Served in Va. and Ga. Took Oath of Allegiance in Maryland. Settled in Nacoochee Valley, Habersham Co., Ga. Married Elizabeth Chadwick.

JOSEPH WESTMORELAND, b. in Va., 1740; d. in Va., 1784. He was a REV. SOLDIER, private in Va. Line. Enlisted Mecklenburg Co., Va., and received land in Ky. for his services. (His brother JESSE WESTMORELAND, REV. SOLDIER of Va., mar. Maria Shores; he d. in Tenn.) Joseph Westmoreland mar. Martha Shores in Va., 1764. After his death, she removed with her family to N. C., then to Fayette Co., Ga., where she d. at a very advanced age in 1838.
Children:
1. Joel, moved west.
2. Joseph, mar. (1) Rebecca Simmons; (2) a Creek Indian Princess and moved west.
3. Reuben, mar. (1) Rebecca Jackson; (2) Keziah Simmons (dau. of JOHN SIMMONS, REV. SOLDIER of Va. and Ga.). He was a Soldier of 1812, and in the Indian War in Ga., 1836.
   Child:
   1. Angelina Westmoreland, mar. William de Graffenreid Tidwell (a descendant of WILLIAM TIDWELL, REV. SOLDIER of S. C. and of TSCHARNER DE GRAFFENREID of Va., REV. SOLDIER).
4. Robert, mar. Louise (Ann) Foreman.
5. John, mar. —. Settled in Pike Co., Ga., Soldier of 1812.
6. Sybilla, mar. Benjamin Moody.
7. Dau., mar. — Linch.
   Two daus.

SAMUEL WHATLEY, b. N. C., 1755; d. 1820, Wilkes Co., Ga. Served as private under Col. Elijah Clarke's Ga. Troops. Received land grant for his services. Widow received Pension for his services. Married Catherine Anglin (1762-1857).

HUDSON WHITAKER, b. in N. C., Oct. 23, 1757; d. Washington Co., Ga., July 5, 1817. Served as Ensign, 7th Reg., N. C. Troops, 1776. Married Susanna Thomas, d. 1839. She mar. (2) Miles Young.
Children:
1. Jordan John, b. 1778.
2. Simon (1780-1849); mar. (1) Elizabeth Mary Irwin (dau. of Gov. Jared Irwin of Ga.); mar. (2) Nancy Pierce.
3. Richard, b. 1782; Soldier of War of 1812; mar. Frances Pace (dau. of NATHANIEL PACE, REV. SOLDIER of N. C. and Ga., and his wife Amelia Mildred Boykin).
4. Samuel, Soldier of War of 1812; married Margaret Young; moved to Fla.
5. William, married Mary Cantey.
6. Willis, married Rebecca Britt.
7. Edwin, married (1) Theresa Goode; (2) Martha Cobb.
8. Nancy, mar. John Davis of Baldwin Co., Ga.
9. Hannah, mar. Mr. Dee of Washington Co., Ga.

SAMUEL WHITAKER (brother of Ensign Hudson Whitaker), was b. in N. C. Came from Halifax Co., to Ga., where he died. Received bounty land in Ga. for his services in N. C. Line. Married Elizabeth Williams.
Children:
1. Winifred Mary, b. 1789.
2. Ooroon Datus (1791-1842); mar. Martha Rivers Harris.
3. John.
4. Katherine Boykin, mar. Major John Broadnax.
5. Elizabeth Carr, mar. James Gray.

EDWARD WHITE, b. in Brookline, Mass., 1758; d. in Savannah, Ga., 1812. Served as Ensign, Mass. Line, 1777; transferred as Lieut. Light Infantry, Yorktown, Va. Married (1) 1792, Mildred Scott Stubbs.

JOHN M. WHITE, b. Spottsylvania Co., Va., 1743; d. Elbert Co., Ga., 1833. Served as Capt. Spottsylvania Co., Va. Troops. Received land 1827, as a REV. SOLDIER, in Cherokee Land Lottery. Married 1775, Mildred Thornton Ballenger (dau. of JOSEPH BALLENGER, REV. PATRIOT, and his wife Sarah Franklin).
Children: (mentioned in will)
1. Milly, mar. John Morris.
2. Mary, mar. — Jones.
3. Nancy, mar. Asa Mann (son of JAMES MANN, SR., REV. SOLDIER of S. C.).
4. Lucy K., mar. Thomas Thornton.
5. Frances, d. before 1832; mar. Robert Roebuck, Jr.
6. Eliza, mar. 1823, Richard Rice.
7. Patsey, mar. Martin White.

RICHARD WHITE, b. 1758 in Va.; d. 1814, Columbia Co., Ga. Served as Lieut., Convention Guards, Va. Continental Line, then as Capt. Married 1782, Mary Meriwether (1763-1840).

THOMAS WHITE, b. in Dublin, Ireland, 1753; d. 1844, Wrightsboro, Ga. Served in the Ga. Line as Captain. Received bounty grant of land in Ga. for his services. Married Mary Annie Hunt.
Child:
1. Susan, mar. Daniel Massenglae.

THOMAS WILBURN, b. in N. C.; d. Greene Co., Ga. Received bounty land in Ga. for services as private, Ga. Troops. Married Martha —.

FREDERICK WILLIAMS, b. 1751 in N. C.; d. 1821, Bullock Co., Ga. Served as private, Ga. Militia, under Col. Elijah Clarke. Married Miss Goff.

JAMES WILLIAMS, b. in England, 1750; d. Wilkes Co., Ga., 1794. Commanded a Co., as Capt., 6th Va. Reg. Married 1788, Elizabeth Blackburn.

JAMES WILLIAMS, b. 1757 in N. C.; d. 1817, Bullock Co., Ga. Served as private under Gen. Elijah Clarke at Battle of Kettle Creek. Married 1777, Elizabeth Callaway (1759-1815), Bullock Co.
Child:
1. Rev. Ezekiel James Williams (1803-1888); mar. Flora McDermid.

JOSEPH WILLIAMS, b. in N. C., 1760; d. in Ga., 1850. Served as Ensign and Lieut., Duplin Co., N. C. Militia, Mar. 1779 to May 1781. Married Mary Erwin in Duplin Co., N. C. He died in Telfair Co., Ga., and is buried at "China Hill" plantation.
Children:
1. William H.   5. Rebecca.
2. Daniel.   6. Phoebe.
3. Joseph, Jr.   7. Nancy.
4. Mary.   8. Elizabeth.

WILLIAM WILLIAMS, allowed pension 1835, while a resident of Washington Co., Ga. Enlisted 1777, served as private in Capt. Isaac Moore's Co., Col. Abraham Shepard, and Col. Thomas Clark's N. C. Reg. Was in Battle of Monmouth; captured at Paramus, N. J., released and captured again, May 12, 1780 at Charleston, S. C.

NOTE: From Dept. of Archives and History, Atlanta, Ga. "The original claims of WILLIAM WILLIAMS, REV. SOLDIER, 2/24/1823, and of FOUNTAIN JORDAN, 2/18/1822, REV. SOLDIER, found in the Office of Clerk of Court, Wilkes Co., Ga.

WILLIAM WILLIAMS, b. 1751 in N.C.; moved to St. Mary's, Ga.
Served as an officer and was killed in S.C. after the War by Tory
sympathizers, at a meeting held in 1799. Married Hannah Blewett.
Children:

1. Sarah, mar. — Thomas of S.C.
2. William, Jr., b. St. Mary's, Ga., 1791; d. Bainbridge, Ga., 1860.
   Married (1) Keziah Ashley; (2) Cassandra Sheppard; (3) Mrs.
   Root of Mass.; (4) Mrs. Cook.

JOHN WILLIAMSON, b. in Ireland; d. 1831, Butts Co., Ga. Served
as private, Va. Troops. Married Margaret (Leslie) Mitchell.
Child:

1. Adam Williamson, mar. 1810, Elizabeth Horton, d. 1868 (dau.
   of PROSSER HORTON, b. 1756; d. 1823, Jackson Co., Ga.;
   served as private, Ga. Line, and his wife Sarah —).

MICAJAH WILLIAMSON, b. Bedford Co., Va., 1735; d. Wilkes Co.,
Ga., 1795. Served as Lieut. Col. and as General in Ga. Army. Served
with Gen. Elijah Clarke to protect the frontier of Ga. Married 1770,
Sally (Sarah) Gilliam, b. Henrico Co., Va., 1745; d. in Ga. They moved
to Wilkes Co., Ga., 1768. She was a REV. PATRIOT. During his ab-
sence in the field, the Tories burned their home and hung their 12
year old son.
Children:

1. Charles, mar. Polly Clarke (dau. of GEN. ELIJAH CLARKE
   of Ga. He made his will Feb. 27, 1800 and left his bounty land
   given to him for his REV. SERVICE to his son.). His widow
   mar. (2) William J. Hobby of Conn. and Augusta, Ga.
2. Micajah, Jr.
3. Thomas Jefferson.
4. Peter.
5. William.
6. Sally, mar. (1) Judge John Griffin; (2) Judge Chas. Tait.
7. Nancy, mar. GEN. JOHN CLARKE (son of GEN. ELIJAH
   CLARKE), a REV. SOLDIER, Soldier of 1812, and Governor
   of Ga., 1819 to 1823.
8. Susan, mar. Dr. Thompson Bird.
9. Martha, mar. Thomas Fitch of New England.
10. Mary, mar. 1808, Duncan G. Campbell (son of Archibald
    Campbell of Orange Co., N.C. and Wilkes Co., Ga.).
11. Elizabeth, mar. Peterson Thweatt.
    Child:
    1. Sarah (1805-1879); mar. Thacker Brock Howard (son of
       JOHN HOWARD, b. 1761 in S.C.; d. 1822, Baldwin Co., Ga.,
       a REV. SOLDIER, and his wife Jane Vivian).

ROBERT WILLIAMSON, b. 1760; d. 1810, Screven Co., Ga. Served with Ga. Troops. Received grant of land in Ga. for his services. Married Lucy Conyers (dau. of JOHN CONYERS (1725-1814 in Ga.); served in the Ga. Line under Col. John Thomas, and his wife Sarah Miller (1737-1834), dau. of ELISHA MILLER, b. 1715 in N. C., d. 1800 in Ga.; served as Capt. of Ga. Militia, and his wife Martha Colson (1720-1790).)
Child:
   1. Benjamin Williamson, Soldier of 1812, b. 1792 in Ga.; d. in Ga., 1881; mar. 1821, Elizabeth Roberts (1790-1879) (dau. of JAMES ROBERTS (1744-1814 in Ga.); served Ga. Line and received bounty grant for his services, and his wife Emily Williamson).

EDWARD WILLS, b. in England, 1758; d. 1820, Clarke Co., Ga. Enlisted 1777, as private in Capt. Thomas Thweatts Co., 10th Va. Reg. Married Sarah Vaughn.

JAMES WILSON, b. 1745 in Ireland; d. 1825, Effingham Co., Ga. Served as Capt., 10th N. C. Reg., and also Capt., 4th S. C. Troops. Was captured at Charleston, S. C., 1780. Received bounty grant of land in Ga. for his services. Mar. (1) Sarah —; (2) Ann (Gordon) (Woodward) Pace.
Children by (1) wife:
   1. John, b. 1768; moved to Texas.
   2. James, Jr. (1773-1833 in Ga.); mar. 1794, Elizabeth Morgan.
   3. Jesse, b. 1774; mar. Eliza Cook. Moved to Ill.
Children by (2) wife:
   4. Luke, mar. (1) Patience Crawford; (2) Ann Catherine Griner.
   5. Allen Fulford, mar. (1) Mary Hurst; (2) Serena Hurst; (3) Margaret Fulford.
   6. Elihu, mar. (1) Catherine Tullis; (2) Ann (Achord) Warren. Child by (1) wife:
      1. Stephen, mar. Tabitha Edwards.
   7. Gabriel, mar. Sarah Oglesby.
   8. Jeremiah, mar. Elizabeth Lucas.

JOHN WILSON, b. Feb. 12, 1755 in Buckingham Co., Va.; married Elizabeth Moore, Sept. 2, 1780 in Prince Edward Co., Va. He d. in Greene Co., Ga., July 24, 1834. She was b. 1761; d. Jan. 1840. He served in Va. Continental Line; received bounty land in Ga. for his services.
Children:
   1. Sally, b. Nov. 25, 1782 in Va.; d. July 2, 1863; mar. Thomas Glass (1769-1846).
   2. John, b. Mar. 14, 1789; mar. Polly Anderson.
   3. Jesse, b. Dec. 14, 1792.
   4. Silas (1795-1818).   5. Polly (1803-1808).

JOHN WILSON, b. in England, 1735; killed in Battle in N.C., 1779 by the British. Married 1766 (2) Martha McKennie (sometimes spelled McKenny or Makennie), b. 1739; d. 1790 (dau. of George McKennie, b. in Ireland; d. in N.C., and his wife Margaret Hutchinson (her sister Elizabeth Hutchinson married Andrew Jackson, Sr., parents of Andrew Jackson, President of the United States. Another sister, Jan Hutchinson, married James Crawford).
Child:
1. John McKennie Wilson (1769-1839); mar. Mary (called Pretty Polly) Erwin (dau. of ALEXANDER ERWIN, REV. SOLDIER of N.C., and his wife SARAH ANN ROBINSON, REV. PATRIOT of N.C.).

JOHN WILSON, b. 1756; d. Feb. 15, 1847. Served as Capt., Ga. Troops. Married Oct. 2, 1783, Mary Robertson. From tombstone in McDuffie Co., Ga., near Thomson, Ga., "Sacred to the Memory of John Wilson who died Feb. 15, 1847, age 91 years, 1 mo. and 15 days, an Officer in the Revolution".
Children:
1. Jonathan, b. Sept. 4, 1784.
2. David, b. April 7, 1786.
3. Sarah, b. Sept. 8, 1788.
4. Elias, b. Nov. 18, 1790; mar. (1) Margaret Scott; (2) Temperance Saxon (mother of all his children); (3) Mary Bacon; (4) Elizabeth Rogers, widow.
5. Rebecca, b. June 9, 1793.
6. Elizabeth, b. July 19, 1795.
7. Mark, b. Dec. 1, 1797.
8. John, b. May 14, 1800.
9. Joel, b. Sept. 13, 1802.
10. Daniel, b. May 13, 1805.

JOHN WIMBERLY, b. in Va., 1755; d. Jones Co., Ga., 1835, and is buried in Twiggs Co., Ga., near Jeffersonville, Ga. Served in N.C. Continental Troops and in Ga. Militia. Married Penelope Perry.
Children:
1. Chloe, mar. Elisah Watson.
2. James, mar. (1) Elizabeth Bryan; (2) Mrs. Cook; (3) Mrs. Jamieson.
3. Abner, mar. Miss Childers.
4. Perry, mar. and moved to Miss.
5. Lewis, mar. Matilda Garrett.
6. William, mar. and moved to Miss.
7. Henry, mar. Miss Childers.
8. John (Jack), mar. Narcissa Garrett.
9. Ezekiel, mar. (1) Sara Mims; (2) Mary (Polly) Bryan in 1809, Washington Co., Ga.

THOMAS WINFIELD, b. in Va., Sept. 17, 1745; d. in Wilkes Co., Ga., July 24, 1797. Served as a REV. SOLDIER. Married 1768, Elizabeth Nelson, b. Sept. 15, 1749; d. Nov. 27, 1802.
Children:
1. Samuel, b. 1772.
2. Mary, b. 1774.
3. Thomas, b. 1777.
4. John, b. 1780.
5. Elizabeth, b. 1782.
6. Charles, b. 1784.
7. Francis Nelson, b. 1787.

JESSE WINFREY, b. 1764, Prince Edward Co., Ga; d. 1808, Columbia Co., Ga. Served as private, Ga. Line. Married 1788, Frances Spencer.
Child:
1. Martha Hughes, mar. 1826, William Drane, Jr. (son of WILLIAM DRANE, SR., a REV. SOLDIER, and his wife Cassandra Magruder).

JOHN WINGFIELD, b. July 20, 1723 in Va.; d. Wilkes Co., Ga., Feb. 3, 1793. Married Frances Oliver Buck, b. May 5, 1725; d. Wilkes Co., Ga., Feb. 25, 1795; in Hanover Co., Va. He was a REV. PATRIOT.
Children:
1. Thomas, b. Sept. 17, 1745; mar. Elizabeth Nelson.
2. Mary, b. Oct. 15, 1747; mar. Peter Terrell.
3. Elizabeth, b. Aug. 30, 1752; mar. Edward Butler.
4. Sarah, b. Aug. 28, 1754; mar. Stephen Petters.
5. Charles, b. Jan. 17, 1756.
6. Garland, b. Oct. 17, 1757; mar. Mrs. Sarah Poullain.
7. Ann, b. May 22, 1759; mar. Rev. Hope Hull.
8. John III, b. July 31, 1761; mar. Mary Darricourt.
9. Frances, b. Feb. 20, 1763; mar. David Meriwether.
10. Rebecca, b. July 12, 1763; mar. John Darricourt.
11. Martha, b. May 30, 1767; mar. John Foster.

THOMAS WINGFIELD, b. in Va.; d. Wilkes Co., Ga., 1806. Served in Va. Continental Line. Married Elizabeth Terrell.
Children: (mentioned in will)
1. John.
2. Sarah G., mar. — Powell.
3. Mary, mar. Richard Worsham.
4. Milly, mar. — Simms.
5. Sarah Garland Poullain.
6. Nancy.
7. Thomas.
Grandchildren: (mentioned in will).
Wm. Garland Grimes; Wm. G., Thomas, Lucy, and John Grimes; Henry P., Thomas W. Grimes; and Benjamin O. Simms.

NOTE: RICHARD WORSHAM, b. in Va., 1746; d. in Wilkes Co., Ga.,

1826. Drew pension for his services as Lieut. in 10th Va. Reg. Married Mary Wingfield.
Child:
1. Elizabeth (1791-1836); mar. as (2) wife, 1822, Samuel Barnett (1775-1843) (son of WILLIAM BARNETT, REV. SOLDIER, and his wife Jean Jack).
Ref: Wilkes Co. Records VI p. 254, p. 70.

JOHN WINN, b. 1720 in S. C.; d. 1781 in Liberty Co., Ga. Member of the First Provincial Congress of Ga. His name appears on the famous "Blacklist" sent by the Royal Governor of Ga. to England. Married (1) Sarah Ann Duval.

PETER WINN, b. 1750, S. C., a Liberty Co., Ga. private, Ga. Mil. Married (1) 1777, Mary Farley.

WILLIAM WISE, b. in Va., 1755; d. in Bullock Co., Ga., May 13, 1816. Served as private, Ga. Line. Certificate signed by Gen. E. Clarke. Married Sarah Margaret —, d. after 1816.
Children:
1. Elizabeth, mar. Nov. 29, 1798, Solomon Groover.
2. Lavinia, b. in Ga., 1787; d. Brooks Co., Ga., 1857; mar. (1) Aug. 17, 1802, Redden, Denmark; b. 1770; d. 1813. She mar. (2) Wm. McNeely.
3. Preston, mar. (1) Margaret Lee; (2) 1808, Amy Jones.
4. Zilpha, mar. Jan. 7, 1811, Jesse Goodman.
5. Henry, mar. 1802, Elizabeth Groover.
6. Susanna, mar. 1802, James Denmark.
7. Rebecca, mar. 1809, Berry Jones.
8. John (1790-1834); mar. 1816, Rachel Jones (dau. of BRIDGER JONES, REV. SOLDIER, and his wife Rachel Barry).
9. Jincey, mar. Mr. Denmark.

JOHN WISENBAKER, served as a PATRIOT from Ga. Died Effingham Co., Ga. Married Ann Dacher.

JESSE WOMACK, b. 1739 in Va.; d. 1815, Madison Co., Ga. Served in Ga. Line, Lieut. under Gen. John Twiggs. Received bounty grant of land for his services. Married Dorothy Prior.
Child:
1. John W. Womack (1776-1848); mar. Frances Coleman (dau. of FRANCIS COLEMAN, b. in Va.; d. in Ala., a REV. SOLDIER, Ga. Line, and his wife Margaret —).

SOLOMON WOOD, b. 1726 in Va.; d. Jefferson Co., Ga., 1815. Moved to N. C., then Ga. Served as Capt. in Ga. Line, and was promoted to General. Built "Wood's Fort" at his own expense. Married (1) Lydia Valentine of Va.; (2) Elizabeth (Eason) Morton (1751-1826).

Children by (1) wife:
1. William, b. 1745.
2. John.
3. Mark.
4. Elizabeth.
5. Solomon, Jr.
6. Willis.
7. Lydia.
8. Joshua.
9. Sally.

Children by (2) wife:
10. Elizabeth, b. 1788; mar. John Mitchell.
11. Eason.
12. Nancy, b. 1781; mar. (1) Henry Willis Braezal; (2) Eason Allen.
13. Mary, mar. — Mitchell.
14. William.
15. Mark Red.
16. John White.
17. Green, b. 1792.

THOMAS WOOTEN, b. 1720 in N. C.; d. 1791, Oglethorpe (formerly Wilkes) Co., Ga. Served as Lieut., under Col. Holman Freeman, 7th Ga. Reg. Received bounty land in Wilkes Co., Ga. for his services. Married (1) Sarah Rabun in 1754; mar. (2) Tabitha Pope (widow of Henry Pope).
Children:
1. Thomas, mar. Millie Smith.
2. Lemuel, mar. Nancy Smith.
3. James, mar. Polly Smith.
4. RICHARD B., b. 1760 in Ga.; d. in Wilkes Co., Ga., 1798. Served as Lieut. in Capt. John Pope's Co., 7th Ga. Batt., Col. Holman Freeman. Married Lucretia Cade (dau. of Drury Cade, b. 1743 in Va.; d. 1809 in Ga., and his wife Winfred —. He was a REV. SOLDIER, served as Capt. under Col. Dooly, Col. Elijah Clarke and Gen. Andrew Pickens).
5. Mary, mar. James Cade.
6. John.
7. Daniel.
8. Robert.

JAMES WRIGHT of 7th Va. Reg., under Col. Dangierfield. Granted land as a REV. SOLDIER, Dec. 26, 1793.

MAJOR SAMUEL WRIGHT, came from England to Frederica, when that town was the military Capital of Ga. He was a REV. SOLDIER of Ga. (His grave has been marked by the Brunswick Chapter, D. A. R., in the Colonial Cemetery at Frederica Church, St. Simons Island, Ga.)

WILLIAM WRIGHT, b. 1736 in Va.; d. Wilkes Co., Ga., 1795. Enlisted as private, Va. Militia, and served until 1781. Married Mary Philpot.

JOHN WYATT, b. in Va., a REV. SOLDIER; moved to Clarke Co., Ga., 1802; then Butts (formerly Henry) Co., where he died, age 99 years.

RICHARD WYLLY, b. 1744 in Coleraine, Ireland; d. 1801, Savannah, Ga. Member of the Provincial Congress, and the Committee of Safety. Commanded a Ga. Brigade, as Colonel. Married Mary Ann Bryan.
Child:
    1. Mary Ann Wylly, mar. Nathaniel Adams.

THOMAS WYLLY, b. in the West Indies, 1762; d. 1846, Effingham Co., Ga. Served as assistant quartermaster to his uncle, COL. RICHARD WYLLY, REV. SOLDIER. Received land for his services. Married (1) Susanna Dawson; (2) Naomi Rosenburg; (3) Sarah (King) Goldwire.
Children by (1) wife:
    1. William C.
Children by (2) wife:
    2. Elisha.
    3. Naomi, mar. 3 times.
    4. Thomas, Jr.
    5. Frederick.   9. Sarah Ann.
    6. Leonidas.
    7. Eliza, mar. Richard Williams.
    8. Maria, mar. 1813, Solomon Dasher.

JOSHUA WYNNE, b. in Va.; d. 1808, Columbia Co., Ga. Served as Major, Ga. Line. Received bounty land for his services. Married Elizabeth Appling.
Child:
    1. WILLIAMSON WYNNE, b. 1760, Pendleton Dist., S. C.; d. 1828, Greene Co., Ga. Served as private, S. C. Line, and in Capt. Dixon's Co., 1st N. C. Reg. Married Eleanor Magruder (dau. of NINIAN OFFUTT MAGRUDER, a REV. SOLDIER of Md. and Ga., and his wife Mary Harris).

WILLIAM YATES (son of WILLIAM YATES, REV. SOLDIER of N. C., and wife Mary), was b. 1762 in Wake Co., N. C.; d. 1850 in Montgomery Co., Ga. (formerly Laurens Co.) Married in N. C., Mary Wimberly, b. 1770, N. C.; d. before 1850 in Ga. He served as private, N. C. Militia, and drew land in Laurens Co., Ga. Lottery of 1827 as a REV. SOLDIER.
Children: (known)
    1. Eli, mar. 1815, Molly Baucom (?).
    2. Joseph, b. 1795 in N. C.; d. 1862 in Brooks Co., Ga. Married Cynthia Swain.
    3. William, b. 1801, Montgomery Co., Ga.; d. 1874, Brooks Co., Ga. Married 1823, Emanuel Co., Ga., Elizabeth Swain (1807-1871)

(dau. of Carmeth Swain and his wife Rebecca Johnson of Emanuel and Thomas Counties, Ga.).

JAMES YOUNG, b. in S. C.; d. 1857, Walker Co., Ga. Served as private, 1776, 6th S. C. Reg. Married Anna Foster.

WILLIAM YOUNG, d. Screven Co., Ga. Was a member, 1775, of the Council of Safety, Savannah, Ga. Also member of the First Provincial Congress. Married Mary Henderson.
Children: (known)
1. James, b. Screven Co., Ga., Sept. 25, 1784; d. 1859 in Ga. Lived in Bullock Co., Ga. Married Lavinia Jones, b. 1795 (dau. of James Jones, b. April 2 4, 1764; d. 1822 in Ga., and his wife Elizabeth Mills, b. 1774). They had 10 children.
2. Michael, b. Screven Co., Ga., 1797; d. Thomas Co., Ga., 1856. Married Sarah Everett (dau. of Joshua Everett and his wife Jane Carter of Bullock Co., Ga.). They had 9 children.

PETER ZACHARY, b. in Va.; d. 1791, Columbia Co., Ga. Served as private, Va. Troops. Married Mary —.
Child:
1. Mary Zackary, b. 1770; mar. 1790, THOMAS WARD, served as private in Capt. Dean's Co., 7th Md. Reg. He was b. in Md.; d. 1800, Jefferson Co., Ga.

APPENDIX

Compiled by

ETTIE TIDWELL McCALL

of

Atlanta, Georgia

Copied and Indexed

by

MRS. J. E. HAYS, STATE HISTORIAN

With the Authority of

JOHN B. WILSON, SECRETARY OF STATE

1938

LIBERTY POLE

The first "Liberty" pole in Georgia was erected on June 4, 1775, the anniversary of King George III, who was born June 4, 1738. It stood in front of Tondee's Tavern in Savannah, Georgia, and became a rallying point for friends of Independence.

After it was raised, two toasts were given: one to the King, and one to "American Liberty". On the 22nd of the same month, upon the occasion of the appointment of the Council of Safety, the Union flag was hoisted upon the pole and thirteen patriotic toasts were drunk, one to each of the 13 Colonies, and each was followed by a salute from two pieces of artillery and martial music.

SOCIETY OF THE CINCINNATI

A meeting was held at the cantonment of the American Army, on June 19, 1783, at the request of General George Washington, to establish the Society of the Cincinnati. At the meeting, attended by the General Officers of the Continental Army and the gentlemen designated by their respective Regiments, this Society was established. (From Historical Sketch of the Society by Charles Lukens Davis.)

CEDED LANDS OF GEORGIA

In the year 1774, Gov. Wright opened a Land Court in Ga., where the Broad River joins the Savannah, a stockade fort was built for protection against the Indians, and here was sold the lands ceded by the Creek and Cherokee Indians. On June 11, 1774, he issued a proclamation stating that the lands would be surveyed and parcelled out in tracts of 100 to 1,000 acres. To the head of each family was to be sold 100 acres; for each child, 50 acres; and 50 acres for the wife.

The "Ceded Lands" (now Wilkes Co.) was almost an unbroken wilderness. Men of energy and enterprise made clearings and built the first homes in Upper Ga. This region is rich in historic memories.

At the point where the Broad River flows into the Savannah, there were three towns bearing the imposing names of Petersburg, Lisbon, and Vienna. These towns constituted a great trading center, where goods could be brought by pole boats from Augusta, and carried by wagons to Upper Ga., and even to Tenn.

The first settlements in the Ceded Lands were at Dartmouth (later the name was changed to Petersburg), located at the confluence of the Broad and Savannah Rivers, * and at Lisbon located on the south side of the Broad River and east side of the Savannah. Across the Savannah River, in S. C., was the town of Vienna. At the present time, Lisbon in Lincoln Co., has only one store; of Petersburg in Elbert, and Vienna in Carolina, not a vestige remains. Petersburg was the third largest town in Ga., second in size only to Savannah and Augusta, and having more than 50 stores and two newspapers.

Many of the men who settled in the "Ceded Lands" were Revolutionary Soldiers, and many received their military training under Gen. Elijah Clarke, who served as Colonel at the Battle of Kettle Creek, Feb. 14, 1779.

Near Coody Creek (now Elbert Co.), stood the home of Nancy Hart, wife of Benjamin Hart, Rev. Soldier, perhaps the most noted woman that the Southern Colonies produced during the Revolutionary War. It was in her home that she performed her celebrated feat of capturing single-handed, a whole squad of British soldiers and holding them at bay until her little daughter Sukey could summon her father and other patriots from the hiding places in the swamps. "A brave intrepid soul was she and a dear lover of Liberty."

From these Ceded Lands (Wilkes Co.), there moved out into the valleys of Ga., Ala., and Miss., small armies of early settlers, the descendants of those early pioneers who settled there before and soon after the Rev. War.

In 1792, there were 82,000 people in Ga.; 36,000 in Wilkes Co.

---

* Point Peter is located in Oglethorpe Co., Ga., near where Petersburg, Ga., was located in the forks of the Savannah and Broad Rivers.

PARISHES OF GEORGIA, 1775

The Colony of Georgia was divided into Parishes.
   Christ Church Parish, including Savannah.
   St. Mathews Parish, including Abercorn and Ebenezer.
   St. George's Parish, including Halifax.
   St. Paul's Parish, including Augusta.
   St. Philips Parish, including Great Ogeechee.
   St. John's Parish, including Midway and Sunbury.
   St. Andrews Parish, including Darien.
   St. James Parish, including Frederica.
Public worship was ordered to be held in all parishes.

When the Colonies found that there was no prospect of a settlement of the dispute between them and England, each of them, following the example of Mass., appointed by action of the Provincial Congress, a committee to resist every attempt at executing the acts of
Parliament. In some cases that Committee was called the "Committee of Safety"; in others as in Georgia, the "Council of Safety". Mass.
set the example in Feb. 1775; Georgia followed suit, June 1775.

Before this, even as early as January, St. John's Parish, dissent-
ing from the action of the Provincial Congress of Ga. in the delay to
positively acquiesce in the proceedings of the other Provinces in re-
gard to the authority of Continental Congress, appointed a committee
to attend the meeting of the General Committee in Charleston, S. C.,
and present the side of St. John's Parish in the questions involved.

The dissatisfaction resulting from such delay, culminated in the
determination of St. John's Parish to send delegates to the Continental Congress before the rest of the Province did so, and on Mar. 21,
1775, Dr. Lyman Hall, afterwards one of the three Signers from Ga.
of the Declaration of Independence, was appointed a delegate to the
Continental Congress from the Parish of St. John. This was the direct
cause of the change of the name of the Parish to Liberty County. The
first County in the Colony of Georgia.

Georgia, at the outbreak of the Revolution, was a Province of
divided households; for while the younger members of the family were
ardent Whigs, the older ones, as a rule, were stout Loyalists, whose
devotion to the Crown stood the supreme test. It required some
courage on both sides to maintain a firm position. Nowhere was this
more noticeable than in Savannah, where the older members of many
of the most prominent families were loyal to the Crown, and where
the "Liberty Boys of Georgia" had as their leader, Archibald Bullock,
President of the First Provincial Congress of Georgia.

COUNTIES IN GEORGIA

Named for Revolutionary Soldiers, and
English friends of the Colonists

BAKER CO. - Created from Early, 1825; named for Col. John Baker, Rev. Soldier of Liberty Co.

BALDWIN CO. - Laid off in the Lottery Act of 1803, organized 1805; named in honor of Abraham Baldwin, born in Guilford, Conn., Nov. 6, 1754. Settled after the Revolution in Savannah, Ga. Was one of the founders of the University of Georgia.

BRYAN CO. - Organized 1793; named for Jonathan Bryan, Rev. Soldier of Ga. On Sept. 16, 1769, he presided over a meeting of merchants and traders in Ga., and was by order of the King, dismissed from the Governor's Council, of which for some time he had been a member. Thus he was the first object of the Royal vengeance in Ga. When the British captured Savannah, Dec. 29, 1778, he was made a prisoner. Because of his deep loyalty to the cause, and notwithstanding his age of nearly four score years, he was confined on one of the British ships. He was very prominent in the affairs of the Colony and took an active part in the stirring events just preceding and during the Revolution.

BULLOCK CO. - Was a part of Screven; created in 1796; named for Archibald Bullock, member of the Provincial Congress, and Governor of Georgia, Jan. 1776 to Feb. 1777. Was called President; also served as Commander-in-Chief of the Army.

BURKE CO. - Was laid out in 1758 as St. George's Parish. It received its present name in honor of Edmund Burke, the great champion of American Liberty in England.

CARROLL CO. - Laid out after Campbell, 1828; named for Charles Carroll of Md., Signer of the Declaration of Independence.

CAMDEN CO. - Was once included in the parishes of St. Thomas and St. Mary's; was formed 1777; and named in honor of the Earl of Camden, a champion of Colonial rights in the English Parliament.

CHATHAM CO. - In the nucleus around which the present State of Ga. has developed. The Colonists first landed at Yamacraw Bluff, site of the present city of Savannah, Feb. 12, 1773. In 1758, this part of Ga. was laid out into St. Philip's and Christ Church Parishes. In 1777, the Parishes were changed into counties. Christ Church Parish, with part of St. Philip's, was erected into a county which was named Chatham in honor of William Pitt, Earl of Chatham, who in the British Parliament, defended the rights of the Colonists. During the Revolutionary War, Chatham Co.

was the scene of a number of engagements between the Americans and the British and their Indian and Tory allies. The first Legislative body ever convened in Ga., assembled at Savannah, Jan. 7, 1755.

CLARKE CO. - Created from Jackson Co., in 1801; named in honor of the rugged Revolutionary Hero of Ga., General Elijah Clarke.

COLUMBIA CO. - Laid out from Richmond Co., 1790; was named for Christopher Columbus, the discoverer of America.

DeKALB CO. - Laid out by Act of Legislature on Dec. 9, 1822, organized on Dec. 22, 1822; named for Baron de Kalb, the German officer who fought with the American forces in the Revolution and was mortally wounded at the Battle of Camden, S. C.

DOOLY CO. - Laid off under Lottery Act of 1821; named for Col. John Dooly, one of Georgia's Rev. Soldiers, born of Irish parents in Wilkes Co., Ga. Commanded a Regiment at the Battle of Kettle Creek; and was murdered by the Tories.

EFFINGHAM CO. - Once a part of the Parishes of St. Matthew and St. Philip which were formed in 1758. It was changed to a county in 1777; named for the Earl of Effingham, who in Parliament, so gallantly defended the interests of the American Colonists, and who resigned his commission in the British Army when his regiment was ordered to America. In 1793, a part of this Co. was given to Screven; and in 1794, a part was given to Bryan Co. Ebenezer was one of the first places outside of Savannah to be founded. Here is found one of the most historic land-marks in Ga., the old "Jerusalem Church of the Salzburgers".

EMANUEL CO. - Laid off from Bulloch and Montgomery, 1812; and named for David Emanuel, Rev. Soldier of Ga., and Governor of the State, 1801.

GLYNN CO. - Formed into a county, 1777; and named in honor of John Glynn, an English nobleman who was an ardent supporter of the Colonists in their demands.

GREENE CO. - Surveyed 1784, laid out from Washington Co., 1786. Named in honor of Gen. Nathaniel Greene, born at Warwick, Rhode Island, May 27, 1742; died at "Milberry Grove", Ga., June 19, 1786. He was Commander of the South during the Revolution.

GWINNETT CO. - Laid out by the Lottery Act of 1818; and named in honor of Button Gwinnett, one of Georgia's Signers of the Declaration of Independence.

HABERSHAM CO. - Laid out by the Lottery Act of 1818; and named for Joseph Habersham of Savannah, born 1751; who as a Major of the Ga. Troops, captured Governor Wright. He was one of the most active and resourceful advocates of Liberty.

HALL CO. - Was created by Lottery Act of 1819; and named for Dr. Lyman Hall, one of Georgia's Signers of the Declaration of Independence. Also Governor of the State, 1783-1784.

HANCOCK CO. - Laid out in 1793; and named in honor of John Hancock of Mass., President of the Continental Congress.

HENRY CO. - Created in 1821 from lands acquired by treaty with the Indians; and was named for Patrick Henry, the renowned Patriot and orator of Virginia.

IRWIN CO. - Laid out by the Lottery Act of 1818; named for Jared Irwin, who distinguished himself as a Rev. Soldier, and served two terms as Governor.

JACKSON CO. - Formed in 1796; and named for James Jackson of Savannah. Brig. Gen. in the Revolutionary army and Governor of Ga., 1798-1801.

JASPER CO. - Formed Randolph Co., 1807; name changed to Jasper Co., 1812; in honor of Sergeant Jasper, who when the flag at Fort Moultrie was shot from the staff, recovered it at the risk of his life, and held it aloft until a new staff could be procured.

JEFFERSON CO. - Laid out from Burke and Warren Counties in 1796; and named for Thomas Jefferson, author of the Declaration of Independence; President of the United States, 1801-1809. Louisville, the county seat, was the first official Capital of the State of Ga.

LAURENS CO. - Laid out in 1807; and named in honor of Lieut. Col. John Laurens of S.C., who was killed near Combahee, S.C., during the Revolutionary War.

LIBERTY CO. - Was formed from the Parishes of St. John, St. Andrew, and St. James, in 1777. Its name is derived from the eagerness of its inhabitants to send a delegate to the Continental Congress before the rest of the Province had decided to join the other Colonies in a fight for Independence. Dr. Lyman Hall was sent as delegate. Liberty Co. is rich in history. Medway (Midway) Church is in this county.

LINCOLN CO. - Was formed from part of Wilkes in 1796; and named for Gen. Benjamin Lincoln of Mass., who for a time commanded the American forces in the South during the Revolutionary War.

MACON CO. - Created 1837; and named for Nathaniel Macon of N.C., who served throughout the Revolutionary War as a private, declining promotion.

MERIWETHER CO. - Created Dec. 1827 from Troup; and named for David Meriwether of Va. and Ga. Served as Brig. Gen. at the Siege of Savannah; captured by the British and held prisoner.

MONTGOMERY CO. - Laid out from Washington Co., 1793; and named in honor of Gen. Richard Montgomery who was killed in an attack upon the fortifications at Quebec in 1775.

MORGAN CO. - Laid out from Baldwin in 1807; and named for Gen. Daniel Morgan, the hero of Cowpens.

PICKENS CO. - Created 1853; and named in honor of Gen. Andrew Pickens of S. C.

PULASKI CO. - Laid out from Laurens in 1808; and named for the Polish nobleman, Count Pulaski, who fell in defense of American Liberty at Savannah, Oct. 9, 1779.

PUTNAM CO. - Laid out in 1807; and named in honor of Gen. Israel Putnam of Mass., the Rev. Hero.

RICHMOND CO. - Laid out as St. Paul's Parish; in 1777, when the parishes were changed to counties, the name of Richmond was conferred on this section of the Province, in honor of the Duke of Richmond, who as a member of the British Parliament, stood as the staunch friend of the American Colonists. Augusta is the County seat.

SCREVEN CO. - Formed from the counties of Burke and Effingham, 1793; was named for Gen. James Screven, who was killed at the Battle of Medway Church. The Battle of Brier Creek was fought in this county.

STEWART CO. - Formed from Randolph, 1830; named for Gen. Daniel Stewart of Liberty Co., who achieved fame as a Soldier of the Revolution and in subsequent Indian wars. He was an ancestor of Mrs. Franklin D. Roosevelt, wife of the President of the United States, 1938.

SUMPTER CO. - Laid out from Lee, 1831; and named for Gen. Thomas Sumpter of Va., who commanded the S. C. Troops during the War of the Revolution.

TALIAFERRO CO. - Formed in 1825; and named for Col. Benjamin Taliaferro of Va., who died in Wilkes Co., Ga., 1821. Served under Morgan during the Revolution and was captured by the British at Charleston.

TATTNALL CO. - Formed from Montgomery, 1801; and named in honor of Josiah Tattnall, Revolutionary Soldier and Governor of Georgia, 1802.

TELFAIR CO. - Laid out in 1807; and named in honor of Edward Telfair, a Son of Liberty, member Council of Safety, and twice Governor of Georgia.

TRENTLEN CO. - Named for John Adam Treutlen, member Provincial Congress, Revolutionary Soldier, Governor of Georgia, 1777.

TWIGGS CO. - Laid out from Wilkinson, 1809; and named for Col. John Twiggs, who during the Revolutionary War won distinction in many battles with the British and their Indian allies.

WALTON CO. - Laid out by the Lottery Act of 1818 and named for George Walton, one of Georgia's Signers of the Declaration of Independence, and Governor of Georgia.

WASHINGTON CO. - Created in 1784 and named in honor of George Washington. At the time of the organization, it included all the land "from the Cherokee corner worth, extending from the Ogeechee to the Oconee, south to Liberty County". It was settled by many refugee Soldiers who were given bounty lands, 287.5 acres for their services in the Revolutionary Army.

WARREN CO. - Laid out in 1793; and named for Gen. Joseph Warren, Revolutionary Soldier of Mass., who fell at the Battle of Bunker Hill.

WILKINSON CO. - Laid out by the Lottery Act of 1803, organized in 1805; named for Gen. James Wilkinson, a Soldier of the Revolution and a Soldier of the War of 1812.

WILKES CO. - Was created in 1777 from land acquired from the Indians in 1773. It was first called the "Ceded Lands of Ga." Named for John Wilkes, a great champion of American Liberty. Washington, the county seat of Wilkes Co., claims the honor of being the first place in the United States to bear the name of the immortal George Washington, the first President of the United States. Wilkes Co. has been divided into Crawford, Taliaferro, Hart, Warren, Greene, Hancock and other counties.

REVOLUTIONARY FORTS IN GEORGIA

FORT BARRINGTON - About twenty miles above the city of Darien, on the east side of the Altamaha River, there is at the present day, a little hamlet called Barrington. Near the site of this village, General James Edward Oglethorpe, the Founder of the Colony of Georgia in 1733, erected a frontier fort in the early days of the Colony and conferred on it the name of Fort Barrington. During the Revolutionary War, the name was changed to Fort Howe, in honor of General Robert Howe of North Carolina, who was for some time the Commander of the American forces in Ga. This old Fort has long since crumbled into ruins.

FORT CORNWALLIS - Was the principal fortification at Augusta during the time of the Revolution. It was erected by the British and named after Lord Cornwallis. Its location was near the center of the town, not far from the Savannah River, and it played a prominent part in the military operations in the several attacks upon and the Siege of Augusta.

FORT HEARD - Or Heard's Fort, located near the headquarters of Fishing Creek, was built 1774 by Stephen Heard, living in the "Ceded Lands", as a protection against the Indians. In 1780, when the British threatened Augusta, then the seat of Government, the Assembly passed a resolution ordering that Heard's Fort in Wilkes Co. be designated as a place of meeting for transacting the business of the Government of Ga. Probably the reason this fort was selected was that Stephen Heard was at that time Acting Governor of Ga.

    The old Fort has long since disappeared, but the part it played in the struggle for Independence forms one of the most interesting incidents in Georgia's Revolutionary history.

FORT MORRIS - This Fort was a heavy earth-work and was located just south of the Town of Sunbury. Named Fort Morris in honor of Capt. Morris, who commanded one of the two artillery companies authorized by a resolution of Continental Congress, 1776. In 1778, the Continental Troops were under command of Col. John McIntosh. After the capture by the British in 1779, the name was changed by the British to Fort Georgia, in honor of the King.

FORT McINTOSH - In the establishment of defenses for the country south of the Altamaha River, Fort McIntosh was erected and named in honor of Gen. Lachlan McIntosh, on the east side of the Satilla River, nearly west of the present village of Tarboro.

FORT TYBEE - After the capture of Savannah by the British, Dec. 1778, Col. Campbell built a fort on the northern end of Tybee Island not far from the site of the present Fort Screven. Sept. 1779, the French fleet and Count D'Estaing made a landing and assault on this Fort, only to find that the British had evacuated at their approach and had taken refuge at the other end of the island.

FORT WAYNE - During the Revolutionary War, an earthwork was thrown up at the eastern end of Savannah and named by a battery of artillery. The name of Fort Wayne was given to the place in honor of Gen. Anthony Wayne. After the Revolutionary War, it was not used until the War of 1812. After this war, it again fell into disuse and disappeared altogether.

FORT GRIERSON - Located half a mile from Fort Cornwallis, it was erected by the British and named after one of their Generals.

BATTLES

In the War of the Revolution, many battles and skirmishes were fought on Georgia's soil. Following is a list of these engagements.

Augusta	Ebenezer	Lockhart's
Beards' Bluff	Etowah River	Matthews' Bluff
Baillon's Causeway	Fishing Creek	Medway Church
Beard's Creek	Fort Charlotte	Ogeechee Ferry
Belfast	Fort Cornwallis	Paris' Hill
Brewton's Hill	Fort Heard	Riceboro
Brier Creek	Fort McIntosh	Savannah
Broad River	Fort Morris	Sharon
Brownsborough	Fort Tybee	Sunbury
Buckhead Creek	Fulsum's Fort	Tybee Island
Bull Town Swamp	Gibbons' Plantation	White House
Burke Co. Jail	Hawk's Creek	Wiggin's Hill
Carr's Fort	Herbert's Place	Wright's Fort
Cherokee Ford	Hickory Hill	Yamacraw Bluff
Cockspur Island	Kettle Creek	Yamassee Bluff

GRAVES OF REVOLUTIONARY SOLDIERS

Located by the Georgia Society,
Daughters of the American Revolution

Following the names will be found the name of County, Cemetery, etc.

Charles Abercrombie, Hancock
James Adams, Elbert
Thomas Adams, Elbert
William Alexander, Elbert
James Allen, Jefferson
William Allen (ae. 112), Lumpkin
Lieut. Col. William Alston, Elbert
Lieut. Col. Nicholas Anciaux,
    Screven
Kenneth Anderson, White
William Anderson, Baldwin
David Andrews, Henry
John Andrews, Oglethorpe
William Andrews, Oglethorpe
Henry Anglin
John Arnett, Screven
John Arnold
William Ash, Franklin
Ica Atkins, Dodge
John Austin, Walton
Samuel J. Axon, Liberty

William Babb, Baldwin
John Bacholts, Glynn
Charles Baker, Bartow
Beal Baker, Hall
John D. Bagwell, Gwinnett
John Ball, Warren
Abner Bankston, Butts
John Barnett, Oconee
Robert Barnett, Wilkinson
Robert Barrett, Irwin
James Barrow, Clarke
Samuel Barrow, Jones
Thomas Barrow, Jackson
William Barrow
George Bassett, Richmond
Cornelius Batchelder, Wilkinson

Jesse Battle, Hancock
Wm. Sumner Battle, Hancock
James Baxter, Baldwin
William Beavers, Coweta
Laban Beckham, Pike
Samuel Beckham, Baldwin
Philip H. Bedford, Washington
Francis Bell, Hall
Jacob Bellew, Habersham
Richard Bennett, near Jesup
John Berrien, Chatham
John Berry, Ebenezer Cemetery
Edward Blackshear, Laurens
Wm. Blackwell, Franklin
Isaac Boring, Jackson
Littleberry Bostick, Jefferson
Francis Boykin, Baldwin
John Brack, Burke
Thomas Bradford, Irwin
Jacob Braselton, Sr., Jackson
Stephen Brock, Burke
John Hanna Brooks, Jones
Andrew Brown, Elbert
Benjamin Brown, Fayette
Benjamin Brown, Elbert
John Brown, Pike
John R. Brown, Camden
Nathan Brownson, Jefferson
John Bull, Baldwin
Hawkins Bullock, Clarke
William Buford, Butts
Jacob Burkalter, Warren
John Burkhalter, Warren
Joshua Burkhalter, Warren
Patrick Butler, Elbert
Zachariah Butler, Elbert

John Calder, McIntosh

Peter Callaway, Laurens
James Cameron, near West Point
Samuel Camp, Hancock
William Candler, near Augusta
James Cantey, Baldwin
Thomas P. Carnes, Baldwin
Patrick Carr, Baldwin
Thomas Carr, McDuffie
Wm. Carraway, Upson
Adam Carson, Jones
William Carson, Wilcox
Alexander Carswell, Burke
David Carter, Hart
James Carter, Richmond
Thomas Carter, Elbert
Wm. Cheek, Bartow
Tully Choice, Hancock
Turner Christian, Elbert
Richard Christmas, Elbert
Christopher Clark, Elbert
William Clark, Hall
Elijah Clarke, Lincoln
Larkin Clarke, Elbert
David Clay, Wilkinson
Jacob Cleveland, Elbert
Ezekiel Cloud, Henry
Daniel Clower, Gwinnett
John Coffee, Telfair
John Coleman, Burke
John Colley, Lincoln
Vines Collier, Oglethorpe
William Cone, Screven
Wilson Conner, Screven
Joshua Cook, Washington
John Cooper, Madison
Richard Cooper, Screven
Samuel Cooper, Muscogee
Thomas Cooper, Jasper
George Cowan, Jefferson
Cary Cox, Putnam
Peter Crow, Bartow
Ansel Cunningham, Jackson
James Cunningham, Elbert

John Daniel, Elbert
Thomas Daniel, Washington
William Daniel, Washington
Cyrus Dart, Glynn

John Davidson, Jasper
Joseph Davidson, Wilkinson
George Dawson, Nancy Hart Chap.
Stephen Day, Columbia
Raymond Demere, St. Simons Is.
James DeLaunay, Baldwin
John Dickinson, Coweta
David Dickson, Clayton
Jesse Dismukes, Baldwin
John Dooly, Lincoln
Thomas Dooly, Lincoln
Andrew DuBourg, Baldwin
Jacob Durden, Emanuel
Daniel Dupree, Oglethorpe
Nathaniel Durkee, Hart
James Duncan, Baldwin
Elisha Dyar, Hart

Peter Early, Clarke
David Edenfield, Emanuel
William Edwards, Bartow
David Elder, Oconee
Joshua Elder, Madison
Samuel Elbert, Chatham
James Espy, Clarke
Hartwell Ezzell, Jasper

Peter Fair, Baldwin
Daniel Fane, DeKalb
Wm. Faris, Walker
Thomas Farrar, Franklin
Jonas Fauche, Baldwin
William Fears, Jasper
William Few, Jefferson
Benjamin Fitzpatrick, Morgan
Lewis Flemister, Wilkes
William Fletcher, Telfair
George Franklin, Wilkes
Wm. Franklin, Irwin
Colquitt Freeman, Madison
George Freeman, Wilkes
Holman Freeman, Wilkes
John Freeman, Wilkes
James Freeman, Richmond

William Gainer, Washington
John Gamble, Jefferson
Jacob Garrard, Baldwin

Lewis Gardner, Randolph
John Gator, Troup
Allen Gay, Coweta
John Gibson, Fulton
Young Gill, Hancock
James Gilmore, Washington
Wm. Giradeau, Liberty
Thomas Gordon, Gwinnett
Nathaniel Greene, Chatham
Thomas Green, Lamar
Aaron Grier, Taliaferro
Charles Griffin, Clinch
James Griffin, Irwin
Moses Guest, Franklin
James Gunn, Jefferson
Jacob Gunn, Baldwin
Richard Gunn, Taliaferro

John Habersham, Chatham
Joseph Habersham, Chatham
Simon Hadley, Thomas
William Haley, Elbert
Lyman Hall, Richmond
John Hames, Murray, now
    Marietta
James Hamilton, Columbia
Stewart Hamilton, Montgomery
Abner Hammond, Baldwin
Henry Hand, Sumpter
William Hardwick, Washington
William Harper, Hancock
Jacob Harrell, Decatur
Absolem Harris, Hancock
Benjamin Harris, Baldwin
John Thompson Harris, Walton
Samuel Harris, Hancock
John Hart, Baldwin
Daniel Hartley, Crawford
Charles Harvie, Gordon
Michael Harvie, Baldwin
Zephaniah Harvey, Jasper
John Hatcher, Wilkinson
Benjamin Hawkins, "Old Agency",
    Crawford
Benjamin Haygood, Monroe
Moses Haynes, Hart
George Haynie, Baldwin
John Hays, DeKalb

Gov. Stephen Head, Elbert
Thomas Heard, Greene
Elisha Hearn, Putnam
Robert Hendry, Liberty
Joseph Herndon, Walton
Ephriam Herrington, Emanuel
Jacob Higgenbotham, Elbert
Samuel Higgenbotham, Elbert
Richard B. Hooper, Banks
James Horton, Jasper
Prosser Horton, Jackson
John Howard, Baldwin
Isaac Howell, Fulton
Isham Huckaby, Coweta
David Hudson, Elbert
Hope Hull, Clarke
James Hunt, Hart
Moses Hunt, Elbert
William Hunt, near Davisboro
Thomas Humphries, Baldwin

Daniel Inman, Burke
Gov. Jared Irwin, Burke
Alexander Irwin, Burke
John Lawson Irwin, Burke
Ephriam Ivey, Baldwin

Charles Jackson, Cumberland Is.
Drury Jackson, Baldwin
John James, Cobb
Sergeant Jasper, Chatham
John Jenkins, Lamar
Levi Jester, Butts
William Jester, Butts
Joseph Jeter, Baldwin
Wm. Johnson, Oglethorpe
Ezell (Ezra ?) Johnston, Jasper
John Johnston, Jasper
Littleton Johnston, Jasper
Daniel Jones, DeKalb
James Jones, Screven
William Jones, Columbia
William Jones, Jasper
John Jordan, Washington
Henry Joyce, near Vidalia

John Kendrick, Pike
Wm. Bibb Key, Elbert

Henry King, Taliaferro
John King, Jackson
Richard King, Taliaferro
Peter Kolb, Meriwether

Abraham S. Lane, Screven
Austin Lane, Screven
Lewis Lanier, Screven
Alexander Latta, Monroe
John Lawrence, Baldwin
Hugh Lawson, Jefferson
"Light Horse" Harry Lee was
    buried Cumberland Island,
    re-interred in Va.
William Lee, Jackson
John Lewis, Bartow
John Lindsey, Wilkes
James Little, Franklin
Wm. Little, Baldwin
Evans Long
Amos Love, Laurens (?)
Col. David Love
James Luckie, Oglethorpe
Jeremiah Lumsden, Jasper
Mayhen Lyle, Jackson
Wm. Lyon, Jefferson

Charles McCall, Bulloch
Thomas McCall, Laurens
Thomas McCall, Bulloch
Thomas H. McCall (McCaule),
    Chatham
William McCall, Screven
Hugh McCauley, DeKalb
Joseph McClendon, Coweta
Samuel McClendon, Henry
Angus McCurry, Hart
John McElhammon, Jackson
John McGough, Greene
Samuel Mackey, Franklin
Charles McKimsey, Jackson
John McMullen, Hart
James McPhail, Liberty
John L. March, Macon
John L. Marsh, Baldwin
Abraham Marshall, Columbia
John Marshall, Columbia
Joseph Marshall, Columbia

Daniel Marshall, Columbia
Levi Marshall, Columbia
Zacheus Marshall, Columbia
Beverly Martin, Elbert
James Mathews, Upson
Isaac Mathews, Jackson
William Mathews, Jackson
George Menifee, Talbot
John Maxwell, Baldwin
Thomas Maxwell, Elbert
Jacob Mercer, Jasper
James Meriwether, Jefferson
Thomas Meriwether, Jasper
Jonathan Miller, Baldwin
John H. Milner, Pike
Henry Mitchell, Hancock
Thomas Mitchell, Henry
William Mitchell, Wilkinson
Claxton Mize, Banks
David Montgomery, Jackson
James Montgomery, Jackson
Clement Moore, Butts
James Moore, Taliaferro
William Moran, Baldwin
Obediah Morris, Butts
William Morris, Newton
William Morris, DeKalb
Oliver Morton, Jones
Samuel Moseley, Stephens
Edmund Murphy, Richmond
Nicholas Murphy, Richmond
John Myrick, Baldwin

Basil Neal, Columbia
John Neely, Coweta
John Nelson, Lincoln
Thomas Nelson, Pike
John Newton, Oglethorpe
Moses Newton, Newton
John Nicholson, Union
Sanders Noble, Clinch
William Norris, Newton
John Nunn, Wilkinson
James Nunnelee, Elbert
John Nunnally, Oconee

Archibald Odom, Pulaski
William Ogletree, Monroe

Dionysius Oliver, Elbert
James Brush Oliver, Richmond
Daniel Orr, Spalding

Richard Parham, Baldwin
James Park, Baldwin
Ezekiel Evans Parke, Baldwin
Henry Parks, Sr., Franklin
Wm. Pate, Turner
Robert Patterson, Baldwin
Wm. Patterson, Baldwin
Seth Peirce, Jefferson
John Peel, Jefferson
William Peters, Loundes
William Penn, Jasper
William Pentecost, Barrow
John Phinazee, Harris
Ferdinand Phinizy, Oglethorpe
James Pittman, Madison
Robert Pollard, near Warrenton
Thomas Pollard, near Warrenton
Henry Pool, Glascock
     (Had 2 daus. living 1936, Real
     Daughters of U. S. D. A. R.)
Oliver Porter, Newton
Antoine Poullaine, Wilkes
John Powell, Jefferson
Josiah Powell, Jefferson
Robert Pullen, Newton or Elbert

Reuben Ransome, Clarke
John Rawlins, Murray
Anderson Redding, Baldwin
Jacob Redwine, Coweta
Samuel Reid, Putnam
Amos Richardson, Hart
James Riley, Elbert
Matthew Rhodes, Habersham
Reuben Roberts, Jones
John Robinson, Hancock
Randall Robinson, Coweta
Hardman Rooks, Washington
Shadrack Rowe, Harris
John Rowell, Haralson
John Rucker, Elbert
William Rucker, Elbert
John Rushin, Macon
William Ryals, Telfair

Philip Ryan, near Athens

Moses Sanders, Clarke
Daniel Schee, Washington
James Scott, Screven
John Eppes Scott, Hancock
James Screven, Liberty
Joseph Sessions, Washington
John Shackelford, Hancock
John Shields, Baldwin
John Shin, Laurens
John Shine, Twiggs
Wm. Studley Shirley, Jones
Stephen Silvey, Silvey Cemetery,
    2 miles from Rayle
Henry Simmons, Camden
John Simmons, Hancock
Thomas Simmons, Jones
Abram Simons, Wilkes
Archibald Simpson, Wilkes
Edward Singleton, Lumpkin
John Sitton, White
Henry Slappey, Jasper
Samuel Slaughter, Baldwin
Hardy Smith, Laurens
Isaac Smith, Monroe
James Smith, Wilkinson
Robert Smith, Sr., Butts
William Smith, Coweta
Wm. (Hell Nation) Smith, Coweta
Lazarus Solomon, Wilkinson
George Snellings, Elbert
Richard Speaks, Butts
John Spearman, Jasper
Rev. John Springer, Baldwin
Robert Stafford, Wayne
George Stapleton
Benton Stark, Jackson
John Steenson, White
Alexander Stephens, Taliaferro
Daniel Stewart, "Midway"
William Stewart, Schley
John Stoneycipher, Stephens
    (Franklin)
Charles Strong, Clarke
John Strong, Clarke
John Stroud, Walton
Peter Strozier, Wilkes

John Stuart, Washington
James Stuart, Washington
Joseph Sumner, Emanuel
John Sutton, White

Matthew Talbot, Washington
John Taliaferro, Wilkinson
Josiah Tattnall, Chatham
Clark Taylor, Oglethorpe
Richard Terrell, Newton
Francis Tennille, Washington
Andrew Thomas, Washington
James Thomas, Butts
Wm. Thomas, Banks
Aaron Thomlinson, Jefferson
Sherrod Thompson, Jackson
Dozier Thornton, Elbert (now Hart)
David Thurmond, Madison
John Thurmond, Coweta
Henry H. Tompkins, Oglethorpe
Andrew Torrance, Baldwin
Parnal Truitt, Wilkes
Richard Turner, Baldwin
Zadoc Turner, Hancock

David Walker, Baldwin
Elisha Walker, Johnson
George Walker II, Bleckley
George Walker III, Bleckley
James Walker, Upson
John Walker, Wilkes
Sanders Walker, Baldwin
George Walton, Richmond
Edward Ware, Clarke
James Ware, Sr., Madison
Francis Ward, Putnam

Eli Warren, Laurens
Jeremiah Warren, Baldwin
Jesse Warren, Hancock
Josiah Warren, Laurens
John Watson, Baldwin
Benjamin Weaver, Greene
Claiborne Webb, Jackson
John Whechel, Hall
Samuel Whateley, Wilkes
James Wheeler, Jackson
Edward White, Chatham
John White, Bartow
John Martin White, Hart
Thomas White, Columbia
Hudson Whitaker, Baldwin
John Williams, Camden
Thomas Williams, Stewart
John Williamson, Sr., Butts
Micajah Williamson, Nancy Hart
  Chapter
John Wilson, Effingham
John Wilson, Greene
Henry Winterwheedle, Wilkinson
William Wise, Bullock
James Wood, Heard
Solomon Wood, Jefferson
William Wood, Coweta
Ambrose Wright, Baldwin
Samuel Wright, Glynn
William Wright, Henry

Jesse Vaughan

Lewis Yancey, Jasper
James Youngblood, Baldwin
Solomon Youmans, Tattnall

Col. Wm. Clark and wife Ruth Goodwin, re-interred in cemetery, Gainesville, Ga.

The above list of Graves of Revolutionary Soldiers and the names of the counties in which they are buried can be found in the "Proceedings of the Ga. Society Daughters of the American Revolution". The lists were compiled for the State Proceedings by Mrs. Howard H. McCall, Atlanta; Mrs. S. V. Sanford, Athens; Mrs. J. L. Beeson, Milledgeville; Mrs. Albert L. Tidwell, Quitman; Mrs. Robert J. Travis, Savannah; Mrs. J. Harold Nicholson, Madison; and others, (1926-1938).

ROLL OF OFFICERS AND PRIVATES
CAPT. PATRICK CARR'S COMPANY OF RANGERS
Burke Co., Ga. 1781-1782

Col. James Mackay's Regiment
Mich'l Jones, First Lieut.

Patrick Carr, Captain
Josiah Hatcher, Second Lieut.

Isaac Ardis
— Ballard
Nath'l Bell
Tephan Bell
Anderson Berryhill
Peter Brown (Besoon)
Edward Bugg
Charles Burch
Edward Burch
William Caletrop
William Collins
Peter Connalley
Henry Doolin
John Doris
Jake Durban
— Epperson
Daniel Evans
George Galphin
Thomas Galphin
Theodk. Goodwyn
Samuel Griffin
Ezekiel Harris
James Harvin
John Hatcher
Urek Hatcher

William Hatcher
— Hill
John Hix
William Holmes
William Hunt
John Jolly
William Jones
John Kitts
John Leith
John McElhoney
Patrick Maloga
John Mammin
John Milledge
William Moore
John Murray
Edward Outlaw
Sud Outlaw
Ezekiel Oxford
Jefse Oxford
William Patterson
Hillery Phillips
Tim Rickerson
Martin Shirley
William Stewart

(Original Record at State Dept. of Archives, Atlanta, Georgia)

ORIGINAL LIST OF DRAWING
OLD IRWIN CO., GA.

Names copied from a copy of "The Original List" of the Drawing of "Old Irwin" Co., Ga., together with a list of the "reverted lots", giving the names, dates of the Grant, and the name of the Counties in which the grantees lived at the time of the issuing of the grants. "Old Irwin" comprised the counties of Irwin, Berrien, Lowndes, and Colquitt, together with portions of Clinch, Worth, Coffee, and Thomas Counties.

(Certified to by E. R. De Graffenreid, and printed at Milledgeville, Baldwin Co., Ga., 1857).

Name	County	Date
Allgood, John	Elbert	Feb. 24, 1831
Bellinger, John	Elbert	Mar. 19, 1825
Binum, Drury	Warren	Oct. 13, 1834
Brantley, Amos	Hancock	Dec. 26, 1828
Brumfield, John	Elbert	Dec. 13, 1830
Bryant, Isaac	Putnam	Sept. 21, 1836
Buford, John, Sr.	Screven	Dec. 19, 1823
Capeheart, John	Jefferson	1824
Casey, Daniel	Elbert	Nov. 11, 1821
Collins, James	Richmond	Dec. 22, 1821
Collins, Joseph	Morgan	Sept. 4, 1837
Conner, Daniel	Clarke	Mar. 1, 1830
Cook, Elisha	Hancock	Nov. 13, 1832
Easterling, James	Twiggs	Dec. 24, 1839
Gilbert, Thomas	Franklin	1824
Gilbert, William	Morgan	Dec. 17, 1829
Goore, Thomas, Sr.	Hancock	Dec. 23, 1828
Grant, Joseph	Hancock	Nov. 3, 1828
Greene, Forrest	Jackson	Nov. 26, 1821
Greer, Robert	Morgan	Nov. 4, 1829
Gully, Richard	Elbert	1828
Harvey, John	Clarke	July 31, 1821
Hendley, John	Morgan	Feb. 2, 1835
Hollinsworth, Isaac	Twiggs	Oct. 30, 1827
Inger, John	Jackson	Dec. 17, 1823
Jarrell, Richard	Baldwin	July 20, 1824
Johnson, Jacob	Twiggs	Oct. 5, 1837
Johnston, John B.	Clarke	Aug. 27, 1841
Judkins, Zachariah	Hancock	Jan. 27, 1840
Kent, John	Warren	Dec. 6, 1820
McCleland, Mack	Screven	Dec. 19, 1825
McGamary, John	Warren	Sept. 30, 1824

Name	County	Date
Mercer, Jacob	Jasper	Jan. 31, 1828
Morris, Wm., Sr.	Jackson	Mar. 31, 1824
Myhand, James	Morgan	Nov. 3, 1822
Nelson, Jeremiah	Hancock	Jan. 12, 1826
Pressnell, William	Jackson	Dec. 21, 1839
Rives, Joel	Hancock	Nov. 23, 1825
Rooks, Hardeman	Jackson	Nov. 5, 1827
Sanders, David	Putnam	Dec. 14, 1836
Smith, John, Sr.	Morgan	Aug. 29, 1841
Smith, William	Walton	Jan. 29, 1821
Snow, Mark	Gwinnett	Nov. 1, 1830
Thompson, William	Jackson	Dec. 29, 1825
Tinney, Ed. R.	Chatham	Dec. 9, 1825
Tison, James	Effingham	Feb. 14, 1833
Webb, Clarence	Jackson	Dec. 19, 1826
Willeby, John	Twiggs	Dec. 19, 1829
Wright, John	Walton	Nov. 4, 1829

APPLICATIONS FOR PENSIONS

Revolutionary Soldiers from Georgia

The following applied for Pensions under Act of Congress, June 7, 1832. From Minutes of Franklin Co., Ga., Court of Ordinary, commencing May 4, 1829 and ending Nov. 4, 1844. (Applications, Abstracts) can be found in Georgia D. A. R. Historical Collections, Vol. I, pages 137 to 182.

Albritton, John	b. Hanover Co., Va., 1747
Bond, Richard	b. Amherst Co., Va., 1763
Cash, James	b. Fairfax Co., Va., 1764
Cheek, William	b. North Carolina, 1752
Clark, Thomas	b. Granville Co., N. C., 1761
Dyer, Elisha	b. on Potomac River, Va., 1763
Downs, Ambrose	b. Richmond Co., Ga., 1761
Edwards, Joseph	b. in Maryland, 1756
Epposon, Thompson	b. Albemarle Co., Va., 1757
Farrar, John	b. North Carolina, 1760
Guest, Moses (Capt.)	b. Fauquier Co., Va., 1750
Glover, William	b. Prince George Co., Md., 1760
Lee, Andrew	b. Augusta, Ga., 1761
Leach, Burdette	b. Virginia, 1760
Murdock, William	b. in Ireland, 1759
Mitchell, William	b. Virginia, 1761
Moseley, Samuel	b. Bute Co., N. C., 1759
Nichols, Julius	b. Granville Co., N. C., 1759
Parks, Henry	b. Albemarle Co., Va., 1758
Stoneycipher, John	b. Culpepper Co., Va., 1756
Smith, Jesse	b. Montgomery Co., N. C., 1765
Stow, Warren	b. Sheffield, Conn.
Smith, Gabriel	b. Montgomery Co., N. C., 1764
Smith, William	b. Moore Co., N. C., 1763
Tate, John	b. in Ireland, 1758
Thomas, William	b. Culpepper Co., Va., 1763
Wilson, James	b. in Pennsylvania, 1758
Wilkerson, Elisha	b. Sussex Co., Va., 1763
Ray, William	Pension No. 19360
York, William	Pension No. 19185

REVOLUTIONARY SOLDIERS
AT THE BATTLE OF KETTLE CREEK

They fought at the Battle of Kettle Creek, through which Georgia was freed of the Tory domination.

(Published by the courtesy of Mrs. Boyce Ficklin, Jr., and the Wilkes County Forum, Georgia.)

Aldridge, James
Alexander, Asa
Alexander, James
Anderson, Alexander
Anderson, Henry
Anglin, William
Anthony, Alexander
Anthony, John
Atkins, John
Austin, Richard
Aycock, Richard
Barnes, Richard
Barnes, William
Barnett, Nathan
Bazelwood, Richard
Beasley, Ambrose
Beasley, James
Beasley, Richard
Beasley, William
Bedell, Absolem
Bedingfield, Charles
Bird, Benjamin
Bird, John
Branham, Samuel
Brannon, Moses
Brown, James
Butler, Edmund
Butler, William
Butts, Solomon
Cade, Drury
Cain, John
Cantey, Jeceriah
Carr, Henry
Carter, James
Catchings, Benjamin
  (Col.)
Catchings, Joseph

Catchings, Merideth
Catchings, Philip
Catchings, Seymour
  (Major)
Chandler, John
Cheshire, John
Clark, John
Clarke, Gibson
Cloud, Ezekiel
Cloud, Jeremiah
Cloud, Nehemiah
Clower, Peter
Cohron, Cornelius
Coleman, Benjamin
Coleman, Daniel
Coleman, James
Coleman, John
Coleman, Thomas
Combs, John
Compton, William
Cook, George
Crain, Spencer
Crosby, William
Crutchfield, John
Dabney, Austin
  (mulatto)
Darden, George
Dautham, Elijah
Davis, Absolem
Davis, Hardy
Davis, Joel
Davis, Samuel
Day, Joseph
Day, Robert
Dooly, George
Dooly, John
Downs, Jonathan

Downs, William
Dullins, Henry
Durkee, Nathaniel
Edison, Shelton
Ellis, Jerry
Evans, Benjamin
Evans, Daniel
Farr, Benjamin
Farr, John
Favour, John
Ferrington, Jacob
Fluker, John
Fluker, Owen
Flynn, John
Foster, Francis
Foster, William
Fowler, Henry
Fowler, Peter
Franklin, David
Franklin, David, Jr.
Freeman, Daniel
Freeman, George
Freeman, Holman, Jr.
Freeman, James
Freeman, John
Freeman, William
Gillons, James
Glass, Joel
Glass, John
Glass, Joseph
Gouze, Henry
Grant, Thomas
Graves, James
Graves, Thomas
Graves, William
Griffin, Randolph
Hamilton, William

Harper, Robert
Harper, Samuel
Harris, Buckner
Harris, David
Harris, John
Hart, John
Harvie, James
Harvie, Joel
Hawkins, Stephen
Heard, Barnard
Heard, George
Heard, Jesse
Heard, Joseph
Heard, Richard
Hill, James
Holliday, William, Sr.
Howard, John
Howard, William
Hubbard, John
Huggins, Robert
Jiles, Samuel
Jiles, Thomas
Johns, Thomas
Johnson, John
Joiner, Benjamin
Joiner, Thomas
Jones, Jesse
Jordan, Dempsey
Jordan, Samuel
Kilby, Daniel
Lamar, Basil
Lamar, James
Lamar, Samuel
Lamar, Zecheria
Lindsey, Dennis
Lindsey, John
Little, Archibald
Little, David
Little, James
Lowe, Jesse
Lowe, William
Loyd, James
McBurnett, Daniel
McCall, Hugh
McCall, Thomas
McLean, James
McLendon, Isaac
McLendon, Jacob, Jr.

McLendon, Jacob, Sr.
McMurray, Frederick
Manaduc, Henry
Marney, Thomas
Mathews, Isham
Mercer, Jacob
Mercer, James
Mercer, Joshua
Mercer, William
Meriwether, Daniel
Morgan, Asa
Morgan, Luke
Morgan, William
Moseley, William
Nelson, John
Oliver, Dionysius
Oliver, John
Oliver, Peter
Ollens, Daniel
Persons, Henry
Persons, Samuel
Philips, Joseph
Philips, Zachariah
Pickins, Joseph
Poullain, Anthony
Poullain, William
Powell, Joshua
Pratt, Edward
Prickett, John
Prickett, William
Reddens, Scott
Rice, David
Rice, John
Rice, Nathan
Roberson, David
Roberson, Hugh
Rogers, Reuben
Sampson, Archibald
Sampson, William
Shannon, Thomas, Jr.
Shannon, Thomas, Sr.
Shepard, Benjamin
Simby, James
Simby, Thomas
Simby, William
Simmons, James
Simmons, William
Simpson, James

Sinquefield, Samuel
Sinquefield, William
Smith, James
Smith, Nathan
Smith, Peyton
Smith, Thomas
Snead, Dudley
Spikes, Nathan
Spurlock, George
Stephens, Benjamin
Stephens, John
Steward, William
Stone, Charles
Stone, Joshua
Stots, John
Stots, Peter
Stripling, Francis
Stroud, Thomas
Strozier, Peter
Stubblefield, Jeter
Summerlin, Dempsey
Summerlin, James
Summerlin, John
Summerlin, Richard
Summerlin, Samuel
Sutton, William
Swan, John
Tate, Richard
Terrell, David
Thompson, Peter
Thompson, Reuben
Triplett, Francis
Tunis, Nicholas
Tyner, Benjamin
Tyner, Richard
Vance, Patrick
Veazey, James
Walker, John
Walker, Thomas
Wallace, John
Waller, Benjamin
Walton, George
Walton, Jesse
Walton, John
Walton, Nathan
Walton, Robert
Watson, Benjamin
Watson, George

Watson, Jacob	Whatley, Walton W.	Willis, Brittain
Watson, John	Wilkinson, Benjamin	Willis, Josiah
Watson, Zacheriah	Wilkinson, Elisha	Willis, Robert
Wellbourne, Daniel	Williams, James	Winn, Benjamin
Wellbourne, David	Williams, John	Wood, James
Weller, Jacob	Williamson, Micajah,	Wooten, Thomas
Whatley, Samuel	Jr. and Sr.	Worth, Thomas

REVOLUTIONARY SOLDIERS OF SOUTH CAROLINA

Found in "Old Records Division", Washington, D.C., Adj. General's Office. No. 30189. (Never Published)

"We whose names are hereunder written, being deeply impressed with the Calamitous Circumstances of the Inhabitants of America from the Oppressive Acts of the British Parliament Tending to Enslave this Continent - Do find it necessary for the Security of our Lives and Fortunes and above all our Liberty and Freedom, to associate ourselves into a volunteer Company under the command of James Jones.

"And that we will hold ourselves in Readiness for our Mutual Security and Defence to obey all such Orders as shall be Directed by our Provincial Congress."

Henry Jourdan, Sr.	Martin Loadholt	Daniel Reaves
Henry Jourdan, Jr.	Jacob Maders	John Morris
Wm. Stanley	Jacob Heir	Wm. Wood
Moses Bennett	Edmund Jones	Mark Tapley
Samuel Pickings	Wm. Wournell	Michael Odom
Josiah Brunston	George Kierse	Joshua Elkins
Gustavus Gulfies	James Morris	Thomas Reavs, Sr.
Thomas Jovas, Sr.	Henry Peoples	Thomas Reavs, Jr.
Jacob Colson	Timothy Caffle	Thomas Lennox, Sr.
Wm. Kierse	John Maders	Thomas Lennox, Jr.
Wm. Brunston	George Brunston	Amos Lennox
John Taylor	William Jones	Jacob Besinger
Joseph Sykes	Henry Taylor	Ephriam Jones
Wm. Lunnix	Jeremiah Brown	Joseph Doelittle
Alexander Brunston	Benjamin Byrd	Daniel Buddest
John Ayers	Lewis Lee	Charles Morris
Wm. Ayers	Solomon Peters	Benjamin Odom
Stephen Frank	John Tedden	William Jones

Original paper in possession of A. S. Salley, State Historian of S. C., No. 503202. Certified to by Mr. Wintermeyer of the Old Records Division Office, Washington, D.C.

FAC-SIMILE SIGNATURES OF
GEORGIA REVOLUTIONARY SOLDIERS' NAMES

Found in Report of Mrs. J. L. Beeson, State Historian, Ga. D. A. R. (1932). (See Ga. D. A. R. Proceedings, 1932).

This list is patterned after Miss Ruth Blair, former State Historian of Georgia, who in her book, "Revolutionary Soldiers Receipts for Bounty Grants 1828", published their fac-simile signatures.

Alexander, Hugh (1822)
Armstrong, Alexander (1815)
Babb, Wm. (1823)
Berrien, John (Major)
  (10/26/1811)
Bostick, Littleberry
Bostick, Nathan (1818)
Beckham, John Y. (1814)
Burney, A. (1820)
Brown, William P. (1813)
Brown, Edward (1810)
Carnes, Thomas P. (1827-8)
Cone, James (1828)
Clarke, Elijah
Carter, J. M. (1819)
Fitzpatrick, Rene (1809)
Cunningham, James
Fair, Peter
Pope, Wylie
(Kendall, Henry)
Powell, John
Herndon, Joseph
Howard, John H.
Howard, Solomon
Howard, Benj.
Irwin, John
Jackson, James
Jackson, Robert
Johnston, Stephen
Marbury, W.
(Marbury, Horatio)
Leonard, John
Lawson, Thomas
Jones, Seaborn
Simmons, Thomas
Smith, Peyton

Talbert, Benjamin
Tennille, Wm. A.
Parks, Ezekiel
Patterson, Robert
Williamson, John C.
Watson, John
Watkins, Robert
Whitesides, John
Wingfield, John
Carswell, A.
Cunningham, Samuel
Campbell, William
Doles, Jesse
Fleming, James
Gamble, John
Hammett, James
Hill, John
Harvey, James
Lamar, Thomas
Pace, Thomas
(Evans, John)
Shelton, Henry
(Brown, Wm. P.)
Jones, Reuben
Flewellyn, Abner
Hines, John B.
Rivers, Joel
Newton, Moses
Thomas, Harris
Hancocke, Isham
Harvey, Michael
Jones, John
Jones, Abraham
Justice, Dempsey
Lawson, Roger
Kendale, Henry

Mathews, Wm.
Martin, Wm.
Merewether, T.
Murphy, Morris
McKee, Wm.
Mitchell, Wm.
Milledge, John
Myrick, John

Moore, Thomas
Martin, Alexander
Meecham, Henry
Pattillo, James
Pitts, John
Redding, Anderson
Scott, John
Stapleton, Geo.

REV. SOLDIERS' GRAVES IN BURKE CO., GA.

Marked by the Shadrack Inman Chapter, D. A. R., Hepzibah, Ga.

JOHN MURPHREE, Served in Collier's Reb. N. C. Militia. Died
March 6, 1798.
BENJAMIN BRACK, d. 1827. Buried near Midville.
MILES MURPHREE, d. Dec. 7, 1815. Buried 14 miles from Waynes-
boro.
LIEUT. JOHN CARSWELL, Lieut., 4th Ga. Reg. Buried on the old
Carswell Plantation.
DANIEL INMAN, d. May 15, 1815. Buried near Midville.

REVOLUTIONARY SOLDIERS
Burke Co., Ga.

Benjamin Brack, d. 1827
Alexander Carswell
Lieut. John Carswell
Daniel Inman
Joshua Inman

Gov. Jared Irwin
Abraham Jones
Col. John Jones
Seaborn Jones
John Lawson

Abraham Lively
Matthew Lively
John Murphree, d. 1798
Miles Murphree, d.1815
Joseph A. Roe

Effingham Co., Ga.
(drew land grants)

Paul Beville
Robert Beville
William Cone
Benjamin D'Aley (Daley)
McKeen Green, Sr.
McKeen Green, Jr.
Samuel Hearn
William Hearn
Caleb Howell

Daniel Howell
David Harris
Robert Hudson, Sr.
Robert Hudson, Jr.
Samuel Hudson
Clement Lanier
Joseph Humphries
Theophilus Lundy
Nathaniel Lundy

Nathaniel Miller
James Moore
Adam Neisler
George Palmer
John Rupert
Solomon Thornton
David Thom
William Willson
Jeremiah Warren

279

LAND GRANTS IN GEORGIA
TO REVOLUTIONARY SOLDIERS

Name	Lived in County	Drew Land in Year,
Henry Averett	Washington	1784
Dempsey Baker	Hancock	1842
Charles Barber	Glynn	1827
David Batson	Pulaski	1829
Joseph Boggs	Washington	1784
John Boyd	Warren	1830
John Brown, Sr.	Franklin	1828
Starke Brown	Walton	1831
John Brumfield	Elbert	1825
James P. Buchanan, Sr.	Jasper	1822
Daniel Bullock	Twiggs	1836
Turner Christian	Elbert	1831
John Crawford	Twiggs	1822
Cary Curry	Baldwin	1823
John Dantigal	Richmond	1832
Jesse Doles	Baldwin	1834
John Duck	Morgan	1837
James Felts	Jones	1823
Thomas Geddins	Pulaski	1842
Thomas Gilbert	Franklin	1838
William Harbin, Sr.	Elbert	1831
Christian J. Heidt	Effingham	1821
Burrus Hickenbotham	Washington	1784
Thomas Hinsley	Jasper	1826
Joseph Hodges	Bulloch	1826
Richard Horn	McIntosh	1837
Manoah Hubbard	Baldwin	1839
David Jameson	Twiggs	
Henry Leverett	Washington	1784
John McCall	Effingham	1820
Thomas McClendon, Sr.	Walton	1822
William McCullers, Sr.	Morgan	1827
Jacob McCullough	Richmond	1836
Rev. Abraham Marshall	Washington	1784
Joseph Moore	Jasper	1833
John Morris	Clarke	1822
William Morris, Sr.	Jackson	1821
Malone Mullen	Hancock	1842
John Parker	Washington	1784

Name	Lived in County	Drew Land in Year,
Robert Patterson	Washington	1784
Joel Perkerson	Jackson	1825
Michael Pilgrim	Franklin	1831
Richard Pollett	Clarke	1824
John Ramey, Sr.	Clarke	1839
James Ridge	Gwinnett	1842
Edward Shavely	Jones	1832
David Shay	Clarke	1823
Sterne Simmons	Wilkes	July 24, 1786
Charles Stewart	Washington	1784
Clement Stewart	Washington	1784
John Taylor	Washington	1784
Thomas Thornby	Pulaski	1829
William Trammell	Elbert	1821
Daniel Usher	Richmond	1821
Lewis Whelons, Sr.	Morgan	1827
Thomas Williams, Sr.	Jackson	1836
Joseph Willis, Sr.	Effingham	1822
Peter Yates	Clarke	1842

Jefferson Co., Ga.

Widows of Rev. Soldiers entitled to draw in Lottery

Lucretia Alford
Rhoda Barber (Joseph)
Jane Bostwick (Nathan)
Esther Brett
Elizabeth Causey
Elizabeth Durougeaux (Peter)
Sarah Fountain
Elizabeth Fort
Mary Patterson
Ann D. Powell
Mary Scott
Nancy Sammons

Mary Spivey (James)
Sarah Thompson
Catherine Warner
Rebecca Garvin (Thomas)
Catherine Goitman
Ann Hall
Mary Haddin (Wm.)
Ann Montgomery
Martha D. Moss
Elinor McNeely (Hugh)
Clvey Pate

NOTE: Rhoda Barber, Elizabeth Durongeaux, Elizabeth Fort, and Catherine Warner were also daughters of Rev. Soldiers.

Rev. Soldiers

Hugh Alexander
John Arrington, d. 1827
John Boutin
Ezekiel Causey
Wm. Clements, Sr., d. 1828

James Cotter
Michael Cowart
James Cook
John Darby, Sr.
Stephen Durougeaux, d. 1833

George Fowler, Sr.
Dempsey Hall, Sr.
Benjamin Green
Hudson Hall, Sr.
John S. Holder
James Johnson
William Lions
Norman McCloud

Morris Murphy
Moses Newton
Seth Pierce
John Thompson
William Thompson
Joshua Watson
Caleb Welch
Jerry Wilsher

Rev. Soldiers - Butts Co.

Joseph Benton, Sr. (Pension)
Wm. Buford
Joseph Dawson
George Eubanks
Alexander Harbin
Levi Jester

E. Price (Pension)
David Ramsdill
Richard Speake (Pension)
Robert Smith, Sr.
John Tillary, Sr.
John Wright

Land Grants for Services - Rev. Soldiers

Name	County
Henry Allison (wife Martha)	Richmond
Henry Averett	Washington
John Averett	Greene
Ephriam Baldwin)	
Owen Baldwin) Records in Greene Co.	
William Baldwin)	
James Bishop (wife Phoebe)	Greene
Joseph Bazdell (wife Phoebe)	Richmond
Joseph Boggs	Washington
William Brady	Wilkes
Starke Brown (6th Va. Reg.) Granted land	
James Buchanan	Oglethorpe
John Burney, Old Town Creek, Oconee River	
John Burford (wife Phoebe)	Wilkes
William Campbell (wife Mary)	Wilkes
Moody Burt, Sr. (from Edgefield, S. C.)	
Hezekiah Bussey (wife Amey)	Wilkes
Owen Carnsby	Wilkes
Laymore Catchings	Wilkes
William Clark (wife Nancy)	Wilkes
Jeremiah Cloud (wife Sarah)	Greene
William Cone (287.5 acres) grant in	Greene
William Daniel, Richland Creek	Greene
Robert Day (wife Fanny)	Wilkes
Reuben De Jarnette	Greene
John Dooly (sold 575 acres to Robert and Lettice Chambers)	

Name	County
John Taylor Dukes	Wilkes
Luke Durban	Greene
William Elder (wife Lydia) (Sold to Turner Hunt of N.C.)	
Stephen Ellis (wife Agnes)	Richmond
James Ferrell (wife Mary)	Greene
Matthew Findley	Greene
John Fluker	Wilkes
Andrew Frazier	Wilkes
George Freeman (wife Frances)	Wilkes
Benjamin Fry (14th Va. Reg.) granted 1793	
Benjamin Gilbert (wife Milly)	Greene
Cary Godbee	Burke
Henry Gabill (wife Mary) (Grabill, Graybill)	Greene
McKeen Green, Sr.) Book G. G. G.	
McKeen Green, Jr. (wife Eleanor) State Capitol	
William Greene, Sr.	Wilkes
John Griffin (brother Chas. Griffin, d. in Va. Service)	Wilkes
James Hall (Capt. John Richel's Co., N.C. Reg.)	
James Hammett	Wilkes
William Hammett	Wilkes
William Hewitt (wife Lacey)	Wilkes
Burrus Hickenbotham	Washington
Thomas Johnson (wife Agnes)	Greene
William Johnson (wife Rosanna) (Sold to Jesse Sanford)	
Robert Jones	Washington
William Lanier (from Anson Co., N.C.)	
Elijah Leonard	Greene
Henry Leverett	Washington
John Lindsay (wife Clarissa)	Wilkes & Greene
John Low	
Abraham Marshall	Washington
Daniel Marshall	Columbia
Solomon Marshall	Richmond
Thomas Marbury (wife Jane) (from S.C.) (Sold to Robt. Flournoy)	
James Mathews (wife Rebecca) grant in	Hancock
William Mims	Greene
James Moore (wife Alys)	Richmond
Leonard Moss	Washington
John McFarland, Jr.	Richmond
Jacob McClendon	Greene
Robert McMullen (Sold to Henry and Martha Allison)	
John McMunn (wife Prudence)	Richmond
John Offutt	Richmond
David Parker	Baldwin

Name	County
John Parker	Washington
Gideon Patterson	Richmond
Robert Patterson	Washington
Dyall Peavey (Sold to John Brewer of Va.)	
John Perkins (wife Sarah)	Richmond
William Ramsey (wife Jemina)	Wilkes
William Ray	Washington
Abraham Reddick (wife Hannah)	
John Shick (in Count Pulaski's Reg., Ga.)	
Thomas Shaw (of 96th Dist., S. C.)	Washington
Sterne Simmons	Wilkes
John Simmons	Wilkes
Charles Stewart	Washington
Clement Stewart	Washington
Graverner Stewart (wife Jane)	Greene
William Strother (12th Va. Reg., Col. Lee's Dragoons)	
John Tanner	Oglethorpe
John Taylor	Washington
James Thompson	Greene
Jesse Thompson	Greene
William Thompson	Richmond
Nathaniel Wake	Richmond
Joseph Walker	Washington
John Wall (wife Mary)	Greene
Edward Weathers (Sold to Richard Simmons of	Wilkes
Isham Williams (3rd Va. Reg.)	
Nathan Wright (1st Detachment, Va. Levies)	
James Wright (7th Va. Reg., under Col. Dangerfield)	
Peter Youngblood (from Edgefield, S. C.)	Washington

Records found in the files, Greene and Wilkes Counties.

LAND RECORDS

WM. DANIELL of Greene Co., Sept. 11, 1787, to Wm. Melton, 500 acres granted him, on Richland Creek, Greene Co.

JOHN WALL and wife Mary, Sept. 16, 1788, to John Cain, 287.5 acres granted him in 1785, in Greene (formerly Washington) Co.

SOLOMON MARSHALL of Richmond Co., to Walton Harris, 287.5 acres granted him.

ROBERT DAY and wife Fanny, sold 287.5 acres of land, granted him in Wilkes Co., 1785.

WILLIAM CLARK and wife Nancy, sold 287.5 acres of land, to Micajah Williamson, granted him Oct. 1, 1784.

GIDEON PATTERSON of Richmond Co., and wife Sophia, sold to Micajah Williamson, 287.5 acres, granted him in 1784.

JOHN TAYLOR DUKES, sold 287.5 acres of land, to Micajah Williamson, granted to him in 1784.

WILLIAM HAMMETT, 287.5 acres.

JAMES HAMMETT, 287.5 acres.

GRAVERNER STEWART and wife Jane, to Amos Stewart, 287.5 acres of land granted him.

JOHN SIMMONS, 287.5 acres, Wilkes Co., Oct. 20, 1785.

JOHN TANNER, 287.5 acres in Oglethorpe Co., July 4, 1796.

JAMES BUCHANAN drew his old warrant of 287.5 acres of land in Oglethorpe Co., Sept. 5, 1796.

ROBERT McMULLEN, granted 287.5 acres of land for services, Sept. 23, 1784; sold it to Henry and Martha Allison of Richmond Co.

JOHN PARKER, granted 287.5 acres for services; sold to Henry and Martha Allison, and sold 1788, to the heirs of Daniel Coleman of Wilkes Co.

LEONARD MOSS, granted 287.5 acres in Washington Co., Sept. 30, 1784.

CHARLES GRIFFIN, dec., a Soldier in 1st Detachment, Va. Levies, commanded by Col. Richard Parker (and who died in said service), his brother John Griffin of Wilkes Co., his heir-at-law, appoints Francis Baldwin of Wilkes Co., his attorney, Jan. 1793.

NATHAN WRIGHT, late a Soldier, 1st Detachment, Va. Levies, appoints Francis Baldwin his attorney. Benj. Taliaferro signs, Jan. 10, 1793. (Book K. K., Wilkes Co.)

JOHN SHIKS (Shick), in Count Pulaski's Reg. of Horse, asks for land, Jan. 2, 1793. Sworn to by Jesse Heard. Granted.

JAMES WRIGHT, 7th Va. Reg., under Col. Wm. Dangerfield, asks for land as Rev. Soldier, Dec. 26, 1793. Granted.

STARK BROWN, 6th Va. Reg., commanded by Col. Mordecai Brown. Asks for land as Rev. Soldier, 1793. Certified to by J. Anthony, J. P.

WILLIAM STROTHER, 12th Va. Reg., Col. Lee's Legion of Light Dragoons. Francis Baldwin, attorney; witnesses John Fannin, Wm. Glenn, June 1793. Appeared in person before Thomas Dukes, J. P. (Book K. K.)

JOHN PERKINS, and wife Sarah, of Richmond Co., sold 287.5 acres in Washington Co., granted 1785, to Ezekiel Smith in 1788.

John Lamar and wife Frances, sold 287.5 acres (granted to JOHN LOW) to John Thomas, in 1788.

Green Co. Records

LAYMORE CATCHINGS of Wilkes Co., 287.5 acres.

MOODY BURT, SR., from Edgefield, S. C., 287.5 acres.

WILLIAM MIMS, 287.5 acres.

WILLIAM LANIER, from Anson Co., N. C., 287.5 acres. Sold to Abram Leapham, Aug. 31, 1785.

WM. RAY, 287.5 acres in Washington Co., Feb. 17, 1786; to Robert Flournoy, 1786.

THOMAS MARBURY and wife Jane, from S. C., sold 287.5 acres, granted him in June 20, 1784, in Washington Co., to Robert Flournoy, Dec. 10, 1785.

NATHANIEL WADE, of Augusta, 287.5 acres in Washington Co., to Robert Flournoy.

PETER YOUNGBLOOD, from Edgefield, S. C., sold 1789, to Howell Harris of Brunswick Co., Va., 575 acres granted him in Washington Co., Feb. 2, 1785.

JAMES MATHEWS and Rebecca Carlton (dau. of Robt. Carlton), his wife, sold 287.5 acres on Denison Creek (now Hancock Co.).

WILLIAM JONES and Abigail his wife, on Oct. 10, 1785, sold to Robert Flournoy of Augusta, Ga., 287.5 acres of land in Washington Co., on Shoulderbone Creek, granted to the said William Jones by his honor the Gov. of Ga., Samuel Elbert, on Oct. 13, 1784, for services as a Rev. Soldier. (Greene Co. Records. Vol. 1. P. 330).

JAMES MOORE and wife Alys of Richmond Co., sold to Thomas Mitchell, 1787, 287.5 acres of land, granted him in Greene Co., Sept. 30, 1784.

P. SULLIVAN, granted 287.5 acres, Aug. 17, 1785; sold by Wm. Sullivan to John Gholson of Wilkes in 1788.

HEZEKIAH BUSSEY and Amey his wife, sold to Jonathan Ragan of Wilkes Co., Jan. 30, 1788, 287.5 acres, granted him on Oconee River, Washington Co., Feb. 4, 1785.

HENRY GRAYBILL and Mary his wife, sold 1788 to Jared Burch, part of 400 acres bounded by Wm. Stewart's land in Greene Co.

REUBEN DE JARNETTE, 287.5 acres of land, to Isaac Borland.

JOHN DOOLY, granted 575 acres of land for Rev. Service; sold to Robert and Lettice Chambers.

WILLIAM GREENE, SR., of Wilkes Co., sold 287.5 acres of land granted him, to Silas Mercer, Dec. 6, 1785, in Washington Co.

JOSEPH WALKER, received 287.5 acres of land, Washington Co., Dec. 31, 1781; sold to Sanders Walker, wittness Nancy Walker.

JAMES THOMPSON, of Greene Co., sold his bounty grant of 287.5 acres in Washington Co., to Robert Carr, of Randolph Co., N. C., Dec. 24, 1791.

JEREMIAH CLOUD, 287.5 acres, Washington Co., 1784, Rev. Soldier living in Greene Co.

JESSE THOMPSON, Greene Co., 287.5 acres of land, bounty grant, sold 1796 to Owen Fluker of Wilkes Co., on Old Town Creek branch Oconee River. Witt. Samuel Coleman, Blake Holliman, J. P. Armor. Rep. Jan. 7, 1784.

EDWARD WEATHERS, 287.5 acres in Washington Co., granted Dec. 15, 1785; sold to Richard Simmons of Wilkes Co., Jan. 16, 1790. Reg. 1809. Witt. John Simmons, Claiborne Maddox, Wm. Huckaby, Robertus Love.

WM. CONE, 287.5 acres in Greene Co.

DANIEL MARSHALL, 287.5 acres land, Columbia Co.

WILLIAM JOHNSON and wife Rosannah, sold 287.5 acres, granted him to Jesse Sanford.

CLAYBORNE BARNETT, 287.5 acres land granted 1785.

JACOB McLENDON, 287.5 acres of land granted June 27, 1786.

ROBERT JONES, 287.5 acres of land in Washington Co., granted 1785, sold to Richard Call.

WILLIAM ELDER and wife Lydia, 287.5 acres granted him, sold to Turner Hunt, of N. C., Jan. 1793.

JAMES HALL, late N. C. Reg., in Capt. John Richel's Co., appoints Francis Baldwin of Wilkes, attorney, to ask and receive pay as Rev. Soldier, N. C. Line.

BENJAMIN FRY, of 14th Va. Reg., commanded by Col. Charles Lewis, before Josiah Jordan, J. P., June 20, 1793, for bounty land.

ISHAM WILLIAMS, 3rd Va. Reg., commanded by Col. Leonard Marbury, applied for land as Rev. Soldier, June 14, 1793.

McKEEN GREEN, received 287.5 acres of land in Washington Co., S. E. bounded by McKeen Green, Sr., and by the Altamaha River. (Book G. G. G., page 567, State Capitol, Atlanta, Ga.)

WM. EPHRIAM and OWEN BALDWIN received bounty land in 1786.

GEORGE FREEMAN, 250 acres of bounty land for Rev. Services, on the waters of Clarke's Fork, Long Creek, Wilkens Co., adjoining lands of Anderson Brown, John Cloud, and Col. Elijah Clarke. (Book E. E. E., page 150) Dec. 4, 1783, mar. Frances Taylor of Va.

The Heirs of ROBERT HOWE, late a Lieut. in U. S. Army, 460 acres in Washington Co., April 8, 1785. (Book G. G. G., page 384)

JOHN FLUKER of Wilkes Co.

OWEN CARNSBY of Wilkes Co., 575 acres in Greene Co.; sold to Isaac Williams, 1788. (See plat, Vol. 1, page 374, Greene Co. Records.)

ISAIAH WRIGHT and wife Rebecca, of Richmond Co., to John Parham, Greene Co.

JAMES BISHOP and wife Phoebe of Wilkes Co., to Samuel Reid of Greene Co.

MATTHEW FINDLEY of Wilkes Co. (Greene).

WILLIAM CAMPBELL and wife Mary, of Wilkes Co., to Abednego Turner of Wilkes, on Oconee River, Washington Co.

CHARLES WATERS of Wilkes Co., to Abednego Turner of Wilkes Co., in Washington Co.

Heirs of JOHN STEWART, dec. Nov. 2, 1786, sold to Joseph Phillips, 287.5 acres in Greene Co., granted to him 1785. Heirs were James, Robert, Charles, and Lydia Stewart.

DAVID PARKER, Baldwin Co., 287.5 acres of land. Paid taxes also, 1809 in Hancock Co.

Rev. Soldiers Land Records, Greene Co., Ga.
(Bounty land of 287.5 acres for Rev. Service)

JAMES FERRELL and wife Mary, sold to Henry Mitchell in Greene Co.

JOHN McMUNN and wife Prudence, of Richmond Co., to James Thweatt, in Greene Co.

WILLIAM HEWETT and wife Lacey, of Wilkes Co., to John Mitchell, in Greene Co.

JAMES MOORE and wife Alis, of Richmond Co., to Thomas Mitchell, in Greene Co.

BENJAMIN GILBERT and wife Milly, to James Garrett of Charlotte Co., Va., in Greene Co.

JOHN McFARLAND, JR. of Richmond Co., to Stephen Horton of Wilkes Co., in Washington Co.

ELIJAH LEONARD of Greene Co., in Greene Co.

LUKE DURBAN of Greene Co., in Greene Co.

ABRAHAM REDDICK and wife Hannah, sold land granted 1786, to James Harvey, 1788.

Land Deeds

THOMAS JOHNSON and wife Agnes, of Greene Co., to Thomas Standley, in Greene Co.

JOHN LINDSEY and wife Clarissa, of Greene (Wilkes ?) Co., sold to Edward and Peyton Wade, in Greene Co.

STEPHEN ELLIS and wife Agnes, of Richmond Co., sold to Thomas Heard of Greene Co.

ANDREW FRAZIER, sold to Thomas Bush, in Greene (formerly Wilkes) Co., adj. Joseph Anthony.

JEREMIAH CLOUD and wife Sarah, of Wilkes Co., to Sanders Walker, on Rocky Creek, Washington Co.

DILL SAPP and wife Lydia, of Burke Co., to Sanders Walker of Wilkes, on Rocky Creek, Washington Co.

Wm. Brady of Wilkes, sold 287.5 acres of land granted to THOMAS SHAW, 96th Dist., S. C., 1785, in Washington Co., to Barney Dunn of N. C.

JOHN BURFORD and wife Phoebe, of Wilkes Co., to James Dozier, in Greene Co.

JOHN AVERETT of Greene, to Daniel McNeil, land in Washington Co.

R. S. Land Records, Greene Co., Ga.

JAMES WEST, 287.5 acres, sold to Jeremiah Reeves, granted 1785.

CARY GODBEE of Burke Co., 287.5 acres, granted Feb. 4, 1785, sold to Robert Flournoy.

JOHN OFFUT of Richmond Co., 287.5 acres, granted Feb. 4, 1785, sold 1786, to Robert Flournoy.

WILLIAM RAMSEY and wife Jemina, 287.5 acres, granted Sept. 18, 1784, of Wilkes Co., sold to Thomas Daniell of Greene Co., May 1, 1787. Witt. Wm. Daniell and Henry Graybill.

DYALL PEAVY, granted 287.5 acres in Washington Co., to John Brewer, planter of Va.

JOSEPH BAZDELL and wife Phoebe, of Richmond Co., 287.5 acres of land, granted Oct. 19, 1785, sold to David Crockett of Wilkes, 1789.

WM. THOMPSON of Richmond Co., sold 287.5 acres of land, granted Mar. 9, 1785, to Robert Flournoy.

CYLASS CHEEK of Mecklenburg Co., N. C., on Dec. 3, 1790, sold to William Holliman of Warren Co., 287.5 acres of land in Greene Co., granted July 29, 1785, to John Burney.

CHEROKEE LAND LOTTERY - OCT. 30, 1825

List of Revolutionary Soldiers who drew in the Land Lottery, and who resided in Major Dobbs and Major Allen's Batallion in Elbert Co., Ga.

Mills, Moses
Maxwell, Thomas, Sr.
Higgenbotham, Jacob
Maxwell, John
Hunt, James
Bond, Nathan
Hilley, Thomas, Sr.
Sandidge, Clairborne
Pulliam, Robert
Adams, Thomas
Adams, James, Sr.
White, William, Sr.
Lockhart, James
Hailey, William
Gaines, Francis
Hinton, Peter
David, John
King, Thomas
Hunt, Moses
Cash, John
Wansley, John, Sr.
Evanson, Eli
Brown, Benjamin
Wheeler, Thomas, Sr.

Thornton, Dozier, Sr.
White, John M.
Burton, Thomas
Cunningham, William
Cook, John
Maupin, Jesse
Key, William Bibb
Allgood, John
Hudson, David
Oliver, Peter
Oliver, Theodosius
Cabeniss, Henry
Rumsey, Richard
Vacray, Joseph, Sr.
Stowers, Lewis, Sr.
Rucker, William
Richardson, Amos
Teasley, Silas
Enlo, John
McCurry, Angus, Sr.
Kelly, William
Alexander, Isaac
Smether, Gabriel
Riley, James

McGuire, Anderson
Grisson, James
Daniel, John, Sr.
Word (Ward), William, Sr.
Harris, John, Sr.
Rucker, John
Ganes, William
Cook, Thomas
Butler, Patrick
Brown, James N.
Dennard, John
Allgood, Spencer
Dillard, James
Wilkins, John —
Child, John
Nunnellee, James F.
Terrell, Joseph
Tate, Enos
Tucker, Godfrey
Tatum, Jesse
Clark, Larkin

LOTTERY OF 1827

Names of Revolutionary Soldiers Who Drew Land In Georgia, and the Counties of Georgia in which they lived. Names of Counties are in parentheses for easy identification.

Adams, Aaron (Hall)
Adams, Dancy (Columbia)
Adams, David (Jasper)
Adams, Thomas, Sr. (Elbert)
Adkins, William (Monroe)
Aiken, John (Morgan)
Aikins, James (Greene)
Ajohns, Eli (Chatham)
Akridge, Ezekiel (Clark)
Akridge, William (Baldwin)
Alberson, William (Newton)
Albritton, John (Franklin)
Alexander, Isaac (Elbert)
Allen, David (Morgan)
Allen, John (Franklin)
Allen, Joseph (Elbert)
Allen, Philip (Clark)
Allen, Robert (Burke)
Allen, Wm. (Elbert)
Allen, Woodson (Walton)
Amison, Jesse (Washington)
Anderson, Henry (Wilkinson)
Anderson, William (Wilkes)
Andrew, John (Clark)
Andrews, Owen (Gwinnett)
Angelly, Alexander (Twiggs)
Anglina, John (Madison)
Armistorph, George, Sr. (Effingham)
Armor, John (Greene)
Arthur, Matthew (Habersham)
Astin, Robert (Greene)
Atkinson, Robert (DeKalb)
Austin, Harris D. (Jefferson)
Austin, Michael (Fayette)
Ayers, Frances (Jackson)

Bachlott, John (Camden)
Bagby, John (Gwinnett)
Bagley, Herman (Gwinnett)
Bailey, Charles (Twiggs)

Bailey, Christopher (Effingham)
Bailey, Henry (Warren)
Bailey, Stephen (Monroe)
Baker, Charles (Habersham)
Baker, Christopher, Sr. (Gwinnett)
Baker, Joshua (Franklin)
Baker, Real (Hall)
Ballard, Frederick (Effingham)
Ballard, James (Greene)
Bandy, Lewis (Morgan)
Banks, Drury (Warren)
Banks, William (Wilkes)
Bankston, Abner (Monroe)
Barker, John (Twiggs)
Barker, Joseph (Crawford)
Barkley, William (Morgan)
Barnett, Robert (Wilkinson)
Barnett, William (Greene)
Barnes, William (Jones)
Barron, Joseph (Houston)
Bates, John (Burke)
Bay, Moses (Henry)
Bazemore, Thomas (Jones)
Beard, Robert (Henry)
Beazley, Henry (Walton)
Beasley, William (DeKalb)
Beckham, Samuel (Baldwin)
Beckham, Sol (Monroe)
Bedgood, John (Washington)
Bellah, Samuel (Morgan)
Bennett, Daniel (Habersham)
Benson, Enoch (Gwinnett)
Benson, Isaac (Jackson)
Bentley, Jesse (Walton)
Benton, John (Liberty)
Benton, Joseph (Henry)
Berry, Isham (Newton)
Bethune, Peters (Richmond)
Bevins, William (Wilkinson)
Biffle, John (DeKalb)

Bird, Thomas (Habersham)
Birdsong, John (Oglethorpe)
Black, Lemuel (Oglethorpe)
Black, Thomas (Habersham)
Black, William (Effingham)
Blackburn, Nathan (Wilkes)
Blakely, William (Jones)
Blanford, Cark (Washington)
Blanks, James, Sr. (Jackson)
Bledsoe, Benjamin (Warren)
Bledsoe, Miller, Sr. (Oglethorpe)
Blount, William (Jones)
Blythe, Rogers (Habersham)
Boen, Stephen (Telfair)
Boggs, Ezekiel (Wilkes)
Boham, Joseph (Putnam)
Boile, Charles (Montgomery)
Bolles, John (Hall)
Bond, Richard C. (Franklin)
Bone, Archibald (Washington)
Booker, John (Wilkes)
Booker, William (Wilkes)
Boon, Jess (Greene)
Boring, Isaac (Jackson)
Bowen, John (Wilkinson)
Bowen, S., Sr. (Wilkes)
Bowling, Edward (Clark)
Boyd, Thomas (Burke)
Brach, Elezur, Sr. (Wilkinson)
Bradberry, Lewis (Clark)
Braddy, Lewis (Warren)
Bradley, John (Jackson)
Bragg, William (Madison)
Bramblett, Henry (Elbert)
Brand, William (Walton)
Branch, William S. (Greene)
Braswell, Britton (Jones)
Braswell, Samuel (Newton)
Braziel, Britton (Jackson)
Brewster, Hugh (DeKalb)
Bridges, Wiseman (Jasper)
Brinkley, Ely (Washington)
Britt, Edward (Henry)
Brockman, Lewis (Oglethorpe)
Brooks, James (Jasper)
Brooks, Micajah (Henry)
Brooks, Robert (Crawford)
Brooks, William, Sr. (Greene)

Brown, Ambrose (Newton)
Brown, Benjamin (Elbert)
Brown, Dempsey (Twiggs)
Brown, Edward (Elbert)
Brown, Edward (Baldwin)
Brown, Elisha (Jones)
Brown, Frederick (Columbia)
Brown, James (Clark)
Brown, John P. (Baldwin)
Brown, Larkin (Richmond)
Brown, Meridith (DeKalb)
Brown, Moses (Newton)
Brown, Samuel (Chatham)
Brown, William P. (Baldwin)
Brown, Uriah (Baldwin)
Bryan, David (Monroe)
Bryan, James (Effingham)
Bryan, John (Franklin)
Bruce, William (DeKalb)
Buchanan, George H. (Jasper)
Buchanan, James (Jasper)
Buckles, Peter (Wilkinson)
Buckner, Benjamin (Putnam)
Bullock, Hawkins (Madison)
Bullock, Richard (Bibb)
Burch, Edward (Houston)
Burgamy, William (Washington)
Burke, Joseph (Wilkes)
Burke, William (Walton)
Burket, Lemuel (Wilkinson)
Burkhalter, Jacob (Warren)
Burkhalter, Michael (Warren)
Burnley, Henry (Columbia)
Burton, John (Franklin)
Burton, Thomas (Elbert)
Bush, Levi (Pulaski)
Bush, Samuel (Burke)
Butler, John (Gwinnett)
Butril, William, Sr. (Henry)
Butt, James (Hancock)
Burwell, William, Sr. (Jackson)
Bynum, Drewry (Warren)
Byrd, John (Hall)

Cabos, John (Chatham)
Camp, Edward (Franklin)
Campbell, William, Sr. (Oglethorpe)

Cameron, James (Jasper)
Cameron, William, Sr. (Oglethorpe)
Candell, Benjamin (Habersham)
Cannon, Allen (DeKalb)
Cannon, Nathaniel (Wilkinson)
Carlisle, Benjamin (Columbia)
Carlisle, Edmund (Morgan)
Carson, Ephriam (DeKalb)
Carr, William (DeKalb)
Carrell, John (Jasper)
Carroll, Brittain (Columbia)
Carroll, Douglas (Greene)
Carroll, Owen (Laurens)
Carter, Charles (Oglethorpe)
Casey, William (Henry)
Cash, Dorson (Columbia)
Cash, Howard (Habersham)
Cash, James (Franklin)
Cash, John (Jackson)
Cason, William (Ware)
Cason, Willis (Ware)
Cason, Willoughby (Ware)
Causey, Ezekiel (Jefferson)
Chambless, Chris (Bibb)
Champion, John (Warren)
Chance, Simpson (Jefferson)
Chandler, John, Sr. (Gwinnett)
Chapman, Abner (Jasper)
Chapman, John (Warren)
Chapman, Nathan (Newton)
Chappell, John (Monroe)
Childress, Thomas (Walton)
Clanton, Holt (Columbia)
Clark, David (Elbert)
Clark, George (Jasper)
Clements, Clement (Bibb)
Cleveland, Absolem (Franklin)
Cleveland, Jeremiah (Habersham)
Cliatt, Isaac (Richmond)
Clore, George (Madison)
Cloud, Ezekiel (Henry)
Clower, Daniel (Gwinnett)
Cobb, Thomas (Columbia)
Cockburn, Ge. (Franklin)
Cockrell, Thomas, Sr. (Newton)
Cockrum, Matthew (Morgan)
Coil, James (Madison)
Colby, Samuel (DeKalb)

Coleman, Abner (Gwinnett)
Coleman, John (Jefferson)
Coleman, Samuel (Walton)
Colley, James, Sr. (Oglethorpe)
Collins, John (Hall)
Collins, Joseph (Twiggs)
Collins, Matthew, Sr. (Lincoln)
Colquitt, James (Oglethorpe)
Cone, John (Bibb)
Congo, Benj. (Gwinnett)
Connell, Daniel (Jefferson)
Connors, William (Putnam)
Cook, Archibald (Franklin)
Cook, Henry (Putnam)
Cook, George (Elbert)
Cook, James (Jefferson)
Cook, John (DeKalb)
Cook, Theodosie (Elbert)
Cook, Thomas (Elbert)
Cooper, Henry (Putnam)
Cooper, James (Madison)
Cooper, John (Wilkes)
Cooper, Richard (Tattnall)
Cooper, Samuel (Putnam)
Copeland, Benj. (Greene)
Corhon, Cornelius (Monroe)
Cornwell, Elisha, Sr. (Jasper)
Cotten, James (Jefferson)
Couch, Shadrach (Putnam)
Cowan, George (Jackson)
Cowan, James (Jackson)
Cowle, Samuel (Monroe)
Cox, John (Hall)
Cox, Moses (Washington)
Cox, Richard (Habersham)
Cox, Thomas (Gwinnett)
Crabb, Asa (Putnam)
Crabtree, William (Houston)
Crawford, Gay (Camden)
Crawford, Lemuel (Clark)
Credilla, William, Sr. (Greene)
Crelington, Jonathan (Rabun)
Crittenden, J. (Twiggs)
Crockett, David (Bibb)
Croison, John (Lincoln)
Cronan, James (Morgan)
Cross, Stephen (Bibb)
Crow, Stephen (Clark)

Crumbley, Anthony (Henry)
Crumbley, Thomas (Habersham)
Culpepper, Malakiah (Morgan)
Culver, Nathan (Hancock
Cummings, F. (Greene)
Cunningham, Andrew (Twiggs)
Curry, Peter (Wilkes)
Cutliff, Abraham (Putnam)
Cutts, Joseph (Houston)

Dabbs, John (DeKalb)
Dalton, Randolf (Gwinnett)
Damron, Charles (Jackson)
Daniel, John (Liberty)
Daniel, Jeptha (Oglethorpe)
David, Isaac (Madison)
Davidson, John (Jasper)
Davidson, Joseph (Pike)
Davis, Clement (Morgan)
Davis, Henry (Gwinnett)
Davis, Samuel (Bulloch)
Davis, Surry (Habersham)
Davis, Thomas (Oglethorpe)
Davis, Toliver (Baldwin)
Davis, William (Warren)
Davis, William (Wilkes)
Davis, Zion (Ware)
Davies, Daniel (Montgomery)
Daughtry, Jacob (Emanuel)
Daughtry, Joseph (Screven)
Dawson, Brittain (Burke)
Dean, Charles (Clark)
Deason, Zacheriah (Henry)
Delk, David (Liberty)
DeLaunay, James (Jones)
DeLoach, Hardy (Liberty)
Denham, Arthur (Fayette)
Dennis, Matthias (Hancock)
Denton, John (Hancock)
DeVeaux, Peter, Major (Chatham)
Dias, John (Tattnall)
Dickerson, Zechariah (Elbert)
Dickinson, Winborn (Hancock)
Dickson, David (Fayette)
Dickson, John (Jones)
Dicky, Patrick (Putnam)
Dillard, James (Elbert)
Dillard, John (Rabun)

Dillon, Thomas (DeKalb)
Dodd, James, Sr. (Oglethorpe)
Dolton, John (Bibb)
Dooly, Thomas (Habersham)
Dossett, Philip (Richmond)
Doster, Jonathan (Wilkes)
Douglass, Stephen (Wilkinson)
Dover, Francis J. (Habersham)
Dowdy, Richard (Chatham)
Downey, Joseph (Gwinnett)
Downs, Ambrose (Wilkes)
Downs, John (Henry)
Drake, Epaphroditus (Hancock)
Drake, James (Telfair)
Dubberly, John (Tattnall)
Dudley, James (Elbert)
Duke, Thomas (Morgan)
Duncan, Edmund (Jones)
Duncan, John, Sr. (Elbert)
Dunham, William (Richmond)
Dunn, Gatewood (Oglethorpe)
Durozeaux, Stephen (Jefferson)
Duty, Thomas (DeKalb)
Dye, Avery (Burke)
Dyess, Winneford (Ware)
Dykes, John (Effingham)
Dyson, John (Wilkes)

Eady, John (Wilkinson)
Eagan, John (Richmond)
Earnest, George (Clark)
Eastwood, John (Newton)
Eavinson, Edi (Elbert)
Edwards, John (Franklin)
Edwards, John (Henry)
Edwards, Joseph (Columbia)
Edwards, Reuben (Henry)
Edwards, William (Madison)
Eidson, Shelton (Oglethorpe)
Eidson, Thomas (Wilkes)
Ellis, Hicks (Putnam)
Elliott, James (Warren)
Elsberry, Benj. (Clark)
Etton, Abram (Washington)
Embry, Joseph (Oglethorpe)
Embry, William
England, Charles (Habersham)
English, Parmenius (Oglethorpe)

Espy, John (Clark)
Evans, Burwell (Early)
Evans, James (Hancock)
Evans, John (Jackson)
Evans, Thomas (Habersham)
Evans, William (Morgan)
Evans, William (Habersham)
Evans, William D. (Baldwin)
Everett, Abraham (Hancock)
Evers, John (Effingham)
Ezell, Hartwell (Jasper)

Faircloth, John (Screven)
Fane, Thomas (Decatur)
Faris, William (Rabun)
Farmer, James (Henry)
Farrar, Francis (Clark)
Feagan, William (Morgan)
Fears, William (Jasper)
Fiveash, Elias (Tattnall)
Finch, William (Oglethorpe)
Findley, John (Fayette)
Flanigan, Wm. (Franklin)
Fleming, Robert (Jefferson)
Fletcher, William, Sr. (Telfair)
Florence, Thomas, Sr. (Lincoln)
Fluker, John (Jasper)
Foster, Arthur (Liberty)
Foster, John (Putnam)
Foster, William (Monroe)
Fownley, Nathan, Sr. (Morgan)
Franklin, David (DeKalb)
Fraser, Simeon (Liberty)
Freeman, Daniel (Jasper)
Friday, Joseph (Montgomery)
Fulcher, James (Richmond)
Fuller, James (Baldwin)
Fuller, William, Sr. (Jackson)
Fulton, Thomas (Twiggs)
Fulwood, John (Laurens)
Funderburk, John (Monroe)

Gaiter, James (Gwinnett)
Gaines, William (Elbert)
Gainer, William (Elbert)
Gainey, Reddick (Tattnall)
Gancy, Bartholomew (Laurens)
Garland, John (Jones)

Garner, Charles (Clark)
Garrotte, Samuel (Washington)
Gates, Hezekiah (Walton)
Gay, Joshua (Emanuel)
Gay, William (Irwin)
Gibson, Henry B. (Wilkes)
Gibson, John (Warren)
Gibson, John (Wilkes)
Gibson, John S. (Butts)
Gideon, Benjamin (Bulloch)
Gilbert, William (DeKalb)
Giles, John M. (Morgan)
Gilleland, William (Fayette)
Gillis, James (Henry)
Glass, Levi (Laurens)
Glaze, Reuben (Oglethorpe)
Glenn, James (Jackson)
Glover, William (Franklin)
Golden, Andrew (Bulloch)
Goodwin, Jacob (Jefferson)
Goodwin, James (Wilkes)
Goodwin, Shadrack (Jones)
Goolsby, Richard (Jones)
Gordon, Thomas (Gwinnett)
Goulding, Palmer (Liberty)
Grady, Arthur (Houston)
Grantham, Nathan (Telfair)
Grantham, William, Sr. (Early)
Grant, Jesse (Burke)
Gray, Allen (Henry)
Greaves, William (Burke)
Greassup, James (Elbert)
Green, Burwell (Jasper)
Green, Richard (McIntosh)
Greer, James (Clark)
Greethouse, John, Sr. (Oglethorpe)
Gresham, John (DeKalb)
Griffin, James (Irwin)
Griffin, John, Sr. (Hancock)
Griffin, Joseph (Monroe)
Griffis, Charles (Ware)
Grimmer, Wm. (Jasper)
Guice, Nicholas (Lincoln)
Gunn, Richard, Sr. (Warren)
Gunter, James (Walton)
Guthrie, John (Gwinnett)
Guthrie, William (Gwinnett)
Guttery, Francis (Morgan)

Hackney, Robert (Greene)
Hadaway, David (Jackson)
Hale, James, Sr. (Clark)
Hall, Benjamin (Jasper)
Hall, Dempsey (Jefferson)
Hall, John (Gwinnett)
Hall, Ignatius (Montgomery)
Hall, Instant (Laurens)
Ham, John (Monroe)
Hamilton, Bartow (Greene)
Hamilton, John (Hall)
Hammond, Abner (Baldwin)
Hamron, Henry (Warren)
Hamrick, Benj. (Jasper)
Hampton, John (Jackson)
Hand, Joseph (Henry)
Hand, William (Baldwin)
Harrington, James (Henry)
Haralson, J. (Greene)
Harbuck, Nicholas (Warren)
Harden, Henry (Walton)
Harkness, Robert (Gwinnett)
Harley, Joseph (Columbia)
Harley, Joseph (Wilkes)
Harley, William (Elbert)
Harper, Samuel, Sr. (Crawford)
Harrell, Simon (Warren)
Harrin, Alexander (Butts)
Harrington, Elijah (Emanuel)
Harris, Benj. (DeKalb)
Harris, Graves (Morgan)
Harris, John, Sr. (Elbert)
Harris, Mathew (Greene)
Harrison, Benj. (Franklin)
Harrison, Edward (Hall)
Harrison, Elijah W. (Jones)
Harrison, Joseph (Wilkes)
Harrison, Reuben (Putnam)
Hartsfield, Richard (Oglethorpe)
Haslett, Wm. (Oglethorpe)
Hatcher, Henry (Richmond)
Hatcher, Thomas (Twiggs)
Hatcher, William (Wilkinson ?
  Washington ?)
Ha(w)thorn, Thomas (Monroe)
Hawthorn, William (Putnam)
Haynes, Moses (Elbert)
Hays, Edward (Gwinnett)

Hays, Jonathan J. (Franklin)
Haval, Hardy (Jefferson)
Head, John S. (Gwinnett)
Heard, John G. (Morgan)
Heard, William (DeKalb)
Heath, Jordan (Burke)
Heaton, James (Gwinnett)
Heeth, Roiston (Warren)
Hemphill, Jonathan (Jackson)
Hendon, Robert (Oglethorpe)
Hendrick, Jesse (Bulloch)
Hendrick, Hezekiah (Monroe)
Hendrick, Siah (Walton)
Hendrix, John (Screven)
Herndon, Joseph (Walton)
Hester, David (Burke)
Hester, Zecheriah (Jones)
Heyman, Stanton (Bryan)
Hicks, David (Pike)
Higden, Daniel (Hancock)
Higgins, Reuben (Gwinnett)
Hill, Isaac (Clark)
Hill, Mordecai (Jasper)
Hill, William (Warren)
Hine, Nathaniel (Greene)
Hines, Lewis (Jackson)
Holbrook, Jesse (Franklin)
Holcombe, James (Richmond)
Holcombe, Sherwood (Habersham)
Hodges, Sherwood (Clark)
Holder, John S. (Jefferson)
Holland, Thomas (Greene)
Holley, William (Washington)
Holman, George (Twiggs)
Holman, Jacob (Richmond)
Holmes, Jonathan (Morgan)
Holt, James (Houston)
Holt, Thomas (Washington)
Holtzclaw, John G. (Oglethorpe)
Hood, John (Wilkes)
Hook, Thomas (Putnam)
Hooper, James (DeKalb)
Hooten, Henry (Upson)
Horn, Sherwood (Bibb)
Hoskins, John, Sr. (Jones)
Howard, Abraham (Hall)
Howard, Solomon (Washington)
Howe, Elisha (Burke)

Howell, John (Houston)
Hornsley, Val (Monroe)
Houston, Samuel (Henry)
Hubbard, Burwell (Oglethorpe)
Hubbard, John (Oglethorpe)
Hubbard, Winaford (Camden)
Huckaby, William (Oglethorpe)
Hudgins, Ansel (Newton)
Hudler, John (Bulloch)
Hudson, Daniel (Elbert)
Huie, James (Jackson)
Hulsey, James (Hall)
Human, Alex (Madison)
Hunt, Daniel (Jones)
Hunt, George (Greene)
Hunt, Turman (Jasper)
Huston, John, Sr. (Jasper)
Hutchinson, James (Franklin)
Hutton, John (Laurens)

Ingram, John (Hall)
Inman, Daniel (Burke)
Ivey, Ephriam, Sr. (Warren)
Ivey, Henry, Sr. (Jasper)
Izely, Philip (Gwinnett)

Jackson, Ebenezer (Chatham)
Jackson, Edward (Gwinnett)
Jackson, Jeremiah (Greene)
Jackson, Moses (Greene)
James, Eliasha (Putnam)
James, George (Gwinnett)
Jarvis, Elisha, Sr. (Morgan)
Jenkins, Francis (Burke)
Jenkins, James (Greene)
Jester, Barnet (Elbert)
Jeter, Andrew (Bibb)
Johns, Eli (Burke)
Johns, Robert (Columbia)
Johnson, Bar (Wilkes)
Johnson, Emanuel (Richmond)
Johnson, Jacob (Burke)
Johnson, John (Oglethorpe)
Johnson, Joseph B. (Wilkes)
Johnson, Martin (Houston)
Johnson, William (Warren)
Johnson, William (Columbia)
Johnson, William (Liberty)

Johnson, William (Morgan)
Johnston, William (Bibb)
Johnston (Johnson), Willis
  (Columbia)
Jones, David (Monroe)
Jones, Harrison (Newton)
Jones, Isaac (Telfair)
Jones, John (Jones)
Jones, Josiah (Dooly)
Jones, Matthew (Liberty)
Jones, Moses (Lincoln)
Jones, Nimrod (Columbia)
Jones, Stephen (Putnam)
Jones, Thomas (Twiggs)
Jones, Thomas B. (Crawford)
Jones, Wm. Jones (Columbia)
Jordan, Aven (Jefferson)
Jordan, Dempsey (Greene)
Jordan, John (Warren)
Jordan, William (Washington)
Jott, Daniel (Greene)
Jourdain, Edmund (Oglethorpe)
Jourdain, Fountain (Elbert)
Joyner, Benjamin (Putnam)
Justice, Aaron (Houston)
Justice, Isaac (Richmond)

Kelly, Lloyd (Hancock)
Kelly, William (Hall)
Kendrick, Hezekiah (Monroe)
Kennedy, Seth (Hancock)
Kendal, William (Jasper)
Kent, Daniel (Oglethorpe)
Kent, Sampson (Oglethorpe)
Kercy, Alcy (Burke)
Key, William Bibb (Elbert)
Key, John Waller (Franklin)
Killard, James (Jones)
Kimball, David (Clark)
King, John (Franklin)
King, John (Putnam)
King, Thomas, Sr. (Putnam)
King, William (Elbert)
King, William (Ware)
Kitchens, Zacheriah (Jasper)
Kits, Henry (Gwinnett)
Knight, Aaron (DeKalb)
Knight, Thomas (Walton)

Knowlton, A. (Oglethorpe)
Kolb, Peter (Jones)

Lacy, Noah (Oglethorpe)
Ladd, Amos (Habersham)
Latta, David, Sr. (Hall)
Lamar, John (Jones)
Lamb, Isaac (Jefferson)
Lambert, Elisha (Fayette)
Lambert, George (Putnam)
Lambert, Thomas (Clark)
Landers, Tarpell (Gwinnett)
Landrum, Timothy (Jasper)
Lane, Wm., Sr. (Morgan)
Langham, James (Upson)
Larissey, William (Screven)
Lassiter, Hansell (Wilkinson)
Lawless, John (Washington)
Lawrence, John (Oglethorpe)
Leathers, Samuel (Hall)
Lee, Andrew, Sr. (Lincoln)
Lee, James (Morgan)
Lee, Jesse (Morgan)
Lee, John (Ware)
Lee, Levi (Ware)
Lee, Sampson (Washington)
Lee, Timothy (Newton)
Leigh, Benjamin (Columbia)
Leshley, Edmund (Columbia)
Lewis, Elizur (Burke)
Lewis, George (Tattnall)
Lewis, Joseph (Hancock)
Lewis, Peter (Henry)
Leverett, Richard, Sr. (Wayne)
Lindsey, Dennis (Warren)
Lindsey, James (Hall)
Lindsey, William (Wilkinson)
Linton, John (Twiggs)
Liverman, Con (Richmond)
Lloyd, James (Fayette)
Lockett, Solomon (Warren)
Loggus, James, Sr. (Hall)
Lokey, William (Madison)
Lord, William (Wilkinson)
Love, James (Walton)
Lowrey, Levi (Jackson)
Lowrey, Simeon (Bulloch)
Lumpkin, Dickson (Jackson)

Lumpkin, John (Oglethorpe)
Lumsden, Jeremiah (Jasper)

Mabry, George (Morgan)
McClain, John (Ware)
McClain, John (Rabun)
McClane, Ephriam
McClelland, McClain (Screven)
McCorkle, Archibald (Lincoln)
McCormick, John (Warren)
McCuller, Thomas (Wilkinson)
McCutcheon, Joseph (Hall)
McDerman, Joseph (Madison)
McDaniel, Jacob (Jones)
McDaniel, Jeremiah (Habersham)
McDonald, Isom (Pulaski)
McDonald, J. (Franklin)
McDonald, James (Bibb)
McDowell, Robert (Jackson)
McDuff, William (Henry)
McFarland, Robert (Franklin)
McGee, Reuben (Warren)
McGlancy, John (Warren)
McIntyre, John (Habersham)
McKee, John (Oglethorpe)
McKie, Samuel (Franklin)
Mackie, Thomas (Franklin)
McKenzie, Samuel (Monroe)
McKinney, Charles (Jackson)
McLain, Thomas (Oglethorpe)
McLendon, Samuel (Henry)
McMichael, John, Sr. (Jasper)
McMillion, Alexander (Franklin)
McNeese, James (Jackson)
McRae, Alexander (Clark)
McRee, William (Clark)
McWhorter, John (Hancock)
Maddox, Charles (Wilkes)
Maddox, John (Fayette)
Maddox, Walter (Wilkes)
Mainer, Samuel (Walton)
Male, John (Warren)
Male, Levi (Habersham)
Malone, William (Clark)
Mallory, Stephen (Wilkes)
Manning, Benjamin
Martin, David (Warren)
Martin, Jesse (Oglethorpe)

Martin, James (Laurens)
Martin, James (Irwin)
Martin, James (DeKalb)
Martin, John (Richmond)
Mash, Nathan (Warren)
Massey, Seaborn (Lincoln)
Mathis, John (Washington)
Matthews, Joel (Warren)
Matthews, John (Twiggs)
Maulden, Amos (Jones)
Maxwell, John (Elbert)
May, Elias (Columbia)
Mayberry, Stephen (Wilkes)
Meacham, Jason (Jones)
Meador, Jason (Jones)
Meadows, Jacob (Oglethorpe)
Meeks, Britton (Gwinnett)
Menefee, George, Sr. (Jackson)
Meriwether, David (Clark)
Meroney, Nathan (Madison)
Merritt, Torem (Elbert)
Middlebrook, John (Newton)
Middleton, John (Washington)
Middleton, Hugh (Houston)
Miles, John, Sr. (Greene)
Miles, Thomas (Baldwin)
Miller, George (Jones)
Miller, Richard (Hall)
Miller, William (Jackson)
Miller, William (Ware)
Miller, William (Bulloch)
Miller, William, Sr. (Jasper)
Mitchell, Henry (Jones)
Moreland, Robert (Jasper)
Monk, John (Monroe)
Monk, Silas (Putnam)
Moore, Francis (Clark)
Moore, John (Upson)
Moore, Joseph (Jasper)
Moore, William (Jackson)
Moore, William (Clark)
Morgan, James (Richmond)
Morgan, John (Morgan)
Morgan, William (Fayette)
Morris, Burrel (Monroe)
Morris, Jesse, Sr. (Columbia)
Morris, John (Baldwin)
Morris, Osten (Gwinnett)

Morris, Nathaniel (Jones)
Morrow, Ewing (Morgan)
Moseley, James (Bibb)
Moseley, Joseph (Bibb)
Moseley, Lewis (Greene)
Mote, William (Warren)
Mott, Nathan (Washington)
Murphy, Edmund (Richmond)
Mushborn, John (Gwinnett)
Myrick, John (Baldwin)

Nash, John (Columbia)
New, Jacob (DeKalb)
Newsome, John (Warren)
Niblack, William (Camden)
Niblet, Tillman (Monroe)
Nichols, James (Franklin)
Norris, Alexander (Wilkes)
Norris, James (Warren)
Norris, William (Monroe)
Norris, William (Gwinnett)
Nunnellee, James F. (Elbert)
Nunnally, Israel (Greene)

Odum, Archibald (Pulaski)
Oglesby, Thomas (Elbert)
Oglitree, William (Monroe)
O'Kelly, Francis (Oglethorpe)
Oliver, James (Pulaski)
Oliver, Peter (Elbert)
Oman, John (Butts)
O'Neal, Ross (Warren)
Osborne, Reps (Henry)
Owens, John (Camden)

Pace, Barnabas (Elbert)
Pace, Thomas, Sr. (Oglethorpe)
Paine, John (Greene)
Palmore, Elijah, Sr. (Greene)
Parker, Aaron (Henry)
Parker, Daniel (Morgan)
Parker, Richard (Hancock)
Parker, Samuel (Morgan)
Parkerson, Levi (Wilkes)
Parr, Benjamin (Clark)
Parris, William (Rabun)
Paschall, George (Oglethorpe)
Paul, Robert, Sr. (Jones)

Paulett, Richard (Clarke)
Paulos, Robert (Greene)
Peace, John (Monroe)
Peacock, Archibald (Washington)
Peacock, Isham (Tattnall)
Peacock, Uriah (Washington)
Pearce, John (Camden)
Peavy, John (Gwinnett)
Peddy, Jeremiah (Monroe)
Penn, William (Jasper)
Penny, Ed (Twiggs)
Perkins, John (Bibb)
Perryman, Herman (Twiggs)
Persons, Jones (Upson)
Peters, Edmund (Walton)
Peters, Moses (Bibb)
Peters, William (Twiggs)
Pettis, Moses (Bibb)
Pharoah, Joseph (Richmond)
Phelps, Thomas (Jasper)
Philips, Daniel (Early)
Philips, Isham (Jones)
Philips, Thomas (Jackson)
Phinazee, John (Monroe)
Pickard, J. H. (Monroe)
Pierce, Hugh (Habersham)
Pierce, Seth (Jefferson)
Pinson, Joseph (Rabun)
Pittman, John (Gwinnett)
Pitts, John (Telfair)
Pledger, Thomas (Elbert)
Poe, Stephen (Habersham)
Polk, John (Wilkinson)
Pollard, John (Jones)
Pool, Henry (Warren)
Pool, Samuel (Monroe)
Pool, Walter (Newton)
Porter, John (Jasper)
Porter, William, Sr. (Jasper)
Porter, William G. (Effingham)
Portwood, B., Sr. (Jasper)
Posey, Bennett (Jasper)
Pose, Henry, Sr. (Walton)
Potter, Augustin L. (Jasper)
Potts, James (Jasper)
Powell, Benjamin (Bulloch)
Powell, Francis (Wilkes)
Powell, Lewis (Columbia)

Powell, Seymour (Newton)
Powledge, George (Effingham)
Presslar, Peter, Sr. (Hall)
Pressley, John (Henry)
Price, Lucius (Crawford)
Prigden, David (Bullock)
Prince, Noah (Clark)
Proctor, Stephen (Monroe)
Prosser, Otey (Washington)
Pryor, John (Jasper)
Pugh, Shadrack (Upson)
Pullen, John (Hancock)
Pulliam, William (Franklin)
Pullin, Thomas, Sr. (Laurens)
Purvis, Needham (Jefferson)
Pye, James (Oglethorpe)

Ragan, Bruce, Sr. (Wilkinson)
Ragen, Buckner (Hall)
Bailey, Charles (Twiggs)
Bailey, Henry (Warren)
Rainey, Isham, Sr. (Oglethorpe)
Ramsdell, David (Burke)
Randolph, Robert (Columbia)
Ransome, Reuben (Clark)
Rawls, Isaac (Jackson)
Rawls, William (Wayne)
Ray, Andrew (Oglethorpe)
Ray, Benjamin (Twiggs)
Ray, John (Wilkes)
Ray, Mark (Monroe)
Ray, Philip (Oglethorpe)
Red, Job (Gwinnett)
Rees, Hugh (Columbia)
Respess, Richard (Upson)
Reeves, John (Columbia)
Reynolds, Benjamin (Jones)
Reynolds, Daniel (Jones)
Reynolds, Thomas (Monroe)
Rhodes, Richard (Oglethorpe)
Rice, Leonard (Elbert)
Rich, John (Hall)
Richardson, John (Oglethorpe)
Rickerson, Benj. (Warren)
Riley, James (Greene)
Roberson, James (Newton)
Robert, Astin (Greene)
Roberts, Aaron (Franklin)

Roberts, Reuben (Jones)
Roberts, Rollin (Screven)
Robinson, Freyer (Clark)
Robinson, James (Newton)
Robinson, John (Irwin)
Roe, John (Hancock)
Rogers, Brittain (Monroe)
Rogers, John (Gwinnett)
Rogers, Robert (Rabun)
Rogers, William, Sr. (Tattnall)
Rooks, John (Wayne)
Ross, George (Jones)
Ross, Jesse (Jones)
Rowe, Joshua (Newton)
Rowe, Shadrack (Putnam)
Royalston, John (Bulloch)
Rucker, William (Elbert)
Rusheon, Specey (Ware)
Russell, George (Madison)
Rutherford, Claiborn (Newton)
Rutherford, James (Irwin)
Rutledge, John (Gwinnett)

Sailors, Christopher (Jackson)
Sandiford, Elim (Wilkes)
Samples, Nathaniel (Jefferson)
Sanford, Jeremiah (Greene)
Sanders, James (Madison)
Sanders, John (Franklin)
Sanders, Thomas (Upson)
Sapp, Shadrack (Tattnall)
Savage, Thomas (Hall)
Sawyer, John Jones (Hancock)
Scott, John (Bibb)
Scott, William (Putnam)
Scroggins, George (Jones)
Scroggins, Thomas (Pike)
Selman, John (Franklin)
Seals, Wm. (Hancock)
Searcy, George (Baldwin)
Sewell, Chris (Franklin)
Sewell, Wm. (Franklin)
Sharp, John (Tattnall)
Sharp, Joshua (Ware)
Shaw, John (Hall)
Sheffield, West (Pulaski)
Sheffield, West (Wayne)
Sheftall, Sheftall (Chatham)

Shelman, John, Col. (Chatham)
Sherley, Edward (Crawford)
Shurling, Ison (Putnam)
Sims, Jeminy
Sims, Robert (Clark)
Simmons, John, Sr. (Pike)
Simmons, Thomas (Ware)
Simmons, William (Jones)
Slack, John, Sr. (Wilkes)
Slocumb, John C. (Jones)
Smalley, Michael (Columbia)
Smether, Gabriel (Elbert)
Smith, Abner (Jasper)
Smith, Ezekiel (Laurens)
Smith, Ezekiel (Richmond)
Smith, Hardy (Laurens)
Smith, Henry (Franklin)
Smith, Henry (Monroe)
Smith, George (Richmond)
Smith, Job (Washington)
Smith, John (Pulaski)
Smith, John (Clark)
Smith, John (Wilkes)
Smith, John (Jones)
Smith, Lawrence (Morgan)
Smith, Leonard (Columbia)
Smith, Mathew (Columbia)
Smith, Nathan (Emanuel)
Smith, Reuben (Greene)
Smith, Robert (Oglethorpe)
Smith, William (Newton)
Smith, William (Jackson)
Smith, William (Gwinnett)
Smith, William (Twiggs)
Smokes, William C. (Jefferson)
Snead, Philip (Jones)
Solomon, Lazarus (Twiggs)
Sowell, Zadoc (Wilkes)
Sparks, Jeremiah (Morgan)
Spearman, John, Sr. (Jasper)
Spinks, Pressly (Warren)
Spurlock, Wm. (Baldwin)
Stanford, Joshua, Sr. (Warren)
Stanton, John (Newton)
Staples, Thomas (Jackson)
Starling, Wm. (Tattnall)
Statham, Wm. (Wilkinson)
Steel, Henry (Jasper)

Stephens, Barnett (Madison)
Stephens, Burrell (Jefferson)
Stephens, James (Burke)
Stephens, John W. (Burke)
Stephens, Joseph (Monroe)
Stephens, Reuben (DeKalb)
Stephens, Richard (Twiggs)
Stewart, Charles (Monroe)
Stewart, James (Forsyth)
Stewart, William (Jones)
Stone, Henry (Ware)
Stoneycipher, John (Franklin)
Stovall, George (Franklin)
Stovall, William (Monroe)
Stowers, Lewis (Elbert)
Strange, John (Franklin)
Strickland, John (Richmond)
Strickland, Joseph (DeKalb)
Strong, Charles, Sr. (Oglethorpe)
Strong, William (Jones)
Stroud, Philip (Jasper)
Sturdivant, Abner (Warren)
Sturdivant, John (Hancock)
Sumner, Joseph, Sr. (Emanuel)
Sutley, James (Franklin)
Sutton, David (Ware)
Sweatman, John J., Sr. (Monroe)
Swan, William (Newton)

Tabor, Zekekiah (Oglethorpe)
Tallant, John (Hall)
Tapley, Adam (Baldwin)
Tarbutton, Joseph (Hall)
Tarver, Absolem (Hancock)
Tate, John, Jr. (Franklin)
Taylor, Clark (Oglethorpe)
Taylor, Dempsey (Irwin)
Taylor, Edward (Monroe)
Taylor, James (Jones)
Taylor, John (Tattnall)
Taylor, Richard (Morgan)
Taylor, Theophilus (Habersham)
Taylor, William (Henry)
Teal, Emanuel (Jasper)
Teal, Ludowick (Jasper)
Teasley, Silas (Elbert)
Tellers, James (Oglethorpe)
Terrell, James (Franklin)

Tidd, David (Jones)
Tilley, William (Monroe)
Tindall, James, Sr. (Burke)
Themby, Thomas (Houston)
Thigpen, Nathan (Warren)
Thomas, Benjamin (Washington)
Thomas, Carl (Tattnall)
Thomas, Ethelred (Laurens)
Thomas, James (Oglethorpe)
Thomas, James (Baldwin)
Thomas, Massa (Putnam)
Thomas, Richard (Monroe)
Thomas, William (Franklin)
Thompson, Andrew (Oglethorpe)
Thompson, James, Sr. (Madison)
Thompson, Moses (Warren)
Thompson, Samuel (Newton)
Thompson, William (Jackson)
Thrasher, George (Habersham)
Tomlinson, Aaron (Washington)
Tomlinson, Nathaniel (Putnam)
Tompson, William (Ware)
Toole, James (Richmond)
Towns, John (Monroe)
Townsend, Thomas (Habersham)
Trimble, John (DeKalb)
Trimble, Moses (Newton)
Triplett, William (Wilkes)
Tripler, William (Tattnall)
Trout, George (Hall)
Truitt, Purual (Wilkes)
Tucker, Henry C. (Montgomery)
Tucker, Robert (Columbia)
Turner, Abrahal (Bulloch)
Turner, Henry (Burke)
Turner, John (Madison)
Turner, Reuben (Wayne)
Turner, Robert (Habersham)

Umphlet, Asa (Warren)
Usurey, John (Wilkinson)

Vanbrackel, John (Bryan)
Varner, George (Oglethorpe)
Vassar, Micajah (Laurens)
Vaughan, Jesse (Wilkinson)
Veal, William (Putnam)
Veasey, Zebulon (Hancock)

Vickery, Hezekiah (Screven)
Vickery, Joseph (Elbert)
Vincent, Isaac (Clark)
Vinson, Elijah (Henry)
Voicle, Lewis (Hancock)

Wade, John W. (Hall)
Wade, John W. (Columbia)
Waggoner, William (Wilkes)
Wagnon, Daniel (Greene)
Wainslow, John (Elbert)
Waldrop, James (Fayette)
Walker, Elijah (Warren)
Walker, James (Irwin)
Walker, Samuel (Jackson)
Walker, Samuel (Jasper)
Walker, Thomas (Gwinnett)
Wall, Henry (Twiggs)
Wall, John, Sr. (Jackson)
Wall, Myall (Greene)
Wallace, John (Putnam)
Wallace, William (Newton)
Waller, Elijah (Warren)
Walls, Charles (Gwinnett)
Walls, Samuel (Franklin)
Walters, Peter (Franklin)
Ward, Nathaniel (Warren)
Ward, Samuel (Oglethorpe)
Watkins, Benjamin (DeKalb)
Watkins, James C. (Hall)
Watkins, William (Washington)
Watson, Ezekiel (Washington)
Watson, John, Sr. (Monroe)
Watson, Joshua (Jefferson)
Webb, John (Jasper)
Weeks, Theophilus (Camden)
Welborn (Wilborn), Elias (Columbia)
Welch, Nicholas (Habersham)
Welsher, Jeremiah (Jefferson)
West, Benjamin (Hall)
West, Willis (Fayette)
Wetherton, Thomas (Walton)
Whateley, Michael (Bibb)
Wharton, Benjamin (Hall)
Wheeler, Amos (Pulaski)
Wheeler, Thomas, Sr. (Elbert)
White, John M. (Fayette)

White, Vincent (Hall)
Whitfield, Lewis (Burke)
Whitington, B. G. (Liberty)
Whitten, Philip (Habersham)
Wiggins, Richard (Warren)
Wilbanks, Gillam (Franklin)
Wilder, Willis (Jones)
Wilder, William (Jones)
Wiley, John (Washington)
Wilhight, Lewis (Elbert)
Williby, William (Clark)
Williams, Abraham (Jackson)
Williams, Benj. Z. (Gwinnett)
Williams, Joseph (Warren)
Williams, Lewis (Franklin)
Williamson, John (Henry)
Williamson, Zach, Sr. (Bibb)
Willingham, Jesse (Madison)
Willis, George (Wilkes)
Willis, John (Walker)
Wilson, James (Franklin)
Wilson, John (Columbia)
Wilson, John (Warren)
Wimberly, John (Jones)
Wilmoth, William (Franklin)
Winburn, Josiah (Pulaski)
Winslett, Samuel (Greene)
Woodall, John, Sr. (DeKalb)
Woodall, Joseph (Oglethorpe)
Woodcock, William (Bulloch)
Wofford, Absolem (Jackson)
Wolf, Andrew (Wilkes)
Womack, A. (Monroe)
Womack, William (Effingham)
Wood, Abraham (Pulaski)
Wood, Ellet (Newton)
Wood, James (Columbia)
Wood, John (Wilkes)
Wood, Thomas (Clark)
Wooten, Thomas (DeKalb)
Wright, Elisha (Jones)
Wright, Reuben (Early)
Wright, William (Clark)
Wright, William (Crawford)
Wyatt, John (Henry)
Wylie, William (Hancock)
Wynne, Clement (Warren)

Yancey, Lewis D. (Jasper)
Yarborough, Benjamin (Laurens)
Yarborough, L. (Morgan)
York, John (Lincoln)

Young, James (Clark)
Young, James (Oglethorpe)
Young, John (Tattnall)
Yates, William (Montgomery)

LOTTERY OF 1827

Names of the Widows of Revolutionary Soldiers who drew land in Ga., and the Counties of Georgia in which they lived. Name of the counties are in parentheses following the name.

Achison, Winnefred (Warren)
Adams, Abigail (Putnam)
Adams, Mary (Jasper)
Adams, Nancy (Jasper)
Akins, Jane (DeKalb)
Aldredge, Elizabeth (Appling)
Alexander, Mary (Elbert)
Alford, Rebecca (Greene)
Allen, Catherine (Jefferson)
Allen, Chloe (Putnam)
Allen, Elizabeth C. (Columbia)
Allison, Chris (Oglethorpe)
Alred, Margaret (Clark)
Also, Elizabeth (Houston)
Amos, Learry (Hancock)
Anders, Mary (Wilkes)
Anderson, Ann (Greene)
Anderson, Mary (Wilkes)
Arendell, Susanna (Franklin)
Armstrong, Mary (Warren)
Armstrong, Sarah (Pulaski)
Arnold, Bethany (Walton)
Atkinson, Martha (Greene)

Babb, Elizabeth (Baldwin)
Baker, Ann (Walton)
Baker, Sarah (Gwinnett)
Barfield, Winny (Morgan)
Bargeson, Elizabeth (Burke)
Barker, Mary (Wilkinson)
Barksdale, F. (Lincoln)
Barnes, Mae (Monroe)
Barrett, Sarah (Fayette)
Baxter, Elizabeth (Madison)
Beall, Rutha (Pulaski)

Beard, Eve (Oglethorpe)
Beavers, Elizabeth (Morgan)
Beck, Sarah (Elbert)
Bell, P. (widow T. Bell) (Burke)
Bell, Sarah (Jackson)
Bellamy, Mary (Franklin)
Bellinger, Mary (Chatham)
Benson, Elizabeth (Wilkinson)
Bentley, Abi (Wilkes)
Benton, Mary (Jones)
Bevers, Jane (Jackson)
Blackwood, Jane (Jasper)
Blair, Nancy (Washington)
Blanchard, Sarah (Columbia)
Blanks, Nancy (Greene)
Bledsoe, Margaret (Morgan)
Blitch, Ann (Effingham)
Blount, Lucy (Jones)
Boatright, Margaret (Emanuel)
Bogan, Elizabeth (Richmond)
Bolton, Chris W. (Wilkes)
Boswell, Sarah (Franklin)
Bradford, Mary (Jackson)
Bragg, Mary (Oglethorpe)
Branham, Elizabeth C. (Putnam)
Brewer, Mary (Pike)
Bridges, Rebecca (Washington)
Bridges, Susanna (Morgan)
Bridges, Susanna (Greene)
Brinson, Mary (Burke)
Brinson, Unity (Pulaski)
Brooks, Mary (Warren)
Brooks, Sarah (Madison)
Brown, Ann (Wilkinson)
Brown, Sarah (Monroe)

Browning, Margaret (Clark)
Brownson, Elizabeth (Screven)
Bryan, Dorcas (Monroe)
Bryan, Mary (Pulaski)
Bryan, Nancy (Gwinnett)
Bryan, Sue (Twiggs)
Bruce, Elizabeth (Wilkes)
Bull, Elizabeth (Pike)
Burden, Hannah (Elbert)
Burney, Elizabeth (Washington)
Burnside, Ann (Columbia)
Burson, Nancy (Warren)
Burton, Rachel (Hall)
Burton, Rhoda (Twiggs)
Busbin, Sarah (Oglethorpe)
Bynum, Silvey (Pulaski)

Calef, Letisha (Jones)
Carden, Milly (Pulaski)
Cargyle, Jane (Columbia)
Carrington, W. (Madison)
Carter, Elizabeth (Wilkes)
Cary, Elizabeth (Warren)
Cates, Hannah (Newton)
Chambless, S. (Jones)
Chance, Mary (Burke)
Chapman, Lydia (Monroe)
Cheatham, Sarah (Franklin)
Christian, Sally (Pulaski)
Christopher, Elizabeth (Greene)
Clark, Lucy (Morgan)
Clark, Rebecca (Elbert)
Clark, S. B. (Baldwin)
Clark, Sarah (Elbert)
Clements, Anna (Putnam)
Clements, Frances (Hall)
Clemmons, Jeninay (Jones)
Cobb, Catherine (Hancock)
Coffee, Nancy (Rabun)
Cofield, S. (Twiggs)
Collins, Bridget (DeKalb)
Collins, Diana (Burke)
Collins, Sarah (Burke)
Comer, Ann (Jones)
Connor, Sarah (Tattnall)
Cook, Elizabeth (Jackson)
Cook, Susannah (Appling)
Cooper, Hollandberry (Oglethorpe)

Cowan, M. (Jefferson)
Cowles, Judith (Monroe)
Crain, Juda (Rabin)
Crawford, Vic (Franklin)
Crosby, Elizabeth (Columbia)
Cruse, Sarah Ann (Chatham)
Culbreath, Jane (Jones)
Cureton, Martha (Hancock)

Dabney, Hannah (Jasper)
Dannielly, Elizabeth (Jasper)
Davenport, Dicy (Clark)
Davis, Elizabeth (Walton)
Davis, Fanny (Oglethorpe)
Davis, Jane (Greene)
Davis, Mary (DeKalb)
Davis, Sarah (Greene)
Dawson, Mary (Twiggs)
Dean, Mourning (Gwinnett)
Defual, Mary (Pulaski)
DeLoach, Elizabeth (Tattnall)
Dennis, Cath. (Warren)
Dickey, Sarah (Putnam)
Dingler, Nancy (Jasper)
Dismukes, Elizabeth (Richmond)
Dixon, Martha (Putnam)
Dodd, Catherine (Franklin)
Dooly, Elizabeth (Habersham)
Douglass, M. A. (Jones)
Duckworth, Christian (Jones)
Duke, Ann (Jones)
Dukes, Sarah (Henry)
Dunn, Winnefred (Columbia)
Dupree, Martha (Twiggs)
Durham, Isabel (Clark)

Eccols, Zippy (Washington)
Ector, Elinor (Monroe)
Eldridge, Jane (Twiggs)
Ellis, Percilla (Crawford)
Evans, Elizabeth (Morgan)
Evans, Elizabeth (Wilkes)
Evans, Lucy (Hancock)

Farley, Delina (Jones)
Featherstone, Jane (Jasper)
Fitzpatrick, Elizabeth (Twiggs)
Fitzpatrick, S. (Morgan)

Fleming, Sarah (Jefferson)
Flemister, E. G. (Jasper)
Flowers, F. Elizabeth (Warren)
Floyd, Sarah (Madison)
Flud, Jane (Greene)
Flynn, Elizabeth (Columbia)
Fogel, Mary (Morgan)
Fountain, L. (Jefferson)
Fountain, Sarah (Jefferson)
Freeman, Mildred (Jasper)

Gadden, Mary (Franklin)
Gailey, Mary (Madison)
Gainer, Elizabeth (Morgan)
Gainer, Phebe (Wilkinson)
Gant, Mary (Bulloch)
Garnett, Elizabeth (Columbia)
Garrard, Elizabeth (Wilkinson)
Garvin, Rebecca (Jefferson)
Giles, Elizabeth (Walton)
Gilmore, Elizabeth (Tattnall)
Girtman, Catherine (Jefferson)
Glover, Drucilla (Jefferson)
Godbee, Mary (Burke)
Goodwin, Elizabeth (Henry)
Goolsby, Caty (Jasper)
Gordon, Mary (Gwinnett)
Grace, Hez (Tattnall)
Gray, Rebecca (Jasper)
Green, Charity (Warren)
Green, Mary (Henry)
Green, Mary (Jackson)
Griffin, Comfort (Richmond)

Hagan, Frances (Appling)
Hale, Drucilla (Burke)
Hall, Ann (Jefferson)
Hall, L. M. (Washington)
Hall, Nancy (Tattnall)
Ham, Betsey (Elbert)
Hambleton, Mary (Monroe)
Hamesburger, Mary (Liberty)
Hamilton, Abigail (Gwinnett)
Hammond, Susanna (Greene)
Hand, Rachel (Henry)
Hand, Sarah (Baldwin)
Haney, Jemina (Oglethorpe)
Hanson, Peggy (Morgan)

Harbuck, Mary (Warren)
Hardagree, Eleanor (Clark)
Hardeman, Zilla (Oglethorpe)
Hardwick, Judith (Jasper)
Hardy, Winnie (Putnam)
Harper, Ann (Morgan)
Harrington, Cath. (DeKalb)
Harris, Catherine (Washington)
Harris, Charity (DeKalb)
Harris, Mary (Rabun)
Harris, Rebecca (Elbert)
Harrison, Charity (Laurens)
Harrison, Elizabeth (Columbia)
Harrison, Mary (Oglethorpe)
Hartley, Fere (Washington)
Harvey, Betsey J. (Burke)
Hasty, Jemina (Jones)
Hatcher, Sarah (Burke)
Haynes, Martha (Monroe)
Haynes, Sarah (Oglethorpe)
Haynie, Elizabeth (Richmond)
Hays, Jane (Greene)
Hays, Nancy (Jasper)
Head, Margaret (Morgan)
Heath, Louisa (Burke)
Heeth, Winnefred (Warren)
Heflin, Sarah (Warren)
Hemphill, Elizabeth (Morgan)
Henderson, Mary (Jasper)
Henderson, Mary (Jones)
Henderson, Sally (Hancock)
Hendrick, Mary (Jones)
Henley, Sarah (Gwinnett)
Herren, Dulcy (Appling)
Herrin, Mary Ann (Habersham)
Herring, Hollin (Morgan)
Hicks, Susanna (Clark)
Hill, Catherine (Jasper)
Hill, Frances (Warren)
Hill, Percilla (Habersham)
Hill, Sarah (Jasper)
Hines, Elizabeth (Laurens)
Hines, Martha (Chatham)
Hinson, Sarah (Jackson)
Hirresly, Elizabeth (Jones)
Hogans, Nancy (Baldwin)
Holbrook, Priscilla (Gwinnett)
Holland, Elizabeth (Jasper)

Hollis, Elizabeth (Jasper)
Holsey, Susanna (Hancock)
Hood, Rebecca (Wilkes)
Horn, Sarah (Greene)
Hoskins, Maryan (Crawford)
Howard, Edith (Baldwin)
Howard, Elizabeth (Baldwin)
Howard, Jane (Columbia)
Howard, Lucretia (Clark)
Howard, Sarah (Jackson)
Howard, Sarah (Wilkinson)
Howell, Franky (Fayette)
Howell, Mary (Houston)
Hughes, Jane (Burke)
Hughes, Sarah (Newton)
Huling, Elizabeth (Wilkes)
Hunter, Elizabeth (Crawford)
Hunter, Martha (Jackson)

Irving, Mary (Greene)
Irwin, Nancy (Bibb)
Irwin, Nancy (DeKalb)

Jackson, Mary (Monroe)
James, Elizabeth (Pike)
Jameson, Mary (Twiggs)
Jarman, Ruth (Greene)
Johnson, Dorcas (Morgan)
Johnson, Elizabeth (Hancock)
Johnson, Mary (Elbert)
Johnson, Molly O. (Jasper)
Johnson, Patty (Pulaski)
Johnson, Rebecca (Morgan)
Johnson, Sivel (Warren)
Jones, Elizabeth (Jones)
Jones, Elizabeth (Rabun)
Jones, Elizabeth H. (Oglethorpe)
Jones, Fanny (Elbert)
Jones, Jane (Gwinnett)
Jones, Jemina (Burke)
Jones, Margaret (Jefferson)
Jones, Nancy (Houston)
Jordan, Milly (Oglethorpe)
Joy, Elizabeth (Jackson)

Kelly, Elizabeth (DeKalb)
Killabrew, Elizabeth (Washington)
King, Elizabeth (Warren)

King, Mary (Jasper)
King, Mary (Monroe)
Kitchens, Sarah (Monroe)

Lantern, Elizabeth (Columbia)
Lavare, Mary (Monroe)
Lawrence, Let. (Oglethorpe)
Lawson, Jane (Wilkinson)
Ligon, Tabitha (Morgan)
Liles, Bathesba (Columbia)
Lindsey, Mary (Wilkes)
Lipham, Elizabeth (Monroe)
Lipham, Nancy (Henry)
Little, Fanny (Screven)
Lockhart, Polly (Wilkes)
Lord, Martha (Tattnall)
Lord, Milly (Wilkinson)
Lurisford, Elizabeth (Putnam)
Lyle, Elizabeth (Jackson)
Lyon, Jemina (Oglethorpe)

McAhaney, Ann (Jasper)
McCants, Darah (Crawford)
McCarty, Mary (Warren)
McCommon, Sue (Clark)
McConnell, Agnes (Gwinnett)
McDonald, Esther (Pike)
McFarling, C. M. (Jones)
McKenzie, N. (Twiggs)
McLelland, Elizabeth (Gwinnett)
McLeod, Muriel (Pulaski)
McLeroy, Christina (Jones)
McLeroy, Sarah (Oglethorpe)
Maclin, Jane (Wilkes)
McNeely, Elinor (Jefferson)
McNeil, James (De Kalb)
McRae, Cath (Telfair)
McWalters, Margaret (Henry)
Malone, Nancy (Clark)
Martin, Edy (Washington)
Massa, Nancy (Walton)
Mathews, Dicey (Wilkinson)
Mathews, Elizabeth (Jefferson)
Mathews, Nancy (Walton)
Mathews, Sarah (Washington)
Mathis, Jane (Jasper)
Maxwell, Hanney (Washington)
Mayo, Susan (Pulaski)

Mayo, Temper (Washington)
Megahee, Susan (Columbia)
Metcalf, Martha (Burke)
Miller, Martha (Warren)
Miller, Sally (Newton)
Mills, Elizabeth (Burke)
Mills, Sarah (Jones)
Mims, Elizabeth (Upson)
Minchen, Martha (DeKalb)
Modiset, Isobel (Monroe)
Montfort, Elizabeth (Laurens)
Montgomery, Mae (Wilkinson)
Moore, Lucy (Walker)
Moore, Nancy (Greene)
Moore, Synthia (Laurens)
Mophit, Mary Ann (Lincoln)
Morgan, Charlotte (Hancock)
Morgan, Elizabeth (Jasper)
Morgan, Mary (Jackson)
Morris, Elizabeth (Gwinnett)
Morris, Hannah (Clark)
Morris, Lucy (Warren)
Morrow, Elizabeth (Franklin)
Moseley, Sarah (Walton)
Munden, Levina (Hancock)
Murphy, Cherry (Jones)
Murray, Elizabeth (Warren)
Murray, Nancy (Elbert)

Nalah, Frances (Elbert)
Nation, Catherine (Gwinnett)
Nelson, Ann (Morgan)
Newsom, Elizabeth (Warren)
Newsom, Lucy (Wilkinson)
Newton, Ann (Screven)
Newton, Catherine (Clark)
Nicholson, Elizabeth (Screven)
Norris, Jemina (Hall)
Nunnally, Mary (Wilkes)
Nunnelee, Elizabeth (Habersham)

O'Kelly, Elizabeth (Habersham)
O'Kelly, Elizabeth (Oglethorpe)
Orrick, Celia (Putnam)
Owens, Barsheba
Owens, Nancy (Burke)
Oxford, Susanna (Jones)

Pace, Meldridge (Wilkinson)
Page, Mary (Warren)
Palmer, Elizabeth (Jackson)
Parham, Asa (Monroe)
Parris, Elizabeth (Warren)
Parrish, Rhoda (Greene)
Payne, Mary (Henry)
Pearce, Lucy (Franklin)
Pearson, Winnefred (Pike)
Penn, Frances (Oglethorpe)
Penn, Martha (Elbert)
Petit, Betsey (Columbia)
Philips, Ruth (Warren)
Philips, Sarah (Pike)
Philips, Sarah (Putnam)
Powell, Ann (Liberty)
Powell, Rachel (Columbia)
Prescott, Fanny (Newton)
Priddy, Judith (Newton)
Pryor, Mary (Jefferson)
Psalmonde, S. (Wilkes)
Purdue, Sarah (Putnam)

Radford, Elizabeth (Walton)
Radford, Patsey (Richmond)
Rahn, Hannah Elizabeth (Effing -
    ham)
Raiford, Patience (Baldwin)
Railey, Ruth (Warren)
Rainer, Sarah (Jones)
Ramsey, Rachel (Franklin)
Reaves, Sarah (Jasper)
Reese, Elizabeth (Columbia)
Reeves, Hanney (Wilkes)
Reynolds, Sarah (Warren)
Reynolds, Susanna (Hancock)
Richards, Lyddy (Greene)
Rickerson, Prucy (Henry)
Right, Alsy (Jackson)
Rivers, Mary Ann (Warren)
Roberts, Tabitha (Camden)
Robertson, Silva (Newton)
Robinson, Jane (Newton)
Rogers, Luraney (Bulloch)
Ross, Sarah (Columbia)
Rouse, Mary (Twiggs)
Rowland, Elizabeth (Oglethorp

Royal, Sarah (Burke)
Rundle, Susanna (Hancock)
Russell, Elizabeth (Monroe)
Rye, Mary (Wilkinson)

Safford, Sarah (Wilkes)
Sanders, Mary (Rabun)
Sapp, Zilpha (Burke)
Saxon, Elizabeth M. (Elbert)
Scarborough, Sarah (Burke)
Seals, Elizabeth (Elbert)
Sharp, Patty (Lincoln)
Shaw, Margaret (Morgan)
Sheerer, Ann (Wilkes)
Shell, Elizabeth (Newton)
Shofner, Elizabeth (Wilkinson)
Simmons, Nancy (Burke)
Simpson, Euphamy (Houston)
Sims, Amis (Franklin)
Sinclair, Mary (Upson)
Sisson, Hannah (Greene)
Skinner, Sarah (Burke)
Smith, Afamy (Liberty)
Smith, Ann (Jackson)
Smith, Elizabeth (Jones)
Smith, Elizabeth (Greene)
Smith, Margaret (Gwinnett)
Smith, Mary (Columbia)
Smith, Mary P. (Clark)
Smith, Rebecca (Walton)
Smith, Sarah (Habersham)
Smith, Sarah (Baldwin)
Smith, Sarah (Jasper)
Smithwick, Elizabeth (Walton)
Sorrels, Mildred (Madison)
Sorrow, Mary (Morgan)
Sosebee, Elizabeth (Franklin)
Spann, Lamey (Jefferson)
Spell, Mary (Laurens)
Spratlin, Winnefred (Monroe)
Stanford, Elizabeth (Washington)
Starr, Mary (Morgan)
Stephens, Caley (Twiggs)
Stephens, Desire (Bulloch)
Stephens, Mary (Bibb)
Stephens, Sarah (Habersham)
Steward, Judith (Jasper)
Stewart, Elizabeth (Greene)

Stinson, Phebe (Wilkes)
Stokes, Sarah (Wilkinson)
Street, Mary (Jackson)
Stringfellow, Amy (Greene)
Summerell, Sarah (Bibb)
Sutton, Sarah (Putnam)
Swan, Nelly (Screven)
Switley, Sarah (Liberty)

Teaver, Rebecca (Madison)
Terry, Priscilla (Morgan)
Tharp, Ruth (Twiggs)
Thomas, E. C. (Clark)
Thomas, Hannah (Gwinnett)
Thomas, Nancy (Twiggs)
Thomas, Polly (Clark)
Thompson, Sarah (Clark)
Thompson, Sarah (Jefferson)
Timmons, Elizabeth (Appling)
Tomlinson, Joanna (Hancock)
Tredeway, Mary (Monroe)
Tumlin, Mary (Gwinnett)
Twiggs, Ruth (Richmond)

Veal, Elizabeth (Putnam)
Veasy, Martha (Greene)
Volloton, Rachel (Burke)

Waldraven, Elizabeth (Gwinnett)
Walker, Rebecca (Jones)
Wall, Ann (Twiggs)
Ward, Charity (Madison)
Ware, Jane (Jackson)
Warren, Unity (Morgan)
Watson, Mae (Richmond)
Webb, Margaret (Elbert)
Whatley, Elizabeth (Newton)
Whatley, Fannie (Jones)
Wheeler, Mourning (Jackson)
White, Barsheba (Jasper)
Whitlock, Elizabeth (Hall)
Wiggins, Almey (Ware)
Wilkerson, Ester (Wilkerson)
Willeford, Lucy (Oglethorpe)
Williams, Dilly (Bulloch)
Williams, Martha (Chatham)
Williams, R. (Fayette)
Williamson, Letysha (Gwinnett)

Williamson, Margaret (Laurens)
Williamson, Sarah (Jasper)
Willis, Sarah (Jones)
Wilson, Ann (Pulaski)
Wilson, Margaret (Hall)
Winburn, Sarah Ann (Gwinnett)
Winn, Ann (Liberty)
Wood, Nancy (Greene)

Woodly, Milly (Hall)
Wooten, H. (Elbert)
Worsham, Nancy C. (Baldwin)
Wyhand, Rosanna (Morgan)
Wyndham (Windham) Permely
  (Laurens)

Yarborough, Margaret (Laurens)
Young, Susan (Laurens)

CHEROKEE LETTERS–LIST

Cherokee Letters–List of Widows of Revolutionary Soldiers who drew in the Land Lottery in Elbert County, October 30, 1835.

Alexander, Mary
Allston, Gilly
Beck, Sarah
Bell, Elizabeth
Blackwell, Sally Chandler
Bryan, Sarah
Bullard, Ann
Burden, Hannah
Clark, Elizabeth
Clark, Rebecca
Colbert, Susannah
Cook, Mary
Coulton, Marian
Crawford, Lucy
Davis, Nancy
Dye, Mary
Easter, Elizabeth
Evans, Elizabeth
Fleming, Margaret
Ford, Mary
Ginn, Transylvania
Gray, Susannah
Harris, Rebecca
Heard, Elizabeth
Hickman, Martha
Highsmith, Milly
Howard, Janet

Hudson, Elizabeth
Hudson, Molly
Jack, Margaret
Johnston, Mary
Jones, Jonnie
Jones, Rebecca
Kerlin, Elizabeth
McCurry, Katherine
Mann, Judith
Murry, Nancy
Naish, Frances
Newberry, Nancy
Owens, Barshaba
Park, Mary
Pritchett, Delpha
Royal, Elizabeth
Saxton, Elizabeth M.
Seals, Elizabeth
Skaggs, Tabitha
Snellings, Rebecca
Tate, Elizabeth
Teasley, Sarah
Terrell, Devisa
Totman, Rebecca
Underwood, Ann
Underwood, Wyneford
Yoes, Katherine

CHEROKEE LAND LOTTERY IN 1838

Names of Revolutionary Soldiers who drew land and the counties in which they lived. Names of the counties are in parentheses following the name of the Revolutionary Soldiers.

Adams, Benjamin (Warren)
Adams, James (Elbert)
Affut, Nathaniel (Washington)
Aikens, James (Fayette)
Alexander, Matthew (Habersham)
Allen, John (Franklin)
Allen, William (Franklin)
Alsabrook, J., Sr. (Jones)
Angley, Conrad (Decatur)
Anthony, David (Franklin)
Arnaud, John Peter (Chatham)
Arnett, John (Thomas)
Arnold, Charles (Tattnall)
Arnold, William (Oglethorpe)
Atkins, Ici (Talbot)
Atkinson, Robert (DeKalb)
Auldridge, Absolem (Houston)
Auldridge, William (Wilkes)
Austin, John (Walton)
Ayers, Baker (Habersham)

Bailey, Stephen (Monroe)
Baker, Charles (Habersham)
Baldassee, Isaac (Tattnall)
Barnett, Joel (Oglethorpe)
Barnwell, John (Henry)
Barnwell, Michael (Houston)
Barnwell, Robert (Hall)
Barton, John (Hall)
Bassett, Richard (Harris)
Beall, Nathaniel (Richmond)
Beard, Moses (Clark)
Bearden, Humphrey (Clark)
Beasley, Thomas, Sr. (Henry)
Blair, James (Habersham)
Boring, Isaac (Jackson)
Bowden, James (Monroe)
Bowen, Elijah (Tattnall)
Bowen, John (Gwinnett)

Bowles, Nathan (Jackson)
Bozeman, Ralph (Thomas)
Bradley, John (Jackson)
Brady, Samuel (Marion)
Branch, James (Laurens)
Branch, William S. (Greene)
Brannon, Michael (Gwinnett)
Brooks, John (Columbia)
Brooks, Robert (Houston)
Brown, James (Clark)
Brown, Jesse (Early)
Brown, Joseph (Rabun)
Brown, Lewis (Monroe)
Brown, Mordecai (orphans of
    (Henry)
Brown, Wallis (Pike)
Bryan, Thomas, Sr. (Franklin)
Burch, Edward (Pulaski)
Burford, Wm. (Butts)
Burgess, Josiah (Jasper)
Burkett, Uriah (Dooly)
Butler, Patrick (Elbert)
Bynant, Sugars (Houston)

Cabaniss, Henry (Elbert)
Caison, Willoughby (Ware)
Callahan, John (Oglethorpe)
Campbell, William, Sr. (Ogle-
    thorpe)
Cannup, Thomas (Habersham)
Cantrell, Charles (Rabun)
Carithers, Robert (Madison)
Carithers, Samuel (Gwinnett)
Carlisle, Benjamin (Columbia)
Carroll, John (Jasper)
Carson, Adam (Jones)
Carter, Charles, Sr. (Oglethorpe)
Carter, James (Elbert)
Carter, Robert (Newton)

311

Cartledge, J., Sr. (Columbia)
Cash, Dorson (Columbia)
Cason, Willis (Henry)
Chestnut, Needham (Houston)
Choice, Tully (Hancock)
Christopher, William (Oglethorpe)
Clark, George (Jackson)
Clayton, Stephen, Sr. (Carroll)
Cobbett, Thomas (Elbert)
Coker, Isaac (Henry)
Coleman, Jesse (Burke)
Collins, Joseph (Twiggs)
Colquitt, Robert (Oglethorpe)
Comer, Hugh M. (Jones)
Comer, James, Sr. (Jones)
Conden, John (Oglethorpe)
Connell, John (Montgomery)
Connor, William (Putnam)
Conyers, John (Screven)
Cook, James W. (Jackson)
Cooksey, John (Newton)
Copeland, Benjamin (Greene)
Cotten, George, Sr. (Warren)
Cowart, Zachariah (Early)
Crabbe, Asa (Putnam)
Crawford, Jay (Chatham)
Crawford, Philip (Newton)
Crosby, Urill (Wilkes)
Cross, John (Muscogee)
Crumbley, Anthony (Henry)

Daniel, Frederick (Pike)
Daniel, Littleberry (Heard)
David, Isham (Madison)
Davidson, Joseph (Pike)
Davies, Daniel (Montgomery)
Davis, John, Sr. (Habersham)
Davis, John (Lowndes)
Davis, William (Fayette)
Dawson, Brittain (Burke)
Dawson, Joseph (Butts)
Dean, Richard (Houston)
Dennis, Josiah (Morgan)
Denson, Joseph, Sr. (Putnam)
Dickerson, Harry (Washington)
Dickey, Patrick (Putnam)
Dillard, James (Elbert)
Dobbs, Nathan (Gwinnett)

Dobson, Henry (Hall)
Doby, John (Jasper)
Dorton, Benj. (Pike)
Dowd, John (Warren)
Downs, Wm. (Effingham)
Drake, James (Telfair)
Dunn, John (Fayette)
Durham, Isaac (DeKalb)
Durvuzieaux, Stephen (Jefferson)
Dyer, Jacob C. (Putnam)

Eagin, John (Richmond)
Elder, Joshua (Fayette)
Elrod, Samuel (Habersham)
Ellis, Shadrack (Talbot)
Elton, Anthony W. (Jackson)
Elvington, Gideon (Lowndes)
Epperson, Thompson (Franklin)
Espy, James (Clark)
Eubanks, George (Butts)
Evans, John

Fain, Ebenezer, Sr. (Habersham)
Fairish, William (Rabun)
Faison, William (Hancock)
Finch, William (Oglethorpe)
Fitzpatrick, Rene (Heard)
Flannigan, Wm. (Hall)
Fould, James (Wilkinson)
Franklin, Zepheniah (Warren)
Funderburk, John (Monroe)

Gainey, Reedy (Tattnall)
Garner, Thomas (Hall)
Gates, Charles, Sr. (Gwinnett)
Gibbs, Cornelius (Rabun)
Gilbert, John (Jackson)
Gilleland, Wm., Sr. (Fayette)
Gilmer, James, Sr. (Hall)
Glasgow, Wm. (Madison)
Glaze, Reuben (Oglethorpe)
Glenn, Thomas (Jones)
Goodwin, Lewis (Twiggs)
Gower, Abel (Gwinnett)
Grace, John (Tattnall)
Gray, James (Pike)
Greene, Daniel (Ware)
Gregory, Richard (Oglethorpe)

Griffin, Joseph (Troup)
Grumbles, George (Burke)
Guise, John (Lincoln)
Guise, Peter (Lincoln)
Gurnill, Wm. (DeKalb)

Habersham, George (Crawford)
Hall, Isaac (Meriwether)
Hall, Wm. G. (Putnam)
Ham, William (Crawford)
Hames, John (Hall)
Hammett, John (Warren)
Hancock, Isaac (Habersham)
Handy, Nathaniel (Habersham)
Harmon, John, Sr. (Elbert)
Harper, George (Jones)
Harper, John (Habersham)
Harper, William (Habersham)
Harrell, Ethelred, Sr. (Pulaski)
Harriden, Joseph (Newton)
Harrington, Ephriam (Emanuel)
Harris, John (Newton)
Harrup, Arthur (Jones)
Hatcher, Henry (Pike)
Hatcher, Josiah (Richmond)
Hayman, Henry (Lowndes)
Hayman, Stephen (Burke)
Hays, John (DeKalb)
Heggie, Thomas
Henderson, Robert (Hall)
Henderson, Robert (Jackson)
Hendrick, John (Pike)
Hendricks, Elias (Madison)
Hendricks, Samuel (Muscogee)
Henry, Robert, Sr. (Walton)
Hewell, Wyatt (Newton)
Hickman, John (Monroe)
Higgs, John (Montgomery)
Higgs, Thomas (Hall)
Hines, John (Burke)
Hinton, Pester (Elbert)
Hodges, Philemon (Muscogee)
Holbrooks, Edy (Franklin)
Holcombe, Moses (Cherokee)
Holliday, William (Twiggs)
Holliman, Samuel (Columbia)
Holmes, Thomas (Franklin)
Hooper, Richard (Franklin)

Hopkins, Isaac (Wilkes)
Horsley, Valentine (Monroe)
Horton, Isaac (Gwinnett)
Hudson, John (Henry)
Huey, Henry (DeKalb)
Hunter, Moses (Habersham)

Jackson, Ebenezer (Chatham)
Jenkins, Lewis (Washington)
Jennings, Robert (Oglethorpe)
Jester, Levi (Butts)
Jett, Daniel (Greene)
Johnson, Angus (Putnam)
Johnson, Hardy (Emanuel)
Johnson, Jesse (Jackson)
Joiner, Abraham (Bibb)
Joiner, Benj. (Pike)
Jones, Gabriel
Jones, William (Bibb)
Jones, William (Jasper)
Jordan, Benjamin (Meriwether)
Jordan, Charles, Sr. (Meri-
    wether)
Jordan, Job (Marion)
Jordan, William (Newton)

Kellmer, George (Talbot)
Kelly, Edward (Pulaski)
Kendall, James Key (Habersham)
Kent, John (Twiggs)
King, John (Jackson)
King, William (Ware)

Lambert, James, Sr. (Burke)
Landrum, John (Wilkes)
Lanier, Lewis (Screven)
Lard, William (Jackson)
Lawrence, John (Putnam)
Leach, Burdette (Franklin)
Leak, James (Jasper)
Leansley, Thomas (Coweta)
Lee, John (Washington)
LeGrand, John (Elbert)
Lesley, Wm. (Oglethorpe)
Lewis, Nathaniel (Chatham)
Liles, Ephriam (Twiggs)
Lindsey, Isaac, Sr. (Hall)
Little, William, Sr. (Putnam)

Litton, John (Habersham)
Lockhart, James (Elbert)
Loyd, Thomas (Jasper)

McCall, Thomas (Laurens)
McClain, John (Ware)
McDade, John (Gwinnett)
McDonald, John (Jackson)
McGinty, John (Pike)
McGruber, W. R. (Richmond)
McKenzie, Wm. (Monroe)
McMullen, John R. (Franklin)
McMurrah, David (Newton)
McNeil, Jesse (Bibb)
McVicker, John (Henry)
Maddox, John (Gwinnett)
Maginty, John (Pike)
Mangham, Howell (Franklin)
Martin, Alexander (Oglethorpe)
Mason, Gideon (Jones)
Massey, Allston S. (Harris)
Matthews, Isaac (Clark)
Matthews, Wm. (Jackson)
Mayes, Thomas (Franklin)
Mead, Minor (Carroll)
Meriwether, Thomas (Jasper)
Middlebrook, John (Newton)
Mikell, James (Bulloch)
Miller, Jesse (Harris)
Miller, Wm. (Habersham)
Millican, Thomas (DeKalb)
Mitchell, Robert (Bibb)
Mitchell, Wm., Sr. (Franklin)
Mitzger, David (Effingham)
Monk, John (Monroe)
Moore, Isaac (Henry)
Moore, John (Hall)
Moore, John (Hancock)
Morgan, John, Sr. (Morgan)
Morris, John (Pulaski)
Moseley, Samuel (Franklin)
Mott, Nathan (Washington)
Murray, Thomas (Columbia)

Nall, Reuben (Tattnall)
Nead, George (Effingham)
Newnan, Thomas (Richmond)
Nix, John (Hall)

Nobles, Lewis S. (Montgomery)
Norman, John (Wilkes)
Nunnellee, James F. (Elbert)

Oates, Richard W. (Harris)
O'Kelly, Francis (Oglethorpe)

Paine, John (Greene)
Palmer, William (DeKalb)
Parker, Daniel, Sr. (Upson)
Patrick, David (Oglethorpe)
Patrick, Wm. (Emanuel)
Peacock, Archibald (Washington)
Peavy, Dial (Fayette)
Pennington, Neddy (Jones)
Pentecost, William (Jackson)
Perkins, Archibald (Greene)
Phillips, Benjamin (Camden)
Phillips, Levi (Carroll)
Pinson, Moses (Hall)
Pledge, Thomas (Elbert)
Pollock, Jesse (Houston)
Potts, John (Habersham)
Price, Ephriam (Greene)
Prince, John (Habersham)

Raines, Edmund (Morgan)
Ratchford, Joseph (Jackson)
Ray, John, Sr. (Harris)
Reddick, Abram (Jasper)
Redwine, Jacob (Elbert)
Renfroe, Stephen H. (Jones)
Rhan, Jonathan (Effingham)
Rice, Leonard (Elbert)
Richardson, Amos (Elbert)
Richardson, Jesse (Habersham)
Roach, Samuel (Early)
Roberts, John (Gwinnett)
Rutherford, John (Baldwin)
Ryles, James, Sr. (Hall)
Ryall, Wright (Telfair)

St. John, James (Newton)
Sanders, James (Madison)
Sanders, John (DeKalb)
Sandridge, Clayborn (Elbert)
Sappington, John (Henry)
Savage, Thomas, Sr. (Hall)

314

Scott, James (Liberty)
Scott, William (Coweta)
Seal, Anthony (Harris)
Seale, William (Hancock)
Sellers, Solomon (Appling)
Selman, William (Upson)
Setzger, Jacob (Franklin)
Shackleford, Edmund (Elbert)
Shockley, Jonathan (Monroe)
Simmons, Richard (Gwinnett)
Simmons, Thomas (Ware)
Sisson, John (Jackson)
Slaton, George (Jackson)
Smith, Benjamin (Coweta)
Smith, Colesby (Washington)
Smith, Ivy (Appling)
Smith, James (Oglethorpe)
Smith, Jesse (Franklin)
Smith, Joshua (Hall)
Smith, Larkin (Oglethorpe)
Smith, Robert (Butts)
Smith, Samuel (Chatham)
Snyder, Godlip (Effingham)
Speak, Richard (Butts)
Spears, John (Newton)
Spears, William (Franklin)
Stacy, Thomas (DeKalb)
Starrell, James (Habersham)
Stewart, Hardy (Wilkinson)
Stewart, Henry (Jasper)
Stewart, John (Monroe)
Stillwell, Jacob (Troup)
Stone, Henry (Ware)
Stone, William (Jasper)
Strauther, James (Rabun)
Stroud, Sherwood (Walton)
Stuart, John (Jasper)
Suttles, William (DeKalb)
Sword, James (Walton)

Tanner, Thomas (DeKalb)
Taylor, Richard C. (Morgan)
Tedder, William (Montgomery)
Telly, Lazarus (Rabun)
Terrell, James (Franklin)
Terrell, William (DeKalb)
Thaxton, James (Greene)
Thomas, John (Troup)

Thomas, Massa (?) (Putnam)
Thompson, Frederick (Walton)
Thompson, Seth (Meriwether)
Thompson, William (Habersham)
Thompson, William (Ware)
Tillary, John (Butts)
Tilley, William (Monroe)
Tomalson, William (Washington)
Treadwell, Stephen (Heard)
Tucker, Allen (Greene)
Tucker, Robert (Elbert)
Tuhett, John (Pike)
Tully, Henry, Sr. (Newton)
Turner, John (Oglethorpe)
Turner, John (Putnam)

Usury, Thomas (Crawford)

Varner, George (Franklin)
Varner, Matthew, Sr. (Oglethorpe)
Vaughan, Felix (Franklin)
Vickers, William (Meriwether)

Waites, George (DeKalb)
Waites, Samuel (Troup)
Walker, James (Upson)
Wallace, William (Greene)
Walton, Josiah (Wilkes)
Warden, Samuel (Madison)
Warthern, William (Washington)
Waters, Clement (Habersham)
Watkins, W., Sr. (Washington)
Watson, Isham (Lowndes)
Watson, Samuel (Troup)
Weatherton, Thomas (Walton)
Weeks, Theophilus (Camden)
West, John (Talbot)
Westbrook, John (Franklin)
Wetter, William (Clark)
Whitaker, Joshua (Richmond)
White, Zeceriah (Effingham)
Whitfield, Lewis (Burke)
Wight, John (Butts)
Wilhite, Lewis (Elbert)
Williams, Anderson (Effingham)
Williams, John (Habersham)
Williams, Solomon (Laurens)
Wills, Leonard (Gwinnett)

315

Wilson, George (Walton)
Wilson, James, Sr. (Jackson)
Wilson, John, Sr. (Greene)
Wilson, John (Columbia)
Wilson, Samuel (Screven)
Wilson, Williams (Jackson)
Wood, James (Monroe)
Woodall, Joseph (Oglethorpe)

Woodruff, Richard (Wilkes)
Wright, John (Butts)
Wright, William (Clark)

Young, George (Oglethorpe)

Zinn, Henry (Richmond

CHEROKEE LAND LOTTERY IN 1838

Names of Widows of Revolutionary Soldiers who drew land, and the counties in which they lived.

Alexander, Sarah (Gwinnett)
Alexander, Susanna (Talbot)
Allison, Martha (Greene)
Arrant, Elizabeth (Upson)

Bacheler, Nancy (Wilkinson)
Bailey, Keziah (Washington)
Baker, Jane (Chatham)
Baker, Sarah (Gwinnett)
Barnett, Caroline (Clark)
Barnett, Margaret (Jackson)
Barr, Elizabeth (Houston)
Barron, Frances (Upson)
Bateman, Tabitha (Houston)
Battle, Sarah (Taliaferro)
Bayless, Sarah (Warren)
Blalock, Eleanor (Upson)
Boggs, Eve (Jackson)
Bohanan, Lydia (Appling)
Bolton, Mary (Warren)
Bostwick, Mary (Morgan)
Brach, Sarah (Wilkinson)
Bradford, Ann (Putnam)
Branch, Hester (Tattnall)
Brantley, Mary (Putnam)
Brewer, Elizabeth (Elbert)
Broadwell, Christian (Jackson)
Brookins, Nancy (Washington)
Brooks, Rachel (DeKalb)
Brown, Elizabeth (Burke)
Brown, Frances
Brown, Laonie (Dooly)

Brown, Mary (DeKalb)
Brown, Mary (Campbell)
Brown, Rebecca (Henry)
Browning, Margaret (Clark)
Bruce, Elizabeth (Wilkes)
Bruson, Frances (Houston)
Bryan, Ann (Burke)
Buchanan, Mary (Jasper)
Buise, Margaret (Newton)
Burnett, Molly (Lowndes)
Butler, Hannah (Lee)
Butler, Marcy C. (Gwinnett)

Cannon, Ann (Walton)
Cannon, Elizabeth (Jasper)
Cannon, Mary (Bulloch)
Carnes, Rosanna (Rabun)
Carroll, Mary (Wilkes)
Cash, Sarah (Jackson)
Chambers, Martha (Fayette)
Cheshire, Sarah (Monroe)
Chesser, Easter (Clark)
Chickonimy, Mary (Monroe)
Childs, Elizabeth (Jones)
Clark, Mary (Jefferson)
Cohom, Elizabeth (Taliaferro)
Coleman, Elizabeth (Bibb)
Coleman, Nancy (Appling)
Connaway, Elizabeth (Hall)
Cook, Deborah (Washington)
Cook, Elizabeth (Jackson)
Cook, Lydia (Effingham)

Copeland, Martha (Bibb)
Crawford, Mary (Carroll)
Crawford, Mary Ann (Columbia)
Creeny, Rebecca (Appling)
Cronich, Rachel (Walton)
Culbertson, Celia (Troup)
Culver, Nancy (Hancock)
Cummings, J. (Washington)
Cumming, Sarah (Greene)
Cunningham, Nancy (Elbert)

Daniel, Mary (Washington)
Daniel, Sarah (Richmond)
Darris, Elizabeth (Jackson)
Davis, Mary (Montgomery)
Davis, Mary Ann (DeKalb)
Deadwyler, Alice (Elbert)
Deason, Hannah (Campbell)
Denton, Emily (Jones)
Dickson, Mary (Screven)
Dobbs, Sarah (Hall)
Doherty, Elizabeth (DeKalb)
Doles, Elizabeth (Baldwin)
Douglass, M. A. (Meriwether)
DuBose, Sarah (Burke)
Duffel, Lucy (Oglethorpe)
Duke, Nancy (Morgan)
Dunnaway, Mary (Warren)
Durracott, Rebecca (Elbert)
Dyson, Esther (Lee)

Edmunds, W. (Wilkes)
England, Margaret (Habersham)
English, Sarah (Franklin)
Estes, Isabella (Putnam)
Eubanks, Susanna (Hall)
Evans, Jane (Fayette)

Fairchild, Elizabeth (Wilkinson)
Faris, Rebecca (Gwinnett)
Fincher, Jemina (Henry)
Fitts, Mary (Elbert)
Fitzpatrick, Elizabeth (Twiggs)
Flood, Jane (Henry)
Floyd, Sarah (Madison)
Fogil, Mary (Morgan)
Fowler, Martha (Morgan)
Fox, Wilmouth (Jasper)

Freeman, Elizabeth (Jasper)
Fuller, Elizabeth (Greene)
Fuller, Keziah (Columbia)

Gaines, Ann (Thomas)
Gamage, Charity (Houston)
Gammill, Jane (Harris)
Garr, Catherine (Morgan)
Gideons, Elizabeth (Talbot)
Giles, Celia (Washington)
Ginn, Sarah (Elbert)
Glazier, Sarah (Newton)
Glenn, Ann (Jasper)
Glenn, Elizabeth (Jackson)
Glenn, Elizabeth (Troup)
Glynn, Lucy (Greene)
Golden, Elender (Walton)
Golden, Frances (Wilkes)
Golightly, S. (Washington)
Goodwin, Nancy (Franklin)
Goolsby, Mary (Oglethorpe)
Grady, Mary (Franklin)
Gray, Diana (Franklin)
Gray, Susanna (Elbert)
Gressam, Sally (Hall)
Grizzard, Susanna (Warren)

Hamilton, C. (Montgomery)
Haney, Elizabeth (Gwinnett)
Haney, Ursula (Putnam)
Hanson, Peggy (Morgan)
Harper, Mary (Hancock)
Harris, Clara (Troup)
Harris, Lavania (Oglethorpe)
Harris, Mary (Rabun)
Hartley, Ferebe (Washington)
Harvey, Sarah (Twiggs)
Head, Sarah (Elbert)
Hendrix, Mary (Screven)
Hendry, Ann (Liberty)
Herndon, Frances (Heard)
Hester, Diana (Jones)
Hewell, Susanna (Clark)
Hicks, Susanna (Upson)
Higgenbotham, Jean (Elbert)
Highsmith, Sarah (Wayne)
Hinds, Martha (Chatham)
Hines, Nancy (Jackson)

317

Hobbs, Margery (Habersham)
Holbrook, Hannah (Gwinnett)
Holbrooke, Prisillon (Gwinnett)
Holcombe, Frances (Chatham)
Holloman, Levicy (Pulaski)
Horn, Dorcas (Pike)
Hubbard, Elizabeth (Oglethorpe)
Hubbard, Susanna (Oglethorpe)
Hunter, Elizabeth (Gwinnett)

Jackson, Mary (Washington)
Jenkins, Rosanna (Oglethorpe)
Johnson, Martha W. (Fayette)
Johnson, Rosannah (DeKalb)
Johnson, Sarah (Heard)
Johnson, Sivel (Warren)
Jones, Margaret (Jefferson)
Jones, Mary (Hall)
Jones, Nancy (Fayette)
Jordan, Winnefred (Washington)
Jourdan, Elizabeth (Warren)

Kellebrew, Elizabeth (Warren)
Kendall, Elizabeth P. (Muscogee)
Kesterson, Nancy (Bibb)
King, Elizabeth (Warren)
King, Mary (Talbot)
Kirklin, Mary (Troup)
Knight, Bethany (Emanuel)

Lacy, Sarah (Newton)
Lambert, Sarah (Jackson)
Lansford, Elizabeth (Jasper)
Lawless, Agnes (Madison)
Lawson, Martha (Wilkinson)
Lewis, Catherine (Henry)
Lewis, Nancy (Coweta)
Lewis, Selia (Gwinnett)
Lindsey, Mary (Wilkes)
Lockland, Charlotte (Monroe)
Long, Louisa (Bibb)
Long, Martha (Hancock)
Lovejoy, Jemina (Pike)
Loyd, Mary (Gwinnett)
Lucas, Mary (Hancock)
Lynn, Sally (Jasper)

McCibben, Margaret (Henry)

McClain, Mary (Gwinnett)
McCollum, Margaret (Franklin)
McCoy, Ann (Taliaferro)
McCutcheon, Jane (Hall)
McDaniel, Elizabeth (Jones)
McDaniel, Mildred (Hancock)
McFail, Judith (Lowndes)
McMinn, Jane (Habersham)
McRee, Mary (Clark)
McWhorter, Margaret (Ogle-
thorpe)
Magbee, Rachel (Butts)
Magee, Elizabeth (Putnam)
Manley, Temperance (Franklin)
Mappin, Mary (Columbia)
Matthews, Elizabeth (Jefferson)
Matthews, Elizabeth (Pike)
Mattox, Amelia C. (Wilkes)
Merritt, Barbara (Jasper)
Middlebrooks, Molly (Newton)
Miller, Lucretia (Early)
Moffett, Mary (Meriwether)
Monk, Susanna (Putnam)
Moody, Anna (Oglethorpe)
Moreland, Frances (Putnam)
Morrow, Ann (Newton)
Morrow, Elizabeth (Franklin)
Murphy, Martha (Wilkes)
Myers, Mary (McIntosh)

Napp, Mary (Greene)
Nash, Mary (Jones)
Newsome, Lucy (Wilkinson)
Newsome, Nancy (Morgan)
Nichols, Mary (Twiggs)
Nix, Rebecca (Talbot)

Oliver, Jane (Elbert)

Paine, Winefred (Crawford)
Paris, Jane (Habersham)
Park, Phebe (Greene)
Parrish, Elizabeth (Warren)
Patterson, Jane (Monroe)
Peacock, Amy (Walton)
Phillips, Mary (Twiggs)
Pool, Dicey (Pike)
Porter, Elizabeth (Columbia)

Proctor, Biddy (Gwinnett)
Pruitt, Peniny (Newton)

Randolph, Dorothy (Wilkes)
Ray, Jane (Talbot)
Reese, Silva (Hall)
Richardson, Clara (Monroe)
Rivers, Mary Ann (Warren)
Roberts, Elizabeth (Walton)
Robinson, Polly (Carroll)
Rooke, Mary (Wayne)
Ross, Mary (Harris)
Ruddell, Lee Ann (Wilkes)
Rudolph, Elizabeth (Camden)
Rushing, Sarah (Washington)
Rutherford, Mary (Gwinnett)
Rye, Elizabeth (Harris)

Sager, Ann (Greene)
Scott, Frances (Greene)
Sett, Susanna (DeKalb)
Shell, Elizabeth (DeKalb)
Simmons, Sarah (Upson)
Sims, Caty (Jasper)
Singletary, Martha (Decatur)
Slatter, Elvira (Twiggs)
Smith, Elizabeth (Greene)
Smith, Mary (Warren)
Smith, Mary (Meriwether)
Smith, Sarah (Morgan)
Smith, Susan (Montgomery)
Sparks, Jane (Troup)
Spence, Mary (Burke)
Springer, Ann (Wilkes)
Stamps, Mary (Warren)
Starr, Mary (Morgan)
Stewart, Tabitha (Screven)
Strad, Priscilla (Monroe)
Stringer, Celia (Burke)
Sutton, Sarah (Putnam)

Tabor, Elizabeth (Franklin)
Talbot, Elizabeth (Clarke)
Tammons, Zipporah (Cherokee)
Tatum, Molly (Monroe)
Terry, Hannah (Warren)
Thomas, Mary (Washington)
Thomas, Sarah (Newton)

Thrower, Sarah (Newton)
Tomlinson, M. W. (Jefferson)
Tool, Jane (Jones)
Trainum, Elizabeth (Morgan)
Turke, Margaret (Franklin)
Twitty, Sally (Fayette)
Tyler, Elizabeth (Newton)

Verdin, Winnie (Oglethorpe)
Vernon, Patsey (Houston)
Vickers, Sarah (Hancock)
Visage, Elizabeth (Rabun)

Walker, Elizabeth (Washington)
Walker, Luraney (Meriwether)
Ward, Elizabeth (Pike)
Ward, Jane (Elbert)
Warren, Mary (Hall)
Waters, Judith (Franklin)
Weaver, Mary (Randolph)
Wense, Mary (Chatham)
Wesson, Sarah (Washington)
Wheeler, Mary (Franklin)
Wheeler, Susanna (Walton)
    (See Gordon Co. History)
Wilcher, Elizabeth (Newton)
Wilkes, Nancy (Elbert)
Williams, Diana (Twiggs)
Williams, Mary (Bulloch)
Williams, Rebecca (Hall)
Williamson, Nancy (Thomas)
Willingham, Jane (Oglethorpe)
Willis, Susanna (Wilkes)
Willoughby, Unity (Bibb)
Willson, Ann (Effingham)
Willson, Rebecca (Greene)
Windham, Lucy (Butts)
Wingate, Mary (Richmond)
Worsham, Mary (Walton)
Wright, Amis (Butts)
Wright, Susan (Hancock)
Wylie, Jane (Pike)

Yates, Susanna (Fayette)
Yarbrough, Rachel (Muscogee)

REVOLUTIONARY SOLDIERS, GEORGIA
WHO APPLIED FOR PENSIONS

Under Act of 1832

David Andrew, Fayette Co.
Absolem Awtry
Thomas Beatty
William Bobbitt, Private
Peter Cash, Henry Co.
Ephriam Cassell, Campbell Co.
Silas Caster, Washington Co.
David Comer, Lieut.
John Conway, Private
James Dawson, Rabun Co.
Joseph Davie, Muscogee Co.
Jeremiah Drew, Private
Alexander Dunn, Monroe Co.
John Halcondale Edge, Bulloch Co.
Arthur Elliott, Private
Liddal Ester, Troup Co.
James Findall, Burke Co.
James Flournoy, Talbot Co.

Christopher Gardner, Private
John M. Griner, Bulloch Co.
Thomas Guthrie, Private
John Hammond, Hall Co.
Arch Henderson, Private
James Hughes, DeKalb Co.
William Merry, Carroll Co.
William Nevis, Early Co.
William Pentecost, Lieut.
Henry Pool, Sr., Baldwin Co.
James Quillen, Habersham Co.
James Sleigh, Camden Co.
Henry Spalding, Columbia Co.
Elisha Talley, Heard Co.
James Town, Madison Co.
James Vassels, Private
Alexander Walden, Coweta Co.
Thomas Wilson, Gwinnett Co.

Widows of Revolutionary Soldiers Applied for Pension

Susan M. Evans (George Evans), Clarke Co.
Harriet Ann Elbert (Lieut. Elbert)
Bethany Fuller, Warren Co.
Drusilla Holbrook (Caleb Holbrook), Gwinnett Co.
Elizabeth Kiker (George Kiker), Cass Co.
Mary G. Levert (Thomas Levert), Walton Co.

Pensioners Upson Co., 1832

Charles Adkins
William Black
Thomas Cannon
William Carraway
William Duke
Henry Garland

Christopher Flannigan
William Hudgins
Benjamin Hamrick
Michael Kelly
Peter McKenzie
Daniel Parker

Samuel Pool
Henry Peeples
Patrick Roach
Wm. Stephens, Sr.
Wm. Shepherd
Thomas E. Sullivan

Pensioners Buried Jackson Co.

Name	Drew Pension
Charles McKenny	1834–1841
Levi Lowry	1835–1841
William Potts	1832
Solomon Saxon	1841
Sherrod Thompson	1841
James Wheeler	1832
Jesse White	1841

Pensioners Buried Jackson Co., Intestate

James Barr	1835	Samuel Knox	
Middleton Brooks	1835	John King	1835
Ansel Cunningham	1832	James McKilgore	1835
Charles Damron	1832	Isaac Matthews	1835
Joseph Harris	1832	William Matthews	1835
Robert Henderson	1835		

Left Wills, but did not draw Pensions

Robert Beavers	John G. Henderson
William Bennett	Philip Ryan, Sr.
Peter Boyle	Henry Stoneham
Isaac Burson	Thomas Stapler
William Deal (Dial)	Levi Wallace
Lewis Hines	Micajah Williamson, Sr.

Pensioners from Lowndes (now Thomas) Co.
Qualified in 1833, under the Veterans' Act of 1832

Simon Hadley	Shadrach Pugh
Joseph Anderson	Ignatius Hall
Ralph Bozeman	

Pensioners from Henry Co., 1835

Francis Adams	Reuben Edwards
Robert Beard	James Hannegan
John Barnhill	Joseph Hand
Ezekiel Cloud	David McCance
John Cash	Isaac Moore, Sr.
Thomas Cook	Charles Upchurch

NAMES AND AGES OF PENSIONERS FROM GEORGIA

For Revolutionary Service, Found in the Census of Pensioners For
Revolutionary Military Service, Under the Act for Taking the 6th
Census in 1840. (From Book of Pensioners, published in Washington,
D.C.)

CAMPBELL CO.

Akins, James	90
Bledsoe, Benjamin	77
Clinton, William	80
Gunnell, William R.	88
Norwood, George	77

CHATTOOGA CO.

O'Rear, Daniel	83

CHEROKEE CO.

Martin, Ephriam	80
Smith, Charles	75
Willaford, Nathan	82

CASS CO.

Baker, Chas.	79
Brewster, Hugh	80
Edwards, Reuben	82
Harris, Benjamin	81
Lewis, John	83

CLARK CO.

Espy, John	84
Farrar, Francis	76
Oliver, John	78
Parr, Benjamin	83
Wilson, George	88

CAMDEN CO.

Wilford, Lewis	95 to 100

COBB CO.

Barnwell, John	88
Collins, John	80
Eastwood, Israel	82
Edwards, Adonijah	73
Groover, Peter	79
McDowell, Robert	86
Nesbit, Jeremiah	105
Sumner, John	77

CRAWFORD CO.

Bailey, James	80
Ethridge, Joel	77
Fudge, Jacob	82
Goodwin, Lewis	74
Hartley, Daniel	97
Mathews, Philip	88
Meador, Jason	81
Turner, Thomas	89

CARROLL CO.

Robinson, John, Sr.	88
Rowell, Jesse	87
Stedman, Zacheriah	89

COWETA CO.

Akens, James	74
Brewster, William	83
Gay, Allen	75
Neely, John	83
Smith, William	91

BURKE CO.

Allen, James	84
Thomas, Abraham	86

BALDWIN CO.

Anderson, William	78
Robinson, Joseph	70
Russell, James G., Sr.	78
Talbot, Benjamin	76

BULLOCH CO.

Banks, John	84

BUTTS CO.

Price, E.	79

DADE CO.

Perkins, Moses	87

DE KALB CO.

Brooks, George	79
Copeland, William	75
Maconeson, John	84
Reeve, William	84
Roberts, Thomas	95
Stowers, Lewis, Sr.	76
Terrell, William	84

ELBERT CO.

Brown, Benjamin	77
Carter, David	82
Cook, John	79
Daniel, John	80
Davis, John	87
Gaines, William	83
Glasgow, William	78
Gulley, Richard	85
Kelly, William	82
Rice, Leonard	81
Richardson, Amos	76
Riley, James	82
Trammell, William	83
Ward, William	82

EMANUEL CO.

Brown, Henry	70
Curl, Matthew	78
Drew, William	75
Durden, Jacob	85
Edenfield, David	79
Sutton, A.	82
Terulauth, Benjamin	83

EFFINGHAM CO.

Rahn, Jonathan	78

EARLY CO.

Baggett, Josiah	78
Jordan, Elizabeth	57
(living with Charles B. Jordan)	
Wells, Redman	58

FRANKLIN CO.

Aaron, William	93
Cash, Ann	75
(living with Howard Cash)	

Clarke, Thomas	79
Dyer, Elisha	77
Fleming, Robert	70
Fuller, Stephen	88
Holbrook, Jesse	76
McCoy, Samuel	79
Mendock, William	81
Mitchell, William	81
Sheridan, Abner	80
Spears, William	95
Stonecypher, John	84

FAYETTE CO.

Black, William	76
Gilleland, Susan	80
Milles, Karew-Harpuck	79
Suddeth, Jared	76
Waldrup, James	85

FORSYTH CO.

Browne, Ambrose	83
Carroll, James	75
Lagraw, John M.	87
Nolen, James	90
Wells, Leonard	84
Whiten, Philip	95

GWINNETT CO.

Andes, Owen	87
Benson, Enoch	84
Bramblett, Reuben	75
Clower, Daniel	79
Conger, Benjamin	84
Curbo, Joseph	86
Davis, John	109
Dobs, Nathan	85
Gowers, Abel	86
Harris, Stephen	86
Herrington, Joseph	77
Horton, Isaac	81
Hunt, Littleton	97
Iseley, Philip	91
Jackson, Edward	86
Lawrence, John	80
McDade, John	93
McRight, William	91
Pateson, Robert	78
Thrasher, George	85

323

Williams, Nathan	89	Upchurch, Charles	85

<table>
<tr><td colspan="2">GILMER CO.</td><td colspan="2">HARRIS CO.</td></tr>
<tr><td>Cox, Richard, Sr.</td><td>79</td><td>Norris, William</td><td>84</td></tr>
<tr><td>Ellis, Mary</td><td>84</td><td>Swan, William B.</td><td>82</td></tr>
<tr><td>(living with Elijah Ellis)</td><td></td><td></td><td></td></tr>
<tr><td>Fain, Hezekiah</td><td>78</td><td colspan="2">HABERSHAM CO.</td></tr>
<tr><td>Kell, James</td><td>81</td><td>McColloms, Daniel</td><td>86</td></tr>
<tr><td>Smith, Enoch</td><td>81</td><td>Pilgrim, Thomas</td><td>74</td></tr>
<tr><td></td><td></td><td>Turner, Robert</td><td>80</td></tr>
<tr><td colspan="2">GREENE CO.</td><td>Vandergriff, Garret</td><td>89</td></tr>
<tr><td>Gaither, Stephen</td><td>?</td><td></td><td></td></tr>
<tr><td>Harris, Matthew</td><td>88</td><td colspan="2">HANCOCK CO.</td></tr>
<tr><td>Pullin, Robert</td><td>85</td><td>Blount, Isaac</td><td>80</td></tr>
<tr><td>Shurr, John</td><td>77</td><td>Brasel, Bird</td><td>70</td></tr>
<tr><td>Slaughter, George</td><td>77</td><td>Dennis, John</td><td>70</td></tr>
<tr><td></td><td></td><td>Faison, William</td><td>70</td></tr>
<tr><td colspan="2">HEARD CO.</td><td>Grant, Joseph</td><td>80</td></tr>
<tr><td>Stewart, James</td><td>75</td><td>Hill, John</td><td>80</td></tr>
<tr><td>(living with John Stewart)</td><td></td><td>Howel, Mills</td><td>70</td></tr>
<tr><td></td><td></td><td>Mullins, Malone</td><td>80</td></tr>
<tr><td colspan="2">HALL CO.</td><td>Rossiter, Timothy</td><td>80</td></tr>
<tr><td>Albread, Elias</td><td>82</td><td>Sheffield, William</td><td>70</td></tr>
<tr><td>Anderson, James</td><td>72</td><td></td><td></td></tr>
<tr><td>Baker, Beal</td><td>84</td><td colspan="2">JONES CO.</td></tr>
<tr><td>Bonds, Joseph</td><td>84</td><td>Morton, Oliver, Sr.</td><td>75</td></tr>
<tr><td>Childers, Milliner</td><td>77</td><td>Roberts, Reuben</td><td>85</td></tr>
<tr><td>Clark, William</td><td>9-</td><td>Slocumb, John C.</td><td>80</td></tr>
<tr><td>Flanigan, William</td><td>91</td><td></td><td></td></tr>
<tr><td>Gilmer, James, Sr.</td><td>80</td><td colspan="2">JASPER CO.</td></tr>
<tr><td>Gunter, Charles</td><td>78</td><td>Barnett, Sion</td><td>79</td></tr>
<tr><td>Hulsey, Jesse</td><td>81</td><td>Davidson, John</td><td>79</td></tr>
<tr><td>Kell, Robert</td><td>89</td><td>Jones, William, Sr.</td><td>82</td></tr>
<tr><td>McClesky, James</td><td>86</td><td>Spears, John</td><td>89</td></tr>
<tr><td>Moore, John</td><td>83</td><td>Waters, David</td><td>105</td></tr>
<tr><td>Nicholson, John</td><td>77</td><td>Yancey, Lewis D.</td><td>78</td></tr>
<tr><td>Pitts, James</td><td>71</td><td></td><td></td></tr>
<tr><td>Reed, Isaac</td><td>87</td><td colspan="2">JEFFERSON CO.</td></tr>
<tr><td>Robertson, Robert</td><td>83</td><td>Sodown, Jacob</td><td>80</td></tr>
<tr><td>Shaw, Basil</td><td>92</td><td></td><td></td></tr>
<tr><td>West, Benjamin</td><td>81</td><td colspan="2">JACKSON CO.</td></tr>
<tr><td></td><td></td><td>Anglin, Henry</td><td>81</td></tr>
<tr><td colspan="2">HENRY CO.</td><td>Cunningham, Ansell</td><td>77</td></tr>
<tr><td>Adams, Francis</td><td>77</td><td>King, John</td><td>85</td></tr>
<tr><td>Chandler, Sheildcake</td><td>88</td><td>Levay, George</td><td>85</td></tr>
<tr><td>Cloud, Ezekiel</td><td>78</td><td>Lowrey, Levi</td><td>76</td></tr>
<tr><td>Cook, Thomas</td><td>88</td><td>Mathews, Isaac</td><td>79</td></tr>
<tr><td>Gilbert, James</td><td>87</td><td>Mathews, William</td><td>77</td></tr>
</table>

Saxon, Solomon 73
Thompson, Sherrod 83
Wheeler, James 85
White, Jesse 79

LIBERTY CO.
Hart, Mary
  (living with Joseph Jones)

LUMPKIN CO.
Allen, William 101
Fleming, William 79
Hames, John 94
Hill, Reuben 69
Ledbetter, Richard 101
Nix, John 75
Pilgrim, Michael 86
Singleton, Edmund 85
  (living with Overstreet
  Singleton)

LINCOLN CO.
Guise, John 79
Linville, William 85

MACON CO.
Baker, Dempsey 77
Passimore, Joseph 79
Whatley, Daniel 87

MORGAN CO.
Barkly, William 80
Campbell, George 86
Cochran, M. 83

MADISON CO.
Cheek, William 89
Hanan, Alexander 80
Tate, Robert L. 76
Thompson, James 77
Tugle, Charles 87

MURRAY CO.
Stone, William

MARION CO.
Buchanan, George 81
Mayo, John 81

McINTOSH CO.
Calder, John 77
White, George 81

MONROE CO.
Davis, Toliver 84
Jones, William
  (living with David Woolsey)
Stewart, William 87

MERIWETHER CO.
Black, John 77
Bowen, Samuel 83
Earnest, George 80
Jenkins, Lewis 87
Keily, Giles 78
Smith, Alexander 81

MUSCOGEE CO.
Christmas, Richard 77
Hodge, Philemon 83

NEWTON CO.
Carter, Robert 84
Fretwell, Richard 87
Hewell, Wyatt 84
McLane, Thomas 80
Terrell, Richmond 80
Weathers, Valentine 76
Webb, John 85

OGLETHORPE CO.
Bledsoe, Miller 78
  (living with Whitfield
  Landrum)
Carter, Charles 88
Dunn, Thomas, Sr. 76
Eberhart, Jacob 83
Finch, William 76
Kidd, William, Sr. 77
Strong, Charles 77
Ward, Samuel 85
Woodall, Joseph 76

UNION CO.
Tanney, Michael 81

UPSON CO.		RABUN CO.	
Chellfinch, Hiram	85	Callahan, Josias	81
		Dillard, John	81
PIKE CO.		Dunlap, Jonathan	81
Gresham, David	83	McLain, John	81
Harper, William	88	Williams, Edward	102
Jenkins, John, Sr.	85		
Whittington, Faddy	87	RICHMOND CO.	
Wise, John	84	Martin, John	103
WILKINSON CO.		RANDOLPH CO.	
Jenkins, William	83	Brown, Ezekiel	75
Meadows, John	78	Brown, John	77
Rosier, Robert, Sr.	84	Bucholler, Peter	77
		Darby, Richard	102
WILKES CO.		Davis, Thomas	85
Combs, John	75		
Williams, William	78	TALIAFERRO CO.	
Woolf, Andrew	88	Evans, William	98
		King, Richard	88
WASHINGTON CO.		McCormack, Thomas	90
Cox, Moses	86	Stewart, Henry	81
Howard, George F.	97		
Jones, Isaac	79	TELFAIR CO.	
Love, Thomas	90	Williams, Joseph	80
Peacock, Uriah	88		
Thompson, Lustatia	74	TALBOT CO.	
(living with Greene H. Warthen)		Ellis, Shadrack	80
Williams, William	86	TWIGGS CO.	
		Keith, John	90
WALTON CO.		Lile, Ephriam	77
Hardin, Henry	89	Taylor, Thomas, Sr.	77
Harris, Benjamin	87		
Swords, James	92	TROUP CO.	
		Johnson, Joseph	86
		Jourdan, Fountain	77
WALKER CO.		Thomason, William	92
Newnan, Daniel			
Story, Robert		PULASKI CO.	
		Parkerson, Jacob	79
WARREN CO.			
Cason, William	93	SUMPTER CO.	
Doud, John	85	Flanigan, Daniel	83
Draper, James	89		
Jackson, John	85	CITY OF SAVANNAH	
Rickerson, Benjamin	80	Bullough, Elias	77
Studivent, Charles	80	Cabos, John	94
Wilson, John	85		

Sheftall, Sheftall	78	Melton, Robert	82
		Smith, Benjamin	88
STEWART CO.		Statham, Nathaniel	76
Bush, Prescot	81		
Elliott, Zacheriah	84	SCREVEN CO.	
Glenn, Thomas	81	Arnett, John	80

WIDOWS OF REVOLUTIONARY SOLDIERS
WHO DREW THEIR PENSIONS MARCH 4, 1859

They were in the directory of 1860. Their husbands were pensioned July 4, 1836. To enable the widows to obtain the pension, the act required that the marriage should have taken place prior to the completion of their husband's service in the Revolutionary War.

North Carolina

Martha, widow of Joseph Elkins; mar. 1780; age 102.
Ann, widow of James Hutchins; mar. 1781; age 99.
Winnefred, widow of J. Holly; mar. 1778; age 104.
Elizabeth, widow of Wm. Lane; mar. 1781; age 98.
Susannah, widow of Wm. West; mar. 1775; age 100.

Tennessee

Sarah, widow of J. Fitzpatrick; mar. 1781; age 105.
Sally, widow of John Goodall; mar. 1775; age 105.
Sally, widow of F. Stewart; mar. 1776; age 100.
Anna, widow of Wm. Taylor; mar. 1780; age 102.

Reference: Proceedings of the Georgia Society D. A. R. 1926. List compiled by Mrs. S. V. Sanford, Athens, Ga., and Mrs. Howard McCall, Atlanta, Ga. Proceedings of the Georgia Society D. A. R. 1932, 1933, 1934, and 1935. Lists compiled by Mrs. J. L. Beeson, Milledgeville, Ga.; Robert J. Travis, Savannah, Ga.; Mrs. Albert L. Tidwell, Quitman, Ga.; and Mrs. J. Harold Nicholson, Madison, Ga.

LIST OF REVOLUTIONARY SOLDIERS

Published in the Book

"McCall-Tidwell and Allied Families"

by

Mrs. Howard H. McCall of Atlanta, Ga.

Alexander, Elias (N. C.)
Ashe, Cato (S. C.)

Bacot, Capt. Samuel (N. C.)
Baker, Col. John (Mass.)
Bankston, Lawrence (Va. and Ga.)
Barnwell, John (S. C. and Ga.)
Barr, James (S. C.)
Benedict, Eliakim (Conn.)
Benjamin, John (Conn.)
Benton, Ephriam (Conn.)
Birdsey, Nathan (Conn.)
Black, James (S. C.)
Blackeman, Edward (Conn.)
Blakeman, Lemuel (Conn.)
Blakeman, Capt. Samuel (Conn.)
Bledsoe, Capt. Miller (Va. and Ga.)
Blythe, Capt. Benjamin (Penn.)
Bobo, Lewis (S. C.)
Bobo, Sampson (S. C.)
Booth, Daniel (Conn.)
Booth, James (Conn.)
Booth, Capt. Nathan (Conn.)
Boykin, Burwell (S. C.)
Boykin, Major Francis (S. C. and Ga.)
Brigham, Capt. William (Mass.)
Brinsmeade, Capt. Abraham (Conn.)
Brooks, John (Conn.)
Brown, Capt. Isaac (Conn.)
Brown, Josiah (Conn.)
Bull, Henry (Conn.)
Bull, John (Penn.)
Bull, Richard (Penn.)
Bull, Col. Thomas (Penn.)
Bull, William (Penn.)
Burroughs, Capt. Stephen (Conn.)
Burtz, Michael (S. C.)

Calwalader, Gen. John (Penn.)
Cantrell, Aaron (N. C.)
Cantrell, Abraham (N. C.)
Cantrell, Isaac (N. C.)
Cantrell, Jacob (N. C.)
Cantrell, John (N. C.)
Cantrell, Joseph (N. C.)
Cantrell, Peter (N. C.)
Cantrell, Simon (N. C.)
Cantrell, Stephen (N. C. and Ga.)
Cantrell, Stephen (N. C.)
Casey, Gen. Levi (S. C. and D. C.)
Clarke, Gen. Elijah (Ga.)
Clark, Jacob (N. C.)
Clarke, Gen. John (Ga.)
Clay, William (Va.)
Cleveland, Aaron (Conn.)
Clontz, Jeremiah (N. C.)
Clymer, George (Penn.)
Culberson, David (N. C.)
Culberson, James (Va.)
Culberson, Joseph (Va.)
Curtiss, Elnathan (Conn.)
Curtiss, Joseph (Conn.)
Curtiss, Stiles, Sr. (Conn.)

Daniell, Lieut. Stephen B. (N. C. and Ga.)
Daniell, William (N. C. and Ga.)
Dell, Lieut. James (Ga.)
Denmark, William (N. C. and Ga.)
Dewees, Col. William (Penn.)
Dixon, Major (N. C.)
D'Oilly (Daley), Benjamin
Dubois, Capt. Zacheriah (N. Y.)
Duncan, John (S. C.)
Duncan, Robert (S. C.)

Emery, Moses (Mass.)
England, Daniel (N.C. and Ga.)
England, Joseph (N.C. and Ga.)
England, William (N.C.)
Erwin, Col. Alexander (N.C.)
Erwin, Col. Arthur (N.C.)
Erwin, Nathaniel (S.C.)
Erwin, William (N.C.)
Evans, Ruel (S.C.)
Ewing, Col. Thomas (Md.)

Fain, William (Tenn.)
Fain, Thomas
Fairchild, Daniel (Conn.)
Fairchild, Robert (Conn.)
Farrar, Capt. Field (S.C.)
Farrow, John (S.C.)
Fletcher, Henry (S.C.)
Fletcher, William (S.C. and Ga.)
Freeman, George (Ga.)

Gage, Major (Mass.)
Garnett, Lieut. Thomas (Ga.)
Giles, Capt. (S.C.)
Gildern, Capt. Daniel (Penn.)
Gillam, Peter (Va. and Ga.)
Green, McKeen (Ga.)
Greene, Solomon (S.C.)
Greene, William (Va.)
Greiner, John Caspar (Ga.)
Griner, Philip (Ga.)
Groover, John (Gruber) (S.C.
   and Ga.)
Graffenried, Tscharner de (Va.)

Hale, Nathan (Mass.)
Hale, Oliver (Mass.)
Hampton, Henry (S.C.)
Harnett, Cornelius (N.C.)
Harlee, Thomas (S.C.)
Harris, Robert (N.C.)
Harris, Samuel (N.C.)
Heard, George (Ga.)
Heard, Henry (Ga.)
Heard, Jesse (Ga.)
Heard, John (Ga.)
Heard, Stephen (Ga.)
Heard, Thomas (Ga.)

Henderson, Capt. Joseph (N.C.
   and Ga.)
Henderson, Capt. Matthew (Penn.)
Henry, Patrick (Va.)
Hill, Henry (S.C.)
Hills, Col. William (S.C.)
Howe, Gen. Robert (N.C.)
Howell, Lieut. Daniel (Ga.)
Hyde, James (Conn.)
Hyde, James, Jr. (Conn.)

Jackson, Amasa (Mass.)
Jackson, Charles (Mass.)
Jackson, Ebenezer (Mass.)
Jackson, Gen. Michael (Mass.)
Jackson, Michael, Jr. (Mass.)
Jackson, Simon (Mass.)
Jaudon, Elias (S.C.)
Jones, William (Va. and Ga.)
Judson, Major Agur (Conn.)
Judson, Agur (Conn.)
Judson, Capt. Daniel (Conn.)
Judson, Daniel (Conn.)
Judson, Isaac (Conn.)
Judson, Silas (Conn.)

Kellogg, — (Conn.)
Kittles, Peter (S.C.)
Kimball, Benjamin (Mass.)
Kimball, Capt. Thomas (Mass.)
King, Philip (Va.)

Landrum, Thomas (Va. and Ga.)
Lawton, Joseph, Jr. (S.C.)
Lea, James (N.C.)
Leacraft, John (S.C.)
Lewis, George (Conn.)
Lewis, Col. Ichabod (Conn.)
Lincoln, Gen. (N.C.)
Lindsay, Col. Reuben (Va.)
Livingston, Philip (N.Y.)
Livingston, Robert (N.Y.)
Livingston, Walter (N.Y.)
Lovett, Thomas (Ga.)
Luttrell, Col. John (S.C.)
Lytle, Col. Archibald (N.C.)

Maner, Samuel (S.C.)

Maner, William (S. C.)
Marion, Gen. Francis (S. C.)
Merrill, Ezekiel (Mass.)
Merrill, Capt. Samuel (Mass.)
Miller, Jesse (S. C. and Ga.)
Morgan, Gen. Daniel (Va.)
Moore, James (S. C.)
Moore, John (S. C.)
Moore, Maurice (S. C.)
Morrow, Robert (Md.)
Morrow, Capt. William (N. C.)
Morton, Joseph (Va.)

McCall, Banajah (Mass.)
McCall, Charles (S. C. and Ga.)
McCall, David (S. C. and Ga.)
McCall, Francis (N. C.)
McCall, George (S. C. and Ga.)
McCall, Henry (S. C.)
McCall, Hugh (N. C. and Ga.)
McCall, James (N. C.)
McCall, James (S. C.)
McCall, James (Penn.)
McCall, James (Va.)
McCall, James (John) (S. C.)
McCall, John (Thomas) (S. C. and Ga.)
McCall, John (Ala.)
McCall, John (S. C.)
McCall, Joseph (N. C.)
McCall, Josiah (Penn. and N. C.)
McCall, Ozias (Mass.)
McCall, Samuel (Va.)
McCall, Thomas (Francis) (S. C. and Ga.)
McCall, Thomas (James) (S. C. and Ga.)
McCall, Thomas (Penn.)
McCall, Thomas (N. C.)
McCall, William (S. C. and Ga.)
McCall, William (N. C.)
McCaule, Thomas (S. C. and Ga.)
McClaghry, Col. James
McCoy, Stephen (Ga.)
McMahan, Archibald (N. C.)
McCall, John (Md.)
McCall, William (Md.)

Newkirk, Col. James (Conn.)
Nichols, Isaac (Conn.)
Nicholls, Nathan (Conn.)
Norton, Capt. Thomas (S. C.)

Ober, Josiah, Sr. (Mass.)
Ober, Josiah, Jr. (Mass.)

Parham, Drury (N. C.)
Payne, Capt. John (N. Y.)
Payne, Thomas (N. C.)
Pearce, Joshua (Ga.)
Pearce, Joshua, Jr.
Pearce, William (Ga.)
Pearce, Stephen (Ga.)
Persons, Thomas (N. C.)
Phifer, John (N. C.)
Phifer, Col. Martin (N. C.)
Phillips, Exum
Pierce, Col. William (Ga.)
Pixlee, William (Conn.)
Polk, Capt. Charles (N. C.)
Polk, Charles, Jr. (N. C.)
Pope, John (S. C.)
Pope, William (S. C.)
Porter, Capt. Billy (Conn.)
Porter, John (Mass.)
Porter, William G. (Ga.)

Quarles, Capt. John (Va.)

Raiford, Capt. Robert (N. C.)
Raines, Capt. John (S. C.)
Ramsey, Ambrose (N. C.)
Ravott, Capt. Abraham (Ga.)
Reade, George (Penn.)
Reid, Robert (S. C.)
Richardson, Daniel
Robert, John (S. C.)
Roberts, Thomas (Penn.)
Roebuck, Benjamin, Sr. (N. C.)
Roebuck, Col. Benjamin, Jr. (N. C.)
Roebuck, George (N. C.)

Schuyler, Gen. Philip (Penn.)
Scott, Capt. Matthew (Penn.)
Sevier, Major Hugh (N. C.)

Shelby, John (N. C.)
Shelby, Moses (N. C.)
Shelby, Reese (N. C.)
Shelby, Thomas (N. C.)
Shelby, Thomas, Jr. (N. C.)
Shephard, Col. Abraham (N. C.)
Silliman, Gen. (Conn.)
Simmons, John (Va. and Ga.)
Stafford, Col. William (S. C.)
Starling, Abijah (Conn.)
Starr, Joseph (Conn.)
Stewart, Matthew (N. C.)
Stuart, David (S. C.)
Stuart, David, Jr. (S. C.)
Stuart, Hardy (S. C.)
Stuart, William (S. C.)

Taylor, Col. Thomas (N. C.)
Tharpe, Vincent A. (S. C. and Ga.)
Thatcher, Col. James (N. C.)
Thompson, George (Conn.)
Tidwell, William (S. C.)
Tidwell, Capt. Francis (S. C.)

Vail, Benjamin, Sr. (N. Y.)
Vail, Benjamin, Jr. (N. Y.)
Vail, John (N. Y.)
Vail, William (N. Y.)
Venable, John (Va. and Ga.)

Walker, Samuel (S. C.)
Walker, Thomas (N. C.)
Ward, Col. Jonathan (Mass.)
Warnock, Andrew (S. C.)
Warnock, John (S. C.)
Water, Thomas (Penn.)
Watson, Capt. Patrick (Penn.)
Watson, Samuel (S. C.)
Westmoreland, Jesse (Va.)
Westmoreland, Joseph (Va.)
Whiting, John (Conn.)
Whiting, Judson (Conn.)
Whiting, Col. Samuel (Conn.)
Whiting, Samuel, Jr. (Conn.)
Whitmire, George F. (Md.)
Wilcox, John (N. C.)
Wilcoxson, David (Conn.)
Wilkerson, John (Ga.)
Wilkins, William (S. C.)
Williams, David (S. C.)
Williamson, Col. Charles (Ga.)
Williamson, Col. Micajah (Ga.)
Woodward, Hezekiah, Sr. (N. Y.)
Woodward, Hezekiah, Jr. (N. Y.)

REVOLUTIONARY PATRIOTS

Clarke, Hannah Arrington (Ga.)
Erwin, Sarah Ann Robinson (N. C.)

Howe, Sarah Grange (N. C.)
Whiting, Elizabeth Judson (Conn.)

INTERESTING ITEMS

Five REV. SOLDIERS buried Decatur Co., Ga. Their widows, Louisa F. Gaines, Hannah O'Brian, Ann Clary, Phebe Pate, and Sarah Brock, were entitled to draw in the Land Lottery of 1827 as the widows of REV. SOLDIERS.

* * * * *

REV. ABRAHAM MARSHALL was the eldest son of eight, all of whom, together with their father, REV. DANIEL MARSHALL, were REV. SOLDIERS. The father was, from 1772-1784, the pastor of Kiokee Church, the First Baptist Church in Georgia. After his death his son Rev. Abraham Marshall carried on his work.

* * * * *

REV. JOHN SPRINGER was the first Presbyterian Minister to be ordained south of the Savannah River, Ga. He was ordained by the S. C. Presbytery at Washington, Ga., 1790.

* * * * *

Found in the Department of Archives, Atlanta, Ga. (1935), Miss Ruth Blair, State Historian:

Claims for Revolutionary Services of JOHN LEFTWICK and JOHN LYNCH, Nov. 7, 1814, in the office of Ordinary, Putnam Co., Ga. Also in the same office, the Claims of ABRAHAM CUTLIFF and WILLIAM J. STEPHENS, Sept. 20, 1823, REV. SOLDIERS of Putnam Co., Ga.

* * * * *

Dr. Alfred Clark Mathews (son of Rev. Philip Mathews), was the grandfather of Corra May White, who married Rev. Lundy Harris. She was the well known Southern author and writer of Georgia — "Corra Harris" of Rydal, Ga.

* * * * *

April 10, 1815, William Wellborn was appointed attorney for the following REV. SOLDIERS "to apply for whatever money was due them for their service in the 5th N. C. Militia, stationed at Norfolk and under the command of Col. Richard Atkinson", SAMUEL MILLICAN, NATHAN WOODRIDGE, THOMAS WHITE, THOMAS LAIN (or Lane), ISAAC COLTRANE, and SETH DIXON.

* * * * *

Notice from the "Augusta Chronicle", Augusta, Ga.:

"Spirit of Seventy-Six Marriage. Another Hero of the Revolution has fallen, before the shrine of Hymen, but even in his fall he triumphs. Thus runs the proud memorial of his glory. On the 25th ult. was united in the holy bonds of matrimony by John McGehee, Esq., MR. DAVID HODGE of Columbia Co., aged 40 years. Mr. Hodge was at Braddock's defeat and served throughout the whole period of the Revolutionary War."

* * * * *

From Georgia Gazette:

"Died July 17, 1788 on his passage from Charleston, S. C. to Martinico - EMANUEL PETER DELEPLAIQUE. A Captain in the late Continental Army, Batt. of Infantry, raised in the State of Georgia during the late War."

* * * * *

WILLIAM DUFFEL, DANIEL SHINE, and CHARLES RALEY, all REV. SOLDIERS of Ga., went to Milledgeville, Ga., 1825 to see Marquis de La Fayette on his visit to America.

* * * * *

On the evening of May 11, 1775, soon after the news of the Battle of Lexington, six adventurers broke into the powder magazine in Savannah, Ga. and took possession of the stores of ammunition. Some of the captured booty was for the use of Ga. Troops, some sent to S. C., and some to Boston, and was used at the Battle of Bunker Hill. The beardless Captain of the band was JOSEPH HABERSHAM. The others were NOBLE W. JONES, EDWARD TELFAIR, JOSEPH CLAY, WILLIAM GIBBONS, and JOHN MILLEDGE.

* * * * *

In Monterey Square, Savannah, Ga., a monument was erected to COUNT PULASKI, the Heroic Pole, who fell mortally wounded fighting for American Liberty at the Siege of Savannah, Oct. 9, 1779.

* * * * *

Eliza (Majors) Carleton, a Real Daughter of the American Revolution Society, born Halifax Co., Va., Dec. 5, 1806; died Senoia, Ga., Oct. 8, 1906. Married Samuel Carleton, came to Oglethorpe Co., Ga., then Coweta Co. She was the daughter of SAMUEL MAJORS, REV. SOLDIER, and his wife Elizabeth Greene, of Va.

* * * * *

Found on a tombstone of a REV. SOLDIER in the "Old Sapp" graveyard on lower River Road to Eastman, Ga., about 4 miles from Hawkinsville, Ga.:

"Sacred to the Memory of ARCHIBALD ODOM, a Minister of the Gospel, a Gentleman, and a REVOLUTIONARY SOLDIER."

* * * * *

"Died Feb. 3, 1797 at Savannah, Ga., Mrs. Elizabeth Wright, widow of the late Mr. William Wright, a charitable and benevolent lady, who during the American Revolution, assisted many of the Officers and Soldiers that were on Board the prisonships in the Savannah River, and through whose means, many valuable citizens were restored to their families. A REVOLUTIONARY PATRIOT."

* * * * *

From Georgia Gazette:

"Died — ANDRE JENVANCEALE, REV. SOLDIER born in Marseilles, France; died 1809, age 78 years, at Savannah, Ga. Left widow at Savannah."

* * * * *

BACHELER, Nancy 316
BACHLOTT, John 15, 291
   Joseph 15
BACHOLTS, John 265
BACKUS, Lucretia 83
BACON, Ann 223
   Catherine 15
   Eliza Winn 15
   Frances 48
   Francis 109
   Henry 15
   John 15
   Capt. John 17
   Col. John 15
   Joseph 15
   Mary 247
   Rebecca 191
   Sarah 15
   Thomas 15
   William 15
BACOT, Capt. 22
   Capt. Samuel 328
BAGBY, Abner 16
   An. 16
   Betty 16
   Dicey 16
   Flumes 16
   George 15
   George W. 16
   Henry 16
   Jeffries 16
   John 16, 291
   Joseph 16
   Mariana 16
   Rachel 16
   Sally 16
   William 16
BAGGETT, Josiah 323
BAGLEY, Herman 291
   Lucy 58
   Susan 58
BAGWELL, John D. 265
   John Daniel 16
BAILEY, — 136
   Capt. — 101
   Abigail 171
   Ann 55
   Bethany 12

BAILEY, Charles 291
   Christopher 291
   Henry 291
   James 322
   Keziah 316
   Mary 220
   Nathaniel 241
   Stephen 291, 311
BAILLIE, Ann Elizabeth 37
BAINES, Thomas 1
BAIRD, Mary 92
BAKER, Miss — 224
   Amelia Rebecca Rudolph 16
   Ann 304
   Beal 16, 265, 324
   Benjamin 16
   Charles 265, 291, 311
   Chas. 322
   Christopher, Sr. 291
   Dempsey 280, 325
   Elizabeth 191
   James 16
   Jane 316
   Col. John 16, 137, 154, 214, 258,
     328
   Joshua 16, 182, 291
   Mary Anne 154
   Mary Ann 16
   Matilda Amanda 17
   Polly 16
   Real 291
   Rebecca 18, 240
   Sarah 15, 16, 76, 304, 316
   William 240
BALDASSEE, Isaac 311
BALDWIN, Mrs. — 94
   Abraham 17, 83, 258
   Augustus 17
   Augustus Collins 17
   David, Sr. 17
   Ephriam 282
   Francis 99, 285, 286, 288
   Louise 17
   Mary Ann (Nancy) 82
   Owen 282, 288
   Polly 185
   William 282
   William Henry 17

BALDWIN, Wm. 17
BALL, — 64
   Annulet 10
   Edward 17
   John 18, 265
BALLARD, — 271
   Miss — 175
   Frederick 291
   James 291
   Mary 78
   Sarah 168
   William 10
BALLENGER, Joseph 243
   Mildred Thornton 243
BALLINGER, William 194
BANDY, Lewis 291
BANKS, Mrs. David 91
   Drury 291
   James 7
   James Jones 7
   John 322
   Mary 45
   Rachel (Jones) 7
   William 291
BANKSTON, Abner 18, 265, 291
   Delphia 18
   Elizabeth 18
   Esther 18
   Hiram 18
   Isabella Lea 18, 68, 123
   Lawrence 328
   Laurence 18, 123
   Martha 18
   Priscilla 18
   Susanna 18
BARBER, Amelia 24, 237
   Charles 280
   Ellen 65
   Joseph 281
   Keziah 58
   Rhoda 281
   William 65
BARFIELD, Winny 304
BARGESON, Elizabeth 304
BARKER, Amey 168
   John 291
   Joseph 291
   Mary 304

BARKLEY, William 291
BARKLY, William 325
BARKSDALE, F. 304
   John 42
BARNARD, Georgia A. 18
   Henrietta 18
   James 18
   Col. John 18
   Major John 18
   John W. 18
   Lucy 18
   Mary E. 18
   Timothy 18
BARNES, Mr.— 1
   Abner 58
   Jincey 49
   Mae 304
   Martha 103
   Mary 208
   Richard 275
   William 275, 291
BARNETT, — 43, 95
   Abraham 18
   Ann 19, 20, 24
   Caroline 316
   Charles 19, 94
   Claiborne 20
   Clayborne 287
   David 20
   Elizabeth 19, 20, 21
   Emily 19
   Frances 21
   Frank 19
   Capt. Jacob 209
   Jane 19
   Joel 19, 20, 94, 155, 311
   John 19, 20, 21, 125, 227, 265
   John F. 19
   Leonard 20
   Lilly 21
   Lucy 21
   Lucy Greene 19
   Margaret 19, 316
   Martha 19, 21, 89
   Mary 19, 21, 56, 95, 125, 169, 221
   Mial 20
   Nathan 19, 20, 227, 275
   Nathaniel 19, 20, 21

BATTLE, Sarah Whitehead 23, 50
    Serena A. Ragan 219
    Susan Faucette 23
    William Sumner 23
    Wm. Sumner 265
BAUCOM, Molly 251
BAXTER, — 196
    Col. — 80
    Andrew 2, 24, 105
    Cynthia 24
    Eli H. 24
    Eliza T. 24
    Elizabeth 304
    Frances 24
    James 24, 265
    John 24
    Mary 24
    Richard 24
    Thomas 24
BAY, Moses 291
BAYLESS, Sarah 316
BAYTOP, Capt. James 211
BAZDELL, Joseph 282, 290
    Phoebe 282, 290
BAZELWOOD, Richard 275
BAZEMORE, Thomas 291
BEAL, Jacob 32
    Rebeckah 32
BEALE, Zephamiah 129
BEALL, Amelia 24
    Amelia Jane 24
    Anna 24
    Elias 24
    Elizabeth 74
    Frederick 24
    Jeremiah 24
    Josiah 24
    Major 24
    Martha 24
    Nancy 21
    Nathaniel 311
    Gen. Resin 24
    Rutha 304
    Samuel 24
    Thaddeus 24
    Walton 24
BEARD, Eve 304
    Moses 311

BEARD, Robert 291, 321
BEARDEN, Humphrey 311
    Sarah 46
BEASLEY, Ambrose 275
    Ann 141
    James 275
    Leonard 2
    Richard 275
    Theodosia Elizabeth 165
    Thomas, Sr. 311
    William 275, 291
BEATTY, Thomas 111, 320
BEAUCHAMP, William 181
BEAVERS, Elizabeth 304
    William 265
BEAZLEY, Henry 291
BECK, Ann J. S. 97
    John 24, 237
    Sarah 304, 310
BECKHAM, Capt. Abner 182
    Albert G. 25
    Amanda 83
    Elizabeth 42
    Elizabeth H. 25
    Erasmus G. 25
    John Y. 278
    Mary B. 25
    Nancy 25
    Rebecca 239
    Samuel 25, 265, 291
    Sol 291
    Susan 25
BECKMAN, Laban 265
BEDELL, Absolem 275
BEDFORD, Philip H. 265
BEDGOOD, Elizabeth 211, 212
    John 291
BEDINGFIELD, Charles 275
BELCHER, Elizabeth 147
    Robert 25
BELFIELD, Frances 241
BELIN, Peter Belin 97
BELL, Ann 36
    Anna 26
    David 25
    Eleanor 26
    Elizabeth 25, 26, 310
    Frances 225

BELL, Francis 25, 265
   George 185
   J. 2
   James 25, 136
   John 25, 225
   Joseph 25, 26, 136, 185
   Joseph Scott 25
   Lucretia 64
   Martha 25
   Mary 25, 26
   Milly L. 26
   Nancy 25, 139
   Nath'l 271
   P. 304
   Peggy (Margaret) 135
   Polly 25
   Rebecca 26
   Sarah 25, 304
   Tephan 271
   Thomas 25, 26, 136
   William 25
BELLAH, James 26
   Morgan 26
   Peggy 26
   Rachel 26
   Robert 26
   Samuel 26, 291
   Steele 26
   Tempee 26
   Walter 26
BELLAMY, Mary 304
BELLEW, Jacob 265
BELLINGER, John 272
   Mary 304
BENEDICT, Eliakim 328
BENJAMIN, Clara 83
   Elizabeth Inman 131
   John 83, 328
BENNEFIELD, John 26
   Martha 26
   Mary Ann 26
BENNETT, Cynthia 120
   Daniel 291
   Elizabeth 76
   Moses 277
   Richard 265
   Sallie 76
   Sarah Ann 88

BENSON, Elizabeth 304
   Enoch 291, 323
   Isaac 291
   John 162
BENTLEY, — 101, 177
   Capt. — 13
   Abi 304
   Chloe 118
   Jesse 291
   William 118
BENTON, Col. — 199
   Annie 87
   Ephriam 328
   George Constantine 26
   Eugenius 26
   John 291
   Joseph 282, 291
   Mary 304
   Nancy 186
   Nathan 26
   Nelson Moore 26
   Parmelia Frances 26
   Susanna 186
   Thomas H. 26
BERGAMONT, Lucretia 63
BERRIAN, John 265
BERRIEN, Eliza 27
   John 164
   Major John 278
   Major Gen. John 26
   Julia 27
   Richard 27
   Ruth Lowndes 27
   Sarah 27
   Thomas 27
   Thomas M. 155
BERNEN, Weems 27
BERRY, Bananza 27
   Isham 291
   John 27, 192, 265
   Naomi 27
   Obediah 27
   Salome 27, 192
   Thomasine 143
BERRYHILL, Anderson 271
BESINGER, Jacob 277
BETHUNE, John 144
   Peters 291

BEVERS, Jane 304
BEVILLE, Claiborne 27
  Clayborne 63
  Frances 27
  Garnett 27
  Granville 27
  James 27
  Paul 27, 279
  Robert 27, 63, 279
BEVINS, William 291
BIBB, Senator B. S. 90
  Benajah Smith 28
  Delia 28
  Dorothy 188
  Elizabeth 28
  Hannah 28
  John Dandridge 28
  Joseph Wyatt 28
  Lucy 28
  Martha 28
  Peyton 28
  Sallie Booker 28
  Sally 84
  Sally Wyatt 20, 21
  Thomas 28
  Dr. William 84
  Wm. 21, 27
  Wm. Wyatt 28
BIFFLE, John 291
BIGGERS, — 192
  Susanna 182
BIGHAM, Joshua 199
BILLINGSLEY, J. 92
  Mary 222
BILLS, Jonathan 191
  Lucy 191
  Martha Goodwin 191
BILLUPS, Ann 72
  Virginia Beverly 106
BINUM, Drury 272
BIRD, Miss — 69
  Ann 67
  Ariana 28
  Benjamin 275
  Betsey (Elizabeth) 29
  Caroline 28
  Catherine 28
  Caty 29

BIRD, Dice 29
  Eliza 28
  Elizabeth 179
  Emily 28
  Fanny 29
  Fitzgerald 28
  James 124
  John 28, 29, 275
  Louisa 28
  Mary (Martha) Elizabeth 179
  Philemon 28
  Price 29
  Tabitha 29
  Thomas 292
  Dr. Thompson 245
  William 28
  Williamson 28, 29
  Wilson 28
BIRDSEY, Nathan 328
BIRDSONG, John 291
  Mary 32
BISHOP, James 282, 288
  John 192
  Phoebe 282, 288
  Simeon 64
  Stephen 78
BIVINS, Martin Luther 29
  Wm. 29
BLACK, James 328
  John 325
  Lemuel 292
  Mary 76
  Thomas 292
  William 292, 320, 323
BLACKBURN, Daniel 168
  Elizabeth 244
  Nathan 292
  Samuel 152
BLACKEMAN, Edward 328
BLACKSHEAR, Ann Elizabeth 29
  David 29
  Brig. Gen. David 100
  Edward 265
  Gen. Edward 170
  Edward Jefferson 29
  Elijah 29
  Eliza Ann 29
  Elizabeth 35

BLACKSHEAR, Everard 29
Floyd 29
James B. 131
James H. 29
John Duke 29
Joseph 29
Mary 29
Wm. T. 29
BLACKWELL, Sally Chandler 310
Wm. 265
BLACKWOOD, Jane 304
BLAIR, Harrison 89
James 29, 311
John 171
Mary 96
Nancy 304
Ruth 18
BLAKE, Benjamin 113
Olive 160
William 160
BLAKELEY, Miss — 19
William 292
BLAKEMAN, Lemuel 328
Capt. Samuel 328
BLALOCK, Eleanor 316
BLANCHARD, Sarah 304
BLANFORD, Cark 292
BLANKS, James, Jr. 292
Nancy 304
BLASENGAME, Benjamin 29
Elizabeth 30
Frances 29
James 29
Nancy 29
Philip 29
Polly 29
BLEDSOE, Benjamin 292, 322
Betsey 30
Eunice 139
Jane 30, 139
Margaret 304
Miller 30, 292, 325
Capt. Miller 328
Moses 30
Nancy 30
Peachy 30
Polly 30
Sarah 103

BLEDSOE, Sidney 30
Unie 30
BLEWETT, Hannah 245
Jean 146
BLITCH, Ann 304
BLOODGOOD, Louisa 91
BLOODWORTH, David Madison 30
Fanny 30
Hiram 30
Lymise Proctor 30
Mary Ann 30
Samuel 30
Simeon 30
Solomon 30
Thomas 30
Thomas S. M. 30
BLOUNT, Captain 94
Gov. — 210
Elizabeth 131
Isaac 324
Lucy 304
Thomas 75
William 292
BLYTHE, Capt. Benjamin 328
Rogers 292
BOATRIGHT, Margaret 304
BOBBITT, William 320
BOBO, Lewis 328
Milly 195
Sampson 328
BOEN, Stephen 292
BOGAN, Elizabeth 304
BOGGESS, Jeremiah 166
BOGGS, Eve 316
Ezekiel 292
Joseph 280, 282, 292
BOHAM, Joseph 292
BOHANAN, Lydia 316
BOILE, Charles 292
BOISFEUILLET, John James
Penfield 12
BOLING, — 209
BOLLES, John 292
BOLLING, Capt. Robert 121
BOLT, Mary 87
BOLTON, — 177
Anna 3
Chris W. 304

346

BOLTON, Elisha P. 31
   Elizabeth 30
   John T. 30
   Lydia 80
   Martha 30
   Mary 30, 78, 316
   Matthew 30
   Millie 30
   Nancy P. 30
   Robert 30
   Samuel 30
   Thomas 30
BOND, Cornelia 91
   Nathan 290
   Richard 274
   Richard C. 292
BONDS, Joseph 324
BONE, Archibald 292
   Susanna 77
BONNELL, Anthony 27, 31, 139
   Daniel 31
   Elizabeth 31
   Jane 139
   Mary 27, 31
   Sarah Ann 27
   William 31
BONNER, Henry 31
   Luranie 43
   Mary Pleasant 217
   Richard 31
   Robert 31
BONTWELL, Mary 89
BOOKER, Mrs. (nee Clark) 28
   Betsey 227
   Betsey Ann 19
   John 292
   Mary Cobb 21, 121
   Simpson 174
   William 292
BOOKES, Martha M. 57
BOON, Jess 292
BOONE, Daniel 171
   Squire 171
BOOTH, Daniel 328
   Edwina 1
   James 328
   John 1
   Capt. Nathan 328

BOOTY, Elizabeth 216
BORING, David 31
   Elizabeth 31, 108
   Isaac 31, 265, 292, 311
   John 31
   Joseph 108
   Phoebe 31
   Rebecca 31
   Robert 31
   Sarah (Senah) 31
   Susanna 49
   Susannah 31, 108
BORLAND, Isaac 287
BOSTIC, Betsey 31
   Elizabeth 235, 236
   Elizabeth (Bostwick) 125
   Littleberry, Jr. 236
   Nathan 236
BOSTICK, Betsey 32
   Caroline 119
   Caroline Verlinda 32
   Chesley 31
   Don Frederick 32
   Elizabeth 31, 32
   Fillmon 32
   Henrietta 31
   Hillery 32
   Homer 32
   Jacob 32
   Jeremiah 32
   John 31, 32
   John Rufus 32
   Littleberry 31, 32, 267, 278
   Mary 32
   Mary Ann 31
   Matilda Golden 32
   Nathan 32, 278
   Nathaniel 32
   Polly 32
   Sarah Maria 31
   Susanna Addison 32
BOSTON, James 32
   John 32
BOSTWICK, Chesley 47
   Elizabeth 47
   Jane 281
   Mary 86, 316
   Nathan 281

BOSTWICK, Sally 190
Samuel 86, 189
BOSWELL, Sarah 304
BOTSFORD, Edmund 32
BOURNE, Ann 97
BOUTIN, John 281
BOUTON, Bridget 111
BOUTWELL, Mary 220, 221
BOWDEN, Emily 100
James 311
BOWDRE, Joicy T. 78
BOWEN, Commodore 33
Elijah 311
Dr. Isaac 10
John 51, 292, 311
Oliver 32
S., Sr. 292
Samuel 325
BOWER, Capt. Michael 56
BOWERS, Elizabeth 234
BOWLES, Nathan 311
BOWLING, Edward 292
(Bolling), Jean 30
BOWMAN, Col. — 193
BOX, Martha 69
BOYD, — 84
Elizabeth 66
Jane 225
John 280
Phoebe 161
Thomas 292
BOYKIN, Amelia Mildred 243
Bius (Bias) 33
Burwell 33, 328
Capt. Burwell 33
Eliza 199
Elizabeth 33
Francis 265
Major Francis 33, 199, 328
James 33
Jeany 33
John 33, 189
Lurania 4
Nancy 33
Samuel 33
Capt. Samuel 33
Solomon 33
Thomas 33

BOYNTON, Miss — 160
BOZEMAN, Mr. — 172
Ralph 311, 321
BRACH, Elezur, Sr. 292
Sarah 316
BRACK, Benjamin 279
Miss — 5
John 265
BRACKENBERRY, Mary 144
BRADBERRY, Lewis 292
BRADDOCK, John 33
BRADDY, Lewis 292
BRADFORD, Ann 316
Margaret 125
Mary 304
Nancy 14, 95
Nathaniel 33
Rebecca (Pace) 139
Thomas 95, 265
BRADLEY, — 65
Dr. — 135
Miss — 217
Avey 211
James 167
John 33, 292, 311
John A. 33
Dr. John A. 155
Mary Ardis 34
Ruth 178
BRADSHAW, — 30
BRADY, Samuel 311
William 282
Wm. 289
BRAEZAL, Henry Willis 250
BRAGG, Mary 304
William 292
BRAINERD, Abigail 66
BRAMBLETT, Henry 292
Nathan 185
BRAMLETT, Reuben 323
BRANCH, Arnistead 34
Emily 34
Hester 316
James 34, 311
John 34
Judith 34
Julia 34
Leah 34

BROCK, Stephen 265
BROCKMAN, Bledsoe 139
  Lewis 292
BROOKINS, Nancy 316
BROOKS, Allen 35
  Charles E. 35
  George 323
  Isaac 35
  James 35, 292
  Jane 119
  Joab 35
  John 35, 311, 328
  John H. 35
  John Hanna 265
  Mary 304
  Micajah 35, 292
  Middleton 321
  Philip H. 35
  Rachel 316
  Robert 292, 311
  Samuel 35
  Sarah 35, 205, 304
  Susan 134
  William, Sr. 292
  William T. 35
  Capt. Zachray Smith 50
BROOMFIELD, — 19
  Mary 19
BROUGHTON, Sarah 34
BROWN, — 132, 173, 192
  Alexander 2
  Ambrose 292
  Anderson 288
  Andrew 265
  Ann 304
  Benjamin 35, 265, 290, 292, 323
  Betsey (Lange) 99
  Dempsey 292
  Edward 279, 292
  Elijah 19
  Elisha 292
  Elizabeth 34, 55, 99, 101, 316
  Eloise 126
  Ezekiel 35, 326
  Frances 316
  Frederick 198, 292
  Henry 323
  Capt. Isaac 328

BROWN, Isabella 48
  Gen. J. Epps 203
  James 275, 292, 311
  James N. 290
  Jeremiah 277
  Jesse 311
  John 35, 55, 221, 265, 280, 292, 326
  John R. 266
  Joseph 311
  Josiah 328
  Laonie 316
  Larkin 292
  Lewis 311
  Lucinda 173
  Mary 316
  Merideth 292
  Mordecai 311
  Col. Mordecai 286
  Moses 292
  Patsey 85
  Rebecca 316
  Reuben 99
  Samuel 292
  Sarah 16, 45, 304
  Sarah J. B. 32
  Stark 286
  Starke 280, 282
  Susan 176
  Teziah 119
  Thomas 80
  Uriah 292
  Wallis 311
  William P. 278, 292
BROWN (BESOON), Peter 271
BROWNE, Ambrose 323
BROWNFIELD, Capt. 4
BROWNING, Clara 62
  Elizabeth 5
  John 31, 62
  Margaret 305, 316
  Phoebe 31
BROWNSON, Elizabeth 35, 305
  Nathan 35, 265
BRUCE, Elizabeth 305, 316
  William 292
BRUMFIELD, John 272, 280
BRUSON, Frances 316

BRUNSTON, Alexander 277
   George 277
   Josiah 277
   Wm. 277
BRYAN, Andrew 130
   Ann 36, 316
   Ann Penelope 56
   Blake 35
   David 292
   Dorcas 305
   Elizabeth 36, 100, 247
   Elizabeth (Pendarvis) 202
   Hannah 36
   Hugh 36
   James 35, 292
   Jason 85
   John 36
   John Hill 56
   Jonathan 36, 258
   Joseph 36
   Josiah 36, 202
   Mary 36, 305
   Mary Ann 251
   Mary (Polly) 247
   Nancy 305
   Sarah 310
   Sarah Jenet 36
   Sue 305
   Thomas, Sr. 311
   William 35, 36
BRYANT, Benjamin 36
   Hugh 36
   Isaac 272
   John 36
   Martha 36
   William Lane 36
BUCHAN, Margaret 163
BUCHANAN, Benjamin 36
   George 325
   George H. 292
   James 282, 285, 292
   James P., Sr. 280
   Mary 316
BUCHER, Ann 95
BUCHOLLER, Peter 326
BUCK, Frances Oliver 248
BUCKLES, Peter 292
BUCKNER, Benjamin 292

BUDDEST, Daniel 277
BUFFINGTON, Mary 91
BUFORD, John, Sr. 272
   William 265
   Wm. 282
BUGG, Edward 271
   Elizabeth 138
   Mary Elizabeth 36
   Obedience 36, 151
   Priscilla 138
   Sarah 129
   Sarah Sherwood 100
   Sherwood 36, 100, 133, 138, 151
   Wm. 36
BUISE, Margaret 316
BULGER, Ann 78
BULL, Elizabeth 305
   Henry 328
   John 265, 328
   Richard 328
   Col. Thomas 328
   William 328
BULLARD, Allen 37
   Ann 26, 37, 310
   Delilah 36
   Elizabeth 37
   Nancy 37
   Sarah 37
   Tapley 26, 37
   Temperance 37
   Thomas 26, 37
   Thomas P. 37
BULLOCH, Anna 39
   Archibald 37, 38, 39
   President Archibald 97
   Archibald Stobo 37
   Charles Irvine 39
   Christina 39
   Feribee 68
   Irvine Stephens 39
   James 37, 39
   James D. 39
   James Stephens 37, 39
   Jane 37
   Jean 39
   John Irvine 37
   Martha 39
   Wm. Bellinger 37

BULLOCK, Alexander Gordon 40
    Archibald 257, 258
    Daniel 280
    David 40
    Frances Roy 40
    Hawkins 265, 292
    Major James S. 214
    Jane 71
    John 40
    John Gordon 40
    Hawkins 40
    Hawkins Sherman 40
    Louise Nance 40
    Lucy L. 40
    Martha (Stewart)(Elliott) 214
    Mary 144
    Mary Wyatt 40
    Nathaniel 40, 144
    Nathaniel H. 40
    Richard 292
    Richard Henley 40
    Susanna 40
    William Gordon 40
    Zacheriah 40
BULLOUGH, Elias 326
BUNCOMBE, Col. — 94
BUNTZ, Christiana 50, 192
    Urban 192
BURBRIDGE, Elijah 31
BURCH, — 25
    Benj. 101
    Blanton 40
    Charles 40, 271
    Edward 40, 271, 292, 311
    Elizabeth 42
    Gerard 42
    Jane 42
    Jared 287
    John 42
    Joseph E. 40
    Kilt 40
    Morton Newman 42
    Richard C. 42
    Seleta 42
    William P. 42
BURDEN, Hannah 305, 310
BURFORD, John 41, 282, 289
    Phoebe 41, 282, 289

BURFORD, Wm. 311
BURGAMY, William 41, 292
BURGE, Nancy 85
BURGESS, Mrs. — 182
    Capt. Edward 24
    Effie 136
    Josiah 311
BURGOYNE, Gen. — 115
BURKALTER, Jacob 265
BURKE, — 19
    Edmund 258
    Capt. John 74
    Joseph 292
    Dr. M. 74
    Michael 142
    Phoebe 94
    William 292
BURKET, Lemuel 292
BURKETT, Uriah 311
BURKHALTER, Barbara 41
    Isaac 41
    Jacob 41, 292
    Jeremiah 41
    John 41, 265
    Joshua 41, 265
    Mary 41
    Michael 41, 292
    Sarah 41
BURNETT, Jeremiah 62, 219
    Molly 316
    Nancy 65
    Naomi 65
    Capt. Peter 72
BURNEY, — 114
    A. 278
    Elizabeth 305
    John 282, 290
BURNLEY, Capt. — 139
    Ann 41
    Elizabeth 41
    Henry 41, 42, 292
    Israel 41
    Lucy Barksdale 41
    Richmond 41
    Sarah 41, 120
    Stephen G. 42
    Susan 42
BURNS, Elizabeth 151

BURNS, Schupert 66
BURNSIDE, Ann 305
BURR, Aaron 63
BURROUGH, Sarah Ann Owen 65
BURROUGHS, Capt. 231
  Rebecca 117
  Capt. Stephen 328
BURRUS, Elizabeth 152
BURSON, Nancy 305
BURT, Moody 42, 282, 286
BURTON, — 120
  Abraham 121, 177
  Elizabeth Neal 211
  John 292
  Nicholas 178
  Rachel 305
  Rhoda 305
  Rhoda (Hubbard) 211
  Richard 121, 211
  Sophia 68
  Susan Virginia 177
  Thomas 42, 178, 211, 290, 292
BURTZ, Michael 328
BURWELL, Capt. — 8
  Annabelle 189
  John 189
  Mary 152, 189
  William, Sr. 292
BUSBIN, Sarah 305
BUSH, Jane 196
  Levi 292
  John 147
  Prescot 327
  Samuel 292
  Thomas 289
BUSSEY, Amey 42, 282, 287
  Hezekiah 42, 282, 287
BUTLER, — 37
  Miss — 155
  Ann 140
  Anne 149
  Barsheba 208
  Constantia 153
  David 42
  Edmund 42, 203, 275
  Edward 42, 248
  Elizabeth 43
  Frances 43

BUTLER, Frances Wade 203
  Hannah 316
  John 43, 138, 292
  Major Col. John 1
  John W. 42
  Kitty 43
  Lucy 43
  Marcy C. 316
  Nancy 43, 211
  Patrick 43, 265, 290, 311
  Peter B. 26
  Peter Patrick 211
  Rebecca 43
  Samuel 208
  Sarah 208
  Susanna 203
  Thomas 140
  Thomas Cooper 131
  William 275
  Capt. Wm. 240
  Zacheriah 42, 265
BUTRIL, William, Sr. 292
BUTRILL, Elizabeth 21
  Martha 21
  Wm. 21
BUTT, Elizabeth 141
  James 292
  Nancy 161
BUTTRILL, Asa 43
  Brittain 43
  Burwell 43
  Elizabeth 43
  Jesse 43
  John 43
  Mary 43
  Nancy 43
  Thomas 43
  William 43
BUTTS, Clara 88
  Solomon 275
  Wm. 88
BUXTON, Samuel 43
  William 43
BYNANT, Sugars 311
BYNE, Ann 106
BYNUM, Drewry 292
  Silvey 305
BYRD, Benjamin 277

BYRD, John 292

CABANISS, Eldridge Guerry 43
  Elijah 43
  George 43
  H. B. 43
  Henry 43, 311
  Mathew 43
  Mary 43
  Nathan 43
  Palatia 43
  Rebecca 43
  Sandall 43, 164
CABENISS, Henry 290
CABOS, John 292, 326
CADE, Capt. — 70
  Drury 250, 275
  James 250
  Lucretia 250
  Mary 146
CAFFLE, Timothy 277
CAIN, John 275, 285
  Nancy 232
CAISON, Willoughby 311
CALDER, A. Seraphina 44
  Alexander 44
  Allen Powell 44
  Ann 44
  Catherine A. 44
  Esther 44
  Eugene M. 44
  George W. 44
  Henrietta 44
  Hugh P. 44
  James Rickey 44
  John 44, 265, 325
  John Morrison 44
  Margery 44
  Maria 44
  Mary 44
  Robert Patrick 44
  Sarah 44
  William Horton Hazzard 44
  William McKay 44
CALDER (CAULDER), John 44
CALDWELL, Col. William 74
CALEF, Letisha 305
CALETROP, William 271

CALHOUN, Charlotte 234
CALICUTT, Dicey Jane 34
CALL, Capt. — 236
  Richard 287
CALLAHAN, John 311
  Josias 325
CALLAWAY, — 192
  Miss — 84
  Addah 45
  Bethany 45
  Clarissa 114
  Elizabeth 244
  Enoch 45
  Eunice 168
  Isaac 44, 192
  Jacob 44
  Jemina 103
  Job 45, 114
  John 44
  Joseph 44, 114, 192
  Mary 45
  Nancy 45, 230
  Peter 266
  Pheribee 45
  Rev. Wm. A. 189
CALLWALADER, Gen. John 328
CAMBER, Dorothy 237
  Sarah Ann 97
CAMDEN, Earl of 258
CAMERON, Alexander 56
  Benjamin H. 45
  David 45
  Flora 45
  James 45, 266, 293
  James Hawthorne 45
  Janie 45
  Margaret 56
  Sarah 45
  Susie 45
  Thomas 45
  William 45, 293
CAMP, Benjamin 45
  Cecilius 45
  Chander 45
  Claudely 46
  Edward 292
  Elizabeth 45, 46
  Gerard 46, 138

355

CASH, Dorson 293, 311
 Howard 293
 James 274, 293
 Jesse 98
 John 290, 293, 321
 Peter 320
 Sarah 316
CASON, William 49, 293, 326
 Willis 293, 311
 Willoughby 293
CASSELL, Ephriam 320
CASTER, Silas 320
CASTLEBERRY, Abigail 87
 Emma 45
CASWELL, Col. — 205
 Col. Lytle 166
CATCHING, Benjamin 49
 Joseph 49
 Philip 49
CATCHINGS, Col. Benjamin 275
 Joseph 49, 275
 Joseph 49
 Laymore 282, 286
 Merideth 275
 Philip 275
 Major Seymour 275
CATE, Ann 31
CATES, Hannah 305
CATLETT, Sarah 228
CATRON, Mr. — 24
CATTEN, Elizabeth 24
CAUSEY, Ezekiel 281, 293
 Elizabeth 281
CEBELLE, Matthews 180
CHADWELL, Capt. Daniel 174
CHADWICK, Elizabeth 242
CHAMBERS, Thomas 7
 Lettice 282, 287
 Martha 316
 Robert 282, 287
CHAMBLESS, Chris 293
 S. 305
CHAMPION, John 293
CHANCE, Mary 305
 Simpson 293
CHANDLER, — 92
 John 275, 293
 Sheildcake 324

CHANEY, — 166
CHAPLAINE, — 79
CHAPLIN, Mary Ann 172
CHAPMAN, — 150
 Capt. — 224
 Miss — 144
 Abner 293
 Benjamin 50, 108
 D. S. 209
 Edward 172
 Isiah 209
 John 49, 293
 Lydia 305
 Mary 30
 Nathan 49, 108, 293
 Polly 101
 Thomas 50, 108
CHAPPELL, John 293
CHAPPELLE, Sophia 126
CHAPTER, Col. Wm. Few 13
CHARLTON, Arthur M. 149
 Thomas 149
CHATFIELD, George W. 128
CHEADLE, Elizabeth 52
 Judith 52
 Lucy 52
CHEATHAM, Sarah 305
CHEEK, Cylass 290
 William 274, 325
 Wm. 266
CHEEKE, William 50
CHELLFINCH, Hiram 325
CHENEY, Aquilla 166, 167
 Levi 167
CHESHIRE, John 275
 Sarah 316
CHESSER, Easter 316
CHESTNUT, Needham 312
CHEWING, Catherine 227
CHICKONIMY, Mary 316
CHILD, Capt. — 127
 John 290
CHILDERS, Miss — 247
 Milliner 324
CHILDRESS, Thomas 293
CHILDS, Edith 200
 Elizabeth 316
 Lucy 127

CHILLERS, John 178
CHISM, Barbara 80
   Ellender 80
   James 80
CHISOLM, Mary 51
   Murdock 18
CHOICE, Ann 50
   Catherine 50
   Fenton 50
   Jesse 50
   John 50
   Martha 50
   Rebecca 50
   Ruth 50
   Tully 50, 266, 312
   William 50
CHRISTER, Wesley 223
CHRISTIAN, Cenas 58
   Elizabeth 58
   Gabriel 89
   John 50
   Mary 50, 178
   Pyrene 58
   Sally 305
   Turner 266, 280
CHRISTIE, Robert 50
CHRISTMAS, — 88
   Mary 212
   Richard 266, 325
CHRISTOPHER, Elizabeth 305
   William 312
CHURCH, Alonzo 51
   Abigail 51
   Timothy 51
CLAIBORNE, Elizabeth 237
CLANTON, Holt 293
CLAPP, Mr. — 239
CLARK, — 112
   Col. — 70, 185, 186
   Agatha 51
   Ann Marie 93
   Ann P. 52
   Barbara 90
   Bathsheba 52
   Benjamin 53
   Bolling 52
   Catherine 52
   Christopher 51, 52, 136, 179, 266

CLARK, Christopher Hill 51
   David 51, 152, 293
   Eliza 52
   Elizabeth 46, 52, 60, 152, 310
   Eunice H. 52
   George 293, 312
   George Washington 57
   Jacob 328
   James 52, 53
   Capt. James 7
   James C. 52
   James Opher 51
   Jeremiah 53
   John 52, 53, 275
   John T. 52
   Joseph 194
   Joseph David 52
   Joshua 51
   Josiah 90
   Judith 51, 52, 53
   Larkin 52, 53, 290
   Lucinda 52
   Lucy 51, 179, 305
   Margaret Ann 51
   Mary 51, 179, 316
   Mary Ann 136
   Mary Lewis 52
   Mary Moore 52
   Micajah 51
   Mildred 52
   Millie 51
   Mourning 25, 51, 136
   Nancy 282, 285
   Penelope 52
   Rachel 51
   Rebecca 305, 310
   Robert 52
   S. B. 305
   Sallie T. 52
   Samuel 51
   Sarah 305
   Sarah Hawkins 54
   Susan 51
   Susanna 53, 179
   Tabitha 52
   Terrell 51
   Thomas 274
   Col. Thomas 244

358

CLOWER, Elizabeth 55
  Geo. 55
  George 55
  Jane 55
  John 55
  Jonathan 55
  Mary 55
  Nancy 55
  Peter 275
  Sarah 55, 232
  Searcy 55
CLUBB, Elizabeth 216
  Thomas 216
CLYMER, George 328
COBB, Catherine 305
  Martha 28, 243
  Mary Willis 82
  Mehitable 49
  Obedience Dutiful (Bugg) 42
  Susanna 31
  Thomas 293
  Capt. Thomas 56
  William A. 166
COBBETT, Thomas 312
COCHRAN, M. 325
COCKBURN, Ge. 293
COCKE, Benjamin E. 56
  Caleb 56
  Isaac Perry 56
  John 56
  Zebulon 56
COCKERMAN, William 232
COCKRELL, Thomas, Sr. 293
COCKRUM, Matthew 293
CODY, Louisa 150
  Louise Amanda 198, 241
  Michael 150, 198
COFFEE, Cynthia 56
  Elizabeth 56
  John 56, 266
  Joshua 56
  Martha 56, 112
  Mary 56
  Nancy 56, 305
  Peter 56
  Sarah 56
  Susanna 56
COFIELD, S. 305

COHEN, Dinah 169
COHOM, Elizabeth 316
COHRON, Cornelius 275
COIL, James 293
COKER, Isaac 312
COLBERT, John 42
  Sarah 19
  Setty 40
  Susannah 310
COLBY, Samuel 293
COLDING, Blanchard 56
  Thomas 57
COLE, — 77
  Martha 172
  Mary 201
  Thomas 56
COLEMAN, Abner 293
  Benjamin 275
  Charles 57
  Daniel 275, 285
  Elisha 57
  Eliza 94
  Elizabeth 316
  Frances 249
  Francis 249
  James 275
  Jesse 312
  John 234, 266, 275, 293
  Jonathan 57
  Kate 74
  Lindsey 57
  Nancy 316
  Samuel 287, 293
  Susan 194
  Thomas 57, 275
COLLERAN, — 61
COLLEY, James, Sr. 293
  John 266
  John W. 57
  Mary 139
  Nancy 99
COLLIER, Ann 57
  Benjamin 57
  Cuthbert 57
  Elizabeth 57
  Elizabeth Wyatt 116
  Frances 57, 163
  Henrietta 154

COX, Bolling 61
  Cary 60, 198, 266
  Elizabeth 61
  Francinia 61
  John, 61, 189, 293
  Letitia 61
  Martha 61
  Mary 61
  Mary (Polly) 199
  Moses 293, 326
  Nancy 73
  Nancy Clark 61
  Orrie 125
  Richard 61, 293, 324
  Thomas 61, 293
  William 190
CRABB, Asa 293
CRABBE, Asa 312
CRABTREE, William 293
CRAFT, — 64
CRAIG, Elizabeth 239
  James 2
  John 2
  Robert 239
CRAIN, Juda 305
  Nancy 114
  Spencer 275
CRAPS, Anna Barbara 61
  Elizabeth 61
  George 61
  John 61
  John Jacob 61
CRATIN, John 61
CRAWFORD, — 19, 194
  Ann 61, 87
  Bennett 62
  Charles 61, 62
  David 62
  Elizabeth 19, 20, 30, 62
  Fannie 62
  Gay 293
  Jay 312
  James 247
  Joel 20, 61, 62
  John 280
  Lemuel 293
  Lucy 62, 310
  Malinda 233

CRAWFORD, Mary 317
  Mary Ann 317
  Nathan 62
  Patience 246
  Philip 312
  Robert 61
  Susanna 20, 26
  Vic 305
  William S. P. 72
  Hon. William Harris 228
  William Harris 62
CREDILLA, William, Sr. 293
CREENY, Rebecca 317
CRELINGTON, Jonathan 293
CRENSHAW, — 78
  Jesse 22
  Patience 22
  Precious Cain 22
CRESSWELL, Col. David 220
  Rev. James 220
  Mary 71
  Susanna 71
  William 71
CRINDER, George 74
CRITTENDEN, J. 293
CROCKER, William 145
CROCKETT, David 290, 293
  Elizabeth 36
CROISON, John 293
CRONAN, James 293
CRONICH, Rachel 317
CROPPER, Capt. John 229
  Lieut. John 113
CROSBY, Elizabeth 305
  Urill 312
  William 275
CROSS, John 312
  Stephen 293
CROSSLEY, Susanna 166
CROW, Frederick 115
  Peter 266
  Rachel 62
  Stephen 62, 219, 293
CROWELL, Henry 47
CRUMBLEY, Anthony 294, 312
  Thomas 294
CRUMP, Elizabeth 154
CRUSE, Sarah Ann 305

CRUTCHFIELD, Emma 182
John 275
Lucy 91
CULBERSON, David 328
James 328
Joseph 328
CULBERTSON, Agnes 62
Celia 317
David 62
Isaac 62
James 62
Jeremiah 62
John 62
Joseph 62
CULBREATH, Jane 305
CULPEPPER, Malakiah 294
CULVER, Nancy 317
Nathan 294
CULVERSON, Capt. — 117
CUMBER, Mary 34
CUMMINGS, Miss — 125
F. 294
J. 317
Sarah 317
Thomas 54
CUMMINS, Alexander 62
Elizabeth 62
CUNDIFF, Peggy 81
CUNNINGHAM, — 64
Alexander 17
Amanda 74
Andrew 294
Ann Pamela 28
Ansel 62, 266, 321
Ansell 324
Drury 114, 128
James 266, 278
Jane 3
John 72
Nancy 317
Capt. Robert 28
Rev. Robert M. 28
Samuel 278
William 290
CUP, Mary 63
Michael 63
CURBO, Joseph 323
CURD, Richard 63

CURETON, Martha 70, 305
Mary 48, 180
CURL, Matthew 323
CURRY, Cary 280
Peter 294
CURTISS, Elnathan 328
Joseph 328
Stiles, Sr. 328
CUTLIFF, Abraham 294, 332
Abram 134
John 134
John M. 134
CUTTS, Joseph 294
CUYLER, Henry 63

DABBS, John 294
DABNEY, Austin 275
Eliza 154
Hannah 305
Mildred 156
Samuel 156
DACHER, Ann 249
DAGGETT, Capt. 55
DALE, — 19
D'ALEY (Daley), Benjamin 279
DALEY, Benjamin 63
Elizabeth 63
John 51
Susanna 63
DALLAS, John 63
DALTON, Catherine 28
Randolf 294
DALY (D'Oilly), Benjamin 27
DALY, Susannah 27
DAMPIER, Daniel 187
John 116
DAMRON, Charles 294, 321
DANGERFIELD, Col. — 284
Col. Wm. 286
DANGIERFIELD, Col. — 250
DANIEL, Allen 63, 64, 127
Benjamin 63
Catherine 64
Charity 63, 127
David 64
Elizabeth 63, 64, 127, 240
Frederick 64, 312
Jack 64

364

DANIEL, James 10, 63, 64
  James J. 64
  Jeptha 64, 294
  Jesse 64
  John 63, 64, 266, 290, 294, 323
  Littleberry 312
  Lucinda 64
  Martha 64
  Mary 64, 317
  Matthew 64
  Moses 64
  Nancy 64
  Polly Ann 112
  Sallie 64
  Sarah 64, 317
  Sophronia 64
  Thomas 266
  William 63, 64, 266, 282
  (Daniell), John 64
DANIELL, — 104
  Abel 66
  Alfred 65
  Amos 65
  Beaden 65
  Cary 65
  Clarissa 65
  Eleanor 65
  Elizabeth 56, 65, 66
  Frances 66
  George 65
  George W. 65
  Isaac 65
  Jeremiah Melton 65
  Josiah 65
  Kenoth 66
  Mary 65
  Masters 65
  Moses 65
  Nathaniel 65
  Olive 65
  Rachel 65
  Rebecca 65
  Robert 65
  Robert Howe 65
  Stephen 65
  Lieut. Stephen B. 328
  Stephen Beadon 65
  Susannah 65

DANIELL, Theophilus 66
  Thomas 66, 193, 290
  Thomas M. 66
  William 65, 66, 328
  Wm. 285, 290
  Young 66
DANIELS, Charles 56
DANMARK, Clarissa 66
  Elizabeth 66
  John 66
  Redden 66
  Sarah 66
  Thomas Irving 66
  William 66
DANNIELLY, Elizabeth 305
DANTIGAL, John 280
DARBY, John, Sr. 281
  Richard 326
DARDEN, — 198
  Elizabeth (Betsey) 111
  George 275
DARK, — 181
DARRACOTT, Cecilia 223
DARRICOURT, John 248
  Mary 248
DARRIS, Elizabeth 317
DART, Alfred 66
  Ann Maria 66
  Cyrus 66, 266
  Edgar C. P. 66
  Eliza Ann 66
  Erastus 66
  Horace 66
  Joseph 66
  Theodore 66
  Urbanus 66
DASHER, Christian 67
  Christopher 67
  John 67
  John Martin 67
  Joshua 67
  Martin 67
  Naomi 67
  Susan 201
  Susanna 67
  Solomon 67, 251
DAUCY, Martha 28
DAUGHTRY, Jacob 294

DAUGHTRY, Joseph 294
DAUTHAM, Elijah 275
DAVENPORT, Dicy 305
    John 41, 108
    Lucy (Barksdale) 41, 42
    Thomas 67
DAVID, D. D. 99
    Isaac 294
    Isham 312
    Ishmael 207
    John 290
DAVIDSON, Gen. 165
    John 266, 294, 324
    Joseph 266, 294, 312
DAVIE, Joseph 320
DAVIES, Daniel 294, 312
DAVIS, — 91, 228
    Capt. 231
    Dr. 241
    Absolem 275
    Benjamin 56, 237
    Catherine 145
    Charles 68
    Charles Lukens 255
    Clement 294
    Cols 67
    Elizabeth 65, 68, 162, 305
    Fanny 305
    Frances 162
    Hardy 275
    Capt. Harman 186
    Henry 294
    James 68, 162
    Jane 68, 305
    Jephtha 68
    Jesse 68
    Joel 275
    John 4, 67, 68, 162, 243, 312, 323
    Jonathan 67
    Rev. Jonathan 68
    Julia 162
    Lewis Lanier 68
    Lucretia 162
    Lucy 162
    Lydia 56
    Maria 68, 177
    Martha 68, 224
    Mary 188, 305, 317

DAVIS, Mary Ann 317
    Mary L. 232
    Mary (Polly) 224
    Melinda 13
    Nancy 3, 162, 310
    Polly 162
    Prudence 22
    Rebecca 51, 68
    Richard 162
    Sallie 3, 188
    Sally 162
    Samuel 275, 294
    Sarah 67, 133, 305
    Surry 294
    Thomas 294, 326
    Lieut. Col. Thomas 80
    Toliver 294, 325
    Ulysses 68
    William 51, 68, 294, 312
    Zion 294
DAWKINS, — 104
DAWSON, Brittain 294, 312
    George 209, 266
    James 320
    Joseph 282, 312
    Malcom 34
    Mary 185, 305
    Robt. 228
    Susanna 251
DAY, Adeline Eliza 69
    Cornelia 69
    Fanny 282, 285
    John 68, 69
    Jonathan 68
    Joseph 68, 275
    Mary (Haile) 220
    Rebecca 68
    Robert 275, 282, 285
    Sarah Rebecca 69
    Stephen 68, 132, 266
    Sylvanus K. 69
    Theodate 69
    Thomas 149
    William A. 69
DAYON, Mary 167
DEADWYLER, Alice 241, 317
    Ann B. 241
    Joseph 241

DEADWYLER, Nancy 241
DEAN, Capt. — 252
  Miss — 117
  Abraham 71
  Charles 294
  Mourning 305
  Richard 312
  Sarah 2
DEASON, Hannah 317
  Zacheriah 294
DEE, Mr. — 243
DEFUAL, Mary 305
DeGAFFENREID, Mary 134
  Tscharner 242
DeJARNETTE, Reuben 69, 282,
  287
deKALB, Baron 199, 259
DeLAUNAY, James 69, 266,
  294
DeLEMOTTA, Sarah 204
DELEPLAIQUE, Emanuel Peter
  333
DELK, David 294
DELL, Ann 57
  Delia 27
  Lieut. James 328
  3rd Lieut. James 86
  Philip 27, 57
DeLOACH, Elizabeth 305
  Hardy 294
DELONEY, Susan J. 73
DEMERE, Ann 69
  John 69
  Joseph 69
  Lewis 69
  Paul 69
DEMERE, Raymond 69, 266
DENHAM, Arthur 294
DENMAN, John 69
DENMARK, Mr. — 249
  James 249
  William 328
DENNARD, Bird 69
  Harriet 69
  Isaac 69
  Jack 61
  Jack (John) 69
  John 69, 290

DENNARD, Shadrack 69
  Thomas 69
  William 69
DENNIS, — 242
  Mr. — 74
  Cath. 305
  John 324
  Josiah 312
  Matthias 294
DENSON, Joseph, Sr. 312
DENTON, Emily 317
DENT, George 69
  Sam 196
  Thomas 24
  William 24
DENTON, John 294
DERBY, — 30
DeROCKE, Hanna Elizabeth A. 148
D'ESTAING, Count 85, 142, 264
DeVEAUX, Mary 39
  Jacob 37
  Harriett 37
  Col. James 37
  Mary (Polly) 37
  Peter 69
  Major Peter 294
DEVEREUX, John A. 46
DEWEES, Col. William 328
DeWILTERINO, Chevalier 7
DEWSE, Samuel 149
DIAMOND, Eleanor 169
DIAS, John 294
DICKEN, Margaret 176
DICKENSON, Elizabeth 55
DICKERSON, Col. 87
  Ann 3
  Harry 312
  Capt. John 208
  Martha 49
  Sarah 208
  Zechariah 294
DICKEY, Rebecca 232
  Patrick 312
  Sarah 305
  Sophronia 170
DICKINSON, John 266
  Capt. John 207
  Sarah 42

DOWSE, Susanna 240
DOZIER, Elizabeth 12, 88
  James 289
  James S. 71
  Leonard Wesley 71
  Margaret 219
  Mary Margaret 12
  William 12
DRAKE, Epaphroditus 294
  Hannah 150
  James 294, 312
DRANE, Eleanor 71
  William 71, 248
DRAPER, James 326
DREW, Jeremiah 320
  William 323
DREWRY, Miss— 240
DUBBERLY, John 294
DUBOIS, Capt. Zacheriah 328
DuBOSE, — 145
  Ezekiel 228
  Harriett E. 228
  Isaac 71
  Louise 28
  Mary Julian 228
  Sarah 71, 317
DuBOURG, Andrew 266
DUCK, John 280
DUCKWORTH, — 10
  Christian 305
DUDLEY, Ambrose 71
  Capt. Ambrose 30
  Col. Ambrose 72
  Edward 230
  James 294
  Sarah 102
DUFFEL, Lucy 317
  William 333
DUGAN, Capt. Thomas 118
DUKE, A. M. 183
  Andrew 71
  Ann 305
  Henry 183
  Nancy 317
  Thomas 294
  William 320
DUKES, John Taylor 283, 285
  Sarah 305

DUKES, Thomas 286
DULLINS, Henry 275
DUNCAN, Delilah 4
  Edmund 294
  James 266
  John 294, 328
  Matthew 173
DUNHAM, William 294
  William A. 149
DUNLAP, Col. 222
  Jonathan 325
DUNN, Alexander 320
  Barney 289
  Gatewood 294
  Isaac 204
  Jane 224
  John 312
  Thomas, Sr. 325
  Winnefred 305
DUNNAWAY, Mary 317
DUNWOODY, Esther 39, 71
  James 37, 71
  John 37, 71
  Mary 71
  (Dinwoody), Mary 71
  Robert 71
DuPONT, Ann 71
DuPONTE, Capt. — 7
  Count 27
DuPREE, Dr. — 66
DUPREE, Daniel 266
  Martha 305
DURBAN, Jake 271
  Luke 283, 289
DURDEN, Jacob 266, 323
DURHAM, Isabel 305
  Isaac 312
DURKEE, Malinda 72
  Nathaniel 266, 275
  Major Nathaniel 72
DUROUGEAUX, Elizabeth 281
  Peter 281
  Stephen 281
DUROZEAUX, Stephen 294
DURRACOTT, Rebecca 317
DURVUZIEAUX, Stephen 312
DUTTON, Henrietta 158
  Rev. Mann 158

369

ELLIS, Stephen 74, 283, 289
 Temperance 66
ELLSBURY, Elizabeth 127
ELROD, Samuel 312
ELSBERRY, Benj. 294
ELTON, Anthony W. 312
ELVINGTON, Gideon 312
EMANUEL, Col. — 204
 Ann 75
 Asenath 75
 David 75, 231, 259
 Martha 75
 Mary 75
 Rebecca 75
 Ruth 75, 231
EMBREE, Jesse 75
 John 75
EMBRY, — 136
 Boley 136
 Delilah 136
 Elizabeth 136
 Joseph 294
 Nancy 75
 William 294
EMERSON, — 198
EMERY, Moses 329
ENGLAND, Charles 294
 Daniel 329
 Joseph 329
 Margaret 317
 William 329
ENGLISH, James 141
 Parmenius 294
 Sarah 317
ENLO, John 290
EPHRIAM, Wm. 288
EPPERSON, — 271
EPPINGER, Anna Magdalina 75
 George 75
 James 75
 John 75
 Margaret 75, 201
 Matthew 75
 Sarah 75
 Wenafoothu (Winifred) 75
EPPOSON, Thompson 274, 312
ERWIN, Alexander 247
 Col. Alexander 329

ERWIN, Col. Arthur 329
 Isabella 124
 Mary 244
 Mary (Pretty Polly) 247
 Nathaniel 329
 Sarah Ann Robinson 331
 William 329
ESPY, James 75, 266, 312
 John 295, 322
ESTER, Liddal 320
ESTES, Isabella 317
ETHRIDGE, Joel 322
ETTON, Abram 294
EUBANKS, — 218
 George 282, 312
 Susanna 317
EUGLAS, Col. 94
EVANS, Annie 76
 Arden 76
 Benjamin 275
 Burwell 295
 Daniel 5, 76, 271, 275
 Elizabeth 76, 305, 310
 James 76, 295
 Jane 317
 Jeanette 5
 John 76, 278, 295, 312
 Capt. John 130
 Lucinda 64
 Lucy 305
 Martha 76
 Rhoda 181
 Robert 173
 Ruel 329
 Sallie 76
 Stephen 76
 Susan 76
 Susan M. 320
 Thomas 295
 William 76, 295, 326
 William D. 295
EVANSON, Eli 290
EVE, Catherine 239
EVERETT, Abraham 295
 Anthony 171
 Cassandra C. 227
 Joshua 252
 Sarah 252

EVERETTE, Sarah 171
EVERS, John 295
EWING, Margaret 88
    Capt. Nathaniel 58
    Thomas 62
    Col. Thomas 88, 329
EXLEY, John William 148
EZELL, Hartwell 295
EZZELL, Hartwell 266

FAIN, Ann 77
    Betty 77
    Clara 77
    David 76
    Ebenezer 76, 312
    Elizabeth 76
    Hezekiah 324
    John 76
    L. 77
    Lavinia 77, 165
    Levice 77
    Luvenicia 77
    Luvincia 160
    Margaret 76
    Mary 77
    Mary Ann 76
    Matthew 77
    Mercer 76
    Nancy 77
    Polly 76
    Rebecca 77, 165
    Rebecca Ann 76
    Sallie 76
    Thomas 76, 77, 160, 329
    William 76, 77, 329
FAIR, Alexander 77
    Effie 77
    Elizabeth 77
    John 77
    Nancy 77
    Peter 77, 266, 278
    Polly 77
    Rebecca 77
    Rhoda 77
    Sally 77
    Susan 77
    William 77
FAIRCHILD, — 23

FAIRCHILD, Ann 37
    Daniel 329
    Elizabeth 317
    Robert 329
FAIRCLOTH, John 295
FAIRFAX, Miss — 168
FAIRISH, William 312
FAISON, William 312, 324
FALKNER, Mary 88
FALL, Henrietta 159
    Dr. John S. 19
FAMBROUGH, Anderson 77
    Elizabeth 77
    Gabriel 77
    Jane 77
    Jesse 77
    Joshua 77
    John Anderson 77
    Lucy 77
    Nancy 77
    Polly 77
    Susanna 77
FANE, Daniel 266
    Thomas 295
FANNIN, Abram 78
    Ann 77
    Eliza 78
    Isham 78
    James 77
    James W. 78
    Jeptha 78
    John 286
    John H. 78
    Joseph Decker 78
    Martha 83
    Sarah 78
    William 78
FANNINS, Margaret (Porter) 23
FARIS, Miss — 49
    Rebecca 317
    William 295
    Wm. 266
FARLEY, Delina 305
    Mary 249
FARMER, James 295
    John 195
FARQUHAS, Robert 78
FARR, Benjamin 275

FITZPATRICK, Sarah 327
   Susan 80
   William 80
   Wm. 94
FIVEASH, Elias 295
FLANIGAN, Daniel 326
   William 324
   Wm. 295
FLANNIGAN, Christopher 320
   Wm. 312
FLEMING, — 241
   James 278
   Jane 12
   Margaret 65, 310
   Robert 295, 323
   Sarah 306
   William 325
FLEMISTER, Catherine 80
   E. G. 306
   Euramie Elizabeth 80
   James 80
   John 80
   Lewis 80, 266
   William L. 80
FLERL, Israel 80
   John 80, 233
   (Floerl), John 80
   Judith 80
   Margaret (Mary) 80
   Mary Virginia 233
FLETCHER, — 112
   Ann (Nancy) 81, 159
   Ann P. 78
   Elizabeth 81
   Frances 179
   George 81
   Henry 329
   John 80, 81
   Joseph 81
   Mary Ann 161
   Nancy 81
   Rebecca 81, 116
   Richard 103
   Sarah 81
   Thomas 81
   Wiley 81
   William 81, 116, 159, 266, 295,
     329

FLETCHER, Zabud 81
   Zecheriah 81
   Ziba 81
FLEWELLYN, Abner 81, 87, 194,
   278
   Fannie 87
   Margaret 194
FLINN, John 190
FLINT, Elizabeth 120
   Mary 139
FLOERL, Israel 233
   Margaret 233
FLOOD, Jane 317
FLORANCE, Mary 132
FLORENCE, Thomas, Sr. 295
FLOURNOY, James 81, 320
   Jane Frances 121
   John 82
   Marcus 32
   Phoebe 115
   Robert 82, 133, 283, 286, 289, 290
   William 120
FLOWERS, Miss — 152
   Mrs. — 152
   F. Elizabeth 306
FLOYD, Caroline L. 29
   Charles 82
   Eliza 84
   Col. John 29
   Gen. John 101
   Major Gen. John 82
   Mary H. 101
   Sarah 306, 317
   Shadrick 131
FLUD, Jane 306
FLUKER, John 275, 283, 288, 295
   Owen 82, 275, 287
   Thomas 82
FLYNN, Elizabeth 306
   John 275
FOGEL, Mary 306
FOGIL, Mary 317
FOLD, Mary 43
FOLSOM, General — 109
FONTAINE, Capt. — 238
FORD, — 43
   Mary 310
   Sallie 3

375

FORDHAM, Benjamin 168
FOREMAN, Louise (Ann) 242
FORSTON, Benjamin 82, 110
   Eason 98
   Eliza (Lane) 98
   Elizabeth 82
   Jesse 82
   John 82, 98
   Millie 82
   Richard 82
   Scott 174
   Thomas 82, 98, 99
   William 82, 98
FORSYTH, Fannie 83
   John 83
   Robert 82, 83
FORT, Arthur 42, 53, 83
   Caroline 102
   Elizabeth 83, 281
   Mary 189
   Moses 83
   Owen Charlton 83
   Sarah 83
   Susanna 83
   Tomlinson 83
   Zachariah C. 83
FOSTER, Mr. — 149
   Anna 252
   Arthur 295
   Emma 233
   Francis 275
   John 83, 240, 248, 295
   Phoebe 130
   Samuel 83
   William 275, 295
FOUCHE, Major Jonas 84
   Susan Jane 5
FOULD, James 312
FOUNTAIN, L. 306
   Sarah 281, 306
FOWLER, George, Sr. 282
   Henry 275
   Martha 317
   Peter 275
FOWNLEY, Nathan, Sr. 295
FOX, Elizabeth 212
   Joseph 215
   Mary 17

FOX, Wilmouth 317
FOXWORTH, Sarah 91
FRANK, Stephen 277
FRANKLIN, — 67
   Benjamin 190
   David 275, 295
   George 84, 266
   Rev. George 84
   Herbert M. (Mrs.) 140
   Owen 84
   Sarah 243
   Sarah Boone 84
   Vashti 84
   Rev. William 84
   Wm. 266
   Zepheniah 312
FRASER, — 127
   Mary Elizabeth 91
   Simeon 295
FRAY, Benjamin 283
FRAZIER, Andrew 283, 289
FREEMAN, Alicy 84
   Allen 84
   Ann 134, 206
   Colquitt 266
   Daniel 275, 295
   Elizabeth 84, 100, 317
   Fleming 28, 84
   Frances 283
   George 84, 266, 275, 283, 288, 329
   Henry 84
   Holman 28, 84, 85, 206, 266, 275
   Col. Holman 250
   James 85, 134, 266, 275
   John 84, 266, 275
   Joseph 84
   Lucy 148
   Mary 28, 84, 119
   Mildred 306
   Nancy 184
   Rebecca 85
   Rhoda 85
   Sally 85
   Wesley 84
   William 69, 85, 275
FRETWELL, Elizabeth 85
   Frances 85
   Leonard 85

FRETWELL, Lucy Clifton 85
    Nancy 85
    Nancy Burge 85
    Patsey Harwell 85
    Philip Z. 85
    Polly 85
    Richard 85, 325
    Wm. A. 85
FRIDAY, Joseph 295
FRY, Benjamin 288
FUDGE, Jacob 322
    Margaret 226
    Martha 166
FULCHER, James 295
FULFORD, Margaret 246
FULKE, Henry 78
FULLER, Bethany 320
    Elizabeth 317
    Keziah 317
    James 295
    Stephen 323
    Treman 65
    William, Sr. 295
FULTON, Thomas 295
FULWOOD, John 295
FUNDERBUCK, John 295
FUNDERBURK, John 312
FURLOW, Charles 85
    David 85
    James 85
    John 85
    Sallie 85
    William 85
FUSSELL, Jane 218

GABILL (Grabill, Graybill),
    Henry 283
    Mary 283
GADDEN, Mary 306
GADDIS, Thomas 58
GAFFORD, — 91
GAGE, Jane 174
    Major — 329
GAILEY, Mary 306
GAINER, Elizabeth 306
    Mary 85
    Penelope 85
    Phebe 306

GAINER, Rebecca 85
    William 85, 266, 295
GAINES, Ann 317
    Archimedes 86
    Bernard 86
    Daniel 85, 86
    Drucilla 195
    Elizabeth 82
    Francis 290
    George 159
    Gustavus 86
    Henry Gilber 86
    Hippocrates 86
    Hiram 3
    Louisa F. 332
    Martha 108
    Mary 10, 122
    William 295, 323
    Zenophen 86
GAINEY, Reddick 295
    Reedy 312
GAITER, James 295
GAITHER, Alice 152
    Nancy 122
    Stephen 324
GALES, Theresy 137
GALLIN, Thomas 170
GALPHIN, George 271
    Thomas 271
GAMAGE, Charity 317
GAMBLE, John 142, 266, 278
GAMMILL, Jane 317
GANCY, Bartholomew 295
GANES, William 290
GANNAY, Ann 99
GANT, Mary 306
GARDNER, Christopher 320
    Elizabeth 13
    Frances 198
    Lewis 267
    Prior 86
GARLAND, Henry 86, 320
    John 295
GARMANY, Jane 111
GARMON, Margaret Eleanor 119
GARNER, Amelia 57
    Charles 295
    Thomas 312

GILBERT, Felix 6, 88, 115
   Henry 86
   Isaac 88
   Jacob 88
   James 324
   John 88, 217, 312
   Maria 88
   Mary 86
   Milly 283, 289
   Nancy 88
   Oliver 88
   Sarah Hillhouse 5
   Thomas 88, 272, 280
   Rev. Thomas 226
   William 88, 217, 272, 295
GILDERN, Capt. Daniel 329
GILES, Capt. 158, 329
   Celia 317
   Elizabeth 306
   Col. Hugh 80
   John M. 295
GILL, — 149
   John 208
   Young 267
GILLAM, Peter 329
GILLELAND, Buddy 183
   Susan 323
   William 90, 295
   Wm., Sr. 312
GILLESPIE, Capt. Daniel 21
GILLESPY, Elizabeth 209
GILLIAM, Ann 89
   Charles 88
   Elizabeth 88
   Ezekiel 89
   Mary 88
   Patsey 88
   Peter 88
   Sally (Sarah) 245
   Sarah 88
GILLIS, — 101
   James 295
GILLISON, Capt. John 12
GILLONS, James 275
GILMER, Betsey 89, 163
   Charles L. 90
   David H. 89
   Mrs. Eliza 45

GILMER, Elizabeth 89
   Frances M. 21
   Francis Meriwether 89
   George 89, 127
   George Oglethorpe 89, 127
   George Rockingham 89
   Harrison Blair 89
   James, Sr. 312, 324
   Jane 89
   John 19, 89, 156, 163
   John Blair 89
   John Thornton 89
   Lucy Ann Sophia 90
   Mary 89
   Nicholas 89
   Peachy 89
   Peachy R. 156
   Peachy Ridgeway 89
   Sally 89
   Sophia Lucy Ann 28
   Thomas Meriwether 89
GILMORE, Capt. — 90
   Elizabeth 306
   James 90, 267
   Rebecca 210
GINDRAT, Abraham 90
   Dorcas 90
   Henrietta 90
   Henry 90
   John 90
   Mary 90
   Rhoda 90
GINN, Sarah 317
   Transylvania 310
GIRADEAU, Mary Ann 14
   Wm. 267
GIRTMAN, Catherine 306
GLASCOCK, Elizabeth 90
   Thomas 90
   William 90
GLASGOW, William 323
   Wm. 312
GLASS, Joel 275
   John 275
   Joseph 275
   Levi 295
   Mary 70
   Thomas 246

GLAZE, Reuben 295, 312
GLAZIER, Sarah 317
GLEN, Sarah 37
GLENN, Ann 317
   Charlotte 37
   Elizabeth 317
   James 295
   Joseph 241
   Nancy 205
   Simeon 136
   Thomas 312, 327
   William 155
   Wm. 286
GLOVER, Drucilla 306
   William 90, 274, 295
GLYMER, George 67
GLYNN, John 259
   Lucy 317
GOBER, Lucy 90
   William 90
GODBEE, Cary 283, 289
   Mary 306
GODFREY, Mary 177
   Polly 230
GODWIN, Elizabeth 118, 168
   Lilliory 205
GOFF, Miss — 244
GOITMAN, Catherine 281
GOLDEN, Andrew 295
   Elender 317
   Frances 317
GOLDING, Thomas W. 218
GOLDSMITH, William 198
GOLDWIRE, James 90, 132
   John 91, 132
   Sarah (King) 251
GOLIGHTLY, S. 317
GOLPHIN, Barbara Rankin 202
GONTO, Mary 65
GOOD, Thomas 136
   Nicholas 136
GOODALL, John 327
   Sally 327
GOODE, Nancy 9
   Samuel 100
   Theresa 243
GOODMAN, Jesse 249
GOODWIN, Amy 173

GOODWIN, Elizabeth 306
   Jacob 295
   James 295
   Lewis 312, 322
   Nancy 317
   Ruth 270
   Shadrack 295
GOODWYN, Theodk. 271
GOOLSBY, Caty 306
   Eliza 19
   Mary 317
   Richard 295
GOORE, Thomas, Sr. 272
GORDON, Col. — 90
   Capt. Alexander 40
   Col. Ambrose 91
   Few 103
   Frances Roy 40
   George 40
   John 162
   John W. 199
   Mary 13, 306
   Sally 199
   Thomas 91, 267, 295
GORDY, Sarah 181
GORMAN, John 88
GOSS, John 179
   Martha 87
GOUDELOCK, Ann 189
GOUGH, Isabella M. 48
GOULDING, Palmer 295
   Sarah 240
   Rev. Thomas 116
GOUZE, Henry 275
GOWER(S), Abel 312, 323
GRACE, Hez 306
   John 312
   Mary 154
GRACIE, James K. 39
GRADY, Arthur 295
   Elizabeth 204
   Mary 317
GRAFFENREID, Tscharner de 329
GRAHAM, Ann (Cuthbert) 39
   Christian 215
   Lieut. Gen. John 93
GRANBERRY, Moses 91
GRANGE, Sarah 65, 331

GRANT, Capt. — 204
  Miss — 88
  Amelia 91
  Anna 91
  Charles 91
  Daniel 91, 234
  Deborah 8
  Elizabeth 92
  Elizabeth Helen 91
  Fannie 91
  Harry 91
  Harry Allen 91
  Hugh F. 91
  Isabella 91
  James Couper 91
  Jesse 295
  Joseph 272, 324
  Mildred 92
  Peter 88
  Dr. Robert 91
  Sarah Ann 91
  Thomas 91, 92, 275
  William 92
GRANTHAM, Nathan 295
  William, Sr. 295
GRATTAN, Eliza Frances 89
  Robert 89
GRAVES, Dorothy 92
  Henry 234
  James 275
  John 92
  Major John 174
  Lewis 92
  Mary 54
  Mary Russell 163
  Ruth 92
  Susanna 214
  Thomas 275
  William 92, 275
GRAY, Allen 295
  Diana 317
  Hezekiah 135
  Isaac 92
  James 92, 243, 312
  Mary 92
  Rebecca 306
  Susan 92
  Susannah 310, 317

GRAYBILL, Henry 92, 287, 290
  Mary 287
GREAVES, William 295
GREASSUP, James 295
GREEN, — 101, 173, 221
  Allen B. 92
  Ann 93, 212
  Benjamin 93, 282
  Burwell 295
  Charity 306
  Dolly B. 92
  Eleanor 283
  Eli 119
  Elizabeth 334
  Hannah 34
  Harris 93
  Hartwell B. 92
  James 92, 93
  Jane 93
  John 93, 194
  Dr. John 177
  Joseph 221
  Julia Elizabeth 177
  McKeen 93, 279, 283, 288, 329
  Martha Rebecca 93
  Mary 306
  Mary B. 92
  Nancy 80
  Polly B. 92
  Richard 295
  Sarah Hull 93
  Selete 93
  Susan B. 92
  Thomas 92, 267
  William 92, 93, 212
  Dr. Willis 10
  Zilpha 101
GREENE, Gen. 40, 85, 149
  Alston Hunter 94
  Augustine 94
  Curtiss 25
  Daniel 312
  Elizabeth 94
  Forrest 272
  George Washington 93
  Lemuel 94
  Louisa Catherine 93
  Martha Washington 93

GREENE, McKeen, Jr. 174
Nancy 94
Nathaniel 94, 259, 267
Nathaniel R. 93
Gen. Nathaniel 40, 43, 46, 72, 90, 113, 134, 166, 180, 185, 199, 220, 224
Major Gen. Nathaniel 93
Philip 94
Ruth Hunter 94
Sarah 94
Sarah Ann (Alston) 93
Sarah Hull 174
Solomon 329
William 93, 94, 283, 287, 329
GREENWOOD, Harry 231
Henry 231
GREER, Aquilla 109
Delia 109
Elisha 43
Elizabeth 109
James 295
Margaret 213
Robert 272
Thomas 61
William 110
GREETHOUSE, John, Sr. 295
GREGORY, Capt. — 120
Col. — 83
Richard 312
GREGG, Capt. James 80
GREINER, John Caspar 329
GRESHAM, David 326
Eliza Williamson 19, 94
John 19, 94, 295
Susan (Barnett) 89
GRESSAM, Sally 317
GRIER, — 111
Aaron 213, 267
Robert 213
Thomas 213
Capt. Wm. 186
GRIERSON, Gen. — 264
GRIEVE, Callender 147
GRIFFEN, Elizabeth (Ray) 192
GRIFFETH, Capt. — 92
John 127
Mary H. R. 40

GRIFFETH, Mary Susan 127
GRIFFIN, — 64
Almeda 56
Andrew 203
Ann Garnett 95
Charles 267, 285
Chas. 283
Comfort 306
David 95
Elizabeth 95
Frances 74, 187
George W. 95
James 94, 95, 267, 295
Jesse Andrews 95
John 19, 59, 95, 283, 285, 295
Judge John 245
Joseph 295, 313
Joshua 95
Lucinda 212
Mary 95, 143
Mary (Polly) 78
Noah 95
Randolph 275
Rhoda 95
Samuel 271
Sarah 95
Shadrack 95
Solomon 95
Susanna 95
Thomas 95
Gen. Thomas 19
William 19, 56, 95
Capt. William 181
Wyatt Andrews 95
GRIFFIS, Charles 295
GRIGGS, Augustua F. 152
Elizabeth 196
GRIMBALL, Ann Marie (Sealy) 108
GRIMES, Henry P. 248
John 172, 248
Lucy 172, 248
Thomas 248
Thomas W. 248
Sidney 1
Wm. G. 248
Wm. Garland 248
GRIMMER, Wm. 295
GRINAGE, Sallie 237

GRINER, Ann Catherine 246
    Caroline 160
    James 160
    John M. 320
    Philip 160, 329
GRISSON, James 290
GRIZZARD, Susanna 317
GRIZZLE, John 136
    Rebecca 136
GROOVER, Amanda 66
    Charles 66
    Elizabeth 249
    James 66
    John 329
    Joshua 95
    Peter 322
    Solomon 95, 249
    William 95
    (Gruber), John 95, 141
GROVER, — 149
GROVES, Elizabeth 162
    Joseph 7
    Stephen 96
GRUMBLES, George 313
GUERARD, Amelia 18
    Catherine 18
GUERIN, Frances 216
GUEST, Annie 96
    Barton 96
    Celia 96
    Cobb 96
    Cynthia 96
    Elizabeth 96
    Giles 96
    Hall 96
    John 96
    Mary 96
    Morgan 96
    Moses 96, 267
    Capt. Moses 274
    Nathaniel 96
    Sanford 96
    Susan 96
    Susanna 96
    William 96
GUGEL, David 233
GUGLE, Mr. — 201
GUICE, Nicholas 295

GUISE, John 313, 325
    Peter 313
GULFIES, Gustavus 277
GULLY, Richard 272, 323
GUNN, Anne 96
    Daniel 96
    Elizabeth 97
    George 96
    Jacob 96, 267
    Major Jacob 96
    James 96, 267
    Jane (Jincy) 96
    John 96, 97
    Jonathan 97
    Larkin R. 97
    Nelson 96
    Radford 97
    Richard 96, 267, 295
    Sarah 96
    William 96, 97
GUNNELL, William R. 322
GUNTER, Charles 324
    Eliz P. 37
    James 295
    John 26
GURNILL, Wm. 313
GUTHRIE, Miss — 46
    John 295
    Thomas 320
    William 295
GUTTERY, Francis 295
GUYTON, John 31
GWINN, Martha 32, 236
GWINNETT, Amelia 97
    Ann 97
    Button 38, 97, 99, 164, 237, 259
    Elizabeth 97

HABERSHAM, Alexander 97
    Ann 98
    Eliza A. 98
    Elizabeth 54
    Esther 97
    George 313
    Isabella 97
    James 97, 98
    James Camber 98
    John 97, 98, 267

HABERSHAM, John Bolton 98
   John Harris 98
   Joseph 97, 98, 259, 267, 333
   Major Joseph 97
   Joseph Clay 97, 98
   Mary 97, 98
   Mary Bulter 98
   Richard 97
   Robert 98
   Susan Ann 98
   Susan Dorothy 98
   William 98
HACKNEY, Robert 296
HADAWAY, David 296
HADDIN, Mary 281
   Wm. 281
HADDOCK, Sarah 58
HADLEY, Mary 103
   Simon 267, 321
HAGAN, Frances 306
HAGOOD, Eliza Ann 178
HAILE, Martha Ann 154
HAILEY, William 290
HALE, Drucilla 306
   James, Sr. 296
   Joe 30
   Nathan 329
   Oliver 329
HALEY, Betsey 98
   James 98
   John 98
   Lucy 98
   Mary 98
   Reuben 98
   Ritta (or Polly) 98
   Sally 98
   Sarah 149
   Tabby (Tabitha) 98
   Thomas 98
   William 267
   (Hailey), William 98
HALL, Capt. — 54, 200
   Alexander 99
   Ann 281, 306
   Anna R. 39
   Benjamin 296
   Bolling 1
   Col. David 230

HALL, Dempsey 282, 296
   Elpheus 99
   Flora 99
   Hudson, Sr. 282
   Hugh 1, 99
   Ignatius 296, 321
   Instance 99
   Instant 296
   Isaac 313
   James 99, 283, 288
   Jemina 4
   John 99, 296
   L. M. 306
   Lewis 99
   Lyman 99, 237, 267
   Dr. Lyman 257, 260
   Mary 99
   Nancy 306
   Polly 99
   Polly Melson 29
   Priscilla 99
   Rebecca 99
   Seaborn 99
   W. L. 99
   Wm. G. 313
HALSEY, Susan F. 113
HAM, Betsey 306
   John 296
   William 313
HAMBLETON, Mary 306
HAMBRICK, Benjamin 99
HAMBY, David 65
   Eliza 65
HAMES, John 100, 267, 313, 325
HAMESBURGER, Mary 306
HAMILTON, Abigail 306
   Major Andrew 7
   Ann Eliza 100
   Bartow 296
   Benjamin 101
   C. 317
   Catherine 7
   Everard 101
   Frances 29, 100
   George 100
   Isabella 144
   James 100, 267
   James Fox 100

HANES, Ephriam 103
  (Haines), James 102, 103
  Joshua 103
HANEY, Elizabeth 317
  Jemina 306
  Ursula 317
HANNA, Robert 2
HANNEGAN, James 321
HANSON, Peggy 306, 317
  Capt. Walter 202
HARALSON, Hugh A. 62
  J. 296
  Jonathan 62
  Kinchen 62
HARBIN, Alexander 282
  William, Sr. 280
HARBUCK, Mary 306
  Nicholas 296
HARBY, Isaac 170
  Solomon 170
HARDAGREE, Eleanor 306
HARDAWAY, F. 241
HARDEE, John 103
HARDEMAN, Zilla 306
HARDEN, Col. — 213
  Henry 296
  Thomas Huston 17
  William 17
HARDIN, Benjamin Cook 103
  Clarrissa Warren 103
  Edward J. 103
  Effie 103
  Elizabeth 103
  Eve 54
  Harriet Hargrove 103
  Henry 103, 221, 326
  John B. 109
  Judith 103
  Margaret (Castleberry) 55
  Mark 103
  Mary 221
  Valentine 55
  William 103, 175
  Col. William 55
HARDMAN, Charles 103
  John 57
  Rhoda 103
HARDWICK, Betsey 104

HARDWICK, Eliza 104
  Franky 104
  Garland 104
  George 104
  James 104, 229
  Jefferson 104
  Judith 306
  Margaret 229
  Martha 104
  Mollie 80
  Molly 104
  Nancy 22, 104
  Nonaly 104
  Patsey 104
  Peggy 104
  Polly 104
  Richard 104
  Sophie Garland 104
  William 80, 103, 104, 267
HARDY, Jesse 104
  John 104
  Penelope 104, 190
  Sutton 104
  Winnie 306
HARGROVE, Ann Matilda 31
  Mary 217
HARGROVES, James 182
HARKNESS, Robert 296
HARLAN, George 104
HARLEE, Thomas 329
HARLEY, Joseph 296
  Capt. Joseph 222
  Margarette 219
  William 296
HARLOW, Sarah Walker 138
  Dr. Southwell 138
HARMAN, Gen. — 240
  Wm. Weare 111
HARMON, Elizabeth 55
  John, Sr. 313
HARNETT, Cornelius 329
HARNEY, Col. — 94
HARPER, Col. — 60
  Miss — 179
  Ann 89, 306
  George 313
  John 313
  Mary 317

HARPER, Polly 74, 149
   Robert 104, 276
   Samuel 276, 296
   William 267, 313, 325
   Wm. 104, 105
HARRELL, — 112
   Ethelred, Sr. 313
   Jacob 105, 267
   John 105
   Simon 296
   W. I. 112
HARRIDEN, Joseph 313
HARRIN, Alexander 296
HARRINGTON, Catherine 306
   Elijah 296
   Ephriam 313
   James 296
HARRIS, — 196
   Abigail 4
   Absolom 105, 267
   Ann 66
   Augustine 106
   Benj. 296
   Benjamin 61, 105, 267, 322, 326
   Benjamin F. 169
   Buckner 72, 106, 276
   Catherine 172, 306
   Charity 306
   Charles 24, 164
   Clara 317
   Corra 332
   Daniel 84
   David 276, 279
   Edwin 106
   Ezekiel 271
   Elizabeth 10, 24, 105, 106, 134
   Elizabeth (Thompson) (Baker) 24
   Fannie 61
   Frances 100
   Graves 296
   Henry 187
   Howell 286
   James 105
   Jane 105
   Janet 159
   Jemina 150
   Jeptha V. 106
   Joel 106

HARRIS, John 105, 203, 276, 290,
   296, 313
   John Thompson 267
   Joseph 321
   Laird 105
   Lavania 317
   Littleton 106
   Rev. Lundy 332
   Martha 105
   Martha Rivers 243
   Mary 69, 122, 147, 251, 306, 317
   Mary Ann 187
   Mathew 105, 296
   Matthew 324
   Nathan 106
   Rebecca 306, 310
   Robert 105, 329
   Sampson 106
   Samuel 105, 267, 329
   Sarah 79, 185
   Simeon 106
   Stephen 323
   Thomas 105
   Walton 72, 105, 106, 285
   William 56, 105
HARRISON, Benj. 296
   Benjamin 10, 134
   Bradley 136
   Charity 306
   Col. Charles 52, 105, 196
   Edward 106, 296
   Elijah W. 296
   Elizabeth 75, 102, 306
   Henry 43
   James 205
   Joseph 296
   Mary 306
   Palatia 43
   Rebecca 10
   Reuben 296
HARRUP, Arthur 313
HARRY, Ann 46
HART, — 19, 104, 194
   Benjamin 106, 107, 139, 171, 256
   Charles T. 202
   Eli 108
   Elizabeth 49, 107, 108, 132
   Elizabeth Screven Lee 202

HART, Esther Mary 201
    Henry William 202
    James 108
    John 106, 107, 108, 132, 139,
        267, 276
    Capt. John 201
    John S. 201
    Keziah 106
    Lemuel 107
    Mark 106
    Martha 108
    Martha Lee 201
    Mary 106, 108, 325
    Mildred 198
    Nancy 70, 106, 107, 139, 171,
        207, 209, 256
    Odingsell W. 202
    Rev. Oliver 107, 201
    Oliver James 201
    Rebecca 173
    Sally 106
    Samuel 49, 108, 146
    Sarah 50, 108
    Smith Screven 202
    Sukey (Susanna) 107, 256
    Susanna 50
    Susannah 108
    Thomas 106
    Thomas Morgan 106
    William 108
HARTLEY, Daniel 267, 322
    Fere 306
    Ferebe 317
HARTON, Lott 238
HARTRIDGE, Elizabeth 153
HARTSFIELD, Andrew 108
    Anna 108
    Becky 108
    Betsey 108
    Haskey 108
    Henry 108
    Jacob 108
    James 108
    John 108
    Mary 108
    Richard 296
    Sally 108
    Tempe 108

HARTSFIELD, William 108
HARVEY, — 114
    Betsey J. 306
    Evan 53
    James 60, 193, 278, 289
    Dr. Jeremiah C. 109
    John 272
    Judith 60
    Mary 53
    Michael 278
    Nancy 199
    Rachel 53
    Sarah 60, 317
    Zephaniah 267
HARVIE, Capt. — 44
    Charles 267
    Daniel 108
    Elizabeth 109, 127, 149
    Genette 109, 135
    James 276
    Joel 276
    John 108
    Martha 108
    Martha Gaines 89
    Mary 108, 156
    Mary Bontwell 89
    Michael 267
    Nancy 89
    Richard 108
    William 108
HARVIN, James 271
HARWELL, Mary 45
    Patsey 85
    Ransom 206
HASKETT, Col. — 181
HASLETT, Wm. 296
HASTY, Jemina 306
HATCHER, — 64
    Henry 296, 313
    James 191
    John 267, 271
    Joseph 109
    Josiah 313
    Lieut. Josiah 271
    Obedience Elizabeth 224
    Sarah 306
    Susan 155
    Thomas 296

HATCHER, Urek 271
  William 109, 178, 271, 296
HAUGHTON (Horton), Phoebe 44
HAVAL, Hardy 296
HAWKINS, Benjamin 67, 109, 208,
  267
  Delia 109
  Jeffersonia 109
  Col. John 109
  Col. Joseph 109
  Col. Josiah 224
  Mary 40
  Philemon 109
  Col. Philemon 109
  Rebecca 120
  Samuel 208
  Sarah 109
  Stephen 276
  Susan 40
  Virginia 109
HAWTHORN, Thomas 296
  William 296
HAWTHORNE, James 109
  John 109
  Stephen 109
  William 109
HAY, Dr. Gilbert 88
  Nancy 145
HAYES, George White 100
HAYGOOD, Rev. — 192
  Benjamin 109, 215, 267
  James 219
  William 219
HAYMAN, Henry 313
  Stephen 313
HAYNES, Ann 52
  Delia 110
  Elizabeth 110
  Henry 109, 110
  Jane 110
  Jasper 110
  Martha 306
  Mary 109
  Moses 110, 267, 296
  Nancy 110
  Parmenas 109, 110
  Polly 110
  Richard 110, 192

HAYNES, Robert 110
  Sally 110
  Sarah 110, 306
  Stephen 110
  Thomas 110
  William 110
HAYNIE, Elizabeth 306
  George 267
HAYS, Miss — 166
  Edward 296
  George 110
  Jane 306
  John 110, 267, 313
  Jonathan J. 296
  Mary 110
  Nancy 306
HAZZARD, Isabella Maria 82
  Major Wm. 202
HEAD, Benjamin 110
  Elizabeth 110
  James 110
  John S. 296
  Lucy 110
  Margaret 306
  Martha 110
  Sarah 4, 110, 317
  Simon 110
  Gov. Stephen 267
HEARD, — 241
  Abram 56, 112
  Ann 88
  Barnard 111, 276
  Col. Barnard 52
  Bridget Carroll 111
  Catherine 111
  Elizabeth 111, 112, 310
  Falkner 112, 197
  George 56, 112, 276, 329
  George Washington 111
  Henry 329
  Isaac Stokes 111
  Jane Lanier 111
  Jesse 111, 276, 286, 329
  Jesse Falkner 111
  John 111, 329
  John Adams 111
  John G. 296
  Joseph 112, 276

HEARD, Judith 111, 210
    Lucy Wilkinson 111
    Mary 111, 112
    Mary Burch 111
    Pamela Darden 111
    Polly 112
    Pressly Watts 111
    Richard 276
    Sarah 111
    Sarah Hammond 111
    Stephen 88, 111, 263, 329
    Col. Stephen 213
    Susan 111
    Thomas 111, 112, 232, 267,
        289, 329
    Thomas J. 111
    William 160, 296
    Woodson 112
HEARN, — 194
    Benjamin 112
    Elisha 112, 267
    Elizabeth Jane 51
    Francis 112
    Huldah 112
    John 112
    Joshua 112
    Polly 112
    Thomas 51, 112
    William 279
HEARST, Salome 171
HEATH, Col. — 139
    James P. 149
    Jordan 43, 296
    Louisa 306
    Rebecca 43
HEATON, James 296
HEETH, Roiston 296
    Winnefred 306
HEFLIN, Sarah 306
HEGGIE, Thomas 313
HEIDT, Christian J. 280
HEIR, Jacob 277
HEMMING, Rev. Mr. — 154
HEMPHILL, Elizabeth 306
    Jonathan 296
HENDERSON, — 189
    Arch 320
    Joseph 18

HENDERSON, Capt. Joseph 329
    Mary 252, 306
    Capt. Matthew 329
    Capt. Michael 93
    Nancy 18, 123
    Nicey 175
    Robert 112, 151, 313, 321
    Sally 306
    Simeon 111
    Susanna 52
HENDLEY, Horton 112
    Jeanet 112
    John 272
    Nancy 112
    Sophia 112
    William 112
HENDON, Robert 296
HENDRICK, Hezekiah 296
    Jesse 296
    John 112, 313
    Mary 306
    Siah 296
HENDRICKS, Elias 313
    Elizabeth 58
    Louisa 81
    Mary 208
    Samuel 313
HENDRIX, John 296
    Mary 317
HENDRY, Ann 317
    Robert 113, 267
HENKS, Susan 229
HENLEY, Sarah 306
    Susanna 232
HENRY, Capt. — 50
    Anna 209
    Capt. John 236
    Patrick 260, 329
    Robert, Sr. 313
    William R. 9
HERITAGE, Capt. — 203
HERLEY, Nancy 171
HERNDON, Frances 317
    Capt. George 109, 215
    Joseph 267, 278, 296
HERREN, Dulcy 306
HERRIN, Mary Ann 306
HERRING, Arthur 185

HILL, Wylie 188
  Wylie Pope 113
HILLARD, Gen. Thomas 168
HILLARY, Mrs. C. 164
  Christopher 115
  Maria 164
  Marie 115
HILLEN, Charity 240
HILLEY, Thomas, Sr. 290
HILLHOUSE, Miss — 5, 88
  David 115
  David Porter 5
  Mary 115
  Sarah Porter 5
HILLS, Col. William 329
HILLY, Polly 73
HILLYER, Asa 85
  Shaler 85
HINDS, Martha 317
HINE, Nathaniel 296
HINES, Drucilla 115
  Elizabeth 306
  James 115, 129
  John 313
  John B. 278
  Lewis 296
  Martha 306
  Nancy 317
  Rhoda 231
HINSLEY, Thomas 280
HINSON, Sarah 306
HINTON, Elizabeth 84
  Nancy 94
  Pester 313
  Peter 290
HIRRESLY, Elizabeth 306
HIX, Elizabeth 151
  John 271
HOBBS, Margery 318
  Polly 228
HOBBY, William J. 245
  Wm. J. 54
HOBBS, Margery 318
HOBSON, Agnes 115
  Mathew 115
HODGE, David 333
  Elizabeth 218
  Elizabeth Mary 224

HODGE, Philemon 325
HODGES, — 65
  Alcy 116
  Benjamin 116
  Catherine 116
  Essenurer 116
  James Carr 116
  John 65
  Joseph 115, 116, 280
  Joshua 81, 116
  Louise 65
  Mary 65
  Patsey 65
  Philemon 313
  Rhoda 116
  Sherwood 296
HODNETT, Benjamin 116
  Jane Brooke 163
HODO, Ann 60
  Peter 60
HOGAN, Col. 190
  Mary 130
  Dr. Robert 91
HOGANS, Nancy 306
HOGG, Capt. 110
  Lewis 116
HOGUE, Mary 224
HOLBROOK, Ann 116
  Drusilla 320
  Hannah 318
  Jesse 116, 296, 323
  Nathan 116
  Priscilla 306
  Susanna 116
HOLBROOKE, Prisillon 318
HOLBROOKS, Edy 313
HOLCOMBE, Capt. — 85
  Frances 318
  Henry 116
  James 296
  Jordan 117
  Moses 313
  Robert 116
  Sarah 15
  Sherwood 296
HOLCOME, Absolem J. I. C. 240
HOLDEN, Jeremiah 96
HOLDER, John S. 282, 296

392

HOLLAND, Elizabeth 306
　　Lavinia 135
　　Thomas 2, 296
HOLLEY, William 296
HOLLIDAY, Abraham 117
　　Ann 2, 117
　　Ayers 117
　　Elizabeth 117
　　Jane 117
　　John 117
　　Margaret 117
　　Margery 117
　　Martha Ann 117
　　Mary 49, 117
　　Mathew 117
　　Robert Alexander 117
　　Sarah 218
　　Thomas 49, 117
　　William 117, 276, 313
　　Wm. 117
HOLLIMAN, Blake 287
　　David 117
　　Elizabeth 117
　　John 128
　　Mark 117
　　Mary 117
　　Nancy 117
　　Samuel 117, 313
　　Sarah 117
　　William 290
HOLLINSWORTH, Isaac 272
　　Thomas 224
HOLLIS, Elizabeth 307
HOLLOMAN, Levicy 318
HOLLY, J. 327
　　Winnefred 327
HOLMAN, Col. — 85
　　George 296
　　Jacob 296
HOLMES, Ann 136
　　Apsylla 118
　　Apsyllah 168
　　Elizabeth 118
　　James 118
　　John 118
　　Jonathan 296
　　Josiah 118
　　Mary 118

HOLMES, Moses 118
　　Patience 202
　　Penelope 118
　　Robert 188
　　Thomas 313
　　William 271
HOLOWAY, William 74
HOLSEY, Susanna 307
HOLT, James 296
　　Thomas 296
　　William 118
HOLTON, Rhoda 14
HOLTZCLAW, John G. 296
HOOD, Christina 118
　　Joel 118
　　John 118, 296
　　Rebecca 307
　　William 118
HOOK, Thomas 296
HOOPER, Elinor 232
　　James 296
　　Richard 313
　　Richard B. 267
HOOTEN, Henry 296
HOPKINS, — 114
　　Elizabeth 132
　　Isaac 313
　　Nancy 25
　　Samuel 106
HOPSON, Elizabeth 36, 100, 138
　　Henry 147
　　Lucy 147
HORN, Dorcas 318
　　Richard 280
　　Sarah 307
　　Sherwood 296
HORNBUCKLE, George 72
HORNE, Mary 60
HORNSLEY, Val 297
HORSLEY, Valentine 313
HORTON, — 173
　　Elizabeth 245
　　Isaac 313, 323
　　James 267
　　John 223
　　Millie Ann 112
　　Prosser 245, 267
　　Stephen 289

HORTON, Thomas 223
HOSKINS, John, Sr. 296
    Maryan 307
HOUGHTON, Elizabeth 25
HOUSTON, John 36, 38, 118
    Gov. John 63
    Margaret 124
    Mary 62
    Sir Patrick 36
    Samuel 297
HOWARD, Abraham 296
    Andrew 176
    Ann 119
    Augustus 119
    Benj. 278
    Benjamin 119
    Edith 307
    Eliza 78
    Elizabeth 119, 307
    George F. 326
    Grover 155
    Hester 119, 228
    Homer 119
    Isaiah 119
    James 119
    Jane 307
    Janet 310
    John 118, 119, 226, 245, 267, 276
    John H. 278
    John Harrison 119
    Joseph 119, 206
    Lucretia 60, 307
    Mark 119
    Mary 119, 129
    Melton 119
    Nancy 119
    Nehemiah 119
    Rhesa 79
    Sarah 119, 307
    Solomon 119, 278, 296
    Thacker 119
    Thacker Brock 245
    William 276
    William Sanders 226
HOWE, Elisha 296
    Judith 116
    Rebecca 65
    Robert 92, 288

HOWE, Gen. Robert 61, 65, 263, 329
    Sarah 102
    Sarah Grange 331
HOWEL, Mills 324
HOWELL, Col. 67
    Caleb 279
    Daniel 279
    Lieut. Daniel 86, 329
    Eleanor 119
    Eli 119
    Elizabeth 119
    Evan 119
    Franky 307
    Isaac 119, 267
    John 119, 297
    Joseph 119
    Margaret 119
    Mary 307
    Michael 119
    William 119
HUBBARD, — 95
    Benjamin 120
    Bennett 120
    Burwell 297
    Elizabeth 43, 120, 318
    John 119, 120, 276, 297
    Joseph 120
    Manoah 280
    Mary 120
    Mildred 120
    Rhoda 120
    Richard 120
    Sally 120
    Susan 58, 120
    Susanna 120, 178, 318
    Thomas 178
    William 120
    Winaford 297
HUBERT, Archibald 120
    Benjamin 120, 199
    Elizabeth 120
    Harmon 115, 120
    Hiram 41, 120
    John 120
    Mary 120
    Mary (Polly) 199
    Matthew 120
    Nancy 120

HUBERT, William 120
HUCHINS, Rebecca 186
HUCKABY, Isham 267
 William 297
 Wm. 287
HUDGINS, Ansel 297
 William 120, 320
HUDLER, John 297
HUDMAN, — 181
HUDSON, Amphelady 121
 Ann Philada 104
 Anne Jones 86
 Bathsheba 121
 Charles 104, 121
 Christopher 121
 Cuthbert 121
 Cuthbert (Cutbird) 120
 Daniel 297
 David 21, 121, 267, 290
 Elizabeth 63, 121, 310
 Frances 3, 121
 Gillam 131
 Gilliom 121
 Irby 3, 121
 Joacim 121
 John 86, 121, 211, 313
 Joshua 121
 Lewellyn 121
 Louise 43, 68
 Madison 52
 Mary 86, 104, 121
 Molly 310
 Polly 21
 Rebecca 211
 Richard D. 211
 Robert 279
 Samuel 104, 279
 Sarah 121
 Sarah Williams 27
 Susanna 121
 Thomas 121
 William 121, 145
 Wm. 121
HUDSPETH, Elizabeth 176
HUEY, Henry 313
HUGGINS, Robert 276
HUGHES, Capt. — 229
 Miss — 101

HUGHES, Elizabeth 237
 Henry 121
 James 320
 Jane 307
 Martha 237
 Sallie 237
 Sarah 307
HUGHS, Mary 90
HUIE, James 297
HULING, Catherine 228
 Elizabeth 307
 James 228
HULL, — 173
 Hope 121, 267
 Rev. Hope 248
 John 122
 Thomas 122
HULSEY, James 297
 Jennens 122
 Jesse 324
HUMAN, Alex 297
HUMES, Harriet 119
HUMPHRIES, Joseph 279
 Judith 140
 Thomas 122, 232, 267
HUNNICUTT, Mary 8
 Polly (Bass) 123
HUNT, Mr. — 217
 Daniel 297
 Drucilla 122
 Elizabeth 122
 George 122, 297
 Henry 122
 Hullium 122
 James 122, 267, 290
 Joel 122
 John S. 122
 Joshua 122
 Littleton 323
 Lucy 112, 222
 Mary 122
 Mary Annie 244
 Moses 122, 267, 290
 Nancy 122
 Richard 122
 Sarah 106
 Sion 122
 Turman 297

HUNT, Turner 122, 283, 287
  William 122, 267, 271
  Willis 122
HUNTER, Col. — 103
  Miss — 171
  Adam 184
  Eliza G. 27
  Elizabeth 231, 307, 318
  Jesse 94
  Martha 307
  Moses 313
  Nancy 80
  Ruth 94
  Samuel 227
  Samuel B. 83
HURST, Miss — 140
  Mary 246
  Serena 246
HURT, Miss — 231
  Emily Elizabeth 195
  William 123
HUSTON, John, Sr. 297
HUTCHINS, Ann 327
  Elizabeth 127
  James 327
  Nancy 13
HUTCHINSON, Elizabeth 247
  James 297
  Jan 247
  Margaret 247
  Mary 188
HUTSON, Mary 111
HUTTON, John 297
HYDE, — 209
  Elizabeth 188, 189
  James 189, 329

INGER, John 272
INGRAM, John 297
  Mary 105
INLOW, Lewellyn 6
INMAN, Alfred 123
  Allen 123
  Daniel 123, 267, 279, 297
  Elizabeth 5, 123
  Jeremiah 123
  Joshua 279
  Mary 123
  Rachel 123

INMAN, Shadrack 123
  Sophie 123
IRVING, Mary 307
IRWIN, Alexander 123, 124, 267
  Elizabeth 124
  Elizabeth Mary 243
  Hugh 123, 124
  Jane 124
  Jared 123, 124, 260
  Col. Jared 124
  Gov. Jared 124, 243, 267, 279
  John 124, 278
  John Lawson 123, 124, 267
  Margaret 123
  Nancy 307
  Thomas 124
  William 123, 124
IRVINE, Anne 37
  Charles Mallory 123
  Christopher 18, 123
  David 123
  Isaiah Tucker 18, 68, 123
  John 123
  Dr. John 37
  Louise Tucker 68
  Prudence 114, 128
  Smith 123
  William 18, 123
ISELEY, Philip 323
ISRAEL, Christinia 124
  David 124
  Hannah Elizabeth 124
  John Godhilp 124
  Joshua 124
  Sarah 124
  Solomon 124
  Susannah 124
IVEY, Ephriam 267, 297
  Henry, Sr. 297
IZELY, Philip 297

JACK, Col. — 175
  Ann 24
  Archibald 125
  Catherine 125
  James 124, 125
  Jean 20, 249
  John 24, 125

JONES, Margaret 173, 307, 318
    Martha 128, 133
    Martha Bugg 129
    Martha Melvina Milledge 133
    Mary 36, 63, 68, 76, 126, 129,
      130, 131, 132, 134, 229, 318
    Mary Amelia 134
    Mary S. 134
    Mary Thomas 129
    Mason 132
    Matilda 130
    Matthew 131, 297
    Mich'l 271
    Minnie 131
    Moses 14, 132, 297
    Nancy 129, 131, 134, 307, 318
    Nathan 132
    Nimrod 297
    Hon. Noble 39
    Noble W. 333
    Noble Wimberly 38, 134
    Obedience 91, 132, 138
    Patsey 120
    Peggy 134
    Philip 129, 133
    Phillipine 132
    Phoebe 130
    Polly 131
    Rachel 129, 249
    Rebecca 310
    Reuben 130, 278
    Reuben H. 161
    Richard 10, 131
    Robert 130, 283, 287
    Russell 63
    Samuel 240
    Capt. Samuel 185
    Sarah 14, 79, 130, 131, 132, 133,
      134
    Sarah Ann 36, 100, 133
    Sarah Keziah Paris 129
    Sarah M. 129
    Sarah Seaborn Rebecca Weed
      133
    Seaborn 119, 128, 129, 130, 131,
      133, 278, 279
    Solomon 132, 133
    Stanby 131

JONES, Standley 6
    Stephen 104, 297
    Susanna 147
    Susanna Ann 140
    Thomas 58, 66, 128, 130, 131,
      297
    Thomas B. 297
    Toliver 132
    William 76, 128, 130, 131, 134,
      267, 271, 277, 286, 313, 324,
      325, 329
    Wm. Jones 297
    Winny (Elder) 130
    Wylie 74, 134
JORDAN, Miss 155, 223
    Aven 297
    Benjamin 313
    Betsey 135
    Britton 135
    Burwell 135
    Charles 127, 135, 313
    Dempsey 276, 297
    Elizabeth 90, 323
    Fleming 135, 155
    Fountain 244
    Green 135
    Job 313
    John 135, 267, 297
    Josiah 113, 288
    Margaret 135
    Martha 135, 170
    Mary 10, 135, 176
    Mary Bates 10
    Milly 307
    Mortimer 135
    Patience 135
    Persilla 135
    Polly 113
    Priscilla 223
    Reuben 127, 135
    Samuel 276
    Samuel Bates 10
    Temperance 170
    William 135, 297, 313
    Winifred 135
    Winnefred 318
    Winny 152
JOSSEY, Henry, Jr. 189

JOTT, Daniel 297
JOURDAIN, Edmund 297
   Fountain 297
JOURDAN, Elizabeth 318
   Fountain 326
   Henry 277
JOVAS, Thomas 277
JOY, Elizabeth 307
JOYCE, Henry 267
JOYNER, Benjamin 297
JUDKINS, Zachariah 272
JUDSON, Major Agur 329
   Capt. Daniel 329
   Daniel 329
   Elizabeth 331
   Isaac 329
   Silas 329
JUSTICE, Aaron 297
   Dempsey 135, 278
   Isaac 297
   Martha 16, 182
KAIGLER, Andrew 61
   Major David 61
KALCHER, Mary Magdalen 95
   Rupert 95
KARR, Eleone 137
KAY, Agnes (McKay) 195
   Robert 145
KEANE, Thomas 103
KEENAN, Col. 70
KEILY, Giles 325
KEITH, John 36, 326
KELL, James 324
   Robert 324
KELLEBREW, Elizabeth 318
KELLMER, George 313
KELLOGG, — 329
KELLY, — 141
   Edward 313
   Elizabeth 307
   Jacob 135
   Lloyd 297
   Mary 162
   Michael 320
   Rebecca 138
   Sims 46
   Susanna 135
   William 290, 297, 323

KELSEY, — 174
KEMP, James 99
KENAN, Amelia (Gray) Powell 136
   James 136
   Lucy 149
   Michael Johnston 135
   Owen 136
   Thomas Holmes 136
KENDAL, William 297
KENDALE, Henry 278
KENDALL, Elisha 118
   Elizabeth P. 318
   Henry 136, 278
   Dr. James 136
   Major John 136
   James Key 313
KENDRICK, Hezekiah 297
   John 68, 69, 267
   Sarah 224
   Thomas 68
KENNEDY, Catherine 148
   Eli 158
   Francis 158
   Hugh 230
   Seth 297
   William 230
KENNON, Frances 85
   M. L. 85
KENNORE, Elizabeth 143
KENSON, Capt. Wm. 60
KENT, Daniel 297
   John 272, 313
   Sampson 297
KERCY, Alcy 297
KERLIN, Elizabeth 310
KERSHAW, Capt. Eli 175
KESTERSON, Nancy 318
KETTLES, Sarah 32
KEY, Agnes 136
   Charles 136
   Elizabeth 136
   George W. 136
   Henry 136
   Capt. Henry 104
   James 136
   Jane 136
   John Waller 297
   John Walter 136

LEWIS, Frances Rhodes 231
George 241, 298, 329
George Baskerville 176
Col. Ichabod 329
James 143
Jane 156
Jesse 143
John 110, 143, 268, 322
Joseph 298
Mary 143, 154, 155
Matthew 143
Meriwether 156
Nancy 318
Narcissa Jane 241
Nathaniel 313
Peter 298
Reuben 156
Richard 143
Samuel 149
Sarah Hines 214, 215
Selia 318
Thomas 89
Ulysses 143
William 156
Wm. 144
Capt. Wm. 128
LIDDELL, Capt. George 167
LIGHTFOOT, Sarah 130
LIGON, Tabitha 307
LILE, Ephriam 326
LILES, Bathesba 307
Ephriam 313
LILYBRIDGE, Mary 178
LINCH, — 242
Rev. Elijah 144
LINCOLN, Gen. — 164, 179, 220, 329
Gen. Benjamin 260
LINDSAY, Ann 119
Benjamin Few Hamilton 144
Clarissa 283
Clarissa Harlow Bullock 144
Jackson Clark Watkins 144
Jennie M. 144
John 80, 144, 283
Matilda Marbury Somerville 144
Munesis Creswell Christmas 144

LINDSAY, Col. Reuben 329
Sallie Collier Billingsea 144
LINDSEY, Clarissa 289
Dennis 276, 298
Isaac, Sr. 313
James 298
John 268, 276, 289
Matilda M. 213
Mary 307, 318
William 298
LINTON, John 298
LINVILLE, William 325
LIONS, William 282
LIPHAM, Elizabeth 307
Nancy 307
LIPSCOMB, Capt. — 139
LITTLE, Archibald 276
Cherry 144
David 276
Ellen 144
Fanny 307
James 144, 268, 276
James H. 144
John 144
John E. 144
Littleberry 144
Micajah 144
Thomas 121
William 144, 313
Wm. 268
LITTLEFIELD, Catherine 93
Edward 93
LITTON, John 314
LIVELY, Abraham 144, 279
Matthew 144, 279
LIVERMAN, Con 298
LIVINGSTON, Adam 144
Philip 329
Robert 329
Walter 329
LLOYD, James 45, 298
LOADHOLT, Martin 277
LOCKETT, Elizabeth 197
Polly 184
Solomon 298
Thomas 198
LOCKHART, James 290, 314

LOCKHART, Polly 307
LOCKLAND, Charlotte 318
LOCKLIN, Nancy 69
LODGE, Sarah 95
LOGAN, Thomas 2
LOGGETT, Mary 14
LOGGUS, James, Sr. 298
LOKEY, William 298
LONG, Capt. — 145
   Anderson 145
   Ann 146
   Col. Bloomfield 196
   Crawford W. 145
   Dr. Crawford W. 145, 146, 238
   Eliza 145
   Eugenia 145
   Evans 53, 145, 268
   Fannie 145
   Frances 121, 145, 196
   Gabriel 145
   Henry 152
   James 145, 238
   John 145
   Joseph 146
   Louisa 318
   Lucinda 145
   Lunceford 145
   Margaret 145, 223
   Martha 318
   Mary 145, 146
   Nicholas 145
   Col. Nicholas 223
   Nimrod 145
   Nimrod Washington 145
   Peggy 145
   Polly 145
   Reuben 145, 196
   Richard H. 145
   Robert 2
   Samuel 145, 146
   Sarah Ann 145
   Sarah Rebecca 145
   Thomas 146
   William 227
LONGSTREET, Capt. — 138
LORD, Hannah 180
   Martha 307
   Milly 307

LORD, William 298
LORRANCE, — 45
LOTT, Cornelia 93
LOURANCE, Catherine 175
LOVE, Acksah 146
   Allelujah 146
   Amos 268
   Beloved 146
   Chaste 146
   David 146
   Col. David 268
   Ingram 203
   James 298
   John 114
   Josephus 146
   Martha 119
   Nancy 119
   Ovid Blewett 146
   Robertus 146, 287
   Sarah 20
   Thomas 326
   Vertus Mary 146
   William 92
LOVEJOY, Jemina 318
LOVETT, Clarky 137
   Fens 137
   Lemuel 183
   Thomas 137, 329
LOVINGOOD, Harmon 25
LOW, Ann 146
   Burrey 146
   Esther 146
   George 146
   Grace 146
   Hickenbotham 146
   Isaac, Sr. 146
   John 283, 286
   William 146
LOWE, Betsey 78
   Col. David 209
   Jesse 276
   Lucinda (Tharpe) 160
   Mary 151
   Sarah 231
   William 276
LOWMAN, Catherine 61
LOWREY, Levi 298, 324
   Simeon 298

McMURPHY, Jane 166
McMURRAH, David 314
McMURRAY, Frederick 276
McNAB, James 30
McNAIR, Anna 166
  Catherine 166
  Daniel 166
  David 166
  Harriet 166
  James S. 166
  John 166
  Martin 166
  Mary 166
  Robert 166
  Samuel 166, 167
McNEELY, Mr. — 66
  Elinor 281, 307
  Hugh 281
  Wm. 249
McNEESE, James 298
McNEIL, Daniel 289
  James 68, 307
  Capt. James 128
  Col. James 146, 234
  Jesse 314
McNEILL, Col. James 31, 32, 63
McNICH, Cornelia Ann 202
MACON, Nathaniel 260
MACONESON, John 323
McPHAIL, James 268
McPHEETERS, Mary 123
McPHERSON, John 26
  Margaret 26
McRAE, Capt. — 70
  Alexander 298
  Cath 307
McREE, Mary 318
  William 298
McRIGHT, William 323
McTYRE, — 23
McVICKER, John 314
McWALTERS, Margaret 307
McWHORTER, John 298
  Margaret 318
MADDEN, Susan 162
MADDOX, Benjamin 147
  Charles 298
  Claiborne 287

MADDOX, Fielding 147
  Henley 147
  James A. 147
  John 147, 298, 314
  Martha 87
  Posey 147
  Sarah 147
  Stansfield 147
  Themie 147
  Walter 147, 298
MADERS, Jacob 277
  John 277
MAGBEE, Rachel 318
MAGEE, Elizabeth 318
  Rebecca 31
MAGINTY, John 314
MAGRUDER, Ann 148
  Archibald 148
  Basil 148
  Cassandra 71, 248
  Eleanor 148, 251
  Elizabeth 148
  George 148
  John 148
  Margaret 148
  Martha 148
  Ninan 147
  Ninian Beall 148
  (McGruder), Ninian Offutt 147,
    251
  Ruth 148
  Samuel 148
  Samuel B. 148
  Sarah 148
  Selina 147
  Sophronia 147
  Zadoc 147
MAINER, Samuel 298
MAJORS, Samuel 334
  Samuel D. 47
MALE, John 298
  Levi 298
MALETTE, Louise 193
MALEY, Johnston 149
MALLETT, Abraham 148
  Daniel 148
  Eliza M. 148
  Gideon 148

MOORE, — 25
   Capt. — 121, 181
   Alice 141
   Alis 289
   Alys 283, 286
   Clement 268
   Dolly 67
   Eliza 66
   Elizabeth 246
   Ellen 66
   Eudliocia Walton 83
   Francis 299
   Isaac 314, 321
   Capt. Isaac 244
   James 170, 268, 279, 283, 286,
     289
   Jane 5
   John 108, 158, 186, 299, 314, 324
   Capt. John 48
   Joseph 280, 299
   Lucy 308
   Margaret 124
   Margaret Catherine 142
   Mary 52
   Maurice 330
   Nancy 308
   Polly 186
   Raney 185
   Robert 73
   Synthia 308
   Thomas 237, 279
   Dr. Thomas 129, 159
   William 25, 271, 299
   Col. Wm. 120
   Williamenia Sarah Eliza 26
MOORMAN, Agnes 232
   Andrew 52
   Charles 232
   Judith 10
   Rhoda 10
MOPHIT, Mary Ann 308
MORAN, William 170, 268
MORDECAI, Rachel 170
   Samuel 170
MORE, Elizabeth 15
MOREL, John 36, 70
   John G. 230
MORELAND, Frances 318

MORELAND, Robert 299
   Tuttle 145
MORGAN, Col. — 49, 139, 145
   Gen. — 71
   Ann (Nancy) 106, 171
   Asa 276
   Charlotte 308
   Col. Daniel 41, 47, 169, 229
   Gen. Daniel 55, 88, 171, 261, 330
   Eleanora 171
   Elizabeth 4, 55, 246, 308
   James 171, 299, 330
   Jane 26
   John 171, 299, 314, 330
   Lemuel 171
   Luke 171, 276
   Mary 201, 234, 308
   Nancy 4, 139
   Rebecca (Alexander) 106
   Sarah 171
   Thomas 106, 171
   William 276, 299
   William C. 178
MORRIS, Capt. — 263
   Burrel 299
   Charles 277
   Edwin 58
   Elizabeth 308
   Hannah 308
   James 277
   Jesse, Sr. 299
   John 243, 277, 280, 299, 314
   Joshua 239
   Lucy 308
   Lydia 10
   Nathan 192
   Nathaniel 299
   Obediah 268
   Osten 299
   William 268, 280
   Wm., Sr. 273
MORRISON, Joseph 81
MORROW, — 241
   Ann 318
   Elizabeth 308, 318
   Ewing 88, 89, 299
   Joseph 89
   Robert 62, 88, 171, 330

MORROW, William 171
  Capt. William 330
MORTON, Ann Elizabeth 171
  Bessie 76
  Daniel E. 171
  Elizabeth (Eason) 249
  Jane 172
  Jesse 171
  Joseph 330
  Lemuel B. (Samuel) 172
  Martha 171
  Mary 171
  Oliver 268, 324
  Oliver H. 171, 172
  Sarah 171
  Silas 171
  Thomas 172
MOSELEY, Celia Ann 143
  Elizabeth 26
  Joseph 299
  Lewis 299
  Marion Elizabeth 43
  Olive 25
  Samuel 268, 274, 314
  Sarah 308
  Capt. William 80
  Col. William 220
MOSELY, James 299
  Phoebe Mary 220
  William 276
MOSES, Meyer 170
  Rebecca 170
MOSS, — 192
  John D. 218
  Leonard 283, 285
  Martha D. 281
MOSSE, Elizabeth 172
  Esther 172
  George 177
  Dr. George 172
  Jane 142, 172
  Martha 142, 172
  Mary 172
  Phoebe 142, 172
  Sarah 172, 177
MOSSMAN, Catherine 182
  Nancy 182
MOTE, William 299

MOTT, Nathan 299, 314
MOULTRIE, Mathilda 173
  Nancy 174
  Nancy Hopson 173
MOUNGER, Caroline 240
  Edwin 54, 172
  Elizabeth 172
  Henry 172
  Julia 172
  Lucy 172
  Mary Ann 172
  Sidney 172
  Thomas 172
MOYE, Miss — 66
  Emma 66
MOYER, Anna Christiana 67
MOZLEY, Samuel G. 18
MUELLER, Anna Margaret 195,
  233
MULLEN, Malone 280
MULLET, James 90
MULLINS, Malone 324
MUMFORD, — 101
MUNDEN, Levina 308
MUNGER, Elizabeth 220
MUNROE, Aramintha Way 213
MURDOCK, William 172, 274
MURPHREE, Martha 172
  John 172, 279
  Miles 279
MURPHY, — 37
  Col. — 92
  Alexander 5, 173
  Betsey Ann 173
  Cherry 308
  Edmund 172, 268, 299
  Edward 173
  Elizabeth Ann 173
  Harriet 173
  James 173
  John 173
  Leroy 173
  Levicy 173
  Maria 173
  Martha 318
  Mary 173
  Morris 279, 282
  Nancy 173

OLIVER, F. McCarty 51
  Florence McCarty 179
  Frances 179
  Francis 179
  Jackson 179
  James 51, 179, 299
  James Brush 269
  Major James Brush 180
  Jane 318
  John 148, 179, 276, 322
  Katherine 161
  Martha 179
  Mary Ann 225
  Mary Xenia 28
  Peter 179, 276, 290, 299
  Theodosius 290
  Thomas 179
  Thomas W. 51
  Thomas Winfrey 179
  William 179
OLLENS, Daniel 276
OMAN, John 299
O'NEAL, Basil 93
  Ross 299
O'NEILL, Malcom 34
O'REAR, Daniel 322
ORR, Daniel 269
ORRICK, Celia 308
OSBORNE, Mary 180
  Reps 299
  William 180
OSBOURNE, Essena 119
OSBURN, Mary 99
OSGOOD, Sarah 240
OSLIN, Jesse 210
OSWALD, Ann Maxwell 216
  Susanna 39, 214, 215
OUTLAW, Alexander 46
  Edward 271
  Elizabeth 46
  Sud 271
OVERTON, Ann (Hannah) 41
OWEN, Frances 91
  Lieut. John 91
  Sarah 17
OWENS, Miss — 33
  Barshaba 310
  Barsheba 308

OWENS, Elisha (?) 119
  John 91, 145, 299
  Mildred 91
  Nancy 308
OXFORD, Ezekiel 271
  Jefse 271
  Susanna 308

PACE, Amy 218, 224
  Ann (Gordon) (Woodward) 246
  Barnabas 299
  Elcie V. (Tankersly) 134
  Elizabeth 180
  Frances 243
  Hardy 180
  James 180
  John 180
  Martha 180
  Mary 180
  Meldridge 308
  Nannie 180
  Nathaniel 243
  Thomas 180, 278, 299
  William 180
PACELEY, Col. John 21
PAGE, Anna Matilda 180
  Martha 236
  Mary 308
  William 6
  Wm. (Buck) 122
  Major William 180
PAINE, Cyrus 66
  John 299, 314
  Winefred 318
PAISLEY, Col. 224
PALMER, Ada 200
  Edmund 5
  Elizabeth 308
  George 48, 180, 279
  Israel 200
  John 193
  Martha 174
  Mary 48
  Priscilla 200
  Susan N. 234
  William 314
PALMORE, Elijah, Sr. 299
PARHAM, Asa 308

PENDARVIS, Alice 202
  Elizabeth 36
PENDER, Martha 213, 215
PENDLETON, Catharine 216
PENN, Col. Abraham 42
  Frances 308
  Col. Gabriel 45
  Joseph 216
  Martha 308
  Mary 221
  Mary (Molly) 215
  Sarah Daniel 238
  William 184, 221, 269, 300
PENNINGTON, Neddy 314
  Samuel 206
PENNY, Ed 300
PENTECOST, William 269,314,320
PEOPLES, Henry 277
PERKERSON, Joel 281
PERKINS, — 193
  Archibald 166, 184, 314
  Dorcas 221
  Elizabeth 166, 184
  John 184, 284, 286, 300
  Martha 233
  Mary 79
  Moses 322
  Sarah 184, 284, 286
PERRY, Mrs. — 142
  James 184
  Josiah 39
  Penelope 247
PERRYMAN, Elisha 234
  Herman 300
PERSONS, Benjamin 184
  Henry 276
  Holly Berry 235
  John 235
  Jones 184, 300
  Josiah 235
  Lovett 184
  Martha 184
  Mary 184
  Obedience 23
  Pinckney 184
  Prudence (Jones) 235
  Rachel 235
  Samuel 276

PERSONS, Sarah 184, 224
  Thomas 184, 330
  Turner 197
PETERS, Edmund 300
  Moses 300
  Solomon 277
  William 184, 269, 300
PETIT, Betsey 308
PETTERS, Stephen 248
PETTIGREW, Capt. — 175
  Mary 232, 233
PETTIS, Moses 300
PETTY, — 78
PEYTON, Capt. John 183
  Lieut. Valentine 67
PHAROAH, Joseph 300
PHELPS, Jane 30, 110
  Lucy 110
  Thomas 300
PHIFER, John 330
  Col. Martin 330
PHILIPS, Anne 92
  Daniel 300
  Isham 185, 300
  Joseph 92, 215, 276
  Ruth 308
  Sarah 308
  Thomas 300
  Zachariah 276
PHILLIPS, — 192
  Benjamin 314
  Exum 330
  George 185
  Hillery 271
  Isaac 185
  Joseph 288
  Levi 314
  Mark 185
  Mary 318
  Sarah 42
PHILPOT, Mary 250
PHINAZEE, Elizabeth 185
  Harris 179, 185
  Hiram 179
  James 185
  John 185, 269, 300
  Mahala 185
  Margaret 185

POWELL, Col. Caleb 93
  Catherine 190
  Charity 190
  Elizabeth 29
  Elizabeth Janet 110
  Evan 190
  Francis 300
  George 190
  John 269, 278
  Joshua 276
  Josiah 269
  Lewis 165, 190, 300
  Martha 190
  Mildred 22
  Moses 190
  Nancy 190
  Rachel 308
  Sarah 190
  Seymour 300
  Simon 110
  Sivility 190
  William 29, 190
  Winifred 29
POWERS, James 190
  Nicholas 89
POWLEDGE, George 300
POYTHRESS, Elizabeth 70
PRATT, Edward 276
PRAY, John 149
PRESCOTT, Fanny 308
PRESSLAR, Peter, Sr. 300
PRESSLEY, John 300
PRESSNELL, William 273
PREWITT (Pruitt), — 64
PRICE, — 89, 225
  E. 282, 322
  Elizabeth (Lindsey) 58
  Elvey 26
  Ephriam 314
  John E. 58
  Lucius 300
  Phoebe 28
  Polly 58
PRICHARD, Peyton 197
PRICKETT, John 276
  William 276
PRIDDY, Judith 308
PRIGDEN, David 300

PRINCE, John 314
  Noah 300
PRITCHET, Isaiah 16
PRITCHETT, Delpha 310
PRIOR, Dorothy 249
  Sarah 148
PROCTOR, Biddy 319
  Francis 30
  Hannah 202
  Stephen 300
  Stephen Royer 202
PROSSER, Otey 190, 300
PROVOST, Peter 229
PRUITT, Peniny 318
PRYOR, John 300
  Mary 308
PSALMONDE, S. 308
PUGH, Shadrack 300, 321
PULASKI, Count 261, 284, 286, 333
PULLEN, John 300
  Robert 269
PULLIAM, Jane (Gilbert) 226
  Matthew 73
  Robert 290
  William 300
PULLIAN, Sarah 182
PULLIN, Robert 324
  Thomas, Sr. 300
PURDUE, Sarah 308
PUREFOY, Stanley 184
PURVIS, Eliza 190
  George 190
  Col. John 118
  Polly 190
  Martha Eliza 191
  Needham 300
  Sarah A. 190
  William G. 191
PURYEAR, — 120
PUTNAM, Capt. — 118
  Gen. Israel 261
PYE, James 300
PYRON, Susan 217
  William 5

QUARLES, Capt. John 330
QUATERMAN, Arlissa 191
  Cynthia B. 191

RANSOME, Dudley 193
   Elizabeth 193
   Jane 193
   Joseph 193
   Nancy 193
   Nancy C. 193
   Polly 193
   Reuben 61, 193, 269, 300
   Richardson D. 193
   William 193
RATCHETT, Susan 188
RATCHFORD, Joseph 314
RAVENS, James 5
RAVOT, Abraham 193
   Elizabeth 193
   Gabriel Frances 193
   Henrietta 193
   Margaret Marie 193
   Mary 193
RAVOTT, Capt. Abraham 86, 330
RAWLINGS, Henry 193
RAWLINS, John 269
RAWLS, Miss — 158
   Arthur 234
   Isaac 300
   William 300
RAY, — 101
   Andrew 300
   Benjamin 300
   Jane 319
   John 134, 300, 314
   Mark 300
   Nancy (Mary) 21
   Philip 300
   Capt. Thomas 214
   William 274, 284
   Wm. 286
READ, Benjamin 185
   Griffin 185
READE, George 330
REARDEN, Tracy 147
REAVES, Daniel 277
   Sarah 308
REAVS, Thomas 277
RED, Job 300
REDD, Frances 180
REDDENS, Scott 276
REDDICK, Abraham 193, 284, 289

REDDICK, Abram 314
   Hannah 193, 284, 289
REDDING, Anderson 193, 194, 269, 279
   Arthur 194
   Charles 194
   Edith 194
   Elizabeth 194
   James M. 194
   Lourania 194
   Mary 194
   Rowland 194
   Thomas 194
   Thomas Parham 8
   William 194
   William Chambless 194
REDMOND, Major 12
REDWINE, Barbara 194
   Elizabeth 194
   Jacob 194, 269, 314
   Jemina 194
   John 194
   Kate 194
   Lewis 194
   Mary 194
   Michael 194
   Nancy 194
   Sally 194
REE, Capt. — 183
REED, Mrs. — 152
   Elizabeth 184
   Isaac 324
REEDER, Mrs. — 226
REES, Hugh 300
   Lycrugus 174
REESE, Miss — 146
   Blanche 81
   Cuthbert 52, 194
   Dr. David 155
   Elizabeth 121, 308
   Henry L. 195
   Isham 194
   John C. 194
   Jordan 195
   Joseph 194
   Percilla 194
   Sarah P. 195
   Silva 319

RUCKER, Lemuel 222
  Mary 174
  William 6, 269, 290, 301
  Willis 6
RUDDELL, Lee Ann 319
RUDICIL, George 199
RUDOLPH, Elizabeth 15, 319
  Mary Frances 15
  Michael 16
  Thomas 15
RUE, Mary 187, 196
RUMSEY, Richard 290
RUNDLE, Susanna 309
RUPERT, John 279
RUSHEON, Specey 301
RUSHIN, Caroline 199
  Elizabeth 199
  Evelyn 199
  James 199
  Joel 199
  John 199, 269
  (Rushing), John 199
  Mary 199
  Matilda 199
  William 199
RUSHING, Sarah 319
  William 227
RUSSELL, Col. — 12
  Caroline 180
  Elizabeth 309
  George 301
  James G., Sr. 322
  John 117
  Nancy 216
RUTHERFORD, Gen. — 100, 165, 195
  Miss — 33
  Ann 208
  Benjamin 200
  Claiborn 301
  Dorothy 199
  Dorothy Wiggins 200
  James 301, 314
  John 199
  John G. 200
  Mary 92, 319
  Nathaniel 200
  Robert 119, 199, 200

RUTHERFORD, Thomas 199
  William 33, 199, 200
RUTLEDGE, John 301
RYALL, Charles 124
  Wright 314
RYALS, Charles 211
  John 59
  Joseph 59
  Penelope 59
  William 59, 200, 269
RYAN, Angelica 200
  Christiana 200
  Matilda 200
  Obedience 200
  Philip 200, 269
RYE, Elizabeth 319
  Mary 309
RYLEE, James 218
RYLES, James, Sr. 314

SAFFOLD, Miss — 21
  Adam Goudylock 189
  Elizabeth 77
  Isom 135
  William 189
SAFFORD, Sarah 309
SAGER, Ann 319
SAILORS, Christopher 301
  Phoebe 57
St. JOHN, James 314
St. MARK, Dr. Benjamin 90
SALLENS, Peter 240
SAMMONS, Nancy 281
SAMPLES, Nathaniel 301
SAMPSON, Miss — 42
  Archibald 276
SAMSON, Col. Simeon 171
SAMPSON, William 276
SANDERS, Miss — 228
  widow — 217
  David 273
  James 301, 314
  Jesse 200
  John 301, 314
  Jonathan 52
  Lucy 118
  Mary 309
  Moses 200, 269

SANDERS, Penelope 128
 Rachel 72
 Thomas 301
SANDIDGE, Clairborne 290
SANDIFORD, Elim 301
SANDRIDGE, Clayborn 314
SANFORD, — 201
 Benjamin 200
 Daniel 200
 Elizabeth 135
 Jeremiah 200, 301
 Jesse 283, 287
 Mildred Washington 94, 200
 Thomas 200
 Vincent 200
SAPP, Dill 200, 289
 Everet 129
 Lydia 200, 289
 Shadrack 301
 Zilpha 309
SAPPINGTON, Caleb 18
 John 314
SAULS, Daniel 93
SAVAGE, Elizabeth 83
 Rev. Loveless 47
 Mary Ann 54
 Thomas 301, 314
SAWYER, John Jones 301
SAXON, — 198
 Benjamin Archelus 71
 Elizabeth M. 309
 Solomon 321, 325
 Temperance 247
SAXTON, Elizabeth M. 310
SAYLOR, Jacob 61
SCARBOROUGH, Sarah 309
SCHADD, Margaret 229
 Col. Solomon 229
SCHAEFFER, Balthazer 75, 200
 Elizabeth 201
 Frederick 201
 George 201
 Hannah Eppinger 201
 Jacob 201
 James 201
 John W. 201
 Margaret 201
 Sarah 201
 Simon Peter 201

SCHAIRER, Marjorie Thomas 211
SCHEE, Daniel 269
SCHMIDT, Louisa F. 5
SCHUYLER, Elizabeth 100
 Gen. Philip 330
SCOTT, Ann Baytop 163
 Annie 201
 Benjamin 201
 Col. Charles 4
 Daniel 201
 Darius 201
 Elizabeth 100
 Frances 319
 Frederick 121, 201
 Isaac 201
 James 201, 269, 315
 Capt. James 57
 Jane 201
 John 94, 201, 279, 301
 Brig. Gen. John 57
 Capt. John 28
 John Eppes 269
 Margaret 128, 247
 Mary 281
 Mary Eliza 219
 Mary L. 57
 Capt. Matthew 330
 Polly 201
 Samuel 201
 Sarah 201
 Thomas 94, 201
 William 201, 301, 315
 Woodlief 121
 Woodliff 201
SCREVEN, Gen. — 202
 Charles O. 18
 Charles Odingsell 202
 Elizabeth 202
 Esther 201
 James 202, 269
 Brig. Gen. James 132, 201
 Gen. James 38, 107, 261
 John 202
 Lieut. John 36
 Martha 202
 Mary 107
 Mary Bedon 202
 Mary Esther 132, 201
 Richard Bedon 202

SCREVEN, Sarah 202
　　Thomas 202
　　Thomas Edward 202
SCREWS, Susan 47
SCROGGINS, George 301
　　Thomas 301
SCRUGGS, Elizabeth 187
　　Gross 187
　　Richard 27
　　Sarah 27
SCURLOCK, William 202
SEAL, Anthony 315
　　John 203
　　Rachel 73
SEALE, William 315
SEALS, Archibald 41
　　Elizabeth 110, 309, 310
　　Ivy 3
　　Martha 231
　　Spencer 41
　　Wm. 301
SEARCY, George 301
　　Maria 193
SEARS, Ella 39
SEAVERS, — 114
SEAWELL, Col. Benj. 177
SEAY, John 202
SELF, Sallie 195
SELLERS, Solomon 315
SELMAN, John 301
　　William 315
SEMMES, Andrew 202
　　Joseph 202
　　Thomas 202
SENTELL, Brittain 203
　　Elizabeth 203
　　Hetty Louise 203
　　John 203
　　Martin 203
　　Nancy 203
　　Nathan 203
　　Samuel 202, 203
　　Sarah 203
　　William 203
SESSIONS, Benjamin 142
　　John 203
　　Joseph 269
　　Mary 203
　　Rebecca 124

SETT, Susanna 319
SETZGER, Jacob 315
SEVIER, Elizabeth 54
　　Major Hugh 330
　　Gen. John 54
SEWELL, Chris 301
　　Eleanor 119
　　Mary 16
　　Wm. 301
SHACKELFORD, Ann 203
　　Betsey 203
　　Cary (Baker) 203
　　Edmund 203, 204, 315
　　Eliza 80
　　Elizabeth 203
　　Fanny 203
　　Frances W. 42
　　Henry 6, 149, 203
　　James 110, 204
　　Jefferson 203
　　Jenny 203
　　John 203, 204, 269
　　Capt. John 47
　　Judith 203
　　Nancy 6, 203, 204
　　Patsey 204
　　Polly 203
　　Philip 203
　　Reuben 203
　　Roger 203
　　Susanna 204
SHAFFER (Schaffer), Belthasas 67
　　Susanna 67
SHANDLEY, Elizabeth 75
SHANKLE, Levi 182
SHANNON, Thomas 276
SHARP, John 301
　　Joshua 301
SHARPE, James 132
　　(Sharp), John 204
　　Mary 132
　　Mary (Newton) 132
SHARP, Patty 309
SHARPE, Thomas 171
SHAVELY, Edward 281
SHAW, Ann 162
　　Basil 324
　　Elinor 148
　　John 301

SLAUGHTER, John 208, 209
  Juda 208
  Lucy 208
  Mary 208
  Patty 208
  Prudence A. 209
  Reuben 46, 208, 209
  Sallie 208
  Sally 209
  Samuel 46, 208, 209, 269
  Sarah 46
  Susanna 208
SLAVEN, Mary Radcliff 2
  Norcut 2
SLEDGE, — 94
SLEIGH, James 320
  Samuel 149
SLOCUMB, John C. 301, 324
SMALLEY, Michael 301
SMALLWOOD, Gen. 2
  Rebecca 191
SMETHER, Gabriel 290, 301
SMITH, — 14, 70, 78, 112, 184, 239
  Capt. — 103
  Col. — 83, 85
  Abner 209, 301
  Afamy 309
  Alexander 209, 325
  Anna 209
  Ann 309
  Ann Adair 211
  Ann Adams 72, 210
  Anthony Garnett 9
  Archibald 165
  Benj. H. 99
  Benjamin 315, 327
  Benjahah 54
  Bonetta 230
  Charity 234
  Charles 209, 322
  Christiana 211
  Clara 116
  Colesby 209, 315
  Daniel 209
  David 175, 211
  Ebenezer 210
  Edith 119
  Edmund 119

SMITH, Edward G. 209
  Eliza 135
  Elizabeth 152, 188, 189, 209, 211,
    309, 319
  Elizabeth Mary Ann 159
  Elizabeth West 71
  Enoch 324
  Ezekiel 286, 301
  Francis 209
  Gabriel 274
  Garnett 175
  George 42, 181, 187, 196, 301
  Hardy 210, 269, 301
  Henry 301
  Hugh 167, 211
  Isaac 210, 269
  Ivy 315
  Jacob 119
  James 209, 210, 269, 276, 315
  Jane 211
  Jemina 209
  Jesse 274, 315
  Job 301
  Johanna 9
  John 46, 188, 209, 210, 273, 301
  John Gottleib Israel 211
  Jordan 85
  Joshua 315
  Judith (Turner) 181
  Julia 175
  Larkin 211, 315
  Lawrence 301
  Leonard 301
  Loftin 210
  Lovett B. 83
  Lucrety 65
  Lucy 72, 141
  Margaret 309
  Martha 187, 208, 235
  Mary 181, 211, 309, 319
  Mary P. 309
  Mathew 301
  Mial 241
  Millie 250
  Morgan 127
  Nancy 186, 250
  Nathan 276, 301
  Noah 209

SMITH, Penelope 46
Peyton 276, 278
Phoeby 211
Polly 250
Rebecca 309
Reuben 210, 301
Rhoda 85
Robert 211, 269, 282, 301, 315
Capt. Robert 165
Robert Wilson 211
Rosannah 211
Samuel 315
Sarah 56, 92, 309, 319
Silas 187
Susan 165, 195
Thomas 201, 210, 211, 236, 276
Thompson 210
Ursula 222
William 72, 111, 211, 215, 269,
273, 274, 301, 322
Wm. 138, 269
SMITHSON, Martha 30
SMITHWICK, Elizabeth 309
SMOKES, William C. 301
SMYTHE, Susan 180
SNEAD, Dudley 276
Philip 301
SNELLINGS, Elizabeth 25, 211
George 211, 269
Hannah 211
John 211
Martha 211
Mary 211
Rebecca 211, 310
Richard Ward 211
Richard Ware 178
Samuel 211
SNOW, Mark 273
SNYDER, Godlip 315
SODOWN, Jacob 324
SOLOMON, Carol 212
Delilah 212
Dicey 212
Elizabeth 212
Fannie 212
Hardy 212
Henry 212
James 212

SOLOMON, John 212
Lazarus 211, 269, 301
Lewis 212
Mary 212
Peter 212
Sarah 212
William 212
SORRELLS, Elenor 40
Milly 40
SORRELS, Mildred 309
SORROW, Mary 309
SOSEBEE, Elizabeth 309
SOWELL, Zadoc 301
SPAIN, Levi 123
Rachel 131
SPALDING, Henry 320
James 164
SPANN, James 212
Lamey 309
SPARKS, Jane 319
Jeremiah 301
John 212
Thomas 146
SPEAK, Richard 315
SPEAKS, Richard 269, 282
SPEARMAN, John 212, 228, 269,
301
SPEARS, — 20
John 315, 324
William 315, 323
SPEER, Moses 142
SPELL, Lucy 193
Mary 309
SPELLER, Capt. Benjamin 85
SPENCE, Mary 319
SPENCER, Charlotte 163
Frances 248
George C. 9
Hannah E. 169
Harriet 125
SPIKES, Nathan 276
SPINKS, Pressly 301
SPIVEY, Col. Eli W. B. 159
James 281
Mary 281
SPLATT, Esther 39
Esther (Dean) 71
SPRATLIN, Henry 114, 128

SPRATLIN, Winnefred 309
SPRATT, Ann 20, 125
  Mary 21
  Thomas 21
SPRINGER, Ann 319
  John 212
  Rev. John 269, 332
  Wm. Green 24
SPURLOCK, widow — 181
  George 276
  Capt. Robert 47
  Wm. 301
STACY, Elizabeth 212
  James 212
  John 191, 212
  Jonathan 212
  Margaret 212
  Mary 212
  Robert 212
  Sarah 212
  Susanna 212
  Thomas 212, 315
  William 212
STAFFORD, — 198
  Dorcas (Williams) 90
  Robert 269
  Col. Samuel 90
  Col. William 331
  Col. Wm. 90
STALLINGS, Capt. James 47
STAMPER, Martin 234
STAMPES, Martin 61
STAMPS, Mary 319
  Sarah 87
STANDLEY, Thomas 128, 289
STANFIELD, — 132
STANFORD, Elizabeth 309
  Joshua, Sr. 301
STANLEY, Ira 159
  Wm. 277
STANTON, John 111, 212, 301
STAPLES, Nancy 71
  Stephen 212
  Thomas 301
STAPLETON, George 269, 279
STARK, Col. — 133
  Benton 269
STARKE, John 213

STARKE, Jonas 76
  Louise 180
  Mary 213
STARLING, Abijah 331
  Winifred 45
  Wm. 301
STARR, Joseph 331
  Mary 309, 319
STARRELL, James 315
STATHAM, Nathaniel 327
  Wm. 301
STEARNS, Hepzibah 242
  Isaac 242
  Martha 150
STEDMAN, Zacheriah 322
STEEL, Henry 301
STEELE, Elizabeth 101
STEENSON, John 269
STELL, John W. 55
STEPHEN, John W. 302
STEPHENS, Col. — 12
  Alexander 269
  Barnett 302
  Benjamin 276
  Burrell 302
  Caley 309
  Desire 309
  James 302
  John 276
  Joseph 302
  Mary 309
  Nancy 45, 203
  Pleasance 96
  Rebecca 64
  Reuben 302
  Richard 302
  Sarah 309
  Thomas 103
  William, Jr. 198
  William J. 332
  Wm., Sr. 320
STERRETT, John H. 240
STEVENS, Aaron 213
  Alexander 213
  Alexander Hamilton 213
  Andrew Baskins 144, 213
  Benjamin 213
  Catherine 213

443

TALBOT, Edward 220
  Elizabeth 319
  Elizabeth Cresswell 220
  Hale 220
  John 220
  Joseph 45
  Mary 220
  Mathew 220
  Mathews 220
  Matthew 172, 270
  Phoebe 220
  Thomas 220
  William 220
TALBOTT, Miss — 147
TALIAFERRO, Miss — 163
  Anna 221
  Benj. 285
  Benjamin 220, 221
  Capt. Benjamin 21
  Col. Benjamin 108, 261
  Betheland 221
  Betsey 221
  Burton 89
  Charles 221
  David 21, 221
  Elizabeth 221
  Emily 220
  Frances 221
  John 221, 270
  Judith 221
  Louis Bourbon 127, 220
  Lucy 221
  Margaret 221
  Martha 221
  Mary 221
  Nicholas M. 221
  Richard 221
  Rosa 221
  Sally 108, 221
  Sarah 143
  Thornton 221
  Warren 89
  Zachariah 220, 221
  Zecheriah 89, 221
TALLANT, John 302
TALLEY, Alexander 221
  Caleb 221
  Elknah 221

TALLEY, Elisha 320
  John Wesley 221
  Nathan 221
  Nicholas 221
  William 221
TAMMONS, Zipporah 319
TANKERSLY, James 134
TANNER, John 284, 285
  Frances 116
  Thomas 315
TANNEY, Michael 325
TAPLEY, Adam 302
  Mark 277
TAPPERLY, John 232
TARBUTTON, Joseph 302
TARPLEY, Mary 45
TARRANT, Capt. Jones 42
TARVER, Absolem 302
  Absolom 222
  Elizabeth (Lowe) 105
TATE, Charity 7
  Elizabeth 196, 310
  Enos 290
  John 222, 274, 302
  Martha 147
  Richard 276
  Robert L. 325
TATTNALL, Commodore Josiah,
    Jr. 222
  Josiah 222, 261, 270
TATUM, Capt. Howell 212
  Jesse 290
  Molly 319
TAYLOR, — 103
  Col. 217
  Benjamin 140
  Clark 222, 270, 302
  Dempsey 302
  Edward 302
  Elizabeth 210
  Frances (Fanny) 84
  Col. Francis 3, 182
  Henry 277
  James 186, 302
  John 88, 211, 216, 277, 281, 284,
    302
  Martha 186
  Mary 216

449

VALENTINE, Elizabeth 184
  Lydia 249
VALKINBURG, Eugene Van 180
VANBRACKEL, John 302
VAN DER BURG, Mary 150
VANCE, Col. — 50
  Patrick 276
VANDERGRIFF, Garret 324
VARDEN, Dolly 182
VARNER, George 302. 315
  Matthew 232, 315
VARNUM, Capt. — 224
VASSAR, Micajah 302
VASSELS, James 320
VAUGHAN, Capt. — 181
  Col. — 55
  Felix 315
  Jesse 270, 302
VAUGHN, Berry 218
  Frances 233
  Sarah 246
VEAL, Elizabeth 309
  Mary 238
  William 302
VEASEY, Zebulon 302
VEASY, Martha 309
VEAZEY, Elizabeth 232
  Ezekiel 232
  Francinia 232
  James 108, 232, 276
  Jesse 232
  John 192, 232
  Mary 232
  Sally 232
  William 232
  Zebulon 232
VEAZY, Mary 111
VEICLE, Lewis 303
VENABLE, Abram 232
  Charles 28, 232
  Jacob 232
  John 232, 331
  John Moorman 55, 232
  Mary 232
  Nathaniel 232
  Robert 232
  William 232
VERDIN, Winnie 319

VERNAL, Ephraim Smith 152
VERNER, Ann 233
  Charles 232, 233
  David 233
  David O. 232
  Dinah 233
  Ebenezer Pettigrew 233
  George 233
  George W. 233
  James 232
  Jane 232, 233
  John, Sr. 232, 233
  John Augustus 232
  Lemuel H. 232
  Mary P. 232
  Nancy 232, 233
  Rebecca 233
  Samuel 233
  William 232
VERNON, Patsey 319
  Sarah 238
VICKERS, Sarah 319
  William 315
VICKERY, Hezekiah 303
  Joseph 303
VIDETTE, Henry 233
VINCENT, Anne 149
  Isaac 303
  Sarah 183
VINES, Mary (Polly) 50
VINING, John 120
VINSON, Elijah 303
  Nancy 227
VISAGE, Elizabeth 319
VIVIAN, Jane 119, 245
VIVIEN, Virgil H. 159
VOLLOTON, Rachel 309
VOSE, Anna 57

WADE, Col. — 232
  Archibald 233
  Edward 233, 289
  Elizabeth 182
  Frances 233
  H. T. 30
  Jesse 166, 233
  John W. 303
  Mary 233

453

WALKER, Sally 235
Samuel 303, 331
Sanders 270, 287, 289
Sarah 234, 235
Sophia 236
Taylor 235
Thomas 76, 276, 303, 331
Col. Thomas R. 210
William 32, 34, 234, 235, 236
William H. 236
WALL, Ann 309
Bud 178
Henry 303
Jesse 59, 85
John 236, 284, 285, 303
Marish 177
Mary 236, 284, 285
Myall 303
Sarah 59
Willis 236
WALLACE, John 276, 303
Lucy 114
Margaret Ann 217
Martha 120
Robert 120
William 2, 54, 303, 315
WALLER, Ann 150
Benjamin 276
Charles R. 237
Daniel 236
Elijah 303
Elizabeth 237
Elizabeth K. 236
Ellis M. 236
Handy 236
Ibby C. 236
Irwin 236
James 236
James B. 236
John 236
Martha 236
Mary Elizabeth 230
Nathaniel E. 237
Phyllis 236
William 236
WALLS, Charles 303
Samuel 303
WALTERS, Mary (Polly) 234

WALTERS, Peter 303
WALTON, Christian 113, 221
Elizabeth 239
George 38, 99, 237, 239, 262, 270, 276
Jesse 276
John 237, 239, 276
Josiah 84, 315
Nathan 276
Nancy Hughes 237
Peninah 84
Robert 237, 276
Sallie 239
Thomas 113
William 237
WANSLEY, John 24, 237, 290
Martha 237
Sarah 24, 237
WARD, — 77
Charity 309
Col. Charles 60
Content 45
Elizabeth 319
Francis 270
Harriet C. 122
Jane 319
Col. Jonathan 331
Nancy 238
Nancy Lavinia 143
Nathaniel 303
Samuel 303, 325
Sarah 238
Thomas 252
Vernon 238
William 238, 323
WARDE, John Peter 164
WARDEN, Samuel 315
WARE, Edward 238, 270
Elizabeth 145, 238
Henry 166, 238
James 238, 270
Jane 309
Letty 238
Mary 166
Nicholas 48, 238
Philip 238
Robert 238
William Alexander 238

WAYNE, Gen. — 6, 57
Anthony 240
Gen. Anthony 96, 202, 222, 264
Elizabeth Clifford 8
WEAKLEY, Miss — 183
Isabella 96
WEATHERS, Edward 284, 287
Valentine 325
WEATHERTON, Thomas 315
WEAVER, Benjamin 240, 270
Henry 240
Isham 34
Mary 319
Travis A. D. 240
William Wylie 240
WEBB, Abner 241
Bathurst 241
Bridges 241
Claiborne 240, 241, 270
Clarence 273
Elijah 241
Evelina 241
Frances 241
Francis 241
James 241
John 241, 303, 325
Lucy 19, 20
Margaret 241, 309
Martha P. 241
Milton Pope 241
Richard W. 241
Thomas 241
William 241
Wm. Meriwether 241
WEEKS, Theophilus 303, 315
WEEMS, Lock 145
WEITMAN, Lewis 80, 233
WELBORN (Wilborn), Elias 303
WELCH, — 201
Capt. 90
Caleb 282
James 75
Lucy Simpson 53
Nicholas 303
WELLBORN, — 14
Abner 242
Abner W. 241
Chapley 242

WELLBORN, Clara 242
Elias 150, 241, 242
Ellias 198
Isaac 242
James 242
James M. 150, 198
James Madison 241
Johnson 242
Lucy 241
Marshall H. 241
Martha 241
Martha Strother 128
Mary 241, 242
Nancy 241
Ruby 241
Samuel 242
Selina H. 241
Thomas 53
William 242, 332
WELLBOURNE, Daniel 277
David 277
WELLER, Jacob 277
WELLES, Elizabeth Worsham 20
Thomas 20
WELLS, Abner 187
Frances 231
Francis 75
Jeremiah 72
Leonard 323
Redman 323
WELSHER, Jeremiah 303
WENSE, Mary 319
WESSON, Sarah 319
WEST, — 5
Miss — 202
Benjamin 303, 324
Catherine 92
James 202, 242, 289
John 315
Susannah 327
Willis 303
Wm. 327
WESTBROOK, John 315
Stephen 121
WESTMORELAND, Angelina 242
Jesse 242, 331
Joel 242
John 242

456

WHITEHEAD, Dr. James 27
   John 27
   Lazarus 23
   Rhoda Henrietta 23
   Richard 83
   Sarah 23
   Susanna Tomlinson 83
WHITEN, Philip 323
WHITESIDES, John 278
WHITFIELD, Miss — 57
   Capt. Bryan 35
   Horatio 88
   Lewis 303, 315
   Sarah 36
WHITING, Elizabeth Judson 331
   John 331
   Judson 331
   Samuel, Jr. 331
   Col. Samuel 331
WHITINGTON, B. G. 303
WHITLOCK, Elizabeth 309
WHITMIRE, George F. 331
WHITTEN, Philip 303
WHITTINGTON, Fuddy 325
WIGGINS, Almey 309
   Richard 303
   Samuel 199, 200
WIGHT, John 315
WILBANKS, Gillam 303
WILBURN, Jack 125
   Martha 125, 244
   Thomas 244
   (Wellborn), Thomas 125
WILCHER, Elizabeth 319
WILCOX, Elizabeth 64
   George 64, 99
   Jane 170
   John 59, 64, 331
WILCOXSON, David 331
WILDER, William 303
   Willis 303
WILEY, James 54
   James Rutherford 54
   John 303
   Mary 24
   Moses 24
   Paulina 178
   Rachel 79

WILEY, William 2
WILFORD, Lewis 322
WILHIGHT, Lewis 303
WILHITE, Lewis 315
WILKERSON, Elisha 274
   Ester 309
   John 62, 331
   Lucy 62, 210
   Sarah M. 62
   William 210
WILKES, Mrs. — 152
   John 262
   Nancy 319
WILKINS, Elizabeth 218
   John 290
   William 331
WILKINSON, Benjamin 111, 277
   Caroline 111
   Elisha 277
   Elizabeth 111
   Gen. James 262
   Judith 111
   Sarah Harwood 133
WILLAFORD, Nathan 322
WILLEBY, John 273
WILLEFORD, Lucy 309
WILLIAM, — 196
WILLIAMS, — 45, 88
   Abraham 303
   Adelaide M. 49
   Anderson 315
   Benj. Z. 303
   Celete Ann 159
   Clarissa 205
   Daniel 244
   David 331
   Diana 319
   Dilly 309
   Edward 325
   Eleanor 165
   Elizabeth 243, 244
   Rev. Ezekiel James 244
   Frederick 244
   Henry 159
   Isaac 288
   Isham 284, 288
   James 244, 277
   John 270, 277, 315

WILSON, Joel 247
  John 192, 246, 247, 270, 303,
    316, 326
  John McKennie 247
  Jonathan 247
  Josiah T. 214
  Lucy 80
  Luke 246
  Margaret 310
  Mark 247
  Mary 118
  Micha 80
  Polly 246
  Rebecca 247
  Sally 246
  Samuel 316
  Sarah 246, 247
  Silas 246
  Stephen 246
  Susan 134
  Thomas 320
  Williams 316
WILTMAN, Lydia 67
WIMBERLY, Miss — 39, 119
  Abner 247
  Chloe 247
  Christian 43
  Ezekiel 208, 247
  Henry 247
  James 247
  John 247, 303
  John (Jack) 247
  Lewis 247
  Mary 251
  Perry 247
  William 247
WINBURN, Josiah 303
  Sarah Ann 310
WINDHAM, Lucy 319
WINFIELD, Charles 248
  Elizabeth 248
  Frances 154, 180
  Francis Nelson 248
  John 248
  Mary 248
  Samuel 248
  Thomas 248
WINFREY, Jesse 248

WINFREY, Jessie 71
  Martha H. 71
  Martha Hughes 248
  Mary Ann 179
  Valentine 179
WINGATE, Mary 319
WINGFIELD, — 203
  Ann 122, 248
  Charles 248
  Elizabeth 42, 94, 172, 248
  Frances 248
  Garland 248
  John 248, 278
  Martha 248
  Mary 197, 248, 249
  Milly 248
  Nancy 248
  Polly 42
  Rebecca 248
  Sarah 248
  Sarah Garland 190
  Sarah Garland Poullain 248
  Thomas 43, 248
  Dr. Thomas 172
WINN, Ann 240, 310
  Benjamin 277
  Catherine 15
  John 249
  Nancy 55
  Peter 249
  Robert 122
WINSLETT, Samuel 303
WINTERSHEEDLE, Henry 270
WISE, Elizabeth 249
  Henry 249
  Jacob 120
  Jincey 249
  John 129, 249, 325
  Lavinia 66, 249
  Preston 249
  Rebecca 129, 249
  Sarah 65
  Sarah Margaret 249
  Susanna 249
  William 66, 249, 270
  Zilpha 249
WISENBAKER, John 249
WITCHER, Capt. William 233

460

WITHERSPOON, George 55
  Mary 212
WITT, — 150
WITTER, Elizabeth 116
WODERWELL, Rev. Mr. — 133
WOFFORD, Absolem 303
WOLF, Andrew 303
  Ida 234
WOMACK, A. 303
  Jesse 249
  John W. 249
  Margaret 249
  Nancy 162
  William 303
WOMBLE, Enoch 234
  Mary 205
WOOD, Miss — 28
  Abraham 303
  Eason 250
  Elizabeth 250
  Ellet 303
  Green 250
  James 270, 277, 303, 316
  Col. James 56
  John 250, 303
  John White 250
  Joshua 250
  Lydia 250
  Mark 250
  Mark Red 250
  Mary 36, 250
  Mary Lee 62
  Nancy 250, 310
  Priscilla 5
  Sally 98, 250
  Sarah 79
  Solomon 249, 270
  Thomas 303
  William 250, 270
  Willis 250
  Wm. 277
WOODALL, — 29
  John 303
  Joseph 303, 316, 325
WOODCOCK, William 303
WOODING, Benjamin 5
  Martha Ann 26
WOODLY, John 36

WOODLY, Milly 310
WOODRIDGE, Nathan 333
WOODRUFF, Mr. — 172
  Huldah 80
  Richard 316
WOODS, Miss 2
  Benjamin 187
  Molly 6
  Rebecca 162
WOODSON, Jane (Ginny) 9
WOODWARD, — 119
  Hezekiah 331
  Susan 175
WOOLF, Andrew 326
WOOLFOLK, Miss — 7
WOOLSEY, David 325
WOOTEN, Daniel 250
  Fathia 6
  H. 310
  James 250
  John 250
  Lemuel 250
  Mary 136, 250
  Olivia Norton 6
  Priscilla 113, 188, 221
  Richard B. 250
  Robert 250
  Thomas 250, 277, 303
  Winfred 250
WORD (Ward), William, Sr. 290
WORSHAM, — 208
  Elizabeth 249
  Mary 319
  Nancy C. 310
  Richard 248
WORTH, Thomas 277
WORTHINGTON, Elizabeth 183
WORTLEY, Sarah 113
WOURNELL, Wm. 277
WRAY, — 139
  Anne 49
  Harriet Bryan 190
WRIGHT, Gov. — 256, 259
  Ambrose 270
  Amis 319
  Dorcas 152
  Elisha 303
  Elizabeth 334

461